Praise for «New Suits»

«To lead change, it is critical to engage emotion, find common purpose and build a sense of urgency. With New Suits, two of the brightest, energetic and creative leaders in the world of legal innovation, Guenther Dobrauz and Michele DeStefano, generously provide legal leaders with the frameworks, data and perspectives they need to build the case for change NOW. By engaging a diverse, cutting-edge team of contributors to New Suits, Guenther and Michele practice, too, what they preach—teamwork and a rigorous, interdisciplinary approach to solving problems. I'm now ready for my New Suit!»

– **Professor Scott A Westfahl**, *Professor of Practise & Director Executive Education, Harvard Law School*

«Those of us interested and involved in today's rapidly changing world of legal services delivery have in recent years had plenty of go-to sources to whet our appetites on the topic. But never before has there been in the «legal world» such an elucidation of the «appetite for disruption» as brought to us by Michele DeStefano and Guenther Dobrauz in their new book. The breadth and depth of the history, in theory and in practice, and the future of legal services transformation one finds in «New Suits» is both welcome and exceptional. It will no doubt be widely referred to by general counsels and outside counsel often and extensively as we all continue this interesting journey into the era of the digital lawyer.»

– **William Deckelmann**, *General Counsel, DXC Technology*

«Lawyers will likely always be lawyers. But the way they work will change fundamentally—to their own and their clients' benefit. Also, we expect a fundamental re-definition of what constitutes actual legal and in particular lawyers' work and what is adjacent and accessory. All of the latter will surely be impacted by technology and other solutions and also the core of our business will face disruption. Michele and Guenther—two recognized legal rebels—have been at the forefront of all of these developments for several years now and have brought together an amazing group of authors to map the current state of the industry and to provide insight into what the future may hold.»

– **Professor Dr Heinz-Klaus Kroppen**, *Global Legal Leader PwC*

«The «Artist Formerly Known as the Legal Profession» isn't what it used to be. You think that you know law firms and the challenges that confront lawyers, but you don't. Legal services providers have spent years resisting change, and now seem determined to pack fifty- or sixty-years of evolution into five. The entire legal services market has been transformed by LegalTech, globalization, and new delivery models—and, until now, there has been no guide to the way that consumers can benefit and providers can profit from the changes. Guenther and Michele have gathered a Who's Who of thinkers to provide a marvelous range of visions of the way that law is changing. They provide a roadmap for the future of law—if only you'll follow it.»

– ***Professor Dan Hunter*** *PhD FAAL, Foundation Dean, Swinburne Law School*

«Lawyers have been trained to look backwards, to precedent, to find the solutions to their client's problems. So it should come as no surprise that the profession is «stuck» when it comes to adapting to technology and the need to understand its transformational impact on the future of legal practice as we know it. This book not only helps the reticent among us better understand why they can no longer stand on the sidelines and hope they finish their careers before being forced to change how they practice, but also gives comfort that client service and satisfaction will improve significantly with its adoption. «New Suits» not only provides the step by step to get to acceptance, adoption and successful implementation of new legal technology, but also helps the reader overcome their fear that the profession's transformation must be seen in a negative light, rather then a unique opportunity for growth.»

– ***Hilarie Bass,*** *Former President American Bar Association and President & Founder at Bass Institute for Diversity and Inclusion*

«For a while now, we have been hearing about digitization, disruption and new delivery models in the world of Big Law. «New Suits» both reassures and gives a wake-up call to all of us in the business of providing legal services. Setting out both the opportunities and the threats engendered by the dynamic change in our industry, the book is an invaluable guide to all lawyers and legal business professionals wanting some insight on the challenges facing them in a globalized and accelerating world.»

– ***Dr Matthias Lichtblau,*** *CMS*

«This book spells massive opportunity… for all those who get excited about change. Legal disruption isn't coming, it has already been here for some time. Michele and Guenther provide an extremely well researched and thoughtful analysis of how that disruption is going to play out in the mid to long term. No scare-mongering here, but a really useful early-warning system for those

wanting to profit from the innovation and efficiencies that market demand is successfully driving into every corner of the global legal sector.»
– **Richard Macklin,** *Partner & Global Vice Chair, Dentons*

«This book comes at a time where we see just the beginning of a transformational change on the legal market. While such transformation is seen as a great opportunity for those participants who endorse change and innovations, others seem to be more frightened by potential disruption of their well-established business models. The structure and comprehensive contributor listing for this book encapsulates many disparate challenges faced by almost all players on the market. The lecture of the book should give good guidance to anyone who is interested in how the legal profession is (finally) modernizing, capitalizing on technology trends and becoming more client-centric.»
– **Dr Cornelius Grossmann,** *Global Law Leader, EY Law*

«New Suits is signaling something different about the staid legal industry—evidence of a sincere appetite to change and potentially switch paradigms. Congrats to DeStefano and Dobrauz for pulling together an important and original work of applied research.»
– **Professor Bill Henderson,** *Indiana University Maurer School of Law, Stephen F Burns Chair on the Legal Profession*

«'Nomen est omen' if you read the book title of 'New Suits'. It encourages, allows and requests lawyers at all levels to rethink their former and existing ways of doing business in many areas of law. In the same, it outlines great opportunities to a new breed of experts in our profession. Thanks to the various authors, one gets a good understanding of how massive the impact of technology has become—and is going to be—to the legal services market. And the authors provide a distinct view of how a rather traditional profession will have to transform their business models to comply with the fast changes in the marketplace.»
– **Jürg Birri,** *Global Head of Legal Services KPMG*

«New Suits provides an excellent overview of how, over the last few years, the legal ecosystem has become increasingly complex and the emergence of new business models has prevailed. From digitalisation to «moreforless» affecting both in-house legal teams and external law firms, New Suits exemplifies what it takes to become a «Modern Legal Services Business». It encapsulates the future of the legal profession through an ensemble of brilliant authors—an educating and thought-provoking read!»
– **Alastair Morrison,** *Partner & Board Member, Pinsent Masons*

«The relevance of «New Suits» to considered thought on the state of the legal industry is profound. Other books predict a brave new world for the legal world, but glaringly offer no markers to when or at what scale such evolution will occur. DeStefano and Dobrauz bring clarity and energy to an area that has confounded most academic and business leaders. «New Suits» provides a single source of deep and broad understanding that is actually actionable–and is a must read for anyone who is or will be a leader in the field of law.»
– ***Daniel Reed,*** *CEO, UnitedLex*

Michele DeStefano & Guenther Dobrauz

New Suits

Appetite for Disruption in the Legal World

Staempfli Verlag

Imprint/Legal notice

«Blurred Lines» cover artwork created for «New Suits» by Billy Morrison in Los Angeles in the summer of 2018 and used with kind permission.

Overall cover design by Tom Jermann of t42design/Los Angeles.

Photography (of cover art and portrait of Dr Guenther Dobrauz-Saldapenna) created by Oliver Nanzig in Zurich 2018 and used with kind permission.

Bibliografische Information der Deutschen Nationalbibliothek
Die Deutsche Nationalbibliothek verzeichnet diese Publikation in der Deutschen Nationalbibliografie; detaillierte bibliografische Daten sind im Internet über http://dnb.d-nb.de abrufbar.

www.staempfliverlag.com

ISBN 978-3-7272-1039-6
ISBN 978-3-7272-1044-0 (E-Book pdf)
ISBN 978-3-7272-1045-7 (E-Book epub)

Table of Contents

The appropriate response to new technology is not to angrily retreat into the corner hissing and gnashing your teeth: it's to ask «Okay, how should we use this?»

– *Burning Man**

* Caveat Magister, *Technology and Immediacy at Burning Man (A slightly less than Socratic dialogue)*, Burning Man (Aug. 18, 2014), https://journal.burningman.org/2014/08/philosophical-center/tenprinciples/technology-and-immediacy-at-burning-man/ (last visited Apr. 30, 2019).

Professor Michele DeStefano and Dr Guenther Dobrauz-Saldapenna

Curators' Foreword

Time to Leave Law-Law Land … and Head Back Into the Jungle

Technological advancements, globalization, and the recent financial crisis have fuelled unprecedented change in the legal industry. Against the backdrop of new business models, altered client expectations, and the fluidity of legal talent, the legal service delivery ecosystem of today and tomorrow is, in some ways, like that of a jungle i.e., difficult to navigate yet vibrant and flourishing. For that reason, we (the co-curators) designed this book to provide an international, multi-cultural map of the *legal jungle*. By putting together the voices of legal thought-leaders from around the world, this book is intended to display the changes unfolding across the legal marketplace today, varied outlooks on the future of the legal profession, as well as potential methods which law/legal professionals might employ for future success in a changed legal environment. To that end, the book is divided into three parts.

Part 1, *Why Do Lawyers Need New Suits?,* contains chapters that focus on the changing legal marketplace and its challenges; it provides various authors' perspectives as to why lawyers need to don *New Suits*. For example, in chapter 1, Professors *David B Wilkins* and *Maria José Esteban Ferrer* demonstrate that what we call *alternative* legal services today is a misnomer and will be the norm in the legal market tomorrow. To meet clients' changing expectations, lawyers need *New Suits* that are customizable and agile and which integrate law into broader business solutions. In chapter 2, Professor *Mari Sako* makes a parallel point about general counsels. In describing their evolving roles around the globe, *Sako* explains why general counsels will need to wear *New Suits* in an even more transient, international, and interwoven marketplace. Professor *Michele DeStefano*, Professor *John Flood*, and *Karl Koller*, in each of their respective chapters (chapter 3, 4, and 6), demonstrate why the wearers of these *New Suits* will need to hone new mindsets, skillsets, and behaviours to thrive.

In Part 2, *What New Suits Might Lawyers Need for the Future?,* the focus turns to predictions; herein, the authors attempt to foresee the impact, risks, and opportunities that technological advancements might have on the legal marketplace overall and, more specifically, on the jobs, roles, and careers of lawyers and law/legal professionals. For example, in chapter 12, *Dr Guenther Dobrauz-Saldapenna* and *Corsin Derungs* share their predictions of how the law marketplace will need to adapt and evolve to survive. In chapters 15, 16, 21, and 22, the authors focus more specifically on the technology they believe will help create the *New Suits* lawyers will wear in the future: e.g., blockchain, automated legal documents, and artificial intelligence. In other chapters, authors including *David Bundi*, *Juan Crosby*, *Mike Rowden*, *Craig McKeown*, and *Sebastian Ahrens* question and sketch the future needs and roles of legal teams and legal functions and what *New Suits* will be required as a result.

In Part 3, *How Will Lawyers Fit into the New Suits of the Future?*, the book turns to chapters that suggest methods and models professionals might leverage to not only meet but to *exceed* the needs and expectations of the critical stakeholders in the future legal marketplace (e.g., business clients, general counsels, and the public at large). In other words, this part is focused on how lawyers will fit into (or fill in) the *New Suits* identified by the other parts of the book. This part begins with a chapter by *Maurus Schreyvogel* (chapter 23). He utilizes the Novartis Journey to describe a model that can be employed by lawyer leaders to drive operational excellence in legal service delivery. *Salvatore Icangelo* outlines the law firm of the future (chapter 30), Professor *Michele DeStefano*, provides a methodology to teach leadership, collaboration, and innovation to law/legal professionals (chapter 31) while *Maria Leistner*, concludes our book fittingly by outlining how the new generations will wear *New Suits* to make more meaningful contributions to the world of law (chapter 32).

To remain authentic to the voices, cultures, views, and scholarly preferences of the authors, we did not edit these articles as traditional editors might; nor did we weave them together so that they read as one contiguous thread. Instead, each author's chapter can be read on its own and represents his/her own research, citation style, and view point. We, the co-curators, analogize the compiling of this book to a quilting bee,[1] a social gathering of legal thought leaders from around the world who have come together to tell stories about our time now (the dynamic state of the current legal marketplace) and to envision a viable future for the legal profession: a future in which we deliver not only more efficient but more effective and comprehensive services and solutions that help our clients and, at the same time, increase access to justice for all. This book, like a quilt, is designed to commemorate where we have been, where we are headed, and the *why* and *how* of both. This is because the future, unlike a jungle, is *not* formidable. The future is filled with fascinating and unfolding opportunities for the law/legal professionals who rise as leaders to hone and own their *New Suits*.

---

1 To understand the heritage of quilts and quilting bees *see* https://www.wonderopolis.org/wonder/how-do-quilts-tell-stories.

Peter D Lederer

Prologue

Thoughts on the Past and the Future of the Legal Profession

What was the practice of law like six decades ago? What is it likely to be in the future?

When Guenther Dobrauz asked me to ponder these questions for this book, he also asked if I would touch on my origins. This is also where, a bit earlier, John Flood had wanted to start the lengthy conversations that led to our work, *Becoming a Cosmopolitan Lawyer*. At first, I wondered why: The facts of my early life were of importance to me, of course, but why should they be to others? And what was their relevance to how I came to embark on a path that led to a career as a «global lawyer»? But of course, such requests caused me to reflect. And over time, what at first seemed to me a random walk through life revealed meaningful patterns and paths. I had largely followed what the Japanese anthropologist Uematsu once called «the aesthetic of drift», but it turns out that drift may be more purposeful than appears on the surface. Let me sketch what mine looked like.

Part I

The story begins in Frankfurt, where I was born of Austrian parents. My early childhood years were spent in 1930s Vienna, and then—separated from my mother—I was forced to emigrate. The destination was to the heartland of the United States, first to Indianapolis and after secondary school to Chicago. There I graduated from college at 19, dismayed to have learned (via undergraduate classes taught by the likes of Fermi, Szilard and Uhry) that I was not cut out to be a scientist of the quality I had aspired to be. Instead, I drifted into working for two years as a community organizer for the United World Federalists, as student director for New York and then as field director for Maine. Skills learned? Public speaking, group dynamics, recruiting volunteers, fund raising—and even lobbying.

Then followed conscription into the U.S. army, and two years of oppressively regimented life (fortunately without physical danger, since I was posted to Germany and not to the Korea of 1951). Here also, benefits flowed: learning to run a small team, how discipline in large groups worked, and how rigid hierarchies operated. In addition, I had the opportunity to relearn some German. Most importantly, it gave me the generosity of the GI Bill—the government stipends that helped pay the cost of attending law school for three years, plus two years of post-doctoral work.

I made the decision to attend law school while in the army. If I was not to work in the «hard» sciences, I would instead chose a discipline where (I thought) there was flexibility as to what one would do after graduation. I was accepted at Yale and the University of Chicago, and I chose the latter. One eye was still on the sciences: The part-time job I took to help pay for law school during the first year was in the University's chemistry department, working for Professor Willard Libby, the Nobel Laureate who developed the carbon-14 dating method. It was no more than glorified bottle washing on a research project of his, but it was fascinating and there is something to be said for working with a genius on a daily basis!

Law school was a good fit for me: challenging, stimulating, and endless intellectual fun. The accident of starting in the summer quarter rather than in the autumn, gave me an elective after three quarters where my classmates had none. The one course that strongly appealed to me was Professor Karl Llewellyn's Jurisprudence; it was only open to 3rd year students, but I asked for an exemption and he was kind enough to grant it. That, again, was an inflection point: at the end of the course, Llewellyn asked me to work for him as his research assistant. I did that for two years, and it is fair to say that the experience shaped my life, more than work on the *Law Review* or any other law school course. It was also, by the way, my first experience of research using data processing—in the form of an ancient IBM punch card sorter!

Exhibit 1: «IBM Card Sorter» [Source: National Institute of Standards and Technology Digital Collections, Gaithersburg (MD)].

The drift continued. Toward the end of my last law school year, the University of Chicago received a large grant from the Ford Foundation to establish a program in foreign legal studies. It sounded perfect for where my interests centered, but the program's start was to be a year in the future. Once again, I took the risk of asking: might the law school be prepared to start early, and take me as the first student for a «trial run»? And Dean Edward Levi said yes! With that began an intense year. Five mornings a week, for two hours each day, I had tutoring in German law from Professor Max Rheinstein. He also arranged for a young Swiss law professor from Bern, Dr. Kurt Naef, who was spending a year at Chicago working on his Habilitationsschrift, to cover the same material with me each afternoon under Swiss law. To make life complete, I still had one regular law school course each quarter, plus the foreign law course, my work as the *Law Review's* book review editor, and 20 hours a week working with Llewellyn. There were fringe benefits, of course. My German became more fluent, my vocabulary grew, and I learned sleep to be an unnecessary luxury!

The year in Switzerland that followed was marvelous, and under less pressure! Though I attended the lectures at the University of Bern, they were somewhat duplicative: the year of private tutoring with Rheinstein and Naef in German and Swiss law had taught me a good deal of what the lectures covered. But Professor Werner von Steiger, Rheinstein's friend who had urged me to come to Bern, had also arranged for me to serve a clerkship at Bern's Commercial Court. That proved a rich experience. The Court was composed of one professional and two lay judges, who heard a broad range of cases. One was a major trademark dispute between two cigarette companies that attracted Switzerland's big-time trial lawyers. Another, my favorite, was an action for the purchase price of a quantity of cow intestines, bought by the defendant butcher for use as sausage casing and argued by him to be unfit for human consumption. The plaintiff, a gentleman who was both a lawyer *and* a cattle dealer, vigorously argued that the goods had been in perfect condition when delivered. He lost. I had a sense that the plaintiff's having chosen to combine these professions influenced the Court very negatively!

I attended all hearings, learned a great deal from the lawyers' arguments and the judges' questions, and tried to predict how the court would decide. Would it be similar to how I thought a U.S. court would rule? Best of all, the court's clerk, or Gerichtsschreiberin, Fräulein Fuerler, let me try writing first drafts of the Court's judgment—and then with incredible kindness took the time to critique my drafts.

All too soon it was time to return to law school in Chicago; there I spent a year «cutting the academic umbilical», before beginning practice with Baker & McKenzie, briefly in Chicago and then in Zurich.

Exhibit 2: «Obergericht/Handelsgericht Bern» [Source: Wikimedia].

Part II

Revenons à nos moutons. What was it like to practice law sixty years ago? In many ways, indistinguishable from what it is today. Clients wanted to sell goods, or expand their operations, or acquire another company. They required help in puzzling through the tax or exchange control implications of a transaction. Occasionally, a dispute had arisen with a business partner that needed to be resolved, whether amicably or through formal dispute resolution. Sometimes they wanted to get married, or divorced, or adopt a child. Sometimes, albeit rarely in my practice, they found themselves in prison—or wished to avoid the risk of landing there.

Obviously, each and every one of these tasks is instantly recognizable to any newly minted lawyer today. But the changes brought about by six decades are profound. Think of the small things. You want to change a few sentences or re-order paragraphs in a draft agreement? That may mean re-typing all of it—word processing and computers didn't exist. (Though a fortunate few had assistants who were artists at «cutting and pasting»; literally, with scissors and paste, though few today realize that this was the genesis of today's keyboard commands.) If a lengthy document had to be re-typed, that often meant losing a day; only the largest of the New York firms had night-typing staff. London law offices went dark shortly after 5pm, and on the Continent the concept of night or weekend work was all but unknown.

Did a client want to talk? Well, trans-Atlantic telephone service existed, but not in a form recognizable today. There was no international direct dialing

(New York became the first U.S. city to have that in 1970), calls had to be placed with an operator and often went through multiple operators at each end. Sound quality was poor, language skills could be a problem, and the cost? A three-minute call might cost as much as an hour of a lawyer's time.

Exhibit 3: «Photograph of Women Working at a Bell System Telephone Switchboard» [Source: The U.S. National Archives/Wikimedia].

This is but a tiny sample of the hurdles and barriers one encountered and, as I said, these were the small things. Much more important were the barriers, seen and unseen, arising out of language, legal system, and culture. Consider: In the late 1950s, when I studied at the University of Bern, I was the first American to study law there in the history of the University. A decade later, when I came to practice in NYC, I thereby doubled the number of lawyers practicing there trained in both U.S. and Swiss law—there had only been one before my arrival. From the late 1940s, well into the 1960s, lawyers who were bilingual, and had trained in more than one legal system were a rare commodity. There were two obvious constraints: the cost of additional years of education, and the limited job openings for those brave few who nevertheless chose this path. Nevertheless, training in more than one legal system had incalculable virtues when counseling in international transactions. The civil law trained lawyer who could understand what a common law lawyer's «needs» were when drafting a contract—and *vice versa*—brought a genuine benefit to the clients in greater efficiency and a sounder agreement. Similar benefits flowed from cultural sensitivity. A lawyer well sensitive to the other party's background could, time and again, smooth negotiation roadblocks or prevent misunderstandings from threatening to wreck a transaction. The role of the lawyer could take on the qualities of a tour guide through strange legal country. Why were Anglo-American contracts so long, and continental European ones so short? Why did Japanese companies not use lawyers? What is a notary, and why is one so important in some countries?

In time, of course, these issues began to diminish in importance. Successive generations of lawyers and business people in steadily increasing numbers began to travel, and study, and work around the world. And by the early years of this century global lawyers and global networks were well established and no longer a novelty. Schools recruited young lawyers from around the world for their graduate law programs; top law firms in many countries began to place a premium on their hires having an LL.M. from abroad; and multi-national corporations hired legal staff from around the globe. At the same time, global business transactions had begun to increase exponentially in number, complexity and speed. Hand in hand with this came ever increasing layers of regulation and oversight: the modern world was upon us.

Part III

So much for the past; what of the present? While much of the world has changed, the legal world does so at what at best can be described as a very measured pace. One gets the sense that many lawyers and legal educators have looked up, blinked, and seen that we have entered the 21st Century. They do not seem to be aware that almost a fifth of it lies behind us. Like most of humanity, they have picked up the shiny things of our age: the cell phones and tablets and other gadgets, the gig-economy services, the Cloud, the apps, the Internet of Things… and, of course, the new vocabulary that comes with this. Look just below the surface, however, and for a large number of those who practice or teach the law very little has changed. Contracts still get written as if each were a case of first impression. Students sit at their classroom desks and often hear lectures so little changed from year to year that course notes are found for sale online.

It is different for the consumers of legal services, at least for that segment of the market that can afford to pay. This is the segment that is increasingly discontent with what is on offer, and has the muscle to enforce change. And change is, indeed, coming apace! For much of history, in much of the world, one went to law firms for legal advice; today, there are alternatives. Let me note three: the expansion of corporate law departments, the growth of law companies, and technological solutions.

The increase in power wielded by «in house» counsel, and the growth in their number, has been steady. One important factor has been management's need for counsel that fully «understands our business» in a way that outside counsel rarely does. Coupled with that is often the need to have inside lawyers work as an integral part of project teams—a role often totally unfamiliar to outside lawyers, but a role that is increasingly demanded by the needs of modern global business. Finally, there is the inexorable pressure to reduce costs, a pressure that is hardly novel, but is made particularly painful by the opaque system used by most lawyers to charge for their services: the billable hour. It is perhaps ironic that corporate counsel, decades ago, fostered this method of charging to obtain greater clarity, a substitute for the terse «For professional services rendered from __ to__». In the event, it has led to an ever-increasing desire to use internal legal resources with much more predictable, and often lower, costs. The big law firms have hardly disappeared, but their number has shrunk and they are under unrelenting pressure.

Law companies, sometimes called alternative legal service providers, are another rapidly growing source of legal help. The Big Four global accounting firms, some twenty years after *Arthur Andersen*'s *Enron* debacle largely put expansion into the legal sphere on hold, are once again on the march. Their scale, capital resources, global reach, and business sophistication make them formidable entrants into the field. All four of these firms have now availed themselves of the UK's Legal Services Act to establish Alternative Business Structures, allowing them to hold professional, management and ownership roles in UK law firms. Penetration into the US market is significantly more difficult to achieve, but it would be shortsighted to say it is impossible. Are the Big Four thus destined to take over the legal world? It is probably too early to tell. The very dominance of their market position, combined with the unresolved tensions of providing both audit and non-audit services, may well prove limiting factors. It is also possible, however, that other pressures may force some separation of these two service branches. If so, the non-audit part might emerge as an even stronger competitor.

But the world of law companies does not stop with the Big Four. The last few years have seen spectacular proliferation and growth of companies that have rethought how—and importantly by whom—legal services can be delivered. They may not yet be household names, but firms such as *Axiom*, *Consilio*, *Elevate*, *LegalZoom*, *PartnerVine*, *Riverview Law*, *Thomson Reuters* and *UnitedLex* are but a small sample of firms that play a significant role in this market. Whether by offering alternative career paths, or utilizing labor arbitrage, or breaking down tasks into legal and non-legal components, or mixing technology with human labor, or re-thinking the workings of law departments, these firms have been successful in «deconstructing» the approach of the conventional law firm. They have been able to rid themselves of many of the burdens that conventional law firms suffer from: archaic management and ownership structures, cost burdens, inflexibility, and—to be blunt—arrogance!

Exhibit 4: «Avocat au parlement de Paris» [Source: Wikimedia].

And then of course there are the changes being brought by technology. As always with new developments, it may be difficult to distinguish solid achievement from hyperbole, or the fully functional from fashionable trappings. The global proliferation of new «crypto» centers, dubious ICOs, roller-coaster behavior of crypto currencies, an endless stream of conferences on AI or Blockchain or big data…all these tend to spur skepticism in many. But make no mistake: the changes in how legal services can be delivered are real, are accelerating, and are profound. When the bulk of the post-millennial generation enters the legal workforce, much of how law is practiced today will seem as quaint as a busy signal, or a fax machine, or a paper pad and a pencil.

The pressure felt by conventional law firms from the emerging competitors and the advent of technological efficiencies is increasing. Some firms seek to gain strength by bulking up via mergers and acquisitions. Others seek to «flatten» their conventional pyramid structures, reducing their hiring of new graduates and increasing their hiring of more seasoned professionals. Some have looked to build global centers for non-lawyer (or lower cost lawyer) support services. Still others have sought to integrate new technologies into their current workflow so as to work more efficiently and effectively. A brave few have even sought to bring legal operations skills into their practice to truly focus on meeting their clients' needs—how successfully they have done so is still too early to judge.

This all, of course, is in its early stages. The investment of a few millions in a new legal enterprise is still enough to make headlines around the world. The behemoths of Big Law continue to dominate much of the legal world. But the horizon is no longer cloudless, and on a very quiet night one can hear creaking noises as these majestic vessels sail.

What then of legal education? For decades, legal education has been a growth business; throughout the world, the number of law schools has increased with ever-larger numbers of students enrolled. Tuition, in much of the world, has been on a similarly dizzying upward spiral. To take a single example, in just twenty-five years tuition at one well-regarded law school, The University of Michigan, has *tripled*. The arguments for why this should be so are many, and often passionate, but on balance unconvincing. This is particularly so in view of the fact that since the financial crisis of a decade ago, enrollment has been declining. Moreover, as is often the case when the practice world feels threatened by the onslaught of something new, here the new entrants and technology, there is a chorus of complaint that the law schools have failed to ready their graduates for the «new world». (There may be a kernel of truth in the complaint; schools rarely lead the professions in anticipating future needs.)

In any event, declining enrollment has caused belt-tightening at a number of schools around the world, as tuition costs skyrocket and job opportunities—in conventional high-paying jobs—shrink. Very slowly, at least to the eye of the outside observer, some schools are beginning to think hard about what the law job of the future might look like. Will every person who works in providing legal services require the identical, costly, training? Are the traditional skills of a lawyer all still required? Does the «one size fits all» approach in training still make sense? How are the new skills to be learned that legal work increasingly requires? To what degree do licensing requirements make sense: are they essential protection of the public or largely anticompetitive entry barriers? The questions are almost endless, the appetite to tackle them is limited, and it is not easy to see a timely and good resolution within reach. The risk of aimless drift is real.

Exhibit 5: «Driftling» [Source: Wikimedia].

To say that change is extremely difficult is not, however, to say that it is impossible. In all corners of the world a growing number of legal educators have seen and acted on the need to enhance and modify existing curricula to better serve the needs of our time. Where in the middle of the last century law schools began to recognize the need for young lawyers to be financially literate, today the need is seen for training in new skills: an understanding of technology, statistics, and data analytics, to name a few. With this has come the rising recognition of the need for the ability to work on teams, often with those of other disciplines, cultures, languages and legal systems. These efforts are embryonic, but a program such as Michele DeStefano's *LawWithoutWalls*, at the University of Miami School of Law, has been in existence nearly a decade. Through its alumni's proselytizing, and demonstrated results, it has helped launch new educational approaches around the globe.

Further pressure for change comes from the client side. Not through the ancient complaint that graduates are not «practice ready»—they never have been—but by way of ever-stronger nudges that what is wanted are young lawyers who have an understanding of the tools of the modern legal and business world. A «hint» from a giant corporation that it prefers to recruit graduates from schools that supply such training can work wonders. Let me also add the obvious: educators, bar associations, and regulators include a great many wise people in their number. They see the problems and use their very best efforts to bring about badly needed change. But educational institutions and bar bodies are slow moving; efforts to change them are to be applauded and supported, but whether they can timely change is an open question.

Part IV

I have spoken of the providers of legal services, and of those whose task it is to educate those providers. Before I turn to the future, something needs to be said about the consumers of legal services: those who require aid in arranging their legal affairs or in seeking justice. Here there is a harsh dilemma: earlier I mentioned «that segment of the market that can afford to pay». This world of large enterprises and institutions, and affluent individuals, can pay the cost of legal services, even if it does so grudgingly and even as it seeks, often successfully, to reduce such costs. Not so, unfortunately, for most of the world which, simply put, cannot afford access to justice. How large is the number so denied access? It varies from place to place, but it is often thought that *80 percent or more* of those requiring legal help may be unable to obtain it. That figure, or anything like it, is a calamity. A just world cannot afford to shut out the vast majority of its peoples from the instrumentalities of justice. Thus, when I consider the future of law, I do so on the premise that correcting this imbalance must be a prime goal. That will not be an easy haul. In a world where the elimination of hunger, the eradication of lethal diseases, or providing adequate shelter for all, are still distant goals, access to justice may strike some as being of lower priority. It is not; it is an essential need of humanity. But how is it to be met?

It is here the technological revolution that we see before us may hold great hope, though at the moment this is more Zukunftsmusik than practical reality. The number of «consumer-facing» software programs and apps is growing, but still small. It is clear, however, that the explosion of digital data available, coupled with advances in data analytics, machine learning, and the decreasing cost of computer power, opens the door to the realization of genuine change. Equally important, there is enhanced pressure from governments, academics, bar groups, and many others to push change. Some of this, obviously, encounters deeply entrenched resistance: few trade guilds welcome the loss of monopoly power with open arms and lawyers are hardly an exception. It is also important to realize that access for all, in law as in medicine, comes at a price. The chatbot may lack the comfort of human warmth; technology has its own values and these may differ from those of law. Nevertheless, there is significant hope to be found in online dispute resolution, law bots and apps that provide easy and free, or modest-cost, solutions to common legal issues, and much more.

What else might technology hold for the future of law? When I look at the marvels—and, alas, the horrors—of the world around us, I am often amazed by how frequently writers of science fiction whom I admired 70 or even 80 years ago were able to predict today's world. Today's crystal balls seem more clouded. There is a burgeoning body of literature that argues, with varying degrees of plausibility, that the singularity—and with it the robot lawyer—is just around the corner. New cottage industries have sprung up to exploit the possibilities to be found in the new universe of distributed ledger technology. Indeed, cities and even small countries vie to be seen as the centers for this new wisdom. Fortunes have been made—and lost—in the space of days or even hours. No week passes without a series of hackathons, meetups, and conferences devoted to exploring the brave new world of technology. Is there a problem seeking a solution? There is an app for that!

This is not said to belittle or scoff at these developments. They carry with them the excitement of new approaches that could truly change *«the world as we know it»*. Nor should the flashier parts of what we see distract us from the fact that significant, sound, and powerful technological advances have been made in the world of law. Some have been broadly adopted, others are being tried, still others await the slow process most innovation goes through before becoming commonplace. But technology is on the march and, as with all genies, unstoppable once out of the bottle.

And so I come to the final question: what is this future that lies before us? As an old Danish proverb notes, it is difficult to make predictions—especially about the future. Moreover, as a colleague recently noted, perhaps it is simply too early in the game to make good calls on what it all means. Still, I will risk one prediction: The world today, tomorrow, and as far out as imagination can reasonably carry us has and will have a need for «lawyers»: as stewards of justice, in the sense of defenders of the rule of law and officers of the court, and as advocates and trusted advisors. Lawyers will not disappear. As a long-forgotten futurist once noted, we will continue to be the warm, wonderful, caring people we have always been, but there will be fewer of us, and more of our remuneration will be psychic rather than monetary. Why? Because much of what now is lawyer's work will indeed be taken over by machines and their algorithms, and workers whose training and thus cost is significantly less than that of a conventional lawyer. That, however, as you will read in my colleagues' essays that follow, is not cause for despair.

While the world we live in is one of extraordinary complexity and lightning fast technological change, the legal world has responded! Whether it is exploring the impact of AI, or analyzing the new structures of law practice, the changing roles of law departments, Blockchain and its progeny, the training of lawyers for the new age…all this and more is thoughtfully explored below. You will find, as you read, that this is a world in flux: there are no long-standing precedents for resolving disputes around an ICO, no years of experience to draw upon in resolving the ethical dilemmas of an artificial intelligence experiment gone awry. No, the urgent need that has evolved is the ability to extract from the past and extrapolate to the future, with sharp awareness that many of the sharpest questions are not *just* legal. Instead, we often find a need to pull together all the wisdom our collective possesses: from science, ethics, and business sense to behavioral psychology, philosophy, and beyond. A popular view today is that we need more T-shaped lawyers, where, in *Wikipedia*'s description

> *«The vertical bar on the T represents the depth of related skills and expertise in a single field, whereas the horizontal bar is the ability to collaborate across disciplines with experts in other areas and to apply knowledge in areas of expertise other than one's own.»*[1]

And that, perhaps, is where I come around full circle to my own shaping. By accident, fortune both bad and good, and drift, I came to be a T-shaped lawyer—though in my day we probably had this in mind when we said «well-rounded». Should others repeat my path? Most obviously not. But there is much to be said for fostering and encouraging schooling, training, and experience that seek to create multi-skilled generalists. We then will have the beginnings of a workforce best equipped to deal with the world before us—a world, it might be added, that needs all the help it can get! Lawyers are well-known for «making haste slowly»; perhaps for once we can do it differently—and when we put on the «*New Suits*» of our title, we will be able to move with the speed our time requires.

> *«Thus, though we cannot make our sun*
> *Stand still, yet we will make him run.»*
> *– Andrew Marvell, To His Coy Mistress (1681)*

1 Wikipedia, T-shaped skills (January 14, 2019, 1:15 PM), https://en.wikipedia.org/wiki/T-shaped_skills.

Sources of Images and Photographs

IBM Card Sorter
Source: https://goo.gl/t88hHr

Obergericht (Handelsgericht) Bern
Source: https://upload.wikimedia.org/wikipedia/commons/1/14/Obergericht_des_Kantons_Bern.jpg

Bell Telephone Operators
Source: https://commons.wikimedia.org/wiki/File:Photograph_of_Women_Working_at_a_Bell_System_Telephone_Switchboard_(3660047829).jpg

Avocat
Source: https://commons.wikimedia.org/wiki/File:20101019-031-Mus%C3%A9e_du_Barreau_de_Paris.jpg

Drifting
Source: https://upload.wikimedia.org/wikipedia/commons/0/04/Japanese_house_adrift_in_the_Pacific.jpg

PART 1:

WHY DO LAWYERS NEED NEW SUITS?

Professor David B Wilkins and Professor María José Esteban Ferrer[1]

Taking the «Alternative» out of Alternative Legal Service Providers

Remapping the Corporate Legal Ecosystem in the Age of Integrated Solutions

TABLE OF CONTENTS

---

1 David B Wilkins is the Lester Kissel Professor of Law, Vice Dean for Global Initiatives on the Legal Profession, and Faculty Director of the Center on the Legal Profession, Harvard Law School. María José Esteban is a Ramon Llull Contracted Doctoral Professor and a Lecturer of Business Law in the Department of Law at ESADE, and Senior Research Fellow and Co-Director (along with Professor Wilkins) of the Big 4 Project at the Harvard Law School Center on the Legal Profession.

I. Introduction

The word «alternative» is definitely trending in the legal zeitgeist. Beginning with the U.K. Legal Services Act and accelerating through the legal tech startup boom, discussion about the growing importance of Alternative Business Structures (ABS) and Alternative Legal Service Providers (ALSP) has become a cottage industry in the legal press, and increasingly in the legal academy as well. And for good reason. According to a recent report by Thomson Reuters, Georgetown Law Center on Ethics and the Legal Profession, the University of Oxford Said Business School, and Acritas (a leading provider of legal market intelligence)—a collaboration that in and of itself is a powerful indication of how widespread the discussion of this topic has become—revenues from ALSPs grew from USD 8.4 billion in 2015 to USD 10.7 billion in 2017—a compound growth rate of 12,9% (Thomson Reuters et al. 2019). Nor is this growth limited to just a few industries or kinds of alternative services. As the Thomson Reuters report documents, more than one-third of companies, and over fifty percent of law firms, report that they are currently using at least one of the top five functions typically performed by ALSPs. At the same time, all four of the Big 4 accountancy networks – PwC, Deloitte, EY, and KPMG—have received Alternative Business Structure licenses to operate as multidisciplinary practices (MDPs) in the U.K. (Evans 2018a). Given the exponential growth in the number of legal startups over the last few years (Law Geek 2018), it is no surprise that practitioners and pundits alike expect that *«competition from non-traditional services providers will be a permanent trend going forward in the legal services market»* (Altman & Weil 2018, at 1).

And yet, for all of the talk about the growing importance of these «alternatives», the very discourse used to cast these new providers as the harbingers of impending dramatic changes in the market for legal services continues to marginalize and mask their true significance. Specifically, by labeling everything from legal tech startups, to long-established outsourcing and electronic discovery providers, to leading information and technology companies and the Big 4 as «alternatives», the current debate reinforces the prevailing wisdom, as succinctly stated by *John Croft*, President and Co-Founder of Elevate, that *«there is one ‹proper› way of providing legal services (i.e., going to a traditional law firm) and any other way is ‹alternative› (i.e., wrong/new/risky!)»* (Artificial Lawyer 2018).

It is not surprising that the discourse has evolved in this fashion. In medicine, for example, *«authorities have devoted significant energy and resources to making sure that alternatives maintain lesser status, power and social recognition either alongside or within the margins of dominant systems»* (Ross 2012, at 6). Given that lawyers exert even more control over the regulatory system that governs law than doctors do in medicine, it is entirely predictable that incumbents have worked hard to cabin the legitimacy of these potentially

«subversive» elements of the legal ecosystem, to borrow Ross's evocative phrase about medicine, as «alternatives» to «real» law firms. Indeed, even the Merriam-Webster Dictionary defines alternative as *«different from the usual or conventional; existing or functioning outside the established cultural, social, or economic system»*. As a result, the only unifying definition that Thomson Reuters et al. (2017, at 1) could muster in their original report on this phenomenon was to say that ALSPs *«present an alternative to the traditional idea of hiring a lawyer at a law firm to assist in every aspect of a legal matter»*. Tellingly, their 2019 report makes no attempt at all to define what constitutes an ALSP (Thomson Reuters et al. 2019).

In this Chapter, we argue that this characterization of the range of new providers competing for a share of the global corporate legal services market is fundamentally flawed. This is not because we believe that we are about to witness «The Death of Big Law» (Ribstein 2010), or even more dramatically, «The End of Lawyers?» (Susskind 2008). To be sure, some law firms will surely «die», and some lawyers will surely lose their jobs. Nevertheless, we believe that so-called «traditional» large law firms will continue to occupy an important place in the legal ecosystem for the foreseeable future—although as we suggest below, the law firms that prosper will be those that harness what we will define as «adaptive innovation» to respond to the changing needs of their clients (Dolin & Buley 2019). But the ecosystem in which both law firms and a wide range of other providers will compete is one that will increasingly require the integration of law into broader «business solutions» that allow sophisticated corporate clients to develop customized, agile, and empirically verifiable ways of solving complex problems efficiently and effectively. As this ecosystem matures, it will both decenter traditional understandings of how to provide high quality legal services, while at the same time raising critical questions about how to preserve traditional ideals of predictability, fairness, and transparency at the heart of what we mean by the rule of law. Understanding the dynamics of this new ecosystem will be critical for all legal service providers seeking to do business in the new global age of more for less.

Our argument proceeds in three parts. In Part II we briefly locate the current demand for ALSPs within the broader context of the large-scale forces that are reshaping the global economy, and therefore inevitably reshaping the market for corporate legal services in which both «traditional» and «alternative» providers compete. These forces, we argue, are producing a market that favors «integrated solutions» and value-based pricing over traditional domain expertise purchased on a fee for service basis. In Part III, we discuss the implications of this trend for legal service providers of all types. Specifically, we argue that corporate clients will increasingly demand professional services that are «integrated», «customized», and «agile». These demands, in turn, will move what are now considered «alternative» providers such as technology companies, flexible staffing models, and multidisciplinary service firms like the Big 4 to the core of the market, while putting pressure on law firms to articulate how the services that they provide contribute to producing integrated solutions for clients. Finally, in Part IV we conclude by identifying some key challenges that this new corporate legal ecosystem poses for legal education, legal regulation, and the rule of law.

II. From Oligopoly to Global Supply Chains: The Evolution of the Corporate Legal Services Market

The first thing that is misleading about the current discourse that seeks to define a set of «alternatives» to traditional law firms is that it frequently equates «alternative» with «new». Thomson Reuters et al. (2017, at 1) original report on ALSPs is typical. After asserting that *«[t]raditionally, clients looked to law firms to provide a full range of legal and legally related services», the report states that «[t]oday, by contrast, consumers of legal services find themselves the beneficiaries of a new and growing number of nontraditional service providers that are changing the way legal work is getting done» (Id.).* But this way of characterizing the current suite of «alternative providers» fails to acknowledge that clients have been looking for alternative ways to source legal services for more than a century—starting with engaging what we now consider to be «traditional» law firms. This historical context is critical to understanding the contemporary market for corporate legal services and its likely future.

A. ALSP 1.0: The Cravath System

Ironically, what we now consider to be the «traditional» mode of providing corporate legal services was once itself an «alternative». Prior to the turn of the twentieth century, there were no large law firms in the United States, or for that matter, anywhere in the world. The overwhelming majority of lawyers were solo practitioners, or worked in small and loosely affiliated law firms, serving a mix of individual and business clients primarily by appearing in court. To the extent that America's businesses had legal needs, they were serviced either by internal lawyers—for example, *David Dudley Field*, Chief Counsel to the Erie and Lackawanna Railroad, who was one of the most powerful (and arguably corrupt) lawyers in the latter decades of the nineteenth century—or by a mix of solo practitioners and self-help. It was not until the early decades of the twentieth century that lawyers like *Paul Cravath*, *Thomas G. Sherman*, and *John W. Davis* created what has come to be known as the «Cravath System»—formally organized law firms consisting of «associates»

and «partners» hired directly from top law schools, providing a full suite of services to big corporations—that we now take for granted as the norm against which all other service providers should be judged (Galanter & Palay 1991). Moreover, like all «alternatives», the Cravath System was considered subversive by the legal elites of the day. Committed to the traditional ideal of lawyers as «independent professionals» modeled on the self-employed English barrister, as late as the 1930s these elites derisively described Cravath and other firms as «law factories» that were destroying the soul of the legal profession (Galanter & Palay 1991). Yet by the 1960s, large law firms following the Cravath System were universally viewed as the gold standard for providing legal services, attracting top talent, and sitting atop the income and prestige hierarchy of the profession (Smigel 1964).

The Cravath System triumphed because it was exceptionally well «aligned» with other key elements of the evolving corporate ecosystem in which these firms operated (Mawdsley & Somaya 2015). Specifically, Cravath System law firms filled an important space in the rapidly expanding «client market» for corporate legal services, and took advantage of a rapidly increasing «labor market» comprised of law school graduates. With respect to the client market, the first half of the twentieth century witnessed the creation of whole new areas of public and private law governing the conduct of corporations. Yet these entities had little or no internal legal resources to address the problems and opportunities that these new laws and regulations created. As a result, corporate clients established long-term and near-exclusive relationships with their principal outside law firms (Gilson 1990). At the same time, a growing number of new law schools were turning out bright young law school graduates who had been taught to «think like a lawyer» but with virtually no training on how to «be» lawyers, and relatively few options for obtaining employment other than «hanging out a shingle» and learning to practice law on their own (or in poorly paid—or even unpaid—and generally unsupervised apprenticeships with established lawyers). As a result, Cravath System firms had no trouble finding an abundance of bright students from top law schools who were eager to join these organizations, and who were willing to work long and demanding hours for the chance of becoming partners with all of the perquisites that this status credibly conveyed (Wilkins & Gulati 1998).

By the latter decades of the twentieth century, however, this beneficial alignment had begun to unravel. It is this unraveling that has created the space for a new generation of «alternatives» to emerge.

B. ALSP 2.0: The In-House Counsel Movement and Its Progeny

As Cravath System law firms proliferated and became more profitable, it became increasing clear that this now traditional way of providing corporate legal services contained the seeds of its own destruction. The form of this disruption to the corporate ecosystem came in the form of the rapid growth of increasingly sophisticated in-house counsel. Beginning in the 1980s, large companies began hiring General Counsels (GCs) to oversee all of the company's internal and external legal needs (Heineman 2016; Wilkins 2012). At the outset, these internal lawyers cast themselves as a straightforward alternative to traditional law firms on the simple ground that it is cheaper to buy wholesale than retail. But this labor arbitrage argument quickly gave way to a substantive claim that in-house lawyers were actually *better* than their law firm counterparts because they are in a better position to «understand the company's business» than outside law firms, and therefore can better align the legal function to achieve these business objectives. As a result, GCs have increasingly become the company's «chief legal purchasing agent», charged with breaking up the long-standing relationships between companies and law firms and requiring firms to compete for every new piece of significant business. At the same time, these increasingly credentialed and sophisticated internal lawyers now act as the company's «chief legal diagnostician», determining the company's legal needs and how these needs fit into the company's overall strategy and goals—thus becoming a credible alternative to the law firm senior partners who traditionally played this «trusted advisor» role (Gilson 1990; Heineman 2016). This «in-house counsel movement», as the legal scholar *Robert Eli Rosen* has aptly labeled this phenomenon, has significantly altered the balance of power within the legal ecosystem by reducing the information asymmetry between corporate clients and traditional law firms (Rosen 1989; Wilkins 2012).

But as legal costs continued to rise even for companies with large and sophisticated in-house counsel departments, the internal lawyers whose initial claim was that they were a low cost alternative to traditional law firms began to face increasing pressure to find even lower cost options to using the expensive fixed cost resource of full-time in-house lawyers. Not surprisingly, many GCs began turning to the same kinds of «alternatives» that their corporate employers were already using to reduce costs and drive productivity in the business as a whole.

Specifically, general counsels began to experiment with three kinds of alternatives to both traditional law firms and in-house lawyers: a) «outsourcing» and «offshoring» low value and repetitive legal tasks to either captured or independent entities; b) «flexible staffing» solutions, either through «secondments» from law firms or through procuring additional human resources from general or specialized temporary staffing firms; and, c) multidisciplinary professional service firms (MDPs), offering efficiencies of scale and scope by bundling legal services together with accounting, tax, and consulting services. Collectively, these three supplemental resources further shifted the balance of power between in-house counsel and law firms, while at the same time blurring the boundary between these two «traditional» legal service providers.

1. ASLP 2.1: Outsourcing and Offshoring

The increasing integration of the global economy during the last decades of the 20th century led many multinational companies to build global supply chains in order to leverage high-quality low-cost resources and competitive opportunities around the world. As both global trade and the speed and sophistication of information technology increased, these companies increasingly resorted to labor arbitrage as a means of cutting costs by *«replacing higher-waged domestic labor with cheaper foreign labor»* (Smith 2015; Spence 2011). It was not long before GCs began to apply this same logic to legal services.

GE, whose legendary GC *Benjamin Heineman* is widely considered the father of the modern in-house counsel movement, was among the first to pursue this strategy. In 2001, GE established *«an in-house legal office in India, staffed by lawyers, to handle issues relating to its plastics and consumer finance divisions»* (Krishnan 2007, at 9). Many other companies and organizations followed, including law firms like Orrick Harrington & Sutcliff which opened a Global Operations Center in Wheeling West Virginia (*Above the Law* 2012). Many more contracted with the growing number of Indian Legal Process Outsourcing firms (LPOs) offering a variety of basic legal tasks, such as legal transcription and legal coding; legal research services and contract drafting; and patent and trademark searching and mapping as well as patent application drafting (Krishnan 2007). By the end of the first decade of the twenty first century, these LPOs were an established part of the corporate legal ecosystem.

If technology enabled companies to use outsourcing and offshoring to efficiently unbundle their production process, these same forces also created a challenge for in-house counsel in their quest to control legal spend. Since 1938, producing company documents and records in response to an adversary's «discovery» request has been a key component of litigation in U.S. federal courts. Until the turn of the twenty first century, responding to such requests was the province of bleary-eyed associates in large law firms manually inspecting boxes of documents in dingy warehouses. But beginning in the late 1990s, these paper records began to be replaced by electronic ones. In 2001, this trend came to a head with the collapse of Enron which brought down the venerable accounting firm Arthur Andersen, largely on the basis of the failure to properly handle electronic records. As *Regan* and *Heegan* (2010, at 2167) report, *«the complexity and expense of electronic discovery has led a large number of firms to rely on e-discovery vendors and information technology specialty companies as key members of litigation teams»*. The result has been the creation of a cottage industry of technology companies and specialty firms creating software to help companies store, categorize, and retrieve electronics records *(Id.)*. Like LPOs, these «alternative service providers» are now a key part of the corporate legal ecosystem.

2. ALSP 2.2: Temporary staffing

The internet revolution and the imperatives of cost control also brought about the emergence of flexible staffing options. For decades, companies have been turning to temporary and contract workers to cut costs, acquire expertise, and increase flexibility (Weil 2014). As legal budgets tightened, general counsels began experimenting with similar tactics. Their first option was to utilize a resource not typically available to other parts of the company: experienced lawyers «seconded» from top law firms for little or no cost (Williams, Platt & Lee 2015). By the second decade of the twenty first century, secondments had become an important alternative to increasing the size of in-house legal departments—an alternative whose appeal comes in part from the fact that it blurs the boundary between law firms and clients (Classen 2011).

In addition, however, both companies and law firms began turning to a variety of temporary staffing companies to hire contract lawyers as an alternative to bringing on more permanent staff (Davis 2015). Although some used traditional staffing companies offering lawyers as part of their suite of services, a growing number of others began turning to a new breed of providers specifically focused on legal services. Axiom Legal Services is the most prominent of these law focused offerings. Founded in 2000 as a more effective way to do secondments, Axiom quickly distinguished itself from traditional temp agencies by recruiting lawyers with blue chip credentials from top law schools and experience in leading law firms and in-house legal departments who were willing to trade income for a more flexible lifestyle. The goal was to provide clients with the same high-quality service that they expected from their own lawyers and outside law firms without the high price tag associated with these «traditional» providers (Turretinni 2004). Although Axiom self-consciously presented itself as an «alternative» to traditional law firms, it has also taken steps designed to blur the distinction between their model and traditional law firms by reassuring both the lawyers who worked for the company and the clients who hired them that Axiom incorporates all of the best features of these traditional service providers but without the costs. Thus, Axiom boasts that it provides its lawyers *«extensive professional development opportunities including mentorship, memberships to Practising Law Institute («PLI») and other professional organizations, and an integrated network of peers just as they would at any traditional firm»* (Williams, Platt & Lee 2015, at 42).

The competitors who followed Axiom's lead have blurred the boundary between «alternative» staffing and «traditional» law firms even further. Consider, for example, Lawyers on Demand (LOD). LOD was originally established in 2007 by the U.K. law firm Berwin Leighton & Paisner (BLP) as a way of offering its clients former BLP lawyers as temporary staff as an alternative to Axiom and other staffing companies. In 2012, BLP spun out LOD as an independent entity, merging it with AdventBalance, an Australian flexible staffing company that itself was initially started by law firms - Balance Legal,

started by the Australian law firm Freehills in 2008, and Advent Legal, founded the same year by Allen & Overy's head of business development in Sydney - (Lawyers on Demand 2019; Johnson 2016). BLP, however, retained an 80% share in the new entity, which it only sold in 2018 when the firm merged with the U.S. firm Bryan Cave (Evans 2018b). Although LOD is now for the first time not affiliated with a «traditional» law firm, like Axiom, LOD has spawned a number of «virtual law firm» competitors, many of which continue to be owned and/or operated by law firms (Ahmed 2014). The fact that these and other similar flexible staffing organizations are now also an established part of the legal ecosystem further blurs the boundary between these «alternative» providers and traditional law firms.

3. ALSP 2.3: MDPs

In addition to putting pressure on costs, the increasing integration of global markets also created a host of managerial and strategic challenges for companies. As noted by the economist *Michael Spence* (2011, at 56), the disadvantage of going global is that *«global supply chains are inherently more complex»* and difficult to manage and control. Corporate clients therefore began seeking ways to ease such complexities—complexities that frequently involved problems at the intersection of business, strategy, finance, technology, and law. In the 1980s, the Big 5 accountancy networks began rebranding themselves as multidisciplinary professional service firms (MDPs) capable of answering this need by bringing together a variety of professionals in a single firm (Wilkins & Esteban 2018).

By the 1990s, it was clear that the Big 5 intended to make legal services a key part of their multidisciplinary offering. Beginning in Continental Europe and spreading to the U.K., Arthur Andersen began building a legal network, subsequently described by the legal publication *The Lawyer* (2007), as the first step in what Andersen *«hoped would be a globally dominant multidisciplinary partnership (MDP)»*. As they trained their sights on the U.S., however, these new entrants took steps to lessen the distinction between themselves and «traditional» law firms. Thus, in order to minimize the appearance of conflicts of interest with their core auditing business, the four firms that had entered the U.K. legal market began to integrate their affiliated law firms under the umbrella of separately branded legal networks—Andersen Legal, Landwell, Klegal and E&Y Law—all led by «star» lawyers recruited from top law firms (Garth 2004). The strategy behind this shift in organization and recruiting was simple: look as much like a traditional law firm as possible (Garth 2004). As a lawyer working at one of these legal networks succinctly explained: *«if you are competing with a law firm, you've got to look like a law firm»* (Garth & Silver 2002, at 917). Once again, this strategy blurred the boundary between these «alternative» providers and their traditional law firm counterparts.

C. The Empire Strikes Back

In sum, by the first decade of the new millennium, the corporate legal services market had already generated two generations of «alternative» providers: Cravath System law firms, as an alternative to solo practitioners and self-help, and in-house legal departments, as an alternative to «traditional» law firms, along with a variety of new «alternative» providers designed to give GCs additional leverage to reduce their use of laws firms even further. Moreover, the lines between these «alternatives» and the traditional modes of delivery to which they were explicitly or implicitly compared have always been ambiguous. Cravath System law firms utilized a variety of mechanisms—e.g., touting their exclusive lawyer ownership, strong commitment to professional values, and strict norms against commercialism—to mimic the norms and practices of «independent» professionals as a means of protecting themselves from the «law factory» critique (Smigel 1964). Similarly, in-house legal departments frequently organized themselves to look and function like internal law firms, while insisting that general counsels were as much «lawyer statesmen» as the private firm lawyers they sought to supplant (Rosen 1989; Heineman 2016). And the new wave of producers from LPOs to temporary staffing companies to the Big 5 all argued that by employing lawyers who used to work at top law firms (as owners and managers, if not always as direct service providers) that they were really just like «traditional» law firms—albeit without the huge cost structure driving corporate clients to look for «alternatives» in the first place. At the same time, as a result of the growing number of secondments to clients, captured LPOs (such as Orrick's facility in Wheeling West Virginia), «ancillary» businesses offering consulting and other related services (such as Arnold & Porter's APCO Associates and Duane Morris's nine consulting subsidiaries), and increased reliance on temporary staffing models (such as Lawyers on Demand), «traditional» law firms had adopted many of the norms and practices of the «alternative» providers with which they increasingly competed.

Partly as a result of «Big Law's revenge» (Williams, Platt & Lee 2015, at 81), the first few years of the new century were not kind to the newest wave of «alternative» providers. Emboldened by the wave of accounting scandals following the collapse of Enron and the resulting demise of Arthur Andersen, the organized bar moved aggressively to press governments and regulators to place severe limits on the ability of the remaining Big 4 accounting firms to offer legal and other non-audit services to their audit clients (Wilkins & Esteban 2018). At the same time, the booming economy that began by the second quarter of 2002 reduced the urgency for many companies to invest in «alternative» providers, which law firms were successfully able to portray as risky and lacking in quality as compared to the often similar (albeit more expensive) services being offered by law firms. As Axiom's CEO *Mark Harris* lamented in a subsequent interview: *«going up against century-old brands in a tradi-*

tion-bound profession was tough, especially since we were targeting the large enterprise segment [with the suggestion to try] something new and untested» (Henderson & Katz 2013). Ultimately, although clients were interested and intrigued with what the ALSPs had to offer, often there was no sense of urgency to change (Wilkins & Esteban 2018).

The Global Financial Crisis (GFC) fundamentally shifted this dynamic.

III. ALSP 3.0: The GFC and the Integration of Law into Global Business Solutions

In the years since the collapse of Lehman Brothers triggered the GFC, legal commentators have engaged in a fierce debate over whether this signal event heralded a fundamental paradigm shift in the corporate legal services market—one that will inevitably produce «The Death of Big Law» (Ribstein 2010), if not «The End of Lawyers?» (Susskind 2008; Susskind & Susskind 2015)—or whether the GFC is more like the painful but ultimately temporary corrections that the corporate legal market endured in 2001 and 1991. Ten years out, the one thing that is clear is that it is unlikely to be either. The fact that many top firms had their most profitable year ever in 2018 (Bruch 2018a) underscores that we are not on the verge of «the death of big law»—although important law firms have failed, and many others have staved off failure by throwing themselves into the arms of more financially solvent firms willing to take on some (but usually in the end, not all) of their struggling partners and associates (The Practice 2017). And after declining for several years, both applications to law school and legal employment in the United States are once again on the rise—although neither has returned to pre-2008 levels (Sloan 2018). Nevertheless, few in the profession think that we are likely to see the levels of exuberant growth that the corporate legal sector enjoyed in the years before the GFC anytime soon. Instead, the large scale forces that have been transforming the corporate legal services market before the GFC—globalization (notwithstanding the important rise of nationalism and protectionism), the acceleration in the speed and sophistication of information technology (notwithstanding important concerns over privacy and security), and the increased «blurring» of the boundaries that used to separate once distinct products and services (notwithstanding regulatory barriers intended to protect competition and prevent the undermining of public norms)—are continuing to put pressure on all legal service providers to produce what *Ron Dolin* and *Thomas Buley* (2019) have aptly called «adaptive innovation» that responds to the demands of the new global age of more for less (Wilkins 2014).

One can see this process of adaptation with respect to each of the «alternative» models that companies began turning to in the years leading up to the GFC.

A. From Outsourcing and Offshoring to Nearshoring and Partnerships

In the years following the GFC, the LPO industry has worked hard to overcome the skepticism with which some clients and law firms still regarded it as a result of its marginal status as an «alternative» service provider. Thus, LPO providers actively lobbied bar officials to clear ethical issues, while instituting rigorous controls taken from the business world such as Six Sigma and ISO certification to reassure end users and regulators about quality, confidentiality, and security concerns (Deloitte 2017; Thomson Reuters 2015). This quest for legitimacy has undoubtedly been aided by the fact that the industry is no longer comprised primarily of small independently owned companies in India, but increasingly consists of captured LPOs owned or under the control of multinational companies and large law firms. The fact that many of these facilities have recently been partly or completely «nearshored» to low cost locations in the U.S. or Europe that are both closer to clients and perceived to be safer has made it even easier for what were once considered radical «alternatives» to be viewed by most clients and law firms as a taken for granted part of the legal supply chain.

Indeed, these now mainstream players are finding themselves increasingly in competition with an even newer breed of technology firms, ranging from legal tech start-ups to established technology giants. As indicated above, there has been an explosion in the number of legal tech start-ups since 2008. Many of these firms are now seeking to leverage technology developments to offer some of the same services offered by LPOs.

One can see this overlap by examining the descriptions in the scholarly literature and popular press of the types of services offered by legal tech companies. Exhibit 1 presents an analysis of the types of services offered by technology companies based on a review conducted by one of us for the International Bar Association of 280 academic papers and professional reports, with particular emphasis on 19 of those documents that addressed the types of services offered by technology companies in the aftermath of the GFC (Esteban 2017). The percentage of total documents citing particular legal services offered by these ALSP provides a rough proxy of the salience of these services in the legal community. As Exhibit 1 demonstrates, the majority of the services described are similar to what was typically sent to LPOs and e-discovery companies in the period prior to the GFC. Software solutions now actively compete with labor arbitrage as the primary mechanism for both companies and law firms to reduce legal costs.

Exhibit 1: Categories of asset-based services provided by ALSPs.

Not surprisingly, in a software-driven competition, established technology companies are likely to have a significant advantage. These companies have the kind of financial and technology resources, brand recognition, and market experience in developing and implementing software solutions that help companies and law firms feel confident that they can deliver on their promises. As a result, companies such as Thomson Reuters, Lexis Nexis, and Wolters Kluwer have become important players in providing software solutions to companies and law firms. But these giants are also competing with a range of legal start-up companies which seek to differentiate themselves from these more established companies by focusing on new or emerging technologies in artificial intelligence and machine learning, by demonstrating greater flexibility and speed in addressing client requirements, and by offering lower costs.

All of these software solutions further blur the line between «alternative» and «traditional» providers. Because software is embedded into the user's existing infrastructure, legal tech companies are as much partners with law firms and in-house legal departments as they are substitutes for these «traditional» services. Indeed, in recent years, law firms such as Clifford Chance (through its new innovation unit Clifford Chance Advance Solutions) and Littler (through its multiple Casesmart products) have begun developing their own software, which they use to streamline their own practices and/or sell directly to clients (Hernandez 2018; Sawnhey 2016).

Oracle's recent entry into the legal managed services business shows just how interconnected all of these providers have become. On January 7, 2019, Oracle announced that it was launching a global «legal practice management system» targeted to law firms in the U.K., with the intention of expanding to the U.S. and other legal markets (Legal Insider 2019a). Oracle's offering is meant to compete directly with similar products currently offered by Thomson Reuters by bringing, in the words of a managing partner who has been briefed on the new product, *«Oracle's cloud and AI technology into it, which makes it a rather different proposition»* (*Id.*). Although the tools Oracle will bring to this service are new, the company's interest in applying its expertise in enterprise management planning to the legal market is not. In 2002, Oracle teamed up with a legal tech start-up to create an early version of a similar system for Clifford Chance, which the global law firm still uses today (*Id.*). That system has now been spun off in a separate company called Aderant, which now actively competes with Thomson Reuters—and now Oracle—in selling practice management systems to law firms. When one adds to this tangled history the fact that Oracle formally launched its new product at an event co-sponsored by PwC, and that in 2015, Oracle experimented with a partnership with the LPO giant Elevate Services to bring another version of managed services to the legal market, it becomes increasingly difficult to draw any sharp distinction between these various participants in the legal ecosystem.

Indeed, the day after its former partner Oracle announced its latest entry into the managed services market, Elevate announced that it had purchased Halebury, a flexible staffing company in the U.K. specializing in providing temporary lawyers for in-house legal departments, but which has increasingly been partnering with law firms such as Hogan Lovells (Legal Insider 2019b). Significantly, the combined firm is now eligible to convert to an «alternative business structure» that will allow it to provide *«both in-house legal teams and law firms with a 360 degree service offering spanning talent, resourcing, consulting, technology, and managed services»* (*Id.*). Coming on the heels of its acquisition of legal AI technology and consulting firm Lex Predict, and contract lifescycle management company Sumati Group, it is clear that Elevate is now poised to both collaborate—and compete—with «traditional» law firms and legal departments in a way that will further blur the boundary between these increasingly linked participants in the legal ecosystem.

The same can be said of UnitedLex's recent outsourcing deals with DXC Technologies and General Electric. Rather than simply outsourcing specific legal tasks, DXC has partnered with Unitedlex to create a unified legal team in which both organizations jointly manage the legal function—including 150 DXC lawyers becoming UnitedLex employees, and 250 Unitedlex lawyers, engineers, and project managers dedicated to supporting DXC globally. The goal, according to DXC's general counsel, is to create a *«One Department mindset...»* providing *«seamless legal services to the business client, regardless of whether the team member is from DXC or Unitedlex»* (Salopek 2017). In 2018, UnitedLex entered into a similar arrangement with GE, which eventually resulted in GE's Executive Counsel and Director of Legal Support Solutions joining UnitedLex as Senior Vice President and Deputy General Counsel

(Kovalan 2018; Spezio 2018). This deal, in turn, follows on the heels of a similar arrangement between GE and PwC in which the Big 4 accounting firm hired more than 600 GE accountants, lawyers, and tax advisors who will continue to do GE's tax work, but who will also help PwC develop tax products that can be marketed to other PwC clients (International Tax Lawyer 2017). As the International Tax Reporter commented: *«The GE-PwC merger sets a bold new precedent for the relationship between big business and law firms»* creating a *«hybrid model in where the company gets a team they know and can trust, supplemented by the capacities of the Big 4»* (*Id.*). In addition to blurring the boundaries between «traditional» internal lawyers and «outsourced» legal resources, all three of these deals underscore how in-house legal departments, LPOs, and the Big 4 are all both competing—and cooperating—in the same market.

UnitedLex's most recent deal with LeClaireRyan further underscores this trend towards what business scholars call «cooptition»—simultaneous cooperation and competition—in the new legal services ecosystem (Wilkins 2010). In June 2018, the outsourcing firm and the AmLaw 200 law firm announced the creation of ULX Partners, which they described as *«a strategic business platform designed to empower a ‹constellation› of law firms with market-leading technology, new sources of capital, project and knowledge management, process innovation, and recourse management to deliver maximum value to clients and improve law firm economics»* (UnitedLex 2018). Lauded by UnitedLex's CEO *«as the most disruptive to the practice and business of law since lawyers began billing their time»,* the venture is intended to be a substitute for prior attempts at *«outsourcing various law firm operations and law-firm owned hybrid staffing options»* which, according to UnitedLex which itself spent the first 10 years of its existence selling exactly these kinds of solutions, *«have largely failed to address urgent client needs and do not ensure that law firms have the right economic structure and high impact training to evolve and thrive in a legal 2.0 environment»* (*Id.*).

Whether ULX Partners will be able to deliver on these ambitious promises, of course, remains to be seen. The fact that LeClaireRyan has been shedding partners since the announcement was made underscores that the success of this and other hybrid models is far from guaranteed (Tribe 2019). What is already clear, however, is that the line between LPOs and traditional law firms is becoming far less clear than the «alternative» label would suggest. The fact that the most recent Thomson Reuters et al. (2019, at 2) report claims that *«about one third of law firms say that they plan to establish their own ALSP affiliate within the next five years»* is certain to blur this boundary even further.

The same trend can be seen in the market for «alternative» staffing arrangements.

B. From Temporary Staffing to Agile Work

The UnitedLex and PwC outsourcing deals highlight the extent to which both companies and law firms are looking for flexibility in the way that they manage their workforce. Although outsourcing tasks—or even personnel—is one way to accomplish this goal, both in-house legal departments and law firms are increasingly looking for ways to create flexibility and encourage creativity among the lawyers and staff who remain. Once again, the software revolution is driving these «traditional» legal service providers to adopt norms and practices pioneered in the «alternative» world of technology.

The increasing prevalence and sophistication of software solutions has done more than decrease the utility of standard labor arbitrage strategies to reduce costs. It has also spurred a revolution in the way that companies manage and deploy human capital. This revolution began in 2001 when a group of software engineers issued «The Agile Manifesto» calling for software development to be redesigned around twelve principles encouraging continuous improvement, collaboration, adaptation, team efforts, and rapid delivery of valuable products and services (Agile Manifesto 2001).Today, this agile approach to project management is now widely used by leading software development companies such as Cisco, Microsoft, Spotify, and Salesforce, and is increasingly being adopted by these and other companies for projects that are not software related (Legal Trek 2016; Leslie 2015). And, since 2008, agile project management is increasingly being applied to legal services (Behnia 2011).

Not surprisingly, in-house legal departments have been the first to embrace this new way of working, creating small, self-governing, cross-functional teams to solve problems and drive results for clients (Bell 2018). A key part of this process is creating flexible staffing and collaborative approaches that allow teams to access expertise and technology from both inside and outside of the company. In response to this trend, companies like Axiom that traditionally specialized in providing temporary staffing for specific projects as a substitute for either internal hiring or engaging external law firms, are increasingly entering into long-term partnerships such as Axiom's recent five year deal with Johnson & Johnson to provide contract management support across the company's entire global platform. Although *«[l]abor arbitrage is an element of this second phase of disaggregated legal delivery»*, the core of Axiom's new value proposition is to *«leverage technology and processes to create ‹agile› workforces that are well-suited to the unpredictable, on-demand, and geographically disparate needs of their customers»* (Cohen 2016). In addition to blurring the boundary between «in-house» and «alternative» providers, this trend also underscores the growing interdependence of «staffing» and «technology» in an agile working environment—a confluence that is likely to blur the boundary between «traditional» and «alternative» providers even further.

Although behind their counterparts in corporate legal departments, a growing number of law firms are also embracing agile approaches to legal work. Responding both to the practices of their technology clients and to the increasingly urgent demand by millennials for greater flexibility and work-life balance, law firms such as Orrick are expressly embracing a version of agile work. Stating that the *«[o]ne size-fits-all approach to legal careers is outdated,»* Orrick promises an «agile» work environment including *«working from home, flexible work arrangements (FWA), job sharing, distinctive parental leave benefits, and even opportunities to work remotely in a location where Orrick does not have an office»*—further promising that *«[w]e don't ask you to make a choice between «agile» working and partnership consideration»* (Orrick 2019).

Once again, like the promises made by UnitedLex, whether either in-house legal departments or law firms will be able to create a truly agile work environment remain to be seen. What is clear, however, is that these agile work practices are further blurring the boundary between «alternative» providers like Axiom and the practices of «traditional» law firms and legal departments.

The evolution of the Big 4's legal model since 2008 reveals a similar dynamic.

C. From MDPs to Integrated Solutions

In the years following the collapse of Arthur Andersen and the passage of the Sarbanes-Oxley Act of 2002 (SOX) and other legislation around the world seeking to limit the Big 4's ability to deliver non-audit services to their audit clients, the near universal consensus among professionals and pundits was that the *«[a]ccountancy firms drive in the legal arena is dead»* (Economist 2003). As the *The Economist* went on to explain, not only did this legislation prevent the Big 4's legal arms from offering services to their *«huge client base»,* but *«law firms have themselves become more global in recent years and many do not need the accounting giants' international reach»* (*Id.*). In the immediate aftermath of SOX, the Big 4 appeared to confirm that they had abandoned their efforts to become important players in the market for legal services, publicly declaring that they were unwinding their legal networks.

Notwithstanding these public pronouncements and some initial actions to disband their legal arms, however, over the last decade the Big 4 have quietly rebuilt their legal networks to the point where they are now larger than they were in 2002. As we have documented elsewhere, by exploiting gaps in the regulatory structure that allow them to sell legal and other non-audit services to companies that they do not audit, and taking advantage of their global reach to grow their legal practices in countries where regulatory restrictions on legal practice are either weak or nonexistent—or where regulatory reforms increasingly allow multidisciplinary practice—the Big 4 legal networks now have a significant presence in every important legal market in the world with the notable exception of the United States (Wilkins & Esteban 2018). Nor are the legal services delivered by these networks confined to tax. Although tax-related advisory services remain an important cornerstone, the Big 4 legal networks are now delivering services in a broad range of legal fields, including premium practices such as finance and M&A, and fast growing ones such as compliance and employment law (*Id.*).

Most importantly, unlike when they entered the legal market in the 1990s, the Big 4 are no longer seeking to brand themselves as «traditional» law firms by mimicking the practices of their Big Law counterparts. Instead their goal is to create a new kind of professional service that integrates law into global business solutions (*Id.*). Thus, rather than establishing free standing legal networks, each of the large accountancy firms have aggressively moved to integrate their legal offering with their other advisory services to build on their strong capabilities in technology, strategy, project management, and global service delivery. This fully integrated MDP model is now legal in the United Kingdom, where each of the Big 4 have now been granted an «alternative business structure» license (Packel 2018).

In championing this new model as an «alternative» to traditional law firms, the Big 4 are following a more general trend toward «integrated solutions» in professional services. Since the 1990s, some of the world's leading companies have been providing integrated solutions rather than selling «standalone» products or services (Davies et al. 2006). For example, IBM, a pioneer of this business model, increased revenues by 50% thanks to its Global Solutions unit (Miller et al. 2002). Originally IBM sold computers as integrated systems. By the mid-1980s, however, specialized firms began to supply modular components. This gave big clients, such as American Express, the buying power to lead the integration of components into a system that would solve their unique business requirements. As *Davies et al.* (2007, at 184) reports: *«Rather than mirroring this trend towards vertical disintegration by turning IBM into a group of individual component suppliers, Louis Gerstner, IBM's CEO, executed a strategy in 1993 to build on the firm's broad base of vertically-integrated capabilities by focusing on the provision of complete integrated solutions for a customers' computing and service requirements».*

The actions of the Big 4 over the last few years make it clear that they are intent on developing a similar set of capabilities. Deloitte's investments in legal technology are illustrative of this trend. In 2014, Deloitte purchased ATD Legal, one of the few providers of managed document review services in Canada. In 2016, they followed with a purchase of Conduit Law, a provider of outsourced lawyers ranked by the Financial Times as one of the *«Most Innovative North American Law Firms»*. Most recently, Deloitte formed a strategic alliance with Kira Systems, which has been described by the company's chief

executive, Noah Waisberg, as *«the largest professional services AI [artificial intelligence] deployment anywhere, period»* (Legal Insider 2016).

But the Big 4 are investing in more than legal technology. Exhibit 2 highlights the Big 4's multiple alliances with leading technology companies disclosed on their websites by May 2017. As Deloitte makes clear on its website, these alliances are meant to co-create solutions to help clients solve *«complex challenges [...] by combining leading technology with [...] time-tested business acumen and strong industry relationships»* (Deloitte 2019a).

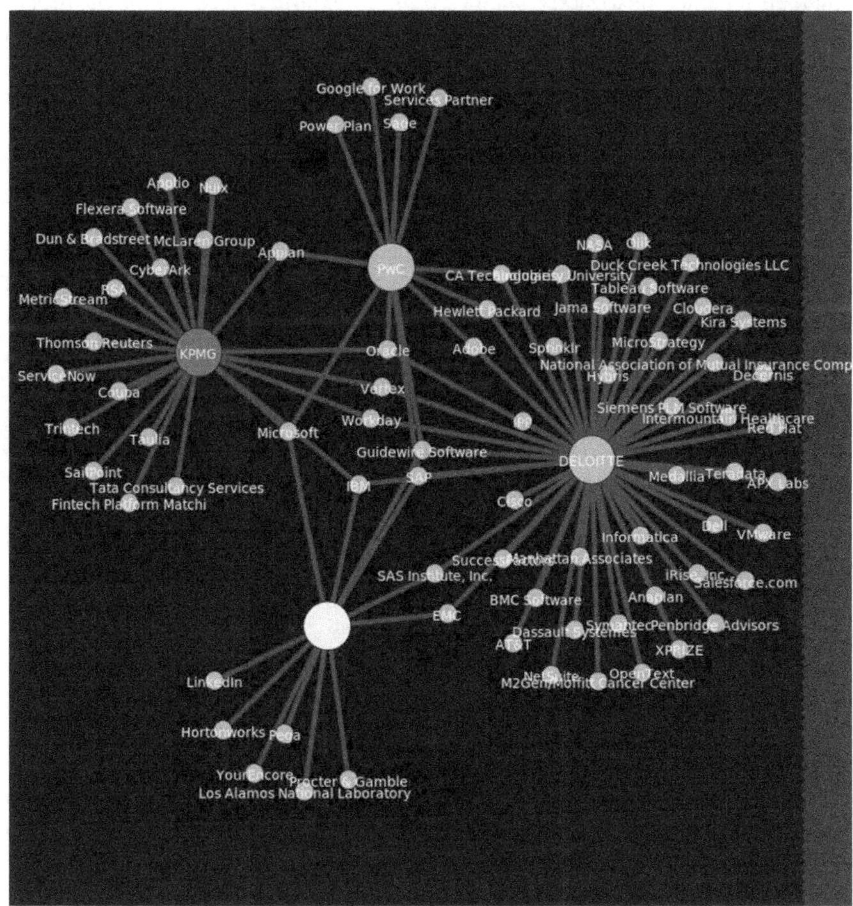

Exhibit 2: Big 4 tech strategic partnerships and alliances [Source: Developed from PwC, Deloitte, EY and KPMG corporate Websites, May 4, 2017].

Nor is technology the only area where the Big 4 are building capacity to deliver integrated solutions. Since 2014, the Big 4 have aggressively expanded their capabilities in strategy consulting, on-demand talent models, digital applications, cyber security, and crisis services. All of these services are increasingly relevant to global companies seeking to deal with complex problems at the intersection of law, business, strategy, and technology, such as data privacy and cyber security, anti-bribery and corruption, and safety and catastrophic risk.

At the same time, the Big 4 are moving aggressively to acquire or develop similar complementary competencies in law. Thus, in 2018 Deloitte launched Deloitte Legal Management Consulting designed to assist companies in helping their legal teams to *«keep pace with the commercial needs of the business»* while assisting them *«to do more with the same or fewer resources»* (Deloitte 2018a). Deloitte followed this launch by forming a strategic alliance with U.S. immigration law firm Berry Appleman & Leiden, which will allow it to help global clients with immigration issues around the world, including in the U.S. market (Deloitte 2018b).

The remainder of the Big 4 have been equally active. Thus, PwC announced in 2017 that it was launching ILC Legal, a U.S. law firm, to help U.S. clients on international matters, as well as Flexible Legal Resources, providing flexible staffing solutions (Packel 2018). At the same time, PwC moved to beef up its own managed legal services business by poaching Clair Hirst, a senior manager from Axiom (Global Legal Post 2017). Ms. Hirst is expected to work closely with the two partners who head up PwC's New Law services—partners that the accounting giant poached the year before from Radiant Law, an awarding winning boutique law firm where they led sales and client delivery (*Id.*). And, in 2018 KPMG hired former King & Wood Mallesons Global Managing Partner Stuart Fuller to launch its Legal Operations and Transformation Services (LOTS) unit, which aims to *«transform the in-house legal function for a more complex future»* (KPMG 2018; Dolor 2018). That same year, EY Legal took over Riverview Law, a managed legal service provider in the U.K. previously funded by the global law firm DLA Piper (EY 2018). To further expand legal services offerings globally, in 2019 EY announced an agreement with Thomson Reuters for the acquisition of Pangea3 – an Indian pioneer in the LPO space which had been acquired by Thomson Reuters in 2003 (Adams 2010; EY 2019).

Not surprisingly, these and other similar moves have finally gotten the attention of «traditional» large law firms, most of which until recently had bought into the prevailing wisdom that the Big 4 were no longer a threat to their market position after the accounting scandals in 2001, particularly in the U.S. where multidisciplinary practice is still formally prohibited (Derbyshire 2018). The fact that the Big 4's integrated solutions model taps into the frequent complaints by general counsels that law firms do not provide commercially relevant advice has undoubtedly contributed to this response. As a recent study by LexisNexis in partnership with the Judge Business School at University of Cambridge underscores, although *«clients repeatedly empha-*

sized that they look to law firms for solutions to business problems, ... forty percent noted that senior partners of their law firms appeared to lack more than a basic knowledge of their business [...] and seventy-five percent mentioned they get little help from law firms when analyzing the complex portfolio of legal work given to them» (LexisNexis 2017). Such sentiments are likely to continue to raise the visibility of the Big 4's legal offerings, which already occupy four of the top five spots in a recent ranking of «alternative service providers» among global general counsels (Packel 2018).

But these same trends underscore how misleading it is to characterize the Big 4's integrated solutions model as an «alternative» to traditional legal services. Just as we are seeing traditional outsourcing and flexible staffing companies blur the boundaries between «alternative» and «traditional» legal services to meet the changing needs of global clients, the Big 4 are building their capacity to provide integrated solutions by acquiring, and partnering with, other legal service providers, including traditional law firms and legal departments. For example, in 2019, Deloitte Legal established an alliance with employment law firm Epstein Becker Green with the goal– as boldly stated by *Piet Hein Meeter*, Deloitte Global Managing Director, Deloitte Legal – of *«bridg[ing] a critical gap in the U.S. market to support clients who require a global solution for employment law and workforce management issues»* (Deloitte 2019b). As PwC's Chairman *Dennis Nally* succinctly put it: *«The idea that as a professional services network we would house all of those capabilities within PwC is a model that's really outdated»* (PwC 2015).

At the same time, many «traditional» law firms are responding by acquiring or creating consulting and advisory networks designed to build multidisciplinary capacity of their own. For example, in 2015, DLA Piper International LLP entered the field of corporate and financial advisory services by incorporating Noble Street Limited in the United Kingdom. While Noble Street and DLA Piper «operate as separate businesses», the focus is on cross-selling financial and consulting services to the law firm's strong international client base (Legal Business 2015; Noble Street 2016). The launch of Noble Street follows a wave of international law firms entering the corporate advisory field since 2010, thus acknowledging clients' demand for external legal advisors who *«understand their issues, focus on delivering solutions to their challenges and share the risks with them»*—as boldly claimed by the law firm Bird & Bird (2015) on the occasion of the creation of a joint venture with ASE Consulting.

The fact that several of the largest and most influential global law firms are now advertising themselves in ways that are indistinguishable from the Big 4's self-presentation is just one more example of the kind of «adaptive innovation» that at least some big law firms are using to respond to the challenges of the new corporate ecosystem. As *Dolin* and *Buley* (2019) argue, even in an age of increasing disruption from «alternative» providers, traditional law firms continue to offer several important advantages in the marketplace. Specifically, *Dolin* and *Buley* point out that large law firms continue to serve an important purpose in providing the kind of specialized services and flexible capacity that led to the original success of the Cravath System, as well as the kind of reputational bonding that mitigates search and monitoring costs particularly in high stakes matters (*Id.*). Given these advantages, it is not surprising, as *Dolin* and *Buley* predict, that we *«see Big Law starting to incorporate disruptive methodologies and migrate their [virtual practice rules] to adapt to changing market demands such as efficiency and evidence based analysis»* (*Id.*).

Whether or not these efforts are successful, they underscore that the move toward an integrated solutions model is no longer an «alternative»—and therefore marginal—part of the legal ecosystem. Instead, it is increasingly clear that in 2019 and beyond, the entire legal ecosystem, including global multidisciplinary professional service firms, established and start-up legal technology companies, international legal talent platforms, top legal process outsourcers, in-house legal departments, and many leading law firms are all focusing their growth strategies on the development of integrated solution platforms which will allow them to increase the value of the legal services they provide. The fact that a growing number of companies now have «legal operations specialists» whose express charge is to drive greater efficiency and rationality in the corporate legal services market—and that these specialists are now coming together, along with a variety of innovation professionals from law firms and «alternative» providers, in the Corporate Legal Operations Consortium (CLOC) to share best practices and create common standards—will undoubtedly accelerate this trend even further (Bruch 2018b; DeStefano 2018).

To be sure, it is far from certain that any of the participants in this increasingly complex ecosystem—let alone all of them—will be able to deliver on their promise of innovation and change. As a subtitle of a 2018 report on «The State of Law Firm Innovation» indicates, *«[a] recent survey shows law firms understand the importance of innovation but are not supporting it enough»* (Parnell 2018). Those attempting to move from «innovation» to a fully integrated solutions model for the delivery of corporate legal services are likely to find the task even more challenging. As we have suggested previously, the Big 4 continue to face important challenges in successfully deploying this model in their core tax and consulting businesses, challenges that raise legitimate questions about whether they will be able to translate whatever they have learned in those fields to the even more complex and regulated terrain of the market for corporate legal services (Wilkins & Esteban 2016). And while CLOC has made great strides, much of the organization's promise to rationalize the legal services market remains unfulfilled (Bruch 2018b). Indeed, IBM's recent problems internally adapting the digital transformation that it espouses for its clients underscores just how difficult it is even for a company formally committed to the integrated solutions model to adopt it fully (Andriole 2017,

Andriole 2018). Nevertheless, even if no legal service provider—whether «traditional» or «alternative»—is able to completely transform itself into an integrated solutions provider, the trends documented in this Chapter are already making this approach to delivering legal services an increasingly important part of the ecosystem. We therefore conclude with a few thoughts about what this evolution might mean for traditional understandings of legal education, legal regulation, and the rule of law.

IV. Conclusion

In a prescient article published in 2002, the American legal scholar *Robert Eli Rosen* hypothesized that changes in the corporate market for legal services were turning both in-house counsel and outside firms into just another «consultant» whose primary task is to integrate legal knowledge into cross-functional teams to better achieve business objectives (Rosen 2002). The movement toward an «integrated solutions» model of the corporate legal ecosystem described in this Chapter will undoubtedly further accelerate this trend. Moreover, it is also clear that this ecosystem involves more than just the «traditional» legal service providers *Rosen* envisioned—and indeed, more than just lawyers. And yet, our current tools for understanding this ecosystem not only divide the world between «traditional» and «alternative» legal service providers, but even more insidiously, between «lawyers» and «non-lawyers».

This framework obscures key challenges that the integration of law into global business solutions poses for core aspects of the «traditional» model of legal services that will not—and should not—be fully disrupted. Although artificial intelligence and machine learning will surely replace some legal jobs, the delivery of corporate legal services is likely to remain a human capital intensive endeavor for the foreseeable future. But these humans must be taught to work effectively with new technologies, in environments where lawyers and other professionals and knowledge workers (who we should stop calling «non-lawyers») must learn to collaborate effectively to deliver value to increasingly sophisticated and cost conscious clients. To focus only on lawyers for the moment, this will require law schools to teach a broad range of «complimentary competencies»—technology and data fluency, business literacy, cross cultural adaptability—along with core legal knowledge and skills to their graduates (Heineman, Lee & Wilkins 2014). Similarly, regulators must move beyond categorical imperatives and blanket invocations of «core values» rhetoric to create «evidence-based regulation» that actually examines the merits of both «traditional» and «alternative» delivery models—and the growing number of hybrid models that incorporate elements of both (Chambliss 2019).

But this does not mean that the «core values» of the legal system should be abandoned entirely. To the contrary, in an era in which the rule of law is under increasing threat around the world—including in the Global North, where allegiance to law and legal institutions has always been presumed robust—it is imperative that we cultivate a legal ecosystem that encourages powerful global companies not only do what is «legal» but what in the end is fundamentally «right» in a world in which these private actors exert as much if not more influence as public governments on a wide range of issues at the heart of human flourishing (Heineman 2017). If we are not ready to fully deregulate the ride hailing market in response to disruptive companies like Uber and Lift, we certainly should not leave the predictability, fairness, and individual rights at the heart of the rule of law solely to market forces.

Needless to say, these are large and difficult issues far beyond the scope of this Chapter. Instead, we end with the modest hope that our analysis will contribute to a new framework for addressing these vital questions. A framework in which we stop viewing the new participants who are reshaping the market for corporate legal services as «alternatives» to some mythical «golden age» when «traditional» law firms defined the epitome of service and professionalism (Galanter 1995). A framework, we hope, in which every legal service provider will be evaluated on their ability to contribute to the creation of real solutions for clients, while also understanding their obligation to help to preserve the core values of the rule of law that creates the infrastructure that makes every solution, private or public, possible.

V. Bibliography

A. Hard Copy Sources

Davies, Andrew, Brady, Tim & Hobday, Michael, *Charting a path toward integrated solutions*, 43 MIT Sloan Management Review 39 (2006).

Davies, Andrew, Brady, Tim & Hobday, Michael, *Organizing for solutions: Systems seller vs. systems integrator*, 36 Industrial Marketing Management 183 (2007).

Galanter, Marc, *Lawyers in the Mist: The Golden Age of Legal Nostalgia*, 100 Dickenson Law Review (1995–1996) 549.

Galanter, Marc & Palay, Thomas, Tournament of Lawyers: The Transformation of the Big Law Firm (University of Chicago Press, 1991).

Garth, Bryant G & Silver, Carole, *The MDP Challenge in the Context of Globalization*, 52 Case W. Res. L. Rev. 903 (2002).

Garth, Bryant G, *Multidisciplinary Practice After Enron: Eliminating a Competitor But Not the Competition*, 29 Law & Soc. Inquiry 591 (2004).

Gilson, Ronald J, *The Devolution of the Legal Profession: A Demand Side Perspective*, 49 MD. L. REV. 869 (1990).

Heineman, Ben W Jr, *The inside counsel revolution: resolving the partner-guardian tension* (ABA, 2016).

Krishnan, Jayanth K, *Outsourcing and the Globalising Legal Profession*, 48 Wm. & Mary L. Rev. 2189 (2007).

Mawdsley, John & Somaya, Deepak, *Strategy and Strategic Alignment in Professional Service Firms*, *in* Oxford Handbook of Professional Service Firms 213–37 (Empson, Laura, Muzio, Daniel, P. Broschak, Joseph & Hinings, Bob, eds., Oxford University Press, 2015).

Miller, Danny, Hope, Quentin, Eisenstat, Russell, Foote, Nathaniel & Galbraith, Jay, *The problem of solutions: Balancing clients and capabilities*, 45 Business Horizons 3 (2002).

Regan, Milton C Jr & Heegan, Palmer T, *Supply Chains and Porous Boundaries: The Disaggregation of Legal Services*, 78 Fordham L. Rev. 2137 (2010).

Ribstein, Larry E, *The Death of Big Law*, 2010 WIS. L. REV. 749 (2010).

Rosen, Robert Ely, *The In-House Counsel Revolution,* Indiana Law Review (1989).

Rosen, Robert Ely, *We're All Consultants Now: How Change in Client Organizational Strategies Influences Change in the Organization of Corporate Legal Services*, 44 Ariz. L. Rev. 637 (2002).

Ross, Anamaria L, The Anthropology of alternative medicine (Berg Publishers, 2012).

Smigel, Erwin O, The Wall Street Lawyer: Professional Organization Man? (Free Press of Glencoe, 1964).

Spence, Michael, The Next Convergence. The Future of Economic Growth in a Multispeed World (Farrar, Straus and Giroux, 2011).

Susskind, Richard, The End of Lawyers? Rethinking the Nature of Legal Services (Oxford University Press, 2008).

Susskind, Richard & Susskind, Daniel, The Future of the Professions. How Technology Will Transform the Work of Human Experts (Oxford University Press, 2015).

Weil, David, The Fissured Workplace: Why Work Became so Bad for So Many and What Can be Done to Improve it (Harvard University Press, 2014).

Wilkins, David B, *Team of Rivals? Toward a New Model of the Corporate Attorney-Client Relationship,* 78 Fordham L. Rev. 2067 (2010).

Wilkins, David B, *Is the In-House Counsel Movement Going Global? A Preliminary Assessment of the Role of Internal Counsel in Emerging Economies*, 2012 Wis. L. Rev. 251 (2012).

Wilkins, David B, *Making Global Lawyers: Legal Practice, Legal Education, and the Paradox of Professional Distinctiveness, in* Tribuna Plural La Revista Cientifica, Acto Internacional, Global Decision making (Royal European Academy of Doctors, 2014).

Wilkins, David B & Esteban-Ferrer, María J, *The Integration of Law into Global Business Solutions: The Rise, Transformation, and Potential Future of the Big Four Accountancy Networks in the Global Legal Services Market*, 43 Law & Soc. Inquiry 981 (2018).

Wilkins, David B & Gulati, G Mitu, *Reconceiving the Tournament of Lawyers: Tracking, Seeding, and Information Control in the Internal Labor Markets of Elite Law Firms*, 84 Va. L. Rev. 1581 (1998).

Williams, Joan C, Platt, Aaron & Lee, Jessica, *Disruptive Innovation: New Models of Legal Practice*, 67 Hastings L. J. 1 (2015).

B. Online Sources

Above the Law, *Why Doesn't Every Big Law Firm have an Office in Wheeling, West Virginia*, Above the Law (Aug. 14, 2012). https://abovethelaw.com/2012/08/why-doesnt-every-biglaw-firm-have-an-office-in-wheeling-west-virginia/ (last visited Apr. 11, 2019).

Ahmed, Murad, *Virtual Legal Teams are Giving Clients a Cheaper, More Efficient Option*, Financial Times (Oct. 8, 2014), https://www.ft.com/content/8bb682fe-39f9-11e4-83c4-00144feabdc0 (last visited Apr. 11, 2019).

Adams, Edward, *Thomson Reuters Acquires Indian Legal Outsourcing Company Pangea3,* ABA Journal (Nov. 18, 2010) http://www.abajournal.com/news/article/report_thomson_reuters_to_acquire_indian_legal_outsourcing_co_pangea3/ (last visited Apr. 11, 2019).

Agile Manifesto 2001, http://agilemanifesto.org/ (last visited Feb. 2, 2018).

Altman & Weil, *Law Firms in Transition 2018*, http://www.altmanweil.com/lfit2018/ (last visited Feb. 2, 2018).

Andriole, Steve, *Since IBM Never Called, Here's the Strategy Anyway*, Forbes (Jun. 5, 2017), https://www.forbes.com/sites/steveandriole/2017/06/05/since-ibm-never-called-heres-the-strategy-anyway/#1ffc19b16fa4 (last visited May 9, 2019).

Andriole, Steve, *IBM's Way Out? Sell Itself!*, Forbes (Mar. 13, 2018) https://www.forbes.com/sites/steveandriole/2018/03/13/ibms-way-out-sell-itself/#15aec0655874 (last visited Apr. 11, 2019).

Artificial Lawyer, *Stop Calling Elevate «Alternative» – We Are a Law Company*, Artificial Lawyer (Nov. 15, 2018), https://www.artificiallawyer.com/2018/11/15/stop-calling-elevate-alternative-we-are-a-law-company/ (last visited Apr. 11, 2019).

Behnia, Roya, *Avoiding Complexity: An Agile Manifesto for Lawyers*, ABA Journal – Legal Rebels (Nov. 15, 2011), http://www.abajournal.com/legalrebels/article/avoiding_complexity_an_agile_manifesto_for_lawyers/ (last visited Apr. 11, 2019).

Bell, Jeff, *Agile Practices in the Legal Industry*, Forbes Technology Council (Aug. 3, 2018), https://www.forbes.com/sites/forbestechcouncil/2018/08/03/agile-practices-in-the-legal-services-industry/#5c55651078a3 (last visited Apr. 11, 2019).

Bird & Bird, *Law Firm Bird & Bird Partners Launch Unique Joint Venture with ASE Consulting, Specialists in IT-Enabled Change Programmes*, *Press release* (Feb. 10, 2015), http://www.twobirds.com/en/news/press-releases/2015/uk/bird-and-bird-partners-launch-joint-venture-with-ase-consulting (last visited Feb. 3, 2019).

Bruch, Nicholas, *Law Firms are More Profitable than ever. How are they Doing it?*, Law.Com (2018a), https://www.law.com/2018/10/03/law-firms-are-more-profitable-than-ever-how-are-they-doing-it/ (last visited Apr. 11, 2019).

Bruch, Nicholas, *CLOC has Scored Some Early Wins – Much Work Remains to be Done*, Law.com (2018b), https://www.law.com/2018/04/18/cloc-has-scored-some-early-wins-much-work-remains-undone/ (last visited Apr. 11, 2019).

Classen, H Ward, *Secondment: A Valuable Option for In-House Staffing*, The Daily Record (Sept. 29, 2011), https://thedailyrecord.com/2011/09/29/secondment-a-valuable-option-for-in-house-staffing/ (last visited Apr. 11, 2019).

Cohen, Mark, *Automated and Agile: The New Paradigm for Legal Services*, Forbes (Dec. 30, 2016), https://www.forbes.com/sites/markcohen1/2016/12/30/automated-and-agile-the-new-paradigm-for-legal-service/#773ba8c64e5d (last visited Apr. 11, 2019).

Davis, Kevin, *Temp Services Offer Part-Time Lawyers for Occasional Needs*, ABA Journal (Jun. 2015), http://www.abajournal.com/magazine/article/temp_services_offer_part_time_lawyers_for_occasional_needs/ (last visited Apr. 11, 2019).

Deloitte, *The Resurgence of Corporate Legal Process Outsourcing Leveraging a New and Improved Legal Support Business Model* (2017), https://www2.deloitte.com/content/dam/Deloitte/us/Documents/process-and-operations/us-sdt-resurgence-of-corporate-legal-process-outsourcing-web.pdf (last visited Jan. 23, 2019).

Deloitte, *Deloitte Legal Launches Legal Management Consulting. New global offering aims to help corporate legal departments to take on the future*, Deloitte Press releases (2018a), https://www2.deloitte.com/global/en/pages/about-deloitte/articles/deloitte-legal-launches-legal-management-consulting.html (last visited Feb. 3, 2019).

Deloitte, *Deloitte UK and Berry Appleman & Leiden LLP (BAL LLP) form alliance to offer best-in-class immigration service for global employers,* Deloitte Press Release (2018b) *https://www2.deloitte.com/uk/en/pages/press-releases/articles/deloitte-uk-and-berry-appleman-and-leiden-llp-form-alliance.html* (last visited May 9, 2019).

Deloitte, *Ecosystems & Alliances. An engine to help carry you forward* (2019a), https://www2.deloitte.com/us/en/pages/about-deloitte/solutions/deloitte-alliances.html (last visited Jan. 15, 2019).

Deloitte, *Deloitte Legal and Epstein Becker Green Announce Alliance to Offer Global Employment Law and Workforce Management Services,* Deloitte News (2019b), https://www2.deloitte.com/dl/en/pages/legal/articles/allianz-deloitte-legal-epstein-becker-green.html (last visited May 9, 2019).

Derbyshire, Jonathan, *Big Four Circle the Legal Profession*, Financial Times (Nov. 14, 2018), https://www.ft.com/content/9b1fdab2-cd3c-11e8-8d0b-a6539b949662 (last visited Apr. 11, 2019).

DeStefano, Michele, *The Law Firm Chief Innovation Officer: Goals, Roles, and Holes* (Nov. 11, 2018), University of Miami Legal Studies Research Paper No. 18–39, https://ssrn.com/abstract=3282729 or http://dx.doi.org/10.2139/ssrn.3282729 (last visited May 9, 2019)

Dolin, Ron & Buley, Thomas, *Adaptive Innovation: Innovator's Dilemma in Big Law*, The Practice, January 2019, https://thepractice.law.harvard.edu/article/adaptive-innovation/ (last visited Apr. 11, 2019).

Dolor, Sol, *KPMG Law's new service helps remake in-house legal department*, Australian Lawyer (Aug. 3, 2018), https://www.australasianlawyer.com.au/news/kpmg-laws-new-service-helps-remake-inhouse-legal-departments-253169.aspx (last visited Apr. 11, 2019).

Economist, *Accountancy and Law: Back to Basics*, The Economist (Nov. 13, 2003), http://www.economist.com/node/2216250 (last visited Apr. 11, 2019).

Esteban, María J, *Drivers of change in legal services*, International Bar Association President's Task Force on the Future of Legal Services (2017), https://www.ibanet.org/Task-Force-on-the-Future-of-Legal-Services.aspx (last visited Apr. 11, 2019).

Evans, Joseph, *Deloitte Becomes the Last of the Big 4 to Get ABS License For Legal Services*, Law.com (2018a), https://www.law.com/americanlawyer/2018/06/22/deloitte-becomes-last-of-big-four-to-get-abs-license-for-legal-services/ (last visited Apr. 11, 2019).

Evans, Joseph, *Post Merger, Bryan Cave Leighton Paisner Sells Stake in Lawyers on Demand*, Legal Tech News (2018b), https://www.law.com/legaltechnews/2018/05/30/bclp-sells-entire-stake-in-lod-as-flexible-lawyer-spin-off-gets-new-majority-shareholder-397-8398/ (last visited Apr. 12, 2019).

EY, *EY to expand legal services offerings globally with acquisition of the Pangea3 business from Thomson Reuters*, Press release (Apr. 3, 2019), https://www.ey.com/en_gl/news/2019/04/ey-to-expand-legal-services-offerings-globally-with-acquisition-of-the-pangea3-business-from-thomson-reuters (last visited Apr. 11, 2019).

EY, *EY expands global legal managed services offering with acquisition of Riverview Law*, Press release (Aug. 7, 2018), https://www.ey.com/en_gl/news/2018/08/ey-expands-global-legal-managed-services-offering-with-acquisition-of-riverview-law (last visited Apr. 11, 2019).

Global Legal Post, *PwC Expands Managed Service Division: PwC has hired a manager from Axiom to continue growing its commercial contracting division*, Global Legal Post (Aug. 15, 2017). http://www.globallegalpost.com/big-stories/pwc-expands-managed-services-division-79767996/ (last visited Apr. 11, 2019).

Heineman, Ben W Jr, Lee, William & Wilkins, David B, *Lawyers as Professionals and as Citizens: Key Roles and Responsibilities for the Twenty First Century* (2014), https://clp.law.harvard.edu/assets/Professionalism-Project-Essay_11.20.14.pdf (last visited Apr. 11, 2019).

Henderson, William & Katz, Dan, *Mark Harris, CEO of managed services provider Axiom, interviewed by William Henderson and Dan Katz in April 2013*, YouTube, https://www.youtube.com/watch?v=Yk4gR011kD4 (last visited Apr. 11, 2019).

Hernandez, Gabrielle Orum, *Clifford Chance Looks to Break Out to Break Through with 2 New Innovation Units*, Legal Tech News (Jul. 13, 2018), https://www.law.com/legaltechnews/2018/07/13/clifford-chance-looks-to-break-out-to-break-through-with-2-new-innovation-units/ (last visited Apr. 11, 2019).

International Tax Lawyer, *Global Tax 50 2017: The GE/PwC Outsourcing Deal* (Dec. 13, 2017), http://www.internationaltaxreview.com/Article/3775137/Global-Tax-50-2017-The-GEPwC-outsourcing-deal.html (last visited Feb. 3. 2019).

Johnson, Chris, *Lawyers on Demand Ramps Up Growth*, American Lawyer (May 17, 2016), https://www.law.com/americanlawyer/almID/1202757842516/ (last visited Apr. 11, 2019).

KPMG, *Legal Operations and Transformation Systems*, (Jul. 2018), https://home.kpmg/au/en/home/services/tax/legal-services/legal-operations-transformation.html, (last visited Apr. 11, 2019).

Kovalan, Steve, *UnitedLex-GE: Barbarians at Big Law's Gate (or... Meh)?*, Law.com (Mar. 29, 2018), https://www.law.com/2018/03/29/unitedlex-ge-deal-barbarians-at-big-laws-gate-or-meh/ (last visited Apr. 11, 2019).

Law Geek, *Three Charts Show the Unstoppable Growth in Legal Tech*, Law Geek (May 22, 2018), https://blog.lawgeex.com/3-charts-that-show-the-unstoppable-growth-of-legal-tech/ (last visited Jan. 30, 2019).

The Lawyer, *20 Years of The Lawyer: 1997*, The Lawyer (Dec. 5, 2007), http://www.thelawyer.com/spanid5red20-years-of-the-lawyer/span-1997/130265.article (last visited Jan. 30, 2019).

Lawyers on Demand, *Our Story* (January 2019), https://lodlaw.com/our-story/S (last visited Jan. 31, 2019).

Legal Business, *A Noble Pursuit—DLA Piper Launches Corp Fin Boutique to Build TMT Profile*, (May 8, 2015), http://www.legalbusiness.co.uk/index.php/lb-blog-view/4124-a-noblepursuit-dla-piper-launches-corp-fin-boutique-to-build-tmt-profile (last visited Feb. 3, 2019).

Legal Insider, *Deloitte Partners with Kira Systems to Bring AI into the Workplace* (Mar. 8, 2016), http://www.legaltechnology.com/latest-news/deloitte-partners-with-kira-systems-to-bring-ai-into-the-workplace/ (last visited Feb. 1, 2019).

Legal Insider, *Exclusive/Trending: Oracle Launches Legal Global Practice Management System* (2019a), https://www.legaltechnology.com/latest-news/exclusive-oracle-launches-legal-global-practice-management-system/ (last visited Feb. 3, 2019).

Legal Insider, *Elevate Acquires Halebury and Converts to Become an ABS*, (2019b), https://www.legaltechnology.com/latest-news/elevate-acquires-halebury-and-converts-to-become-an-abs/ (last visited Feb. 2, 2019).

LegalTrek, *How to Make a Strong Legal Team with Agile Project Management* (Dec. 27, 2016), https://legaltrek.com/blog/2016/12/how-to-make-a-strong-legal-team-with-agile-project-management/ (last visited Feb. 3, 2019).

Leslie, John, *Agile Project Management Software User Report – 2015*, Software Advice https://www.softwareadvice.com/resources/agile-project-management-user-trends-2015/ (last visited Feb. 1, 2019).

LexisNexis, *Amplifying the voice of the client in law firms*, (2017), http://cert-www.lexisnexis.co.uk/research-and-reports/voice-of-the-client-thanks.html (last visited Feb. 3, 2019).

Nanda, Ashish, Rohrer, Lisa & Wilkins, David B, *Axiom Getting Down to Business*, Harvard Law School Case Development Initiative (2012), https://casestudies.law.harvard.edu/axiom-a-getting-down-to-business/ (last visited Apr. 11, 2019).

Noble Street, *2016 FAQs*, http://www.noblestreet.com/?page_id554 (last visited Feb. 3, 2019).

Orrick, *Agile working 2019*, https://www.orrick.com/Careers/Agile-Working (last visited Jan. 29, 2019).

Packel, Dan, *Big 4 Dominate as Law Firm Alternatives Press their Brand*, American Lawyer.Com (Oct. 4, 2018), https://www.law.com/americanlawyer/2018/10/04/big-four-dominate-as-law-firm-alternatives-press-their-brands/ (last visited Apr. 11, 2019).

The Practice, *Bank on More Failures: A Conversation with Dan DiPietro of Citi Private Bank*, 3 (3) The Practice 2017, https://thepractice.law.harvard.edu/article/bank-on-more-failures/ (last visited Apr. 11, 2019).

PwC, *Chairman's interview. Dennis Nally. Annual Review 2015*, http://www.pwc.com/gx/en/about/global-annual-review-2015/chairmans-interview.html (last visited Feb. 1, 2019).

Salopek, Jennifer, *Taking Managed Services to a New Level*, ACC Value Challenge 2017, https://www.acc.com/valuechallenge/valuechamps/dxc-technology-and-unitedlex.cfm (last visited Feb. 3, 2019).

Sawhney, Mohanbir, *Putting Products into Services*, Harvard Business Review September (2016), https://hbr.org/2016/09/putting-products-into-services (last visited Apr. 11, 2019).

Sloan, Karen, *Number of Law School Applicants Surges, Especially Among High Scorers*, Law.com (Jul. 30, 2018), https://www.law.com/2018/07/30/number-of-law-school-applicants-surges-especially-among-high-scorers/ (last visited Feb. 2, 2019).

Smith, John, *Imperialism in the Twenty-First Century*, Monthly Review (Jul. 1, 2015), https://monthlyreview.org/2015/07/01/imperialism-in-the-twenty-first-century/ (last visited Jan. 27, 2019).

Spezio, Caroline, *GE Lawyer Christine Hasiotis Now Deputy GC at UnitedLex*, Law.com (Jan. 25, 2018), https://www.law.com/corpcounsel/sites/corpcounsel/2018/01/25/ge-lawyer-christine-hasiotis-now-deputy-gc-at-unitedlex/ (last visited Jan. 23, 2019).

Thomson Reuters, *The Next Phase of the Legal Process Outsourcing (LPO) Industry* (2015), https://store.legal.thomsonreuters.com/law-products/ns/solutions/legal-outsourcing-services/outsourcing-insights/lpo-industry (last visited Jan. 24, 2019).

Thomson Reuters, Georgetown Law Center for the Study of the Legal Profession & the University of Oxford Said Business School, *Alternative Legal Service Providers: Understanding the Growth and Benefit of These New Providers* (2017), https://legal.thomsonreuters.com/en/insights/reports/alternative-legal-service-provider-study-2017? (last visited Jan. 24, 2019).

Thomson Reuters, Georgetown Law Center on Ethics and the Legal Profession, the University of Oxford Said Business School & Acritas, *Alternative Legal Service Providers 2019: Fast Growth, Expanding Use and Increasing Opportunity* (2019), https://legal.thomsonreuters.com/content/dam/ewp-m/documents/legal/en/pdf/reports/alsp-report-final.pdf?cid=9008178&sfdccampaignid=7011B000002OF6AQAW&chl=pr (last visited Apr. 6, 2019).

Turretinni, John, *Cut the Partners: Axiom Legal Eliminates the Expensive Middleman in Corporate Legal Work*, Forbes (Jul. 26, 2004), https://www.forbes.com/forbes/2004/0726/136.html#645c3c1e4443 (last visited Jan, 23, 2019).

Tribe, Meghan, *As 5-Lawyer IP Group Bolts for Pepper Hamilton, Shrinking LeClaireRyan plans «Law Firm 2.0»*, American Lawyer (Jan. 25, 2019), https://www.law.com/americanlawyer/2019/01/25/leclairryan-ip-group-bolts-for-pepper-hamilton-adding-to-losses/?kw=LeClairRyan%20IP%20Group%20Bolts%20for%20Pepper%20Hamilton%2C%20Adding%20to%20Losses&et=editorial&bu=TheAmericanLawyer&cn=20190125&src=EMC-Email&pt=AfternoonUpdate (last visited Jan. 25, 2019).

UnitedLex, *UnitedLex and LeClairRyan Achieve a «Tour de Force» with the Launch of ULX Partners*, (Jun. 13, 2018), https://www.unitedlex.com/news-and-insights/press-releases/2018/unitedlex-and-leclairryan-achieve-%E2%80%9Ctour-de-force%E2%80%9D-launch-ulx (last visited Jan. 23, 2019).

Wilkins, David B & Esteban Ferrer, María José, *The Reemergence of the Big Four in Law. Their rise, transformation, and potential triumph*, The Practice (2016), https://thepractice.law.harvard.edu/issue/volume-2-issue-2/ (last visited Apr. 11, 2019).

C. Other Sources

Chambliss, Elizabeth, Evidence-Based Lawyer Regulation (2019) (unpublished manuscript) (on file with the author at Harvard Law School).

Professor Mari Sako

The Changing Role of General Counsel

Break on Through (To the Other Side)[1]

TABLE OF CONTENTS

---

1 THE DOORS, BREAK ON THROUGH (TO THE OTHER SIDE) (Elektra Records, 1967).

I. Abstract

The General Counsel (GC) performs multiple roles, namely service support, risk control, and business partnering. The mix of roles changes over time, and differs across companies and countries. How and why has the mix of these roles changed over time in different parts of the world? This chapter addresses this question by reviewing evidence—contemporary and historical—in the United States, Germany, and Japan. In-house lawyers face similar pressures across different locations, but significant differences remain. In the US, the rise in the power of General Counsel was triggered by top management's demand for business partnering. By contrast, German GCs are on the cusp of building a strategic role for themselves in response to corporate demand for a robust internal risk control system. In Japan, in-house lawyers are a recent phenomenon as corporate law departments had been staffed by non-lawyers; some lawyers work in-house and are appointed on corporate boards. The chapter makes sense of these variations, and draws implications for global corporations, law firms, and legal careers.

II. Introduction

Law has, for centuries, attracted the best minds to contemplate profound issues facing society, such as the problem of «the more laws, the less justice» attributed to the Roman philosopher, *Cicero*. What would *Cicero* make of today's legal scene, with the image of legal services as an industry with buzzwords like innovation and disruption overshadowing its image of a world of contemplation about justice? Today, lawyers are pressurized to do «more for less», to adopt process mapping and legal technology to enhance efficiency, and to use alternative legal service providers (ALSPs) including the Big Four accounting firms. And who is behind the wheel to drive such transformation? Many observers would agree that it is the corporate client. These clients are typically large business corporations and financial institutions with international presence. And the General Counsel, heading their legal function, is in charge of articulating his or her demand on law firms and ALSPs, and executing the necessary changes inside the in-house department.

The aim of this chapter is to analyze the changing role of General Counsel in different parts of the world. The next section elaborates the three distinct roles that in-house lawyers generally and the General Counsel in particular play inside business corporations. With this analytical lens at hand, I evaluate the changing role of General Counsel in the United States over the last century. I then go onto examine the situation in Germany and Japan, two giant industrial nations with many prominent corporations.

Based on evidence garnered from public sources and the author's interviews with lawyers in the three countries, analysis suggests that the General Counsel has become more powerful across different locations. While similarities in the reasons for this phenomenon abound, one should be mindful of subtle differences across the United States, Germany, and Japan. These differences are here to stay for the foreseeable future. This fact points to the likely continuation of a semi-globalized world for lawyering that is not flat.[2]

III. What do In-house Lawyers do?

In-house lawyers wear multiple hats in their day-to-day work. They provide service support to their internal clients; they are also expected to lead in company-wide risk control; last and not least, they act as business partners who advise and steer business decisions. All three roles are important across a variety of companies and sectors.

A. Service Support

The *service support* role applies to all in-house lawyers, and is about facilitating business transactions in a cost-effective and efficient manner. This may take the form of drafting and negotiating contracts and agreements; it also involves handling routine day-to-day legal matters such as updating leases and regulatory filings. Service support also includes dealing with disputes, and dealing with the legal aspect of mergers, disposals or acquisitions of business units. As business corporations consider entering new geographic markets, in-house lawyers may be also involved in advising on country-specific laws and regulations. Last and not least, service support involves the selection, retention, and supervision of external law firms and lawyers. Legal scholars have referred to a business lawyer as a «transaction cost engineer»,[3] noting first and foremost this service support role.

---

2 The notion of «the world is flat» was popularized by Thomas L Friedman, The World Is Flat: A Brief History of the Twenty-First Century (2007). Technology has enhanced global integration, but existing approaches to making rules that guide global integration—the legal infrastructure—are inadequate (*see* Gillian K Hadfield, Rules for a Flat World (Oxford University Press, 2017). The aim of this chapter is to demonstrate one aspect of an unevenly integrated global economy by focusing on legal practice within global corporations.

3 Ronald J Gilson & Robert H Mnookin, *Symposium on business lawyers and value creation for clients*, 74 (1) Oregon Law Review 8–10 (1995).

B. Risk Control

The *risk control* function of in-house lawyers is potentially extensive. Although risk has both upside (risk-taking) and downside (i.e., risk avoidance), lawyers are trained and conditioned to focus on the latter. As a result, risk control in this context has emphasized the latter, as is evident from the definition of legal risk as «the risk that a business faces in connection with a negative legal event such as sitting on an *unenforceable contract or collateral, paying damages to a third party, ... or indictment of the company or its executives.*»[4] In-house lawyers have responsibilities, and work with other departments, to ensure legal compliance with respect to anti-trust, anti-corruption, data protection, export control, and technical compliance. Moreover, risk has become increasingly more multi-disciplinary. That is, risk is not just legal or financial, but also a matter of corporate reputation. The multi-disciplinary nature of risk control compels in-house lawyers to work closely with other functions including communications and public affairs.

C. Business Partnering

The *business partnering* role applies to the general counsel and lawyer-directors on corporate boards. As the term «partnering» implies, these in-house lawyers at the top do not just advise, but participate in decisions about the strategic direction of the company.[5] In this role, the general counsel and lawyer-directors must navigate a fine line between being lawyers first and foremost with professional ethics as guide for their conduct on the one hand, and being business managers endorsing and pursuing business opportunities on the other. Acting simultaneously as independent lawyers and as managers pursuing business opportunities evidently requires skilled judgement. Not surprisingly, this role has created much controversy on whether or not inside counsel could wear two hats and remain independent.[6]

---

4 Peter Kurer, Legal and Compliance Risk (Oxford University Press, 2015).

5 Veasey E Norman & Christine T Di Guglielmo, Indispensable Counsel: The Chief Legal Officer in the New Reality (Oxford University Press, 2012).

6 Joseph Auerbach, *Can inside counsel wear two hats?* Harvard Business Review September-October 80–86 (1984). *See* also Philippe Coen & Christophe Roquilly, eds., *Company Lawyers: Independent by Design*: *in* European Company Lawyers Association (ECLA) White Paper (LexisNexis 2014).

D. Where does GC Power come from?

In gauging the changing role of General Counsel in different parts of the world, the rest of this chapter tracks how and why the mix of the three roles spelt out—service support, risk management, and business partnering—has changed over time in different country locations. Moreover, attention will be paid in particular to the General Counsel, the chief legal officer, and this focus warrants asking more explicitly what is the bases of power that the General Counsel has been able to exercise? Without power, the General Counsel would not be able to bring about changes in a sustainable manner. Here, it makes sense to distinguish between *external GC* power and *internal GC* power. The former is with respect to external law firms and other providers of legal services, and the latter is GC power inside the business corporation.

1. External GC Power

External GC power is about bargaining power with respect to law firms and other providers of legal services. At any particular point in time, external GC power depends on the size of the in-house legal department; the bigger the legal department with its own lawyers across different practice areas, the stronger and the more credible the GC's threat to replace external lawyers by in-house lawyers. The most temporary of external GC power lies in being in a buyers' market during an economic downturn. Much of the bargaining power resulting from an adverse economic climate, however, is likely to erode when the economy picks up. This implies that to exert sustained external GC power, making law firms compete with each other may be necessary but not sufficient. External GC power for the long term is based on proactively managing a network of law firms, so that they are made to collaborate as much as compete.

2. Internal GC Power

GC power inside the corporation depends on the capabilities of the GC and his or her staff in the legal department. More specifically, the general counsel may enhance his internal power to become a sustainable force for change by proactively investing in capabilities such as project management and risk management. In relation to top management, the test of internal GC power lies in the general counsel's ability to influence CEO's strategic decisions. This requires offering advice based on deep legal knowledge in the business context of the corporation. It is also predicated on the legal department holding legal information in the form of meta-data and analytics to enable the general council to provide evidence-based strategic advice. The managerial theory of the firm states that managers have a propensity to grow their firm for reasons of prestige and status. We might apply this theory to company lawyers, with the general counsel wishing to grow their legal department to signal their power. For sustainable internal GC power, however, we would expect the large size of the legal department to be underpinned by in-house lawyers' broad capabilities (encompassing service support, risk control, and business partnering) to execute legal work effectively for internal clients.

IV. United States: Past and Present

The legal profession has been a highly prestigious one in the United States, where nearly half of the framers of the constitution and two-thirds of Presidents to date have been lawyers. Within the legal profession, however, the relative prestige of in-house counsel relative to external counsel has ebbed and flowed over the past century. I rely on existing scholarship to outline how GC power rose with the emergence of the modern business corporation in the early twentieth century, then declined in midcentury before re-emerging in response to the increasing regulatory burden of businesses in the late 1970s. I can trace the century-long trend to a changing mix of GC roles, starting with service support, and shifting more and more to risk control and business partnering.I present some data on GC compensation to demonstrate how general counsel incentives have become increasingly aligned to the business strategy of the corporations for which they work.

A. Long-term Trends in GC Power

1. «Golden Years of Corporate Counsel» in the 1920s and 1930s

Corporate counsel were mighty powerful in the early part of the twentieth century. During the period dubbed the «golden years of corporate counsel» by *Carl Liggio*,[7] management sought professional and business advice from corporate counsel. Liggio marshals two pieces of evidence to back up the preeminence of corporate counsel: first, that they were usually among the three highest paid executives in the company; and second, that over 75 percent of the CEOs in corporate America had legal backgrounds.

This period immediately followed an era when newly incorporated modern corporations required legal input to draft and implement the articles of incorporation. Not surprisingly, the best and the brightest in the legal profession were hired into prestigious in-house positions, and these corporate counsel became part of senior management which crafted and developed major modern corporations as we know them today. Of the three roles, business partner-

---

7 Carl D Liggio, *The changing role of corporate counsel*, 46 Emory Law Journal 1201–1222 (1997).

ing, combining legal and business advice, ruled the day; it was the most prominent part of the identity of corporate counsel.

2. Decline of Corporate Counsel from the 1940s to the 1960s

By the middle of the twentieth century, and certainly by the end of the Second World War, senior management positions in major corporations shifted to non-lawyer graduates, triggering a decline in the status of corporate counsel. This decline, according to Liggio, was set in motion by one fact, namely the rise of business schools, leading to marketing and finance types displacing lawyers in senior management.

At the same time, legal careers became more institutionalized with top-tier law firms able to take a first pick at recruiting associates from law schools. In the «up or out» promotion system in law firms, associates aspired to make it to partner, and in-house lawyers came to be stereotyped as second-class lawyers who had not quite made their grade as partner. Liggio goes as far as to state: «the outside bar treated the employed corporate legal community with disdain» as a result of the decline in compensation and a narrower role given to corporate counsel than in an earlier period.

3. Renaissance of Corporate Counsel since the late 1970s

Since the late 1970s, however, corporate counsel re-emerged in prominence due to greater use of litigation by businesses, higher external counsel fees, and ever-increasing legal complexity facing businesses. One could trace the origin of the legal complexity brought about by the more recent Sarbanes-Oxley Act to the proliferation of regulatory agencies with broad legal responsibility, beyond the Securities and Exchange Commission (SEC), the Fair Trade Commission, the Department of Justice, and the Inland Revenue. To navigate through the alphabet soup of laws and regulations, business corporations needed capable in-house lawyers who were well versed in both the law and the specific business context.

Consequently, major corporations began to hire more in-house lawyers and build their in-house legal teams.[8] In-house lawyers began to do SEC filings and part of the work in litigation cases, taking work away from external counsel. The need to combine legal expertise and business knowledge led to a new breed of corporate counsel who could apply business techniques and tools to manage the legal process. Increasingly, corporate counsel is involved in the corporate strategic planning process, alerting management to the level of legal risks involved in specific strategic decisions. And this time, business schools

---

8 Bejarne P Tellmann, Building an Outstanding Legal Team Battle-Tested Strategies from a General Counsel (Globe Law and Business, 2017).

are supporting, rather than undermining, the rise of General Counsel and in-house lawyers who seek business education beyond their legal training.

B. Business Partnering and the Rise since the 1990s

In the United States, the General Counsel at major corporations have wielded significant power via business partnering, going beyond their «trusted advisor» role. As joint risk managers, US general counsel front-load legal inputs, not only to pre-empt disputes and anticipate likely government investigations, but also to endorse upside risk-taking in new market entry decisions or large M&A deals. Around 80% of General Counsel at *Fortune 500* companies carry the managerial titles of Executive Vice President or Senior Vice President, and many are incentivized with stock options. Not surprisingly, GCs at major US companies would be content with stating: «I'm a business person who happens to be a lawyer, a business partner who brings legal background to business problems.»[9]

The advice GCs give and how they are party to actual business decisions inside business corporations are not visible. But we can explore the extent to which GCs are incentivized to act as business partners by looking at two things. One is whether or not the General Counsel carry a managerial title of Senior Vice President (SVP) or Executive Vice President (EVP). The other is the level and the composition of compensation that the General Counsel receives. The data from Compustat Executive Compensation (Execucomp) for companies included in Compustat, show interesting trends as follows:

a, In major US companies, the proportion of General Counsel with managerial titles (SVP or EVP) increased steadily from 53% in 1993 to 75% in 2014 (*see* Exhibit 1).

b, While the ratio of GC salary to CEO salary has not advanced much over time (46% in 1993; 50% in 2014), the non-salary portion of GCs' total compensation has increased from 48% in 1993 to 68% in 2014. The non-salary income consists of bonus plus payment from stock options (*see* Exhibit 2).

c, General Counsel with managerial titles are paid slightly higher relative salaries (the GC to CEO salary ratio was 49% for GC with managerial titles, 46% for those without during this period). More notable is the ratio of non-salary payment to total compensation, which is significantly larger for GCs with managerial titles than for those without. In 1993, GCs

---

9 A US general counsel interviewed for a study of general counsel in the US and Britain. *See* Mari Sako, *General Counsel with Power?*, SAID BUSINESS SCHOOL, UNIVERSITY OF OXFORD (Oct. 13, 2018, 4:33 PM), http://eureka.sbs.ox.ac.uk/4560/1/General_Counsel_with_Power.pdf (last visited Apr. 11, 2019).

with SVP or EVP titles received 49% of total compensation in non-salary payment, compared to 46% for GCs without these titles. By 2014, the non-salary to total compensation ratio rose to 69% for GCs with SVP/EVP titles, and to 65% for GCs without such titles (*see* Exhibit 2).

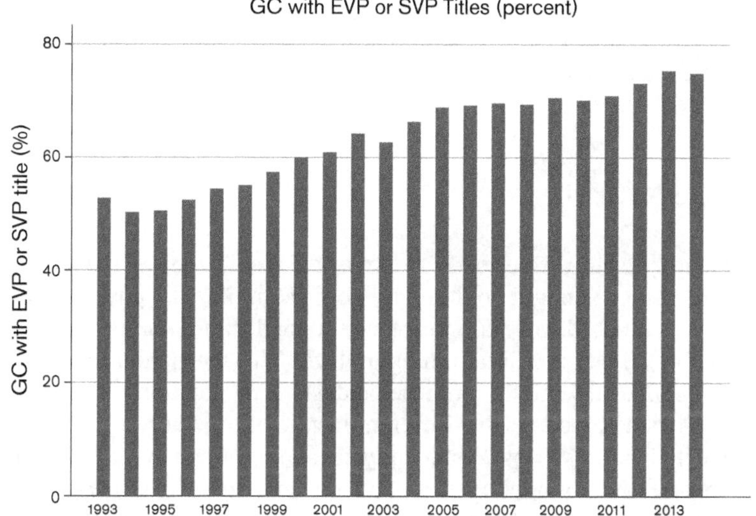

Exhibit 1: General Counsel with SVP (Senior Vice-President) or EVP (Executive Vice-President) Titles in the United States 1993–2014.

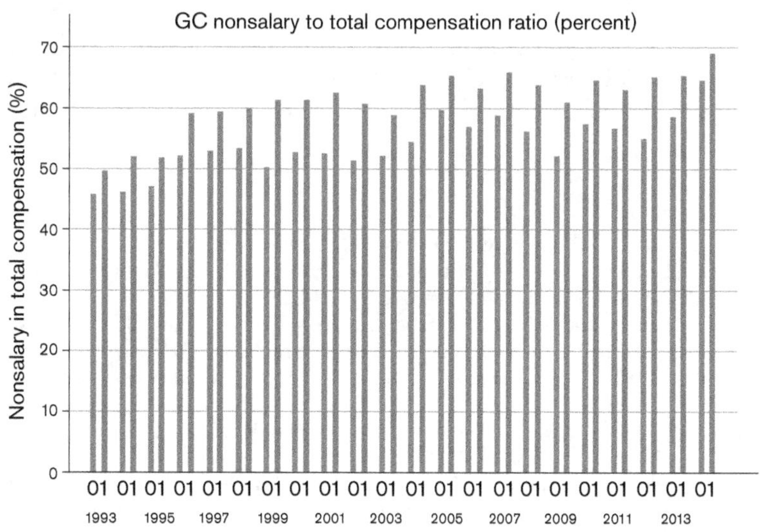

Exhibit 2: General Counsel Compensation: Non-salary in Total Compensation Titled vs. Non-Titled 1993–2014.

Thus, in the last two and a half decades, corporate expectation on US General Counsel to act as business partners has increased steadily. This is evident from GCs being rewarded with executive management titles—a status signal to other members of the top management team and to all company employees—and incentivized via compensation to contribute to the profit-making enterprise of the business corporation. At the same time, CEOs who are lawyers—lawyer CEOs—are a non-trivial but not very prominent phenomenon in Corporate America (9% of Standard & Poor 1500 firms had CEOs with a JD or another law degree during 1992–2012).[10]

V. Germany[11]

The predominantly Anglo-American account of the inside counsel movement with its longer history[12] should not blind us from examining the phenomenon in other parts of the world. Germany represents a good starting point for comparisons with the US, given similar timing in developing as a major industrial nation, resulting in legal work for renowned industrial corporations. Nevertheless, Germany has had a somewhat different historical trajectory of lawyers' touch points with business firms. Historically, legal education in Germany was geared towards training for public service and the judiciary. But business firms have drawn on the expertise of lawyers not only as external counsel, but also as chairs and members of the two-tier boards. Moreover, it is said that as recently as in the early 1990s, one in three CEOs of large German companies was a lawyer.[13] Now, one in five CEOs at DAX30 companies is said to have started his career as a management consultant. Times have changed. This might be another instance of business schools supplanting law schools in providing executive talent. But in what ways is this decline of lawyer-CEOs related to

---

10 *See* Todd Henderson, Irena Hutton, Danling Jiang & Matthew Pierson, *Lawyer CEOs*, University of Chicago Law School Working Paper (Oct. 13, 2018, 4:37 PM), http://www.law.nyu.edu/sites/default/files/Lawyer%20CEOs.pdf (last visited Apr. 11, 2019).

11 This section is based on a study of 33 in-house lawyers in Germany, reported *in* Mari Sako, *Changing Role of General Counsel in Germany*, Said Business School, University of Oxford (Oct. 13, 2018, 3:45 PM), http://eureka.sbs.ox.ac.uk/6870/. This work will be referred to in the main text as «the study».

12 Robert E Rosen, *The inside counsel movement: professional judgment and organizational representation*, *in* 64 Indiana Law Journal 479–533 (1989).

13 Tillmann Neuscheler, *Jeder fünfte DAX-Chef begann seine Karriere als Unternehmensberater*, *in* Frankfurter Allgemeine Zeitung (Sept. 13, 2018, 4:37 PM) at 7, http://www.faz.net/aktuell/beruf-chance/beruf/jederfuenfte-dax-chef-startete-seine-karriere-als-unternehmensberater-15624400.html. By 2017, only two of the DAX30 companies had lawyer- CEOs, namely E.ON and HeidelbergCement (author's data based on company websites).

the changing role of in-house lawyers and general counsel working in German firms?

I address this question by examining how German in-house lawyers are enhancing their importance inside the companies, by taking on the challenges of (a) managing legal and non-legal risks, (b) improving service support by systematizing relationships with law firms, and (c) figuring out how best to be part of, or apart from, top management teams. One GC who was interviewed for the study stated the nature of his challenge succinctly: «we must be risk managers of course, *but also opportunity managers*».[14]

A. Risk Control as a Major Trigger

It is probably not an overstatement to assert that the need for an enhanced risk control function has been the primary trigger in empowering the general counsel in Germany. As is well known, the 2010s saw some German companies suffer major compliance challenges due to bribery cases, anti-trust violations, and the emissions scandal. These compliance breaches heightened the strategic importance of risk control. Moreover, «mediatization» (media attention) of such corporate events necessitates dealing with legal and non-legal risks together.

In major German corporations, new CEOs may be appointed. These CEOs may restructure the firm to make business units more visible to the corporate headquarter. Risk control becomes a board-level issue, and corporate boards may make more explicit which director is responsible for Legal & Compliance. Above all, the general counsel is on the frontline to implement a robust risk control and compliance system. In restructuring the legal function, they must walk a tightrope between providing independent advice to business units and retaining intimacy with internal clients. This requires culture change, not just structural and procedural changes. The latter may be announced overnight, but the former takes time, years in many cases.

In-house lawyers have always had responsibilities to ensure legal compliance with respect to anti-trust, anti-corruption, data protection, export control, and technical standards. But as mentioned above, risk is increasingly not just legal or financial, but also a matter of corporate reputation. The multi-disciplinary nature of risk control poses an extra challenge, as in-house lawyers must work closely with other functions including communications and public affairs.

There is no doubt that the legal and compliance function has become more important in the survival of German corporations. There is, however, no

---

14 Mari Sako, *Changing Role of General Counsel in Germany*, Said Business School, University of Oxford (Oct. 13, 2018, 3:45 PM), http://eureka.sbs.ox.ac.uk/6870/ (last visited Apr. 11, 2019).

consensus on whether or not the legal department should incorporate, or be separate from, the compliance function. This debate is, of course, not unique to Germany. Proponents of the view that the two—legal and compliance—should be separate emphasize the need to have a separate investigative body when in-house lawyers may have been party to business transactions and decisions under investigation. Supporters of combining the two assert that it makes sense because of the necessity for tight coordination and communication in executing the lines of defense.

B. Preference for Insourcing

General Counsel in German companies also oversee the relationships with law firms, and are party to deciding the relative balance between sourcing legal services from them and from in-house resources. German companies are in the midst of systematizing their relationships with law firms, by establishing panels with formal performance reviews, insisting on greater cost transparency by practicing alternative billing arrangements, and accessing boutique law firms. Boutiques are preferred for better focus, greater flexibility, and lower fees, in practice areas such as employment law and real estate. The recent emergence of boutique law firms is perhaps a uniquely German phenomenon, not seen in the United States where law firms are, if anything, consolidating to become full-service providers. It is not clear what the future holds for boutique law firms in the face of competition from alternative legal service providers, but for now, they present viable alternatives to global law firms whose branches are located in major German cities.

Apart from systematizing relationships with law firms, German general counsel expressed a preference for insourcing legal work, to consider using in-house resources first before going out-of-house. This preference for insourcing is due to a mix of reasons, including in-house lawyers' greater knowledge about the company compared to external lawyers. The other two reasons, growing attention to legal budget control and better risk management are worthy of further discussion, and the two are intricately intertwined.

The 2008 financial crisis had a major impact on all global corporations. Back then, soaring billable hours led major corporations to insource in order to cut legal spending. Legal department heads of German companies said they also preferred to insource legal work as much as possible. But the reasons given were less to do with avoiding extremely high fees law firms charge, and more to do with the aforementioned concern for better risk control and greater transparency. Tighter legal budget control leads to better risk control. In particular, greater central oversight is intended to prevent local business unit managers paying legal fees for external lawyers who were consulted informally, for example over playing golf. This amounts to having a central approval system for legal spending, so that in-house lawyers must think twice about the necessity of putting work out to external lawyers. The resulting practice of considering the use of in-house resources first before going out-of-house has the dual benefit of cost efficiency and risk control. In short, the policy to prefer insourcing gives the general counsel centralized oversight at the headquarter.

C. A Variety of Business Partnering

We are now in a position to draw implications for the role of general counsel in relation to top management teams in Germany. Senior German managers generally expect the general counsel to boost risk control, but their expectations on business partnering vary from company to company. This is in contrast to the United States, where business partnering among major corporations has spread widely in the past few decades.

It is worth keeping in mind a different historical trajectory. Remember that until recently, lawyer-CEOs had been prominent in Corporate Germany. Remember also that licensed lawyers are present on the two-tier boards. If we define «lawyers» broadly as those who passed at least the first state exam (some with a doctorate in law, and others with experience of practicing law), 14 (47%) of the DAX30 companies have lawyers on their Executive Boards, and 22 (73%) of the DAX30 companies have lawyers on their Supervisory Boards.[15] It is also worth remembering the context in the European Union of which Germany is a part. In particular, in-house lawyers in the European Union still faces the need to lobby and clarify their independent status in relation to the 2010 European Court of Justice (ECJ) ruling in the Akzo case. The ECJ ruling confirmed that in-house lawyers, because they are in an employment relationship with his or her client, are not independent and therefore cannot claim legal professional privilege.[16] Arguably, this makes it easier for in-house lawyers to uphold the philosophy that one can wear two hats (as a lawyer and as a senior executive of a company) at the same time. But giving independent advice remains dear to the heart of many in-house lawyers, including in Germany.

Against this backdrop, the study found a variety of attitudes and practices towards business partnering. At one extreme, some GCs regarded themselves as fully part of the executive team and acted as business managers entitled to speak up on all types of business issues that they consider important for the company. At the other extreme, traditional attitudes persist, with GCs adopting

15 Author's own calculation based on websites of DAX30 companies, accessed in early 2018.

16 Philippe Coen & Christophe Roquilly, eds., *Company Lawyers: Independent by Design, in* European Company Lawyers Association (ECLA) White Paper (LexisNexis, 2014).

the role of independent lawyers who speak in executive meetings primarily to address legal issues. Companies continue to hire lawyers as lawyers, not as managers. The study identified three patterns.

In the first pattern, the general counsel keeps an arms-length distance from the Management and Supervisory Boards. Only if the CEO requests the presence of the general counsel on a specific agenda item with a legal angle would the general counsel be asked to be present at the Board meeting, but just for that item. One GC said that he had no loyalty to any specific board member, and the most important thing about boards is transparency. He attributed this view to his career of having spent longer than his predecessor as an external lawyer.

In the second pattern, the general counsel is the Company Secretary who prepares the agenda and takes minutes of the board meetings. This provides an opportunity for the general counsel to know the nature of board discussion intimately. But the board members do not expect him/her to speak much, unless asked by the CEO for comments primarily from a legal angle. The intimate knowledge of the business of the company is the basis for one GC asserting that «we are becoming more and more advisors to the board, and to the management of the company.»

In the third pattern, the general counsel is fully part of the Executive Board (Vorstand), or else an executive committee (normally consisting of the CEO, the CFO, and one or two other functional heads in some cases). In this situation, the general counsel is a full-blown business partner, and is considered part of the executive management team. The rationale for the general counsel becoming closer to the executive management team may arise from the need to prevent the company from running foul of compliance, so the GC does «not have to preach the importance of legal to the company.» However, a seat at the table has opened up an opportunity to go beyond this. According to one GC, *«we are all managers, ... legal managers in the business»*. The general counsel interviewed in this category rubbed shoulders with the CEO regularly not just because they report to the CEO, but by dint of having a seat on the corporate executive committee.

Thus, a variety of roles were identified for the general counsel in relation to the company's top management team. The most involved were fully part of the executive team and saw themselves as business managers entitled to speak up on all types of business issues which they consider important for the company; by contrast, the least involved adopting the role of a lawyer who focused on dealing primarily with legal issues. This variety in the involvement of general counsel in top management teams is likely to persist. This is because in Germany, Legal became a top management issue via the need to control risks better, and not necessarily via the business partnering route.

VI. Japan

Compared to Germany where major corporations remain privately held, Japanese corporations are more likely to be publicly listed in stock exchanges, and are therefore subject to similar pressures from investors and securities regulators to those that US corporations face. Nevertheless, the in-house counsel is a very recent phenomenon in Japan since the 2000s, driven by supply side factors as much as demand factors. This section portrays the nature of Japanese corporate legal departments, and presents an overview of in-house lawyers in the late 2010s. Reasons for why more lawyers are going in-house are spelt out. Since the 2000s, lawyers are also interacting with business corporations in a different capacity, as nonexecutive directors on corporate boards. We investigate what types of companies are adopting this practice, and the impact their appointment has had on corporate performance.

A. Corporate Legal Departments in Japan

A brief historical perspective on Japanese corporate legal departments is instructive in understanding the contemporary picture, a sharply different world from the US norm. Major Japanese corporations, many with international presence, have in-house legal departments, but they tend not to be staffed by licensed lawyers. The in-house legal department staff may have studied law at top universities, but an overwhelming majority do not sit for the bar exam and therefore are not admitted to the bar. Just a handful of corporations have a licensed lawyer (*bengoshi*) heading the legal department. A career in a corporate legal department is considered a life-long job, on a par with any other white-collar lifetime employment jobs in large corporations. In this context, it is senior colleagues in the legal department who provide on-the-job training necessary to be able to draft contract documents and to comply with government regulations. One consequence of this system is that corporate legal department staff have deep knowledge and understanding of the business of the company for which they work.

With a long-term perspective, the internationalization of Japanese business has been a key factor in the creation and expansion of corporate legal departments at various points in history. In the early part of the twentieth century, general trading companies, such as Mitsubishi Corporation and Mitsui & Co., spearheaded cross-border international trade, and were the first among Japanese companies to create an early form of an in-house legal function, typically known as *bunsho-ka* or a documentation department. Trading companies recruited university graduates with a B.A. degree in law, and nurtured them on-the-job so that they could draft legal documents, including contracts and licensing agreements.

After the Second World War, and by the 1960s, this practice spread to manufacturing companies, which created their own legal documentation departments to facilitate the rapid expansion of exports. Gradually, in the 1980s and beyond, documentation needs shifted from drafting sales contracts for overseas clients to drafting more complex agreements for foreign direct investment, project finance, and cross-border mergers and acquisitions. Throughout these decades, in-house legal department staff have remained in charge of drafting documents, and not considered part of the team for business negotiations. Thus, by satisfying the day-to-day legal needs of business corporations, the Japanese legal department staff have focused primarily on the service support function.

B. Growth of In-house Lawyers in Japan

1. Current situation

In 2017, there were 1931 in-house lawyers who were employed by business corporations, out of a total of 38,930 licensed lawyers in Japan, so roughly 5.0% of all lawyers were in-house. In order to appreciate how recent the in-house lawyer phenomenon is, there were only 188 in-house lawyers in 2007.[17] Similar to situations in other countries, in-house lawyers are more likely to be diverse in gender (40% of in-house lawyers were women in 2016) than the lawyer population as a whole (only 18.4% of total lawyers were female in 2017).

A questionnaire survey of in-house lawyers conducted by the Japan Federation of Bar Associations in 2016 (based on responses from 461 in-house lawyers or 27% response rate) makes their career intention clear. In particular, 61% of respondents became in-house after a period of working in private practice, and 60% became in-house because of better work-life balance, while 54% because they wanted to do work that was closely linked to business. In fact, 54% had the ambition to be promoted to top management in order to participate in corporate strategy making, and 28% were already in senior managerial position employed in functions other than the legal function. However, those in legal departments were more junior, with only 31% reported to a superior who was a licensed lawyer.

In-house lawyers have their own association called the Japan In-house Lawyers Association (JILA), which collects data on the top ten companies that employed the largest number of in-house lawyers. Over-time changes in the companies listed give a good picture of which companies have led the in-house lawyer phenomenon in Japan. In 2017, the top ten companies with the

17 Data from the Japanese Federation of Bar Associations.

number of in-house lawyers in brackets, were: *Yahoo* (28), *Nomura Securities* (20), *Mitsui Sumitomo Bank* (20), *Mitsubishi Corporation* (20), *Marubeni* (15), *Mizuho Securities* (15), *SMBC Nikko Securities* (14), *Mitsui Bussan* (14), *Mitsubishi Tokyo UFJ Bank* (14), and *Yucho Bank* (14). Thus, apart from Yahoo, companies are predominantly in financial services or in general trading. Ten years earlier in 2007, this list was dominated by foreign subsidiaries, such as *Goldman Sachs*, *IBM Japan*, *Morgan Stanley*, *Microsoft* and *General Electric*.[18]

2. Why have in-house lawyers increased in numbers?

The reasons why Japanese lawyers started to consider an in-house career, and why such opportunities became available, may be divided into demand-side and supply-side factors. Most existing accounts, confirmed by the author's interviews, place more emphasis on the supply side than the demand side.

The supply side account starts with the perceived need to improve the efficacy of the legal system to better serve societal needs, for example by reducing the very long waiting time for plaintiffs to have their case heard. Attributing this to the scarcity of judges and lawyers, the Japanese government implemented reforms in legal education, creating law schools and increasing the number who sit the bar exam. The result was an acceleration in the number admitted to the bar every year, contributing to a stock of just under 40,000 licensed lawyers (in a country of 120 million people). The increase in the number of lawyers led to a diversification in the career aspiration of freshly minted lawyers beyond becoming a judge or a partner in a law firm, to include going in-house.

The legal education reform began to impact corporate legal departments gradually. First, a trickle of experienced attorneys went in-house, mostly for the Tokyo offices of foreign banks and subsidiaries of foreign multinationals such as *IBM* and *GE*. Japanese lawyers used to have to seek permission from their professional association to go in-house until the 1970s, but this permission system was changed to a notification and registration system more recently. In the 2010s, junior lawyers may consider going in-house only after a few years' experience as external attorneys, or even straight after passing the bar exam. It is this last career route that has led to a debate on whether or not Japan has an excess supply of lawyers; this assertion is underpinned by a rigid view that true lawyers should only work either in the judiciary or as external attorneys.

Although not yet well articulated, Japanese corporations appear to have a situation similar to German corporations for insourcing legal services. Just like their German counterparts, some Japanese corporations facing compli-

18 Japan In-house Lawyers Association (JILA).

ance challenges see the need to better manage their risk and reputation. A common reaction following a corporate scandal or mismanagement is to increase the size of their legal departments significantly to enforce compliance. Hiring more in-house lawyers is also on the cards of senior management at companies whose sales markets have shifted more and more from the domestic market to overseas, and as they look to the legal function not only for service support but for risk management inherent in their investment decisions.

In sum, Japanese companies in the late 2010s typically have a legal department whose head came up through the old system of internal training and promotion without qualifying as a lawyer, staffed by a small number of younger licensed lawyers. The jury is still out on how the balance between non-lawyers and lawyers will pan out in the future. A small number of Japanese legal department heads are lawyers, but more likely than not, junior lawyers reporting to a non-lawyer department head face uncertainty as to the extent to which they could use their legal expertise on a day-to-day basis. In a work environment in which lawyers and non-lawyers are treated equally, it concentrates our mind on what it is that only qualified lawyers can do, or permitted to do, in corporate legal services.

C. Lawyers on Corporate Boards

Another way in which lawyers are interacting with business corporations recently is thanks to recent corporate governance reforms in Japan. Japanese corporate boards used to be nearly entirely staffed by managers who were promoted from within. But the proportion of firms listed in the first section of Tokyo Stock Exchange with at least one outside or non-executive director rose gradually from 35% in 2005 and 48.7% in 2010, to 64.4% in 2014 and 95.8% in 2016. One talent pool for non-executive directors is the legal profession. Lawyers provide valuable expertise on laws and regulations; they are also seen to excel in being independent.

Examining all publicly quoted companies in Japan, the proportion of companies with either lawyers and/or accountants on their boards increased from 2.67% in 2004 to 17.09% in 2015. The ratio of lawyers to total directors has, however, been still very small, increasing from 0.18% in 2004 to 1.64% in 2015. Lawyers are more likely to be on corporate boards in regulated industries than in unregulated industries. Hence, this is still early days to judge what impact lawyers' presence on boards has had on the nature of strategic discussion and performance impact. That said, there is some evidence to suggest that particularly in regulated industries, lawyer-directors endorse, rather than prevent, risk-taking by companies, when they consider major projects such as mergers & acquisitions.[19]

VII. Implications for an Unflat World

A tour around the world of three major countries indicates that the mix of roles in-house lawyers and general counsel play has changed over time, and in different ways from country to country. In the United States, business partnering was prominent in the early twentieth century; after a period of being service support-focused «transaction cost engineers», business partnering re-emerged as a focal role for the general counsel. The recent practice to appoint Legal Operations Directors or Chief Operations Officers (COOs) of the legal department reinforces this focus, as GCs can offload their responsibilities for service support to COOs. In Germany, lawyers have long been CEOs and board directors, but more recently, the decline of lawyer CEOs coincided with the enhanced role of general counsel and in-house lawyers as risk managers. In Japan, lawyers operated largely as external attorneys advising companies; only since the 2000s have there been gentle winds of change with a few thousand lawyers going in-house, and another group who, as external lawyers, sit on company boards as non-executive directors. Thus, the service support role in Japan is largely carried out by legal department staff who are non-lawyers, while corporate lawyers and lawyer-directors focus on risk management. I can also summarize trends in each of the three roles as follows:

- *Service support* has become increasingly subjected to business tools and techniques to improve efficiency. The appointment of COOs and the formalization of relations with law firms through the establishment of law firm panels have become more common in the US. In Germany also, systematizing relations with law firms is beginning to spread. But in Japan, with a few exceptions by multinational and domestic companies with a heavy reliance on overseas markets, efficiency-enhancing drives are less common and are led by non-lawyers in legal departments.
- *Risk control* has explicitly come to the fore in German companies, but it is also important in Japanese and US companies. In all locations, a preference for insourcing is driven as much by this concern, as the need to control legal cost. In-house lawyers can take a lead in educating employees about compliance and prevention of incidents, in the way that external attorneys would not be able to. As risks become multi-disciplinary, and

19 For further details, *see* Mari Sako & Katsuyuki Kubo, *Professionals on Corporate Boards: How do they affect the Bottom Line?*, RIETI DISCUSSION PAPER (2019), https://www.rieti.go.jp/en/publications/summary/19020011.html (last visited Apr. 11, 2019).

as companies focus on prevention as much as dealing with risks once violations or scandals break out, the general counsel in all locations are compelled to work closely with other corporate functions.

- *Business partnering*, with the general counsel and lawyer-directors participating in strategic decisions of corporations, is steadily on the rise in the United States. By contrast, Germany has seen a decline in lawyer-CEOs in the last few decades, but the continued presence of lawyers on the two-tier boards has set the tone for Legal & Compliance being a board-level issue. By contrast, business partnering in Japan is a much more recent phenomenon, with the appointment of lawyers as non-executive directors.

Thus, the world is not flat with respect to the mix of roles that general counsel play. This fact has implications for global corporations, law firms, and lawyer careers. For global corporations headquartered in different countries, their headquarter practice is likely to dominate global practice as the group legal function becomes more centralized. Nevertheless, as they enter new emerging markets and create in-house teams in these new locations, they are likely to be have to be sensitive to local practices. For law firms, their corporate clients demand legal services of consistent quality in different parts of the world, and expect law firms to provide lawyer talent to work closely with in-house teams, on temporary placements or transfers to in-house teams. This implies that lawyers who wish to be internationally mobile benefit not only from being qualified in multiple jurisdictions, but also from being flexible with respect to their careers, working as external and internal attorneys in different sequence at different stages in their careers.

VIII. Bibliography

A. Hard Copy Sources

Auerbach Joseph, *Can inside counsel wear two hats?* HARVARD BUSINESS REVIEW September-October 80–86 (1984).

Liggio, Carl D, *The changing role of corporate counsel*, 46 EMORY LAW JOURNAL, 1201–1222 (1997).

Coen, Philippe & Roquilly, Christophe, eds., *Company Lawyers: Independent by Design*: *in* EUROPEAN COMPANY LAWYERS ASSOCIATION (ECLA) WHITE PAPER (LexisNexis 2014).

FRIEDMAN, THOMAS L, THE WORLD IS FLAT: A BRIEF HISTORY OF THE TWENTY-FIRST CENTURY (Penguin Books, 2007).

Gilson, Ronald J & Mnookin, Robert H, *Symposium on business lawyers and value creation for clients*, 74 (1), OREGON LAW REVIEW 8–10 (1995).

HADFIELD, GILLIAN K, RULES FOR A FLAT WORLD (Oxford University Press, 2017).

KURER, PETER, LEGAL AND COMPLIANCE RISK (Oxford University Press, 2015).

Rosen, Robert E, *The inside counsel movement: professional judgment and organizational representation,* 64 Indiana Law Journal 479–533 (1989).

Sako, Mari & Kubo, Katsuyuki, *Professionals on Corporate Boards: How do they affect the Bottom Line?*, Rieti Discussion Paper (2019), https://www.rieti.go.jp/en/publications/summary/19020011.html (last visited Apr. 11, 2019).

Tellmann, Bejarne P, Building an Outstanding Legal Team Battle-Tested Strategies from a General Counsel (Globe Law and Business, 2017).

Veasey, E Norman & Di Guglielmo, Christine T, Indispensable Counsel: The Chief Legal Officer in the New Reality (Oxford University Press, 2012).

B. Online Sources

Henderson, Todd, Hutton, Irena, Jiang, Danling & Pierson, Matthew, *Lawyer CEOs*, University of Chicago Law School Working Paper (Oct. 13, 2018, 4:37 PM), http://www.law.nyu.edu/sites/default/files/Lawyer%20CEOs.pdf (last visited Apr. 11, 2019).

Neuscheler, Tillmann, *Jeder fünfte DAX-Chef begann seine Karriere als Unternehmensberater* [Every fifth DAX-CEO had a career start as management consultant], *in* Frankfurter Allgemeine Zeitung (Sept. 13, 2018, 4:37 PM) at 7, http://www.faz.net/aktuell/beruf-chance/beruf/jeder-fuenfte-dax-chef-startete-seine-karriere-als-unternehmensberater-15624400.html (last visited Apr. 11, 2019).

Sako, Mari, *Changing Role of General Counsel in Germany*, Said Business School, University of Oxford (Oct. 13, 2018, 3:45 PM), http://eureka.sbs.ox.ac.uk/6870/ (last visited Apr. 11, 2019).

Sako, Mari, *General Counsel with Power?*, Said Business School, University of Oxford (Oct. 13, 2018, 4:33 PM), http://eureka.sbs.ox.ac.uk/4560/1/General_Counsel_with_Power.pdf (last visited Apr. 11, 2019).

C. Other Sources

The Doors, Break On Through (To the Other Side) (Elektra Records, 1967).

Professor Michele DeStefano

Innovation

A New Key Discipline for Lawyers and Legal Education

TABLE OF CONTENTS

I. Intro: The Innovation Tournament in Law and Why We Should Care About It

Over the past two years, I have interviewed hundreds of in-house and law firm lawyers from around the globe to explore the changing legal marketplace, expectations of clients, and innovation in law. One of my main conclusions is that we are experiencing an Innovation Tournament in Law and almost everyone is playing in it. What do I mean by that? As I explain in more detail in my book, *Legal Upheaval: A Guide to Creativity, Collaboration, and Innovation in Law,*[1] driven by a combination of technology, socio-economics, and globality, we are witnessing innovation on almost every legal dimension, including how legal services are priced, packaged, sourced, and delivered. Importantly, this innovation is not only coming from legal tech startups and alternative legal service providers (now called «law companies»).[2] Law firms, the Big Four, and corporate legal departments are creating some innovations of their own—including new services, products, tools, and, importantly, new processes. For example, big firms have purchased LPOs, created new tools to provide self-service to clients, and developed innovation incubators. Even those that aren't creating the innovations are playing in the Innovation Tournament by utilizing the innovations (or exapting[3] them) to become more efficient and effective—

---

1 Michele DeStefano, Legal Upheaval: A Guide to Creativity, Collaboration, and Innovation in Law (Ankerwycke, 2018).

2 Thomson Reuters Legal Executive Institute, Georgetown University Law Center, Oxford University Säid Business School and Acritas, *Alternative Legal Service Providers: Understanding the Growth and Benefits of These New Legal Providers* (Jan. 2019), https://legal.thomsonreuters.com/content/dam/ewp-m/documents/legal/en/pdf/reports/alsp-report-final.pdf?cid=9008178&sfdccampaignid=7011B000002OF6AQAW&chl=pr (last visited Aril 13, 2019) at 5–6 (reporting that nearly small, medium, and large law firms use ASLPs) [hereinafter «ALSP Report»]; Vicky Waye, Martie-Louise Verreynne & Jane Knowler, *Innovation in the Australian Legal Profession,* 25 (2) International Journal of the Legal Profession 213–242 (2017).

3 Exaptation is a word generally used in the field of evolutionary biology. The term was originally coined by evolutionary biologists *Stephen Jay Gould & Elizabeth S Vrba* to describe a change in the biology of a species other than adaptation. *See* Stephen Jay Gould & Elizabeth S Vrba, *Exaptation—A Missing Term in the Science of Form,* 8 (19) Paleobiology 4–15 (1982), http://www2.hawaii.edu/~khayes/Journal_Club/fall2006/Gould_&_Vrb_1982_Paleobio.pdf (last visited Apr. 12, 2019). However, it is also a term to describe how scientific inventions are made. Exaptation is when something is borrowed from one field and used to solve a problem in a totally unrelated field. *See* Steven Johnson, Where Good Ideas Come From: The Natural History of Innovation (Riverhead Books, 2010) at 159–61; Nicolas Dew, Saras D Sarasvathy & Sankaran Venkataraman, *The Economic Implications of Exaptation*, 14 (1) J. Evol. Econ. 69–84 (2004), https://link.springer.com/article/10.1007/s00191-003-0180-x (last visited Apr. 12, 2019). («[N]ew markets develop as the result of the application of an existing technology to a new domain of use … When an entrepreneur flips a technology into an adjacent possible market this is truly an exaptation of the technology, not an adaptation.») Exaptation is different than (but related to)

and deliver better service.[4] Further, the Innovation Tournament is attracting significant investment. In July 2018, Legal Zoom received $500 million dollars from Francisco Partners and GPI Capital.[5] In September 2018, CVC capital partners announced a majority interest investment in UnitedLex, valued at approximated at $200 million.[6]

The law market sky, however, is not falling. Consider that these new legal services companies only make up $10 billion of what is a $700–800 billion-dollar legal marketplace.[7] Many of the newcomers could be coined «Legal Freegans» because they are eating Big Law's leftovers and serving it to clients in the form of new technology driven solutions that may not be Rolls Royce bespoke solutions but that increase efficiency and are good enough. True, that sounds a little bit like the beginnings of a path to disruption. Yet, I'm not the only one to believe that this is not a *Kodak Moment*. We are not seeing disruption in the law marketplace in the Clayton Christensen sense; that is, in the way that Eastman Kodak was disrupted by digital film. Perhaps this is in part because by entering the Innovation Tournament, law firms are taking what *Ron Dolin* and *Thomas Buley* identify as an «adaptive innovation» approach. That is, they are «acknowledging the peculiarities of the industry that prevent

---

association in that exaptation is a result of the cross-fertilization of different disciplines; association skills help us make the exaptation leap. I first wrote about the importance of exaptation for creating innovation in law in 2012. *See* Michele DeStefano, *NonLawyers Influencing Lawyers infra* note 16. Further, I created an exaptation exercise that others now use when they teach design thinking to lawyers and law students.

4 ALSP Report, *supra* note 2; Altman Weil, *2018 Chief Legal Officer Survey*, http://www.altmanweil.com//dir_docs/resource/154F22DC-E519-4CE2-991D-492A0448C74F_document.pdf (last visited Apr. 11, 2019) at iv (reporting that 47% of law departments outsource work to vendors that they used to give to law firms); Thomson Reuters and Georgetown University Law School, *2019 Report on the State of the Legal Market*, http://ask.legalsolutions.thomsonreuters.info/LEI_2019-State_of_Legal_Mkt (last visited Apr. 9, 2019) at 15 (reporting that corporate legal spend has been rising steadily while law firms are losing market share because more work is being brought in-house and corporate law departments have transferred work to ALSPs); *id.* at 13 («Over the past 10 years, clients have become ever more willing to disaggregate matters … [and] to move matters down market», i.e., to smaller firms or to non-traditional providers).

5 *See,* e.g., LegalTech News, *LegalZoom Announces $500 Million Investment, Among Largest in Legal Tech History*, (Jul, 31, 2018), https://www.legalzoom.com/press/press-mentions/legal zoom-announces-500-million-investment-among-largest-in-legal-tech-history (last visited Apr. 12, 2019).

6 *See,* e.g., Roy Strom, *UnitedLex, Big Deals in Hand, Sells Majority Stake to European Buyout Firm*, The American Lawyer (Sep. 20, 2018), https://www.law.com/americanlawyer/2018/09/20/unitedlex-big-deals-in-hand-sells-majority-stake-to-european-buyout-firm/ (last visited Apr. 4, 2019); Reghu Balakrishnan, *CVC Capital in talks to buy UnitedLex for $200 million*, Economic Times (Jul. 17, 2018), https://economictimes.indiatimes.com/industry/services/consultancy-/-audit/cvc-capital-in-talks-to-buy-unitedlex-for-200-million/articleshow/65159083.cms (last visited Apr. 9, 2019).

7 ALSP Report, *supra* note 2, at 1; Ray Worthy Campbell, *Rethinking Regulation and Innovation in the U.S. Legal Services Market*, 9 N.Y.U.J. L. & Bus. 1 (2012); Brian Sheppard, *Incomplete Innovation and the Premature Disruption of Legal Services*, 2015 Mich. St. L. Rev. 1797 (2015).

total disruption while embracing tenets of disruptive innovation to help cement the incumbents' position in the market, augmenting and amplifying the services they provide».[8] Legal service providers that are playing in the Innovation Tournament are not doing so simply to increase business or services; rather, they are embracing the new business models that are being developed as the new way of doing business.[9] For now, then, we don't need to be afraid that the wolf is coming (like the Boy Who Cried Wolf), or that the sky is falling (like Chicken Little).

So why should we care about this Innovation Tournament, or the «legal upheaval» that is occurring in the law marketplace, if it is not leading to disruption? We should care because lawyers of all types—from big law to small and mid-size firms, from government to in-house, and even solo lawyers—are being challenged to change the way they work. Clients are asking their lawyers to innovate (and often with others outside their organization or departments), and lawyers don't know what their clients are asking for when they ask for innovation or how to do it or both. This is frustrating and confusing lawyers all over the world. A common response I hear from law firm lawyers when I ask about the call for innovation is as follows:

> *As more and more work is being transferred to in-house legal teams, we are being asked to innovate and I don't know what that means or how to do it or how to get resources from my firm if I have a great idea or know how to do it. We keep getting told to go do these great innovative things but we don't have any tools or a path do it. And we don't even know what «it» is or if our clients will really want it in the end, anyway.*

Over the course of conducting hundreds of interviews and working with teams of lawyers and their clients on innovation journeys, I can't help but conclude that what clients are really asking for with «the call to innovate» is a new type and level of collaboration and client service. It's a call for service transformation in disguise. What they are asking for is the mindset, skillset, and behavior of innovators. The problem with this is that many lawyers are ill-equipped to meet these new demands. A combination of their temperament, training, and professional identity works against honing the DNA of

---

8 *See* e.g., Ron Dolin & Thomas Buley, *Adaptive Innovation: Innovator's Dilemma in Big Law*, 5 (2) HARVARD LAW SCHOOL'S THE PRACTICE (Jan.–Feb. 2019) («Neither the disruptive nor sustaining innovation described in Christensen's work seems to adequately characterize the changes occurring.»).

9 Scott D Anthony, *Kodak's Downfall Wasn't About Technology*, HARVARD BUSINESS REVIEW (Jul. 15, 2016), https://hbr.org/2016/07/kodaks-downfall-wasnt-about-technology (last visited Apr. 4, 2019) (explaining that this was why Kodak failed).

innovators.[10] This is why, for practicing and aspiring lawyers, the new discipline in legal education needs to be innovation.

Part II of this chapter begins by demonstrating that clients' call for innovation is really a call for transformation in service from their lawyers. Part III explores why answering this call can be problematic for lawyers. It seeks to show that lawyers' professional identity, training, and temperament (along with extrinsic and intrinsic motivation) make it difficult for lawyers to adopt the collaborative, creative mindset of innovators. Part IV begins by recommending that innovation be adopted as a new key discipline at the law school and executive education (continuing education) level because in the process of learning how to innovate, lawyers hone the mindset, skillset, and behaviors that clients desire. It provides some suggestions that may help lawyers overcome the hurdles that may be restricting their individual ability to hone the DNA of an innovator. It concludes with some pie-in-the-sky suggestions to ensure that innovation becomes the new key discipline for lawyers.

II. The Call for Innovation in Law: A Call for Service Transformation in Disguise

True, some clients who ask for innovation from their lawyers *really* want innovation—for example, the forward-thinking CEOs of companies like DXC[11] who partner with their General Counsels (hereinafter «GCs») in their charge to innovate are, as part of that charge, asking their GCs to innovate how they run their legal departments—and they mean business (in every sense of the phrase!). However, over the course of conducting hundreds of interviews of GCs, law firm partners, and heads of innovation at law firms all around the world, I have concluded that when clients ask for innovation, they are not asking for shiny new toys; instead, what they are really asking for (but not *directly*) is a new type and level of service. Even if clients truly desire for their lawyers to create new products, apps, or platforms, my research suggests that clients crave the new way of collaborating with their lawyers and the new kind of service that comes from the undergoing of the innovation process. Whether the client really wants innovation or not, in most cases, at a minimum, the call for innovation is also a call for service transformation in disguise. It's a sexy

10 Jeff Dyer, Hal Gregersen & Clayton M Christensen, The Innovator's DNA: Mastering the Five Skills of Disruptive Innovators (Harvard Business Review Press, 2011) at 23–7.

11 DXC is a multinational IT services corporation with revenues of $25 billion operating in 70 countries. It is the result of a merger between Computer Sciences Corporation (CSC,) Electronic Data Systems (EDS), and a spin-off of Hewlett Packard Enterprise. *See* Wikipedia, *DXC*, https://en.wikipedia.org/wiki/DXC_Technology (last visited Apr. 7, 2019).

spin on a request that should have been made ages ago: clients want full-service client service from their lawyers. They want lawyers to put the emphasis on the word «services» in the offering of legal services and they are asking for it under the mask of innovation. I am led to this conclusion for the following three reasons:

A. Reason #1: The Ask for Innovation from Lawyers Is for Inches Not Miles

Our clients are being pressured to innovate the products and services that they provide and the processes by which they provide them in order to be more efficient and add value. In response, these same clients are looking to their lawyers to innovate—and looking to do so *with* them. My GC interviewees commonly stressed this point: They want to co-collaborate towards innovation alongside and with their law firm lawyers. In-house legal clients need help running their legal departments more like businesses so that they are not «just» cost centers. Innovation is a way to to enhance efficiency, measure value, create profit-generating tools and resources, and create a value-add (even if not measurable). Professor *David B. Wilkins* has referred to this ask as one that is about «operationalizing innovation in legal organizations».[12] Part of this operationalization includes structural change as well. Today, big corporate legal departments often include someone as the Head of Legal Operations, which could be considered the mirror image to the Chief Innovation Officer at law firms. As discussed in my recent article, *The Chief Innovation Officer: Goals, Roles, and Holes*, both of these roles have been developed to help suppress demand from clients, provide more self-service, and create a culture of innovation within their respective organizations.[13]

Most would agree that the call for innovation has not been met with big bang innovative products and services from lawyers. The good news is that because the law marketplace has been slow to change (up until the last decade), small changes make a big difference. Simply mapping out processes and client journeys can help in-house legal departments and law firms alike recognize areas for improvement. Therefore, at the moment, the call to innovate (even when the GC means it) is not one for big bang impact. It is a smaller ask for incremental changes that create lasting value. My colleague, client, and now great friend, *James Batham*, Partner at Eversheds Sutherland, coined the

---

12 David B Wilkins, *Operationalizing Innovation in Legal Organizing*, Harvard Law Today (Aug. 29, 2018), https://today.law.harvard.edu/operationalizing-innovation-legal-organizations (last visited Apr. 11, 2019).

13 Michele DeStefano, *The Law Firm Chief Innovation: Goals, Roles, and Holes*, Modern Legal Practice (Oct. 2018–Jan. 2019).

client ask for innovation as one for «TNT»—not the explosive powder—but instead for T as in Tiny, N as in Noticeable, and T as in Things, or Tiny Noticeable Things that make lasting value. In one of my favorite books of all time, *A Man Without Qualities*, *Robert Musil* writes that it is easy «to think in miles when you've no idea what riches can be hidden in an inch».[14] My research suggests clients are relishing any inches they are receiving and, therefore, that the kind of innovation that clients are asking for is in inches, not miles. My research also suggests that the lawyers who understand and embrace this are experiencing riches; that is, they are being compensated for delighting their clients with TNT and the new mindset and behaviors they have adopted and bestowed upon clients in the process of innovating.

B. Reason #2: The Focus is Changing from *What* Lawyers Do to *How* They Do It

My research suggests that clients' focus is changing from *what* services and expertise lawyers provide to *how* they provide those services and expertise. In the past, clients may have been delighted to receive the highest quality legal expertise (at the best price). That is not the case anymore. In today's competitive market, lawyering skills alone are not enough. Clients want more than what might be considered traditional, high-quality legal advice and services from their lawyers. They want lawyers who bridge the gap between private practice and full-service client service. Clients are calling on lawyers to leverage tech differently, to innovate, cross-collaborate, and partner together to solve problems. To be adept at lawyering today, at a minimum, lawyers must be business-focused and business-minded, readily able to harness technology and social media to their employer and clients' advantage. They must be leaders who are experts in their market sector (not just specialized area of practice). They must excel at project management, business planning, communicating, presenting, mentoring, and giving feedback. Clients want lawyers to approach legal services like business services. They want lawyers who communicate the way a business person communicates—with branding and target audience in mind and much (much) more succinctly. They want lawyers to at least understand the impetus behind the twenty-first century acronym TL;dr (too long; don't read). Further, they want their outside lawyers to be an extension of the legal department to go so far as to behave and write like client i.e., deliver legal advice in the client's specific corporate-culture style. And they want more than that:

---

14 Robert Musil, The Man Without Qualities, Vol. I: A Sort of Introduction and Pseudoreality Prevails into the Millennium (Vintage Books, 1996) at 62.

1. Lawyers Who Are Proactive Co-Collaborators

My research indicates that clients are demanding not only that lawyers collaborate[15] but that they proactively co-collaborate «together» with the client. In order to prevent and solve the problems of today, clients of all kinds and sizes need their lawyers to collaborate with other lawyers and business professionals from different backgrounds, industries, and locations. This is because today's problems are more complex and, if not multidisciplinary at their core, can still benefit from a multidisciplinary approach. Arguably, this is just as true for the solo practitioner as for the big law attorney.[16] Although lawyers have learned how to cross-sell, as Harvard Law Fellow *Heidi Gardner* points out, collaboration is not cross-selling.[17] Cross-selling is telling your corporate client after negotiating a contract, «I have a partner that does great litigation work. Let me introduce you.» Collaboration is telling your banking client during an M&A deal, «My partner is an expert in deal-making. She works in our real estate area, but she might be able to help us think through our deal from a different angle. Do you want me to set up lunch for the three of us to brainstorm?»

Collaboration is *not* attempting to claim credit and identify individual contributions when working with other law firms on a panel, a client-service-horrible (i.e., a worst practice), I have heard in too many variations too many times. Clients want lawyers to collaborate internally and externally—together with the client—in real time. An example of a client-service-honorable (i.e., a best practice) also comes from one of my GC interviewees. The GC explained that his law firm panel of five firms met on their own impetus prior to the first «official» meeting with him in order to get to know each other, identify and divvy areas of expertise, and create a new brand and identity so that they could present themselves to the GC as one entity. This showed great understanding of why GCs put together «dream teams» and demonstrated em-

---

15 Heidi K Gardner, *When Senior Managers Won't Collaborate*, 93 (3) Harvard Business Review 74–82 (Mar. 2015); Heidi K Gardner, Smart Collaboration: How Professionals and Their Firms Succeed by Breaking Down Silos (Harvard Business Review Press, 2016) at 8; Henry N Nassau, *Collaboration as Superpower: Optimizing Value to Lead in the Future*, New York L.J. (Apr. 24, 2017), https://www.newyorklawjournal.com/id=1202784074939/Collaboration-as-Superpower-Optimizing-Value-to-Lead-in-the-Future (last visited Apr. 5, 2019).

16 Consider that academics have been researching and writing about the need for collaboration in law practice since as early as the 1990s, if not earlier. *See,* e.g., Susan Bryant, *Collaboration in Law Practice: A Satisfying and Productive Process for a Diverse Profession*, 17 Vt. L. Rev. 459 (1993) (espousing on the benefits of collaboration among lawyers in terms of skillset, mindset, inclusiveness, judgment, effectiveness, and work satisfaction); *see also* Michele DeStefano, *NonLawyers Influencing Lawyers: Too Many Cooks in the Kitchen or Stone Soup*?, 80 Fordham L. Rev. 2791 (2012) (touting the importance of multi-disciplinary collaboration for creative problem solving and innovation).

17 Gardner, *Smart Collaboration, supra* note 15, at 8.

pathy for the GC; i.e., how hard it is for GCs to manage law firm partners from five different firms when they act like competitors instead of collaborators. During the first official meeting, they introduced themselves as the client's «virtual dream firm» made up of partners with five different areas of expertise who would work together to deliver the services *as if* they were from one firm. It was a bright spot in my many interviews that often seemed to uncover only pain points.

The ask for collaboration from lawyers' clients isn't for the normal run-of-the-mill collaboration that most people talk about. Instead, it is for what *Carlos Valdes-Dapena*, former director of organization and group effectiveness at Mars, Inc., calls «proactive collaboration».[18] *Valdes-Dapena* maps out the interactions of professionals on a progressing scale from «disruptive politics»—and eventually to that which begins to be more collaborative: «co-operation—coordination—reactive collaboration—proactive collaboration».[19] Evidently, most professionals spend most of our time in «co-operation» and «coordination» mode. Further, even when we collaborate, we usually only do so reactively.[20] My interviews suggest that lawyers are being asked to collaborate and to do so differently than before, to do so proactively. And in my interviews inhouse lawyers emphasize the word «together». Clients want their outside lawyers to proactively collaborate with them «together» in real-time.

2. Lawyers Who Are Consiglieres Who Focus on Problem Finding and Help Predict the Future

Our clients' needs have changed. Clients want more than the collaboration of the past. They are asking for us be counselors again. They want us to collaborate towards decision-making and work through risk assessment in business language from a business mindset. They want help making decisions and working through issues beyond law. And they want tailored advice. Think: The consigliere from the Godfather (but an ethical one, of course).

The difference is also in the willingness to admit that we might not have all the answers and that talking to lawyers from different industry groups and business professionals outside of law might create a better solution and, importantly, help us uncover problems we might not have found. Clients are asking their lawyers to spend more time on the front end in problem-finding exploration so that the solution is a snug fit—as opposed to over- or under-delivering. As *Tina Seelig* and *Daniel Pink* have made clear, this is because, the

---

18 Carlos Valdes-Dapena, Lessons from Mars: How One Global Company Cracked the Code on High Performance Collaboration and Teamwork (Change Makers Books, 2018) at 54–61.

19 *Id.* at 55 (identifying the non-collaborative interactions on the following scale: «destructive politics; unhealthy competition; passive aggression; benign neglect»).

20 *See* Part IV *infra*.

best problem solvers are the best problem finders.[21] So, the big difference is a shift in *how*. It is a change in the way we approach problem solving (i.e., by problem finding), the we communicate, the way we present ideas, the way we actually problem solve and, more than that, it is a shift toward a client-centric provision of services. Consider the difference between cross-selling and collaborating noted above. In the first scenario, the offer to involve the lawyer's partner wasn't based on needs or pain points of the client. In the second, it was. It was a shift toward empathy with the client. It was a shift towards full-service client service.

Our clients' businesses are changing in unpredictable ways. Clients need lawyers to be the «innovation consiglieres» who look around the corner to help their clients map their future industries (and resulting risks). They need lawyers who will research and recommend what types of legal, technological, and other resources they will need to support their future undertakings. A client that was once a rental car company may now consider itself a company in the business of big (and profitable) data; a real estate and construction company may soon be considered a tech company. Simply put, clients want business advice in addition to legal advice from their lawyers. They want lawyers to be counselors, not just advisers. Some may question whether lawyers should be counselors who provide a mix of legal and business advice and services. Clients, however, think the answer to that question is absolutely yes!

Clients are asking for this transformative service when they ask their lawyers to «innovate». What they really need, whether they want their lawyers to actually create innovations or not, is for their lawyers to learn *how* to innovate. This is because, in the process of learning how to innovate, lawyers hone the mindset, skillset, and behavior that delight clients. This is the third reason I suggest that the call for innovation is more aptly described as a call for service transformation.

C. Reason #3: In the Process of Learning How to Innovate, Lawyers Transform How They Collaborate with and Provide Service to Clients

As suggested above, my main finding from conducting hundreds of interviews and leading hundreds of multi-disciplinary teams on 16-week innovation journeys is that clients are calling for lawyers to innovate because the innovation process transforms how lawyers collaborate with and service clients. This is

---

21 Daniel H Pink, To Sell Is Human: The Surprising Truth About Moving Others (Riverhead Books, 2012) at 5; 88–9; Tina Seelig, What I Wish I Knew When I Was 20: A Crash Course on Making Your Place in the World (Harper One, 2009) at 20.

why some of the biggest and best corporations, law firms, and professional service providers pay money to send their lawyers on 16-week innovation journeys in LawWithoutWalls and to get trained in the 3-4-5 Method of Innovation I designed especially for lawyers (and that is described in my other chapter in Part 3 of this book). True, these teams are charged with solving a real problem faced by the corporate legal department or law firm. Many of the teams create viable innovations at the intersection of law, business, and technology that are brought to life in some shape or form. But the innovation is just the icing. The cake? The cake is the transformation of the individual on the journey. Generally, the lawyers I lead on these journeys don't want to quit their day jobs to create the innovations. They don't want to be entrepreneurs. At most, they may want to be intrapreneurs.[22] The better part of these lawyers, however, desire the change in mindset, skillset, and behavior that comes with learning how to innovate. They realize they can't just change by deciding to change. They realize that they can't take a few classes to teach them how to collaborate, give feedback, mentor, or lead. They go on an innovation journey to become more creative and more innovative, and to transform how they collaborate with others in creative problem solving. In the process, they transform how they lead, how they practice, and how they provide service to clients.

This is why I call learning how to innovate «the new value equation in law».[23] I often argue that lawyers should learn how to innovate because it makes cents and sense—that is, it makes economic sense (equates to money in lawyers' pockets) and logical sense. My research along with research by others demonstrates that clients reward lawyers (inhouse and external lawyers) for collaborating towards innovation: 1) internal business clients reward inhouse lawyers by returning the collaboration and including inhouse earlier on (both of which enable inhouse to create processes and solutions and ways of working that add more value); and 2) inhouse lawyers reward law firms by putting them on panels, giving them more business, talking about them in the press, and recommending them to others.[24] That's the «cents» in innovating with clients. The sense is the value-add that is baked in; i.e., in the process of learning how to innovate, even if the innovation (itself fails), the value equation delivers.

---

22 An intrapreneur is someone who has the qualities and skills of an entrepreneur but seeks to create innovation internally—within the organization or company or firm in which she/he works. *See generally* Vjay Govindarahan & Jatin Desai, *Recognize Intraprenuers Before they Leave*, Harvard Business Review (Sep. 20, 2013), https://hbr.org/2013/09/recognize_intrapreneurs (last visited Apr. 2, 2019).; but *see* Andrew Corbett, *The Myth of the Intrapreneur*, Harvard Business Review (Jun. 26, 2018), https://hbr.org/2018/06/the-myth-of-the-intrapreneur (last visited Apr. 14, 2019).

23 DeStefano, *Legal Upheaval, supra* note 1, at Chapter 4: The New Value Equation in Law: An A, B, C, Primer.

24 DeStefano, *Legal Upheaval, supra* note 1, at 70–82; *see also* Gardner, *Smart Collaboration, supra* note 1, at 72–8,

I call this the ABC primer.[25] This is because in attempting to innovate, we change our attitude (A) about what is innovation. Innovation is no longer daunting and unattainable. Everyone, you, me, he, she, and they can be an intrapreneur. Our attitude about leadership shifts just an inch with an increased emphasis on creativity, collaboration, inclusion, and empathy. Second, in learning how to innovate, we hone new skills and that equates to new behaviors (B) like those I outline in the *Lawyer Skills Delta:* skills that are necessary to meet clients' expectations (project management, business acumen, communication, mentoring, giving and receiving feedback, technology) and those that help us exceed them (like empathy, listening, curiosity, resilience, cultural competency, association, audacity, humility, self-awareness).[26] Lastly, in changing our attitude (A) and behavior (B), we begin to create culture change (C) that is a little like wacky-tack (a repositionable liquid adhesive). It sticks, it's catchy, and that's how culture change works when teams innovate. Traditional thought dictated that culture change should come from the top down, like pushing down the filter of a French Press. Or we were told that it has to come from the bottom up, like bubbles in soda water; or, say others, from the middle out, as I have contended in the context of creating a culture of compliance.[27] Recent research around culture change, however, has suggested what LawWithout-Walls teams have been doing for almost 10 years: culture change occurs with small interventions designed to get one small group to collaborate differently and that team then motivates others to do the same over time.[28] I fondly call it the bonfire approach, because *Chris White*, Chief Information Officer at HFW, once told me that when it came to innovation, he liked to light bonfires at his firm. Who can resist the lure from the bonfire's light, or the scent from roasted marshmallows? Everyone knows that when fires burn, they spread. So that's the «sense»: in learning how to innovate, we hone these new skills and behaviors. We become creative, collaborative, leaders and we delight our clients.

But it is not so simple. Lawyers aren't taught how to innovate in law school or afterwards in practice—or in most continuing education programs. In fact, we are taught to hone attitudes and behaviors that are inapposite to innovators. This leaves a big gap between what clients want and what we deliver. Further, this gap isn't easily over come as the next Part of this chapter explains.

---

25 DeStefano, *Legal Upheaval, supra* note 1, at 70.

26 *Id.* at 28–44.

27 DeStefano, Michele, *The Chief Compliance Officer: Should There Be a New «C» in the C-Suite*? Harvard Law School's The Practice (Jul. 2016), https://thepractice.law.harvard.edu/article/the-chief-compliance-officer/ (last visited Apr. 2, 2019); Michele DeStefano, *Creating a Culture of Compliance: Why Departmentalization May Not Be the Answer*, 10 Hastings Business L.J. 71–182 (2013).

28 Jon R Katzenbach, Ilona Steffen, & Caroline Kronley, *Culture Change That Sticks,* 90 (7–8):110–7 Harvard Business Review 162 (July–Aug. 2012), https://hbr.org/2012/07/cultural-change-that-sticks (last visited Apr. 4, 2019).

III. The Two «i's» in Innovation: Why Collaborating and Innovating Can Be Hard for Lawyers

Everyone likes to tout that there is no «i» in team. Although that is undeniably true, I like to point out that there are two «i's» in innovation and that these two «i's» wreak havoc on successful teaming and collaboration by lawyers. Let's face it: learning to collaborate and innovate isn't easy for anyone but, arguably, it is especially hard for lawyers. This is due, in part, to our training (how we are taught in law school and in practice). It is also due to the temperament that we (naturally or over time) have developed in our practice. Although this temperament makes us really good at being lawyers, it might, at times, impede our ability to innovate and meet these new client expectations. It might make it really hard for us to «team» in the way that today's multi-disciplinary, global world is requiring. This is why I argue that lawyers who want to learn how to innovate need to keep their eye on the two «i's» in innovation. These two «i's» are: the lawyer's *Identity* as a legal professional and the lawyer as an *Individual.* Without recognizing how these «i's» impact lawyers' ability to team and collaborate, our efforts at innovation will be stymied—that's why the future of legal training needs to keep an eye on the «i's» in innovation.

A. Identity: The Lawyer's Professional Identity is Inapposite to the DNA of Innovators

Although, of course, all lawyers are different, research shows that we often share some common characteristics, that we view ourselves differently than other types of professionals—and that we are trained to develop and/or exhibit these characteristics.[29] There has been literature about lawyers' professional identity vis-a-vis other types of professionals since almost the beginning of the

---

29 *See* Larry Richard, *Herding Cats: The Lawyer Personality Revealed,* 29 (11) Altman Weil Report to Management 1–12 (2002), http://www.managingpartnerforum.org/tasks/sites/mpf/assets/image/MPF%20-%20WEBSITE%20-%20ARTICLE%20-%20Herding%20Cats%20-%20Richards1.pdf (last visited Apr. 2, 2019); *see also* Larry Richard, *The Lawyer Personality: Why Lawyers Are Skeptical,* What Makes Lawyers Tick? (Feb. 11, 2013), https://www.lawyerbrainblog.com/2013/02/the-lawyer-personality-why-lawyers-are-skeptical/ (last visited Apr. 9, 2019); *see also* Jathan Janove, *Can Risk-Averse Lawyers Learn to Embrace Change? An Interview with Dr. Larry Richard,* Ogletree Deakins (Jan. 12, 2016), https://ogletree.com/insights/2016-01-12/can-risk-averse-lawyers-learn-to-embrace-change-an-interview-with-dr-larry-richard/ (last visited Apr. 9, 2019); *see also* Robert Eli Rosen, Christine E Parker & Vibeke Lehmann Nielson, *The Framing Effects of Professionalism: Is There a Lawyer Cast of Mind? Lessons from Compliance Programs*, 40 (1) 14 Fordham Urb. L.J. 297–367 (2013).

time: think Shakespeare.[30] The title of an article by *Ben W Heineman, Jr., William F Lee*, and *David B Wilkins* says it all: «Lawyers as Professionals and as Citizens: Key Roles and Responsibilities in the 21st Century».[31] As professionals, lawyers have special responsibilities that other professionals do not. Consider the first sentence in the ABA's Model Rules of Professional Conduct: «A lawyer, as a member of the legal profession, is a representative of clients, an officer of the legal system and a public citizen having special responsibility for the quality of justice».[32] Perhaps in contradiction to some of our other duties, historically in the United States and UK, lawyers have been taught that their role is to represent their clients with zeal and that the client is king (taking precedent over even the reigning monarch themselves). Consider the speech of Henry Lord Brougham in early 1800s:

> *An advocate by the sacred duty which he owes his client, knows, in the discharge of that office, but one person in the world, that client and none other. To save that client by all expedient means—to protect that client at all hazards and costs to all others, and among others to himself—is the highest and most unquestioned of his duties.*[33]

Despite that Brougham's call for zealous advocacy has since been criticized and rejected in England and elsewhere, it «has had a lasting effect across the pond[,] [i]n the United States.»[34] Since the 1800s, the lawyer identity has been equated to saver and servant of the client.

All of these duties (plus our training) help form our professional identity as lawyers. Thus, it is unsurprising that there is research demonstrating that lawyers often display a similar disposition, nature, character, makeup, mind, spirit, and attitudes (and that this «temperament» is different than other types

---

30 William Shakespeare, Shakespeare's King Henry the Sixth, Part II (ed. William J. Rolfe, Harper & Brothers, 1895), Act IV, Scene II, at 107; *see also* Robert S Redmount, *Attorney Personalities and Legal Consultation,* 109 U. Pa. L. Rev. 972 (1961).

31 Ben W Heineman, Jr. et al, *Lawyers as Professionals and as Citizens: Key Roles and Responsibilities in the 21st Century*, Harvard Law School Center on the Legal Profession (November 2014).

32 American Bar Association, *Model Rules of Professional Conduct, Preamble & Scope* (Aug. 15, 2018), https://www.americanbar.org/groups/professional_responsibility/publications/model_rules_of_professional_conduct/model_rules_of_professional_conduct_preamble_scope/ (last visited Apr. 10, 2019).

33 Henry Brougham, Speeches of Henry Lord Brougham, (A and C Black, 1838).

34 Lawrence J Vilardo & Vincent E Doyle III, *Where Did the Zeal Go?*, ABA Litigation Journal (Fall 2011), https://www.americanbar.org/groups/litigation/publications/litigation_journal/2011_12/fall/where_did_zeal_go/ (last visited Apr. 11, 2019).; *see also* Fred Zacharis & Bruce Green, *Reconceptualizing Advocacy Ethics*, 74 Geo. Wash. L. Rev. 1 (2005); Monroe H Freedman, *Henry Lord Brougham and Zeal*, 34 Hofstra L. Rev. 1319 (2006).

of professionals).[35] Of course, there are variations by lawyer and context,and it may be forever unclear whether people who choose to go to law school are more likely to enter with a certain temperament, or whether the training they receive in law school and beyond makes them a certain way (the classic chicken/egg situation). However, recognizing how our identity as lawyers impacts how we behave is essential to any type of change effort. True, the idea that we need to be self-aware in order to grow as leaders is not new.[36] For lawyers, however, there is an additional level of awareness needed and that is of our self-concept as lawyers because we rely on that concept when we are acting as lawyers and it filters our preferences, tendencies, and practices.[37]

Although not all lawyers are alike and indeed there are differences based on the type of practice, research about lawyers shows that the way we behave, how we view ourselves, and how we are trained can be inapposite to the mindset, skillset, and behaviors of innovators. Consider, for example, what *Jeff Dyer*, *Hal Gergersen*, and *Clayton M Christensen* identify as the five essentials skills that make up the DNA of innovators: 1) Observing; 2) Questioning; 3) Associating, 4) Networking: and, 5) Experimenting.[38] Research suggests that the lawyer's professional identity (which I define as a combination of temperament and training) may make all five especially hard for lawyers.[39] Let me unpack why this may be so. In section 1 below, I will analyze DNA 1 (observing) and 2 (questioning); then in section 2, I will move on to DNA 3 (associating) and 4 (networking). Section 3 will address with DNA 5 (experimenting). I caveat this entire chapter by saying that the purpose of this exploration is not to say that lawyers cannot be creative, collaborative, and innovative. To the contrary, they can be and I know many who are! Instead, I enter this analysis in order to support my main contention of this chapter: we need to spend time training lawyers and aspiring lawyers how to be proactively collaborative and innovative in the way that clients desire today.

1. Why Observing (DNA 1) and Questioning (DNA 2) Like Innovators Can Be Hard for Lawyers

Research demonstrates that lawyers are great at complex problem solving.[40] Although this is a strength, it can also lead lawyers to rush to solve and, as a

35 *See* Research by Dr Larry Richard, *supra* note 29.

36 *See*, e.g., Peter F Drucker, Managing Oneself (Harvard Business Press, 2008).

37 Paul J Brouwer, *The Power to See Ourselves*, Harvard Business Review (Nov. 1964), https://hbr.org/1964/11/the-power-to-see-ourselves (last visited Apr. 7, 2019) (explaining that we have multiple self-concepts that change based on the role we are playing).

38 Dyer, Gregersen & Christensen, *supra* note 10, at 23–7.

39 *See* Research by Dr Larry Richard, *supra* note 29.

40 *See id.*

result, we sometimes solve for symptoms instead of problems. We don't spend enough time doing what both *Daniel Pink* and *Tina Seelig* tout in their respective books: problem/need finding.[41] *Albert Einstein* has a famous quote: *«If I had an hour to solve a problem, I'd spend 55 minutes thinking about the problem and five minutes thinking about solutions.»* And that's the point. Lawyers don't spend enough time upfront in the problem exploration and this is, in part, because we are trained that the client is king and we should drop everything to help our clients because our job is to solve their problems. We are taught that the order of events is: first, clients tell us their problems; then, we go off and solve them. The irony is that in trying to give the clients the royal treatment, to treat them like kings and do *all* the work for them, we do them a disservice.

This behavior is so baked in that even I still do it—even after 10 years teaching innovation to lawyers and leading over 200 multi-disciplinary teams on an innovation journey emphasizing problem finding over problem solving. Just a couple weeks ago, I rushed to solve and missed the mark with my Microsoft client (for whom I have led, for the past four years, an experiential learning innovation/collaboration program targeting the corporate and legal affairs department). This year, we decided to change the program from a part-virtual, three-month format to an intensive, in-person, five-day format. People from Microsoft offices all over the world were scheduled to fly in for the program to join professionals that work at Microsoft's headquarters located close to Seattle, Washington. On the Friday morning before the program's launch scheduled for Monday, I received an urgent email from my client. My client explained that a huge, historic snowstorm was expected to hit the greater Seattle area on Sunday and Monday. My client asked (with a red exclamation point) if I had some time to hop on a call to discuss our options given that the program was supposed to begin on Monday. I immediately called my team. «Drop everything! This is urgent! This is Microsoft! And the client wants to talk ASAP.» We brainstormed in a rabid frenzy:

> *Might we include a live stream so that those whom couldn't make it physically could attend virtually? Might we record the live stream so that those stuck in transit could watch after hours and thereby catch up? Might we re-arrange the teams so that those flying in were grouped together so that they would be similarly situated? Might we have some of the participants fly in earlier to ensure that they arrive before the snowstorm hits?*

41 Daniel H Pink, To Sell Is Human: The Surprising Truth About Moving Others (Riverhead Books, 2012) at 5; 88–9; Tina Seelig, What I Wish I Knew When I Was 20: A Crash Course on Making Your Place in the World (Harper One, 2009) at 20.

Thirty minutes later, abuzz and prepared, we were on the phone with my client. I started by asking: «how are you? I bet this is really hard.» And then I listended. *Empathy right?* I explained that my team had jumped when we received his email and that we had a few options to share to begin a joint brainstorm to come to the right solution together. *Collaborative, problem solving with the client? Check?* WRONG. In the middle of option 2, my client interrupted me and said:

> *I'm not worried about the people flying in from out of town. I'm worried about the people here already, who live in the surrounding suburbs. The greater Seattle area is not built for a snowstorm this size. People that live here won't be able to get to Microsoft Headquarters. And even if they could, the schools will likely close so they won't have child care …*

His words jarred me like the sound of a record needle being dragged across my favorite album. I had committed the ultimate *problem-solver sin*. In my rush to please the client by solving his problems, I missed the mark. Smacking myself, I thought: *What I should have done is started the call by asking questions like: «Why are you worried about the snow impacting our program? Why is that your biggest worry?» Seriously, what is wrong with me? I'm the one who starts every presentation touting Simon Sinek's «Start with Why». And this is what I do?*

True, lawyers are trained to question everything (in a critical manner to ensure we are accounting for all risks), but that type of questioning is different in kind from the open-ended questioning in problem finding. It is different than asking the 5 Whys to get to the root cause of the problem.[42] Lawyers aren't trained to spend time observing (DNA 1) and questioning (DNA 2) in the same way that innovators do. This type of questioning is almost in contradiction to our problem-solver role. We are taught that our clients count on us to prevent problems and to solve those we cannot prevent. When we put the saver/solver together with the historical professional rules of conduct that teach us that we are the servants of the client (who is king), it is no wonder we rush to perform. As mentioned above, since the beginning of time, lawyers' codes of conduct have ordered us to represent with zeal, to use our «judgement *solely* for the benefit of [our] client[s]» and that nothing (not our own personal interests or the interests of others) should dilute our loyalty to the client.[43] Although the same words may no longer be used in our professional codes of

---

42 For a simple explanation of the «5 Whys», *see* Wikipedia, *The 5 Whys*, https://en.wikipedia.org/wiki/5_Whys (last visited Mar. 30, 2019).

43 *See ABA Model Code of Professional Responsibility* (first adopted in 1970 and then replaced by the Model Rules of Professional Conduct in 1983), Canons 5,7; *see also* ABA Model Rules of Professional Conduct, *supra* note 32.

conduct for many of us, they remain as part of our professional identity and training.[44] So, it is perhaps at least understandable why we might not be inclined to spend that time up-front observing and questioning the client.

The sad thing is, my heart was in the right place. I wanted my client to know how dedicated we were to him and I wanted to help ease his worries by finding a solution that could save the program. But we don't get paid for having big hearts that fail to empathize with the client's true situation. And that's the other reason why lawyers have trouble observing and questioning like innovators. Even if we are trained to conduct the type of open-ended pain point discovery interviews that are needed to really understand the problem, we are at a disadvantage because research shows that lawyers score lower on empathy than other professionals and prefer matters of the mind over matters of the heart.[45] It is not that we don't like intimate, strong, relationships—we do—but it could be that we like the intimate relationships we already have (and have grown for years) as opposed to building more. This makes sense given that part of our professional identity is the idea that lawyers are supposed to be the trusted advisors that build long-lasting relationships with clients. Research supports that we are very good at that.[46] Yet, it is problematic for the observing and questioning parts of the innovator's DNA. Observing and questioning are only valuable if they are done with empathy—which is all about understanding and connecting with the heart.[47] If we don't have empathy for the subject we are observing, we won't ask the right questions in the right way. Therefore, our observations won't help us create the right, innovative solutions. This is one reason why empathizing is a key component to any training programs related to design thinking or collaboration.[48] Only when we empathize with the target audience experiencing the problem can we create a solution that resonates.

---

44 Vilardo & Doyle, *supra* note 34.

45 *See* Richard, *Herding Cats*, *supra* note 29.

46 Research I co-conducted with *John Coates*, *Ashish Nanda*, and *David B Wilkins* demonstrates that relationships between law firm lawyers and their clients are strong and long-lasting and take a lot of time to cultivate. *See* John C Coates, Michele B DeStefano, Ashish Nanda, David B Wilkins, *Hiring Teams, Firms, and Lawyers: Evidence of the Evolving Relationships in the Corporate Legal Market*, 36 (4) Law & Soc. Inquiry 999–1031 (Fall 2011) (analyzing interview and survey data from 166 chief legal officers of S&P 500 companies from 2006–2007).

47 For more detail and support, *see* DeStefano, *Legal Upheaval*, *supra* note 1, at 102–4.

48 Charles Duhigg, *What Google Learned From Its Quest to Build the Perfect Team*, The New York Times Magazine (Feb. 28, 2016), https://www.nytimes.com/2016/02/28/magazine/what-google-learned-from-its-quest-to-build-the-perfect-team.html (last visited Apr. 10, 2019); Anita Williams Woolley, Christopher F Chabris, Alex Pentland, Nada Hashmi & Thomas W Malone, *Evidence for a Collective Intelligence Factor in the Performance of Human Groups*, 330 Science 686–688 (2010); Anita Williams Woolley, Christopher F Chabris & Thomas W Malone, *Why Some Teams Are Smarter Than Others*, NY Times (Jan. 16, 2015), https://www.nytimes.com/2015/01/18/opinion/sunday/why-some-teams-are-smarter-than-others.html (last visited Apr. 12, 2019); Young Ji Kim et al., *What Makes a Strong Team? Using Collective Intelligence to Predict Team Perfor-*

2. Why Networking (DNA 3) and Associating (DNA 4) Can Be Hard For Lawyers

Research shows that lawyers are often introverted,[49] competitive,[50] and that we prefer autonomy.[51] This combination often means we like to work behind closed doors (that's when out best work gets done). It also means that we might find it hard (and more exhausting) to co-collaborate with others in innovators' desing-thinking sessions. Moreover, for various reasons, including professional rules and regulations (particularly in the United States) and our professional identity (temperament and training), lawyers tend toward independent (versus collaborative) work[52] and strong, long lasting relationships[53] as opposed to weak alliances.[54] Therefore, we don't work or create networks in the same way that successful entrepreneurs do, which is the third piece of the DNA (networking DNA 3). Studies show that the most successful and innovative entrepreneurs have wide, eclectic networks.[55] As a result, we miss out

---

mance in League of Legends, CSCW 2017 (Feb. 25–March 1, 2017), http://mitsloan.mit.edu/shared/ods/documents/?DocumentID=2710 (last visted Apr. 11, 2019). (finding that cognitive intelligence is positively correlated with the presence of a female team member).

49 Leslie A Gordon, *Most Lawyers Are Introverted, and That's Not Necessarily a Bad Thing*, ABA Journal (Jan. 2016), http://abajournal.com/magazine/article/most_lawyers_are_introverted_and_thats_not_necessarily_a_bad_thing (last visited Apr. 12, 2019) (citing to Eva Wisnik, who has administered Myers-Briggs personality tests to more than 6,000 attorneys since 1990 and found that more than 60% of lawyers are introverts).

50 Gardner, *Smart Collaboration, supra* note 15, at 37–8 (demonstrating that when lawyers are working on complex volatile and ambiguous problems, they become even more risk-averse and protective of client relationship, thereby limiting access to diverse viewpoints of experts within and outside the law firm).

51 *See* e.g., Lawrence S Krieger & Kennon M Sheldon, *What Makes Lawyers Happy? A Data-Driven Prescription to Redefine Professional Services?*, 83 George Washington Law Review 554 579–584 (Feb. 2015) (confirming that importance of autonomy for lawyers well-being and that it increased satisfaction); *see also* Kennon M Sheldon & Krieger, Lawrence S, *Understanding the Negative Effects of Legal Education on Law Student: A Longitudinal Test of Self-Determination Theory*, 33 Personality & Soc. Psychol. Bull. 883, 884–85 (2017).

52 *See* DeStefano, *NonLawyers Influencing Lawyers, supra* note 16.

53 *See* Richard, *Herding Cats, supra* note 29.

54 For more detailed analysis and support, *see* DeStefano, *Legal Upheaval, supra* note 10, at Chapter 4.

55 Martin Ruef, *Strong Ties, Weak Ties and Islands: Structural and Cultural Predictors of Organizational Innovation*, 11 Indus. & Corp. Change 427, 429–30, 432, and 443 (2002) (studying Stanford business school graduates and finding that the most successful entrepreneurs were those with diverse social networks); *see also* Rob Cross & Andrew Parker, The Hidden Power of Social Networks: Understanding How Work Really Gets Done in Organizations (Harvard Business School Press, 2004) 81–3 («Research has shown that people with more diverse, entrepreneurial networks tend to be more successful.»).

on what *Mark S Granovetter* calls «the strength of weak ties.»[56] Weak interpersonal ties create dotted lines between diverse groups and form a conduit for the wide dissemination of ideas. The ideal is to have a combination of both.[57]

Without both, we can miss that diverse interaction that enables association (DNA 4), the fourth piece of the innovator's DNA. Association is the connecting of things that might otherwise not be connected and the migration of ideas that Stephen Johnson points out is how we get to the «pearl of the oyster».[58] We might never find the pearl, however, if we don't open our doors (literally) to other people who are different than us and that have diverse view points. As a result, not only might we solve the wrong problem, but we might not get as far as we might in our solutions. As discussed at greater length in *Legal Upheaval,* innovative solutions stem from the act of building on each other's ideas with a growth mindset and the inclination to say «yes and» as opposed to «no, but.» Lawyers, however, are trained and paid to critique, unpack, and say «no» and «but»—they save their clients a lot of money (and prevent risks) in so doing. So to ask lawyers to suddenly switch their mindset to that of the associative innovator who seeks to connect ideas (in what is often a format that is designed for the extrovert) is a lot to ask without training or the ability to practice. Research shows that executives who are great at analyzing, implementing, and delivering results against defined goals (like lawyers) don't connect things like innovators do.[59] An example of associating like innovators is the puffer fish pill. By associating/connecting the attributes of puffer fish to cancerous tumors, scientists created a pill that inflates inside the body so that it can track a tumor's growth, and then easily deflate when ready for it to pass safely out of the body.[60] Lawyers, like many other senior executives, may have trouble making the leap from fish to pill; they have trouble leaping from the possible to the what Stephen Johnson and Stuart Kauffman call «the adjacent possible».[61]

---

56 Mark S Granovetter, *The Strength of Weak Ties*, 78 Am. J. Soc. 1360, 1361–66 (1973), https://sociology.stanford.edu/sites/default/files/publications/the_strength_of_weak_ties_and_exch_w-gans.pdf (last visited Apr. 8, 2019).

57 Richard Ogle, Smart World: Breakthrough Creativity and the New Science of Ideas (Harvard Business School Press, 2007) 87–8. A combination of weak and strong ties is exactly what lawyers have after they have gone on a 16-week innovation journey in LawWithoutWalls.

58 Steven Johnson, Where Good Ideas Come From: The Natural History of Innovation (Riverhead Books, 2010) at 159–61.

59 Dyer, Gregersen & Christensen, *supra* note 10, at 31–2.

60 BBC, *Inflatable puff fish pill «could track patient's health»,* BBC News (Jan. 30, 2019), https://www.bbc.com/news/health-47059079 (last visited Apr. 3, 2019).

61 Johnson, *supra* note 58, at 174.

3. Why Experimenting (DNA 5) Can Be Hard for Lawyers

Experimenting (DNA 5) also proves difficult for lawyers. Here's why: Research on lawyers demonstrates that lawyers are more skeptical and less trusting than other professionals and lower on psychologic resilience (which is a fancy way of saying we are thin-skinned).[62] This is problematic because without trust and thick skin, we won't collaborate (because we don't trust that the other person will do their job or that they won't jeopardize ours by critiquing us).[63] Further, we won't take risks because doing so opens us up to failure, which our thin skin can't handle.[64] Taking risks is also the opposite of what we have been trained to view as our core job, which is often to help prevent risk for our clients and to identify *any* and *all* risks that might arise (regardless of their severity or probability). This aversion to risk, then, contradicts the innovator's essential need to experiment.

The literature on design thinking and innovation that touts failure as something to be celebrated likely contributes to lawyers' lowered appetite for the type of experimentation that innovation requires. Yes, I have written about the importance of learning from failure. Yet, as I explain in my book, *Legal Upheaval*, failure is not a necessity to innovating.[65] There is research that suggests that failure doesn't make entrepreneurs more likely to succeed in their next ventures. In fact, it suggests the opposite: Entrepreneurs who had previously failed were more likely to fail than first-time entrepreneurs.[66] So, failure for failure's sake is overrated, not to mention unpalatable to lawyers. The failures I recommend celebrating are competent failures. Like Harvard Business School Professor *Gary P Pisano*, I believe «failure should be celebrated only if it results in learning».[67] In LawWithoutWalls, we have a low tolerance for mediocrity and sloppy work, both of which can cause team dysfunction and incompetent failures. We have extremely high expectations and deliverables. When an individual fails to meet these, we don't celebrate that. We work to correct the action. We have a teaming coach, *Susan Sneider*, whose job is essentially to prevent these kinds of incompetent failures. We have found (as others have) that dysfunctional teams generally stem from an «individual per-

---

62 *See* research by Dr Larry Richard, *supra* note 29.

63 For more detailed analysis and support, *see* DeStefano, *Legal Upheaval*, *supra* note 1, at Chapter 3: Lawyers' Crutches: The Source of the Gap in Skills, Behavior, and Mindset.

64 Rosen, Parker & Lehmann, *supra* note 29.

65 DeStefano, *Legal Upheaval*, *supra* note 1, at 73.

66 Walter Frick, *Research: Serial Entrepreneurs Aren't Any More Likely to Succeed*, HARVARD BUSINESS REVIEW (Feb. 20, 2014), https://hbr.org/2014/02/research-serial-entrepreneurs-arent-any-more-likely-to-succeed (last visited Apr. 3, 2019) (finding that successful entrepreneurs were just as likely not to have failed the first time as to have failed the first time).

67 Gary P Pisano, *The Hard Truth About Innovative Cultures*, HARVARD BUSINESS REVIEW (Jan.–Feb. 2019), at 66.

formance problem.»[68] That said, we try to do what *Pisano* recommends: strike the right balance between a culture of unbridled tolerance for failure and one that is completely intolerant of any incompetence.[69] But this balance is hard to find, and most lawyers who dip their toe into any kind of design thinking experience aren't taught about that balance. They believe design thinking or innovation sessions are silly or a waste of time or, worse yet, flirt too dangerously with failure. Before I lead design thinking or innovation sessions at a law firm, I interview some of the partners to get a gauge on how they feel about these types of sessions at their law firm retreats or in their training programs. A common response by lawyers goes something like:

> *Well, let me say, I certainly wouldn't want to be in charge of organizing a collaborative innovation session for the lawyers at my firm. Most lawyers are skeptical and generally, lawyers are not fun at all. I think you have a hard job because most of he lawyers are going to question its value and believe it doesn't mean anything. And its value can be difficult to prove which makes it difficult to convince the lawyers that it is going to be useful and not just a waste of time. And, I think lawyers are not all the time open enough to understand the value of such work.*[70]

The way we are trained in law school does not help increase lawyers' appetite for experimentation either, especially the type of collaborative experimentation that innovation requires. Generally, we are assessed for our own work in law school, even if it has some collaborative component (like a brief.) Therefore, a lot rides on us individually. Further, given that a course's entire grade is often based off of one test, and that grades equate to jobs, there is little room for failure. This emphasis on the individual in law school doesn't stop on graduation day; in fact, its perpetuation leads directly to the second «I» in innovation, the «I» that focuses on the lawyer as an individual.

B. Individuality: The Individual Lawyer May Not Be Motivated to Collaborate or Innovate

Experts in collaboration, like *Carlos Valdes-Dapena*, have pointed out that «the key to unlocking and enhancing collaboration lies in accounting for the needs and drives of the typical individual team member.»[71] This is because, as

---

68 Valdes-Dapena, *supra* note 18, at 77.

69 Pisano, *supra* note 67, at 71.

70 This comment was made to me by a law firm partner who heads up the Paris office of an international, global law firm.

71 Valdes-Dapena, *supra* note 18, at 81.

Chris Avery observes in his aptly named book, «teamwork is an individual skill.»[72] In other words, if the success of collaborating depends on the individual's motivation to develop a collaborative mindset, skillset, and set of behaviors, without the right level of intrinsic and extrinsic motivation, individuals won't focus on honing those teaming skills; and collaboration efforts will fail.

1. Lawyers and Intrinsic Motivation

The reality is that we are not born collaborative. Instead, we are born really, really self-absorbed. If you have ever spent any time with children who are three years old, it becomes very clear that we are born caring most about ourselves. This is why *Carlos Valdes-Dapena* claims that «the individual achievement motive eats the vague goal of collaboration for breakfast.»[73] This is also why we, like children aged three, remain side-by-side in «parallel play»; that is, each doing our thing in close physical proximity instead of collaborating. *Valdes-Dapena* explains that «[c]ollaboration is second- or third-nature for a large majority of us and this predisposes us to consistently revert to our more selfish ways, especially where we're rewarded and recognized to do so.»[74] Further, according to *Daniel H Pink*, humans aren't entirely rational; we are motivated by both extrinsic motivation and intrinsic motivation.[75] This makes overcoming the natural instinct to look out for only ourselves especially hard to overcome for lawyers. Here's why:

The research on lawyers' temperament and training (described above) makes it hard to believe that the majority of lawyers are intrinsically motivated to collaborate or innovate. Intrinsic motivation is «[w]hen the reward is the activity itself—deepening learning, delighting customers, doing one's best.»[76] We know from research that lawyers are intrinsically motivated to complex problem solve and excel at their work and meet individual goals. However, research by others (and by me) does not suggest that most lawyers are intrinsically motivated by collaboration for collaboration's sake or innovation for innovation's sake. (And yes, there are people who *love* innovation for innovation's sake, and some of them are lawyers, like me.) Although we will never know the answer to the chicken-egg question posed above, it is hard to believe that law school students who entered with an innate intrinsic motivation to collaborate or innovate *actually* graduate with that intrinsic motivation to collaborate intact. We've already walked through the typical law school collabo-

---

72 Christopher M Avery, Teamwork is an Individual Skill: Getting Your Work Done When Sharing Responsibility (Berret-Koehler Publishers, 2001).

73 Valdes-Dapena, *supra* note 18, at 193.

74 *Id.* at 20.

75 *See generally* Daniel H Pink, Drive: The Surprising Truth About What Motivates Us (Riverhead Books, reprt. ed., 2011).

76 *Id.* at 51.

ration example: «You take your part of the brief, and I'll take mine.» As mentioned above, even when students do collaborate on something, they are often graded individually. Further, a parallel-work model has been the norm of law school teaching for decades.[77] In this model, each lawyer makes his/her own independent decisions about how to handle his/her piece of the work and is assessed on such.[78] The combination of: 1) this style of training; 2) the lawyer's vision of their identity; and, 3) the lawyer's preference for autonomy and matters of the mind over the heart may work together to squash intrinsic motivation towards collaboration and innovation.[79]

True, not all law school students who come in with their intrinsic motivation to collaborate lose it. True, introverts (although they may not prefer the real-time ping-pang collaborative ideation that innovators do), can still be great collaborators and like collaborating in different ways.[80] True, there are lawyers who are genuinely intrinsically committed to collaboration and innovation.

However, even if it were true that most lawyers have an intrinsic motivation to collaborate and innovate, it would likely not be enough to lead to consistent, effective collaborative behaviors at law firms at least. This is because research shows we need both intrinsic and extrinsic motivation.

2. Lawyers and Extrinsic Motivation

It appears that (more often than not) lawyers are not provided the extrinsic motivation (rewards and punishments) to incent collaboration.[81] This is true in law school and beyond. Moreover, in the United States, for example, our model rules provide extrinsic motivation towards independence, not collaboration.[82]

Many countries outside the United States are more forward thinking and seek to enable lawyers to collaborate with people who are often pejoratively called *«non-lawyers.»* Yet, even in those countries where lawyers can share profit with other types of professionals, lawyers working in traditional law

---

77 Bryant, *supra* note 16, at 498 (describing model and its inefficiencies especially when not combined with another model of working like the «input model» or the «collaborative model»).

78 *Id.*

79 For further discussion, *see generally*, DeStefano, *NonLawyers Influencing Lawyers*, *supra* note 16.

80 Susan Cain, Quiet: The Power of Introverts in a World That Can't Stop Talking (New York: Crown Publishing Group, 2013) at 7–11, 61.

81 Pink, *supra* note 75; Nik Kinley & Shlomo Ben-Hur, Changing Employee Behavior: A Practical Guide for Managers (Palgrave MacMillan, 2015); Shlomo Ben-Hur & Nik Kinley, *Changing Employee Behavior: Do Extreinsi Motivators Really Not Work?*, IMD: Tomorrow's Challenges (May 2015), https://www.hrdsummit.eu/wp-content/uploads/sites/4/2016/10/TC035-15-EXTRINSIC-MOTIVATION.pdf (last visited Apr. 12, 2019).

82 ABA Model Rules of Professional Conduct, *supra* note 43.

firms or legal departments are, for the most part, paid and recognized for their *individual* contributions. Although there are a few outlier law firms (like Dentons, Reed Smith, Mischcon de Reya, and HSF), many firms do not *really* count and compensate for time spent on collaboration or innovation programs.[83] Instead, at best, they consider collaboration as a soft factor in deciding a partner's compensation. As mentioned in my article, *Law Firm Chief Innovation Officers: Goals, Roles, and Holes*, law firms often fail to adequately support and reward innovation efforts.[84] It doesn't appear to be *that* different in legal departments. Although collaboration is a necessity to the professional success of inhouse counsel and, therefore, part-in-parcel to their compensation, hard metrics on collaboration and innovation are not ubiquitous.[85] If *Peter Drucker*, management thinker and consultant, was right in his conclusion that «[p]eople in organizations ... tend to act in response to being recognized and rewards—everything else is preaching», then it is unsurprising that lawyers fail to collaborate or innovate or spend time learning how to do both.[86] Further, what *Valdes-Dapena* says about all professionals is even more true for lawyers: «The collaboration-versus-individual-achievement problem is a bit like broccoli versus ice cream. We know collaboration is a good thing but will nonetheless, if given a choice, go for the tasty treat of individual achievement.»[87] Adding to this is the fact that many Lawyers' business models are not broken i.e., they don't need income from collaboration.

Moreover, the way lawyers are motivated extrinsically (i.e., the way they are rewarded and punished based on their individual contributions) may cause additional damage: it may counteract efforts towards collaboration and innovation. Research shows that goals set by organizations can actually decrease co-

---

83 HSF, Reed Smith, Mischcon de Reya, and Dentons are examples of outliers. HSF has just introduced a program that enables their lawyers to utilize (and get paid for) up to 10 working days working on innovation projects. Reed Smith gives some lawyers the chance to spend 50 hours working on innovation projects and that time counts towards the lawyers' billable hour targets. Mischcon de Reya offered some attorneys the opportunity to focus 20% of their billable time targets on innovation initiatives. Dentons amended its European partnership agreement to link partner remuneration to individual contribution to innovation. For a short description of each, *see* Cristiano Dall Bona, *HSF Hands All Staff «Innovation Fortnight»*, The Lawyer (Feb. 13, 2019), https://www.thelawyer.com/hsf-hands-all-staff-innovation-fortnight/ (last visited Apr. 12, 2019).

84 DeStefano, *The Law Firm Chief Innovation Officer*, *supra* note 13.

85 *Cf.* Heidi K Gardner, *Harness the Power of Smart Collaboration for In-House Lawyers*, Harvard Law School's Center on the Legal Profession White Paper (recommending that GCs «[d] efine clear metrics that capture in-house lawyers' collaborative behaviors and outcomes and identifying hard metrics efforts by one GC as best practice»), https://clp.law.harvard.edu/assets/Gardner_Smart-Collaboration-for-In-House-Lawyers_HLS-white-paper.pdf (last visited March 29, 2019).

86 Peter F Drucker, *Don't Change Corporate Culture—Use It!*, Wall St. J., Mar. 28, 1991, at A14 («Changing habits and behavior requires changing expectations and rewards.»).

87 Valdes-Dapena, *supra* note 18, at 86.

operation.[88] Worse yet, external rewards and punishments have a devasting impact on our ability to see the bigger picture, think broadly, and to be creative.[89] Essentially, the way lawyers are compensated and recognized can literally fix their mindsets and prevent them from developing the DNA of innovators, the growth mindset that questions, the thick skin that enables experimentation, the trust and preference for matters of the heart that enable wide networks, and the ability and desire to associate to get to the «adjacent possible». So, it is no wonder that lawyers are found more likely to have fixed mindsets versus growth mindsets.[90] If you add in our training and the research on path-dependency, it is no wonder that lawyers don't collaborate but, instead, remain in a loop of «parallel play» on repeat.[91]

IV. Conclusion: Innovation Should be a Required Discipline for Lawyers and Lawyers Should Keep An Eye on the «i's» in Innovation

My research indicates that the top two calls by lawyers' clients are to proactively co-collaborate and innovate; but, essentially, they are one in the same. They represent the clients' desire for lawyers to adopt new mindset, skillset, and behaviors so that lawyers can provide transformative client service. The kind of service they are looking for incorporates the innovator's DNA: questioning towards problem finding; listening with empathy to diverse viewpoints; communicating with self-awareness; collaborating proactively; experimenting despite risks; and associating that which might otherwise not be associated to predict future risks and find more creative solutions. The kinds of skills clients are looking for are those on the *Lawyer Skills Delta*, ranging from the concrete

---

88 *Id.* at 51.

89 Pink, *supra* note 75 («[E]xternal rewards and punishments—both carrots and sticks—can work nicely for algorithmic tasks. But they can be devastating for heuristic ones. Those sorts of challenges--solving novel problems or creating something the world didn't know it was missing—depend heavily on Harlow's third drive.») (citing researcher Teresa Amabile and explaining that «Amabile calls it the intrinsic motivation principle of creativity, which holds in part: «intrinsic motivation is conducive to creativity; controlling extrinsic motivation is detrimental to creativity.» In other words, the central tenets of Motivation 2.0 may actually impair performance of the heuristic, right-brain work on which modern economies depend.»).

90 Marcie Borgal Shunk, *Fixed Mindset or Growth Mindset? How Learning Mindsets May Be Stifling Law Firm Change,* LawVision Insights (blog) (Sep. 1, 2014), lawvisiongroup.com/fixed-mindset-or-growth-mindset-howlearning-mindsets-may-be-stifling-law-firm-change/#.WisJQrQ-eF0 (last visited Apr. 11, 2019).

91 *See,* e.g., Ruth & David Collier, Critical Junctures and Historical Legacies, Shaping the Political Area: Critical Junctures, the Labor Movement, and Regime Dynamics in Latin America (Princeton University Press, 1991).

to the more abstract, including technology, project management, branding, social networking, business planning, mentoring, giving/receiving feedback, leadership, cultural competency, growth mindset, and multidisciplinarity.[92] Essentially, clients want their lawyers to have the mindset, skillset, and behavior of innovators. And, as this chapter attempts to show, that is a problem to the third degree: First, a lot of lawyers don't have that DNA. Second, our temperament and training, along with the attributes and skills that make us (laywers) great at the actual practice of law, make it hard for us to adopt the mindset and behavior of the innovator. Third, innovation is generally not taught at law school or in the continuing education, learning and development, executive education courses designed for practicing lawyers. And, even when it is taught, it isn't taught extensively enough (experientially enough) to hone the innovator's DNA and develop the lawyer's intrinsic motivation towards collaboration.

This is why innovation should be a *required* key discipline in legal education and training for both practicing and aspiring lawyers. The bonus is that in learning how to innovate, lawyers not only develop into the type of service providers clients desire, but they also develop as leaders. As my second chapter in this book points out, teaching innovation is another way of teaching leadership to lawyers because the traits of an innovator overlap with those of a collaborative, inclusive leader.[93] So, by adding innovation to lawyer education curriculums, we get a «twofer»: an offer that is comprised of two things, but offered as one. More than that, is has the potential to be a hat trick. In 10 to 20 percent of cases, the innovation curriculum might result in a real innovation: a creative, viable solution that can be brought to life to solve real problems.[94] So, adding innovation to any legal training curriculum? It's the best deal going in legal education.

True, not all lawyers are going to find the time take a course on innovation let alone to go on a four-month innovation journey like that offered in LawWithoutWalls. Given the obstacles created by the lawyer's identity, the predisposition to be self-focused, and our tendency towards parallel play, how do we move to the new type of «proactive collaboration» that clients want?

---

92 DeStefano, *Legal Upheaval, supra* note 1, at 28–44.

93 Bernadette Dillon & Juliet Bourke, *The Six Signature Traits of Inclusive Leadership*, Deloitte, (Apr. 14, 2016), https://www2.deloitte.com/insights/us/en/topics/talent/six-signature-traits-of-inclusive-leadership.html (last visited Apr. 11, 2019).

94 I say this because we can never guarantee that a viable innovation will be developed during the process of trying to innovate. In my experience, if you have ten teams working at once, generally two of them create innovative, viable solutions that can be brought to life. Two of them are so awful that we hope that the teams can pull off a decent presentation without embarrassment. And the rest of them are somewhere in-between.

I include more specific recommendations on the right way to collaborate towards innovation in my second chapter in this book; however, my first (and most practical) recommendation to lawyers is to keep an eye on the «i's» of Innovation. Because «[t]eamwork is an [i]ndividual [s]kill», lawyers will only get better at collaborating if we commit—individually—to being better at teaming.[95] The only way we can do that is if we keep an eye on the «i's» in innovation that are making it hard for us to team, to collaborate, and to hone the DNA of innovators like our clients desire. Recognizing that our professional identity and our innate *Darwinian* inclination to look out for ourselves (along with all the extrinsic motivators) are working against any individual or intrinsic commitment or intention to collaborate towards innovation is essential for us to make change. The power of self-awareness research that has proven true in other areas works here too. Keeping an eye on the «i's» that bias us against collaborating can help us counteract those biases. Adopting new habits related to collaboration and innovation are no different (or less difficult) then adopting new eating habits. As *Valdes-Dapena* points out, for the same reasons we fail at dieting (i.e., we choose French fries over broccoli), when given the choice, our inclination will likely be not to collaborate.[96] Only by recognizing and embracing that truth will we be able to move forward. Without this concession, we won't do the requisite soul searching. If we aren't self-aware that we lack some inclinations of the innovator, we don't accept that the onus is on us to do something about it, and we won't change.

My second (albeit less practical recommendation) is to actually *require* lawyers to learn to collaborate towards innovation. This could be done at the country level i.e., much like a training contract in the UK; or it could be done at the state level. For example, similar to how New York requires that all lawyers do 50 hours of pro bono legal services before they can be licensed to practice in New York, states might require that all lawyers spend a certain number of hours collaborating towards innovation (perhaps in conjunction with a pro bono case) before getting a license. Alternatively, given that we can easily resort back to our Darwinian selves—especially as we gain more responsibility and have less and less time to focus on being great leaders or collaborators—states or countries might require collaboration as continuing education requirement.[97] Firms and legal departments might unilaterally require the same or, at least, start compensating (outwardly and boldly and substantively) those lawyers who do collaborate. Regardless, the reality is that if

95 *See* Avery, *supra* note 72.

96 Valdes-Dapena, *supra* note 18, at 106–11.

97 I'm not the only one to believe that this recommendation might have legs. Recently, after writing the first draft of this chapter, at a conference on the Legal Profession, hosted by Miami Law and the University of St. Gallen School on Technology, Management, and the Law, Jason Barnwell, Assistant General Counsel of Operations and Strategy at Microsoft, suggested the same.

we want to convince lawyers to collaborate towards innovation, we must provide the extrinsic motivation and a convincing explanation of its value. And if we don't do this for ourselves, our clients will do it for us.

V. Bibliography

A. Hard Copy Sources

AVERY, CHRISTOPHER M, TEAMWORK IS AN INDIVIDUAL SKILL: GETTING YOUR WORK DONE WHEN SHARING RESPONSIBILITY (Berret-Koehler Publishers, 2001).

BROUGHAM, HENRY, SPEECHES OF HENRY LORD BROUGHAM, (A. and C. Black, 1838).

Bryant, Susan, *Collaboration in Law Practice: A Satisfying and Productive Process for a Diverse Profession*, 17 VT. L. REV. 459 (1993).

CAIN, SUSAN, QUIET: THE POWER OF INTROVERTS IN A WORLD THAT CAN'T STOP TALKING (New York: Crown Publishing Group, 2013) at 7–11, 61.

Campbell, Ray Worthy, *Rethinking Regulation and Innovation in the U.S. Legal Services Market*, 9 N.Y.U.J. L. & BUS. 1 (2012).

Coates, John C, DeStefano, Michele B, Nanda, Ashish, Wilkins, David B, *Hiring Teams, Firms, and Lawyers: Evidence of the Evolving Relationships in the Corporate Legal Market*, 36 (4) LAW & SOC. INQUIRY 999–1031 (Fall 2011).

RUTH & DAVID COLLIER, CRITICAL JUNCTURES AND HISTORICAL LEGACIES, SHAPING THE POLITICAL AREA: CRITICAL JUNCTURES, THE LABOR MOVEMENT, AND REGIME DYNAMICS IN LATIN AMERICA (Princeton University Press, 1991).

CROSS, ROB & PARKER, ANDREW, THE HIDDEN POWER OF SOCIAL NETWORKS: UNDERSTANDING HOW WORK REALLY GETS DONE IN ORGANIZATIONS (Harvard Business School Press, 2004) 81–3.

DESTEFANO, MICHELE, LEGAL UPHEAVAL: A GUIDE TO CREATIVITY, COLLABORATION, AND INNOVATION IN LAW, (Ankerwycke, 2018).

DeStefano, Michele, *The Law Firm Chief Innovation: Goals, Roles, and Holes*, MODERN LEGAL PRACTICE (Oct. 2018–Jan. 2019).

DeStefano, Michele, *Creating a Culture of Compliance: Why Departmentalization May Not Be the Answer*, 10 HASTINGS BUSINESS L.J. 71–182 (2013).

DeStefano, Michele, *NonLawyers Influencing Lawyers: Too Many Cooks in the Kitchen or Stone Soup?*, 80 FORDHAM L. REV. 2791 (2012).

Dolin, Ron & Buley, Thomas, *Adaptive Innovation: Innovator's Dilemma in Big Law*, 5 (2) HARVARD LAW SCHOOL'S THE PRACTICE (Jan.–Feb. 2019).

Peter F Drucker, *Don't Change Corporate Culture—Use It!*, WALL ST. J. (Mar. 28, 1991).

DRUCKER, PETER F, MANAGING ONESELF (Harvard Business Press, 2008).

DYER, JEFF, GREGERSEN, HAL & CHRISTENSEN, CLAYTON M, THE INNOVATOR'S DNA: MASTERING THE FIVE SKILLS OF DISRUPTIVE INNOVATORS (Harvard Business Review Press, 2011).

Freedman, Monroe H, *Henry Lord Brougham and Zeal*, 34 HOFSTRA L. REV. 1319 (2006).

GARDNER, HEIDI K, SMART COLLABORATION: HOW PROFESSIONALS AND THEIR FIRMS SUCCEED BY BREAKING DOWN SILOS (Harvard Business Review Press, 2016).

Gardner, Heidi K, *When Senior Managers Won't Collaborate*, 93 (3) HARVARD BUSINESS REVIEW 74–82 (Mar. 2015).

JOHNSON, STEVEN, WHERE GOOD IDEAS COME FROM: THE NATURAL HISTORY OF INNOVATION (Riverhead Books, 2010).

KINLEY, NIK & BEN-HUR, SHLOMO, CHANGING EMPLOYEE BEHAVIOR: A PRACTICAL GUIDE FOR MANAGERS (Palgrave MacMillan, 2015).

Krieger, Lawrence S & Sheldon, Kennon M, *What Makes Lawyers Happy? A Data-Driven Prescription to Redefine Professional Services?*, 83 GEORGE WASHINGTON LAW REVIEW, 554, 579–584 (Feb. 2015).

MUSIL, ROBERT, THE MAN WITHOUT QUALITIES, VOL. I: A SORT OF INTRODUCTION AND PSEUDOREALITY PREVAILS INTO THE MILLENNIUM (Vintage Books, 1996).

OGLE, RICHARD, SMART WORLD: BREAKTHROUGH CREATIVITY AND THE NEW SCIENCE OF IDEAS (Harvard Business School Press, 2007).

PINK, DANIEL H, TO SELL IS HUMAN: THE SURPRISING TRUTH ABOUT MOVING OTHERS (Riverhead Books, 2012).

PINK, DANIEL H, DRIVE: THE SURPRISING TRUTH ABOUT WHAT MOTIVATES US (Riverhead Books, reprt. ed., 2011).

Pisano, Gary P, *The Hard Truth About Innovative Cultures*, HARVARD BUSINESS REVIEW (Jan.–Feb. 2019)

Redmount, Robert S, *Attorney Personalities and Legal Consultation,* 109 U. PA. L. REV. 972 (1961).

Rosen, Robert Eli, Parker, Christine E & Lehmann Nielson, Vibeke, *The Framing Effects of Professionalism: Is There a Lawyer Cast of Mind? Lessons from Compliance Programs*, 40 (1) 14 FORDHAM URB. L.J. 297–367 (2013).

Ruef, Martin, *Strong Ties, Weak Ties and Islands: Structural and Cultural Predictors of Organizational Innovation*, 11 INDUS. & CORP. CHANGE, 427, 429–30, 432, and 443 (2002).

SEELIG, TINA, WHAT I WISH I KNEW WHEN I WAS 20: A CRASH COURSE ON MAKING YOUR PLACE IN THE WORLD (Harper One, 2009).

SHAKESPEARE, WILLIAM, SHAKESPEARE'S KING HENRY THE SIXTH, PART II (ed. William J. Rolfe, Harper & Brothers, 1895).

Kennon M Sheldon & Krieger, Lawrence S, *Understanding the Negative Effects of Legal Education on Law Student: A Longitudinal Test of Self-Determination Theory*, 33 PERSONALITY & SOC. PSYCHOL. BULL. 883, 884–85 (2017).

Sheppard, Brian, *Incomplete Innovation and the Premature Disruption of Legal Services*, MICH. ST. L. REV. 1797 (2015).

VALDES-DAPENA, CARLOS, LESSONS FROM MARS: HOW ONE GLOBAL COMPANY CRACKED THE CODE ON HIGH PERFORMANCE COLLABORATION AND TEAMWORK (Change Makers Books, 2018).

Waye, Vicky, Verreynne, Martie-Louise and Knowler, Jane, *Innovation in the Australian Legal Profession*, 25 (2) INTERNATIONAL JOURNAL OF THE LEGAL PROFESSION 213–242 (2017).

Williams Woolley, Anita, Chabris, Christopher F, Pentland, Alex, Hashmi, Nada & Malone, Thomas W, *Evidence for a Collective Intelligence Factor in the Performance of Human Groups*, 330 SCIENCE 686–688 (2010).

Zacharis, Fred & Green, Bruce, *Reconceptualizing Advocacy Ethics*, 74 GEO. WASH. L. REV. 1 (2005).

B. Online Sources

Altman Weil, *2018 Chief Legal Officer Survey*, http://www.altmanweil.com//dir_docs/resource/154F-22DC-E519-4CE2-991D-492A0448C74F_document.pdf (last visited Apr. 11, 2019).

American Bar Association, *Model Rules of Professional Conduct, Preamble & Scope* (Aug. 15, 2018), https://www.americanbar.org/groups/professional_responsibility/publications/model_rules_of_professional_conduct/model_rules_of_professional_conduct_preamble_scope/ (last visited Apr. 10, 2019).

Anthony, Scott D, *Kodak's Downfall Wasn't About Technology*, Harvard Business Review (Jul. 15, 2016), https://hbr.org/2016/07/kodaks-downfall-wasnt-about-technology (last visited Apr. 4, 2019).

Balakrishnan, Reghu, *CVC Capital in talks to buy UnitedLex for $200 million*, Economic Times (Jul. 17, 2018), https://economictimes.indiatimes.com/industry/services/consultancy-/-audit/cvc-capital-in-talks-to-buy-unitedlex-for-200-million/articleshow/65159083.cms (last visited Apr. 9, 2019).

BBC, *Inflatable puff fish pill «could track patient's health»,* BBC News (Jan. 30, 2019), https://www.bbc.com/news/health-47059079 (last visited Apr. 3, 2019).

Ben-Hur, Shlomo & Kinley, Nik, *Changing Employee Behavior: Do Extreinsi Motivators Really Not Work?,* IMD: Tomorrow's Challenges (May 2015), https://www.hrdsummit.eu/wp-content/uploads/sites/4/2016/10/TC035-15-EXTRINSIC-MOTIVATION.pdf (last visited Apr. 12, 2019).

Borgal Shunk, Marcie, *Fixed Mindset or Growth Mindset? How Learning Mindsets May Be Stifling Law Firm Change,* LawVision Insights (blog) (Sep. 1, 2014), lawvisiongroup.com/fixed-mindset-or-growth-mindset-howlearning-mindsets-may-be-stifling-law-firm-change/#.WisJQrQ-eF0 (last visited Apr. 11, 2019).

Brouwer Paul J, *The Power to See Ourselves*, Harvard Business Review (Nov. 1964), https://hbr.org/1964/11/the-power-to-see-ourselves (last visited Apr. 7, 2019).

Corbett, Andrew, *The Myth of the Intrapreneur*, Harvard Business Review (Jun. 26, 2018), https://hbr.org/2018/06/the-myth-of-the-intrapreneur (last visited Apr. 14, 2019).

Dall Bona, Cristiano, *HSF Hands All Staff «Innovation Fortnight»,* The Lawyer (Feb. 13, 2019), https://www.thelawyer.com/hsf-hands-all-staff-innovation-fortnight/ (last visited Apr. 12, 2019).

DeStefano, Michele, *The Chief Compliance Officer: Should There Be a New «C» in the C-Suite*? Harvard Law School's The Practice (Jul. 2016), https://thepractice.law.harvard.edu/article/the-chief-compliance-officer/ (last visited Apr. 2, 2019).

Dew, Nicolas, Sarasvathy, Saras D & Venkataraman, Sankaran, *The Economic Implications of Exaptation*, 14 (1) J. Evol. Econ. 69–84 (2004), https://link.springer.com/article/10.1007/s00191-003-0180-x (last visited Apr. 12, 2019).

Dillon, Bernadette & Bourke, Juliet, *The Six Signature Traits of Inclusive Leadership*, Deloitte, (Apr. 14, 2016), https://www2.deloitte.com/insights/us/en/topics/talent/six-signature-traits-of-inclusive-leadership.html (last visited Apr. 11, 2019).

Duhigg, Charles, *What Google Learned From Its Quest to Build the Perfect Team*, The New York Times Magazine (Feb. 28, 2016), https://www.nytimes.com/2016/02/28/magazine/what-google-learned-from-its-quest-to-build-the-perfect-team.html (last visited Apr. 10, 2019).

Frick, Walter, *Research: Serial Entrepreneurs Aren't Any More Likely to Succeed*, Harvard Business Review (Feb. 20, 2014), https://hbr.org/2014/02/research-serial-entrepreneurs-arent-any-more-likely-to-succeed (last visited Apr. 3, 2019).

Gardner, Heidi K, *Harness the Power of Smart Collaboration for In-House Lawyers*, Harvard Law School's Center on the Legal Profession White Paper, https://clp.law.harvard.edu/assets/Gardner_Smart-Collaboration-for-In-House-Lawyers_HLS-white-paper.pdf (last visited Mar. 29, 2019).

Gould, Stephen Jay & Vrba, Elizabeth S, *Exaptation—A Missing Term in the Science of Form,* 8 (19) Paleobiology 4–15 (1982), http://www2.hawaii.edu/~khayes/Journal_Club/fall2006/Gould_&_Vrb_1982_Paleobio.pdf (last visited Apr. 12, 2019).

Gordon, Leslie A, *Most Lawyers Are Introverted, and That's Not Necessarily a Bad Thing*, ABA Journal (Jan. 2016), http://abajournal.com/magazine/article/most_lawyers_are_introverted_and_thats_not_necessarily_a_bad_thing (last visited Apr. 12, 2019).

Govindarahan, Vjay & Desai, Jatin, *Recognize Intraprenuers Before they Leave*, Harvard Business Review (Sep. 20, 2013), https://hbr.org/2013/09/recognize_intrapreneurs (last visisted Apr. 2, 2019).

Granovetter, Mark S, *The Strength of Weak Ties*, 78 Am. J. Soc. 1360, 1361–66 (1973), https://sociology.stanford.edu/sites/default/files/publications/the_strength_ of_weak_ties_and_exch_w-gans.pdf (last visited Apr. 8, 2019).

Heineman, Ben W Jr., Lee, William F, Wilkins & David B, *Lawyers as Professionals and as Citizens: Key Roles and Responsibilities in the 21st Century*, Harvard Law School Center on the Legal Profession (November 2014), https://clp.law.harvard.edu/assets/Professionalism-Project-Essay_11.20.14.pdf (last visited Feb. 14, 2019).

Janove, Jathan, *Can Risk-Averse Lawyers Learn to Embrace Change? An Interview with Dr. Larry Richard*, Ogletree Deakins (Jan. 12, 2016), https://ogletree.com/insights/2016-01-12/can-risk-averse-lawyers-learn-to-embrace-change-an-interview-with-dr-larry-richard/ (last visited Apr. 9, 2019).

Katzenbach, Jon R, Steffen, Ilona & Kronley, Caroline, *Culture Change That Sticks,* 90 (7–8):110–7 Harvard Business Review 162 (July–Aug. 2012), https://hbr.org/2012/07/cultural-change-that-sticks (last visited Apr. 4, 2019).

Kim, Young Ji, Engel, David, Williams Woolley, Anita, McArthur, Naomi, Lin, Jeffry Yu-Ting, Malone, Thomas W, *What Makes a Strong Team? Using Collective Intelligence to Predict Team Performance in League of Legends*, CSCW 2017 (Feb. 25–Mar. 1, 2017), http://mitsloan.mit.edu/shared/ods/documents/?DocumentID=2710 (last visted Apr. 11, 2019).

LegalTech News, *LegalZoom Announces $500 Million Investment, Among Largest in Legal Tech History*, (Jul. 31, 2018), https://www.legalzoom.com/press/press-mentions/legalzoom-announces-500-million-investment-among-largest-in-legal-tech-history (last visited Apr. 12, 2019).

Nassau, Henry N, *Collaboration as Superpower: Optimizing Value to Lead in the Future*, New York L.J. (Apr. 24, 2017), https://www.newyorklawjournal.com/id=1202784074939/Collaboration-as-Superpower-Optimizing-Value-to-Lead-in-the-Future (last visited Apr. 5, 2019).

Richard, Larry, *The Lawyer Personality: Why Lawyers Are Skeptical,* What Makes Lawyers Tick? (Feb. 11, 2013), https://www.lawyerbrainblog.com/2013/02/the-lawyer-personality-why-lawyers-are-skeptical/ (last visited Apr. 9, 2019).

Richard, Larry, *Herding Cats: The Lawyer Personality Revealed*, 29 (11) Altman Weil Report to Management 1–12 (2002), http://www.managingpartnerforum.org/tasks/sites/mpf/assets/image/MPF%20-%20WEBSITE%20-%20ARTICLE%20-%20Herding%20Cats%20-%20Richards1.pdf (last visited Apr. 2, 2019).

Strom, Roy, *UnitedLex, Big Deals in Hand, Sells Majority Stake to European Buyout Firm*, The American Lawyer (Sep. 20, 2018), https://www.law.com/americanlawyer/2018/09/20/unitedlex-big-deals-in-hand-sells-majority-stake-to-european-buyout-firm/ (last visited Apr. 4, 2019).

Thomson Reuters Legal Executive Institute, Georgetown University Law Center, Oxford University Säid Business School and Acritas, *Alternative Legal Service Providers: Understanding the Growth and Benefits of These New Legal Providers* (Jan. 2019), https://legal.thomsonreuters.com/

content/dam/ewp-m/documents/legal/en/pdf/reports/alsp-report-final.pdf?cid=9008178&sfdc-campaignid=7011B000002OF6AQAW&chl=pr (last visited Apr. 13, 2019).

Thomson Reuters and Georgetown University Law School, *2019 Report on the State of the Legal Market*, http://ask.legalsolutions.thomsonreuters.info/LEI_2019-State_of_Legal_Mkt (last visited Apr. 9, 2019).

Vilardo, Lawrence J & Doyle, Vincent E, III, *Where Did the Zeal Go?*, ABA Litigation Journal (Fall 2011), https://www.americanbar.org/groups/litigation/publications/litigation_journal/2011_12/fall/where_did_zeal_go/ (last visited Apr. 11, 2019).

Wikipedia, *DXC*, https://en.wikipedia.org/wiki/DXC_Technology (last visited Apr. 7, 2019).

Wikipedia, *The 5 Whys*, https://en.wikipedia.org/wiki/5_Whys (last visited Mar. 30, 2019).

Wilkins, David B, *Operationalizing Innovation in Legal Organizing*, Harvard Law Today (Aug. 29, 2018), https://today.law.harvard.edu/operationalizing-innovation-legal-organizations (last visited Apr. 11, 2019).

Williams Woolley, Anita, Chabris, Christopher F & Malone, Thomas W, *Why Some Teams Are Smarter Than Others*, NY Times (Jan. 16, 2015), https://www.nytimes.com/2015/01/18/opinion/sunday/why-some-teams-are-smarter-than-others.html (last visited Apr. 12, 2019).

04

Professor John Flood

Legal Professionals of the Future

Their Ethos, Role, and Skills

TABLE OF CONTENTS

I. Introduction[1]

Lawyers traditionally look to the past, choosing their idols—such as Abraham Lincoln, Lord Denning, Clarence Darrow, Marshall Hall—for their capacity to conjure up virtue, tenacity, and wisdom. Yet each of these idols is specific to his historical moment despite displaying a vision of professionalism that superficially appears enduring. But if the legal profession were to reproduce itself along the lines indicated by these four, it would fail miserably in the modern world. Our world is no longer so rigid in its values like the societies occupied by them; we live in a diverse and intersectional world that needs capacities for specialised skills, organisational adaptability, and cosmopolitanism. Try to picture either Denning or Darrow in a large corporate law firm: it's impossible to imagine. Neither would be able to hack it since they would be in constant rebellion against the bureaucracy and hierarchy of modern organisations. While the past is not really that long ago, the future creeps up on us far more quickly than we imagine.

In order to go beyond the stereotypes we need to understand the essentials of professionalism and professional knowledge. With this in hand we can speculate on the future(s) of legal professionals. The term future(s) is preferred to future because theoretically the future is open and dependent on actions taken in the present and past. It is a series of stochastic processes and given this unpredictability, at best, we can provide glimpses of the futures of legal professionals. To arrive there, it is necessary to appreciate the nature or essence of professionalism because professionalism has been built over hundreds of years. And part of the reason I emphasise essence is because the title of this chapter contains the term ethos.

Ethos concerns credibility and character. It is one of the three forms of persuasion mounted by Aristotle along with pathos (emotion) and logos (logical argument) (*Braet* 1992). Ethos is deeply incorporated into professionalism. Professionals have to establish their character, their authority. They will also use pathos and especially logos in representing their expertise and knowledge, but without ethos the other two will not take the professional far (*Higgins and Walker* 2012). In an earlier article I argued that one of the key roles of lawyers was to manage complexity for their clients (*Flood* 1991, 2013). To achieve success in this role, lawyers had to present themselves convincingly to their clients as knowledgeable and competent and sure of the outcome. The problem with the appeal to ethos is that it is difficult to say what it is or how it can be characterised within professions. It almost seems chimerical in form in the way *Homer* described it in *The Iliad*, «a thing of immortal make, not human, lion-fronted and snake behind, a goat in the middle, and snorting out the breath

---

1 This paper borrows from three earlier papers of mine, Flood (2017, 2018a, with Robb 2019).

of the terrible flame of bright fire (*Lattimore* 1952:179–82).» How then do we identify the ethos of a profession?

Professions are a significant and important part of civilised society. *Toynbee* (1948) remarked how civilisation advanced by the move towards elite professions. *Freidson* (2001) claimed the professions were the third logic between market and bureaucracy. *Adair Turner* (2018) classifies the professions as distributive in that while they may not necessarily create value themselves, they create the spaces for others to generate value. *Gilson* (1984) calls lawyers value transaction engineers managing the Coasian transaction costs in business. Unlike most occupations, expert or otherwise, professions are distinct. And it is this distinction that will give them the capacity to tackle the future, whatever they face.

II. The Nature of Professions

Leaving aside the simplistic descriptions of professions as collections of traits, or taxonomies, such as lengthy education, codes of practice, self-regulation, and the like (*Greenwood* 1957), professions do possess particular types of knowledge and the practice of that knowledge occurs in social networks. Students of work like *Hughes* (1958) and *Becker* (1970) understood this and focused on the actual work and the actors involved. Small groups were their key sites of study; *Goffman* (1952) showed, for example, how professional conmen cooled out their marks with exquisite dexterity when they were completing their stings. This approach is micro-oriented examining the small and subtle exchanges that take place rather than looking at larger social structures based on power. Later theorists moved that way by being more Marxist (*Larson* 1977) or Weberian (*Abel* 1989) in their outlooks, focusing on monopoly rents and market closure sought by professions as part of their professional project. Ecologists, such as *Abbott* (1988), examined how professions are in constant conflict with each other aggressively attacking the other's jurisdictions and attempting to capture their work. We only have to look at the near constant battles between accountants and lawyers over who possesses the mandate to do tax work. And in the case of accountants that attack has, in the 21st century, spread to the core areas of legal work as well. The 19th century struggles between mainstream allopathy and homeopathy in the US to determine who should be the primary diagnostician are well documented (*Starr* 1982). The allopaths were able to mobilize stronger political resources, combined with the might of the hospital, to gain dominance, a position still strongly defended today. The arrest and imprisonment of midwives in Hungary is another example of professional domination as the state sided with doctors to outlaw midwifery. The medicalization of births, to be carried out in hospital, is the only professional activity sanctioned by the state.[2]

The taxonomic approach to professions hasn't completely disappeared. *Eliot Freidson* (2004) argued that professions constituted a third logic between the market and bureaucracy where market refers to consumer control and bureaucracy control by managers. Professionalism is therefore an organized occupation that has the power to determine who will perform certain tasks. *Julia Evetts* (2014:33) has provided a more modern approach:

> *«Professionals are extensively engaged in dealing with risk, with risk assessment and, through the use of expert knowledge, enabling customers and clients to deal with uncertainty...professions are involved in birth, survival, physical and emotional health, dispute resolution and law-based social order, finance and credit information, educational attainment and socialization, physical constructs and the built environment, military engagement, peace-keeping and security, entertainment, the arts and leisure, religion and our negotiations with the next world.»*

Law in most countries appears to fit this model. Lawyers are granted monopolistic powers by the state, which places them *primus inter pares* among those who work in the legal industry. The last part of the 20th century has seen this market closure eroded and authority given to a growing paralegal body of workers as the division of legal labour has intensified.

III. The Nature of Knowledge and Expertise

The many studies of professionals, professionalism, and professionalisation, from *Carr-Saunders and Wilson* (1933) onwards, tell us that professions are characterised by specialist knowledge. It is not something acquired quickly but takes time and experience. The use of the term «to practice» reinforces this idea.

There are two defining features of professional knowledge: it takes time to learn and also must be continually monitored and rejuvenated; it can't be learnt in isolation—professions are concerned about how their knowledge is used and in what contexts. One way to represent these features is through the use of a three-dimensional model developed by *Harry Collins*. *Collins* has categorised knowledge from its most simplistic (beer mat knowledge) to the esoteric (practitioners) (*Collins and Evans* 2007). The «simple» approach won't ever approximate full understanding, while closeness to the «esoteric»

2 *See* Royal College of Midwives (2018).

will enable understanding. And this is because professional knowledge, at heart, is based on discourse and so facility with discourse and language promotes closer proximity to professional practice. This latter facility is made up of tacit and interactional expertise. It is the kind of expertise that isn't shared lightly. And, according to *Michael Polanyi* (1966), all knowledge is ultimately based in tacit knowledge so a complete explicit knowledge is impossible.

In Exhibit 1 we see a typical learning process based on three dimensions, namely, the depth dimension which is here the individual's learning; the horizontal dimension represents one's acquaintance with tacit knowledge of the group; and the vertical dimension shows how esoteric the domain can be (*Collins* 2010). This is learning to drive, for example. A driver must become acquainted with the mechanics of the car insofar as they are necessary to drive it. There is a body of knowledge to learn which is both empirical (e.g., how to negotiate turns) and theoretical (e.g., braking distances at various speeds). The normal starting point for learning in this situation is point zero. Through practice, the driver gains in competence and expertise as shown by the broken line in the box. There is a tacit knowledge or interactional expertise aspect since driving is social and there will be informal as well as formal rules that are learned by exposure to others. This is shown by the broken line veering to the right as it rises but not too far. If the driver were, say, training to be a Formula

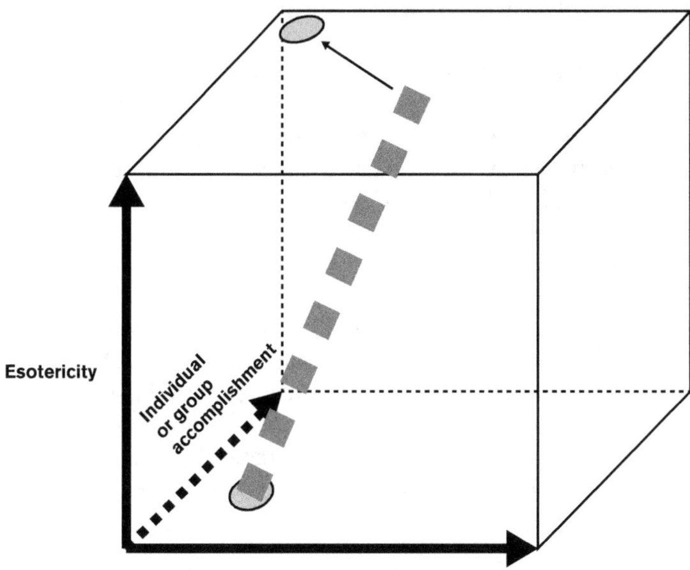

Exhibit 1: A three-dimensional model of the acquisition of knowledge—the «Collins Expertise-Space Diagram» [Source: Harry Collins, Three Dimensions of Expertise (no date) at 18.]

1 racing driver then there would have been a massive increase in the acquisition of tacit knowledge since the pool of drivers becomes highly specialised.

Is professional knowledge or expertise any different? In order to understand this question I look at how French doctors managed the Debré reforms, after the Second World War, which attempted to consolidate practice, teaching and research within university hospitals. According to *Jamous and Peloille* (1970) since the French Revolution of 1789 and following the establishment of the teaching hospital the medical profession found itself caught between two extremes. If it defined its work in terms of the technical complexities, it would become accessible to others—it could be written into a manual—and their control over medicine would be diminished. Instead, doctors argued that there was a significant indeterminant element (i.e., uncertainty) to their work which required the deployment of tacit knowledge, or judgment, and was gained through social exposure to the profession.

However, there are limits to how far individuals can promote indeterminacy. The rise of rationalism along with the rise in print culture evidences the decline of Church authority during the Enlightenment in the face of scientific knowledge (*White* 2018).[3] French doctors were able to argue that the combination, or ratio, of indeterminacy and technicality (I/T) is what makes the medical profession, and by extension other professions, the most suitable and appropriate way of organising control over medicine. They allowed for technicians and other medical workers whose work would always be under the authority of the doctors.

With the help of the I/T ratio, it is possible to represent professional knowledge in the three-dimensional space used above. In some ways Exhibit 2 could also incorporate racing car drivers mentioned above as well. For most professionals, there is an extensive training period (e.g., acquiring a university degree) which raises them into the esoteric category early in their careers. The knowledge and expertise of lawyers starts with a novice lawyer already in possession of esoteric knowledge acquired in law school. And this is why the professional is at the top of the esotericity axis instead of at zero. By moving from the front top left to the rear top left point, the individual acquires greater knowledge but can never be totally competent unless tacit knowledge is acquired by moving rightwards (*Collins* no date). According to this model, the most expert lawyer will be located at the rear top right corner—maximal combinations of primary source knowledge and tacit knowledge. There are two lots of white space in the diagram at the left and right-hand sides of the top.

---

3 John Cage in his piano work, Music of Changes (1951), employed indeterminacy by using the divination process of the *I Ching* as a means of determining which piece should be performed next. In other compositions the musicians would be required to cast sticks to find the hexagram that would direct them next, which would sometimes upset the musicians who were used to formal linear scores (*Pritchett* 1993).

The left is blank because in order to go beyond competence and acquire true expertise tacit knowledge is necessary so there are limits beyond which an individual can go alone. While at the right-hand side void is there because if one has some exposure to the tacit knowledge of the domain but fails to make progress one is likely to be expelled from the community of those who have it. Thus, to maintain a position within a profession interaction with other members is required (*Collins* no date).

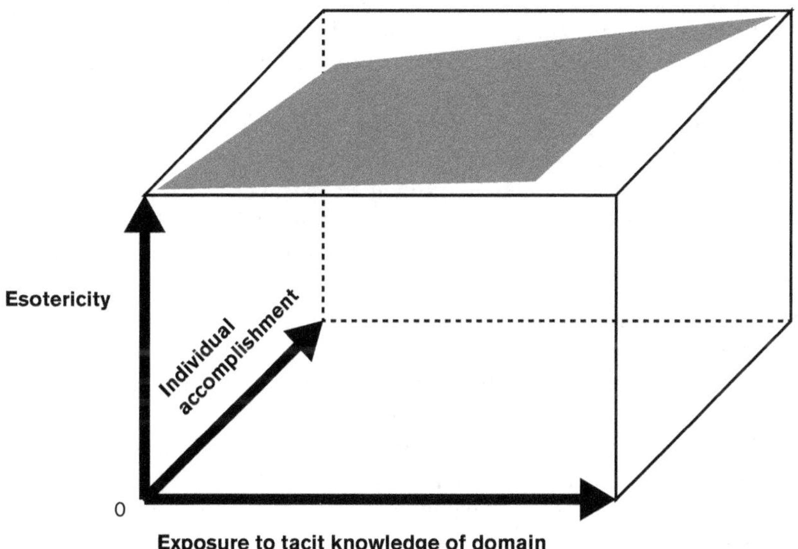

Exhibit 2: A three-dimensional model of the acquisition of professional knowledge [Source: Harry Collins (no date)].

IV. Professionalism and Knowledge

Knowledge, and especially professional knowledge, is a more complex phenomenon than some might have imagined. *Richard Susskind*, for example, considers professionalism as a set of tasks that can be decomposed and, therefore, allocated to the most efficient «handler». In a recent paper for the British Academy Review (*Susskind* 2018), which reflects his general approach to professional work, he argues an instrumental view of work. Work, he says, should be measured by its outcomes not its internal meanings to those who engage in it. While it is reasonable to examine outcomes, they can't be the only measure, especially for professions. It reduces them to being technicians. Among the reasons *Susskind* inclines to this conclusion is that he ignores the social and cultural aspects of professions within society. There are monopolistic aspects to professional work, but the bargain professions strike with society is that they won't exploit their clients and patients (*Carr-Saunders and Wilson* 1933). To enforce this, professions put in place codes of ethics, disciplinary bodies, and inculcate their members with professional values *(id.)*. Moreover, professions have played a civilizing and altruistic role in societies for many years (*Tawney* 1921; *Marshall* 1950). In a study of speeches by the leaders of professions including lawyers, doctors, engineers, architects, educators, among others, there were consistent themes articulated around the topics of access to justice, public health, and the virtues of the built environment (*Brint and Levy* 2004). Of the groups studied, lawyers were the most persistent in pursuing these ideas and ideals considering them an essential part of their community values. Indeed, *Susskind* (2018:31) himself provides an example which I think proves the point. He conjectures that scientists discover an affordable cancer vaccine that could reduce their work and so affect their livelihoods. Would they choose not to introduce the vaccine because it could reduce their incomes? It does seem inconceivable that oncologists might consider this as a valid plan of action because it would be quite contrary to their ethos and impossible to justify to their public.

The collective endeavours, therefore, of professions are crucial to their development. And this is why, unlike *Susskind* contends, we can't focus on outcomes alone. It is likely *Susskind* has conflated the change in professionalism with a more instrumental approach to professional work. *Evetts* (2014) and others have pointed out how professional work is being increasingly bureaucratised as professional work coalesces in larger organisations. Professionalism has to co-exist with bureaucracy wherein its autonomy as a coordinating principle is diminished as management hierarchies within organisations issue directives. The result is often that professionals have to deal with the problem of double deontology; whose rules count? The answer is that all rules count, but some will have greater significance than others. If organisational rules were to run counter to professional ethics, for example, the professional could be sanctioned for not abiding by the ethical code. A consequent removal of professional status could render the professional unemployable by the organisation that created the situation. Therefore, the ethos of professionalism has to adapt to new milieu; and similarly, organisations have to consider carefully their relationships with professionals.[4] We have seen this tension played out in the finance industry where regulators have placed additional reporting duties on lawyers outside the normal lines of authority within financial institutions.[5]

---

4 *See*, however, *Elizabeth Chambliss* (2005) who argues that bureaucratic centralised management could be beneficial to law firms.

5 The Sarbanes-Oxley Act of 2002 section 307 requires lawyers to report wrongdoings up the company chain of command. *See Patterson* (2003) on Sarbanes-Oxley as an instrument of the

V. Future Roles for Lawyers

There will always be a demand for lawyers, or at least someone versed in skills related to law such as dispute resolution, handling complex, cross-border transactions, or dealing with crime. What roles lawyers will play is an open question. And to some degree the equivalent question applies to other professions like architecture and medicine. The extent to which professionals will continue as they have done is unlikely.

The starting point for this section is the analysis put forward by *Adair Turner* (2018) in a paper on «Capitalism in the Age of Robots: Work, Income, and Wealth in the 21st Century». Turner's starting point is that automation—robots, artificial intelligence, blockchain—will have an irreversible and dramatic effect on society that will nullify our present understanding of economics and economies. Countries that rely on low-paid, low-skilled work as a way of climbing the economic ladder will not be able to do this in the future. And automation is a matter of *when* not *if*. According to *McKinsey* (2017), full automation of jobs could occur between 2060 and 2100. At present *Frey and Osborne* (2017) estimate 47% of all jobs are susceptible to automation. *McKinsey* (2017:7) locates these jobs mainly in the repetitive sectors and less so in management and professional ones where judgment tends to be the critical function. The automation potential for professionals and management is 35% compared to the 60% of manufacturing and transport (id).

The jobs *Turner* (2018:10) believes will thrive are what he terms the «zero-sum» or «distributive» activities. That is, they not so much create as distribute resources throughout the economy. Among these, for example, are lawyers «who protect intellectual property rights»; tax accountants and lawyers who minimise tax payments; and «financial regulators and the increasing army of compliance officers and auditors» (*Turner* 2018:11). The effects of relentless automation are growth in personal service jobs, e.g., nurses, chefs, care aides, some of which might be able to command higher salaries, others not, as people leave the jobs which are being automated. There will also be an increase in returns to monopoly capital, of all kinds, and rent seeking skills whether they be in property, sport, creative industries, or exploiting intellectual property (*Turner* 2018: 21). These shifts and outcomes raise the demand for professionals, the zero-sum specialists, who will be managing the distribution of rights and property. Lawyers are essential to these activities and so will not fade away. A key question will be: what is the optimum number of lawyers and other professionals in an automating economy? *Turner* argued that zero-sum activities will increase, but over time the tasks being done by such specialists will themselves become subject to automation through developments in AI,

erosion of lawyers' self-governance.

blockchain and the like. Thus, an increase in professionals could be followed by an eventual decrease in numbers.

In the future lawyers' roles will still be dependent on the social structure of the societies in which they function. *Heinz and Laumann* (1982), following *Johnson* (1972), theorised that lawyers' practices and mores are a function of the type of client they serve. Elite lawyers who work with corporate clients are in a «patronage» relationship. Their control of the relationship with clients is heavily moderated by the expertise and repeated use of legal services by clients. While the lawyers enjoy high status and incomes, they depend for these on the continuing employment of corporations and companies who are willing to spend large sums on the legal liabilities that surround them. Accountants and management consultants are in similar situations. For lawyers who serve individual clients the situation is quite different. Most of their clients are «one-shot» clients who use law as a distress good—a matter of compulsion rather than choice. The incomes and status of such lawyers is more parlous than their corporate colleagues. Both are susceptible to automation.

VI. Lawyers and Automation

Corporate lawyers are already investing in and using all kinds of automation such as chat bots, machine learning, and smart contracts (*Goodman* 2016). A number of machine learning processes for contract analysis, due diligence, and legal research are in existence and in use (id). For example, ROSS Intelligence started by using IBM Watson to act as a research database for insolvency law (https://rossintelligence.com/). ROSS now encapsulates all areas of practice. Some law firms are creating incubators for startups that might assist in their business in the future (id).

The types of work being automated fall within the parameters set out by *Turner*, *McKinsey*, and *Frey and Osborne* (2017). These are the jobs that involve high degrees of repetition and relatively simple processes such as finding key words in a document. Junior associates and paralegals are the endangered species in the law firms. The effect of automation here could be dramatic in that if junior associates were to be gradually culled from firms, the entire reproduction of the legal profession could be jeopardised since law firms are structured around associates being promoted to partnership, in the classic «tournament» model of partner selection in law firms (*Galanter and Palay* 1991). In addition to this effect is the decline in paying for the use of first year associates by corporate clients (*Zaretsky* 2014). Who then will train junior lawyers if law firms are reluctant to undertake this? We know law firms operate multiple tracks where some juniors are «trained» with prospects of making partner and other tracks where associates are churned through the organisation without training (*Wilkins and Gulati* 1998). In all probability, elite big law

firms will retrench to a model closer to the nineteenth century one with a small number of partners and a large cohort of mostly underqualified or uncredentialled clerks who have little or no possibility of rising through the firm.

For individual-client-lawyers the threats from automation don't come from within but rather without. There is the rise of the online legal services supplier such as LegalZoom and more specialist suppliers like OnlineDivorce. These tend to offer less expensive services than Main or High Street lawyers and are often delivered in a more efficient manner. In addition, there are an increasing number of chatbot lawyers that use artificial intelligence to provide the service. DoNotPay is a known example which started as a parking appeals service and has expanded into law suits, travel disruption and more, and which runs from a mobile app (https://itunes.apple.com/app/id1427999657). The thrust of these services is to promote self-help among claimants without the use of lawyers. And for small businesses there are companies like RobotLawyerLisa which assist in drafting non-disclosure agreements (http://robotlawyerlisa.com/nda/). This type of company will also extend its services into other areas of business. Government too promotes self-help by creating online courts such as the UK Money Claim Online which is designed to be user-friendly (https://www.moneyclaim.gov.uk/web/mcol/welcome). An increasing number of previously lawyer-provided services are moving into digital formats that negate the use of extensive paper trails that lawyers would typically do. Areas like conveyancing are being intensively digitised and utilised online.[6] Lawyers may be needed to moderate and monitor these activities but not to carry out the tasks themselves—that is the ambit of the machine.

VII. Lawyers' Skills

Can lawyers continue with the traditional portfolio of skills and knowledge carefully cultivated over the centuries into the 21st century? The answer is of course not clear. They will still have to possess an understanding of the principles of law, but it might not need to be to the same extent as regulators presently prescribe. If the answer were to veer towards no, then we would have to enquire what skills and competencies would be necessary either as substitutes or additions, and which skills would have to be subtracted from the curriculum. I am not going to delve into this topic in details in this chapter as I have dealt with it in elsewhere *(see Flood* 2015, 2018b). But I would accept *Turner's* (2018:29) argument that increasing the extensity and intensity of coding skills among non-IT people might seem attractive, but the main rewards for

6 The Chicago real estate title transfer pilot project, for instance, successfully transfers a title peer-to-peer on the Bitcoin Blockchain using a colored coin. *See Lifthrasir* (2017).

good coding will necessarily go to the best coders not those with barely adequate skills. And, in any case, teaching coding widely may well result in being a redundant exercise as machines learn to code themselves and so become self-sustaining.

Robb and I have argued (*Flood and Robb* 2019) that the essential skill for future lawyers is that of trusted advisor. Throughout the 20th century, this particular skill has been downplayed in contrast to that of the transaction expert (*Maister et al.* 2000). Because of the changing nature of law practice from enduring, long-term relationships with clients to ad hoc transactionalists focusing on series of discrete tasks, the demand has been for lawyers with particular sets of skills, e.g., securitisation or mergers and acquisitions, at the expense of the counselor and advisor (see *Flood and Lederer* 2012; *Flood* 2013). Tasks that depend on document production, as do both securitisation and M&A, lend themselves to automation through machine learning. As Google's AlphaGo has demonstrated in the game of Go, even complex tasks that have minimal rules can be taught to machines through a self-learning reinforcement process. Combine this with the global effects of international associations creating international templates for these activities, e.g., International Swaps and Derivatives Association documentation, and machine learning associated with a series of smart contracts executed on the Blockchain seem logical outcomes.

With the possible reduction in future numbers of lawyers and the automation of more and more tasks, there will be rising needs for people who can see the «big picture» and undertake comprehensive risk analyses—a new kind of generalist. If this is the result of the changes filtering through the professions and law in particular, then this brings us back to the start of this chapter where I discussed the ideals of professionalism and ethos. There are potentially two directions: one following the path of automation and the other taking the human course. The first has implicit within it a necessary disinterest that negates the need for human emotions or feelings such as the idea of trust. Machines execute code without the need for trust since trust is in the code i.e., *Lessig's* idea of the code as law (*Lessig* 2006). This is suitable for tasks such as compliance where much of what is done is effectively box ticking. The second, however, reintroduces the ideals of trust through the counselor/advisor relationship; it is necessarily built on interaction, exchange, even affective relationships comparable to *guanxi.*[7] Ethos takes us back to the characteristics of credibility and character, neither of which appears unbidden. Both must be developed and nurtured. At present, few of these kinds of skills, or an appreciation of them, is taught in law schools. Lawyers need to create and expand their capacity for ethos within the context of professionalism. Trusted advisors

---

7 *Guanxi* is a Chinese concept of forming relationships outside the family built on reciprocity, gift exchanges, with an affective dimension (see *Buderi and Huang* 2007).

and trusted brokers will be in high demand in a world wracked with populism and nationalism; someone must be able to communicate over these boundaries and connect with those on the other side. Lawyers, because their basic tool is language, are ideally suited for these roles.

VIII. Bibliography

A. Hard Copy Sources

Abbott, Andrew, The System of Professions: An Essay on the Division of Expert Labor (University of Chicago Press, 1988).

Abel, Richard, American Lawyers (Oxford University Press, 1989).

Becker, Howard, *The Nature of a Profession*, *in* Sociological Work 87–103 (Becker, Howard I, ed., Aldine Publishing, 1970).

Braet, Antoine, *Ethos, Pathos and Logos in Aristotle's Rhetoric: A Re-Examination,* 6 Argumentation 307–320 (1992).

Brint, Steven & Levy, Charles, *Professions and Civic Engagement: Trends in Rhetoric and Practice, 1875–1995*, *in* Civic Engagement in American Democracy (Skocpol, Theda and Fiorina, Morris P, eds., Brookings Institution Press, 2004).

Buderi, Robert & Huang, Gregory, Guanxi (The Art of Relationships): Microsoft, China, and the Plan to Win the Road Ahead (Simon & Schuster, 2007).

Carr-Saunders, Alexander & Wilson, Paul, The Professions (Clarendon Press, 1933).

Collins, Harry & Evans, Robert, Rethinking Expertise (University of Chicago Press, 2007).

Evetts, Julia, *The Concept of Professionalism: Professional Work, Professional Practice and Learning*, *in* International Handbook of Research in Professional and Practice-based Learning, (Billett, Stephen et al., eds., Springer International Handbooks of Education, 2014).

Flood, John, *Doing Business: The Management of Uncertainty in Lawyers' Work*, 25 (1) Law & Society Review 41–71 (1991).

Flood, John, What Do Lawyers Do? An Ethnography of a Corporate Law Firm (Quid Pro Books, 2013).

Flood, John, *Global Challenges for Legal Education: Competing for the World's Law Students*, 24 Nottingham Law Journal 79–93 (2015).

Flood, John, *Foreword: Professions as Contingent Structures in a Perilous World*, 40(1) UNSW Law Journal 211–217 (2017).

Flood, John, *Professions and Professional Service Firms in a Global Context: Reframing Narratives*, *in* Professions and Professional Service Firms: Private and Public Sector Enterprises in the Global Economy 26–45 (Saks, Mike and Muzio, D, eds., Routledge, 2018a).

Flood, John, *The Rule of Law and Legal Education: Do They Still Connect?*, *in* Handbook on the Rule of Law (May, Christopher & Winchester, Adam, eds., Edward Elgar. 2018b).

Flood, John & Lederer, Peter, *Becoming a Cosmopolitan Lawyer*, 80(6) Fordham Law Review 2523–2539 (2012).

Flood, John & Robb, Lachlan, *Professions and Expertise: How Machine Learning and Blockchain are Redesigning the Landscape of Professional Knowledge and Organisation*, *in* University of

Miami Law Review's 2018 Symposium, Hack to the Future: How Technology is Disrupting the Legal Profession 443–482 (2019).

Freidson, Eliot, Professionalism: The Third Logic (Polity, 2001).

Frey, Carl & Osborne, Michael, *The Future of Employment: How Susceptible are Jobs to Computerisation?*, 114 (3) Technological Forecasting and Social Change (2017).

Galanter, Marc & Palay, Thomas, Tournament of Lawyers: The Transformation of the Big Law Firm (University of Chicago Press, 1991).

Gilson, Ronald, *Value Creation by Business Lawyers: Legal Skills and Asset Pricing*, 94 (2) Yale Law Journal 239 (1984).

Goffman, Erving, On Cooling the Mark Out, 15 (4) Psychiatry 451–463 (1952).

Goodman, Joanna, Robots In Law: How Artificial Intelligence is Transforming Legal Services (Ark Group, 2016).

Greenwood, Ernest, *The Attributes of a Profession*, 2 Social Work 44–55 (1957).

Higgins, Colin & Walker, Robyn, *Ethos, Logos, Pathos: Strategies of Persuasion in Social/Environmental Reports,* 36 Accounting Forum 194–208 (2012).

Hughes, Everett, Men and Their Work (Free Press, 1958).

Jamous, Haroun & Peloille, Bernard, *Professions or self-perpetuating system; changes in the French university-hospital system, in* Professions and Professionalisation 111–152 (Jackson, J, ed., Cambridge University Press, 1970).

Johnson, Terence, Professions and Power (Macmillan, 1972).

Larson, Margali, The Rise of Professionalism (University of California Press, 1977).

Lattimore, Richard, Homer: The Iliad (University of Chicago Press, 1951).

Lessig, Lawrence, Code: And Other Laws of Cyberspace, Version 2 (Basic Books, 2006).

Maister, David, Green, Charles & Galford, Robert, The Trusted Advisor (Free Press, 2000).

Marshall, Thomas, Citizenship and Social Class and Other Essays (Cambridge University Press, 1950).

Patterson, Stephanie, *Section 307 of the Sarbanes-Oxley Act: Eroding the Legal Profession's System of Self-Governance,* 7 North Carolina Banking Institute 155–176 (2003).

Polanyi, Michael, The Tacit Dimension (University of Chicago Press, 1966).

Pritchett, James, The Music of John Cage (Cambridge University Press, 1993).

Starr, Paul, The Social Transformation of American Medicine (Basic Books, 2017).

Tawney, Richard H, The Acquisitive Society (Harcourt Bruce, 1921).

Toynbee, Arnold, Civilization on Trial (Oxford University Press, 1948).

Wilkins, David & Gulati, Mitu, *Reconceiving the Tournament of Lawyers: Tracking, Seeding, and Information Control in the Internal Labor Markets of Elite Law Firms*, 84 Virginia Law Review 1582–1681 (1998).

B. Online Sources

Chambliss, Elizabeth, *The Nirvana Fallacy in Law Firm Regulation Debate*, 33 Fordham Urban Law Journal 119 (2005), https://ir.lawnet.fordham.edu/ulj/vol33/iss1/1 (last visited Feb. 3, 2019).

Collins, Harry, *Three Dimensions of Expertise* (no date), http://sites.cardiff.ac.uk/harrycollins/draft-papers/ (last visited Feb. 3, 2019).

Lifthrasir, Ragnar, *Permissionless Real Estate Title Transfers on the Bitcoin Blockchain in the USA!–Cook County Blockchain Pilot Program Report,* Medium (Jun. 28, 2017), https://medium.

com/@RagnarLifthrasir/permissionless-real-estate-title-transfers-on-the-bitcoin-Blockchain-in-the-usa-5d9c39139292 (last visited Feb. 3, 2019).

McKinsey Global Institute, *A Future that Works: Automation, Employment and Productivity* (2017), https://www.mckinsey.com/~/media/McKinsey/Featured%20Insights/Digital%20Disruption/Harnessing%20automation%20for%20a%20future%20that%20works/MGI-A-future-that-works_Full-report.ashx (last visited Feb. 1, 2019).

Royal College of Midwives, *Home Birth: A Universal Fear?* (2018), https://rcm.org.uk/news-views-and-analysis/analysis/home-birth-a-universal-fear (last visited Feb. 2, 2019).

Turner, Adair, *Capitalism in the Age of Robots: Work, Income and Wealth in the 21st Century* (2018), https://www.ineteconomics.org/research/research-papers/capitalism-in-the-age-of-robots-work-income-and-wealth-in-the-21st-century (last visited Feb. 2, 2019).

White, Matthew, *The Enlightenment*, https://www.bl.uk/restoration-18th-century-literature/articles/the-enlightenment (Jun. 21, 2018) (last visited Feb. 3, 2019).

Zaretsky, Staci, *Biglaw Firm Figures Out a Way for Clients Not to Pay for First-Year Associates*, Above the Law (Sep. 16, 2014), https://abovethelaw.com/2014/09/biglaw-firm-figures-out-a-way-for-clients-not-to-pay-for-first-year-associates/ (last visited Feb. 3, 2019).

Christoph Küng

Legal Marketplaces and Platforms

The New Playground

TABLE OF CONTENTS

I. Introduction[1]

Marketplaces are long-established concepts of trading. They are places where supply and demand meet in a concentrated manner. The reference to historical marketplaces dates back to the Minoan culture (2200–1400 B.C.),[2] to ancient Greece through the Agora[3] as well as to the Bible.[4] Even today there are countless physical marketplaces. The potential of the Internet has had a major impact on online marketplaces especially, as it has massively reduced costs per transaction unit, search costs for information, trading and communication partners as well as time and regional restrictions on trading. In addition, network effects potentially lead to a disproportionate growth of online marketplaces & platforms.[5]

Online marketplaces exist nowadays in practically all industries: Books, music, movies, electronics, tickets, book building, real estate, food, clothes, cars, drugstores, HR, artisans, private equity, doctors/health, loans, taxis, lodging, etc. Over the past 20 years, this has led to a change in consumer habits when purchasing goods. There are increasing signs that this development is also having an impact on services.[6] If online marketplaces have proved to be accepted and successful, there are practically no constraints.[7] In this context,

1 Note: This chapter is a translation of a contribution originally penned in German.

2 As early as the Minoan period (approx. 2200–1400 B.C.), archaeological findings can be used to determine Aegean trade routes. The eastern route ran from Eastern Crete via Karpathos to Rhodes and from there eastwards via Cyprus to the Levant and northwards to Kos, Miletus and Samos. Wikipedia, *Mykenische Palastzeit,* https://de.wikipedia.org/wiki/Mykenische_Palastzeit (last visited Jul. 15, 2018).

3 The Agora (ancient Greek ἀγορά, «Marketplace») in Athens was a meeting place of the polis in Greek Antiquity and was used for the army, court and public assemblies of the free citizens. Wikipedia, *Agora (Athen)*, https://de.wikipedia.org/wiki/Agora_(Athen) (last visited Jul. 15, 2018).

4 Luther 1912, Von den Arbeitern im Weinberg, Matthäus, Chapter 20 Verses 1–16.

5 Often the benefit of a particular good to the consumer depends on the number of other consumers using the same good, and it increases disproportionately with each additional consumer due to increasing economies of scale. For each individual user, the value of a network generally increases proportionally to the number of users, whereas from the point of view of social welfare the overall benefit of a network increases disproportionately to the number of users, Fiona Savary, *Regulierung dominanter Internetplattformen*, Dissertation University of St. Gall, at 34 (2017).

6 Li Jin & Andrew Chen, *What's Next for Marketplace Startups?*, https://a16z.com/2018/11/27/services-marketplaces-service-economy-evolution-whats-next/, (last visited Dec. 10, 2018), see a huge potential in the marketplace offer of services, because while 69% of consumer spending in the US concerns services, according to an estimate of the Bureau of Economic, only 7% of it is digitized.

7 The turnover of the listed online mail order company *Amazon*, based in Seattle, amounted to around 56,5 billion USD in the 3rd quarter of 2018. Amazon's worldwide turnover in the 2017 financial year was around 177.87 billion USD, statistica, *Umsatz von Amazon weltweit vom 1. Quartal 2007 bis zum 4. Quartal 2018,* https://de.statista.com/statistik/daten/studie/197099/

the big winners of digitization are the platforms that have largely eliminated their competitors through direct and indirect network effects. *Google, Apple, Facebook, Amazon, eBay* and *Alibaba*, for example, have grown into powerful monopolists.[8] In 2017, USD 1.55 trillion were spent worldwide on the 75 largest online marketplaces. This represents 90 percent of the revenue generated on online marketplaces. How important the marketplaces are for online merchants is reflected in their share of total worldwide e-commerce sales: 50 percent of all worldwide sales on the Internet are to be generated by the rise of Internet retailers via online marketplaces.[9]

The immense forces of the marketplaces will not leave the market for legal services untouched. Despite regulation, isolation and a partially protected profession—or perhaps just because of it—the temptation to change the growing USD 849 billion legal service market[10] with the power of network effects, technology and customer-centric legal service provision is too big. The need for a large or even global legal marketplace has already been articulated several times. I am sure that some giants are already working on this in the background. Fasten your seatbelt!

II. Legal Marketplaces & Platforms

Legal marketplaces & platforms are primarily aimed at bringing together clients and legal experts in a more goal-oriented manner. They lead to more price-, performance-, and fulfilment transparency. They are aimed both at end customers (B2C) and at legal departments or law firms (B2B). Although a study by CLI Corporate Legal Insights and Wolters Kluwer Germany shows that legal marketplaces & platforms are still used relatively rarely,[11] many factors point to an exponential increase in their level of popularity and operating

---

umfrage/nettoumsatz-von-amazoncom-quartalszahlen/ (last visited Jun. 3, 2018). In the 3rd quarter of 2018, Zalando was able to generate sales amounting to around 1.2 billion EUR, STATISTICA, *Umsatz von Zalando vom 1. Quartal 2012 bis zum 3. Quartal 2018 (in Millionen Euro)*, https://de.statista.com/statistik/daten/studie/301245/umfrage/umsatzentwicklung-von-zalando-quartalszahlen/ (last visited Jun. 3, 2018).

8 Florian Glatz, *Für einen more technological approach in der Plattformökonomie,* in RETHINKING LAW, 0.2018, at 50–55.

9 Digital Commerce 360, *Internet Retailer*, https://www.digitalcommerce360.com/2018/01/11/infographic-largest-online-marketplaces-world/ (last visited Jul. 15, 2018).

10 In 2017, the legal services market worldwide was valued at 849 billion U.S. dollars, STATISTICA, *Size of the Global Legal Services Market*, https://www.statista.com/statistics/605125/size-of-the-global-legal-services-market/ (last visited Jan. 1, 2019).

11 According to the study «Legal Technology 2018» by CLI Coporate Legal Insights and Wolters Kluwer Germany, legal Marketplaces such as job exchanges, the search for lawyers and law firms and legal forums are only used by 3.57% of the respondents.

field. The terminology of legal marketplaces & platforms still has a certain vagueness,[12] which is why I recommend making the following distinction in terms of category:

Multi-sided legal marketplaces & platforms are online platforms that act as pure intermediaries providing technological infrastructure (services) to bring together supply and demand in the market for legal services. The classic multi-sided legal marketplace is transparent, bilateral, and open, i.e., interdependent from different providers and buyers and not limited to individual participants. In other words, these marketplaces solve the customer's legal needs through different providers, such as law firms, individual legal experts, in-house experts or alternative legal service providers. The services provided by the marketplace operator enable an efficient and targeted matching of supply and demand a specific subject-matter. The platform operator is neither involved in the provision of legal services nor decides which parties are to be matched. This is the sole responsibility of legal experts and customers. A major challenge for multi-sided legal marketplaces & platforms is the so-called «chicken or egg problem». Both customers, on the demand side, and experts, on the supply side, need a critical mass so that the matching function of the platform works.

Single-sided legal marketplaces & platforms are web portals that meet a specific customer need, but on the supply side they are dependent on one or more predefined legal service providers, who offer their services via this online channel. The services offered by these legal platforms are very different in nature and now cover a large part of the legal services and legal technology market. What they have in common is that their offers help customers select the appropriate legal experts or services and satisfy a specific customer need on the demand side. Single-sided legal marketplaces & platforms are thus one-sided and (partially) closed. The role of the platform operator is not limited to a pure intermediary function.

A third category are the so-called **legal networks**. These are collaboration platforms that improve cooperation between providers of legal services and usually aim to achieve the broadest possible geographical and high quality coverage of providers within the market for legal services. In addition, they rely on economies of scale to reduce the cost base of the participating lawyers. With their collaboration model of independent law firms, they sometimes compete with large international law firms.[13]

---

12 Thus *Roland Vogl* rightly points out that according to Wikipedia online marketplaces are a type of e-commerce site, where product or service information is provided by multiple third parties, whereas transactions are processed by the marketplace operater, *see* Roland Vogl, *Changes in the US Legal Market Driven by Big Data/Predictive Analytics and Legal Platforms*, *in* LEGAL TECH, DIE DIGITALISIERUNG DES RECHTSMARKTS (Markus Hartung et al., eds., 2018) at 61.

13 Michael Siebold, *The Downfall of Traditional Law Firms: The Struggle in Finding Good Legal Advice*, LAWYER MONTHLY, at 40, 41, https://www.lawyer-monthly.com/2018/04/the-downfall-

According to the Tech Index of the CodeX Center for Legal Informatics at Stanford University, more than 200 companies are already listed under the category «marketplace»; but this figure is likely to be significantly higher worldwide.[14]

A. Specificities of Legal Marketplaces & Platforms

The specificities of legal marketplaces & platforms can typically be divided into three categories. **Interdisciplinary** legal marketplaces & platforms are thematically oriented towards several consulting sectors (legal, tax, management consulting, HR, etc.) both on the demand and on the supply side. **Single-disciplinary** legal marketplaces & platforms, on the other hand, are exclusively aimed at the classical legal sector. **Thematic** legal marketplaces & platforms serve specific customer needs that could not traditionally be solved efficiently and cost-effectively in the legal field due to the small amount in litigation. These legal marketplaces concentrate on solving similar standard cases but not necessarily legally trivial, online, efficiently, cost-effectively, and transparently. The providers of such marketplaces include not only the private sector, but also the administration.[15] The business models of these legal marketplaces work because they exploit the same legal challenges and can offer their customers automated processes much faster and cheaper than in individual cases. In addition, these legal marketplaces have a DNA that focuses on the customer, which makes them very successful and relevant. The law is therefore a means to an end and not an end in itself.[16] Economically, these legal marketplaces are interesting in two respects. On the one hand, there

---

of-traditional-law-firms-the-struggle-in-finding-good-legal-advice/ (last visited May 30, 2018).

14 CodeX Techindex, http://techindex.law.stanford.edu/ (last visited Jul. 14, 2018).

15 In particular, the UK administration is keen to offer certain standardised services with online platforms: A new digital service is allowing people to submit appeals over their tax bill entirely online, a new online service to make it quicker and easier for people to claim money owed, resolve disputes out of court and access mediation has gone live, https://www.gov.uk/government/news/quicker-way-to-resolve-claim-disputes-launched-online and the stress of applying for a divorce could be eased thanks to a new online service that removes the need for paper forms, Gov. uk, *Fully digital divorce application launched to the public*, https://www.gov.uk/government/news/fully-digital-divorce-application-launched-to-the-public (last visited Jul. 14, 2018).

16 Mark A Cohen summarizes this phenomenon as follows: «The legal industry has the tools to expand access and improve the delivery. The «profession» will continue to provide differentiated legal knowledge, skills, expertise for matters that demand it. The industry—«business of law»—will be dominated by providers whose delivery capability responds to the pace and needs of business. Traditional delivery paradigms, notably law firms and corporate legal departments—many of whom still operate like law firms, not businesses—will either be reengineered or become marginalized by a new breed of alternative legal service providers that is culturally and operationally aligned with business.», Mark A Cohen, *Legal Delivery at The Speed of Busi-*

is the aspect of «Access to Law», since customers are increasingly trying to enforce their rights because of the low marginal costs. On the other hand, they have the potential to contribute to a higher quality-of-service in the legal professions.[17] Many of these legal marketplaces are not open on the supply side, i.e., they are controlled by one or a group of legal service providers, which is why they usually belong to the category of single-sided legal marketplaces & platforms.

B. Types of Legal Marketplaces & Platforms

The following six types of legal marketplaces & platforms are worth mentioning:[18] Marketplaces which offer «**Subject Matter Matching**», i.e., the matching of supply and demand of individual legal needs, a «**Contingent Staffing**», i.e., the flexible lending of experts for a limited period of time, the «**Standardized Legal Products**», i.e., the offering of Standardised Legal Products at fixed prices, «**Legal Process Outsourcing**» (LPO), where tasks previously performed by internal legal departments are now taken over by external legal service providers, «**Lawyer Specific Platforms**», which through their technological services help law firms and legal departments to overcome inefficiencies and achieve a better return on investment (ROI) and «**Expert Portals & Legal Networks**», where clients can search for and find lawyers quickly and specifically online. Of course, there are some mixed forms and also other models, which, despite different names and characteristics, can usually be assigned to one of these types in terms of content.[19]

---

ness—And Why It Matters, LegalMosaic (Jun. 28, 2018), https://legalmosaic.com/2018/06/28/legal-delivery-at-the-speed-of-business-and-why-it-matters/ (last visited Jul. 19, 2018).

17 Stephan Breidenbach & Florian Glatz, *Einführung, in* Rechtshandbuch Legal Tech, (Stephan Breidenbach & Florian Glatz eds., 2018) at 3.

18 I intentionally deviate here from the most recent classifications of some jurisdictions, including the EU, as my experience has shown that these classifications are too vague and do not reflect the categories and types of legal marketplaces sufficiently. For example, the EU, which defines only three types of online platforms and apparently also lists them under the category «multi-sided legal marketplaces & platforms», *see* Council of Bars & Law Societies of Europe, https://www.ccbe.euifileadmin/speciality_distribution/publicidocuments/DEONTOLOGY/DEON_Guides_recommendations/EN_DEON_20180629_CCBE-Guide-on-lawyers-use-of-onlinelegal-platforms.pdf (last visited Dec. 10, 2018).

19 Based on the Hastings College of Law School Study, published in 2015 with the title «*Disruptive Innovation: New Models of Legal Practice*» Roland Vogl mentions 5 categories within alternative legal service providers, *Changes in the US Legal Market Driven by Big Data/Predictive Analytics and Legal Platforms, in* Legal Tech, Die Digitalisierung des Rechtsmarkts (Hartung et al., eds., 2018) at 63.

1. Subject Matter Matching

Here supply and demand of a concrete need for legal advice are brought together. **Thematic** legal marketplaces & platforms have been very successfully positioned in this area. They provide very efficient, cost-effective and customer-specific legal advice for similar problems faced by end consumers.

Certain **multi-sided** legal marketplaces & platforms in the area of Subject Matter Matching, which also provide legal advice themselves in addition to making the platform available, were increasingly confronted with criticism or bans by lawyers' associations.[20] Consequently, the provision of legal advice bundled with service packages was abandoned.[21] Other platforms which focus solely on their intermediary role will more and more establish themselves. These platforms enable private individuals or corporate clients to efficiently solicit legal advice from legal experts or law firms.

The creation of Law Department Operations (LDO) or Legal Operations (LO), i.e., a unit in legal departments that manages the efficient sourcing of external legal service providers,[22] facilitates such multi-sided legal marketplaces. It is expected that such publicly accessible platforms will soon be used by legal departments of large corporations to more efficiently mandate external service providers. To this end, both parties (customers and legal experts) are typically guided through the mandate process in a structured manner and supported by an integrated workflow management, safe document storage, interaction and measurement tools (chat, metrics and ROI analyses, etc.). These multi-sided legal marketplaces are not merely about comparing prices, but about applying individual business practices of companies to the purchase of legal services and ensuring the exchange of information and data between legal departments in the same role as customers and law firms.[23] Such market-

---

20 Rhys Dipshan, *On-Demand Legal Providers Want to Put State Battles Behind Them*, LegalTech News (Jun. 15, 2018), https://www.law.com/legaltechnews/2018/06/15/on-demand-legal-providers-want-to-put-state-battles-behind-them/ (last visited Jun. 30, 2018).

21 Gabrielle Orum Hernàndez, *Avvo to Discontinue Controversial Legal Services Offering*, Law.com, https://www.law.com/legaltechnews/2018/07/09/avvo-to-discontinue-controversial-legal-services-offering/ (last visited Jan. 1, 2019). Cohen criticizes this as follows: «Fundamentalists have also led the resistance to new professional business models, inter-disciplinary practice, tech-driven companies like *LegalZoom* and *Rocket Lawyer* (via a multiplicity of failed unauthorized practice of law claims), and *foment* fear that technology—notably artificial intelligence— will replace lawyers», Mark A Cohen, *Legal Innovation ist the Rage, But there's Plenty of Resistance,* LegalMosaic (Sep. 4, 2018), https://legalmosaic.com/2018/09/04/legal-innovation-is-the-rage-but-theres-plenty-of-resistance/ (last visited Sept. 4, 2018).

22 Brad Blickstein, *Law Department Operations Professionals Are Flexing Their Purchasing Power*, law.com (Jun. 27, 2018), https://www.law.com/legaltechnews/2018/06/27/law-department-operations-professionals-are-flexing-their-purchasing-power/ (last visited Jun. 30, 2018).

23 Chris Pullen, *Does the Rise of Legal COOs Spell Trouble for Law Firms?*, LinkedIn, https://www.linkedin.com/pulse/does-rise-legal-coos-spell-trouble-law-firms-chris-pullen/ (last visited Nov. 18, 2018); Mark A Cohen, *Procurement and The New Legal Buy/Sell Dynamic,* LegalMo-

places will professionalize legal procurement in companies because they will enable legal departments to provide the best possible mix of resources (internal and external lawyers) for the tasks/transactions or projects to be handled.[24] Until now, Request for Proposals (RfP) software solutions were often closed, i.e., not accessible to everyone (single-sided), or they were tailor-made for the needs of large companies and only accessible to a closed circle of users (usually large law firms).[25] For law firms, getting involved with such RfP software applications is very time-consuming and involves complex issues.[26] However, the number of large companies using traditional RfP software applications is relatively low. Furthermore, according to several surveys that were conducted multiple times in Europe and the UK, small and medium-sized companies are typically still using excel lists of their preferred law firms. In my opinion, there is a lot of potential for a multi-sided legal marketplace approach for Subject Matter Matching in the legal services industry.

2. Contingent Staffing

Legal marketplaces of this kind enable the temporary provision of a legal expert for a predetermined time period in the organisation of a company or in the legal department of a larger corporation (often referred to as project lawyers or liquid workforce[27]). A contingent worker is someone who does work for a company, business, or person on a temporary basis. In contrast to LPO, Contingent Staffing leases flexible legal resources and does not outsource the solution of a legal problem to an external law firm. Through the flexible placement of external specialists within the company, the company can receive the necessary legal support quickly and without having to search the labour market. These services help companies and law firms to minimize the problem of under- and over-capacity. In this area, there are both **single-sided** and **multi-sided** legal marketplaces & platforms.

SAIC (Apr. 4, 2018), https://legalmosaic.com/2018/04/18/procurement-and-the-new-legal-buy-sell-dynamic (last visited Aug. 16, 2018).

24 Benno Quade, *Legal Tech in Rechtsabteilungen*, *in* LEGAL TECH, DIE DIGITALISIERUNG DES RECHTSMARKTS (Hartung et al., eds., 2018) at 173.

25 JENS WAGNER, LEGAL TECH UND LEGAL ROBOTS. DER WANDEL IM RECHTSMARKT DURCH NEUE TECHNOLOGIEN UND KÜNSTLICHE INTELLIGENZ, EINSATZBEREICHE VON LEGAL TECH (Springer Gabler, 2018) at 13.

26 Typical disadvantages of traditional legal panels include the time required to structure and operate the panel professionally, the dependence on a few existing law firms in the panels, reduced competition between panel firms, the risk of wrong aggregation in large firms because they still have to hire local firms, and inefficiency because only large and expensive law firms get into the panel. BRUNO MASCELLO, BESCHAFFUNG VON RECHTSDIENSTLEISTUNGEN UND MANAGEMENT EXTERNER ANWÄLTE (Schulthess, 2015) at 209, 210.

27 Markus Hartung, *Digitalisierung*, at 10 and Hariolf Wenzler, *Big Law & Legal Tech*, both *in* LEGAL TECH, DIE DIGITALISIERUNG DES RECHTSMARKTS (Hartung et al., eds., 2018).

3. Standardized Legal Products

A Standardized Legal Product is the result of a partial or full automation of a legal consulting process. This is done using automation software that logically structures performance fulfilment with a workflow and decision tree. The result of this is an efficient internal service creation process, which is offered to customers externally as a «product».[28,29] Thanks to the automation and time traceability, the provider knows the price of his services and can provide legal advice with a fixed price, which leads to greater price- and service transparency for the customer. This includes both **single-sided** and **multi-sided** legal marketplaces & platforms. In the latter case, different law firms and legal service providers appear on the supply side. Simple processes can be fully automated, which is why a legal expert is no longer required to perform the service. The customer is guided through the decision tree and receives the finished product after completion (e.g., an employment contract or an NDA). More complex processes are typically semi-automated. The expert still has to work in the background, be it because a step cannot (yet) be automated (e.g., opening a blocked account at a bank in order to found a company, notarization, etc.) or because the lawyer does not want to give up customer relations in order to maintain high client retention or to offer the customer an optional additional legal service on an hourly rate basis. Typical Standardized Legal Products include insolvency applications, out-of-court divorces, lease cancellations and eviction suits, NDAs, simple shareholder agreements, company inceptions, compensation claims due to flight delays or appeals against fines.

4. Legal Process Outsourcing (LPO)

This type of legal marketplaces enables temporary or constant legal outsourcing. Through legal outsourcing, responsibilities are transferred to an external legal service provider or a law firm so that the company does not have to hire a lawyer of its own via the labour market.[30] In principle, the mandate remains within the law firm or legal department of the company, while individual tasks are carried out by third parties.[31] In contrast to Contingent Staffing, here a purchase of a concrete consulting service takes place, which usually comprises clearly defined performance requirements. Modern LPOs exchange information via electronic collaboration tools and communicate online independently of time and terri-

---

28 Dominik Tobschall & Johann Kempe, *Der deutsche Legal-Tech-Markt*, *in* Rechtshandbuch Legal Tech (Stephan Breidenbach & Florian Glatz, eds., 2018) at 25.

29 Markus Hartung, *Gedanken zu Legal Tech und Digitalisierung*, *in* Legal Tech, Die Digitalisierung des Rechtsmarkts (Hartung et al., eds., 2018) at 9.

30 Tobschall & Kempe, *supra* note 28.

31 Jens Wagner, Legal Tech und Legal Robots. Der Wandel im Rechtsmarkt durch neue Technologien und künstliche Intelligenz (Springer Gabler, 2018) at 12.

tory.[32] The type and manner of cooperation is often laid down in a so-called Service Level Agreement (SLA). These modern LPOs successfully use technology in the provision of legal services in order to be able to offer the customer an optimal resource mix, price transparency and flexibility. The portfolio of services is much more modern and progressive than in conventional law firms.[33] LPO platforms are mostly **single-sided** legal marketplaces & platforms.

5. Lawyer Specific Platforms

These platforms allow law firms and legal departments to achieve, with the use of technological services, «more for less» or a higher ROI.[34] Lawyer Specific Platforms are **single-sided** legal marketplaces & platforms until today but could be multi-sided in the future[35]. They cover the entire legal tech spectrum. From eDiscovery to Legal Practice Management Software, Machine Learning, Legal Research, Data Analytics, Predictive Legal Analytics, Online Dispute Resolution (ODR), Document Analysis, Research Databases, Compliance, Archiving & Data-rooms, various technologies are usually offered in the form of Software-as-a-service (SaaS). While platforms that cover the core area of legal practice directly lead to a more efficient, client-oriented way of working for the legal experts, services that li.e.,outside the core area of legal practice are indirectly responsible for a more digital and decentralized way of working.[36]

6. Expert Portals & Legal Networks

Expert Portals provide clients with detailed information about legal experts. In most cases, experts can also upload publications via these portals and can be found more easily through online searches via Google or other search engines. The actual legal advice, however, is usually provided bilaterally between clients and legal experts.[37] Legal Networks are associations of legal experts who specialise in different jurisdictions and fields with a focus on collaboration.

---

32 Markus Hartung, *Digitalisierung*, *in* Legal Tech, Die Digitalisierung des Rechtsmarkts (Hartung et al., eds., 2018) at 10.

33 Gabriel Buigas, *Legal services entity in digital transformation*, *in* Minutes of the Conference on the Future of Legal Services 2018 (Leo Staub ed., 2018) at 7, 11.

34 Ilhana Redzovic, *The «Uber for Legal Services» and Faster Divorces: How Legal Tech Is Changing the Game,* https://medium.com/the-mission/the-uber-for-legal-services-and-faster-divorces-how-legal-tech-is-changing-the-game-c3c26cc00919 (last visited Jul. 31, 2018).

35 A group of leading global law firms is participating in a consortium to support the launch of the Reynen Court platform. Reynen Court aims to make it easy, secure, and efficient for law firms to deploy heavy computing applications, Reynen Court, https://reynencourt.com/ (last visited Jan. 2, 2018).

36 Jens Wagner, Legal Tech und Legal Robots. Der Wandel im Rechtsmarkt durch neue Technologien und künstliche Inteligenz, *Legal Tech als Teil der rechtlich relevanten Rahmenbedingungen* 15, 25–30 (Springer Gabler, 2018).

37 Tobschall & Kempe, *supra* note 28, at 26.

Due to the tendency of geographical fragmentation of legal departments, such networks will become more important in the future.[38]

C. Regulation of Legal Marketplaces & Platforms

Legal marketplaces & platforms must comply with the country-specific rules and regulations governing the practice of the legal profession. When structuring their business model and providing consulting services or arranging the services of legal experts, the requirements laid down in statutory and private regulations must be adhered to. These include, in particular, attorney law, personality rights, unfair competition law, price monitoring law, data protection law and, above a certain size and spread, probably also antitrust law. In this context, the term «gatekeeping regulations» is often used. In the USA, for example, the ABA Model Rules of Professional Conduct[39] are relevant for most states. In Switzerland, these are the codes of conduct of the Swiss Bar Association.[40] In Germany, the Federal Lawyers' Act (BRAO) and the Legal Services Act (RDG) are relevant.[41]

The clash between, from today's point of view, partly antiquated rules and requirements for the practice of the legal profession and the developing new consulting concepts in the legal market, weakens innovation or sometimes makes innovation impossible. These rules and requirements arose at a time when the technological evolution of legal advice could not yet be foreseen. As a result, law firms may not be able to be active in the areas of alternative legal service providers and alternative legal service providers may not be able to penetrate the areas of law firms protected by the lawyer's monopoly. The sufferers are the customers. *Li Jin & Andrew Chen* therefore assume that aggre-

---

38 In this way, Amazon plans to no longer have its legal department run centrally but from different geographical locations, *see* Caroline Spezio, *Amazon Announces 2 New HQs: How to Manage a Dispersed Department*, LAW.COM (Nov. 7, 2018), https://www.law.com/corpcounsel/2018/11/07/a-legal-team-geographically-divided-how-to-manage-a-dispersed-department/ (last visited Nov, 12, 2018).

39 ABA, *ABA Model Rules of Professional Conduct,* https://www.americanbar.org/groups/professional_responsibility/publications/model_rules_of_professional_conduct.html (last visited Jul. 17, 2018).

40 SAV FSA Swiss Bar Association, *National Rules of Professional Conduct*, https://www.sav-fsa.ch/en/anwaltsrecht/berufsregeln-national.html (last visited Jul. 17, 2018).

41 Markus Hartung, *Legal Tech und anwaltliches Berufsrecht, in* LEGAL TECH, DIE DIGITALISIERUNG DES RECHTSMARKTS (Hartung et al eds., 2018) at 245–247 and Markus Hartung, *Legal Tech und anwaltliches Berufsrecht*, THE LEGAL®EVOLUTIONARY (Sep. 4, 2018) at 137–146, https://legal-revolution.com/images/pdf/Legal-Tech-und-anwaltliches-Berufsrecht.pdf (last visited Dec. 12, 2018), where Markus Hartung is of the opinion that the rigid professional requirements and structures of the legal profession lead to the fact that it is rather the non-lawyer service providers who offer novel legal tech services and are therefore very successful.

gated trust in online marketplaces in the form of feedback, ratings, guarantees and other mechanisms could obsolete regulation in the field of legal advice, in particular exercise licences.[42] *Nicolas Torrent* also sees this scenario in the distant horizon: *«In addition, I would not rule out the possibility—given the current populist trends—that a demagogue would abolish the lawyer monopoly on client representation. It may be remote, but we should definitely make sure that, if this scenario occurs, we have a good relationship with our clients and an agreeable public image».*[43] Furthermore, *Leo Staub* points out that certain jurisdictions, with the aim of strengthening the international competitiveness of domestic providers, seek to liberalise the legal market by admitting law firms that are not controlled by lawyers, even in the monopoly area of legal profession.[44]

D. Success Factors of Legal Marketplaces & Platforms

There are several factors that are relevant for legal marketplaces & platforms to work.

1. Trust

The service offered must function flawlessly so that customers go to the legal marketplace and trust that their legal consulting needs will be met. Large cooperation partners, rating and feedback features or satisfied customers support and promote this trust.

2. Customer Satisfaction

Successful online marketplaces usually improve customer satisfaction, compared to traditional physical marketplaces, or complement their offering by letting the platform operator or third parties handle unwanted or administratively complex elements of the purchasing process. This also includes the integration of further elements in the marketplace value creation process, which the buyer or seller typically had to offer himself in the traditional business. These elements are typically handled by intelligent online legal marketplaces for the customers.

---

42 «For instance, most of us were taught since childhood never to get into cars with strangers; with Lyft and Uber, consumers are comfortable doing exactly that, millions of times per day, as a direct result of the trust those platforms have built», Li Jin & Andrew Chen, *What's Next for Marketplace Startups?*, https://a16z.com/2018/11/27/services-marketplaces-service-economy-evolution-whats-next/ (last visited Dec. 10, 2018).

43 Nicolas Torrent, *Lawyers & AI: A comprehensive overview*, LinkedIn, https://www.linkedin.com/pulse/lawyers-ai-comprehensive-overview-nicolas-torrent/ (last visited Oct. 10, 2018).

44 The United Kingdom or Australia are regarded as pioneers of this development, *see* Leo Staub, *Geschäftsmodelle der Schweizer Anwaltschaft im Wandel, in* in dubio 4_17, at 235, 236, https://www.alexandria.unisg.ch/253198/1/in%20dubio_Leo_Staub.pdf (last visited Nov. 1, 2018).

3. Quality

The quality of the legal consulting service must meet the customer's requirements. For single-sided legal marketplaces & platforms, this is quite easy to ensure by tailoring the processes, experts, technologies and structures for the provision of services to the customer's needs and ensuring that the final result always meets the customer's expectation. It is more difficult to maintain the quality of multi-sided legal marketplaces & platforms because the supply side is not controlled by one or a group of service providers. Therefore, suitable quality controls of the service providers or suitable feedback and rating features from the customer's side reduce or make it impossible to offer services of inferior quality.[45]

4. Security

The marketplace must be secure. The exchange of documents may only take place in secure document repositories, chat functionalities must be encrypted and the re-registration process for customers and providers must meet the high security requirements of the services provided on the Internet.

5. Technology

The technology must be very customer-oriented, i.e., the marketplace must have a very high intuitive usability, so that the customer feels understood and finds his way around the marketplace quickly and easily.

6. Traction

The chicken egg problem is an almost unsolvable problem for many online marketplaces, especially the multi-sided legal marketplaces & platforms. Only with enough legal services providers will the marketplace become interesting for customers, because they will be getting a large selection of legal service providers, services or products. Conversely, the marketplace only becomes interesting for providers with a certain number of new or returning customers.

7. Momentum

The momentum for legal marketplaces & platforms did not exist a few years ago. Customers were not well informed and providers of traditional legal services refused to provide services via an online channel. But times have changed. Alternative legal service providers now provide a wide range of legal services with different business models via online platforms. Customers are increasingly demanding service, fulfilment- and price transparency and are

---

45 Of course, multi-sided legal marketplaces & platforms have other advantages with regard to scaling the provision of services and the free market, which, with the exception of certain market failures (which are less relevant here), deliberately tends to lead to the best offer.

willing to make use of small legal matters via online legal marketplaces & platforms.[46] The range of services offered by future lawyers has expanded and this change will continue to increase. The use of technology in legal consulting means that the focus is no longer only on expertise or reputation, but on the type of service provided as a whole. The use of suitable technology and business and economic knowledge now also flow into the service provision process. The topic «do more with less» has found its way into legal consulting.[47]

The trend to consider alternative legal service providers rather than just law firms for external legal sourcing is also calling for legal marketplaces & platforms, which appear as service providers in these areas. In some cases, a shift in negotiating power from the provider (e.g., law firm) to the customer (e.g., legal department) is already evident. This shift makes it clear that customers are better informed and increasingly demand transparency before and during the mandate, regarding price expectations, insight into expert profiles, determination of services- and delivery times. At best, they are also guided by a «net promoter score». It is precisely these needs that are typically met by innovative legal marketplaces & platforms.

III. The New Playground

Above all, however, legal marketplaces & platforms not only promote these new alternative areas of legal consulting (in the below exhibit light grey). The law firm, which provides legal services in its traditional field (dark grey in the below exhibit), will have to consider whether it also wants to be active in the new alternative areas of legal consulting by joining platforms that provide these new services or developing platforms in these areas itself. Conversely, the alternative legal service providers are also active in the traditional consulting area of the law firm, as far as they are allowed to. On the demand side, legal departments will increasingly consider services from these new alternative areas when sourcing legal advice. So will private individuals and SMEs allocate their consulting needs to the new alternative areas.

A **possible resource mix** of a law firm is illustrated in the red rectangle. Of course, a law firm does not have to be active in all new alternative areas.

---

46 Victoria Hudgins, *Survey: 69 Percent of People Would Use Online Legal Services Over Attorneys*, LAW.COM (Dec. 12, 2018), https://www.law.com/legaltechnews/2018/12/12/survey-69-percent-of-people-would-use-online-legal-services-over-attorneys/ (last visited Dec. 19, 2018), which evaluated a survey by *The Harris Poll* that found that 76% of the Americans between 18 and 54 that were questioned prefer online legal services to traditional legal advice.

47 Mark A Cohen, *Legal Operations is Hot. But Legal Culture is Lukewarm Toward It*, LAW.COM (May 15, 2018), https://www.law.com/2018/05/15/legal-operations-is-hot-but-legal-culture-is-lukewarm-towards-it/ (last visited Jul. 17, 2018).

Within the framework of a digital strategy, however, it should analyse every area and make a conscious business decision as to how its resource mix should be composed.[48] In addition, it will be represented in Expert Portals & Legal Networks and will either source solutions from Lawyer Specific Platforms or itself be represented with services on such platforms. There is nothing to be said against offering internal process optimizations or intelligent interfaces to legal departments as innovative legal products to other service providers.

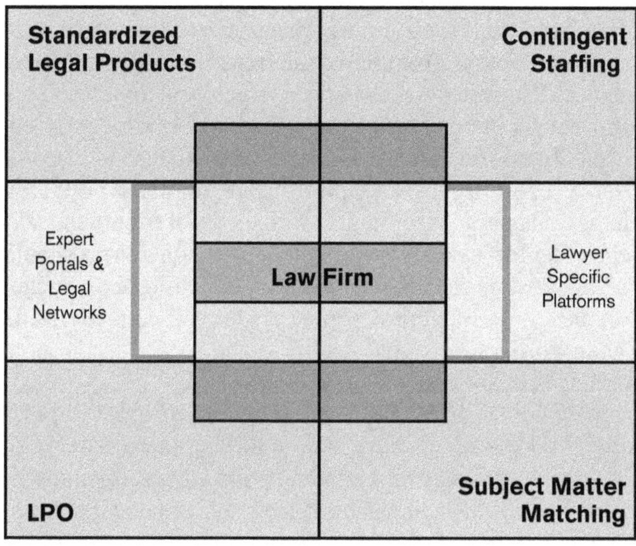

Exhibit 1: The New Playground.

IV. Advantages of Legal Marketplaces and Platforms

Legal marketplaces & platforms, which bring supply and demand together in digital form, **open up new customer access** for providers of legal services and tend to **reduce acquisition costs**. They also facilitate **interactions** between legal professionals and customers. The latter does not necessarily have to be of a digital nature. A visit to a marketplace is usually only the first step to inform oneself and to make a decision, and often ends in a personal consultation. From other industries, we know all too well how a visit to a marketplace has turned into a

---

48 According to *Christopher Schutz:* «Law firms that are focused on offering to their clients defensible, repeatable processes with robust quality and cost control built in are the firms of the future», *in* Ari Kaplan, *The Expanding Impact of Legal Procurement*, LAW.COM (Sep. 12, 2019), https://www.law.com/legaltechnews/2018/09/12/the-expanding-impact-of-legal-procurement/ (last visited Oct. 17, 2018).

purchase decision.[49] For some time now it has also been noticed that younger potential customers in particular are proactively informing themselves via the web and tend to expect that **more information about legal experts** and law firms is available than can currently be seen on law firm websites. And the digitally experienced customer will hardly visit different law firm websites for this purpose but expects a consolidated presentation on a legal marketplace.

Legal marketplaces & platforms also improve **access to law**.[50] Clients who have previously shied away from contacting a lawyer and as a result have undermined or lost their legal rights, can inform themselves on the legal marketplace and in many cases obtain **greater transparency** in terms of costs, services and performance. The pretext legal advice is a personal matter and the personal legal advisor that should be considered for every further legal need, will not be able to hold.[51] The digitalisation of legal advice will lead to customers informing themselves about legal marketplaces & platforms, **comparing products and services**, exchanging information with the legal expert and taking advantage of and paying for legal advice directly online. Law firms should therefore focus on digital customer acquisition and digital customer management. For certain complex cases, the conventional model will certainly stand the test of time, but a large proportion of consumers'—and SMEs' needs could shift to digital marketplaces in the future.[52]

This development will also affect the **legal sourcing of legal departments**. I expect that legal departments have a need to take more account of legal marketplaces & platforms. The cost pressure on the successful and efficient sourcing of external law firms and legal service providers and the disadvantages of the traditional lawyer panel, such as the time and effort required to structure a panel, the assurance of professional operation, the dependence on a few law firms, the low allocation efficiency, the reduction in competition be-

---

49 *Micha Bues*, for example, points out that in Germany already about 70% of the population regularly buys on the Internet, which will increase further due to the expansion of digital media, *see* Micha Bues, *Auswirkungen und Erfolgsfaktoren der Digitalisierung von Kanzleien*, *in* Legal Tech, Die Digitalisierung des Rechtsmarkts (Hartung et al., eds., 2018) at 25, 26.

50 Markus Hartung, *Gedanken zu Legal Tech und Digitalisierung*, *in* Legal Tech, Die Digitalisierung des Rechtsmarkts (Hartung et al., eds., 2018) at 10, 11.

51 Specialization and transparency have also ensured that the patient, with the support of his health insurance company, has a right to a free choice of medical doctor and regularly makes use of it, even in the field of medical advice which always is linked to very personal matters. It is not the personal relationship to the medical doctor, but the specialization, experience and the type of service provided that are decisive.

52 Micha Bues, *Auswirkungen und Erfolgsfaktoren der Digitalisierung von Kanzleien*, *in* Legal Tech, Die Digitalisierung des Rechtsmarkts (Hartung et al., eds., 2018) at 25, 26.

tween the law firms accepted in the panel, will encourage legal departments to obtain digital services from legal marketplaces & platforms.[53]

A survey by Legal Week Intelligence clearly revealed the need for a global legal marketplace that would provide customers with rapid access to high-quality legal experts. The General Counsels surveyed confirmed that it is becoming increasingly difficult to centralize investigations in multiple jurisdictions through a large international law firm; there is often a lack of quality, network, collaboration and knowledge of local practices.[54] According to an analysis by ALM Intelligence, the distribution of headcounts at leading global law firms is very one-sided, with around 83% of headcounts stationed in the USA, UK, and Europe. Only 17% are still located in the rest of the world, 2% in Central and South America, 1% in Sub-Saharan Africa, 2% in Middle East & North Africa, 2% in Southeast Asia, 6% in East Asia and 4% in Oceania.[55] A first indication that confirms this imbalance is the trend of international companies to no longer let their legal department act from their country of domicile for the rest of the world, but to allocate their legal resources in very different jurisdictions (so-called geographical fragmentation).[56]

Reasons	Description	Customers
Threshold theory	This group of customers is very reluctant to consult a lawyer for legal advice. The reason for this is the high cost associated with it. Therefore, they usually conduct unmonitored self-help in order to avoid a lawyers consultation. On legal marketplaces & platfonns this group receives transparent and competitive services or non-binding offers.	Micro Small Individuals
Comparability	This group of customers uses legal marketplaces & platforms to compare offers and services from law firms and legal service providers. Thanks to legal marketplaces, the services of lawyers and legal service providers are more comparable and easy to obtain.	Big Middle Individuals
More for less	This group of customers is disturbed by the intransparency and the high costs associated with legal advice and is exerting increasing pressure on law firms and legal service providers to become more efficient and cost effective. The best means of exerting pressure are offers that are comparable and show that problem solving by other law firms or legal services providers is more efficient. This comparison can be achieved via legal markteplaces & platforms.	Big Middle Individuals
Allocation efficiency	This group of customers wants to find specialised lawyers or legal service providers and and select those who are best suited to solve their legal need. Without legal marketplaces & platforms the allocation efficiency cannot be increased because the client has too little consolidated information about lawyers and legal service providers.	Small Micro Individuals Middle
Usability	If the assignment of legal experts or the purchase of legal products is easy to handle online, not tied to opening hours and time zones and fully supporting online devices, the customers will increasingly request these services on legal marketplaces & platforms.	Small Middle Micro

Source: Christoph Küng   Headcounts: Micro <9; Small <50; Middle 50-250; Big 2So+

Exhibit 2: Reasons for Legal Platforms

---

53 For the disadvantages of panels *see* Bruno Mascello, Beschaffung von Rechtsdienstleistungen und Management externer Anwälte (Schulthess, 2015) at 79–84 and 209–210.

54 Legal Week Intelligence on behalf of Interlaw, *Global Legal Services in a Disruptive World*, at 4–7, http://www.interlaw.org/global-legal-services-in-a-disruptive-world/ (last visited May 24, 2018).

55 Legal Week Intelligence on behalf of Interlaw, *id.*, at 9.

56 Caroline Spiezio, *Amazon Announces 2 New HQs: How to Manage a Dispersed Department*, Law.com (Nov. 7, 2018), https://www.law.com/corpcounsel/2018/11/07/a-legal-team-geographically-divided-how-to-manage-a-dispersed-department/ (last visited Nov, 12, 2018).

Some reasons for the increased use of legal marketplaces & platforms are shown in the chart above. The assignment of needs differs according to the size and the nature of the customers.

In the new online world, legal marketplaces & platforms are the **gateway to legal experts and services**. Marketplaces are knowledge mediators and help the customer make an initial self-assessment. This new digital sales channel has great advantages for innovative law firms. Through their presence on marketplaces, they reach a **better visibility** for their experts and also **improve their experts findability** on the leading search engines (such as Google). Marketplaces also **promote the branding** and thought leadership of law firms and legal experts (e.g., through publications or blogs). They also give law firms access to **effective rating systems**[57] which, unlike traditional lawyer rankings[58], transparently demonstrate the quality of the advice and the legal expert.

V. Token-based Marketplaces and Signature Platforms

Distributed Ledger technology is changing the way assets are transferred, documents enforced and records retained. Using Smart Contracts[59] or the Internet of Things,[60] transactions can be automated and legally executed on online marketplaces. This could lead to platforms becoming more user-centric and participatory in the future. According to *Glatz*, such decentralised platforms could also show the large platform operators their limits. He points out that the power and economic potential of these giants are based on the application layer, thanks to their data collection on buyer behaviour. On the other hand, block-chain technology means that the data collected on the protocol layer is basically available to all participants in the network, which could shift

57 Rating engines can be used to harness the efficiency gains and quality advantages of certain external legal consultants for ongoing quality improvement, *see* Benno Quade, *Legal Tech in Rechtsabteilungen*, *in* LEGAL TECH, DIE DIGITALISIERUNG DES RECHTSMARKTS (Hartung et al eds., 2018) at 179.

58 With questionable, financially driven rating methods and recommendations that are less meaningful for the end consumer (e.g., Legal 500, Chambers ect.).

59 Smart Contracts are automated business processes on a platform in a digital environment that check and enforce their terms themselves and, if necessary, report to the contracting parties whether certain contractual conditions have been met or not, *see* Tom Braegelmann, *Der klügere Vertrag vollstreckt sich selbst*, *in* RETHINKING LAW, 0.2018, at 34–37.

60 The term «Internet of Things» generally describes a network of computers, smartphones, vehicles, household appliances and other Internet-enabled devices that are equipped with sensors and actuators and are connected to each other in such a way that these devices can exchange data, *see* Nico Kuhlmann, *Smart Contracts & Embedded Legal Knowledge, in* RETHINKING LAW, 01.2018 at 32.

the added value to the protocol layer and weaken the giants.[61] This thesis is also referred to as «creative destruction». Token-based legal marketplaces & platforms would therefore not only bring the advantages of the legal marketplace, but would also make the data collected on it available to customers.

In the future, **e-signatures** will have a decisive influence on the execution of customer transactions when transactions are processed via online legal marketplaces and platforms. The UK Law Commission's consultation on «Electronic Execution of Documents» suggests that we will see a major shift towards signing platforms in 2019 that law firms—from the rare Magic Circle to the modest High Street—will use electronic and digital signatures as the standard method to execute customer transactions.[62]

VI. Concluding Remarks

Online legal marketplaces & platforms will result in customers being better informed, able to compare legal offers and legal experts, as well as in high transparency with regard to price, performance and fulfilment. **Legal departments** of big corporate customers will move to tendering a large part of their external legal advice via legal marketplaces. They will demand both traditional legal advice and alternative legal consulting services. Negotiating power shifts from the legal service provider to the corporate customer.

Private individuals and **smaller companies** will use legal marketplaces to obtain a better basis for decision-making and a faster and customer-centric legal service. The lower barriers to access legal advice mean that they tend to address legal issues earlier than today. Clear processes and transparency will provide the customer with a better understanding of his legal problem. Customers will place their consulting needs provider-agnostically. In other words, they will take into account all the characteristics of legal service providers when assigning mandates.

Providers of legal services inevitably have to orient themselves more strongly to the customer's needs. To this end, they will have to adapt their range of products and services, their service provision processes, and their structure. In order to do this, they must be willing to invest part of their revenue in new technologies.[63] The traditional differentiation criteria, expertise

---

61 Florian Glatz, *Für einen more technological approach in der Plattformökonomie*, *in* RETHINKING LAW, 0.2018, at 50–55.

62 Richard Oliphant, *Why e-signatures should be the de facto standard for executing deals*, LAWYER FIRM NEWS (Oct. 31, 2018), https://lawyerfirmnews.com/2018/10/31/why-e-signatures-should-be-the-de-facto-standard-for-executing-deals/ (last visited Dec. 10, 2018).

63 *Wolfgang Weiss* formulates this with very clear words: «Only those capable of investing significant amounts of their current revenue into digital support technologies (contract building, AI,

(assumed), and classical rankings (no longer relevant) are not sufficient to assert oneself as a successful legal expert in the digital age. Differentiation, mobility, service mentality, technology, online access, fulfilment efficiency, and customer satisfaction will be the new success factors.

VII. Bibliography

A. Hard Copy Sources

Braegelmann, Tom, *Der klügere Vertrag vollstreckt sich selbst*, *in* REthinking Law, 0.2018 at 34–37.

Breidenbach, Stephan & Glatz, Florian, *Einführung*, in Rechtshandbuch Legal Tech (Breidenbach & Glatz eds., 2018).

Micha Bues, *Auswirkungen und Erfolgsfaktoren der Digitalisierung von Kanzleien*, *in* Legal Tech, Die Digitalisierung des Rechtsmarkts (Hartung et al eds., 2018).

Buigas, Gabriel, *Legal services entity in digital transformation*, *in* Minutes of the Conference on the Future of Legal Services 2018 7, 11 (Leo Staub ed., 2018).

Hartung, Markus, *Digitalisierung*, *in* Legal Tech, Die Digitalisierung des Rechtsmarkts (Hartung et al eds., 2018).

Hartung, Markus, *Gedanken zu Legal Tech und Digitalisierung*, *in* Legal Tech, Die Digitalisierung des Rechtsmarkts (Hartung et al eds., 2018).

Hartung, Markus, *Legal Tech und anwaltliches Berufsrecht*, *in* Legal Tech, Die Digitalisierung des Rechtsmarkts (Hartung et al eds., 2018).

Kuhlmann, Nico, *Smart Contracts & Embedded Legal Knowledge*, *in* REthinking Law, 01.2018.

Mascello, Bruno, Beschaffung von Rechtsdienstleistungen und Management externer Anwälte, (Schulthess, 2015).

Quade, Benno, *Legal Tech in Rechtsabteilungen*, *in* Legal Tech, Die Digitalisierung des Rechtsmarkts (Hartung et al eds., 2018).

Savary, Fiona, *Regulierung dominanter Internetplattformen*, Dissertation University of St. Gall, (2017).

Siebold, Michael, *The Downfall of Traditional Law Firms: The Struggle in Finding Good Legal Advice*, Lawyer Monthly, https://www.lawyer-monthly.com/2018/04/the-downfall-of-traditional-law-firms-the-struggle-in-finding-good-legal-advice/ (last visited May 30, 2018).

Tobschall, Dominik & Kempe, Johann, *Der deutsche Legal-Tech-Markt*, at 25, *in* Rechtshandbuch Legal Tech (Breidenbach, Stephan & Glatz, Florian eds., C. H. Beck 2018).

Vogl, Roland, *Changes in the US Legal Market Driven by Big Data/Predictive Analytics and Legal Platforms*, *in* Legal Tech, Die Digitalisierung des Rechtsmarkts (Markus Hartung et al, eds., 2018).

Wagner, Jens, Legal Tech und Legal Robots. Der Wandel im Rechtsmarkt durch neue Technologien und künstliche Intelligenz. Einsatzbereiche von Legal Tech (Spriner Gabler, 2018).

Weiss, Wolfgang, *How are legal services going to develop in the future?*, *in* Minutes of the Conference on the Future of Legal Services 2018 (Leo Staub ed., 2018).

---

workflows) with the aim of being able to deliver the best content with the best price, will survive in that market», Wolfgang Weiss, *How are legal services going to develop in the future?*, *in* Minutes of the Conference on the Future of Legal Services 2018, (Leo Staub ed., 2018) at 73.

Wenzler, Hariolf, *Big Law & Legal Tech, in* LEGAL TECH, DIE DIGITALISIERUNG DES RECHTSMARKTS (Hartung et al., ed., 2018).

B. Online Sources

ABA, ABA Model Rules of Professional Conduct, https://www.americanbar.org/groups/professional_responsibility/publications/model_rules_of_professional_conduct.html (last visited Jul. 17, 2018).

Blickstein, Brad, *Law Department Operations Professionals Are Flexing Their Purchasing Power*, LAW.COM (Jun. 27, 2018), https://www.law.com/legaltechnews/2018/06/27/law-department-operations-professionals-are-flexing-their-purchasing-power/ (last visited Jun. 30, 2018).

CLI Coporate Legal Insights & Wolters Kluwer Germany, *Legal Technology 2018*, https://www.wolterskluwer.de/unternehmen/presse/detail/rechtsabteilungen-deutscher-unternehmen-halten-legal-tech-fuer-unverzichtbar/ (last visited Jul. 15, 2018).

Council of Bars & Law Societies of Europe, *CCBE Guide on Lawyers use of online legal platforms* (Jun. 29, 2018), https://www.ccbe.eu/fileadmin/speciality/speciality_distribution/public/documents/DEONTOLOGY/DEON_Guides_recommendations/EN_DEON_20180629_CCBE-Guide-on-lawyers-use-of-online-legal-platforms.pdf (last visited Dec. 10, 2018).

CODEX TECHINDEX, http://techindex.law.stanford.edu/ (last visited Jul. 14, 2018).

Cohen, Mark A, *Legal Operations is Hot. But Legal Culture is Lukewarm Toward It*, LAW.COM (May 5, 2018), https://www.law.com/2018/05/15/legal-operations-is-hot-but-legal-culture-is-lukewarm-towards-it/ (last visited Jul. 17, 2018).

Cohen, Mark A, *Legal Innovation is the Rage, But There's Plenty of Resistance*, LEGALMOSAIC (Sep. 4, 2018), https://legalmosaic.com/2018/09/04/legal-innovation-is-the-rage-but-theres-plenty-of-re sistance/ (last visited Sept. 4, 2018).

Cohen, Mark A, *Procurement and The New Legal Buy/Sell Dynamic,* LEGALMOSAIC (Apr. 4, 2018), https://legalmosaic.com/2018/04/18/procurement-and-the-new-legal-buy-sell-dynamic (last visited Aug. 16, 2018).

Cohen, Mark A, *Legal Delivery at The Speed of Business—And Why It Matters,* LEGALMOSAIC (Jun. 28, 2018), https://legalmosaic.com/2018/06/28/legal-delivery-at-the-speed-of-business-and-why-it-matters/ (last visited Jul. 19, 2018).

Digital Commerce 360, *Internet Retailer*, https://www.digitalcommerce360.com/2018/01/11/infogra phic-largest-online-marketplaces-world/ (last visited Jul. 15, 2018).

Dipshan, Rhys, *On-Demand Legal Providers Want to Put State Battles Behind Them*, LEGALTECH NEWS (Jun. 15, 2018) 50–55, https://www.law.com/legaltechnews/2018/06/15/on-demand-legal-providers-want-to-put-state-battles-behind-them/ (last visited Jun. 30, 2018).

Glatz, Florian, *Für einen more technological approach in der Plattformökonomie*, RETHINKING LAW (Jun. 1, 2018), https://rethinking-law.owlit.de/document.aspx?docid=REL1283317&authen tication=none (last visited Dec. 13, 2019).

GOV.UK, *Fully digital divorce application launched to the public*, https://www.gov.uk/government/news/fully-digital-divorce-application-launched-to-the-public (last visited Jul. 14, 2018).

Hartung, Markus, *Legal Tech und anwaltliches Berufsrecht*, THE LEGAL®EVOLUTIONARY (Sep. 4, 2018) 137–146, https://legal-revolution.com/images/pdf/Legal-Tech-und-anwaltliches-Berufsrecht.pdf (last visited Dec. 12, 2018).

Hudgins, Victoria, *Survey: 69 Percent of People Would Use Online Legal Services Over Attorneys*, LAW.COM (Dec. 12, 2018), https://www.law.com/legaltechnews/2018/12/12/survey-69-percent-of-people-would-use-online-legal-services-over-attorneys/ (last visited Dec. 19, 2018).

Jin, Li & Chen, Andrew, *What's Next for Marketplace Startups?*, https://a16z.com/2018/11/27/services-marketplaces-service-economy-evolution-whats-next/, (last visited Dec. 10, 2018).

Kaplan, Ari, *The Expanding Impact of Legal Procurement*, LAW.COM (Sep. 12, 2019), https://www.law.com/legaltechnews/2018/09/12/the-expanding-impact-of-legal-procurement/ (last visited Oct. 17, 2018).

Legal Week Intelligence on behalf of Interlaw, *Global Legal Services in a Disruptive World*, http://www.interlaw.org/global-legal-services-in-a-disruptive-world/ (last visited May 24, 2018).

Oliphant, Richard, *Why e-signatures should be the de facto standard for executing deals*, LAWYER FIRM NEWS (Oct. 31, 2018), https://lawyerfirmnews.com/2018/10/31/why-e-signatures-should-be-the-de-facto-standard-for-executing-deals/ (last visited Dec. 10, 2018).

Orum Hernàndez, Gabrielle, *Avvo to Discontinue Controversial Legal Services Offering*, LAW.COM (Jul. 9, 2018), https://www.law.com/legaltechnews/2018/07/09/avvo-to-discontinue-controversial-legal-services-offering/ (last visited Jan. 1, 2019).

Pullen, Chris, *Does the Rise of Legal COOs Spell Trouble for Law Firms?*, LINKEIN, https://www.linkedin.com/pulse/does-rise-legal-coos-spell-trouble-law-firms-chris-pullen/ (last visited Nov. 18, 2018).

REYNEN COURT, https://reynencourt.com/ (last visited Jan. 2, 2018).

Redzovic, Ilhana, *The «Uber for Legal Services» and Faster Divorces: How Legal Tech Is Changing the Game*, https://medium.com/the-mission/the-uber-for-legal-services-and-faster-divorces-how-legal-tech-is-changing-the-game-c3c26cc00919 (last visited Jul. 31, 2018).

SAV FSA Swiss Bar Association, *National Rules of Professional Conduct*, https://www.sav-fsa.ch/en/anwaltsrecht/berufsregeln-national.html (last visited Jul. 17, 2018).

Spezio, Caroline, *Amazon Announces 2 New HQs: How to Manage a Dispersed Department*, LAW.COM (Nov. 7, 2018), https://www.law.com/corpcounsel/2018/11/07/a-legal-team-geographically-divided-how-to-manage-a-dispersed-department/ (last visited Nov, 12, 2018).

STATISTICA, *Size of the Global Legal Services Market*, https://www.statista.com/statistics/605125/size-of-the-global-legal-services-market/ (last visited Jan. 1, 2019).

STATISTICA, *Umsatz von Amazon weltweit vom 1. Quartal 2007 bis zum 4. Quartal 2018*, https://de.statista.com/statistik/daten/studie/197099/umfrage/nettoumsatz-von-amazoncom-quartalszahlen/ (last visited Jun. 3, 2018).

STATISTICA, *Umsatz von Zalando vom 1. Quartal 2012 bis zum 3. Quartal 2018 (in Millionen Euro)*, https://de.statista.com/statistik/daten/studie/301245/umfrage/umsatzentwicklung-von-zalando-quartalszahlen/ (last visited Jun. 3, 2018).

Staub, Leo, *Geschäftsmodelle der Schweizer Anwaltschaft im Wandel*, *in* IN DUBIO 4_17, at 235, 236, https://www.alexandria.unisg.ch/253198/1/in%20dubio_Leo_Staub.pdf (last visited Nov. 1, 2018).

Torrent, Nicolas, *Lawyers & AI: A comprehensive overview*, LINKEDIN, https://www.linkedin.com/pulse/lawyers-ai-comprehensive-overview-nicolas-torrent/, (last visited Oct. 10, 2018).

WIKIPEDIA, *Agora (Athen)*, https://de.wikipedia.org/wiki/Agora_(Athen) (last visited Jul. 15, 2018).

WIKIPEDIA, *Mykenische Palastzeit*, https://de.wikipedia.org/wiki/Mykenische_Palastzeit (last visited Jul. 15, 2018).

06

Karl Koller

PropTech

How the Practice of Real Estate Transactions is Altered by Technology

TABLE OF CONTENTS

«What can be digitized will be digitized;
what can be networked, will be networked;
what can be automated, will be automated.»
– Karl-Heinz Land (2018)[1]

I. Disclaimer

Of course, it is not possible for a lawyer to write anything without a proper disclaimer. Consequently, this chapter needs to be read with the following caveats in mind:

- I was born, raised, and mostly educated in Vienna, Austria.
- I spent most of my professional career in Vienna.
- I have worked on commercial real estate transactions since starting as an intern at one of Austria's most prominent law firms in 1999, again, mostly in Austria.

In summary: this essay is quite subjective from the point of view of an Austrian lawyer having worked on Austrian real estate transactions for almost two decades.

The first part will give a condensed overview of real estate and real estate transactions ending with a description of issues resulting from the characteristics of real estate, followed by a short history of real estate transactions. We finish with the second part, which aims to give a primer on property technology or PropTech in general, followed by a discussion of two specific and potentially disruptive technologies. We conclude with the consequences of such disruption on real estate and real estate transactions.

II. Part 1—Real Estate and Real Estate Transactions

A. Real Estate

Real estate has physical characteristics that give land an inherent value:

- Real estate is unique: Each piece of land and each building is said to be a different piece of real estate; no two are the same. Even if two buildings look the same, they are different because of their different location. Since more land cannot be created in a given location, it is a scarce commodity. Value is derived from this perceived scarcity due to uniqueness.

---

1 *Karl-Heinz Land* at «Breakfast Briefing» presentation given on Sep. 21, 2018 in Vienna.

- Real estate is immobile: A piece of land and a building cannot be moved from one location to another location.
- Real estate is indestructible: A piece of land cannot be consumed, does not wear out and cannot be destroyed.

Only real estate has this combination of physical attributes and, as a result, they can affect value.[2]

In April 2017, Savills—one of the global leading property agents—reported that global asset price inflation had increased the amount of global real estate values to USD 228 trillion up from USD 217 trillion in early 2016.[3] Subsequently, Savills reported that the value of the world's real estate reached USD 280.6 trillion at the end of 2017.[4] All stocks, shares and securitized debt combined amounted together to USD 170 trillion as of April 2017 and to USD 188.6 trillion at the end of 2017. Consequently, real estate is the world's largest asset class by quite a margin.

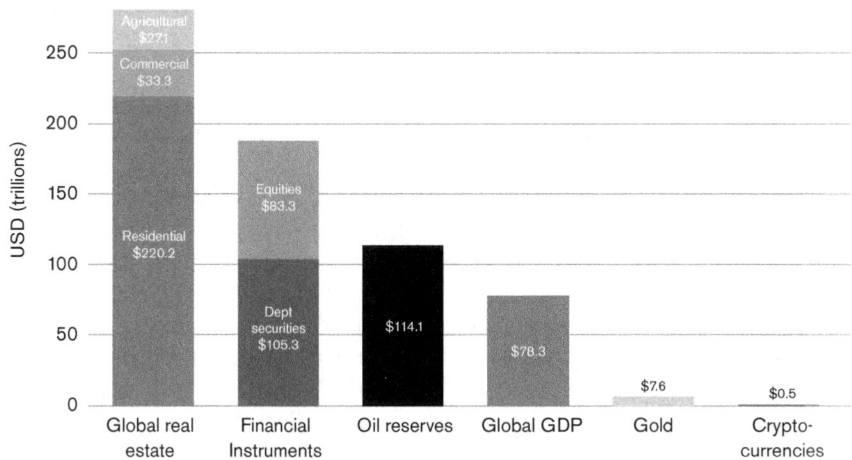

Exhibit 1: Global Real Estate Market [Source: Savills World Research].

The asset class real estate consists mainly of the sub-classes residential and commercial real estate. In essence, residential means owner-occupied real estate for personal use as a dwelling. Whereas, for institutional investment purposes,

2 Learn Mortgage, *Chapter 11 The Value of Real Estate*, https://mortgage.fastclass.com/docs/mortgage/MLPP4e_Ch11_PP.pdf (last visited Feb. 4, 2019).

3 The Savills Blog, *How much is the world worth* (Apr. 10, 2017), https://www.savills.com/blog/article/216300/residential-property/how-much-is-the-world-worth.aspx (last visited Feb. 9, 2019).

4 Yolande Barns, *Economic Trends, 8 things you need to know about the value of global real estate*, Savills (2018), https://www.savills.com/impacts/economic-trends/8-things-you-need-to-know-about-the-value-of-global-real-estate.html (last visited Feb. 3, 2019).

commercial real estate usually refers to the commercial sectors of office, retail, industrial (including logistics) and the leased, rather than owner-occupied, residential sector.

The point of investing in real estate is that owning real estate encompasses not only the physical asset but also the rights to the future income stream from that land and building, which provides additional value to the real estate. Consequently, real estate is traded either due to its inherent value and/or due to the income stream that it is able to generate.

But it is also the above characteristics that made real estate seem immune from digitalization … until now.

B. Real Estate Transactions

1. Asset Deals

At its core, a real estate transaction is an agreement between a seller and a purchaser to transfer a specific piece of real property (asset) for a specific consideration.[5]

Depending on the jurisdiction, the actual conveyance of real property, i.e., the actual transfer of ownership, is subject to a particular process and certain formalities.

For example, in Austria transfer of ownership takes place according to the Roman system of *titulus* (title) and *modus* (conveyance/transfer).[6] In an Austrian real estate transaction the typical title is a (valid) purchase contract with the aim to transfer the real estate[7], whereas the transfer has to be performed by the registration of the title in the land register[8].

The Austrian Civil Code as well as the Austrian Land Register Act set forth strict formalities that need to be adhered to, such as the purchase contract containing a declaration of conveyance, i.e., the seller's express consent to the transfer of his title to the purchaser, and a notarial certification of the signatures of the seller and the purchaser.[9]

2. Share Deals

Now, in case of commercial/institutional investments it is quite common to sell/purchase real estate by way of share deals, i.e., an agreement between a seller and a purchaser to transfer (usually) all shares of the entity (in such settings usually a special purpose vehicle) that owns a specific piece of real prop-

---

5 Austrian Civil Code, § 1054 No 2.

6 Cf. § 380 Austrian Civil Code.

7 Cf. § 424 Austrian Civil Code.

8 Cf. § 431 Austrian Civil Code.

9 Cf. §§ 432 and 433 Austrian Civil Code; §§ 26, 27, and 31 to 33 Austrian Land Register Act.

erty for a specific consideration. Simplified, the consideration in such a share deal is calculated on the basis of an agreed upon value of the real estate (usually equal to the purchase price that would have been paid in an asset deal) plus any (other) assets of the entity less any liabilities of the entity. Also, in this case, Austrian law provides for a specific process and specific formalities, depending on the type of entity that owns the real estate. For example, the sale and transfer of all shares in an Austrian limited liability company requires a notarial deed.[10] Even though the validity of such transfer is not subject to the registration in the Austrian commercial register, the managing directors of the company have an obligation to notify any transfer of shares with the commercial register.[11]

3. Asset Deals vs. Share Deals

At least in Austria, the decision on whether to employ an asset deal or a share deal is mostly tax driven. Since a detailed examination would go way beyond the scope of this chapter, just the following example: In Austria, an asset deal triggers 3.5% real estate transfer tax and 1.1% registration fee, both based on the gross purchase price. Conversely, assuming the same property is held by a limited liability company, a share deal aimed at transferring all shares in such limited liability company only triggers 0.5% real estate transfer tax based on the property value, which in turn is usually also less than an agreed purchase price; further, there is no registration fee in this case. However, there are generally also some other factors at play when deciding what kind of transaction to employ in a specific situation.

4. Types

Considering the real estate asset classes mentioned above, there are many types of real estate transactions. For example, all of the following would be viewed as a real estate transaction:

- Sale of land for the purchaser to build his family home on the land (residential real estate).
- Sale of land for the purchaser to develop an apartment building or (after subdivision of the land) a number of family homes on the land (commercial real estate).
- Sale of land for the purchaser to develop offices or a shopping center (commercial real estate).
- Sale of an apartment or a single-family home for the purchaser to live in (residential real estate).

---

10 Cf. § 76, para 2 Austrian Limited Liability Company Act.

11 Cf. § 26 Austrian Limited Liability Company Act and § 10 Austrian Commercial Register Act.

- Sale of an apartment or a family home for the purchaser to lease the apartment/home to a lessee to live in (commercial real estate).
- Sale of an office building or shopping center or logistics center or hotel for the purchaser to lease these assets to a third party (again commercial real estate).

5. Professionals

In a study commissioned by the EU,[12] four broad categories of regulatory systems of conveyancing have been identified:

- The lawyer system of the British Isles, Hungary, the Czech Republic and Denmark, which is characterized by quality control of professionals through licensing and professional exams only, negotiable fees and a low level of regulation on market structure and conduct.
- The Nordic licensed agent system under which estate agents provide legal services too. This model is also characterized by quality control of professionals through professional exams and licensing only, negotiable fees and a low level of regulation on market structure and conduct.
- The traditional, highly regulated Latin notary system, characterized by mandatory involvement of notaries, *numerus clausus*, fixed fees and strict regulation on market structure and conduct.
- The deregulated Dutch notary system, which reflects a more modern vision of the notary as a private entrepreneur fulfilling public tasks. Under this model no *numerus clausus* exist, fees are negotiable, and market structure and conduct regulation are generally less strict.

The key finding of this study was a clear statistical correlation between higher levels of regulation and higher prices (see also below).

In Austria, there is no professional legally mandatory to intervene in the conveyancing of real estate. All steps of conveyancing can be done by the parties themselves, including the mandatory certification of signatures (which can be done at court) and the application for recording the title with the land register.

---

12 Preliminary Findings from the ongoing Study on «Conveyancing Services Regulation in Europe», commissioned by the European Commission and undertaken by Centre of European Law and Politics, University of Bremen (ZERP): Christoph Schmid (Project Leader) International Real Estate Business School, University of Regensburg: Gabriel. S. Lee and Steffen Sebastian Institute for Advanced Studies (IHS): Marcel Fink and Iain Paterson. *See* Directorate for Financial and Enterprise Affairs Competition Committee, *Improving Competition in Real Estate Transactions (DAF/COMP/WP2/WD/(2007)6)* (Jan. 8, 2008), available at http://www.oecd.org/officialdocuments/publicdisplaydocumentpdf/?cote=DAF/COMP(2007)36&docLanguage=En (last visited Dec. 27, 2018).

However, in practice, in most real estate transactions, a notary or attorney will

- carry out some preliminary checks (due diligence),
- draft the purchase contract,
- provide some additional legal advice,
- certify the signatures (notary only),
- coordinate the execution and registration of the purchase contract,
- take a role in taxation, i.e., calculate the real estate transfer tax or file the transaction with the financial authority for assessment of the real estate transfer tax.

Especially when a bank is financing the purchase price, it will most certainly insist on the involvement of a notary or attorney as a professional escrow agent. This means that the purchase price will be deposited on an escrow account held by the notary or attorney acting as escrow agent for all parties involved in the transaction, including the bank. According to common escrow rules, the escrow agent will only make the payment to the seller once it has been ensured that in the land register the purchaser will be registered as owner of the property and the financing bank will be registered as the beneficiary of the mortgage, which usually secures the financing provided by the bank.[13] Quite typically, a real estate transaction will also involve real estate agents (matching seller with purchaser), tax advisors (usually providing advice on the structuring of a transaction), and technical experts (surveyors, architects, engineers providing technical advice).

6. Legal Process

For this chapter let us examine the current legal process of a rather typical residential real estate transaction, such as the sale of a condominium apartment within a newly developed building, as compared to the same process for a commercial real estate transaction, such as the sale of a newly developed logistics project.

a) Residential

The developer/seller will have retained an attorney for advising on the development of the apartment building. Usually, this attorney will be exclusively tasked with the sale of all units in such building, and any interested purchaser will have to agree to use and pay this attorney, who is not necessarily representing the interests of the purchaser. Should the purchaser choose to retain his or her own legal counsel, he will have to pay two lawyers.

---

13 Christoph Schmid, Gabriel S Lee, Steffen Sebastian, Marcel Fink & Iain Paterson, *Study COMP/2006/D3/003, Conveyancing Services Market, Country Fiches* (Dec. 2007), http://ec.europa.eu/competition/sectors/professional_services/studies/csm_study_fiches.pdf (last visited Dec. 27, 2018).

This attorney will already have prepared the entire transaction documentation, which—except for the description of the unit and identification of the purchaser—will be mostly identical for every sale of an apartment in such a building. Such documentation will consist of the purchase contract, a condominium agreement, and some powers of attorney. Further, either the purchase contract will contain an escrow clause, or there will be a separate escrow agreement.

In such cases and a healthy real estate market, the purchaser of a single apartment will have only negotiation power concerning the factual specification of the apartment but not in relation to the legal content of the transaction documents. Therefore, even if the purchaser retains his or her own lawyer, the effect of such an advisor on the transaction will be quite negligible in most cases.

Subsequently, the purchase contract and any ancillary documents will be printed out and signed in notarized form; usually, after the purchaser has secured financing for the purchase price. The financing bank will insist on security, generally in the form of a mortgage agreement, which also will be printed out and which also needs to be signed in notarized form.

The purchaser, respectively his financing bank, will deposit the purchase price on the escrow account held by the attorney acting as escrow agent. The escrow agent will then proceed with the registration of ownership and registration of the mortgage, both in the land register and both by electronic filing of a scan of these documents with the land register. Once the registration has been effected, of which the escrow agent is informed by electronic delivery of the decree of registration by the land register at the competent district court, the escrow agent will then pay out the purchase price to the seller.

In case that during this process the apartment building is still under construction, the payment to the seller will be effected in tranches depending on the progress of construction. Upon making the (last) payment, the attorney/escrow agent has performed his function.

b) Commercial

Also, in this case, the developer/seller will have retained an attorney for advising on the development of the project.

Usually, the legal process will start with the negotiation of a letter of intent or a similar instrument between the seller and the purchaser. Such LOI will set forth a summary of the intended transaction, including transaction structure and—most importantly—an exclusivity period during which the purchaser agrees to carry out his due diligence, while the seller agrees to not market or sell the project to any other party. Depending on the state of the market, such LOI might be more or less detailed. As of the writing of this chapter, it is quite common for sellers to use more extensive LOIs, e.g., already providing the representations and warranties that—subject to the results of the due diligence—will also be used in the final transaction documents.

Within the LOI or around its execution, seller and purchaser will agree on whose legal counsel will provide the first draft of the transaction documentation, which at that time might or might not already exist and which will be standardized only insofar as the attorney drafting this documentation will use his or her own or the seller's precedents. The types of transaction documents will be quite similar to those utilized in a residential transaction; however, for the reasons explained below, they will be quite individualized and tailored to the specific transaction.

During the period of exclusivity, the purchaser and its advisers will carry out legal, tax, and technical due diligence. For these purposes the seller and its advisers will prepare a data room, containing the documents pertaining to the project.

When I started my career in 1999 it was common to establish a physical data room, i.e., all documents were collected, printed, and deposited in a more or less orderly fashion at some office, which was called the data room. The purchaser's legal counsel then sent some lawyers into the data room, who in a worst–case scenario were not allowed to make copies or use any advanced technical equipment such as laptops and, thus, proceeded to dictate their finding on tape recorders. These tapes were then typed up by assistants, and the lawyers then turned the resulting documents into a due diligence report. Fortunately, this process was replaced by electronic data rooms, which can be accessed from virtually any computer with an internet connection.

At some point, the first draft of the transaction documentation is shared with the other party, e.g., the purchaser and its legal counsel, who will proceed to review and as the case may be, immediately, markup the documentation to suit their needs.

In many if not most cases, the parties and their legal counsel will subsequently meet for negotiations of the transaction documentation. Whether this occurs before or after the first markup and in person or on the telephone is highly diverse and depends on many factors. I advised on transactions where the entire documentation was negotiated by exchanging markups via email but equally on transactions, which required numerous rounds of negotiations in person with subsequent multiple exchanges of markups of the transaction documents.

Once the content of the documentation is agreed, the parties will set a signing date. In most cases, a signing meeting will be attended by authorized representatives of all parties, the respective legal counsel, and a notary, and, as the case may be, by representatives of any banks involved in such transaction, i.e., the bank providing the development financing to the seller and the bank providing the acquisition financing to the purchaser. How long such a signing may take depends a lot on the structure of the transaction, the diligent preparation of the signing, and any arising complications. Same as in a residential transaction, the entire documentation will be printed out and signed in notarized form. Again, I have been involved in signings that took two days to complete as well as in signings that were executed within half an hour.

The next step is what is mostly referred to as «closing» or «completion». Primarily, depending on whether there are conditions precedent to be fulfilled and what type such conditions precedent are, a closing might happen either at the same day of signing or only after quite some time has passed since signing. Generally, closing will be the transfer of risk and benefit of the project (i.e., commercial transfer of ownership) and ideally as close as possible to the legal transfer of ownership, i.e., registration of title.

Also, in such settings, it is quite likely that there will be an escrow mechanism, which opposed to a residential transaction will be quite individualized and tailored to the specific transaction.

The transaction mechanism together with the escrow mechanism will (also) result in (i) the purchaser being registered as owner, (ii) the development financing bank receiving its outstanding financing, (iii) the acquisition financing bank being registered as beneficiary of the mortgage, and (iv) the seller receiving the purchase price.

c) Differences

Considering the above, the major differences between residential and commercial real estate transaction can be summarized as follows from a purely legal/procedural view:

- In general, residential transactions tend to be more uniform, whereas commercial transactions are more individualized.
- Consequently, also the content of residential transaction documents will be highly similar if not almost identical, whereas the content of commercial transaction documents will be more diverse.
- In a residential transaction, there is generally way less room to negotiate than in a commercial transaction.
- In a residential transaction, the documentation will be less extensive than in a commercial transaction.
- The legal process will be highly similar in most residential transactions, whereas commercial transactions can be structured in a number of different ways.
- The number of professionals involved in a residential transaction will be quite limited, whereas in a commercial transaction, quite many different professionals will be involved, mostly in the course of the due diligence.
- Due to these facts, residential transactions tend to be performed somewhat faster and relatively cheaper than commercial transactions.

C. Issues

The characteristics of real estate as such, the type and number of professionals, and the process, lead to some issues, the two most important ones being time and money.

1. Time

Due to their rather straightforward and uniform process, residential transactions can be completed quite fast. In Austria, depending on where the property is located and, thus, which district court is competent for performing the registration, the most likely bottleneck will be the actual registration of title and the delivery of the decree of registration. The reason is that even though the process is electronic, the land register officials scrutinize the title so that the Austrian land register principles, e.g., principles of trust (§ 1500 Austrian Civil Code), registration (§ 4 Austrian Land Register Act), and public access (§ 7 Austrian Land Register Act), can be maintained. For example, in Vienna, a registration decree might be delivered within one week at one district court, but it might also take six weeks at a different district court.

In theory, it is possible also to perform an entire commercial transaction within one week. Then again, a transaction might be structured on purpose in a way that signing and closing have a gap of one to two years.[14] As a rule of thumb, a commercial transaction will currently require the following timeframe:

- About two weeks until the signing of the LOI,
- Around eight weeks to perform the due diligence,
- Additional two to four weeks for negotiating and finalizing the transaction documents,
- About another two weeks until signing,
- Another two to four weeks until closing (unless there are time-consuming conditions precedent to perform).

Therefore, the total timeframe will be around 18 weeks or two to three months.

During my research for this chapter, I found an eye-opening statement by Harvard Business School professor *Arthur Segel*, referring to the work of the Peruvian economist *Hernando de Soto*. According to this work, it takes 17 years on average to buy a home in Peru. This is attributed to the fact that most of the world lacks a tradition of property rights as well as courts and title insurance to enforce those rights.[15]

---

14 E.g., in forward purchases of real estate projects.

15 Sarah Jane Johnston, *Real Estate: The Most Imperfect Asset*, Harvard Business School Working Knowledge (Aug. 30, 2004), https://hbswk.hbs.edu/item/real-estate-the-most-imperfect-asset (last visited Dec. 27, 2018).

2. Costs

In 2006, the European Commission had chosen to examine the market of conveyancing services (i.e., services associated with buying and selling property) in more detail with a particular focus on legal related conveyancing services, to explore the economic impact of such restrictive professional regulation on specific markets.[16]

The reasoning was that this market was and still is of direct interest to consumers and of high overall economic significance, since at that time it was estimated that property turnover in the EU27 for 2005 was almost EUR 1,800 billion (about 16% of the EU27 GDP) with the corresponding turnover in property related legal services being approximately 16.7 billion Euro. Consequently, in August 2006, DG Competition commissioned a consortium of research institutions coordinated by the Centre of European Law and Politics at Bremen University (ZERP) to undertake a comparative study into the EU conveyancing services market.[17]

Summarizing, this and other studies[18] concluded that in the EU member states for a property value of (only) EUR 250,000, the following (non-adjusted) transaction costs apply:[19]

- Professional fees (nominal) ranging from 1% on the low end[20] to 9% on the high end[21] with an EU average of 4.62%
- Legal fees (nominal) ranging from 0% on the low end[22] to 1% and above on the high end[23] with an EU average of 0.79%
- Total transaction costs (nominal) ranging from 3% on the low end[24] to 15% and above on the high end[25] with an EU average of 9.8%

---

16 Christoph Schmid, Gabriel S Lee, Steffen Sebastian, Marcel Fink & Iain Paterson, *Study COMP/2006/D3/003, Conveyancing Services Market, Final Report* (Dec. 2007), http://ec.europa.eu/competition/sectors/professional_services/studies/csm_study_complete.pdf (last visited Dec. 27, 2018).

17 Christoph Schmid, Gabriel S Lee, Steffen Sebastian, Marcel Fink & Iain Paterson, *Study COMP/2006/D3/003, Conveyancing Services Market, Final Report* (Dec. 2007), http://ec.europa.eu/competition/sectors/professional_services/studies/csm_study_complete.pdf (last visited Dec. 27, 2018).

18 E.g., Directorate for Financial and Enterprise Affairs Competition Committee *supra* note 12 ff.

19 Christoph Schmid, Gabriel S Lee, Steffen Sebastian, Marcel Fink & Iain Paterson, *Conveyancing Services Regulation in Europe, Presentation at DG-Competition: «The Economic case for professional services reform»* (Dec. 13, 2006), http://ec.europa.eu/competition/sectors/professional_services/conferences/20061230/lee.ppt (last visited Dec. 27, 2018).

20 England, Ireland, Scotland, Poland and the Netherlands.

21 Austria, France, Greece, Hungary, Italy, and Spain.

22 Czech Republic, Denmark, Finland and Sweden.

23 Belgium, France, Greece, and Italy.

24 Czech Republic, Denmark, England, Ireland, Scotland, Slovenia and Sweden.

25 Belgium, Greece and Spain.

Such total transaction costs are composed of taxes (about 43%), registration fees (about 5%), and professional fees (about 52%). Thus, taxes amount to 4.8%, registration fees to 0,4% and professional fees to about 4,6% of the transaction value.[26]

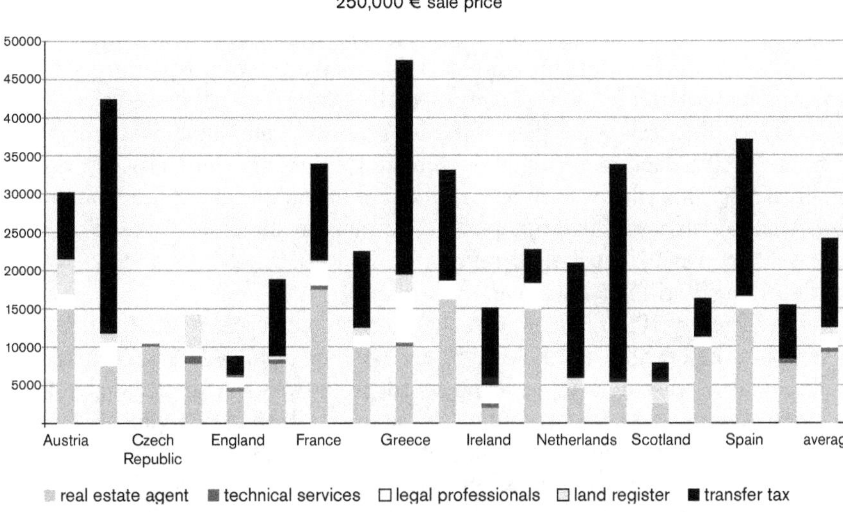

Exhibit 2: Total Transaction Costs [Source: Conveyancing Services Regulation in Europe, Presentation at DG-Competition: «The Economic case for professional services reform» 13 December 2006].

I am not aware of any such detailed studies concerning the transaction costs for commercial real estate transactions, but based on my experience the budgets for professional and legal fees can quite easily reach six-figures per transaction.

26 DAF/COMP/WP2/WD(2007)6, Preliminary Findings from the ongoing Study on «Conveyancing Services Regulation in Europe», commissioned by the European Commission and undertaken by Centre of European Law and Politics, University of Bremen (ZERP): Christoph Schmid (Project Leader) International Real Estate Business School, University of Regensburg: Gabriel S Lee and Steffen Sebastian Institute for Advanced Studies (IHS): Marcel Fink and Iain Paterson.

III. Interlude—A Short and Highly Subjective History of Real Estate Transactions

When I first stepped into a law firm as an intern in the fall of 1999, every lawyer and every assistant had his or her own workstation and staff was communicating via email, but only internally. Externally, the law firm could only be reached via one «office@» email address, and only three workstations were connected to the internet, one for receiving email and two library workstations to do legal research in the first commercially available legal databases.

Due diligences were performed in physical data rooms utilizing tape recorders. Transaction documents were drafted using word processors, but interestingly markups were made by hand on printouts and, quite a novum in the Austrian market at that time, exchanged via fax machine. I like to call this the second wave of technical revolution in legal right after the typewriter replaced handwriting (first wave).

In the early 2000s, every workstation received access to the internet, and every lawyer became reachable via an external email address. Transaction documents were still drafted using word processors, but increasingly track change modus was used for markups and email quickly replaced the fax machine for the exchange of documentation (third wave).

In the last years, collaboration tools have matured sufficiently to be used at law firms already internally for document production, and I believe that in quite a short time, collaborative writing and document production between all parties to a transaction will be utilized on a regular basis (fourth wave).

My perception is that, at least in Austria, we are at the tail end of the third wave and are already looking straight ahead at this fourth wave of technical revolution in legal.

There are two interesting things to note: First, is the acceleration of change:

- The first typewriters were placed on the market in 1874.[27]
- The first workable model of an electric typewriter was introduced in the 1920s and became mainstream in the business community in the 1930s.[28]
- The first word processing machine was launched in 1964 and became prevalent with the invention of the floppy disk in the 1970s.[29]

---

27 Encyclopaedia Britannica, *Typewriter*, https://www.britannica.com/technology/typewriter (last visited Feb. 3, 2019).

28 Brian Kunde, *A Brief History of Word Processing (Through 1986)*, https://web.stanford.edu/~b-kunde/fb-press/articles/wdprhist.html (last visited Dec. 27, 2018).

29 *Id.*

- Starting in the 1980s, word processing on personal computers became mainstream.[30]

Roughly, it took each stage half of the time of the previous stage, and there is no reason, why any further changes should happen more slowly. In fact, I would expect these changes to happen even more quickly going forward.

Second, is the impact these developments had and have on client expectations:

- For example, before the fax age, it was necessary and customary to wait many days or even weeks until mail was delivered by the post service to exchange transaction documents.
- After the rise of the fax machine, the turn-around periods turned into days.
- The advent of email accelerated the turn-around period into a couple of hours or the next day principle.
- Since the rise of smartphones and instant messaging platforms, clients sometimes expect responses within minutes.

  Again, there is no reason, why this should not accelerate further.

IV. Part 2—Property Technology—«Proptech»

First, before defining what «PropTech» (i.e., Property Technology) is, here are some facts about the use of the term:

- As of 15 December 2018, neither the Austrian legal database rdb.manz.at nor the other prevalent legal database 360.lexisnexis.at contained any references to the search term «PropTech»; in contrast, at the same time there where 135, respectively 70, hits for the search term «blockchain», the oldest hits of which were both from May 2016.
- On 19 December 2018, a Google search for «proptech» produced about 1,270,000 results, whereas a search for «blockchain» led to about 201,000,000 results.

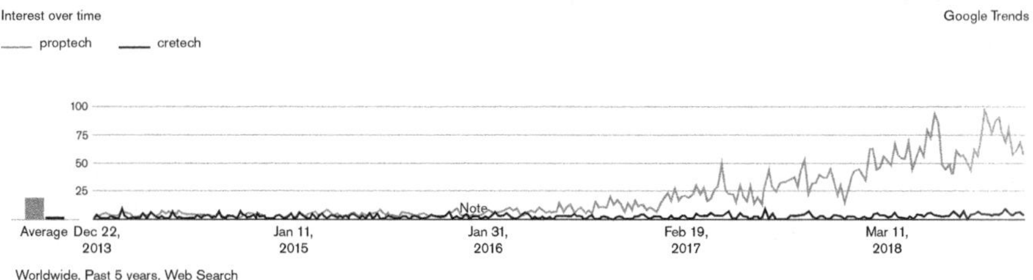

Exhibit 3: The Rise of Interest in PropTech and CREtech [Source: Google Trends].

30 MARTIN CAMPBELL-KELLY, COMPUTER, A HISTORY OF THE INFORMATION MACHINE (Westview Press, 3rd ed., 2013).

– Google trends for the past five years for the terms «proptech» and the occasionally also used «cretech»[31] show steadily rising interest since the end of 2016. However, once compared with the trend of the term «blockchain» within the same period, «proptech» is an almost invisible blip in mid-2018.

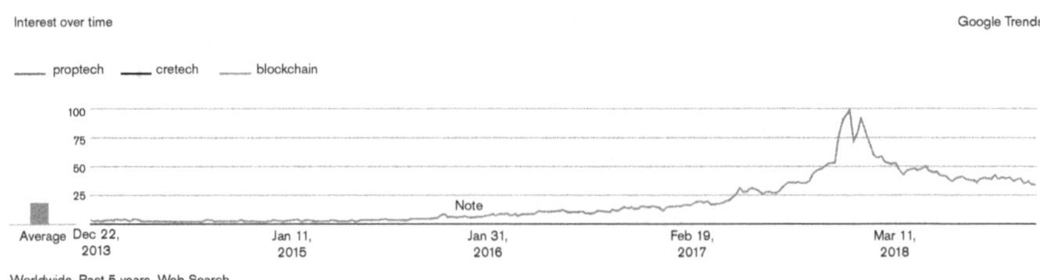

Exhibit 4: The Rise of Interest in PropTech, CREtech and Blockchain [Source: Google Trends].

Even though PropTech or rather investing in PropTech is a significantly growing business,[32] it seems safe to say that currently, outside of a circle of PropTech enthusiasts, not that many people are aware of this topic and what impact it will have on the future of real estate and real estate transactions.

However, any impact of PropTech will be an impact on the world's largest asset class with potentially equally vast consequences.

A. Definition

In April 2017, Professor Andrew Baum published «Proptech 3.0: The Future of Real Estate» mapping the emerging sector of PropTech and focusing on the impact of tech change on the character of the enormous asset class of real estate.[33]

In the August 2018 blog post «What is Proptech?»[34], the serial entrepreneur *James Dearsley*, also referred to as «the original *PropTech blogger»* and «the

31 Short for «Commercial Real Estate Technology».

32 PwC & Urban Land Institute, *Emerging Trends in Real Estate®, United States and Canada 2019*, https://www.pwc.com/us/en/asset-management/real-estate/assets/pwc-emerging-trends-in-real-estate-2019.pdf (last visited Dec. 27, 2018): *«Proptech—a portmanteau of «property technology»—has already hit the mainstream, adding USD 1.9 billion in new investment globally in 2017 after reaching a record USD 2.6 billion in 2016.»*

33 Andrew Baum, *Proptech 3.0: The Future of Real Estate,* University of Oxford Saïd Business School (2017), https://www.sbs.ox.ac.uk/sites/default/files/2018-07/PropTech3.0.pdf (last visited Dec. 27, 2018).

34 Juwei, *What PropTech means for you* (Dec. 18, 2018), https://list.juwai.com/de/news/2018/12/what-proptech-means (last visited Feb. 22, 2019).

most influential person in *PropTech*»[35], writes that after having been asked to define PropTech at a conference, together with his fellow panelist *Professor Baum*, they decided on the following definition:

> *«PropTech is one small part of the wider digital transformation of the property industry. It describes a movement driving a mentality change with the real estate industry and its consumers regarding technology-driven innovation in the data assembly, transaction, and design of buildings and cities.»*

Interestingly, in the same blog post *James Dearsley* states that

> *«PropTech is not the replacement of humans with machines; it is the utilization of modern technology to enhance the abilities, speed, and efficiency of those who sell, buy, maintain, manage, work within, live within and make their living from property.»*,

which I think is a better definition.

Similarly, a market report by *Jones Lang LaSalle* from April 2018 stated:

> *«Proptech, a blend of the words property and technology, refers to the utilization of technology as a solution to challenges in the real estate sector. Specifically, technology is used to create or renovate services offered in real estate to buy, sell, rent, develop, market and manage property in a more efficient and effective way.»*[36]

In any case, these definitions encompass a plethora of different technology applications in the real estate sector. Over the past several years, startups around the world developed numerous business models:

- Organizing, analyzing, and extracting key data from lengthy rental documents
- Virtually walking through homes and apartments without leaving the couch
- Finding a dream home match quicker than ever
- Splitting rent amounts easily
- Working from (and living in) shared office spaces
- Managing properties using simple digital dashboards

---

35 LENDINVEST, *Top 25 PropTech Influencers 2016*, https://www.lendinvest.com/blog/2016/11/top-25-proptech-influencers-2016/ (Nov. 30, 2016) (last visited Feb. 21, 2019).

36 JLL, *Clicks and Mortar: The Growing Influence of Proptech* (2018), http://www.ap.jll.com/asia-pacific/en-gb/research/950/proptech-2018-refreshed-with-new-insights-apr2018#.XHLw-pyVbDt4 (last visited Feb. 13, 2019).

- Crowdfunding real estate projects[37]

According to Professor *Baum* there are three PropTech sub-sectors (verticals), and three drivers (horizontals). The verticals are Real Estate FinTech, Shared Economy, and Smart Real Estate. The horizontals are information, transactions (or marketplaces), and control:

- Real Estate FinTech describes technology-based platforms which facilitate the trading of real estate asset ownership. The assets can be buildings, shares or funds, debt or equity; ownership can be freehold or leasehold. The platforms may simply provide information for prospective buyers and sellers, or they may more directly facilitate or effect transactions of asset ownership or leases with a (negative or positive) capital value. This sector supports the real estate capital markets.
- The Shared Economy describes technology-based platforms which facilitate the use of real estate assets. This sector supports the real estate occupier markets.
- Smart Real Estate describes technology-based platforms which facilitate the operation and management of real estate assets. This sector supports real estate asset, property and facilities management.[38]

Considering the above and building upon a definition of the more mature FinTech[39] as «the use of technology and innovative business models in financial services» in the 2015 World Economic Forum report «The Future of *FinTech*», I propose the following more general definition of PropTech:

> *«PropTech is what happens at the intersection of digitalization and real estate.»*

B. Origins

On the one hand, PropTech is developed by the players in the real estate industry, focusing on the streamlining of workflows and best practices (endogenous technology). On the other hand, there is a lot of technology created outside of the real estate industry, which will still have an effect on the industry (exogenous technology).

For example, Virtual Reality will completely change the way that properties are marketed and designed, Artificial Intelligence will disrupt the

---

37 German PropTech Initiative, *What is PropTech? A brief history* (Aug. 19, 2016), http://gpti.de/blog/2016/08/19/what-is-proptech-a-brief-history/ (last visited Feb. 7, 2019).

38 Baum, *supra* note 33.

39 I.e., financial technology.

way we understand and interpret our data, and Blockchain has the potential to entirely change how real estate is sold and transferred.[40]

C. Disruption

Looking at the issues of real estate transactions and the underlying legal process, I believe that two technologies have the potential to disrupt real estate transactions as we know them today.

1. Blockchain

Assuming that my prediction about the fourth wave of technical revolution in legal holds true, this will result in an exclusively digital production process for transaction documents. Since at least in Austria, also the conveyancing has to happen electronically[41], it seems like a no-brainer that the analog step of notarization will be replaced in the future.

In February 2018, a paper with the title «Real Estate Transactions via Blockchain» was published in the legal magazine *Immolex*.[42] Summarizing, the authors propose a system based on smart contract and blockchain, which would essentially replace the function of the notary but keep the working Austrian land register intact. Under this proposal, it would be the job of the clerk at the land register to check whether the document deposited by the blockchain represents the actually digitally concluded contract, which is necessary to be able to keep the land register in sync with the blockchain system.

While I appreciate the ingenuity of the proposal, it does not solve for the identified issues of time (i.e., the time it takes the land register to actually register the title and issue a decree) and cost (since the costs of notarization are negligible). At the same time, it requires quite extensive changes to the existing system, such as a re-training of all land register clerks, without replacing the existing and, arguably, well working system.

However, in countries that have no land register, or an archaic paper-based land register, or a land register that is not governed by the principles of

---

40 Juwei, *supra* note 34 and *Baum*, *supra* note 33.

41 Austria has a fairly advanced land register: Since the 1980s the Austrian land register has been a database maintained at the Federal Computing Center. Since 1999 it has been possible to make external inquiries into the land register via the internet and since November 2009 notaries and attorneys are obliged to make filings with the land register only in electronic form. In 2012 the «old» land register was replaced with a new and modernized database. Since May 2012 a failure to use electronic filings is a lack of form.

42 Thomas Seeber, Manuel Schweiger & Martin Schachner, *Immobilientransaktionen über die Blockchain*, 2 IMMOLEX (2018) at 38.

trust, registration and public access, I can imagine a tremendous potential for the application of a blockchain based system as an open, distributed ledger that can record transactions between two parties efficiently and in a verifiable and permanent way.

I was involved in many transactions that also encompassed real property in CEE countries, i.e., countries that might not have had a working land register with the additional risk that a purchaser might face restitution claims. These issues were usually solved by a title search and title insurance. Title search means that during the due diligence process, every single transaction in relation to a piece of land was traced back for at least ten years and every such transaction was reviewed as regards its validity. Title insurance essentially means taking out insurance against certain risks possibly affecting the real property, such as restitution claims. It goes without saying that both these instruments added substantial additional costs to a real estate transaction.

It is not hard to imagine that in such countries, a blockchain based land register and conveyancing system would solve some time consuming and expensive issues.

For example, *Lantmäteriet* (the Swedish Mapping, Cadastre and Land Registration Authority), *Telia* (a Swedish telephone company and mobile network operator), *SBAB* (a Swedish Bank), *Landshypotek Bank* (another Swedish Bank), *ChromaWay* (a Swedish blockchain company), and *Kairos Future* (a Sweden-based research and management consulting firm) are currently working on a development project to study and test the possibilities of using blockchain as a technical solution for real estate transactions and the mortgage deed processes. The end result shall be a secure process for real estate transactions and mortgage deeds with, among others, the following characteristics:

- All involved actors will have a digital file representing the agreement of ownership of the real estate, mortgage deeds and the transaction process.
- The authenticity of the process, the signatures, the file confirming ownership, mortgage deeds etc. will be secured with a blockchain. The Swedish Mapping, Cadastre and Land Registration Authority will store the blockchain with the proofs, but the blockchain will also be stored and validated by other actors. It will, therefore, be easy for authorized third parties to verify information. These third parties would usually be actors who are part of the process: banks, buyers, sellers, real estate agents etc.
- The records and files that should be public according to Swedish law will be public and those which should be confidential will stay confidential.[43]

---

43 Kairos Future, *The Land Registry in the blockchain – testbed*, https://chromaway.com/papers/Blockchain_Landregistry_Report_2017.pdf (2017) (last visited Dec. 27, 2018).

2. Artificial Intelligence (AI)[44]

In February 1996, as *Luis Ackermann* outlines in a chapter herein, *Garry Kasparov* beat IBM's Deep Blue chess computer 4-2 in Philadelphia. Deep Blue won the first game, becoming the first computer ever to beat a world chess champion at tournament level under serious tournament conditions. On 11 May 1997, Deep Blue defeated *Garry Kasparov* in a 6-game match held in New York. This was the first time a computer defeated a reigning world champion in a classical chess match.[45]

In 2016 Google's AlphaGo computer program won at the Chinese board game Go against Korean *Lee Sedol,* one of Go's most dominant players, marking significant developments in artificial intelligence.

Right now, I am using tools such as *DeepL,*[46] an AI machine translation service, to translate texts between German and English and Grammarly,[47] Another AI application, which automatically detects grammar, spelling, punctuation, word choice, and style mistakes to avoid errors in what is not my native language. At the time of writing, these applications are not necessarily «better» than a human, but they are definitely quicker by orders of magnitude.

The point that I am making is that AI has already arrived in the mainstream. Especially as regards commercial real estate transactions, the issue that makes lawyers still very necessary is that there exist vast amounts of data related to a property, such as land register data (e.g., title, encumbrances), data from the lease of the property (imagine a shopping center with hundreds of lease agreements), data from the operation of the property (e.g., supply agreements, utilities consumption records, bills), and technical data (e.g., maintenance logs). Most of this data is available in data silos, unstructured, and sometimes only in hardcopy, which then will be scanned, and made available in an electronic data room once a real estate transaction is imminent. This is precisely the reason why sellers spend a lot of time collecting such documents, and lawyers and other advisors then again spend weeks sifting through these documents, assessing whether the content of such documents might have any impact on the transaction. To put that into perspective: a commercial lease for

---

44 «AI means machines that imitates human capabilities, such as driving cars, reading text or playing chess. Machine learning is a subfield of this, meaning computers that can learn without being explicitly programmed—i.e., we don't write rules for the program, the program writes its own rules. Deep learning is a class of machine learning algorithms programmed to imitate functions of the human brain, so called artificial neural networks, with the aim of solving complex problems the way human brains do.» LEVERTON, *AI for Real Estate—Turning Myth into Reality*, LEVERTON BLOG (Apr. 11, 2017), http://blog.leverton.ai/2017/04/11/ai-real-estate-myth-reality-0 (last visited Dec. 27, 2018).

45 CHESS.COM, *Computers and Chess—A History* (Aug. 7, 2007), https://www.chess.com/article/view/computers-and-chess—a-history (last visited Dec. 27, 2018).

46 https://www.deepl.com/home.

47 https://www.grammarly.com/.

a unit in a shopping center, together with annexes can have easily up to a hundred pages with potentially relevant provisions, such as change of control clauses, strewn throughout the entire document. If done diligently, the review of one such lease agreement can take easily about two hours. Austria's largest shopping center has a bit over 250 shops; reviewing all leases would, therefore, take about 500 hours, which results in legal due diligence costs for only this part of about EUR 125,000 at a modest blended rate of EUR 250 per hour. Due to various circumstances, investors are increasingly less willing to pay such amounts.

Now, AI technology can be used to identify and understand text and to automatically extract data from documents, such as leases. Furthermore, such a platform can then structure the data, making it accessible and understandable for big data analytics. Such AI technology might not be perfect yet, but it is already definitely faster and cheaper than paying a lawyer for 500 hours.

D. Consequences

Generally, I am convinced that PropTech will affect every step of a real estate transaction. Depending on circumstances, such as the applicable legal framework, and the type of real estate asset class, these effects will have varying degrees of impact on the legal profession.

It is clear that the New Suits of real estate law will have to have a far greater understanding of current technology and future developments than the old guard. They will have to stay open for the increasing acceleration of technological advances and its impact on the legal profession. They will have to compete not only against lawyers but also against new market entrants, such as software engineers and data scientists, who attempt to build the next PropTech unicorn start-up.

It remains to be seen, which profession will adapt quicker: Will lawyers acquire the skillset of the Science, Technology, Engineering and Mathematics crowd faster than vice versa?

> *«It is difficult to make predictions, especially about the future.»*
> – *Danish Proverb*[48]

48 *Cf.* K. K. Steincke, Farvel Og Tak: Minder Og Meninger, (Farvel Og tak: Ogsaa en Tilvaerelse IV (1935–1939)), Quote Page 227, Forlaget Fremad, København as reported by Garson O'Toole, https://quoteinvestigator.com/2013/10/20/no-predict/ (Oct. 20, 2013) (last visited Apr. 22, 2019).

Notwithstanding the above proverb and the undeniable risk that predictions might not age well, I will still make some statements relating to the consequences of PropTech and the future of real estate law:

1. Land Registers

On the one hand, countries with advanced, electronic land registers will most likely not have a sufficient economic incentive to replace a properly working system with another system. However, countries without an established and trustworthy land register will utilize blockchain-based technology, which could be the easiest and most cost-efficient way to unlock, respectively raise the value of available real estate.

There is also no reason why blockchain systems should not encroach on the entire transaction chain up to the filing with the land register. As regards Austria, it is not hard to imagine a system that translates a «regular» purchase contract written by a lawyer into a smart contract which populates any individual information with data from existing public databases such as the commercial or land register, and then produces exactly an output equal to the input for the mandatory electronic filing with the land register.

A further side effect of «putting real estate onto the blockchain» will be the essentially inherent tokenization of real estate, i.e., the conversion of rights to an asset into a digital token resulting in a digital representation of a real-world asset on a blockchain. This process will result in many additional possibilities and applications, such as streamlining the voting process in a condominium association or the trade in such real estate backed security tokens, which opens an entirely new way of investing in real estate.[49]

2. Structuring of Transactions

Currently, the structuring of a transaction, in particular whether it shall be a share deal or an asset deal happens by a back and forth discussion between the parties to the transaction, and their tax and legal advisers. Recently, I have seen a tax technology tool, which upon actually drawing a corporate structure as little boxes, connected with arrows, and the input of some data, is able to show accurately what tax consequences a given structure has. It is quite easy

---

49 Fortune reported in August 2018 that instead of going the IPO route, the owner of the St. Regis Aspen Resort in Colorado began to sell real estate security tokens on a blockchain with help from Indiegogo, a crowdfunding site. To conduct the sale, the owner of the Aspen St. Regis has created a single-asset real estate investment trust, or REIT, called Aspen Digital, that is selling tokenized equity in the form of Aspen Digital Tokens (Aspen Coin), which are not registered with the SEC, and represent common stock with no voting rights. Aspen Digital planned to sell 18 million tokens at an initial valuation of US$1 apiece, converting a slice of the property's US$224 million valuation into crypto coins. Robert Hackett, *Ritzy Aspen Hotel Sells Real Estate on Blockchain with Indiegogo's Help*, FORTUNE (Aug. 23, 2018), http://fortune.com/2018/08/23/hotel-real-estate-aspen-blockchain-ethereum-st-regis-indiegogo (last visited Dec. 27, 2018).

to imagine to combine such tool with AI so that the results do not only show possibilities but also recommendations, taking into account not only numbers but also unstructured data, such as personal preferences of one of the parties to the deal. Here, there is a strong possibility that lawyers and tax advisors will have to acquire a skill set, which allows to «teach» the AI and do a sanity check on the results.

3. Data Rooms

Data rooms will be established using blockchain technology. According to an October 2018 press release, one data room provider already offers a blockchain secured data room, i.e., it is substituting traditional archiving that comes in the form of DVDs, CDs, USBs and hard drives, with secure data rooms validated via blockchain for the warranty period of a transaction.[50] In a world of smart buildings studded with sensors and IoT technology, it is not a big leap to imagine that all the data produced by such building will be automatically recorded into a blockchain, which then can immediately constitute the technical data room. The same applies for the electronic conclusion of (smart) contracts relating to such a building, which can also be recorded directly into a blockchain. The use of blockchain will have a severe impact on legal concepts, such as disclosure. Can everything that is recorded on such blockchain be considered as disclosed even if it might be impossible for a human to cope with the sheer amount of recorded data or to make sense of it, without utilizing yet another technology?

4. Due Diligences

As mentioned, AI is faster and more accurate when reading and extracting data from unstructured documents. Currently, even if such AI tools are employed, it is still the job of the lawyer to assess possible risks from the then structured data and «translate» a mitigation of such risks into a purchase agreement in a way that in the end satisfies both the seller and the purchaser. Again, I will not be surprised if the job of analysis and coming up with suggestions for mitigation of risk will keep shifting to the AI, since the AI platform provider with its access to far more and also competing datasets will have a better basis for suggestions than a lawyer who will have (limited) access to the datasets of his clients only.

---

50 Drooms, *Drooms—The first data room with blockchain technology* (Oct. 4, 2018), https://drooms.com/en/pressrelease/drooms-the-first-data-room-with-blockchain-technology (last visited Apr. 22, 2019).

5. Transaction Documents

The age of exchanging markups or comparing versions of transaction documents via email will come to an end soon. The future is cloud-based solutions, where the parties to the transaction and their advisors will collaboratively draft provisions and documents and where it will be evident (at any time) who made what change. I suggest that this will lead to more uniform contracts within each of the real estate asset classes. Once such collaborative writing platforms will be connected with AI platforms, it is just a small step to image the AI asking questions to the parties, making suggestions, and amending any connected provisions in real time. The provisions of a purchase contract that are usually negotiated the most are representations and warranties, and the liability provision, respectively limitations thereof. If a property and its owner are recorded on a blockchain, which per definition is a permanent and immutable ledger, why would it be necessary for the seller to agree to a warranty for clear title or any other circumstances (such as lack of encumbrances)? In many cases, the monetary and temporal limitations of liability result from gut feelings of the involved parties and some equally gut-driven negotiations and are usually argued with the statement «this is market standard».[51] In a future including AI, with access to an incredible amount of data, it will be likely that the AI will indeed be in a position to make suggestions for limitations that actually are current market standard.

6. Conveyancing

The conveyancing process including escrow services will be mostly automated and shifted to non-legal intermediaries. Therefore, the function of the lawyer will be relegated to the design of transactions and the underlying (smart) contracts, to the maintenance of such designs, and, maybe to an arbiter role if things go wrong. To some extent, this is already true for the sale of residential apartments, where the lawyer will draft a master transaction documentation, which is then used in each sale. At the same time, the day to day work, like contact between seller and purchaser, minor amendments of the contract, preparation of signing, filing with the land register, is performed by back-office staff or very junior lawyers. Also, with a fully electronic transaction process and the advance of electronic signatures and similar technology, actual signing and closing meetings will become increasingly rare and in the case of smart contracts will be replaced by automatic performance, once any conditions have been fulfilled.

---

51 Some lawyers are of the opinion that once opposing counsel argues with the phrase «market standard» it simply means that this opposing counsel is out of «real» arguments.

V. Concluding Remarks

The net result of PropTech will be that clients will demand even quicker real estate transactions at even lower costs, which is insofar a conundrum since PropTech solutions are quite capital intensive in their initial deployment. Even though the rise of PropTech might make the future of the legal profession working in real estate look quite bleak, one thing should not be underestimated: in part due to 1) the education of lawyers, and 2) the regulation of the legal services market, a lawyer, or a notary, respectively, law firms have one thing that any startup first has to earn over a long period of time: *trust*. Therefore, real estate lawyers still have the chance to avoid being thoroughly disrupted by PropTech if they embrace the coming change, upskill their technological capabilities, and leverage the trust in them either by establishing PropTech solutions or by partnering with PropTech innovators.

VI. Bibliography

A. Hard Copy Sources

CAMPBELL-KELLY, MARTIN, COMPUTER, A HISTORY OF THE INFORMATION MACHINE (Westview Press, 3rd ed., 2013).

Seeber, Thomas, Schweiger, Manuel & Schachner, Martin, *Immobilientransaktionen über die Blockchain*, 2 IMMOLEX (2018).

B. Online Sources

Barns, Yolande, *Economic Trends, 8 things you need to know about the value of global real estate*, SAVILLS (Impacts—The Future of Global Real Estate) (2018), https://www.savills.com/impacts/economic-trends/8-things-you-need-to-know-about-the-value-of-global-real-estate.html (last visited Feb. 3, 2019).

Baum, Andrew, *Proptech 3.0: The Future of Real Estate*, UNIVERSITY OF OXFORD SAÏD BUSINESS SCHOOL (2017), https://www.sbs.ox.ac.uk/sites/default/files/2018-07/PropTech3.0.pdf (last visited Dec. 27, 2018).

CHESS.COM, *Computers and Chess – A History* (Aug. 7, 2007), https://www.chess.com/article/view/computers-and-chess—a-history (last visited Dec. 27, 2018).

Directorate for Financial and Enterprise Affairs Competition Committee, *Improving Competition in Real Estate Transactions (DAF/COMP/WP2/WD/(2007)6)* (Jan. 8, 2008), http://www.oecd.org/officialdocuments/publicdisplaydocumentpdf/?cote=DAF/COMP(2007)36&docLanguage=En (last visited Dec. 27, 2018).

DROOMS, *Drooms—The first data room with blockchain technology*, (Oct. 4, 2018), https://drooms.com/en/pressrelease/drooms-the-first-data-room-with-blockchain-technology (last visited Apr. 22, 2019).

Encyclopaedia Britannica, *Typewriter*, https://www.britannica.com/technology/typewriter (last visted Feb. 3, 2019).

Garson O'Toole, (Oct. 20, 2013), https://quoteinvestigator.com/2013/10/20/no-predict/ (last visited Apr. 22, 2019).

German PropTech Initiative, *What is PropTech? A brief history* (Aug. 19, 2016), http://gpti.de/blog/2016/08/19/what-is-proptech-a-brief-history/ (last visited Feb. 7, 2019)

Hackett, Robert, *Ritzy Aspen Hotel Sells Real Estate on Blockchain with Indiegogo's Help*, Fortune (Aug. 23, 2018), http://fortune.com/2018/08/23/hotel-real-estate-aspen-blockchain-ethereum-st-regis-indiegogo (last visited Dec. 27, 2018).

JLL, *Clicks and Mortar: The Growing Influence of Proptech* (2018), http://www.ap.jll.com/asia-pacific/en-gb/research/950/proptech-2018-refreshed-with-new-insights-apr2018#.XHLwpyVbDt4 (last visited Feb. 13, 2019).

Johnston, Sarah Jane, *Real Estate: The Most Imperfect Asset*, Harvard Business School Working Knowledge (Aug. 30, 2004), https://hbswk.hbs.edu/item/real-estate-the-most-imperfect-asset (last visited Dec. 27, 2018).

Juwei, *What PropTech means for you* (Dec. 18, 2018), https://list.juwai.com/de/news/2018/12/what-proptech-means (last visited Feb. 22, 2019).

Kairos Future, *The Land Registry in the blockchain – testbed*, https://chromaway.com/papers/Blockchain_Landregistry_Report_2017.pdf (2017) (last visited Dec. 27, 2018)

Kunde, Brian, *A Brief History of Word Processing (Through 1986)*, https://web.stanford.edu/~bkunde/fb-press/articles/wdprhist.html (last visited Dec. 27, 2018).

Learn Mortgage, *Chapter 11 The Value of Real Estate*, https://mortgage.fastclass.com/docs/mortgage/MLPP4e_Ch11_PP.pdf (last visited Feb. 4, 2019).

lendinvest, Top 25 PropTech Influencers 2016, https://www.lendinvest.com/blog/2016/11/top-25-proptech-influencers-2016/ (Nov. 30, 2016) (last visited Feb. 21, 2019).

Leverton, *AI for Real Estate—Turning Myth into Reality*, Leverton Blog (Apr. 11, 2017), http://blog.leverton.ai/2017/04/11/ai-real-estate-myth-reality-0 (last visited Dec. 27, 2018)

PwC & Urban Land Institute, *Emerging Trends in Real Estate®, United States and Canada 2019,* https://www.pwc.com/us/en/asset-management/real-estate/assets/pwc-emerging-trends-in-real-estate-2019.pdf (last visited Dec. 27, 2018).

The Savills Blog, *How much is the world worth* (Apr. 10, 2017), https://www.savills.com/blog/article/216300/residential-property/how-much-is-the-world-worth.aspx (last visited Feb. 9, 2019).

Schmid, Christoph, Lee, Gabriel S, Sebastian, Steffen, Fink, Marcel & Paterson, Iain, *Conveyancing Services Regulation in Europe, Presentation at DG-Competition: «The Economic case for professional services reform»* (Dec. 13, 2006), http://ec.europa.eu/competition/sectors/professional_services/conferences/20061230/lee.ppt (last visited Dec. 27, 2018).

Schmid, Christoph, Lee, Gabriel S, Sebastian, Steffen, Fink, Marcel & Paterson, Iain, *DAF/COMP/WP2/WD(2007)6, Preliminary Findings from the ongoing Study on Conveyancing Services Regulation in Europe*, http://ec.europa.eu/competition/international/multilateral/2007_feb_realestate.pdf (last visited Dec. 27, 2018).

Schmid, Christoph, Lee, Gabriel S, Sebastian, Steffen, Fink, Marcel & Paterson, Iain, *Study COMP/2006/D3/003, Conveyancing Services Market, Country Fiches* (Dec. 2007), http://ec.europa.eu/competition/sectors/professional_services/studies/csm_study_fiches.pdf (last visited Dec. 27, 2018).

Dr Marc O Morant

Gig Economy Lawyers and the Success of Contingent Workforce Models in Law

TABLE OF CONTENTS

I. Fundamentals and issues—upheavals in the world of work

Since the advent of digitisation, the world of work has undergone a major change. The era in which employees served an employer faithfully for many years (or even decades) seems to be a thing of the past. Employers and employees have changed dramatically—as have their expectations.[1] In the last two decades, employers have faced growing cost pressure against a backdrop of increased competition and market volatility.[2] This has forced them, among other things, to restructure their workforce to maintain or regain the necessary competitiveness, flexibility and cost efficiency. Conversely, expectations and perceptions of employment have changed with regard to digitisation, the rapid development of new technologies and the «flexibilisation» of the world of work.[3]

Firstly, the development of new technologies and new working methods, sometimes accompanied by cuts in workers' rights, is incompatible in some cases with the right to protection of service providers. From the point of view of labour law, there is therefore a widespread call to limit temporary work, especially as an independent «freelancer»[4] has the same need for protection in many cases as an employee.[5] The *gig economy* (or *«Uber» economy*) is held responsible for robbing millions of workers of time, space, and wages through the use of technology-based methods.[6] Yet, this exploitation is not sufficiently regulated by law or even sanctioned under criminal or administrative criminal law.[7] These critical voices agree that labour law must actually reach those it

---

1 Note: For ease of reading, the masculine form of nouns and pronouns is used in the following text to refer to members of both sexes.

2 Wendy R Boswell, Marla Baskerville Watkins et al., *Second-class citizen? Contract workers' perceived status, dual commitment and intent to quit*, 80 JOURNAL OF VOCATIONAL BEHAVIOUR 454–463 (2012) at 454; Ahmad Karim, *The Increasing Usage of Professional Contingent Workers: A Review*, 10 (1) THE JOURNAL OF GLOBAL BUSINESS MANAGEMENT 33–37 (2014) at 33.

3 Boswell & Watkins et al., *supra* note 2, at 454; *see* also Ryan Calo & Alex Rosenblat, *The Taking Economy: Uber, Information, and Power*, 117 (6) COLUMBIA LAW REVIEW 1623–1690 (October 2017) at 1626.

4 The term «freelancer» is generally understood to mean a freelance, independent, entrepreneurial activity. The type of cooperation can legally be structured in different ways.

5 *See* the critical view of the former President of the German Federal Labour Court on new developments in temporary agency work, temporary employment and personnel service agencies and on the transfer of competences to enforce workers' rights (equal pay etc.), Hellmut Wissmann, *Zur Entwicklung des Arbeitsrechts in Deutschland und Europa*, 62 (2) AUR 46–51 (2014).

6 *See* the critical view *in* Laureen Snider, *Enabling Exploitation: Law in the Gig Economy*, 26 (4) CRITICAL CRIMINOLOGY 563–577 (2018).

7 *Id.*

seeks to protect.[8] However, in the gig economy and platform economy,[9] it is not just a question of enforcing workers' rights. Rather, it is about reconciling work, needs, changing lifestyles, and employment models.

On the one hand, the gig economy has not only promoted the exploitation of synergies from an economic point of view and the global exchange of services (e.g., through platforms such as «*UpWork*»), but has also produced «real-time flexibility» in employment relationships and new choices that traditional employer-employee relationships cannot offer.[10] On the other hand, companies in the *new economy* and the platform economy continue to maintain traditional employment relationships, demanding a high willingness to work substantial hours from their salaried employees, but in return granting these employees considerable flexibility in the organisation of working hours and a large number of benefits and bonuses. Compared with gig workers, whose advantage is primarily limited to flexible working hours, this makes these companies appear to be true *corporate paradises.*[11] The much-praised flexibility of gig workers and their freedom to choose their clients stands and falls with the question of how economically dependent a gig worker is with respect to the type of gig work in question.[12]

As a rule, gig workers display elements of both employment and self-employment in performing their work, although the distinction between an employment contract, a contract for work and services and an agency contract is sometimes difficult to see in individual cases, as exemplified by *Uber* taxi drivers (starting in 2010) and the case law that has been passed in various countries on this subject in the meantime.[13] The loss of *affective commitment*

---

8 *See* Wissmann *supra* note 5, at 50.

9 Platforms, one sometimes reads, are the railways of the 21st century. Today, so-called platform companies constitute the majority of the ten most valuable companies in the world. Of the ten most valuable brands, half is in the platform economy: Google, Apple, Amazon, Facebook and, to some extent, Microsoft. It is no longer about producers who «push» supposedly desirable services and products into the market and try to attract customers with them. Rather, the focus is on the end customer whose conscious and unconscious desires are precisely measured and predicted by self-learning intelligence and algorithms in order to communicate the increasingly precisely determined need to all stages of the production chain from end to end. In the future, there will no longer be any business solely between companies, but all businesses will be based on consumers. *See* also below, II.

10 *See* Maureen Soyars Hicks, *Flexible jobs give workers choices,* Monthly Labor Review 1–2 (2017) at 1.

11 *See* Martin Kenney & John Zysman, *The Rise of the Platform Economy*, 32 (2) Issues in Science and Technology University of Texas at Dallas 61–69 (2016) at 66.

12 *See* Calo, Ryan & Rosenblat, *supra* note 3, at 1638.

13 *See* Seth D Harris &, Alan B Krueger, *Is Your Uber Driver an Employee or an Independent Contractor?,* 80 Perspectives on Work 30–33, http://www.lerachapters.org/OJS/ojs-2.4.4-1/index.php/LERAMR/article/download/3098/3073 (2016) (last visited Nov. 15, 2018) at 31 and Soyars Hicks *supra* note 10.

and loyalty to the employer, combined with a stronger relationship with the client, is accepted as a compromise (at least in such irregular tripartite relationships) provided the client does not have to accept any loss of expertise or quality and gains more transparency—especially in regard to the work processes and the cost structure.[14] Irrespective of the legal characterization of Uber, the key features for offering said business model can be applied to emerging legal services and legal outsourcing, likewise. Namely, when splitting the legal industry into services and products, one comes to the identical pattern of work provision as is the case with Uber. The technology of reaching the customer and delivering a particular output is different, but the functional relation between the service provider and the client is nearly identical.[15] What matters is the fact that, in line with the clients′ expectations, certain service standards are met and that the network operates efficiently.[16] In other words: Taking Uber as a surrogate for new forms of delivery means that legal practice is not going to disappear, it is «just going to forms of delivery that can combine the competence and flexibility of an old-fashioned firm with the efficiency and scale of a just-in-time cloud-computing company.»[17]

The present paper aims to address the impact and influence of gig economy on the provision of legal services, discussing the question of how it will transform the provision of legal services in the future. As a general observation, the law market has escaped the gig economy in many respects—at least in Europe. This question will be dealt with in the context of legal tech against the backdrop that traditional legal services are reluctant to change work methods that have worked quite well in the past. Accordingly, the first chapter will take a look at the fundamentals of legal services as traditional employment relationships, followed by reflections on old and new concepts of rendering services. Chapter III focuses on the culture and self-image of the legal profession, whereas chapter IV examines the compatibility of legal services and the gig economy from a strategic management workforce and risk perspective. Finally, in a summarized assessment, future paths for the provision of legal services and possible focus areas of the legal profession will be outlined.

---

14 *See* Boswell et al., *supra* note 2, at 462 and Michael Skapinker, *Breaking the Law,* Financial Times (Apr. 11, 2016), at 73.

15 Eric Tucker, *Uber and the Unmaking and Remaking of Taxi Capitalism: Technology, Law, and Resistance in Historical Perspective*, in Law and the «Sharing Economy» (Derek McKee, Finn Makela & Teresa Scassa eds., University of Ottawa Press, 2018), at 378 et seq.

16 Tucker, *supra* note 15, at 379.

17 *Oliver Goodenough* cited in Rachel M Zahorsky &William D Henderson, *Who's eating Law Firm's Lunch?*, 99 (10) ABA Journal 32–38 (October 2013) at 35.

II. Legal services as a bedrock of traditional employment relationships

The fact that traditional branches of industry, such as the media (especially the newspaper industry) as well as the telecommunications and medical sectors, have long been claiming new business models for themselves and providing their services in an increasingly standardised form is not new. The trend towards the use of external labour, body leasing and the general increase in the *contingent workforce* within tripartite contractual relationships has also been confirmed in recent years. From the workers' point of view, primarily in the USA, the idea of securing one's livelihood by means of a series of jobs *(gigs)* lined up one after the other, rather than a steady stream of income, has prevailed—not only among the working class, but also among university graduates and highly qualified freelancers.[18]

One of the few industries that appears thus far to have resisted successfully the new trends outlined above—whether because of its historical importance or because of the nature of the services provided—is legal services. In fact, it can be observed worldwide that in numerous law firms the practice of the legal profession has hardly changed in recent decades and consistently follows the pattern of providing *tailor-made, high-priced* advice.[19] A billing system based on fixed lawyer's rates, the amount of the disputed claim, and hourly rates does not incentivise a lawyer or a legal service provider to provide services faster or more efficiently—on the contrary. The perception of the lawyer as a conservative, change- and risk-averse, service provider who sees no need for change in the traditional working environment is, therefore, very common.[20]

There is a lot to be gained from the idea of standardised and cost-efficient provision of legal advice services, if one overcomes the traditional models and the disadvantages—predominantly from the point of view of (labour) law, liability law, and data protection law—are weighed up realistically. At first glance, it is difficult to understand why time-consuming legal research and the creation of repetitive master agreements or standard contracts and processes[21]

---

18 *See* Barbara Durkin, *Whole New World: Gigonomics, Human Resource Development and the Brave New Lawyer*, 83 (7) New York State Bar Association Journal 34–40 (September 2011) at 34 et seq. and Malcolm Sargeant, *The Gig Economy and the Future of Work*, 6 (2) E-Journal of International and Comparative Labour Studies 1–12 (2017), http://eprints.mdx.ac.uk/22247/1/422-1007-1-PB.pdf (last visited Nov. 16, 2018) at 2.

19 *See* Skapinker, *supra* note 14, at 73.

20 *See*, Ashish Nanda, David Wilkins & Lisa Rohrer, *Axiom (a): Getting Down to Business*, 09-20 Harvard Law School 1–17 (2012) at 3 and Durkin *supra* note 18, at 35.

21 For example, the creation of standardised swap contracts for banks and, in general, all kinds of commercial, standardised and sometimes not individually negotiated contracts such as non-dis-

would not be accessible to standardisation, both with regard to aspects of content, in general, and the way in which the work is performed[22], in particular.[23]

These aspects would be very interesting, for example, in class actions brought under international investment protection law. These may involve several hundred plaintiffs, whose claims and the admissibility of a lawsuit in accordance with precedent would first need to be determined by means of a separate *database verification procedure* undertaken by external experts in painstaking detail before the major questions were dealt with.[24] It should be remembered that, to date, *lawyers* have been appointed to perform data reviews relating to such investment protection lawsuits, but their mandate from the court was merely to ascertain the facts and *not* to draw any legal conclusions from the data collected.[25] It is legitimate to ask, therefore, why these and similar activities, which could also be carried out by legal laypersons or even automated tools, require expensive, externally purchased *legal* expertise. In this context, it is also justified to ask why the court called upon to resolve the dispute, instead of having the evidence examined on the basis of a random sample—as was the case in the well-known international arbitration proceedings before the ICSID Tribunal in 2012, *Abaclat versus Argentina*—does not, instead, carry out a complete examination of evidence with the aid of *LegalTech*. The last option would certainly be more in line with the *rule of law* and would provide plaintiffs with increased legal protection than the solution currently used in practice.

The fact that outsourcing and technology-based efficiency enhancements are possible in the field of legal services and that the demand for new business models for legal services also undoubtedly exists has been demonstrated by alternative, non-lawyer providers of legal services, primarily in the USA, but now also in Switzerland and Germany.[26] In the meantime, legal service provid-

---

closure agreements or subscription contracts or components for demerger or merger agreements and similar transactions.

22 With regard to processing, the focus is on technological solutions (e.g., data analysis supported by artificial intelligence), which perform manual legal work more efficiently and accurately, and on outsourcing to external employees.

23 *See* Daniel Fisher, *Legal-Services Firm's $73 Million Deal Strips The Mystery From Derivatives Trading,* FORBES (Feb. 12, 2015), https://www.forbes.com/sites/danielfisher/2015/02/12/legal-services-firms-73-million-deal-strips-the-mystery-from-derivatives-trading/_(last visited Nov. 16, 2018).

24 For example, in the arbitration proceedings Abaclat versus Argentina from 2012, ICSID Case # ARB/07/5 and, in particular, Procedural Order No. 17 of Feb. 8, 2013 for the appointment of a legal expert for the data verification of the plaintiffs; *see* STACIE I STRONG, CLASS, MASS, AND COLLECTIVE ARBITRATION IN NATIONAL AND INTERNATIONAL LAW (Oxford University Press, 2013) at 79.

25 *See* Strong, *supra* note 24, at 80.

26 *See* Nanda et al., *supra* note 20, at 1 et seq.; in addition to PwC Legal, companies such as Thomson Reuters, EY Law, Deloitte Legal or Axiom Law are the main alternative providers of legal

ers can make use of a wide range of technologies that serve the *screening, analysis,* and *evaluation* of previously unprecedented data volumes. According to a study by the *Boston Consulting Group* from 2016, it is precisely these three options that will in the future be at least as important for the continued existence of the legal profession as the «classical» art of providing legal advice and legal representation.[27] In addition, the *Boston Consulting Group* surveyed legal partners and found that legal technology solutions could already handle between 30% and 50% of the tasks currently performed by junior lawyers, even though a significant portion of the legal profession still prefers to conduct a manual data review and analysis as part of the laborious processing of each individual document.[28] The reason why there are few incentives to invest in new technologies is again noted as the billing system of chargeable hourly rates and the profit-sharing agreements between the law partners.[29] A certain cautious attitude towards the implementation of new technologies, which are still under development and which require radical changes in workflows and a need for additional training measures, is also unmistakable.[30]

III. Old and new concepts—Contingent workforce, gig economy and new contract models

The term «*gig economy*» appears in the literature as a sometimes vaguely defined relation of the *sharing*, *collaborative* or *platform economy*.[31] However, a distinction must be made because the sharing, collaborative and platform economy designates a number of techniques and practices that enable intermediation between strangers on a digital platform. However, the gig economy, as a generic term, encompasses a wide range of industries and professions that do not necessarily benefit from a platform.[32] The term gig economy was born as a necessity and, as it were, a reaction to the global financial crisis and the frag-

---

services; *see* Acritas, *Global Alternative Legal Brand Index 2018*, https://www.acritas.com/global-alternative-legal-brand-index-2018 (last visited Feb. 3, 2019).

27 *See* BCG & Bucerius Law School eds., *How Legal Technology Will Change the Business of Law*, http://www.bucerius-education.de/fileadmin/content/pdf/studies_publications/Legal_Tech_Report_2016.pdf, (Jan. 2016) (last visited Nov. 23, 2018) at 1–20.

28 *See* BCG 2016 *supra* note 27, at 3.

29 *Id.*

30 *Id.*

31 *See* Calo & Rosenblat *supra* note 3, at 1625.

32 *See* Chris F Wright, Nick Wailes, Greg J Bamber & Russell D Bamber, *Beyond National Systems, Towards a «Gig Economy»? A Research Agenda for International and Comparative Employment Relations*, 29 Employee Responsibilities and Rights Journal 247–257 (2017) at 253.

mented business world in 2009.[33] The main pillars of the gig economy are the use of underutilised or unused assets and the avoidance of downtime.[34]

The gig economy, thanks particularly to the low barriers of entry to work via platforms, etc., has created a new breed of self-employed, who exert considerable competitive pressure on traditional service providers to reduce consumer costs and improve quality.[35] These new forms of employment must be accompanied, of course, by social provisions for the employee or service provider in terms of social security and pensions, so that legislators and social partners are called upon to act.[36]

The *US Department of Labor* has reported that, in May 2017, 3.8% of workers in the US (5.9 million people) were employed as part of the *contingent workforce,* a term used to refer to persons whose work is not expected to be permanent or for whom the provision of labour is inherently temporary.[37] While these figures alone do not show a dramatic increase, between 1986 and 1996, employment in the US as a whole rose by only 1.7%, while employment under temporary contracts grew by 10.3% over the same period and the number of freelancers increased rapidly.[38] In addition, the gig economy, in combination with other forms of employment, shows a marked increase.[39] A study conducted by Ernst & Young for the American market in 2016 concludes that 50% of the organizations surveyed had seen a significant increase in their use of contingent workers employed over the last five years, confirming the findings of a previous Harvard study according to which at the same time, the contingent workforce in the USA grew by 66% between 2005 and 2015.[40] At the same time, the *contingent workforce* in the USA grew by 66% between 2005 and 2015. In Switzerland, there has been no increase in the proportion of precarious employment relationships to date. At a global level, however, there

---

33 *See* PwC, *Workforce of the future—The competing forces shaping 2030*, https://www.pwc.com/gx/en/services/people-organisation/publications/workforce-of-the-future.html (2018) (last visited Nov. 23, 2018) at 39.

34 *See* Kristopher Jones, *Three Gig Economy Trends To Watch For In 2017*, Forbes (Dec. 29, 2016), https://www.forbes.com/sites/forbesagencycouncil/2016/12/29/three-gig-economy-trends-to-watch-for-in-2017/ (last visited Nov. 24, 2018) at 1.

35 Calo & Rosenblat, *supra* note 3, at 1626.

36 *See* Natalie Gratwohl, *Freelancer sind die Angestellten der Zukunft*, in: NZZ (Nov. 9, 2018), https://www.nzz.ch/meinung/freelancer-sind-die-angestellten-der-zukunft-ld.1435216 (last visited Nov. 24, 2018).

37 US Department of Labor/Bureau of Labor Statistics, *Economic News Release—Contingent and Alternative Employment Arrangements Summary* (Jun. 7, 2018), https://www.bls.gov/news.release/conemp.nr0.htm (last visited Nov. 24, 2018).

38 *See* Ahmad Karim, *The Increasing Usage of Professional Contingent Workers: A Review*, 10 (1) The Journal of Global Business Management 33–37 (2014) at 33.

39 *See* Wright, *supra* note 32, at 253.

40 *See* Ernst & Young, *Is the gig economy a fleeting fad, or an enduring legacy*, https://gigeconomy.ey.com/Documents/Gig%20Economy%20Report.pdf (2016) (last visited Dec. 11, 2018) at 6.

is a trend towards more flexible employment models and working with freelancers.[41] This trend is underpinned by the fact that employers are increasingly providing their employees with greater freedom of action and are looking specifically for «internal entrepreneurs» in the company in order to increase their ability to innovate. However, there is little discussion that the incentives for a company to invest in the training and further education of the existing «regular» workforce are reduced at the same time.[42]

More and more companies are opting to buy in specialists on a contingent worker basis, for increased flexibility, as these types of specialists often have broad expertise that would either not be attainable at all with a regular employment contract or would be far too expensive for companies to maintain in the long term.[43] In line with this, there are already numerous internet marketplaces specially designed for highly qualified consultants, which give them access to a large number of engagements. These are proving to be economically more lucrative for service providers than entering into an employment contract.[44] Nevertheless, the question arises as to whether these «income options» can generate the same workload as employment by a large company or law firm, and whether the higher revenue amounts per contract can compensate for the potential fluctuations in demand for the consulting services.[45] In principle, however, lawyers are also faced with the same decision when they ask themselves whether they want to remain employed in a large, renowned law firm or whether they should open their own firm.[46] In any case, access to potential employment is extended via platforms and the cost risk of establishing oneself as an independent expert is lower.[47]

IV. Culture and self-image of the legal profession

Usually (especially in the USA), law firms have a typically hierarchical structure, led by one or a few senior partners at the top of the pyramid, frequently referred to as «profit center model».[48] These partners have the highest hourly rates and they are followed by teams of junior lawyers concentrating on de-

41 *See* Gratwohl, *supra* note 36, at 1.
42 *Id.*
43 *See* Karim, *supra* note 2, at 33.
44 *See* Wright, *supra* note 32, at 253.
45 *Id.*
46 *See* Wright, *supra* note 32, at 253.
47 Calo & Rosenblat, *supra* note 3, at 1625, 1634.
48 David A Steiger, *The Rise of Global Legal Sourcing: How Vendors and Clients Are Changing Legal Business Models*, 19 (2) Business Law Today 38–43 (November/December 2009) at 41 et seq.

tailed legal work, legal research, and the drafting of contracts.[49] The client is usually charged hourly rates for the vast amount of working hours spent on «small-scale» legal work like document review, discovery consulting or even merely administrative tasks like organizing file documents.[50] The client also pays for downtime and for unproductively invested working time.[51] It is not surprising that, in times of digitisation, legal tech and standardised procedures, clients are no longer willing to pay such opaque fees piled up in this manner.[52]

The inflexibility and defensive attitude of the legal profession towards new technologies, structures, and employment models is understandable if one considers the exclusivity (in the sense of an exclusivity of service provision by lawyers trained and licensed for this purpose only) and the monopolisation of the legal profession.[53] For law firms, there is virtually no need or pressure for any action to support change, especially since the traditional model of providing legal services would also be economically viable even if—sooner or later—lawyer's fees were reduced due to the increasing number of alternative providers. As a result of an increase in supply, law firms could react by reducing their staff, but still retain the high-priced segment.

This rather rigid approach by law firms is an obstacle to current developments. In general, there is an increasing need for legal advice and other legal services, especially by large companies. This need is partly covered by internal lawyers or, in selective cases, by the deployment of an entire team of external lawyers, depending on the requirements and the legal system in which the company operates.[54] Legal disputes are no longer exclusively settled in court in the form of litigation, but are terminated at an earlier stage through settlement, mediation, or arbitration.[55] In addition, there is a trend towards companies increasingly seeking advice from alternative providers, such as tax consulting firms, management consultants and banks, as well as *multidisciplinary practice firms (MDPs).* The landscape of legal service providers has therefore changed radically and created new competition.[56]

---

49 *See* Skapinker, *supra* note 14, at 73.

50 Steiger, *supra* note 48, at 39, 41.

51 *See* Skapinker, *supra* note 14, at 73; Steiger *supra* note 48, at 39, 41; Andrew Bruck & Andrew Canter, *Supply, Demand, and the Changing Economics of Large Law Firms*, 60 (6) Stanford Law Review 2087–2130 (Apr. 2008) at 2089.

52 *See* Skapinker, *supra* note 14, at 73 and Richard E Susskind & Daniel Susskind, The Future of the Professions. How Technology will transform the Work of Human Experts (Oxford University Press, 2015) at 30, 66 et seq.; Greenberg, Michael D & McGovern, Geoffrey, *An Early Assessment of the Civil Justice System After the Financial Crisis* (2012) at 34.

53 *See* Susskind & Susskind, *supra* note 52, at 67.

54 *See* Dzienkowski, *supra* note 57, at 2999.

55 *See* Dzienkowski, *supra* note 57, at 3000; Calo & Rosenblat, *supra* note 3, at 1626 et seq.; Susskind, Tomorrow's Lawyers, at 109 et seq., 130 et seq.

56 *See* Dzienkowski, *supra* note 54, at 3001.

Only a few legal systems, such as that in England and Australia, have succeeded in liberalising the legal market, so that non-lawyers can now also open companies to provide legal services and the monopoly of the legal profession has been penetrated.[57] Naturally, this also has an impact on the behaviour and preferences of clients, who are increasingly being advised by management consultants or external service providers rather than by conventional lawyers.[58]

This assessment is consistent with the findings of a 2012 survey conducted by *Eversheds/Sutherland (UK)* and *RSG Consulting* of 1,800 mostly young lawyers (aged 26–35) in 73 countries around the world, on the culture of the legal profession, career opportunities, and employment in law firms.[59] The future expectations and prospects for the coming 10 years were examined. According to this survey, many young lawyers feel that the model of the law partner in a law firm is outdated and unsuited to the 21st century. Additionally, they feel that the training period is too long and there is an exaggerated focus on providing services on an hourly basis. Criticism of the traditional legal profession is leveled at a lack of *work-life balance* and an outdated working environment, with one sixth of respondents wanting a more «human» and positive corporate culture.[60]

The renowned British lawyer and author *Richard Susskind,* who has promulgated the demise of the traditional legal profession and the advance of legal tech since the early 1980s, sees three major areas as central drivers for the erosion and transformation of the legal market in the future:

- the global economic downturn, which is accompanied by a reduction in the legal workforce and a simultaneous increase in the workload, especially of in-house lawyers, in line with the need for «more legal services at lower cost»;[61]
- the liberalisation of the legal market, which in England and Wales, for example, led to the *Legal Services Act of* 2007, which allowed *alternative business structures (ABSs)* to be established and permitted the provision of legal services by non-lawyers; and,
- as a third driver, the advance of technology in the legal profession.[62]

57 *See* Susskind & Susskind, *supra* note 52, at 67.

58 *Id.*

59 Eversheds Sutherland, *21st Century law firm—Inheriting a new world,* https://www.eversheds-sutherland.com/global/en/what/publications/21stclawyers/index.page (2012) (last visited Nov. 24, 2018).

60 Eversheds Sutherland, *supra* note 59.

61 *See* Susskind, *supra* note 55 note 55, at 4 et seq.

62 *See* Susskind, *supra* note 55, at 6 et seq.

According to *Susskind*, alternative legal service providers are not characterised by outdated work structures nor are they stuck in a billing system based on hourly rates. Traditional, outdated work models and status symbols, which were once expected from law firms, such as representative office premises with prestigious corporate locations in urban business centres, are now a thing of the past.[63] «Virtual» litigation and online dispute resolution are just two examples of the future prospects that *Susskind* sees as a result of the reduced demand for legal services and the outsourcing of global, internet-based legal services as well as online document creation, mass service provision and the standardisation of procedures.[64] Not only the work processes and methods, but also the fields of activity of lawyers will change radically in the coming years and new job profiles will emerge—from legal project managers to technology managers, analysts, designers, and legal engineers.[65]

V. Considerations on the compatibility of legal services in the form of alternative legal service providers

A. Strategic Workforce Management from the HR Perspective

The «technologisation» of the legal profession and the trend towards the specialisation of services and the associated outsourcing of certain services to alternative providers will require new staffing models, both in law firms and in corporate legal departments. Ideally, for legal departments, with a view to these new developments, *legal operations teams* will be formed for the acquisition or outsourcing of legal services which address five strategic tasks—supplier management, risk management, knowledge management, financial management and technology management—using data analysis tools, technology, strategic planning, inter- and intra-functional collaboration, and process standardisation.[66] By linking up these areas, a higher quality of work, optimised resource utilisation, increased cost efficiency, and time savings, a better legal

63 *See* Susskind 2017, *supra* note 55, at 8, 10 et seq.

64 *See* Susskind 2017, *supra* note 55, at 10 et seq.

65 *See* Markus Hartung, Micha-Manuel Bues & Gernot Halbleib eds., Legal Tech – Die Digitalisierung des Rechtsmarkts (C. H. Beck, 2017) at 237 et seqq.

66 BCG & Bucerius Law School, eds., *Legal Operations: Getting More from In-House Legal Departments and Their Outside Counsel*, http://www.bucerius-education.de/fileadmin/content/pdf/studies_publications/Buc_BCG_Legal_Operations_Studie_2019.pdf 1-28 (Nov. 2018) (last visited Nov. 24, 2018) at 7.

risk profile and a higher employee retention rate can be achieved.[67] Standardisation and optimisation are key, both in legal departments and in law firms, in order to automate processes successfully in the legal profession. Again, a legal operations team can evaluate the existing processes and determine whether and which procedures can be standardised and optimised. The team members check workflows within the department, identify bottlenecks that hinder the efficiency of processes and implement new processes to eliminate weaknesses as required. Relevant methods, such as *Lean* or *Six Sigma,* are used for process optimisation and process management.[68]

In return, the use of legal operations can drive the outsourcing of certain activities to alternative legal service providers. In a study conducted in 2018, the *Boston Consulting Group/Bucerius Law School* outlined the outsourcing of legal services in particular by corporate legal departments to big law firms, on the one hand, and to new, alternative legal service providers, on the other. While complex, high-risk legal work that cannot be performed efficiently within a company is outsourced to large law firms, the low-risk and large-scale work, which cannot be performed as efficiently within the company itself, is outsourced to alternative legal service providers that utlize technology tools.[69] This outsourcing to alternative legal services providers is intended to provide legal practitioners with cost savings according to the recommendations of the *Boston Consulting Group* (2018) and, at the same time, provide the opportunity to offer their own clients lower prices and better service.[70]

The 2016 study by the *Boston Consulting Group* in collaboration with *Bucerius Law School* on how technology will change the legal profession, proposes a legal technology framework that can be divided into three broad categories or levels:[71] The first level of *enabler technology* is the cornerstone and unites the infrastructure of the platform *(security, cloud* and *connectivity)*. The second level comprises supporting process solutions, with the Case Management module at the top, followed by the Document and Knowledge Management, Human Resources, Business Development and CRM, as well as Accounting and Finance modules. Finally, the top level covers solutions for the treatment of substantive law (litigation and transactions/contracts), which includes the collection and analysis of facts relating to a case and their evaluation.[72]

The use of legal tech started solely with the automation of standard legal tasks, but is currently developing in the direction of the automation of special-

67 BCG & Bucerius Law School, *supra* note 65, at 7.

68 BCG/Bucerius Law School 2018, *supra* note 66, at 14.

69 BCG/Bucerius Law School 2018, *supra* note 66, at 21.

70 *Id.*

71 BCG/Bucerius Law School 2016, *supra* note 27, at 4.

72 *Id.*

ised fields of activity right up to tailor-made automation solutions.[73] *Hartung et al.* (2017) cite *Clearspire* as an example of the successful use of legal tech, which overcomes the traditional pyramid structure of law firms and creates a de facto office for lawyers via the proprietary *Coral* technology platform.[74] Although *Clearspire* failed to achieve the predicted financial success and went out of business in 2014 after four years in operation, it had implemented a groundbreaking model of service company replicated by others in the marketplace.[75] As the first legal services provider, *Clearspire* had combined legal, technological and process expertise, stripping out typical cost-escalators like expensive offices, real estate and a personnel surplus.[76] At the same time, *Coral* enables worldwide, location-independent collaboration between lawyer and client as well as real-time communication while eliminating both unnecessary staff and expensive business premises.[77]

At the same time, outsourcing is not limited by nature to legal aid activities or temporary activities *(legal temp services).* Alternative, non-lawyer legal service providers are commissioned for comprehensive legal services either by law firms or directly by (large) companies. In addition, «*onshore outsource attorneys*» are primarily used in the USA for their specialised expertise, without the need to call on a workforce abroad.

In practice, several innovative models of alternative legal services for corporate clients have established themselves that pursue different approaches in the provision of services. For example, *Clearspire* used multi-disciplinary teams led by lawyers and its remuneration system is not based on a partnership hierarchy. Compensation is generally made up of a salary and an incentive component, which is based on customer satisfaction and used to reward excellent performance.[78] Other providers consist exclusively of lawyers, some with decades of experience, who have previously worked in large American law firms and offer advice on complex legal issues in virtual law firms for demanding clients. The remuneration is fixed by each individual partner, but not by the company, and is determined either by hourly rates or by flat rates. The client expressly purchases the legal assessment and expertise of an *experienced* lawyer without having to purchase the administrative apparatus and representative insignia of the large law firms. In return, the location-independent, decentralised working method provides lawyers with greater job satisfaction and a free hand in scheduling appointments.[79]

---

73 BCG/Bucerius Law School 2016, *supra* note 27, at 6.

74 Hartung et al., *supra* note 65, at 130 et seq.; Dzienkowski, *supra* note 54, at 3002.

75 Mark A Cohen, *in* Hartung et al., *supra* note 65, at 130 et seq.

76 *Id.*

77 Hartung et al., *supra* note 54, at 130 et seq.

78 Dzienkowski, *supra* note 54, at 3005.

79 Dzienkowski, *supra* note 54, at 3007.

A third large provider of alternative legal services (*Axiom Law*) was founded in the USA explicitly as a non-legal service and sees itself more as a comprehensive management consultancy and provider of complete solutions for clients, offering insourcing and outsourcing options.[80] With this model, lawyers and other consultants are employed directly by the company for a project or an agreed period of time on the basis of a secondment contract, or they work from another location for the client using an intranet set up by the provider. The outsourced services include complex legal procedures, such as commercial contracts, derivatives and compliance matters. A workflow is created in advance for each task, involving systems engineers, IT professionals and project managers, and often involving the clients to best serve their interests.[81]

A fourth model (*VistaLaw*) operates through a network of lawyers in various locations worldwide. The lawyers are available on a fee basis for specific projects. Their competitive advantage lies primarily in an innovative billing system, with low operating costs and the fact that no inexperienced junior partners are hired. Another provider provides lawyers for short-term projects who are often used as a substitute for the unplanned loss of the client's own internal legal counsel.[82]

A central aspect of all these models is the prior assessment of the proposed cases and their unbundling: legal and non-legal tasks are systematically separated so that non-legal items can be outsourced and processed by an alternative provider at considerably lower cost in order to avoid the high hourly rates according to the lawyer's tariffs. If staff are sent directly to the client's business location to perform work locally, the client's infrastructure and resources are used, which contributes to additional cost efficiency. Most alternative providers work with fixed prices or a price cap system.[83]

B. Risks associated with the use of alternative legal service providers and the employment of gig lawyers from a legal point of view

In the USA, especially, the practice of *legal outsourcing* is already well established in order to increase efficiency and profitability.[84] Among other things, legal research and activities are outsourced that are time-consuming, recurring

---

80 *See* Dzienkowski *supra* note 54, at 3008.

81 *See* Dzienkowski *supra* note 54, at 3010.

82 *See* Dzienkowski *supra* note 54, at 3014.

83 *See* Dzienkowski *supra* note 54, at 3022.

84 *See* William L Jr Pfeifer, Privacy and Legal Outsourcing, 29 (6) American Bar Association, GP Solo, Privacy and Confidentiality 30–33 (2012) at 30 et seq.; Greenberg & McGovern *supra* note 52, at 33–35; Steiger *supra* note 48, at 39; Bruck & Canter *supra* note 51, at 2094.

or serve to prepare proceedings or procedural steps.[85] It is already common practice in the USA for insolvency and asylum lawyers, for example, to engage *paralegals* living in India to prepare various forms.[86] Among others, civil lawyers outsource the review of documents, law firms specialising in damages outsource the collection and review of data as well as the classification of claims or the dispatch of client documents in class actions, and contract lawyers outsource the drafting of contracts and due diligence activities.[87] In the USA, outsourcing can and may be legally carried out by both legal and non-legal personnel, as long as certain data protection regulations are complied with to guarantee data security when exchanging data and the client has ensured that, taking into account the nature of the legal transaction, the contractor complies with the data protection regulations and is trustworthy.[88]

More generally, according to *Dzienkowski,* possible concerns regarding the use of alternative legal service providers that may raise issues in terms of confidentiality, ethics or quality arise in four areas, in particular:

1. the unbundling of client representation or client advice;
2. the training and supervision of lawyers;
3. the training and supervision of non-lawyers; and,
4. dealing with client data and documents.[89]

Responsibility for the unbundling of agendas usually remains with the client, i.e., the corporate entity or the internal lawyers, but here, too, informed consent is required from the client that, for example, documents containing confidential data may be transmitted via the internet. Some vendors have established their own privacy policies for *managed (legal) services*.[90]

A further important aspect is the risk of *conflicts of interest*[91] due to the numerous consulting opportunities, the rapid expansion of business areas and the diversification of the client base. Conflicts of interest in law firms are usually eliminated by a system of checks and balances or, as is widespread in

---

85 Steiger, *supra* note 48, at 41 et seq.

86 *See* Pfeifer, note 84, at 30 et seq.; Steiger, *supra* note 48, at 41 et seq.

87 *See* Pfeifer, *supra* note 84, at 31. The outsourcing of legal activities outside the USA is understandable when one considers, for example, that foreign providers are often under the professional supervision of law firms domiciled in the USA or that employees abroad are subject to a more or less strict background check before being commissioned. The Indian legal service provider, SDD Global Solutions, for example, is subject to an international law firm based in the USA; *see* Pfeifer, *supra* note 84, at 33.

88 In accordance with Resolution 105C of the ABA adopted in August 2012 and amended ABA Model Rules 1.1, 5.3 and 5.5, see Pfeifer, *supra* note 84, at 32 et seq.

89 Dzienkowski, *supra* note 54, at 3024.

90 Dzienkowski, *supra* note 54, at 3030.

91 Dzienkowski, *supra* note 54, at 3031.

Europe, by the supervision of the bar associations and their trust system.[92] Questions also arise as to whether providers that explicitly operate as non-legal service providers are subject to strict professional ethics and rules of conduct, as is the case with lawyers. The information, including trade secrets, obtained by external service providers in the course of their work (in particular, at the client's business location) is likely to be substantial. In addition, in light of the cross-border provision of the services, it is doubtful that each service provider on a project has the authorisation and licences required by law for the provision of the legal or business consulting services.[93] Finally, the independence required of the lawyers or legal advisors employed could conflict with the profit motive of the non-legal advisors involved.[94]

VI. Concluding Remarks

The market for legal services is in a state of upheaval. An overcapacity of lawyers, a lack of flexible resources, and outdated procedures suggest that staffing models are outdated. The gig economy has produced new lawyers who, through the use of legal tech, have found a broad spectrum of activity away from the traditional advisory and remuneration models. Not only the working processes and methods, but also the fields of activity of lawyers will change radically in the next few years and new job profiles will emerge.[95] The traditional legal market today is in competition across a wide range of services with alternative, non-lawyer service providers and *managed legal service providers*, which operate globally and provide more cost-effective and efficient solutions as a complete package for corporate clients.

Through the use of new technologies and management consulting services, on the one hand, and drawing on legal expertise, on the other hand, alternative service providers split consulting services into routine *(commodity)* tasks and those tasks that require sound legal advice based on real-life experience.[96] In global terms, large law firms will need to invest more in new technologies in the future, increase their outsourcing of certain tasks, expand their product portfolios and focus on specific areas of activity. For smaller law firms, their specialisation and the use of legal tech and fixed-price offers will be key.[97] From a HR perspective, the efficient allocation of resources, the establishment of strategic partnerships and the outsourcing of routine legal work

92 Dzienkowski, *supra* note 53, at 3012, 3024, 3027; Greenberg & McGovern, *supra* note 52, at 35.

93 Dzienkowski, *supra* note 53, at 3034 et seq.

94 Dzienkowski, *supra* note 53, at 3032.

95 *See* Hartung et al., *supra* note 65, at 237 et seq.

96 Dzienkowski, *supra* note 54, at 3037.

97 BCG & Bucerius Law School 2016, *supra* note 27, at 6.

and non-legal work to alternative providers will be crucial to achieving the necessary efficiency and performance levels.

VII. Bibliography

A. Hard Copy Sources

Boswell, Wendy R, Baskerville Watkins, Marla et al., *Second-class citizen? Contract workers' perceived status, dual commitment and intent to quit, in* 80 Journal of Vocational Behavior 454–463 (2012).

Bruck, Andrew & Canter, Andrew, *Supply, Demand, and the Changing Economics of Large Law Firms*, 60 (6) Stanford Law Review 2087–2130 (April 2008).

Calo, Ryan & Rosenblat, Alex, *The Taking Economy: Uber, Information, and Power*, 117 (6) Columbia Law Review 1623–1690 (October 2017).

Durkin, Barbara, *Whole New World: Gigonomics, Human Resource Development and the Brave New Lawyer*, 83 (7) New York State Bar Association Journal 34–40 (September 2011).

Dzienkowski, John S, *The Future of Big Law: Alternative Legal Service Providers to Corporate Clients,* 82 (6) Fordham Law Review 2995–3040 (2014).

Greenberg, Michael D & McGovern, Geoffrey (2012), An Early Assessment of the Civil Justice System After the Financial Crisis. Something Wicked This Way Comes? (RAND Corporation, 2012).

Hartung, Markus, Bues, Micha-Manuel & Halbleib, Gernot (2017) Legal Tech – Die Digitalisierung des Rechtsmarkts (C. H. Beck, 2017).

Karim, Ahmad, *The Increasing Usage of Professional Contingent Workers: A Review*, 10 (1) The Journal of Global Business Management 33–37 (2014).

Kenney, Martin & Zysman, John, *The Rise of the Platform Economy*, 32 (2) Issues in Science and Technology University of Texas at Dallas 61–69 (2016).

McKee, Derek, Makela, Finn, & Scassa, Teresa, The Law and the «Sharing Economy». Regulating Online Market Platforms (University of Ottawa Press, 2018).

Nanda, Ashish, Wilkins, David & Rohrer, Lisa, *Axiom (a): Getting Down to Business*, Harvard Law School 09-20, 1–17 (2012).

Pfeifer, William L Jr, *Privacy and Legal Outsourcing*, 29 (6) American Bar Association, GPSolo, Privacy and Confidentiality, 30–33 (2012).

Skapinker, Michael, *Breaking the Law,* Financial Times (Apr. 11, 2016) at 73.

Snider, Laureen, *Enabling Exploitation: Law in the Gig Economy*, 26 (4) Critical Criminology 563–577 (2018).

Soyars Hicks, Maureen, *Flexible jobs give workers choices*, May 2017 Monthly Labor Review 1–2 (2017).

Steiger, David A, *The Rise of Global Legal Sourcing: How Vendors and Clients Are Changing Legal Business Models*, 19 (2) Business Law Today 38–43 (November/December 2009).

Strong, Stacie I, Class, Mass, and Collective Arbitration in National and International Law (Oxford University Press, 2013).

Susskind, Richard E, Tomorrow's Lawyers: An Introduction to Your Future, (2 Oxford University Press, 2017).

SUSSKIND, RICHARD E & SUSSKIND, DANIEL, THE FUTURE OF THE PROFESSIONS. HOW TECHNOLOGY WILL TRANSFORM THE WORK OF HUMAN EXPERTS (Oxford University Press, 2015).

Tucker, Eric, *Uber and the Unmaking and Remaking of Taxi Capitalisms: Technology, Law and Resistance in the Historical Perspective, in* LAW AND THE «SHARING ECONOMY» (McKee, Derek, Makela, Finn & Scassa, Teresa, eds., University of Ottawa Press, 2018).

Wissmann, Hellmut, *Zur Entwicklung des Arbeitsrechts in Deutschland und Europa*, 62 (2) AuR 46–51 (2014).

Wright, Chris F, Wailes, Nick, Bamber, Greg J, & Lansbury, Russell D, *Beyond National Systems, Towards a «Gig Economy»? A Research Agenda for International and Comparative Employment Relations*, 29 EMPLOYEE RESPONSIBILITIES AND RIGHTS JOURNAL 247–257 (2017).

Zahorsky, Rachel M & Henderson, William D, *Who's eating Law Firm's Lunch? The legal service providers, law schools and new grads at the table*, 99 (10) ABA JOURNAL 32–38, 40 (October 2013).

B. Online Sources

Acritas, *Global Alternative Legal Brand Index 2018*, https://www.acritas.com/global-alternative-legal-brand-index-2018 (last visited Feb. 3, 2019).

BCG & Bucerius Law School, eds., *How Legal Technology Will Change the Business of Law*, http://www.bucerius-education.de/fileadmin/content/pdf/studies_publications/Legal_Tech_Report_2016.pdf 1–20 (Jan. 2016) (last visited Nov. 23, 2018).

BCG & Bucerius Law School, eds., *Legal Operations: Getting More from In-House Legal Departments and Their Outside Counsel*, http://www.bucerius-education.de/fileadmin/content/pdf/studies_publications/Buc_BCG_Legal_Operations_Studie_2019.pdf 1–28 (Nov. 2018) (last visited Nov. 24, 2018).

Ernst & Young, *Is the gig economy a fleeting fad, or an enduring legacy*, https://gigeconomy.ey.com/Documents/Gig%20Economy%20Report.pdf (2016) (last visited Dec. 11, 2018).

Eversheds Sutherland, 21st Century law firm—Inheriting a new world, https://www.eversheds-sutherland.com/global/en/what/publications/21stclawyers/index.page (2012) (last visited Nov. 24, 2018).

Fisher, Daniel, *Legal-Services Firm's $73 Million Deal Strips The Mystery From Derivatives Trading*, FORBES (Feb. 12, 2015), https://www.forbes.com/sites/danielfisher/2015/02/12/legal-services-firms-73-million-deal-strips-the-mystery-from-derivatives-trading/ (last visited Nov. 16, 2018).

Gratwohl, Natalie, *Freelancer sind die Angestellten der Zukunft*, in: NZZ (Nov. 9, 2018), https://www.nzz.ch/meinung/freelancer-sind-die-angestellten-der-zukunft-ld.1435216 (last visited Nov. 24, 2018).

Harris, Seth D & Krueger, Alan B, *Is Your Uber Driver an Employee or an Independent Contractor?* 80 PERSPECTIVES ON WORK 30–33 http://www.lerachapters.org/OJS/ojs-2.4.4-1/index.php/LER-AMR/article/download/3098/3073 (2016) (last visited Nov. 15, 2018).

Jones, Kristopher, *Three Gig Economy Trends To Watch For In 2017*, FORBES (Dec. 29, 2016), https://www.forbes.com/sites/forbesagencycouncil/2016/12/29/three-gig-economy-trends-to-watch-for-in-2017/ (last visited Nov. 24, 2018).

PwC, *Workforce of the future—The competing forces shaping 2030*, https://www.pwc.com/gx/en/services/people-organisation/publications/workforce-of-the-future.html (2018) (last visited Nov. 23, 2018).

Sargeant, Malcolm, *The Gig Economy and the Future of Work*, 6 (2) E-Journal of International and Comparative Labour Studies, 1–12 http://eprints.mdx.ac.uk/22247/1/422-1007-1-PB.pdf (2017) (last visited Nov. 16, 2018).

US Department of Labor/Bureau of Labor Statistics, *Economic News Release—Contingent and Alternative Employment Arrangements Summary* (Jun. 7, 2018), https://www.bls.gov/news.release/conemp.nr0.htm (last visited Nov. 24, 2018).

Dr Eva Maria Baumgartner

Virtual Lawyering– Lawyers In The Cloud

A Survival Kit for Lawyers in the Cloud Computing Universe

TABLE OF CONTENTS

I. Introduction: What is «virtual» or «digital» lawyering?

Articles, blog posts and legal press comments defining what a «*digital*» or «*virtual lawyer*» is, have sprung up online. What we seem to know so far is that the *digital* or *virtual lawyer* touches all layers of lawyers' work. *Richard Susskind*, with his more-for-less challenge has shown the path.[1] Others[2] have evolved it and helped to increase our understanding of the impact technology has (and will have) on the (i) business model of legal work;[3] (ii) organization of legal work processes;[4] (iii) value chain within the legal market and the allocation of revenue within the market players;[5] and, finally the (iv) way lawyers communicate with their clients.[6]

The way (digital) lawyers are *different* has accurately been described in an important work on legal education for digital lawyers which was published some time ago by pioneer, tech optimist and university professor *Oliver Goodenough* and *Marc Lauritsen.*[7] There, *Brian Donelly*[8] from Columbia University states that digital lawyers focus on the *gathering, managing and presenting* (legal) information (and law can be seen as informational order[9]) *as much* as on *the legal issues* relevant to the dispute itself.

Thus, lawyers working in the cyberspace and changing their work processes *thereby* can impact law and jurisdiction, so that actually the way of performing legal work, availability and technical skill changes the *result* of lawmaking itself, case law, and established law practice. This seems to happen because a change in gathering information *strongly impacts* the relevance of sources (which are the basis of legal decision makers)[10].

Talking education, digital lawyer educators seek to teach not only classical lawyer skills, but also the mechanics of internet search engines, fact finding and techniques to understand and filter relevant information via technology.

The use of a cloud in legal work is part of digital lawyering. Not only for lawyers the cloud is a place of organizing processes, gathering, saving, producing, and sharing of information. It impacts accessibility of information for

---

1 Richard Susskind, Tomorrow`s Lawyers (Oxford University Press, 2013) at 4.

2 Markus Hartung et al. eds., Legal Tech Die Digitalisierung des Rechtsmarkts (2018) at § 87.

3 Susskind, *supra* note 1, at 3.

4 Hartung et al., *supra* note 2, at § 87.

5 Hartung et al., *supra* note 2, at § 92.

6 Hartung et al., *supra* note 2, at § 97.

7 Oliver Goodenough & Marc Lauritsen, Educating the Digital Lawyer (Lexis Nexis, 2012) at § 1.03.

8 *Id.*

9 Goodenough & Lauritsen, *supra* with reference to Frederick Schauer & Virginia J Wise, *Legal Positivism and Legal Information,* 82 Cornel Law Review 1080 (1996).

10 Goodenough & Lauritsen, *supra* note 7.

lawyers, team members, and clients and can change communication channels with clients directly. This in turn can lead to different liability scenarios for lawyers too, as documentation and legal work can become more transparent. Ultimately, it can also be of relevance when it comes to strategic decision making. Depending on electronic resources provided by the state in which lawyers are practicing and if communication with courts happens via electronic legal data exchange (or e-justice)[11], accessibility, momentum, and the way in which information is presented and transmitted to court can actually impact the result of a proceeding. As an example, note the Austrian pilot of an electronical file being maintained by court and used by all parties on touch screens to the effect that court hearings are paperless and relevant words or phrases can be found in real time during the court hearing by using the search tools available in the pilot program[12].

Cloud computing is one of the upcoming mega trends[13] for all industries; specifically in the legal industry more and more lawyers and legal service providers (in the following «LSPs») are using the cloud.[14] The most relevant driver of it all is price.[15] LSPs view the cloud as a way to use legal technology tools without a significant upfront investment in hardware, software and especially, support services.[16] Many cloud services are offered by cloud service providers («CSPs») in the form of subscription models[17], where support service is included.[18] The cost of the cloud is 1/10th of the cost of individual, local, on-premise IT-solutions, which is why cloud usage grew more than 40 % from 2016 to 2017 (from 37% to just over 52%).[19]

---

11 Only 8 of 22 countries handle 50% or more communication between courts and lawyers electronically so far; see the 2018 EU Justice Scoreboard, Figure 30, https://ec.europa.eu/info/sites/info/files/justice_scoreboard_2018_en.pdf (last visited Dec. 16, 2018).

12 Maria Sterkl, *Der langsame Abschied vom Gerichtsakt auf Papier*, DER STANDARD (Nov. 19, 2018), https://derstandard.at/2000090757655/Der-langsame-Abschied-vom-Gerichtsakt-auf-Papier (last visited Apr. 25, 2019).

13 The biggest three cloud service providers *AWS*, *Microsoft* and *Google* will account for revenues of cloud computing amounting to 411 bn worldwide in 2020; *see* Cisco Global Cloud Index, 2016–2021 (Nov. 19, 2018), https://www.cisco.com/c/en/us/solutions/collateral/service-provider/global-cloud-index-gci/white-paper-c11-738085.html (last visited Dec. 16, 2018).

14 Dennis Kennedy, *2017 Cloud Computing*, ABA Techreport 2017 (Dec. 01, 2017), https://www.americanbar.org/groups/law_practice/publications/techreport/2017/cloud_computing/ (last visited Dec. 17, 2018).

15 Kennedy, *supra* note 14.

16 *Id.*

17 Examples of legal cloud service providers offering subscription models are *Clio*, *Rocket Matter*, *NetDocuments*, *PracticePanther*, *Bill4Time*, and *MyCase*.

18 Kennedy, *supra* note 15. Also note examples of legal cloud service providers such as Clio, Rocket Matter, NetDocuments, PracticePanther, Bill4Time, MyCase and others.

19 Kennedy, *supra* note 14.

Small and mid-size firms are leading[20] when it comes to cloud usage, as individual on-site solutions are not scalable when it comes to cost.[21] In the US approximately 56% of solos and small firms (made up of 2–9 lawyers) use the cloud (up from the mid-forty percentile in 2016).[22] However, also larger firm «Yes» responses ranged from 39–53%, showing substantial increases from 2016.[23]

The following article is designed to help LSPs or other players in the legal industry who are developing new ways to work in the cloud to better understand their obligations, duties, and risks. It shall lead LSPs to understand what questions to ask when considering a cloud service. The article is intended to be a resource and inspiration for the certification of standards and the designing of contracts with CSPs. For this purpose, the article considers specific obligations for LSPs and focuses on cloud security measures and best practices on cyber security, as those cause concern for lawyers who are willing to innovate and want to move to the cloud.

II. Cloud Computing models for LSPs

LSPs need to understand *what type of cloud computing service* they will use. As stated by ABA[24], there can still be some confusion on the standard definitions for cloud computing, where the terms «SaaS» (Software-as-a-Service), «IaaS»(Infrastructure-as-a-Service) and «PaaS» (Platform-as-a-service) are the most common types of cloud services used by LSPs.[25] LSPs might not need to *technically* understand the difference of those models; however LSPs might run into different obligations in function of the cloud service model they employ for legal work[26], research, communication and storage or management of files.

The three most common types of models can be characterized in a nutshell:

---

20 *Id.*

21 *Id.*

22 *Id.*

23 *Id.*

24 *Id.*

25 Extremely helpful overview in the white paper by IT Tech Law Pioneer Richard Kemp: *Cloud Computing and Data Sovereignity*, Richard Kemp (2016), http://www.kempitlaw.com/cloud-computing-and-data-sovereignty/ (last visited Dec. 19, 2018).

26 Note that legal tech software also might include cloud use; e.g., the Austrian software system provided for lawyers communicating with courts provided by MANZ maintains a cloud service where all legal data transmitted by the system is stored in addition to the cloud of the respective law firm.

- LSPs need to engage into more software management competence, when employing a **IaaS**[27] model where CSPs (only) provide physical processing, storage, networking and the hosting environment as well as virtualization; so LSPs don´t need to purchase servers, software or equipment to store. LSPs in these models however are responsible for creating and installing, managing and monitoring software and operating systems, and services for IT operations[28].
- In the **PaaS**[29] model, CSPs' responsibilities grow, so that it handles not only networking, storage, servers, virtualization but also comes to handling middleware and provides also development, deployment and admin tools, operating systems, and middleware. Infrastructure providers can adopt platforms for their customers' needs. LSPs still have to develop, test, and manage apps hosted in the cloud environment.
- In the **SaaS**[30] model, CSPs provides everything from networking, storage and servers, virtualization to middleware, operating services and apps for use. It does also install, manage and support the software app on the cloud infrastructure; where LSPs only interact with the relevant applications or services for the process operations.

These different types of cloud services can be deployed in different ways, such as «private» and «community» clouds (infrastructure, platform and software use only used by private customer or a group of private cloud customer), «public» clouds (where any customers can access the service) or «hybrid» clouds (which are private clouds using public clouds to get on top of peaks.

When engaging into one of the three mentioned cloud service models, LSP shall consider the following:

A. Questions LSPs should ask when moving to the cloud

1. Issues and stakeholders

When looking into the stakeholders[31] of cloud use in the legal field, several are to be addressed: (i) cloud service providers; (ii) cloud users (e.g., legal professionals); (iii) clients of such cloud users; and, (iv) public institutions (the government) or other institutional organizations. All of these stakeholders have

---

27 Example: Open Stack.

28 Sergio Maffioletti, *Cloud middleware* (Apr. 25, 2014), https://www.sif.it/static/SIF/resources/public/files/va2014/Maffioletti_1.pdf (last visited Dec. 19, 2018).

29 Google App Engine, Apache Stratos, or AWS Elastic Beanstalk.

30 Example: Gmail, Facebook, Flickr.

31 Richard Kemp, *Legal Aspects of Cloud Computing: Cloud Security* (2018), http://www.kempitlaw.com/wp-content/uploads/2018/06/Cloud-Security-White-Paper-KITL-v1.0-June-2018.pdf, Table 1 (last visited Dec. 19, 2018)

different interests to manage, which leads to different questions related to cloud use.

Richard Kemp outlines the various areas of cloud computing law, which touch on the following aspects and interests: (i) Cloud/data security refers to the legal, technical, operational and governance controls to make sure cloud data security is provided; (ii) cloud contracting touches the various aspects on how agreements between CSPs and customers look like, (iii) data rights refers to IP in relation to data, (iv) data protection rights; mostly referring to the rights of «data subjects», using GDPR language, and finally (v) data sovereignty, referring to rights of third parties to control and access data (mostly governmental agencies).[32]

Cloud service providers are concerned about their reputation and market position (which entails efficiency needs, pricing, security and customer need satisfaction), as well as compliance with legal requirements that are in a changing landscape. **Cloud users** (specifically lawyers) are concerned about specific professional compliance legislation, disciplinary measures, confidentiality, security, data control (how to get hold of data), usability of the respective cloud product, and, of course, pricing. Also, a significant reputational risk comes with it, as potential leaks and security issues may be vital for reputation in the legal field too. **Clients of such cloud users** (i.e., clients of attorneys) are concerned about confidentiality and accessibility to data, as many law firms exercise administrational tasks when it comes to managing contracts and securing delicate information). Finally, **government agencies** are mainly concerned about data sovereignty issues, meaning the ability to access data by enforcing orders provided by courts or other authorities. The issue of data sovereignty entails issues also bigger than that; as due to the *Snowden* revelations[33] the question is, if data access is granted to other states by the mere existence of technical facilities and networks, too.

In terms of risk management, it seems obvious that there is a significant remainder of risk about securing of sensitive data in the cloud; on the other hand the incredible opportunities and benefits granted by the cloud, such as flexibility, cost savings, access to new services, new client relationships and, ultimately innovation and changes in organization and communication within

---

32 *Id.*

33 Note the analysis in the whitepaper: Richard Kemp, *Cloud Computing and Data Sovereignity* (2016), http://www.kempitlaw.com/cloud-computing-and-data-sovereignty/ (last visited Dec. 19, 2018), pursuant to which, as an example by TEMPORA, a program to be said to intercept all data transmitted over underwater fibre optic cables landing in the UK; apparently between 10 % and 25 % of the global telecoms and internet traffic is estimated to transit the country via these cables. Comparable programs include PRISM, a surveillance program operated by the NSA, to which 9 IT giants are providing data: AOL, Apple, Facebook, Google, Microsoft, Paltalk, Skype Yahoo and Youtube. Another example of governmental surveillance programs include UPSTREAM, which is said to collect data from communication service providers.

law firms and between firms and clients urges LSPs to at least balance such risk.

The following frameworks shall help lawyers to get orientation and maneuver when moving their practice to the cloud.

2. Determine LSP obligations and duties on cloud security

A way to manage the risk of leaks or losing data sovereignty when storing sensitive data in the cloud is to classify it, and—where it comes to uncontrollable factual circumstances (think about TEMPORA footnote 30)—to control risk contractually and operationally (if possible). For these purposes, *Richard Kemp*[34] provided a very useful tool (leaning into UK law) which helps to classify questions and issues especially in view of cloud security which can be used as outline for enterprises, and of course, also law firms. It helps to collect and establish a catalogue of duties based on the respective operating jurisdiction, and, in a second step establish a best practices to-do to implement such duties. In the following this model is put in context to the legal profession, also citing examples from other European countries (such as Austria, Germany, France) when it comes to regulation examples. For firms or companies operating in several jurisdictions the task has to be adopted to the respective jurisdiction.

a) Regulatory Duties of LSPs

Potential regulatory duties of LSPs, and non-sector specific regulatory duties are outlined, as all of them might apply to LSPs or companies working in the legal industry.

aa) LSP-Sector specific

Lawyers must research regulatory laws setting duties on risk management, outsourcing and confidentiality based on the respective countries' laws on the *profession of lawyers* (e.g., the German BRAO,[35] regulating duties and obligations of lawyers in Germany including security measures, data storage and confidentiality obligations; the Austrian RAO[36], including the respective implementation regulations and whitepapers of the bar associations on the execution, such as the Austrian handbook on IT Security issued by the Austrian Chamber of Lawyers pursuant to which it is imperative that the cloud data is

---

34 Richard Kemp, *supra* note 33, at Table 1 (last visited Dec. 19, 2018).

35 Bundesrechtsanwaltsordnung, https://www.gesetze-im-internet.de/brao/ (last visited Dec. 19, 2018).

36 Rechtsanwaltsordnung, https://www.ris.bka.gv.at/GeltendeFassung.wxe?Abfrage=Bundesnormen&Gesetzesnummer=10001673 (last visited Dec. 19, 2018).

stored within Austrian territory;[37] the UK's SRA Code of Conduct, relating inter alia to outsourcing which applies to cloud computing;[38] for notaries things may be different; note specific regulations on risk management, outsourcing and confidentiality based on e.g., the Austrian Law on Notaries[39] or the French rules on the exercise of notarial services[40]). In many countries, such laws do not (yet) provide reliable resource for lawyers to make sure cloud use is actually compatible with the disciplinary frameworks, as legislators remained silent so far. In such cases, it is advisable to turn to regulatory laws or guidelines by international legal/disciplinary organizations or associations, such as e.g., the CCBE guidelines[41] on the use of cloud computing services by lawyers, which can be a useful tool when arguing with the respective bar association on the use of cloud computing. Also, recommendations for the financial sector, such as e.g., the regulations on outsourcing to cloud service providers by the European Banking Authority[42] can be a helpful tool as well. Most relevant for LSPs in this regard might be provisions focusing on data residency/domiciliation related requirements.

Note that some countries provide particular regulatory laws or duties on general risk management, outsourcing and confidentiality for *legal service providers* who are *not* lawyers (e.g., in Germany such legal service providers are separately recognized and regulated by law; the RDG[43], providing for specific laws on data security, Sec. 5).

Additional topics which might be addressed by regulatory laws are: system availability obligations, lock- in of data and exit/deletion obligations, including term, termination duties (rights), and return obligations of data after termination as well as data destruction and deletion (now also covered by

---

37 The Austrian Chamber of Attorneys (Österreichischer Rechtsanwaltskammertag), *Handbuch IT-Sicherheit in Rechtsanwaltskanzleien*, http://www.archivium.at/index.php/news/90-handbuch-it-sicherheit (last visited Dec. 19, 2018).

38 Solicitors Regulation Authority, *Code of Conduct 2011* (Dec. 6, 2018), https://www.sra.org.uk/solicitors/handbook/code/content.page (last visited Dec. 19, 2018).

39 Notariatsordnung, https://www.ris.bka.gv.at/GeltendeFassung.wxe?Abfrage=Bundesnormen&Gesetzesnummer=10001677 (last visited Dec. 19, 2018).

40 Conseil Supérieur du Notariat, Reglement National et Reglement Inter-Cours (Jul. 22, 2017), https://www.notaires.fr/sites/default/files/reglement_national_-_reglement_intercours_-_arrete_du_22_07_2014_-_jo_du_01_08_2014.pdf (last visited Dec. 19, 2018).

41 Council of Bars and Law Societies of Europe, *CCBE Guidelines on the use of cloud computing services by lawyers* (Sept. 7, 2012), https://www.ccbe.eu/NTCdocument/07092012_EN_CCBE_gui1_1347539443.pdf (last visited Dec. 19, 2018).

42 European Banking Authority, *Recommendations on outsourcing to cloud service providers* (Mar. 28, 2018), https://www.eba.europa.eu/documents/10180/2170125/Recommendations+on+Cloud+Outsourcing+%28EBA-Rec-2017-03%29_EN.pdf/e02bef01-3e00-4d81-b549-4981a8fb2f1e (last visited Dec. 19, 2018).

43 Gesetz über außergerichtliche Rechtsdienstleistungen, https://www.gesetze-im-internet.de/rdg/ (last visited Dec. 19, 2018).

GDPR on a more general level; see below Sec C.b). Note that regulatory laws may impede LSPs to enter into agreements that enable the CSP to change service features unilaterally; they might explicitly contain provisions on access rights and location of servers and data. Regulatory laws usually provide for insurance duties of LSPs; note that it might be crucial to consult LSPs' insurance company before engaging into cloud computing to make sure professional insurance remains valid also in cases where cloud specific risks might materialize.

Finally, regulatory laws might also contain provisions on applicable law and jurisdictions lawyers have to consider when entering into outsourcing agreements; note the mandatory applicability of GDPR also for companies (lawfirms) which are located outside the EU (see below Sec C.g).

ab) Laws applicable to all sectors

GDPR is a main source of concern for all companies operating in the EU, offering services in the EU, or processing data in the EU (e.g., Articles 5, 24, and 28 GDPR); in Sec C we set out GDPR specific scenarios and duties for further consideration. Note that for any enterprise, local laws on data protection are relevant too: most countries have enacted local legislation on data protection stipulating obligations and duties which may go beyond GDPR duties or specify such; e.g., the German BDSG[44] or the Austrian DSG.[45] Regulatory laws which might apply to lawyers/LSPs, but also other companies working in the legal field are local laws on IT-security such as the German IT-Security Act[46] (IT-Sicherheitsgesetz), enacted in 2015 which provides a national IT security standard for IT infrastructures which are of critical importance to the public; such sectors (at the time this article is written) include energy, IT, communications, transport, finance and insurance. The scope of such national IT security legislation may well be extended to legal service providers or lawyers in near future.

Local laws on telecommunication might be specifically applicable to CSPs: as an example, the UK Communications Act[47], the Austrian TKG including regulations[48] or network legislations can be cited; such legislations build the regulatory framework CSPs have to abide to. In most cases such laws

---

44 Bundesdatenschutzgesetz, http://www.gesetze-im-internet.de/bdsg_2018/ (last visited Dec. 19, 2018).

45 Datenschutzgesetz, https://www.ris.bka.gv.at/GeltendeFassung.wxe?Abfrage=bundesnormen&Gesetzesnummer=10001597 (last visited Dec. 19, 2018).

46 Federal Office for Information Security, *Das IT-Sicherheitsgesetz*, https://www.bsi.bund.de/DE/Themen/Industrie_KRITIS/KRITIS/IT-SiG/it_sig_node.html (last visited Dec. 19, 2018).

47 Communications Act 2003, https://www.legislation.gov.uk/ukpga/2003/21/contents (last visited Dec. 19, 2018).

48 Telekommunikationsgesetz 2003, https://www.ris.bka.gv.at/GeltendeFassung.wxe?Abfrage=Bundesnormen&Gesetzesnummer=20002849, Datensicherheitsverordnung, https://www.ris.bka.gv.at/

might not be applicable to LSPs directly, however compliance should be taken into account when it comes to choosing the right CSP.

For purposes of data sovereignty and investigatory powers (specifically in penal procedural laws or laws regulating the rights of security police / investigating authorities), local laws might provide for a professional privilege for LSPs which limits investigatory powers. However, note that such privilege might be circumvented by investigation authorities if CSPs maintain international structures (in terms of data storage and accessibility), so that the professional privilege is not recognized. LSPs should thus be aware of the CSPs architecture and regulatory frameworks CSPs are subject to. As an example, the case *Microsoft Corp. v. United States*, during which it was questionable if US investigation authorities required a search warrant for data stored outside the country (in the case at hand: Ireland). Lately, the case was put on moot, as new US legislation (the CLOUD Act[49]) was passed, which finally enabled investigatory authorities basically to access data held by US communication providers. This shows, that the structure chosen should be enabling the LSP to actually provide the privilege to his client as granted by (national) law. Other laws, applicable due to CSPs structure, might interfere with such specific professional privilege.

Finally, national criminal law provisions on illegal sharing, saving or forwarding of personal data should equally be reviewed by LSPs but also other companies working in the legal industry.

b) Non-Contractual Civil Law Duties of LSPs

Statutory duties might result in claims towards LSPs/CSPs by data subjects, e.g., in cases of a data leak or hacking; damage restitution might be based on the violation of professional obligations such as organizational and technical measures which must be met, or GDPR legislation, which might apply specifically to third-party data. Data leaks and possibly also copyright or IP law infringements, may lead to damage claims which should ideally be taken care of by adequate insurance contracts. Also potential fiduciary duties, if any, might result in damage claims.

c) Contractual Duties of LSPs

Note that LSPs might be exposed to contractual duties already in place when cloud computing is introduced; such obligations might need to be translated into the LSP-CSP agreement or the scope of data introduced into the cloud solution.

GeltendeFassung.wxe?Abfrage=Bundesnormen&Gesetzesnummer=20007596 (last visited Dec. 19, 2018).

49 The Claryfing Lawful Overseas Use of Data Act, H.R.4943, 115th Cong., https://www.congress.gov/bill/115th-congress/house-bill/4943).

aa) LSP – Client

LSPs need to understand their client's policies and needs on data security, physical/logical security, data retention, disaster recovery/business continuity, business conduct, audit, and potential needs based on the legal mandate in general. Also note potential requirements in connection with prosecution and securing of proof clients may have. Clients might further be subject to «appropriate technical and organizational measures»-clauses (which consequently LSPs' need to be able to be respond to), and data sovereignty/residency-domiciliation requirements (also when it comes to format and lock-in/ delivery of data), in particular but not limited to international proceedings and possible data seizure scenarios across countries. Finally, LSPs need to understand their client's status and duties under GDPR (note cases where LSPs need to do automated work on data in mass-cases or e-discovery) as well as their role towards the client under GDPR (determination of status of controller and processor) and reflect such requirements clients are subjected to in negotiating the contract with CSP.

ab) LSP – Supplier

LSPs might have specific suppliers of services with particular requirements, which need to be considered when moving all data to the cloud.

d) Internal duties of LSPs

LSPs might have specific requirements set out in handbooks, employee privacy policies, GDPR implementation policies et al. Note that this also might encompass encryption requirements which need to be clarified when working with a CSP; especially what type of encryption is in place, and who manages the encryption keys.

3. Relationship between LSP and CSP

Based on the abovementioned duties and obligations of the LSP and its clients, and suppliers, the relationship and scope of the service provided by the respective CSP must be determined. The following should help to design a contractual relationship with CSPs appropriate for LSPs needs and provide help to determine criteria when choosing the CSP.

a) Useful certifications and standards for CSPs

Most lawyers or legal service providers don´t have the knowledge to self-assess the quality of cloud services provided to them, especially when it comes to security measures. A good and helpful way to find out whether a cloud service provider is fit, is to look for certifications that aim to confirm a minimum quality standard. Please note however that certifications do not necessarily reflect the very specific requirements set out above. Also note that the certifications do not all cover the same topics; we tried to outline main topics of the respective certifications below.

The federal office of information security (Bundesamt für Sicherheit in der Informationstechnik) in Germany has issued the very useful «Catalogue of Cloud Computing Compliance», also called «C5»[50] which derives its certification principles from a list of other useful certifications and best practices for cloud computing on the market. If lawyers or legal service providers do not find a C5 certification, useful best practices they should look for when going virtual are:

- ISO/IEC 27001:2013, ISO 27018 Information Security and Protection of personal data, as well ISO 20000-1 (on IT Service Management), ISO/IEC 38500 (on IT Governance), ISO/IEC 38505 (on Data Governance), SSAE 16/18 SOC II.
- CSA3 CCM – Cloud Controls Matrix 3.01 (Cloud Security Alliance, a non-profit organization for the distribution of security standards in the field of cloud computing).
- ICPA4 – Trust Services Principles Criteria 2014 (TSP) by the American Institute of Certified Public Accountants (focus on he technical accuracy of the Trust Services Criteria (TSC), assessing security, availability, processing integrity, confidentiality, privacy).
- IDW6 ERS FAIT 5, are generally accepted accounting principles for the outsourcing of accounting-related services, including cloud computing, version of Nov. 4, 2014 by the Institute of Certified Public Accountants in Germany; note that this is not a certification itself, but a standard, certification of which might be granted by auditors; this also applies to the IDW PS 880 standard, focusing on storage of documents.
- Eurocloud Star Audit[51]
- MoReq stands for «Model Requirements for the Management of Electronic Records» and aims to standardize creation and storage of business documents in digital form.

For implementation/due diligence purposes, questions to be asked to cloud service providers regarding certifications should include whether the certifications has been issued by an approved certifier and is currently/will be in place during the entire contractual relationship. It shall also be clarified, if the certification is accompanied by the full, relevant report and all other necessary

50 Federal Office for Information Security, *Compliance Controls Catalogue*, https://www.bsi.bund.de/EN/Topics/CloudComputing/Compliance_Controls_Catalogue/Compliance_Controls_Catalogue_node.html;jsessionid=49BC275931E2103BBD5A6A2F9D08528E.2_cid369 (last visited Dec. 19, 2018).

51 StarAudit, https://staraudit.org (last visited Dec. 17, 2018).

supporting documentation, if the certification is still in force and if it covers the CSP service that is actually to be contracted for.

In addition, the LSP needs to understand if the certification covers all data centres/locations at which the provided data will be stored and what would be the consequences if the CSP loses any relevant committed certification (in such case: if LSP can terminate for CSP breach of contract in these circumstances). Finally it needs to be stated that certifications don't replace accurate contractual agreements, but crucial issues regarding certifications shall be reflected in the cloud service agreement between LSPs and CSPs. For LSPs, certifications certainly help argue compliance standards set out by disciplinary organizations, bar associations and other quality standards if challenged.

b) Best practices for implementation of cloud security based on NCSC framework

Now, once the LSP has figured out its duties in terms of cloud computing, the challenge is to understand the architecture the CSP uses, and to design the contractual arrangement accordingly. In terms of best practices for this process, Kemp[52] provides a very useful checklist for implementation of cloud security which is based on the NCSC's (the UK National Cyber Security Centre) cloud security principles.[53] It was adapted for lawyers (as NCSC's principles are for the public sector) and resulted in a very useful tool for LSPs to understand what questions to ask their CSP to address the respective NCSC principle. We took the overview and slightly adapted it for purposes of this article, sticking to its structure and topics very tightly:

aa) Data classification

Data classification is deemed to be one of the critical (and first) steps[54] to be taken when moving towards cloud security best practices. In general, it is advisable to classify a company`s data assets to the effect that an organization can «determine and assign specific values to the data they possess».[55] In general, data is structured in states (at rest, in transit, in process) or can be structured or unstructured, and subject to different states of access control. Also, it can be differed between the nature and level of confidentiality. For lawyers, in terms of classification, it can be assumed that data will often be deemed per-

52 Richard Kemp, *supra* note 33.

53 NCSC, *Implementing the cloud security principles* (Sept. 21, 2016), https://www.ncsc.gov.uk/guidance/implementing-cloud-security-principles (last visited Dec. 17, 2018).

54 Richard Kemp, *Legal Aspects of Cloud Computing: Cloud Security* (2018), Table 1,http://www.kempitlaw.com/wp-content/uploads/2018/06/Cloud-Security-White-Paper-KITL-v1.0-June-2018.pdf (last visited Dec. 19, 2018).

55 Microsoft, *Classification for Cloud Readiness,* https://www.microsoft.com/en-us/search/result.aspx?q=data+classification+for+cloud+readiness (last visited Dec. 19, 2018).

sonal and confidential, and, in case of legal work provided, propriety of the law firm.

ab) Cloud security principles checklist with questions to CSP

The below NCSC schedule[56] can be used for the CSP due diligence process and be adapted to respective jurisdictions; the topics addressed should enable LSP to cover the most relevant issues when it comes to assessing the right CSP. Note that the NCSC provides very detailed information on each and every principle including goals, relevant standards and best practices recommendations.

Cloud Security Principle	Checklist Question
1. Data in transit protection	Is the LSP's data transiting network adequately protected against tampering and eavesdropping by the CSP? Note that the NCSC provides guidance on the respective types of network such as private WAN, Legacy SSL and TLS, IPSec or TLS VPN or bonded fibre optic connections.
2. Asset protection and resilience	Is LSP's data and the assets storing or processing it protected against physical tampering, loss, damage or seizure by the CSP? The principle aims to help understand the physical storage situation (note that this can be relevant for data sovereignty issues in case other jurisdictions are applicable to CSP; refer to Sec ab).
3. Separation between consumers	Will a malicious or compromised service user be able to affect the service or data of another user? The goal of this principle is to understand the types of users LSP shares the platform with; also, to build confidence in the separate management of the service of CSP.
4. Governance framework	Does CSP have a security governance framework which coordinates and directs its management of the service and information within it? Are any technical controls deployed outside of this framework?
5. Operational security	Does CSP operate/manage the service securely in order to impede detect or prevent attacks? Good operational security should not require complex, bureaucratic, time consuming or expensive processes; within operational security configuration and change management, vulnerability management, protective monitoring and incident management is covered.
6. Personnel security	Does CSP screen/adequately train its staff? Where CSP personnel have access to LSP data and systems LSP needs a high degree of confidence in CSP trustworthiness. Thorough screening, supported by adequate training, reduces the likelihood of accidental or malicious compromise by CSP personnel.

56 Mostly headline points; note the NCSC's full document at https://www.ncsc.gov.uk/guidance/implementing-cloud-security-principles (last visited Dec. 17, 2018).

7. Secure development	Are your CSPs development services in line with evolving threats and in line with industry good practice regarding secure design, coding, testing and deployment? Is your CSP either implementing a security standard such as e.g., ISO/IEC 27034 or other (corresponding) security standards?
8. Supply chain security	Does CSP ensure that its supply chain satisfactorily supports all of the security principles which the service claims to implement?
9. Secure consumer management	Does CSP make the tools available for secure management of the law firm's use of CSP's service? Management interfaces and procedures are a vital part of the security barrier, preventing unauthorized access and alteration of LSP's resources, applications and data.
10. Identity and authentication	Is all access to service interfaces constrained to authenticated and authorized individuals?
11. External interface protection	Are all external or less trusted interfaces of the service identified and appropriately defended?
12. Secure service administration	Do all administration systems for CSP's service have highly privileged access to that service? Their compromise has significant impact, including the means to bypass security controls and steal or manipulate large volumes of data.
13. Audit information provision to consumers	Does CSP undertake to provide the LSP with the audit records it needs to monitor access to the service and the data held within it? The type of audit information available to the LSP will have a direct impact on its ability to detect and respond to inappropriate or malicious activity within reasonable timescales.
14. Secure use of the service by LSP	Does the LSP have to undertake reasonable, specific (so measurable) responsibilities when using the service in order for the law firm's data to be adequately protected? Note that this depends strongly on the service deployment model (e.g., when deploying IaaS and PaaS, LSP is largely responsible for security of data and workloads, whereas in a SaaS scenario, the burden is on CSP). LSPs should also consider which devices are used to adapt End User Device Security.

To translate the information collected when assessing duties and going through the data protection principles, best practices do combine a combination of factors which help to provide cloud security; such include the combination of contractual commitments, accredited standards certifications, and rights to to carry out independent testing.

B. Cloud computing and GDPR

1. Typical constellations: LSP–CSP

LSPs and lawyers operating in areas where GDPR applies[57] need to determine which status under to GDPR the contracting parties meet; most relevant is the question who is deemed «data controller» and «data processor»[58]. For purposes of this article it is assumed that data processed by LSPs will in all cases qualify as «personal data», in most cases also as «special categories of personal data»[59]. For purposes of personal data relating to criminal convictions[60], it is assumed that processing is allowed to lawyers if they are subject to appropriate diligence laws (which are usually provided by the relevant disciplinary rules or codes of conduct published by bar associations). Note that processing is deemed quite anything one does to or with data; GDPR[61] defines *inter alia* collection, recording, organization, structuring, storage, adaptation or alteration, retrieval, consultation, use, disclosure by transmission of personal data as processing.[62]

CSPs will typically qualify as processors: «a natural or legal person, public authority, agency or other body which processes personal data on behalf of the controller»[63]; wherever CSP has (1) potential access to the personal data provided by the controller and (2) processes such data solely on the instruc-

57 GDPR Regulation (EU) 2016/679 of the European Parliament and of the Council of 27 April 2016 on the protection of natural persons with regard to the processing of personal data and on the free movement of such data, and repealing Directive 95/46/EC (General Data Protection Regulation) Official Journal of the European Union, Vol. L119 (4 May 2016), pp. 1–88 Art 2 (Material Scope,) Art 3 (Territorial Scope). Transferring data to a CSP storing personal data in a member state of the Union or the EEA does not require any additional limitations but the processing agreement (note potential additional requirements under local disciplinary laws for lawyers/legal service providers, see 2.b. A1. e.g., prohibiting transfer out of national territory).

58 GDPR, *supra* note 57, at Art 4 (Definitions).

59 GDPR, *supra* note 57, at Art 9, stipulating a general prohibition of processing such special categories of data (data revealing racial or ethnic origin, political opinions, religious or philosophical beliefs, or trade union membership, and the processing of genetic data, biometric data for the purpose of uniquely identifying a natural person, data concerning health or data concerning a natural person's sex life or sexual orientation); however such prohibition shall not apply in cases where the data subject has given consent to such processing (Art 9 Sec 2 para a), or processing is necessary for certain specific purposes serving data subjects' interests (Art 9 Sec 2 para b–h), or in public interest (Art 9 Sec 2 para I, j).

60 GDPR, *supra* note 57, at Art 10.

61 GDPR, *supra* note 57, at Art 4 Sec 2.

62 Note that in cases where CSP would argue that personal data transmitted and stored with him is encrypted and therefore not accessible to him, qualification as processing is likely as the mere possibility of decryption in processors' sphere renders a processing agreement obligatory.

63 GDPR *supra* note 57, at Art 4 (8).

tions of the controller, a **data processing agreement** is required[64]. LSPs using cloud computing services will most likely qualify as data controllers; to the effect that LSPs are subjected to all typical «controller» obligations laid down in GDPR (including but not limited to (i) the necessity to enter into data processing agreements with CSPs, (ii) obligations to exercise the rights of data subjects[65], (iii) notification obligations in case of data breach and (iv) the obligation to maintain the records of data processing activities[66]).

Note that from a practical perspective, data controller (in the case at hand the respective LSP) needs to be able to respond appropriately to data subject requests; in other words, the cloud architecture and application software must effectively enable LSPs to retrieve and provide all data on a data subject in a presentable format within a 4 weeks term.[67] This needs to be depicted appropriately in the data processing agreement.[68] Direct obligations of data processors (usually CSPs) resulting from GDPR[69] include ensuring a level of security in terms of encryption of data, restoring data and availability and access to data. Note that processing data beyond instructions of data controller would render CSP himself a data controller, subjecting him to the «controller» obligations. From the LSP's perspective, entering into a data processing agreement is crucial as non-compliance with said provisions entail significant exposure to penalties[70] executed by the respective supervisory authority.

2. Duties towards data subjects and duration of data processing

Pursuant to Art 6 personal **data must not be processed longer than necessary[71] for the purpose of processing**. This requires detailed retention and deletion schedules held and pursued by data controller. For implementation purposes, an option might be appropriate processing instructions to processor to the effect that processor is in charge of scheduling and deletion; possibly also shifting controller`s liabilities to processor. However, also note that local or disciplinary law based data retention/restoring obligations might require

64 GDPR *supra* note 57, at Art 28 Abs 3; this article stipulates mandatory content of processing agreements.

65 GDPR *supra* note 57, at Art 12–23.

66 GDPR *supra* note 57, at Art 30.

67 GDPR *supra* note 57, at Art 12 Sec 3.

68 GDPR *supra* note 57, at Art 28 Sec 3 lit e.

69 GDPR *supra* note 57, at Art 32.

70 GDPR *supra* note 57, at Art 83 Sec 4.

71 In cases where the consent of the data subject was withdrawn or the contractual grounds have terminated, processing still is necessary when (i) there is an overriding legitimate interest of the controller to further process, e.g., to exercise or defend legal claims (e.g., in Austria the statute of limitations is 3 or 30 years), (ii) the processing is necessary for compliance with a legal obligation the controller is subject to (e.g., tax purposes, in Austria 7yrs, or a disciplinary law obligation to maintain records of clients for 5 years).

complex deletion and data management schedules, so that delegation to processor can be costly. In any case the processing agreement should address that at the end of a retention period the contracted CSP shall delete all copies of the data in question, including backups.

As LSPs will usually be deemed data controllers, they are also bound by other duties towards data subjects[72], such as (i) responding to claims by data subjects without undue delay (usually a term of 4 weeks), the so-called right of «access», (ii) rectifying inaccurate personal data, (iii) respond to claims for restricting the data processing, and (iv) the duty to convey personal data of the data subject in a commonly used and machine-readable format. The right of access by the data subject[73] cannot be rejected by the controller, provided that he actually processed the personal data in question, elsewise the data subject is still to be notified that there has not been any processing of his/her personal data. The right to be forgotten[74] and the right to rectification and portability are crucial from a controllers' perspective, as significant technical and human resources may be required to be able to respond to large-scale data subject claims. This will mandate a technical and organizational infrastructure the controller needs to implement with processor for most efficient retrieval of all data concerning the claiming data subject.

3. Record of processing obligation

Both controller and processor need to maintain a record of processing activities[75] but are free to design format and organization of such record. LSPs usually are provided with sample records by their bar associations.

Note that GDPR recital provides for a specific application As a LSP particular attention should be payed to the fact that supervisory authorities have no competence for covering processing of personal data by «courts acting in their judicial capacity».[76] This leads to the (at this point not very clear and quite surprising) consequence that all processing of judicial files is *not* subject to the duty of recording processing, however all things leading up to processing judicial files (so everything to prepare a claim etc.) and not particularly within the judicial files need to be recorded in the record of processing file.

72 GDPR *supra* note 57, at Art 15–22.

73 GDPR *supra* note 57, at Art 15.

74 GDPR *supra* note 57, at Art 17.

75 GDPR *supra* note 57, at Art 30 Sec 1 lit a-g; GDPR provides for the mandatory content of such record; GDPR Art 30 Sec 2 for processors.

76 GDPR *supra* note 57, at recital 20.

4. Security measures

GDPR provides a basic framework for security measures to be undertaken when processing personal data.[77] GDPR requires implementation of appropriate security measures by controller and processor. When contracting CSPs, a reliable way to ensure compliance with GDPR is to look into the security framework set out above and choose a provider that has recognized certifications (see above Sec Ba)).

5. Data Breach

In the event of a personal data breach controller is obliged to either inform the supervisory authority[78] or the data subject directly[79], depending on the risk to the rights and freedoms of natural persons. In addition, processor himself must notify controller in the event of a breach.[80] This requires the processing agreement to (i) define breach events (ii) set out a protocol for such events.

6. Data transfers to third countries outside the EU/EEA

A data transfer to a country or an international organization outside the EU/EEA requires that the European Commission has decided that the country, a territory of such country or the international organization in question has an adequate level of protection[81], in which case a transfer to such does not necessitate additional safeguards than a transfer within EU/EEA, thus the controller only is bound to his «regular» controller duties (see above Sec Ba) under GDPR.

In case such adequacy decision is lacking, appropriate safeguards have to be ensured by controller.[82] The most relevant and common safeguard instrument are the standard contractual clauses[83][84], provided by the European Commission which are (still) used for protection for personal data processing to third countries. In respect of the US, the Safe Harbour Framework was chal-

---

77 GDPR *supra* note 57, at Art 32 Sec 1 lit a-d.

78 GDPR *supra* note 57, at Art 33.

79 GDPR *supra* note 57, at Art 34.

80 GDPR *supra* note 57, at Art 33 Sec 2.

81 List of countries under which such level of protection is assumed (as per Dec. 14, 2018): The European Commission has so far recognised Andorra, Argentina, Canada (commercial organisations), Faroe Islands, Guernsey, Israel, Isle of Man, Jersey, New Zealand, Switzerland, Uruguay and the United States of America (limited to the Privacy Shield framework) as providing adequate protection; currently adequacy talks are ongoing with South Korea; https://ec.europa.eu/info/law/law-topic/data-protection/data-transfers-outside-eu/adequacy-protection-personal-data-non-eu-countries_en

82 GDPR *supra* note 57, at Art 46 Sec 2 lit a–f.

83 GDPR *supra* note 57, at Art 46 Sec lit c.

84 European Commission, Model contracts for the transfer of personal data to third countries, https://ec.europa.eu/info/law/law-topic/data-protection/data-transfers-outside-eu/model-contracts-transfer-personal-data-third-countries_en (last visited Dec. 17, 2018).

lenged and invalidated during the *Schrems vs Facebook* case[85] where CJEU ruled that supervisory authorities of member states may examine claims by persons of which data has been transferred to a third country when such third country does not ensure an adequate data protection level, to the effect that a new solution was found: For data exchange between Europe and the US, the EU-US Privacy Shield decision was adopted on 12 July 2016, and the framework became operational on 1 August 2016[86]. Subject matter is in particular that access to data managed by private (US) companies by public authorities shall be more transparent and is subject to limitation, safeguards and oversight mechanisms; and that data subjects shall have rights to access and correct data on them, as well as obtain remedy free of cost. In the first review report the commission to the European parliament and the Council on the functioning of the EU-US Privacy Shield, published on October, 18, 2017 it stated that the US continues to ensure an «adequate level of protection» for personal data transferred under the Privacy Shield, and 2400 US companies have certified under the Privacy Shield so far. However, when it comes to companies referring to their Privacy Shield Certifications, the DoC currently seems to not (yet) be able to rectify false certification claims. However, it has to be noted that access to personal data by public authorities for (US) national security purposes is still possible, and, although Sec 702 of the U.S. Foreign Intelligence Surveillance Act (FISA) was set to expire on 31 December 2017, it has been renewed by the FISA Amendments Reauthorization Act of 2017 under the Trump administration.[87] Section 702 of the Foreign Intelligence Surveillance Act authorizes the Intelligence Community to target the communications of non-U.S. persons located outside the United States for foreign intelligence purposes.[88]

In general, however it has to be reiterated that to render such data transfer to third countries legal, controller has three possibilities: (i) consent of the data subject that his/her personal data is transferred to such country or international organization[89], (ii) necessity of the data transfer for the performance of a contract[90] (which is usually the case when clients mandate LSPs) and controller has **no other option** than to transfer to a third country[91], or (iii) necessity of the

---

85 C 362-14.

86 European Commission, EU-US Privacy Shield, https://ec.europa.eu/info/law/law-topic/data-protection/data-transfers-outside-eu/eu-us-privacy-shield_en (last visited Dec. 20, 2018).

87 FISA Amendments Reauthorization Act of 2017, https://intelligence.house.gov/fisa-702/ (last visited Dec. 20, 2018).

88 *Id.*

89 GDPR *supra* note 57, at Art 49 Sec 1 lit a.

90 GDPR *supra* note 57, at Art 49 Sec 1 lit b.

91 Rainer Knyrim, *DatKomm* Art 49 DSGVO § 25 (2018).

data transfer for the establishment, exercise or defense of legal claims[92] and controller has **no other option** than to transfer to a third country.[93]

CSPs commonly operate multiple servers, sometimes in multiple countries and jurisdictions. LSPs must clarify where the personal data will reside when contracting a CSP, to advert conflicts with union or national law. In this scope a thorough assessment of how the CSP processes the data (e.g., some might backup their servers in different countries than where the original copy resides) can minimize potential gateways for GDPR violations.

7. Data transfers from third countries to the EU/EEA

Even in cases where a data controller processes personal data **outside** the EU, GDPR can applicable if controller has been made in the context of the *activities* of an *establishment* within the EU. For example, if a Canadian LSP has a branch office in France and uses a South American cloud service provider for data *in the context of such establishment*, such processing would need to be GDPR-conform; more over most likely French data protection laws would have to be observed as well[94]. At least, establishment understands a minimum staffed office with a degree of performance and stability;[95] whereas the term «in the context of such establishment» remains still vague.

Note that GDPR also applies to data subjects which are non EU citizens or residents, if the aforementioned constellation is in place. Also, wherever personal data of data subjects who are in the Union is processed by a controller or processor who has *no* establishment in the Union but (i) offers goods or services in the EU or (ii) monitors data subjects behavior in the EU, GDPR might apply. Thus if a US enterprise has no establishment in the Union but contracts a CSP established in the EU, which does not actually process data in the Union, GDPR still applies. For companies who do **not** have an establishment in the Union but fall within the territorial scope because they offer goods or services on the European markets it is mandatory to designate a representative in the Union.[96] This provision ought not to be derided, as penalties are excessive.[97]

---

92 GDPR *supra* note 57, at Art 49 Sec 1 lit e.

93 Rainer Knyrim, DatKomm Art 49 DSGVO § 25 (2018).

94 W Kuan Hon, et al., *Which Law(s) Apply to Personal Data in Clouds, in* Cloud Computing Law (Christopher Millard, Oxford University Press, 2013) at 221.

95 *Id.*

96 GDPR *supra* note 57, at Art 27 Sec 1.

97 GDPR *supra* note 57, at Art 83 Sec 4 lit a.

C. Bring it all together–for LSPs

The CCBE[98] guidelines highlight lawyer—specific topics and aspects, which should be considered when contracting a CSP. Based on regulatory, civil law and potential duties of LSPs which were explored during this article, as well as the respective results of the security due diligence based on the cloud security principles, and considering additional typical negotiation topics[99] when contracting a CSP, cloud computing **contracts** should at least cover the following topics (unfortunately it is impossible to provide detailed guidance on each and every section):

- scope of service, service levels, system deployment model, system availability and deadlines for error corrections, contractual fines for delays and non-performance (see above Sec II.A),
- commitments of CSP to sector-specific regulations of the client/lawyer/LSP, also commitments on system adaptions based on changing regulatory provisions (see above Sec 2),
- provisions on/notification obligations in cases of involuntary intrusion by government agencies
- provisions covering the security duties (see above Sec 2 the LSP has to abide to),
- exclusion or limitation of liability and remedies, particularly regarding data integrity and disaster recovery,
- IP/ownership of data provisions including access rights, also regulating licensing of software, including tailor made solutions for clients who may want to own such,
- agreements reflecting the data protection legislation (in case GDPR is applicable: data processing agreements, Sec B) including how to handle data subject rights re deletion or change,
- provisions on the use of sub-contractor and the security standard requested for those (including potential notification obligations, or consent obligations, if desired; also note GDPR requirements on sub-contractors as processors),
- back-up, lock-in and deletion plans including provision on physical location of data (reflecting particular requirements of LSP/client), termination rights, notice periods and return of data in exit rights
- provisions on disclosure/transparency of the CSPs services, governance models and, internal compliance procedures

---

98 Council of Bars and Law Societies of Europe; many local bar associations in Europe refer to when it comes to cloud computing recommendations, if any.

99 W Kuan Hon et al., *Negotiated Contracts for Cloud Services*, in CLOUD COMPUTING LAW (Christopher Millard, Oxford University Press, 2013) at 73.

- provisions on providers' ability to change terms and features unilaterally (which is a common phenomenon in standard terms mostly unacceptable to LSPs)
- insurance terms
- applicable law / jurisdiction / mediation / arbitration clause.

III. Concluding Remarks

The way new technologies impact management is by creating new opportunities for innovation; this applies also to LSPs. With cloud computing, gathering and distribution of information is excessively enhanced, making it more impactful than any other information technology of our time.

It makes for much faster collection, interchangeability and analysis of data, enabling more flexible and client focused solutions that can be iterated constantly and seamlessly over the air. LSPs can profit substantially from outsourcing their proprietary data centers and using cloud-based software subscriptions- updated daily.

Clearly, it makes sense from LSPs perspective to analyze obligations and duties particular to the legal industry and reflect such in the respective cloud computing service agreements. The market grows, and cloud—use based on general terms will be, for most LSPs not an option. There is still—in most countries—lots of room for organizations such as the bars and disciplinary organizations to move towards the cloud and help members to clearly understand requirements to be able to move forward with their clients.

IV. Bibliography

A. Hard Copy Sources

MILLARD, CHRISTOPH, CLOUD COMPUTING LAW (Oxford University Press, 2013).

HARTUNG, MARKUS et al. eds., LEGAL TECH DIE DIGITALISIERUNG DES RECHTSMARKTS (C. H. Beck, 2018).

Hon, Kuan, et al., *Which Law(s) Apply to Personal Data in Clouds, in* CLOUD COMPUTING LAW (Christopher Millard, Oxford University Press, 2013) at 221.

GOODENOUGH, OLIVER & LAURITSEN, MARC eds., EDUCATING THE DIGITAL LAWYER (Carolina Academic Press, 2012).

KNYRIM, RAINER ed., DATKOMM (LexisNexis, 2018).

SUSSKIND, RICHARD, TOMORROW`S LAWYERS (Oxford University Press, 2013).

B. Online Sources

CISCO, *Global Cloud Index 2016–2021* (Nov. 19, 2018), https://www.cisco.com/c/en/us/solutions/collateral/service-provider/global-cloud-index-gci/white-paper-c11-738085.html (last visited Dec. 16, 2018).

Conseil Supérieur du Notariat, *Reglement National et Reglement Inter-Cours* (Jul. 22, 2017), https://www.notaires.fr/sites/default/files/reglement_national_-_reglement_intercours_-_arrete_du_22_07_2014_-_jo_du_01_08_2014.pdf (last visited Dec. 19, 2018).

Council of Bars and Law Societies of Europe, *CCBE Guidelines on the use of cloud computing services by lawyers* (Sept. 7, 2012), https://www.ccbe.eu/NTCdocument/07092012_EN_CCBE_gui1_1347539443.pdf (last visited Dec. 19, 2018).

Dennis Kennedy, *2017 Cloud Computing*, ABA Techreport 2017 (Dec. 01, 2017), https://www.americanbar.org/groups/law_practice/publications/techreport/2017/cloud_computing/ (last visited Dec. 17, 2018).

European Banking Authority, *Recommendations On Outsourcing to Cloud Service Providers* (Mar. 28, 2018), https://www.eba.europa.eu/documents/10180/2170125/Recommendations+on+-Cloud+Outsourcing+%28EBA-Rec-2017-03%29_EN.pdf/e02bef01-3e00-4d81-b549-4981a8fb2f1e (last visited Dec. 19, 2018).

European Commission, *Adequacy Decisions*, https://ec.europa.eu/info/law/law-topic/data-protection/data-transfers-outside-eu/adequacy-protection-personal-data-non-eu-countries_en (last visited Dec. 19, 2018).

European Commission, *EU-US Privacy Shield*, https://ec.europa.eu/info/law/law-topic/data-protection/data-transfers-outside-eu/eu-us-privacy-shield_en (last visited Dec. 20, 2018).

European Commission, *Model Contracts for the Transfer of Personal Data to Third Countries*, https://ec.europa.eu/info/law/law-topic/data-protection/data-transfers-outside-eu/model-contracts-transfer-personal-data-third-countries_en (last visited Dec. 17, 2018).

European Commission, *The 2018 EU Justice Scoreboard* (2018), (https://ec.europa.eu/info/sites/info/files/justice_scoreboard_2018_en.pdf (last visited Dec. 16, 2018).

Federal Office for Information Security, *Compliance Controls Catalogue*, https://www.bsi.bund.de/EN/Topics/CloudComputing/Compliance_Controls_Catalogue/Compliance_Controls_Catalogue_node.html;jsessionid=49BC275931E2103BBD5A6A2F9D08528E.2_cid369 (last visited Dec. 19, 2018).

Federal Office for Information Security, *Das IT-Sicherheitsgesetz*, https://www.bsi.bund.de/DE/Themen/Industrie_KRITIS/KRITIS/IT-SiG/it_sig_node.html (last visited Dec. 19, 2018).

HANDBUCH IT-SICHERHEIT, http://www.archivium.at/index.php/news/90-handbuch-it-sicherheit (last visited Dec. 19, 2018).

Koetsier, John, *Cloud Revenue 2020: Amazon's AWS $44B, Microsoft Azure's $19B, Google's Cloud Platform $17B*, FORBES (Apr. 30, 2018), https://www.forbes.com/sites/johnkoetsier/2018/04/30/cloud-revenue-2020-amazons-aws-44b-microsoft-azures-19b-google-cloud-platform-17b/#4c95d20c7ee5 (last visited Dec. 16, 2018).

Columbus, Louis, *Cloud Computing Market Projected to Reach $411B by 2020*, FORBES (Oct. 18, 2017), https://www.forbes.com/sites/louiscolumbus/2017/10/18/cloud-computing-market-projected-to-reach-411b-by-2020/#55b69f6878f2 (last visited Dec. 16, 2018).

Kaminska, Magdalena & Smihily, Maria, *Cloud computing—Statistics on the Use by Enterprises* (Dec. 13, 2018), https://ec.europa.eu/eurostat/statistics-explained/index.php/Cloud_computing_-_statistics_on_the_use_by_enterprises (last visited Dec. 19, 2018).

NCSC, *Cloud Security Principle 1: Data in Transit Protection* (Sept. 21, 2016), https://www.ncsc.gov.uk/guidance/cloud-security-principle-1-data-transit-protection (last visited Dec. 20, 2018).

NCSC, *Cloud Security Principle 5: Operational Security* (Sept. 21, 2016), https://www.ncsc.gov.uk/guidance/cloud-security-principle-5-operational-security (last visited Dec. 20, 2018).

NCSC, *End User Device Security Collection* (Apr. 17, 2018), https://www.ncsc.gov.uk/guidance/end-user-device-security (last visited Dec. 20, 2018).

NCSC, *Implementing Cloud Security Principles* (Sept. 21, 2016), https://www.ncsc.gov.uk/guidance/implementing-cloud-security-principles (last visited Dec. 17, 2018).

NCSC, *Implementing the Cloud Security Principles* (Sept. 21, 2016), https://www.ncsc.gov.uk/guidance/implementing-cloud-security-principles (last visited Dec. 17, 2018).

Mell, Peter & Grance, Tim, *The NIST Definition of Cloud Computing* (September 2011), https://csrc.nist.gov/publications/detail/sp/800-145/final (last visited Dec. 19, 2018).

Kemp, Richard, *Cloud Computing and Data Sovereignity* (2016) http://www.kempitlaw.com/cloud-computing-and-data-sovereignty/ (last visited Dec. 19, 2018).

Kemp, Richard, *Legal Aspects of Cloud Computing: Cloud Security* (2018), http://www.kempitlaw.com/wp-content/uploads/2018/06/Cloud-Security-White-Paper-KITL-v1.0-June-2018.pdf (last visited Dec. 19, 2018).

Maffioletti, Sergio, *Cloud Middleware* (Apr. 25, 2014), https://www.sif.it/static/SIF/resources/public/files/va2014/Maffioletti_1.pdf (last visited Dec. 19, 2018).

Microsoft, *Classification for Cloud Readiness,* https://www.microsoft.com/en-us/search/result.aspx?q=data+classification+for+cloud+readiness (last visited Dec. 19, 2018).

SRA, *SRA Code of Conduct 2011* (Dec. 6, 2018), https://www.sra.org.uk/solicitors/handbook/code/content.page (last visited Dec. 19, 2018).

Staraudit, https://staraudit.org (last visited Dec. 17, 2018).

Sterkl, Maria, *Der langsame Abschied vom Gerichtsakt auf Papier*, Der Standard (Nov. 19, 2018), https://derstandard.at/2000090757655/Der-langsame-Abschied-vom-Gerichtsakt-auf-Papier (last visited Apr. 25, 2019).

The World Justice Project, *The WJP Rule of Law Index 2017–2018* (2018), https://worldjusticeproject.org/sites/default/files/documents/WJP-ROLI-2018-June-Online-Edition_0.pdf (last visited Dec. 16, 2018).

C. Legislative Material

Bundesdatenschutzgesetz, BGBl. I S. 201 as amended BGBl. I S. 2097, http://www.gesetze-im-internet.de/bdsg_2018/ (last visited Dec. 19, 2018).

Bundesrechtsanwaltsordnung, BGBl. I S. 565 as amended BGBl. I S. 3619, https://www.gesetze-im-internet.de/brao/ (last visited Dec. 19, 2018).

Datenschutzgesetz, BGBl. I Nr. 165/1999 as amended BGBl. I Nr. 24/2018, https://www.ris.bka.gv.at/GeltendeFassung.wxe?Abfrage=bundesnormen&Gesetzesnummer=10001597 (last visited Dec. 19, 2018).

Datensicherheitsverordnung, BGBl. II Nr. 402/2011 as amended BGBl. II Nr. 228/2016, https://www.ris.bka.gv.at/GeltendeFassung.wxe?Abfrage=Bundesnormen&Gesetzesnummer=20007596 (last visited Dec. 19, 2018).

FISA Amendments Reauthorization Act of 2017, H.R. 4478, 115th Cong.

General Data Protection Regulation (EU) 2016/679 of the European Parliament and of the Council of 27 April 2016 on the protection of natural persons with regard to the processing of personal data

and on the free movement of such data, and repealing Directive 95/46/EC (General Data Protection Regulation) Official Journal of the European Union, Vol. L119 (4 May 2016).
Gesetz über außergerichtliche Rechtsdienstleistungen, BGBl. I S. 2840 as amended BGBl. I S. 1121, 1143, https://www.gesetze-im-internet.de/rdg/ (last visited Dec. 19, 2018).
Notariatsordnung, RGBl. Nr. 75/1871 as amended BGBl. I Nr. 71/2018, https://www.ris.bka.gv.at/GeltendeFassung.wxe?Abfrage=Bundesnormen&Gesetzesnummer=10001677 (last visited Dec. 19, 2018).
Rechtsanwaltsordnung, RGBl. Nr. 96/1868 as amended BGBl. I Nr. 32/2018, https://www.ris.bka.gv.at/GeltendeFassung.wxe?Abfrage=Bundesnormen&Gesetzesnummer=10001673 (last visited Dec. 19, 2018).
Telekommunikationsgesetz 2003, BGBl. I Nr. 70/2003 as amended BGBl. Nr. 78/2018, https://www.ris.bka.gv.at/GeltendeFassung.wxe?Abfrage=Bundesnormen&Gesetzesnummer=20002849 (last visited Dec. 19, 2018)
The Claryfing Lawful Overseas Use of Data Act, CLOUD Act, H.R. 4943, 115th Cong.
UK Parliament Acts, Communications Act 2003 (2003 c 21), https://www.legislation.gov.uk/ukpga/2003/21/contents (last visited Dec. 19, 2018).

D. Case Law

C-362/14, Maximilian Schrems v. Irish Data Protection Commissioner, 2015 ECJ.

Michael Grupp and Micha-Manuel Bues

The Status Quo in Legal Automation

50 years of automation in the legal industry—looking back and ahead

TABLE OF CONTENTS

I. Introduction

«There may be a more indirect way of saying this, but perhaps it is better to simply say it like it is: law firms are inefficiency factories and automation is the cure.»[1]
– Richard Tromans

While public media muses on the question if and when lawyers will be replaced by algorithms,[2] file trolleys are still pushed through the corridors of many courts and law firms. In the legal industry, automations are still rare. Applications are limited to well defined tasks and niches. Automation is not being used across the board in the legal sector, academic and scientific contributions on the topic have stalled. Other fields on the intersection of law and technology have risen in importance: Data privacy and security have become more relevant and the label «legal tech» has emerged in to a distinct industry, assembling platforms, research and analytics platforms as well as digital legal headhunting tools. The core of legal digital transformation, however, remains untouched, it seems. Legal automation continues to be a complex and unclear field with little visibility. Other industries have fostered innovation and the development of automation in many, if not most fields of work: from the automation of simple manual processes to the development of machine learning.

Legal automation has a rich history—often unknown and untold. In recent years, it has, however, experienced increased attention both in theory and practice—with greatly diverging expectations in its benefits and limitations. This article summarizes the status quo and gives an outlook of future developments and their likely influence on the legal industry. This article will attempt to show that the underpinning technology has been broadly and thoroughly researched and described by legal informatics starting from the 1960s. Rule-based applications have emerged from this phase as a well-established technology. The complexity of legal semantics allows for data-driven approaches only in very narrow niches.

This article will also attempt to show that recent developments in legal automation are largely possible due to the all-encompassing digital transformation (in the legal industry). Part II provides a succinct overview of the history and status quo of automation in the legal area. Part III serves as a guide to navigate the different notions of automation and highlight the differences be-

---

1 Richard Tromans, *Law Firms are Inefficiency Factories, Automation is the Cure*, ARTIFICIALLAWYER (Jun. 11, 2018), https://www.artificiallawyer.com/2018/06/11/law-firms-are-inefficiency-factories-automation-is-the-cure/ (last visited Jan. 12, 2019).

2 Oliver Voß, *Will lawyers become obsolete?*, WIRTSCHAFTSWOCHE (Mar. 24, 2017), https://www.wiwo.de/erfolg/gruender/legal-tech-werden-anwaelte-obsolet/19523172.html (last visited Jan. 3, 2019).

tween approaches, technologies, and concepts. Part IV focuses on the application of automation technology in the legal field—examining both technological feasibility on legal content as well as market-related factors.

II. A Short History of Legal Automation

Public perception may give the impression that the legal sector is unrivalled by technical innovations. But this might be misleading: legal automation has a long tradition in the field of legal informatics and a research-rich past.

A. Early Days

From the very early days of computer science and the first computer systems in the 1950s, legal work was in the spotlight of (legal) research,[3] starting from the comparability of legal and information technology logic and with the help of logical programming languages.[4] The *prima facie* comparability of both, strongly rule-based areas[5] motivated a whole generation of young jurists to experiments in the field of formal logic with the goal of a veritable automatic law machine on the basis of prototypical experiments in criminal law[6] and administrative law.[7] The early work on the algorithm suitability of legal decision-making processes and the formalization of complex semantic structures is still unrivalled today. As an interface function,[8] legal informatics[9] has given rise to projects, chairs, and considerable research activities at many universities with links to (computer) linguistics, cognitive sciences, and mathematics.[10]

The development directions could be broadly summarised as follows: on the one hand, rule-based systems were, literally speaking, mechanical repre-

---

3 Ulrich Klug, Juristische Logik (Springer, 1951) at 157 et seq.

4 In particular PROLOG and COBOL, e.g., Herbert Fiedler, *Juristische Logik in mathematischer Sicht*, ARSP (1966) at 93 et seq.

5 Herbert Fiedler, *Automatisierung im Recht und juristische Informatik*, JuS 228 et seq. (1971).

6 Fritjof Haft & Hein Lehmann, The LEX Project. Entwicklung eines jurstischen Expertensystems (Attempo Verlag, 1989) at 60 et seq.

7 Herbert Fiedler, *Rechenautomaten in Recht und Verwaltung*, JZ 689, 692 et seq. (1966).

8 Examples e.g., L Throne McCarthy, *TAXMAN for the review of tax rules in M&A, An Experiment in Artificial Intelligence and Legal Reasoning*, 90 Harvard Law Review 837 et seq. (1977).

9 In the states of the former Soviet Union «right-wing cybernetics», in the Anglo-American area as a rule «Artificial Intelligence and Law», more rarely «Legal Informatics».

10 Svenja L Gräwe, Die Entstehung der Rechtsinformatik (Verlag Dr Kovac, 2011) at 69, 220; Roland Traunmüller & Maria A Wimmer, eds., Informatik in Recht und Verwaltung: Gestern – heute – morgen. Ehrenband Prof Dr Dr Herbert Fiedler zum Achtzigsten Geburtstag (Köllen Verlag, 2009) at 22 et seq.

sentations of human decision-making patterns. On the other hand, data-based, statistical approaches emerged with self-learning components.[11]

Several projects with a rule-based, statistical, or hybrid focus achieved at least prototype status,[12] partly also in cooperation with industrial companies and significant financial support.[13] The only legacy of legal informatics with a broad impact was the legal information systems such as JURIS[14].

If technology is absent in the day-to-day business of the legal industry, this is less due to the lack of innovation in the industry than to then existing technological hurdles that have only recently been overcome in a few individual areas.[15]

B. The Forgotten Tech: Rule Based Systems and Hybrids

Rule based systems and related have been feasible early on. The lack of adaptation of rule-based systems was not due to inadequate technological feasibility. The development of rule-based decision support systems and expert systems for legal content was not surprising.[16] The (theoretical) feasibility was determined early on in extensive conceptual preparatory work.[17] From the 1980s onwards, several projects were put into practice (in Germany, for exam-

---

11 Overview e.g., *in* Michael Grupp, *Legal Tech – Impulse für Streitbeilegung und Rechtsdienstleistung*, AnwBl 660, 480 et seq. (2014).

12 Overview *in* Thomas Jandach, *Juristische Expertensysteme* (Springer, 1993) at 22 et seq.; summary also in: Elmar Bund, Einführung in die Rechtsinformatik (Springer, 1991) at 284 et seq.

13 LEX/LEX-1 at the University of Tübingen with IBM, Haft & Lehmann, *supra* note 6, at 60; KOKON, Detlef L Kowalewski, Josef Schneeberger & Susanne Wiefel, *KOKON-3: A prototypical system for knowledge-based contract configuration*, 223 Informatik-Fachberichte 79 et seq. (1989); DFG project «Analysis of Legal Language» at the DRZ Darmstadt, Hans Brinckmann, Janos S Petőfi & Hannes Rieser, *Paraphrasen juristischer Texte II*, 73 DVR 257 (1972).

14 Herbert Fiedler, Friedrich Gebhard, Bernd S Müller, Joachim Poetsch & Imant Stellmacher, *Methodological Requirements of Legal Information Systems—Remarks on the Development of JURIS*, Supplement 5 to the DVR 7 (1976).

15 The two practical manuals Markus Hartung, Micha-Manuel Bues & Gernot Halbleib, Legal Tech – die Digitalisierung des Rechtsmarktes (C. H. Beck, 2017/2018) and Stephan Breidenbach & Florian Glatz, Legal Tech (C. H. Beck, 2017) also provide an overview of current feasibility at the interface between law and technology.

16 An expert system is here understood as a computer program that attempts to construct a machine system on the basis of collected trains of thought and experiences of experts in a certain field, which provides users with aspects of problem-solving competence, *see* Ipke Wachsmuth, *Expertensysteme, Planen und Problemlösen*, *in:* Einführung in die Künstliche Intelligenz (Günther Görz, ed., (2nd ed., Oldenbourg Wissenschaftsverlag, 1995) at 713 et seq.

17 Roland Traunmüller, *Rechtsinformatik auf dem Weg ins nächste Jahrtausend*, in: Informatik in Recht und Verwaltung – Entwicklung, Stand, Perspektiven, Festschrift für Herbert Fiedler zur Emeritierung (Klaus Lenk, Heinrich Reinermann & Roland Traunmüller, eds., 1997) at 3 et seq.

ple, the XPS by Nilgens, Jurex), which, however, only illustrated individual rule-based application cases as examples and (with the exception of labour law information system ARBIS by Haufe publishers) never really left the university sector.[18]

The development of decision support systems is subject to particular difficulties and limitations: for example, the systems cannot self-referentially determine their area of application (plateau-cliff problem[19]) or reach their limits of knowledge acquisition (Feigenbaum's bottleneck[20]). Care and maintenance are costly and increase exponentially with larger systems.

In the 1980s and 1990s, expert systems research was consistently criticized. Beyond the content aspects, the development of automated decision making was sometimes considered «inhumane» or untrustworthy.[21] Conversely, the often-exaggerated expectations of automation possibilities had to lead to disappointments.[22] At the beginning of the 1990s, several legal informatics specialists noted the failure of the concept,[23] *Jandach's* comprehensive overview denies the development concept's lasting success,[24] and one speaks of the «AI winter» of legal informatics.

In fact, the criticism was not based on the technical challenges mentioned (which also existed in other sectors) or on the general feasibility or benefits. It should be understood in its temporal context. The technological framework for the dissemination of interactive legal systems did not emerge until the 1990s, with the most homogeneous operating system landscape and the mass dissemination of end devices in households, companies and law firms.[25] It was not until the 2000s that the technological foundations required for a professional legal software landscape were successively created.[26] In addition to the digitisation of essential aspects of legal typesetting and data processing, the neces-

---

18 Maximilian Herberger, *Arbeitskreis «Entscheidungsunterstützungssysteme»*, 3 JurPc 121 (1996).

19 John Alvey, *The problems of designing a medical expert system*, 83 Proceedings of Expert Systems (1983).

20 Rinke Hoekstra, *The Knowledge Reengineering Bottleneck*, Semantic Web Journal (2010) http://www.semantic-web-journal.net/sites/default/files/swj32.pdf (last visited Feb. 2, 2019).

21 Haft, Fritjof, *Computer-aided decision making*, in: Informatik in Recht und Verwaltung – Entwicklung, Stand, Perspektiven. Festschrift für Herbert Fiedler zur Emeritierung 95–119 (Klaus Lenk, Heinrich Reinermann & Roland Traunmüller, eds., R von Decker's Verlag, 1997) at 589.

22 Arndt Bohrer, *Development of an Internet-based expert system to examine the scope of copyright agreements* 20 et seq. (2003).

23 Fritjof Haft, *The Second Birth of Legal Informatics*, in: Informatik in Recht und Verwaltung – Entwicklung, Stand, Perspektiven. Festschrift für Herbert Fiedler zur Emeritierung (Klaus Lenk, Heinrich Reinermann, & Roland Traunmüller, eds., R von Decker's Verlag, 1997) at 95–119.

24 Thomas Jandach, Juristische Expertensysteme. Methodische Grundlagen ihrer Entwicklung (Springer, 1993).

25 Elmar Bund, Einführung in die Rechtsinformatik (Springer, 1991) at 129.

26 Alexander Konzelmann, *Tagungsbericht Internationales Rechtsinformatik Symposion Salzburg (IRIS)*, 110 JurPC § 36 (2003).

sary data basis and digitised external services such as company registers are also available.

In particular, the spread of the Internet, i.e., an active ecosystem of a «network economy», and server-based computing changed the landscape and made it economically feasible to develop, deploy and sell rules-based applications. Recent developments show that the now established IT infrastructure allows for rule-based applications on large scale. One example is the tool developed by the commercial law firm CMS Hasche Sigle for social selection or the deployment of external personnel, or the information tools provided by the consulting companies for the Federal Office for Migration and Refugees.[27]

Recently, systems have been made available, to facilitate the creation and maintenance of rule-based systems. Vendors from the USA, the Netherlands or Germany also offer so-called no code applications, which allow the development of rule-based applications even without programming knowledge.[28]

III. The Concept of Automation

A. Definition

The term automation is difficult to grasp due to its linguistic breadth and requires the demarcation of different application categories and areas for its more detailed containment. A uniform definition has not emerged. Every effort at definition, however, is ultimately based on the same core idea already coined by Aristotle (384–322 BC) in his work *Politeia*:

> *«If every instrument could accomplish its own work, obeying or anticipating the will of others, like the statues of Daedalus, or the tripods of Hephaestus, which, says the poet, «of their own accord entered the assembly of the Gods» if, in like manner, the shuttle would weave and the plectrum touch the lyre without a hand to guide them, chief workmen would not want servants, nor masters slaves.»*[29]

---

27 *See* for further examples: Gernot Halbleib, *Der Weg zur Legal Tech Strategie*, 31–43 in: LEGAL TECH – DIE DIGITALISIERUNG DES RECHTSMARKTES (Markus Hartung et al., eds., (2017/2018) at §128 31.

28 *See* for example BRYTER (www.bryter.io) or KnowledgeTools (www.knowledgeteools.de) in Germany.

29 Aristotle, *Politeia,* 1253b. The word automation/automation has its own Greek roots and is derived from the goddess *Automatia* (Greek: αυτοματια, the one that comes by itself).

The generic term automation thus encompasses systems that are capable of solving tasks or problems of a constant or changing nature with varying degrees of individual autonomy, i.e., without human participation.[30] The less a person has to intervene, the higher the degree of automation. To reduce the human component to achieve a task is the goal of any automation.

The main drivers of automation today are software programs that perform certain tasks independently. The object of automation can be an activity, a process (several steps) and material decisions («thinking»).[31] The predominant part of software-supported automation refers to linear processes, i.e., the sequence of certain process steps (e-mail dispatch, approval processes, storage in databases, etc.). The sequence of the process steps is always the same but could vary depending on the tasks at hand. Increasingly, more complex processes interdependent on conditions and complex scenarios can also be automated. A new field applies this to automate complex decision paths for material problem solving, especially in business decisions.[32]

In contrast to processes, decision automation requires the automation of complex, content-related, domain-specific questions (e.g., in the legal field), while processes require domain-agnostic work steps. In the legal field, for example, a process would involve the creation of a new mandate file, a material decision would involve the admissibility of a lawsuit.

Automation is predominantly based on so-called rule-based approaches, which subdivide a particular problem into individual predefined rule logics and automate them. Automation works according to these rules without the system requiring any training data (see the distinction between this and automatic learning procedures later). Rule-based automation is therefore completely predictable and comprehensible.

B. Automation Dimensions

Usually different types of automation fields are distinguished, which address different problem fields and—despite often very similar names—can only be used in certain domains. There is a certain Babylonian confusion of language which does not facilitate the understanding of the individual fields.

The following automation types might be distinguished:

---

30 Transfer of functions of the production process to artificial systems according to GABLER WIRTSCHAFTSLEXIKON at https://wirtschaftslexikon.gabler.de/definition/automatisierung-27138/version-250801 (last visited Apr. 11, 2019).

31 SHIMON NOF, SPRINGER HANDBOOK OF AUTOMATION (Springer, 2009) at 780.

32 Robert O'Keefe & Tim McEachern, *Web-based customer decision support systems*, 41 COMMUNICATIONS OF THE ACM ARCHIVE 73 (1998).

Automation of processes
- Simple processes (= Workflows): Workflow Automation
- Repetitive (UI-based) processes: Robotic Process Automation
- Complex processes (+ simple decision processes regarding content): Business Process Automation

Automation of (content-related, cognitive) decision-making processes
- Complex decision-making processes regarding content: decision automation

C. Business Process Automation

For years, Business Process Automation (BPA) has been a vital part of the digital strategies of many companies.[33] Process automation refers, in simple terms, to the use of rule-based technologies to perform one or more processes to execute a workflow or function. So this includes planning, modelling, visualization and finally the automation of processes (e.g., BPMN or classical workflow automation). Process automation is often used in areas with important <u>linear</u> processes and workflows. A typical automated process is, for example, an invoice receipt management process.

D. Robotic Process Automation

Robotic Process Automation (RPA) makes it possible to imitate and automate human interactions with user interfaces of rule-based software systems with so-called bots (software robots).[34] In other words, RPA can automate repetitive and rule-based processes and tasks that are currently performed manually by users—via mouse and keyboard—on the frontend of different software systems.[35] RPA is a robot for the hand, mouse or keyboard. Or in other words, a digital mechanic workflow.[36]

---

33 Gero Decker et al., *The Business Process Modelling Notation*, in: *Modern Business Process Automation: YAWL and its Support Environment* (Arthur H M ter Hofstede, Wil M P van der Aalst, Michael Adams, Nick Russell, eds., 2010) at 12.

34 The field of robotics, which deals with the design, the control, the production and the operation of physical robots—in contrast to pure software robots—is to be seen as a separate area.

35 Berruti, Federico, Nixon, Graeme, Taglioni, Giambattista & Whiteman, Rob, *Intelligent process automation: The engine at the core of the next-generation operating model*, McKinsey Study (2017), https://www.mckinsey.com/business-functions/digital-mckinsey/our-insights/intelligent-process-automation-the-engine-at-the-core-of-the-next-generation-operating-model? reload (last visited Apr. 12, 2019) at 3.

36 Santiago Aguirre & Alejandro Rodriguez, *Automation of a Business Process Using Robotic Process Automation (RPA): A Case Study*, in: Workshop on Engineering Applications 65 (2017).

RPA processes rule-based, structured data via the user interface of the process-supporting robot software without accessing the backend of a system.[37] The spectrum of bots used ranges from simple workarounds to complex software on a virtual machine. A frequent application of RPA is, for example, the repeated input of data into systems. If systems cannot be connected easily through APIs, data needs to be transferred manually—almost mechanically—between the systems.[38] Hence, if data is copied from one system to another («Copy&Paste»), this activity can be replaced by RPA by a bot (macro) that automatically performs this task, i.e., the operation of mouse and keyboard.[39]

RPA aims to automate processes without changing existing applications. This explains the outstanding success of RPA in recent years. In contrast to classical process automation, existing processes and workflows do not have to be changed or analysed. This means that rapid automation success can be achieved across applications at relatively low cost. The advantage, however, is also a disadvantage: existing (bad) processes are perpetuated and conserved in this way. More complex actions and (frequently) changing interfaces represent a major challenge for RPA.

Recently, the rule-based RPA tools have been combined with machine learning to hybrid approaches in order to better address these problems.[40] The approaches are called «Cognitive Automation», «Intelligent Automation» or «Intelligence Process Automation» (IPA) and represent the next development step. However, fields applications focus on supporting the core function other than operating truly intelligent systems.

RPA/IPA plays a subordinate role in the legal field. It can have a meaningful area of application where existing law firm and mandate management systems are to be automated in partial areas. RPA/IPA cannot be applied to the genuine field of activity of lawyers, where semantically complex decision making is the rule.[41]

---

37 Esko Penttinen, Henje Kasslin & Aleksandre Asatiani, *Choice between lightweight and heavyweight IT*, Twenty-Sixth European Conference on Information Systems (ECIS2018) 1 (2018).

38 Federico Berruti et al., *supra* note 35, at 3.

39 Mary Lacity, Leslie Willcocks & Andrew Craig, *Robotic Process Automation at Telefónica O2,* The Outsourcing Unit Working Research Paper Series 21–35 (2015); Mary Lacity, Leslie Willcocks & Andrew Craig, *Robotizing Global Financial Shared Services at Royal DSM,* The Outsourcing Unit Working Research Paper Series 122 (2016); Jonathan Love, Process Automation Handbook: A Guide to Theory and Practice (Springer, 2007) at 42.

40 Federico Berruti, Graeme Nixon, Giambattista Taglioni & Rob Whiteman, *supra* note 36, at 3.

41 Phil Fresht & James R Slaby, *Robotic Automation Emerges as a Threat To Traditional Low-Cost Outsourcing*, HfS Research 1–18 (2012).

Anti-Money-Laundering-Check-Process as an example for Automation

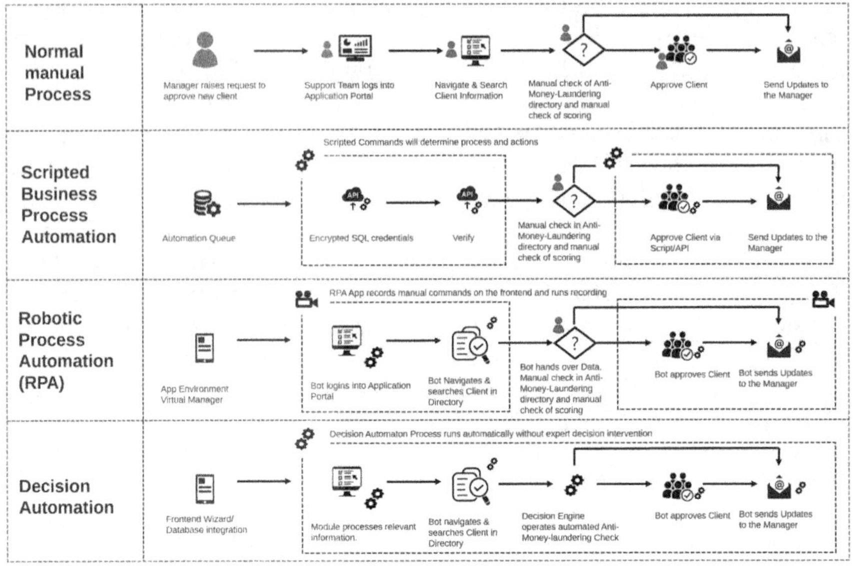

Exhibit 1: NMP vs SBPA vs RPA.

E. Decision Automation

A new and rapidly developing field is the so-called decision automation, which in turn has to be distinguished from process automation and RPA. Decision automation involves different concepts, technologies and methods to reduce the human component in complex, content-, judgement- and scenario-based decision processes. The focus of decision automation is on imitating, modelling and automating a cognitive decision-making process in order to make it more transparent and comprehensible. Decision automation is thus to some extent RPA for the brain and not just for «manual» processes.[42]

Decision automation is used in complex decision scenarios in which different, interdependent, mechanical, and complex conditions have to be evaluated in a cognitive process in order to decide.[43] BPA and RPA, by contrast,

42 Robert O'Keefe & Tim McEachern, *Web-based customer decision support systems*, 41 Communications of the ACM Archive 73 (1998).

43 Thomas Davenport & Jeanne Harris, *Automated Decision Making Comes of Age*, 46 MIT Sloan Management Review 4 (2005).

focus primarily on linear processes and simple human tasks that do not require a complex assessment process, as encompassed by decision automation.[44]

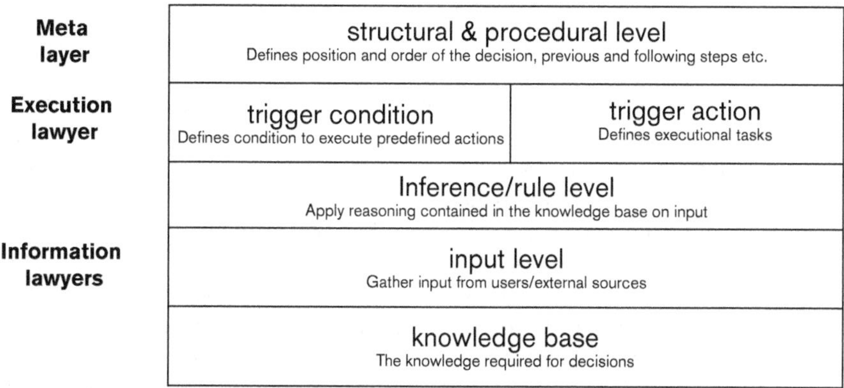

Exhibit 2: Key Levels for Decision Automation.

Decisions contain more than meta elements of workflows—determining only structure of the workflow and possible integrated actions. Core elements of decision and digitally transformed decisions are the inference levels that combine the input level and the knowledge base.[45] Only through applying a set of rules the trigger conditions are set in motion. This turns Decision automation into sub-forms of knowledge management software.

However, decision automation is different from decision support systems that assist and interact.[46] Decision automation is based on rule-based systems able to map complex and conditional decision scenarios and make them understandable.[47] Here, too, there are approaches to develop hybrid systems that make use of machine learning procedures in order to make predictions based on the automated data. Routine decision situations can be analyzed and «programmed» significantly and can be supported in most situations by technology. The potential rewards from improving routine, recurring decisions are usually very large.[48]

---

44 Jay Nunamaker, Lynda Applegate & Benn Konsynski, *Computer-Aided Deliberation: Model Management and Group Decision Support*, 36 Operations Research 826–848 (1988).

45 Thomas Jandach, *Juristische Expertensysteme. Methodische Grundlagen ihrer Entwicklung* (Springer, 1993) at 30.

46 Daniel J Power, *Decision Support Systems: Concepts and Resources for Managers* (Greenwood Publishing Group, 2002) at 39.

47 Nils J Nilsson, Principles of Artificial Intelligence (Morgan Kaufmann, 1982) at 37–43.

48 Power, *supra* note 46, at 39.

F. Expert Systems

In the 1970s, the concept of expert systems emerged as an independent category of machine decision support systems. This refers to systems that have certain defined components in a typical structure (usually five).[49]A knowledge base contains explicitly formulated the mostly textual and rule-based knowledge of the system, a component through which the legal rules are entered into the knowledge base («knowledge acquisition component»), mostly used by the to expand the knowledge base of the system, an interface (mostly a frontend or chat-window) through which the rules and the intermediate results and results derived from them are displayed to the user («explanation component») as well as interfaces that allow a dialog to take place between the user and the program («dialog component»).[50] One of the essential components is an inference engine, which infers the legal consequences («inference engine», «problem-solving component») from the set of Rules. If programmed, it also enable the system to learn further knowledge independently.[51] The structure is visualized classically as follows:

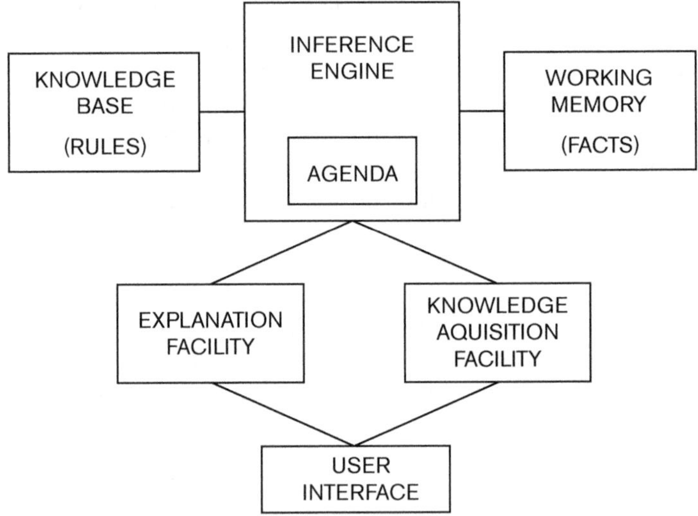

Exhibit 3: Schematic structure of classical (rule-based) expert systems [Source: Herbert Fiedler, Orientierung über juristische Expertensysteme, CR (1987) at 325].

49 Overview by Jandach, *supra* note 24 and Herbert Fiedler & Roland Traunmüller, *Formalisierung im Recht und Ansätze juristischer Expertensysteme*, 21 Working Papers Rechtsinformatik (1986) on classical expert legal systems.

50 Herbert Fiedler, *Orientierung über juristische Expertensysteme*, CR (1987) at 325.

51 *Id.*

By using powerful inference engines, classical expert systems were able to provide a self-learning and flexible decision support comparable to machine learning, which within their domain were even superior to neural networks or possibilities of so-called fuzzy logic due to their hybrid character.[52]

However, their scope of application was small—and hardly any system reached market-readiness.[53] In contrast to decision automation, expert systems tried to capture and automate all the relevant knowledge and logic of a particular domain—eliminating the human factor altogether. It has proven almost impossible to encapsulate and automate a whole knowledge domain. Modern decision automation focuses on standardised and well-contained problems that allow for automation with human interaction.

G. Machine Learning

In contrast to (rule-based) automations, machine learning (in short ML, also commonly referred to as AI[54]) uses an opposite approach. In contrast to rule-based methods, machine learning uses statistical probability models rather than deterministic rules. The basic functioning of a machine learning process assumes that certain outputs (*will it rain tomorrow?*) can be described by a combination of input variables (also called «features») and other parameters (e.g., temperature, humidity etc.).

Machine learning (usually based on neural or Bayesian networks) does not learn «independently» (autonomously) but must be trained on historical data. Through the training, the ML algorithm should independently derive (deduce) rules from the feature data. The resulting model is derived from the data itself and not from externally provided, explicitly formulated information (rules). The ML algorithm therefore tries to draw the right conclusions from the historical data in order to make predictions for the future. The better the model (ML algorithm) is trained, the better the prediction of the results.[55]

Self-learning systems require a sufficient amount of high-quality data.[56] Machine learning also requires the annotation of the data records with data describing contents. For a ML algorithm to distinguish between cat and dog

---

52 Nikolaus Petry, *Fuzzy Logik und neuronale Netze*, 1–54 JurPC Web-Doc. 187/1999 (Mar. 4, 2003), http://www.jurpc.de/aufsatz/19990187.htm (last visited Feb. 2, 2019).

53 *See* details below.

54 Technically speaking, machine learning is merely a technique that is summarized under the generic term AI.

55 Yangqing Jia et al., *Caffe: Convolutional architecture for fast feature embedding*, Proceedings of the 22nd ACM International Conference on Multimedia 675 (2014).

56 Geoffrey Hinton & Ruslan Salakhutdinov, *Reducing the Dimensionality of Data with Neural Networks*, Science 504–507 (2006).

pictures, it does not only require a large number of training pictures of both kinds, but an annotation of the pictures after animal kind. Only in this way can the mathematical model in the form of a network derive which image properties can be assigned to the respective animal work.[57]

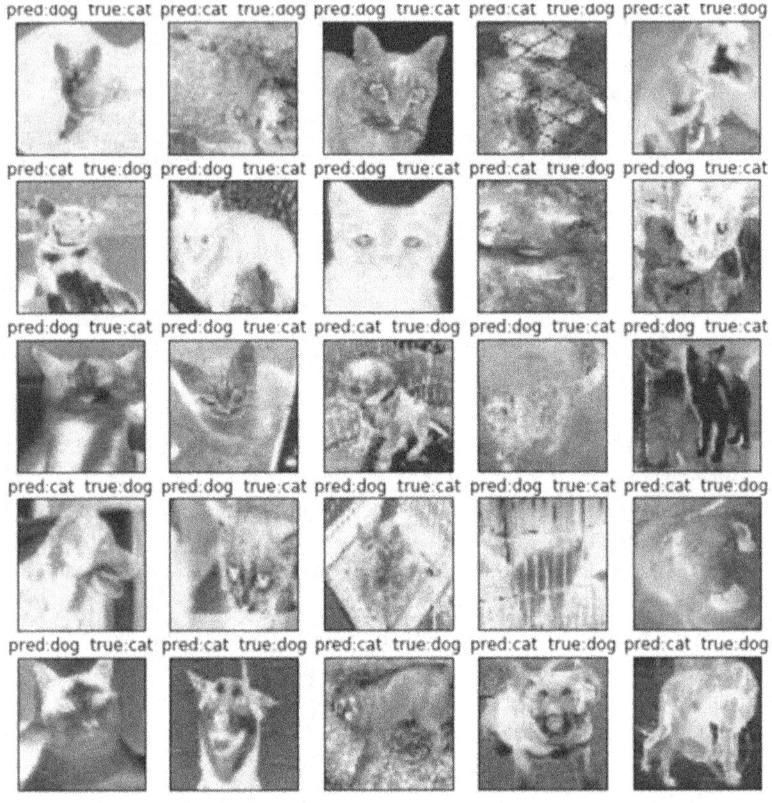

Exhibit 4: Cats and dogs as probably seen today from an AI perspective. Still a blurry picture but the fog is starting to clear [Source: Sandipan Day, Dogs vs. Cats (2017)].

By means of several training cycles and data sets, the ML algorithm is increasingly able to align the image content with the statements of the models. The mathematical models generated by the network through constant corrective revision are increasingly approaching a desired accuracy value through more or better training data or manual corrections during the training process.

57 *See* further pictures/examples *in* Sandipan Day, *Dogs vs. Cats*, DATA SCIENCE CENTRAL (Aug. 14, 2017), https://www.datasciencecentral.com/profiles/blogs/dogs-vs-cats-image-classification-with-deep-learning-using (last visited Feb. 3, 2019).

IV. Automating the Law

A. Legal Automation Today: Between Hopes and Hoops

Times have changed significantly. Automations can be used in the legal sector in very different areas. Legal automation could be defined as the design, management, execution, and automation of repetitive legal tasks, workflows and processes. The core idea of legal automation is to transfer recurring tasks into a technology-based repeatable process. In the area of non-legal administrative processes, BPA, workflow automation and RPA (rather subordinate) can be used. For example, the client receipt process, scheduling or invoicing can be automated.

Legal automation is possible in almost all legal areas. Some areas of law are more prone to automation than others. Areas of law with a high vicinity to automation are those with

- clearly defined (legal) rules and processes
- with a not too complex scenario or logic
- questions and problems often recurring
- low levels of required fact finding

For legal advice automation has played a subordinate role thus far.[58] For legal work, the focus is on the automation of complex decision-making processes. Historically, the field of document automation has emerged as the first subset of decision automation. The «document» (in the legal context this refers to the MS Word document) is traditionally the core product of legal practice and has been compiled after extensive consideration. Therefore, it was obvious to be the first to automate this area. Document automation means that documents are assembled from ready-made text modules according to a certain rule-based logic. Many other areas of decision automation are currently emerging, which are described below and in the larger context of this issue.

By automating legal work significant improvements can be made in:

- Efficiency
- Productivity
- Accuracy
- Audibility
- Job Satisfaction

58 Michael Grupp, *Legal Tech – Impulse für Streitbeilegung und. Rechtsdienstleistung*, AnwBl 660 (2014); Michael Grupp & Bernhard Fiedler, *Legal Technologies: Digitalisierungsstrategien für Rechtsabteilungen und Wirtschaftskanzleien*, Der Betrieb 1071 (2017).

Machine learning methods are not applicable in the field of process automation, since automation must take place in clearly comprehensible and repeatable steps and not in probabilities. Therefore, machine learning approaches can only support or enrich a rule-based framework (hybrid approach). For some areas of legal activities, however, ML-based tools can be used that lead to sufficiently precise results, especially if there is sufficient data and formalizable content. This is the case, for example, with contract analyses with a numerical focus, e.g., in real estate law. But machine learning also plays a role in forensic areas, for example in (economic) criminal investigations.

However, even here, it is no longer possible to manually check the completeness or correctness of the results, which are only a fraction of the size of the original part. In any case, the deployment was legitimized for the area of criminal law in the USA in initial decisions.[59] In the United Kingdom, the use of predictive coding was also permitted in two decisions, in 2016 and by the Highest Court in 2018.[60]

B. Machine Learning for Lawyers: What to Automate?

The lack of adaptation of statistical, self-learning systems in the legal field is often due to inadequate technological feasibility. In contrast to rule-based decision systems, which are relatively easy to develop, the development of machine learning systems has not been successful despite some interesting niches. This is due to a number of reasons:

First, there is a lack of clearly formalised data with legal content. Legal content often cannot be easily translated into clear, objective value schemes, which then become the basis for formalisation. For example, the vendor-friendliness characteristic of a sales contract cannot be classified as a numerical degree.

Corresponding attempts to create clear, formalized legal terms have been made at the international level, for example by the projects of the RuleML community,[61] partly with the Legal *Legal Knowledge Interchange Format LKIF,* but have so far been limited to standard terms only.[62]

---

59 Southern District Court of NY, Moore v. Publicis, Beschl. v. 25.04.2012, 11 Civ. 1279 (ALC) (AJP).

60 Notice of the BLP Plenipotentiaries, available via: Artificial Lawyer, *Law Firm BLP Claims Landmark Predictive Coding 1st in English Courts,* Artificial Lawyer (Mar. 12, 2018), https://www.artificiallawyer.com/2018/03/12/law-firm-blp-claims-landmark-predictive-coding-1st-in-english-courts/ (last visited Feb. 4, 2019).

61 Available at www.legalxml.org.

62 European Project for Standardised Transparent Representations in order to Extend Legal Accessibility, available at www.estrellaproject.org.

Secondly, the semantic complexity of the legal content prevents computer-understandable modelling, and consequently the automatic subsumption.

> *«While there are functions of AI that are very well-suited to replacing many of the more defined tasks, legal practice requires advanced cognitive abilities and problem-solving skills in environments of legal and factual uncertainty.»*
> *– Dr. Xuning Tang, Chief Data Scientist, Vista Analytics*

Machine learning requires numerical and thus clearly formalised input. However, legal content requires semantic comprehension which cannot be formalised easily (sometimes it is not possible at all). Machine learning is satisfied with data, i.e., objective and formalized information, and gets by with simple data syntax. Legal thinking usually does not take place on a syntactic level, but on a semantic level.

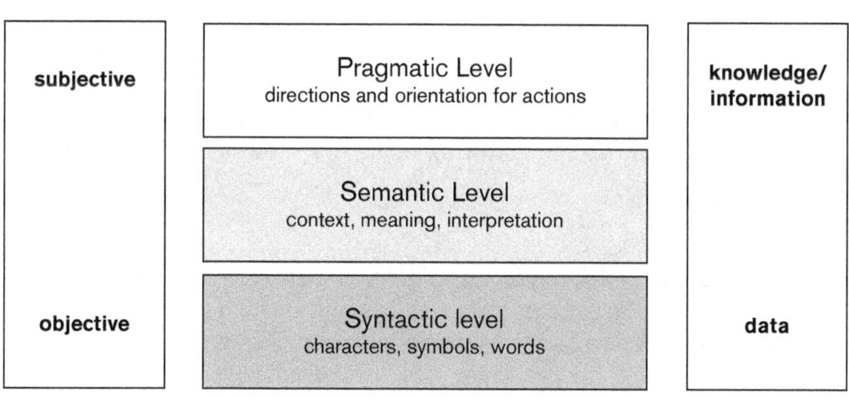

Exhibit 5: Levels of Legal Thinking.

Context and interpretation of terms play a role and leave a lot of room for subjective considerations. Further, aspects of the semantic level that are relevant for the legal evaluation are contextual developments and the understanding of implicit contents. This also includes hierarchies and content structures that are currently not comprehensible to machines without detailed instructions. The main difficulty is the insufficient formation of ontologies in the legal field. Only apparently can normative structures be transformed into a knowledge structure comparable to an ontology. However, this is necessary for error-free interpretation by artificial systems.

The techniques of machine learning are often unsuitable for legal applications because of their lack of transparency: A neural network can often provide no explanation for derivation of results and can only provide a mathematical analysis of the evaluation process.[63]

C. Challenges for Feasible Automation Applications

The challenge of legal automation today is not such much the technology but how to deliver an automated legal product on a digital marketplace.

As soon as legal services are released from the (regulated) protection zone of personal and analogue service provision and offered on the market as a digital product, they have to compete in the digital arena. The digital marketplace obeys its own rules without taking the legal industry into account. It is not enough to simply automate a legal process or content. A successful legal automation requires to have a realistic and holistic understanding of the digital playground that automated legal services will enter into.

One challenge is to meet the «digital demands» of modern users. This requires a «new» way of thinking in comparison to the traditional application and delivery form of legal services. The path might be especially long in the legal industry, considering that in many countries there are still regulations in place that limit marketing efforts. And automated products might collide with the self-image of lawyers. Legal work ought not to be sold on the digital bazaar.

1. Bundled Access

Another challenge is that the access to digital products tends to bundle or monopolise strongly. The successful establishment of digital products presupposes that these can be found by potential users. This is anything but easy. Digital products must appear on the radar of potential users. The radar of the digital user is extremely narrowed.

Access to digital products is mainly via a few search engines and platforms (Facebook, Amazon, etc.). Due to search and behaviour patterns, the search concentrates on a few contact points. For example, 90% of successful search queries are found on the first Google search page, 70% on the top five positions.[64] Almost all organic search queries are from one provider—Google.[65] Active advertising of content is possible, but very expensive and costly. Legal digital products must, therefore, find ways to stand out from the mass of digital products.

---

63 Bohrer, *supra* note 22, at 20 et seq.

64 Jeff Bullas, *10 Facts Reveal The Importance of Ranking High In Google*, https://www.jeffbullas.com/10-facts-reveal-the-importance-of-ranking-high-in-google/ (last visited Feb. 1, 2019).

65 GlobalStats, *Search Engine Market Share Worldwide Jan 2018–Jan 2019*, http://gs.statcounter.com/search-engine-market-share (last visited Feb. 2, 2019).

2. Convenience vs Content

The automation of legal content can only be successful if it takes the behaviour of the average consumer into account and takes it seriously. For the digital user, convenience, i.e., user-friendliness, is a central qualitative factor in the use of digital services. While the rather quantitative evaluation standard «content is king» applies to legal content, the average consumer wants a product that is as low-threshold, easy to understand, graphically appealing, easy to use, and as quick to consume as possible. The digital user makes it easy for himself.

Reading time is somehow the tipping point between the two concepts: while good legal content requires a long reading time, the modern, average user increasingly wants to read less. On average, Internet users spend only a few minutes on a homepage or in an app to consume content.[66] Only those who adapt to this user behaviour can be successful with a digital solution.

3. Automation is for the Volume Market

Digitization and automation aim for volume. If you want to benefit from the advantages of automation, you have to be prepared for the inherent conditions: Through automation, bespoke services loses importance—in favour of mass processing.

Mass processing cannot and does not need to be perfect. An off-the-shelf product does not claim to be the best product. The tailor-made suit is a better product than the off-the-shelf suit. A mass-produced suit will not perfectly fit. It comes in certain sizes and grids. The carrier (=user) has to be satisfied with what he or she finds on the shelf. The same applies to all products manufactured in mass processing. The decisive factor is that the average user accepts less quality, as the products are much cheaper and easier to obtain. There are cases where a tailor-made suit is desired. However, custom-made products are the (expensive) exception.

The fact that the user is satisfied with (automated) legal off-the-shelf products is difficult for many lawyers to accept. The legal activity has a different self-image. It strives for individualised, tailor-made advice; the client receives individualised legal advice after a thorough examination of all facts and legal facets—ideally in personal contact. The aim is to present the best legal assessment in terms of quality and illuminating all eventualities and to help the client to obtain justice in the existing (state) structures.

---

66 eMarketer, *Consumers Spent Less Time With Publisher Articles* (Jan. 29, 2018), https://www.emarketer.com/content/consumer-time-spent-on-publisher-sites-fell-in-2017 (last visited Feb. 3, 2019) and statista, *Most popular mobile social networking apps in the United States as of July 2018, by average session duration (in minutes)*, https://www.statista.com/statistics/579411/top-us-social-networking-apps-ranked-by-session-length/ (last visited Feb. 3, 2019).

There have been hardly any off-the-shelf products in the legal market so far. Efficiency and products suitable for mass production—and thus also the topic of automation—were not the focus of attention. Our thesis is that legal bar products—as in the clothing industry, for example—will assert themselves, even if the quality of the result cannot compete with tailor-made advice.

In principle, the only thing that counts for the customer is «getting the right answer». As soon as standardised and automated solutions are offered on the market, customers will decide in particular on the basis of the following three criteria whether they prefer a tailor-made or an automated (standardised) solution:[67]

- Convenience, i.e., user-friendliness
- price
- Trailability, i.e., possibility to try out the offer without obligation
- Speed of service provision

If an automated legal service in these three areas performs significantly better than a manual, tailor-made solution, customers will opt for it—regardless of whether the result is as high-quality as an individual solution.

Lawyers need to adapt to this level of «quality» and design to compete with cheaper digital products. The process also makes it possible to identify automation potentials in the provision of services. Lawyers often have a wrong understanding of automation. An automated legal advice is often equated with a fully automated one. A complete automation is not possible, advisable, or necessary in many areas. As in other industries, however, automation makes sense when parts of an activity or product are highly standarized. To stick with the example of the suit: Here the cutting was first automated, then the sorting, then the assembling of the parts, then the sewing together, etc. Automation therefore means shifting different automation potentials in production stages. If advantages in price can already be created through partial automation, it is irrelevant if smaller or larger parts are still produced by hand. Automation, therefore, begins in the small and where it is easily possible.

Automation does not only concern the area of substantive law finding, i.e., the area of substantive legal decision making, but the whole process of service provision from the initial search for the service to payment. The digital user is increasingly accustomed to being guided in an overall process and to carry out all necessary steps in a standardized manner. At Amazon, the customer receives automation of the entire purchasing process. The legal industry

---

67 Chuang-Chun Liu et al., *Physical or Digital? Factors drive consumers to purchase digital music (2008),* https://pdfs.semanticscholar.org/6e6c/1602afd083700a0eb8cbcb6926000e37c77c.pdf (last visited Feb. 1, 2019).

must think in the same direction. For those seeking legal advice, it would often be a great advantage if the appointment could be made online or the legal advice could be provided via an online video call. Automation therefore means a comprehensive but step-by-step automation of the material but also formal (process-technical) aspects of service provision.

This process of the total automation of «shopping worlds» is complex and requires substantial and continuous investments. The example of Amazon shows an interesting effect that could be described as the exponential concentration effect of automated service delivery. The more users use an offer, the more providers can invest in «convenience» and increasing automation. The better the offer, the more it will be used. The result is a «virtous circle», which leads to the fact that (also in connection with the searchability on the Internet) offers are concentrated on a few providers. Only a few suppliers will gain substantial market shares. This effect can be observed in all areas of software and online solutions.

As a result, it can be said that automation solutions will be particularly successful if—compared to individual solutions—they are cheaper, more user-friendly, faster, and easier to try out. In many cases, users will opt for legal off-the-peg products. Qualitative considerations will not deter them. The user-friendliness and experience of the customer, and thus the assessment criteria according to which he decides between a tailor-made and a standardised solution, are the entire service provision process and not the purely substantive process of finding a law. The entire process is automated in steps. Successful overall processes will be able to concentrate a high number of users on themselves.

V. Summary

Legal automation is still in its infancy, but the stage is set for exponential growth. While the technological foundation has been laid in the 1980s, it is only now that the technological eco-system is sufficiently developed to expedite future adoption and implementation. Law firms and corporate legal departments have begun to automate simple, recurring and—increasingly also more complex cognitive processes. New tools will facilitate a wide-spread use and implementation. The field of decision automation yields early and promising results. An increased automation will foster a data-driven approach to law. The more legal processes are automated, the more structured data is available for analytics or machine learning. Automation provides the foundation for a data-driven approach. This is another reason why it is quintessential for the legal industry to kick-start its automation efforts. The article has shown, it's not that much about the technology itself. It has been available for more than 30 years. Easy-to-use automation tools and a new attitude towards automation will be essential for the future development of the legal industry.

VI. Bibliography

A. Hard Copy Sources

Aguirre, Santiago & Rodriguez, Alejandro, *Automation of a Business Process Using Robotic Process Automation (RPA): A Case Study*, Workshop on Engineering Applications (2017).

Alvey, John, *The problems of designing a medical expert system*, 83 Proceedings of Expert Systems, Churchill College (Cambridge 1983).

Bohrer, Arndt, *Development of an Internet-based expert system to examine the scope of copyright agreements* (Dissertation, 2003).

Breidenbach, Stephan & Glatz, Florian, Legal Tech (C. H. Beck, 2017).

Bund, Elmar, Einführung in die Rechtsinformatik (Springer, 1991).

Davenport, Thomas & Harris, Jeanne, *Automated Decision Making Comes of Age*, 46 MIT Sloan Management Review 4 et seq. (2005).

Decker, Gero et al., *The Business Process Modelling Notation*, in: Modern Business Process Automation: YAWL and its Support Environment (ter Hofstede, Arthur H M, van der Aalst, Wil M P, Adams, Michael & Russell, Nick, eds., 2010).

Fiedler, Herbert, *Automatisierung im Recht und juristische* Informatik, JuS 228 et seq. (1971).

Fiedler, Herbert & Traunmüller, Roland, *Formalisierung im Recht und Ansätze juristischer Expertensysteme*, 21 Working Papers Rechtsinformatik (1986).

Fiedler, Herbert, *Orientierung über juristische Expertensysteme*, CR (1987).

Fresht, Phil & Slaby, James R, *Robotic Automation Emerges as a Threat To Traditional Low-Cost Outsourcing*, HfS Research 1 et seq. (2012).

Görz, Günther ed., Einführung in die Künstliche Intelligenz (2nd ed., Oldenbourg Wissenschaftsverlag, 1995).

Gräwe, Svenja L, Die Entstehung der Rechtsinformatik (Verlag Dr. Kovac, 2011).

Grupp, Michael, *Legal Tech – Impulse für Streitbeilegung und Rechtsdienstleistung*, AnwBl 480 et seq. (2014).

Grupp, Michael & Fiedler, Bernhard, *Legal Technologies: Digitalisierungsstrategien für Rechtsabteilungen und Wirtschaftskanzleien*, Der Betrieb 1071 et seq. (2017).

Haft, Fritjof & Lehmann, Hein, The LEX Projekt. Entwicklung eines jurstischen Expertensystems (Attempo Verlag, 1989).

Haft, Fritjof, *Computer-aided decision making, in:* Informatik in Recht und Verwaltung – Entwicklung, Stand, Perspektiven, Festschrift für Herbert Fiedler zur Emeritierung 95–119 (Lenk, Klaus, Reinermann, Heinrich & Traunmüller, Roland, eds., 1997).

Halbleib, Gernot, *Der Weg zur Legal Tech Strategie*, 31 et seq., *in:* Legal Tech – die Digitalisierung des Rechtsmarktes (Hartung, Markus, Bues, Micha-Manuel, Halbleib, Gernot, eds., 2017/2018).

Hartung, Markus, Bues, Micha-Manuel & Halbleib, Gernot, Legal Tech – die Digitalisierung des Rechtsmarktes (C. H. Beck, 2017/2018).

Herberger, Maximilian, *Arbeitskreis «Entscheidungsunterstützungssysteme»*, 3 JurPc 121 (1996).

Hinton, Geoffrey & Salakhutdinov, Ruslan, *Reducing the Dimensionality of Data with Neural Networks*, Science 504–507 (2006).

Jandach, Thomas, Juristische Expertensysteme. Methodische Grundlagen ihrer Entwicklung (Springer, 1993).

Jia, Yangqing, et al, *Caffe: Convolutional architecture for fast feature embedding—Proceedings of the 22nd ACM international conference on Multimedia* (2014).

Klug, Ulrich, Juristische Logik (Springer, 1951).

Konzelmann, Alexander, *Tagungsbericht Internationales Rechtsinformatik Symposion Salzburg (IRIS)*, 110 JurPC § 36 (2003).

Kowalewski, Detlef L, Schneeberger, Josef & Wiefel, Susanne, *KOKON-3: A prototypical system for knowledge-based contract configuration*, 223 Informatik-Fachberichte (1989) 79.

Lacity, Mary, Willcocks, Leslie & Craig, Andrew, *Robotic Process Automation at Telefónica O2*, The Outsourcing Unit Working Research Paper Series 21 (2015).

Lacity, Mary, Willcocks, Leslie & Craig, Andrew, *Robotizing Global Financial Shared Services at Royal DSM,* The Outsourcing Unit Working Research Paper Series 122 (2016).

Love, Jonathan, Process Automation Handbook: A Guide to Theory and Practice (Springer, 2007).

McCarthy, L Throne, *TAXMAN for the review of tax rules in M&A, An Experiment in Artificial Intelligence and Legal Reasoning*, 90 Harvard Law Review 837 et seq. (1977).

Nilsson, Nils J, Principles of Artificial Intelligence (Morgan Kaufmann, 1982).

Nof, Shimon, Springer Handbook of Automation (Springer, 2009).

Nunamaker, Jay, Applegate, Lynda & Konsynski, Benn, *Computer-Aided Deliberation: Model Management and Group Decision Support*, 36 Operations Research 826 (1988).

O'Keefe, Robert & McEachern, Tim, *Web-based customer decision support systems*, 41 Communications of the ACM archive 73 (1998).

Penttinen, Esko, Kasslin, Henje & Asatiani, Aleksandre, *Choice between lightweight and heavyweight IT*, Twenty-Sixth European Conference on Information Systems (2018).

Power, Daniel J, Decision Support Systems: Concepts and Resources for Managers (Greenwood Publishing Group, 2002).

Traunmüller, Roland, *Rechtsinformatik auf dem Weg ins nächste Jahrtausend, in* Informatik in Recht und Verwaltung – Entwicklung, Stand, Perspektiven, Festschrift für Herbert Fiedler zur Emeritierung (Lenk, Klaus, Reinermann, Heinrich & Traunmüller, Roland eds., 1997) 3 et seq.

Traunmüller, Roland & Wimmer, Maria A eds., Informatik in Recht und Verwaltung: gestern – heute – morgen. Ehrenband Prof. Dr.Dr. Herbert Fiedler zum Achtzigsten Geburtstag (Köllen Verlag, 2009).

Wachsmuth, Ipke, *Expertensysteme, Planen und Problemlösen, in*: Einführung in die Künstliche Intelligenz 713 et seq. (Görz, Günther, ed., Oldenbourg Wissenschaftsverlag, 2nd ed. 1995).

B. Online Sources

Artificial Lawyer, *Law Firm BLP Claims Landmark Predictive Coding 1st in English Courts,* Artificial Lawyer (Mar. 12, 2018), https://www.artificiallawyer.com/2018/03/12/law-firm-blp-claims-landmark-predictive-coding-1st-in-english-courts/ (last visited Feb. 4, 2019).

Berruti, Federico, Nixon, Graeme, Taglioni, Giambattista & Whiteman, Rob, *Intelligent process automation: The engine at the core of the next-generation operating model*, McKinsey Study (2017), https://www.mckinsey.com/business-functions/digital-mckinsey/our-insights/intelligent-process-automation-the-engine-at-the-core-of-the-next-generation-operating-model?reload (last visited Apr. 12, 2019).

Bullas, Jeff, *10 Facts Reveal The Importance of Ranking High In Google*, https://www.jeffbullas.com/10-facts-reveal-the-importance-of-ranking-high-in-google/ (last visited Feb. 1, 2019).

Day, Sandipan, *Dogs vs. Cats*, DATA SCIENCE CENTRAL (Aug. 14, 2017), https://www.datasciencecentral.com/profiles/blogs/dogs-vs-cats-image-classification-with-deep-learning-using (last visited Feb. 3, 2019).

eMarketer, *Consumers Spent Less Time With Publisher Articles* (Jan. 29, 2018), https://www.emarketer.com/content/consumer-time-spent-on-publisher-sites-fell-in-2017 (last visited Feb. 3, 2019).

GlobalStats, *Search Engine Market Share Worldwide Jan 2018–Jan 2019*, http://gs.statcounter.com/search-engine-market-share (last visited Feb. 2, 2019).

Hoekstra, Rinke, *The Knowledge Reengineering Bottleneck*, SEMANTIC WEB JOURNAL (2010), http://www.semantic-web-journal.net/sites/default/files/swj32.pdf (last visited Feb. 2, 2019).

Liu, Chuang-Chun et al., *Physical or Digital? Factors drive consumers to purchase digital music* (2008), https://pdfs.semanticscholar.org/6e6c/1602afd083700a0eb8cbcb6926000e37c77c.pdf (last visited Feb. 1, 2019).

Petry, Nikolaus, *Fuzzy Logik und neuronale Netze*, 1–54 JurPC Web-Dok. 187/1999 (Mar. 4, 2003), http://www.jurpc.de/aufsatz/19990187.htm (last visited Feb. 2, 2019).

Statista, *Most popular mobile social networking apps in the United States as of July 2018, by average session duration (in minutes),* https://www.statista.com/statistics/579411/top-us-social-networking-apps-ranked-by-session-length/ (last visited Feb. 3, 2019).

Tromans, Richard, *Law Firms are Inefficiency Factories, Automation is the Cure,* ARTIFICIALLAWYER (Jun. 11, 2018), https://www.artificiallawyer.com/2018/06/11/law-firms-are-inefficiency-factories-automation-is-the-cure/ (last visited Jan. 12, 2019).

Voß, Oliver, *Will lawyers become obsolete?,* WIRTSCHAFTSWOCHE (Mar. 24, 2017), https://www.wiwo.de/erfolg/gruender/legal-tech-werden-anwaelte-obsolet/19523172.html (last visited Jan. 3, 2019).

C. Case Law

Southern District Court of NY, Moore v. Publicis, Beschl. v. 25.04.2012, 11 Civ. 1279 (ALC) (AJP).

Karl J Paadam and Priit Martinson

e-Government & e-Justice: Digitizations of Registers, IDs and Justice Procedures

The Estonia Example

TABLE OF CONTENTS

Across the world, the modern state is experiencing a substantial transformation. In a connected society, how people want to deal with the government is changing, driven by evolving technology. Both at home and work, we are used to communicating online, ordering services, purchasing goods and sending out formal requests without having to leave the room or meet the other party face-to-face. More and more, people expect the same from governments. How come in a world with virtual assistants and self-driving cars, even the most basic interactions with the public sector still cannot be carried out online in many developed countries? Even in the Silicon Valley that is otherwise obsessed with disruption, the interaction with the public sector is of old-school.

However, there is a post-Soviet country in Northern Europe where the way a state engages with its citizens is diferent—Estonia. Virtually all state-related operations except marriage, divorce, and real estate transactions can be carried out digitally. Its e-government is so unique that Wired Magazine called it the most advanced digital society in the world[1] and *Barack Obama* had been quoted saying: «I should have called the Estonians when we were setting up our health care website.»[2]

The Estonians take it for granted that filing a tax return takes less than five minutes and all patients have electronic medical records. Both, selling a car and establishing a company can be carried out online. The standard services that government is involved with—legislation, justice, voting, education, banking, taxes, and so on—have been digitally connected across one platform, wiring up the nation. The Estonian government estimates that its e-governance ecosystem enabled by digital signatures saves the country the equivalent of 2% of GDP annually.

An American scientist *Carl Sagan* has famously said: «If you want to make an apple pie from scratch, you must first invent the universe.»[3] Estonia, after regaining its independence in 1991, began building its digital society through an e-governance system to provide public services online in 1997. Estonia never had a central office for digital transformation but thrived upon agile digital agendas of ministries and government agencies.

According to OECD, the term e-government focuses on the use of new information and communication technologies (ICTs) by governments as ap-

---

1 Ben Hammersley, *Concerned about Brexit? Why not become an e-resident of Estonia*, Wired (Mar. 27, 2017), https://www.wired.co.uk/article/estonia-e-resident (last visited Dec. 30, 2018).

2 Ben Wolfgang, *Obama: «Should've called the Estonians» to help with Obamacare website*, The Washington Times (Sep. 3, 2014), https://www.washingtontimes.com/news/2014/sep/3/obama-shouldve-called-estonians-help-obamacare-web/ (last visited Dec. 28, 2018).

3 Carl Sagan, *If you wish to make an apple pie from scratch, you must first invent the universe*, YouTube, https://www.youtube.com/watch?v=7s664NsLeFM (last visited Dec. 30, 2018).

plied to the full range of government functions.[4] The European Commission defines e-government as «the use of ICTs in public administrations combined with organizational change and new skills in order *to improve public services and democratic processes and strengthen support to public policies*.»[5]

There is a hope in many countries that ICTs will increase the degree of interest and involvement of citizens in politics and thus act as an aid to representative democracy.[6]

A common error is that e-governance is mainly about computer software and hardware. Instead, moving from analogue to digital is not only about technology. Public services have to be re-invented which requires new strategy, policy and legislation. Both, the mindset of the officials and citizens has to change. This involves challenging long-held assumptions and having to rethink processes and products with a goal to make public services more efficient and user-friendly.

Countries need to set a clear digital strategy, enable electronic identification, digital signatures and data interoperability and constantly analyse and review the legislation to remove obstacles to digitization. The performance of e-Government is most clearly revealed in terms of the working time the citizens and officials save, that would otherwise be spent on bureaucracy and document handling. It also increases citizen engagement.

A global transformation towards digital society and e-government demands new skills and a fresh mindset from all market participants. For lawyers, it is a brand new era whether they would be designing national legislation for countries looking to digitize their services, or representing their clients in dispute resolution and court proceedings. In societies where technology has become part of everyday lives, interdisciplinary skills are of utmost importance. Estonia's case study shows that for e-government initiatives to develop even further, significant support is needed from the private sector including legal professionals, computer scientists and management consultants.

---

4 California Department of Technology, *eGovernment (eGov) Reference Architecture (RA)*, (Jan. 2014), https://cdt.ca.gov/services/wp-content/uploads/sites/2/sites/2/2017/04/EA-eGovernment-eGov-V2.pdf (last visited Dec. 30, 2018).

5 Elisabetta Raguseo & Enrico Ferro, *E-Government & Organizational Change: Towards and Extended Governance Model*, Researchgate (2011), https://www.researchgate.net/publication/256979622_E-Government_Organizational_Change_Towards_and_Extended_Governance_Model (last visited Dec. 30, 2018).

6 Lourdes Torres, Vicente Pina et al., *E-government and the transformation of public administrations in EU countries: Beyond NPM or just a second wave of reforms?* (Jan., 2005), http://www.dteconz.unizar.es/DT2005-01.pdf (last visited Dec. 30, 2018).

I. e-Government Enablers

A. e-Government Strategy and Legal Framework

The legislation that regulates government and its operations also concerns e-government. The development of the e-government requires binding legal force to ensure the legitimacy and credibility of the e-government policies implemented. In some countries, the ability of governments to adapt existing laws or issue new laws involves a lengthy procedure of debate. It is essential to engage legal experts early in the planning process to avoid regulatory obstacles and enable smooth digitization of government services. According to research by *Kiškis and Petraukas*, legal framework initiatives for e-Governance has followed several different paths, which may be merged into two parallel approaches[7]:

The first is the development of separate laws and regulations covering individual questions regarding e-Government. Issues addressed within such separate regulations include various user groups with different service needs and interaction requirements, distinct government processes etc.

The second is a holistic framework, which could identify and address all relevant issues impacting e-Government development under a single principal law or regulation. This approach may notably be applied to cross-border issues and challenges common within any e-government implementation environment.[8]

Legal system changes should be seen as typical elements of e-Government, similar to the conditions of organizational change. A survey from 2009 among lawyers in Norwegian Government administration showed that 55.1% of the respondents disagreed with a statement saying legal questions related to government use of ICT received sufficient attention. Only 11.4 % agreed. The survey also found that majority of the respondents confirmed a high number of unsolved basic legal questions within e-Government.[9]

The Estonian government was one of the first movers in developing an e-government strategy. In 1998, the government adopted the Principles of the Estonian Information Policy and the Information Policy Action Plan. These

---

7 Mindaugas Kiškis & Rimantas Petrauskas, *e-Governance: Two Views on Legal Environment*, *in* PROCEEDINGS OF THE SECOND INTERNATIONAL CONFERENCE ON ELECTRONIC GOVERNMENT (EGOV 2003) (Traunmüller Roland ed., Springer, 2003), https://doi.org/10.1007/10929179_73 (last visited Dec. 30, 2018).

8 Kiškis & Petrauskas, *supra* note 7.

9 Dag Wiese Schartum, *Developing E-government Systems—Legal, Technological and Organizational Aspects*, SCANDINAVIAN STUDIES IN LAW (2015), http://www.scandinavianlaw.se/pdf/56-6.pdf (last visited Dec. 30, 2018).

policy documents formed the foundation for effective policy-making decisions and set up ongoing action plans designed to create a momentum in the advancement of Information Society projects.[10] Estonia does not have specific e-governance legislation, but several legal acts are fundamental to e-governance. The Estonian e-government ecosystem is governed by legal norms that provide a structure for usage, security and protection of the personal data stored within Population Register and other associated government data registers. Collectively, these norms regulate the process by which organizations, individuals and companies can request and receive access to information stored in government databases and thereby build new public e-services by using the information already stored in state's databases.[11] Estonia's Public Information Act prohibits government bodies from asking Estonian citizens and businesses for information they have already provided to other parts of the government (the «Once-Only» principle). When personal information, such as the marital status or address changes, the change only needs to be entered into the system once, thus saving citizens the time and effort that would otherwise be required. According to *Vassil*, the following legal norms are most relevant regarding Estonian e-governance and collectively provide the foundation for the entire range of data protection, application development and security issues in the field of e-governance:[12]

Personal Data Protection Act: The Act aims to protect the fundamental rights and freedoms of natural persons upon processing of personal data. The Act provides: 1) the conditions and procedure for processing of personal data; 2) the procedure for the exercise of state supervision upon processing of personal data; and, 3) liability for the violation of the requirements for processing of personal data.[13]

Public Information Act: The Act covers national and local government agencies and other legal entities that are responsible for the delivery of public services in areas such as health care and education. The purpose of the Act is to guarantee that every person has the opportunity to access information des-

10 Colin Combe et al., *E-Government in Estonia: Development and Best Practice Background Paper*, World Bank (Aug. 2006), www.siteresources.worldbank.org/INTSLOVAKIA/Resources/eGovernmentEstonia.doc (last visited Dec. 30, 2018).

11 Kristjan Vassil, *Estonian e-Government Ecosystem: Foundation, Applications, Outcomes. Background Paper, Digital Dividends, World Development Report*, World Bank (Jun., 2015), http://pubdocs.worldbank.org/en/165711456838073531/WDR16-BP-Estonian-eGov-ecosystem-Vassil.pdf (last visited Dec. 30, 2018).

12 Vassil, *supra* note 11.

13 Personal Data Protection Act, RT I 2007, 24, 127,https://www.riigiteataja.ee/en/eli/ee/512112013011/consolide/current.

ignated for public use, based on the principles of democracy, the rule of law and open society, and to enable monitoring the performance of public duties.[14]

Population Register Act: The Act sets out the principles for the unique personal identification code. The ID code is a crucial element of the electronic authentication process and is obligatory for everyone living and working in Estonia. This Act provides for the formation and processing of data in the population register and exercise of supervision over the maintenance of the register.[15]

Digital Signatures Act: The Act grants the same legal status to both digital and handwritten signatures and stipulates the requirement for all public sector institutions to accept digitally signed documents. The Act provides the conditions necessary for using digital signatures and digital seals, and the procedure for supervising the provision of certification services and time-stamping services. It is superseded by the EU regulation No 910/2014 on electronic transactions in the European internal market (eIDAS).[16]

Electronic Communications Act: The purpose of this Act is to 1) create the necessary conditions for the development of electronic communications: 2) promote the development of electronic communications networks without giving preference to specific technologies: and, 3) to ensure the protection of the interests of users of electronic communications services.[17]

B. Personal Identification Code

Personal Identification Code (ID-code) is another enabler of e-government. It is a unique number, created on the basis of the sex and date of birth of a person, which allows the specific identification of the person. It is granted to all Estonian citizens by birth when the birth certificate is entered in the population register. ID-Code is used as a primary key in the majority of databases holding personal information.[18]

Without a unique ID-code, the state could not identify its citizens online with 100% certainty as it is common for more than one person to carry the

14 Public Information Act, RT I 2000, 92, 597, https://www.riigiteataja.ee/en/eli/ee/514112013001/consolide/current (last visited Dec. 30, 2018).

15 Population Register Act, RT I 17.11.2017, https://www.riigiteataja.ee/en/eli/ee/Riigikogu/act/522032019005/consolide (last visited Dec. 30, 2018).

16 Digital Signatures Act, RT I 2000, 26, 150, https://www.riigiteataja.ee/en/eli/530102013080/consolide.

17 Electronic Communications Act, RT I 2004, 87, 593, https://www.riigiteataja.ee/en/eli/ee/Riigi kogu/act/501042015003/consolide (last visited Dec. 30, 2018).

18 Population Register Act, *supra* note 15.

same name and even be born on the same date. Identifying them in a digital environment is essential.

The Estonian ID-code is also granted to a person who has been issued the e-residency. An e-resident is a foreign citizen for whom Estonia has created a digital identity and issued a digital identity card.[19]

C. Electronic Identity

To receive public services online, citizens need to be able to identify themselves and provide a legally binding digital signature. Electronic identity (e-ID) is the key enabler and a gateway to functioning e-government.

In Estonia, every citizen has a plastic ID-card that is the only obligatory state-issued personal identification document. Due to the built-in microchip, the ID-card also provides digital access to all of Estonia's e-services. According to legislation, a qualified electronic signature is equal to a hand-written signature, stamp, or seal and all Estonian authorities are obliged to accept electronic signatures. Having a personal identification code is a prerequisite of the ID-card and the enabler of the e-ID.

e-ID can be used to give digital signatures, establish a company online, submit tax declarations, use e-Prescription service, and to vote in national elections to name a few. During the past 15 years over 400 million digital signatures have been given in Estonia—more than in all the other EU member states combined, helping to lower both direct and indirect cost of signing documents on paper.

Having the digital ID infrastructure alone is not enough. There have to be enough relevant services to support it and getting the private sector onboard is of crucial importance. In Germany, people were not keen to adopt the e-ID system because to log in to public databases, a physical ID-card reader was needed that many did not have. In Finland, e-ID has not become popular mostly because of its high cost and voluntary adoption. In Estonia, the ID-card readers were given to people for free by the banks and telecom companies in cooperation with Look@World Foundation because by enabling customers to log in via the state-issued e-ID, the banks did not need to develop their elec-

19 Ministry of the Interior, *Population Register*, https://www.siseministeerium.ee/en/population-register (last visited Dec. 30, 2018).

tronic identification solutions saving both on cost and time.[20] As a result, 99% of all banking transactions in Estonia are carried out online.[21]

A person with an ID-card is not obliged to carry a physical driver's license since a police officer can check via X-Road from the database of the Road Administration if the license is valid.

Estonia has developed an e-ID that can be used on mobile phones—Mobile-ID. It has the same functionality as the plastic ID-card enabling its owner to use it for authentication and give digital signatures while not requiring a card reader. Mobile-ID system is based on a special SIM card, which the customer must request from the mobile phone operator.[22]

An even further development—Smart ID—is an identification solution for anyone that does not have a SIM card in their smart device but needs to prove their online identity. Smart-ID can be used both on smartphones and tablets. To use Smart-ID, only a Wi-Fi network or mobile internet connection is needed, no special SIM cards are necessary.[23]

D. X-Road

In Estonia, public organisations have their unique information systems to process data relevant to the state and its citizens to provide public services. They often run on different systems that suit the role of the organisation. X-Road is a distributed information exchange platform that makes it possible for these different systems to communicate all across the governmental sector; for example, the police can access data from the tax board or business registry and vice versa.[24]

To do this, X-Road must satisfy three criteria. First, the platform must be interoperable and technically easy for each member of the system to access the data they need. Second, the data cannot be corrupted in transit by the system or an external third party. And third, the data must be protected from prying

20 Vaata Maailma Sihtasutus, *Hansapanga pressiteade* (Jun. 2008), http://vaatamaailma.ee/uudised/hansapank-koostoos-vaata-maailmaga-jagab-sel-nadalal-paide-kontoris-tasuta-id-kaardilugejaid (last visited Apr. 15, 2019).

21 Invest in Estonia, *Banking & Financing*, https://investinestonia.com/business-in-estonia/financing/e-banking/ (last visited Apr. 15, 2019).

22 SK ID Solutions, *Mobile ID*, https://www.sk.ee/en/services/digital-identity/mobile-id/ (last visited Apr. 15, 2019).

23 E-Estonia, *Smart ID*, https://e-estonia.com/solutions/e-identity/smart-id (last visited Dec. 30, 2018).

24 E-Estonia, *X-Road*, https://e-estonia.com/wp-content/uploads/facts-a4-v02-x-road.pdf. (last visited April. 15, 2019).

eyes so that unauthorised individuals cannot view the content of the data *en route*.[25]

X-Road is based on an interoperable ecosystem meaning that there is no single central database, but the X-Road connects all the decentralized components of the system through end-to-end encrypted pathways.[26] There is no single point of failure making it impossible for hackers to take down the entire system. X-Road enables the functioning of the «Once-Only» principle, meaning that if one of the databases already has specific information about the citizen, the others can pull it from there, instead of asking the citizen to provide it again.[27]

Estonia's Information System Authority has mapped all data owned by the national government and provides a standardized technical environment for secure information sharing with all users in public and private sectors such as banks and telecommunication companies. To ensure the safety of data usage, all activities on the platform are logged, and citizens can check the logs to see who has accessed their information. All outgoing data from the X-Road is digitally signed and encrypted. All incoming data are authenticated and logged. X-Road members can request access to any data services provided through X-Road. Exchanging data through X-Road does not affect the availability, confidentiality or integrity of the data.[28]

Today, if a state or private sector organization wants to offer automated e-services, it has to connect its databases to X-Road which is the basis for the automation of public services in Estonia.

Initially, X-Road was a system used for making queries to the different databases. It has now developed into a mechanism that can also write to multiple databases, transfer large data sets, and perform searches across several databases.[29]

Finland recently began using X-Road as well, enabling its citizens to pick up their e-prescription medicine from Estonia's pharmacies and vice versa.[30] Both countries will make their databases reciprocally available, that will en-

---

25 E-Estonia, *supra* note 24.

26 Information System Authority, *X-Road*, https://www.ria.ee/en/state-information-system/x-tee.html (last visited Apr. 15, 2019).

27 Ministry of Economic Affairs and Communications, *Digital Agenda 2020 for Estonia*, https://www.mkm.ee/sites/default/files/digital_agenda_2020_estonia_engf.pdf. (last visited Apr. 15, 2019).

28 Information System Authority, *supra* note 26.

29 E-Estonia, *X-Road*, https://e-estonia.com/solutions/interoperability-services/x-road/ (last visited Apr. 15, 2019).

30 E-Estonia, *Estonia and Finland to start sharing patient data. And that's just the start!*, https://e-estonia.com/estonia-and-finland-to-start-sharing-patient-data-and-thats-just-the-start/ (last visited Dec. 30, 2019).

able cross-border access to digital prescriptions and full patient medical history. This measure should increase the quality of healthcare in both countries.[31]

One of the critical features of Estonia's e-governance system is the ability of citizens to see all the information the government has collected on them and to make corrections if necessary. Estonians are also able to see who else has accessed their information and, if this accessing was inappropriate, it could be reported to law enforcement with severe legal consequences for the offender. The system is built on a principle that the citizens are the owners of their data and the X-Road technology only offers a secure data exchange.[32]

X-Road connects more than 600 institutions and enterprises, enabling the usage of 2700+ e-services. Human users submit only 5% of the requests on X-Road.[33] Assuming that every request saves 15 minutes—those requests have saved 1400+ years of working time during one calendar year.[34] Putting it in a different context—if the same system were applied in Germany—citizens could gain 64 million hours of free time per year, companies could reduce their administrative costs by €1 billion per year, and public authorities could save 59% of the work hours spent processing cases.[35]

II. e-Registers

A. Population Register

The Population Register is the database for collecting and holding fundamental information about each person living in Estonia. It holds a person's name, ID-code, date of birth, place of residence, and other statistical data like native language, nationality, education, and profession. Each subject can review and correct their data in the register.[36]

State and local government agencies can access information in the Population Register in order to perform public duties. Natural and legal persons with a legitimate interest can also access the information. Additionally to personal information, the Register contains information on the processing of the

---

31 E-Estonia, *supra* note 30.

32 Information System Authority, *X-Road*, https://www.ria.ee/en/state-information-system/x-tee.html (last visited Dec. 30, 2018).

33 Information System Authority, *X-Road Factsheet*, https://www.x-tee.ee/factsheets/EE/#eng (last visited Apr. 15, 2019).

34 Information System Authority, *supra* note 33.

35 Matthias Daub, Axel Domeyer et al., *Digitizing the state: Five tasks for national governments*, McKinsey & Company (Nov. 2017), https://www.mckinsey.com/industries/public-sector/our-insights/digitizing-the-state-five-tasks-for-national-governments (last visited Dec. 30, 2018).

36 Ministry of the Interior, *supra* note 19.

register data; for example, on the time of entry in the register, the person entering the data and persons making inquiries about the data.[37] Adults have the right to access all present information about themselves, their minor children and individuals under their guardianship entered in the Population Register.[38] A person has the right to restrict access to his or her personal data and related information.[39]

The Population Register is connected to other databases via X-Road, and numerous other state registers depend on its data for their services.[40] For example, if a person applies for child support or study allowance, data is retrieved from the Population Register. The information is retrieved by the system automatically—no extra documents need to be submitted, or online forms filled out.

B. e-Land Register

The e-Land Register is a one-of-a-kind online application that holds data on all ownership relations and limited real rights for properties for the benefit of third persons.[41] The information on the e-Land Register is public—one can easily find the owner of the real estate by just searching by the address of the property.[42] The search also functions by the owner's name without a difference whether the owner is a natural person or a legal entity.[43]

The Estonian Land Register is a title-based electronic register. Only the titles inserted into the Land Register are considered to be valid, and the entries made in the Land Register are presumed accurate.[44]

The e-Land Register, paired with a geographical information system (GIS), delivers real-time geographical data through the X-Road, enabling advanced map-based visualizations and allowing one to view the exact location and size of the property on a map.[45] It has electronic data interchange with

---

37 Population Register Act, *supra* note 15.

38 Ministry of the Interior, *supra* note 19.

39 Ministry of the Interior, *supra* note 19.

40 E-Estonia, *Population Registry*, https://e-estonia.com/solutions/interoperability-services/population-registry/. (last visited Apr. 15, 2019).

41 E-Estonia, *e-Land Register*, https://e-estonia.com/solutions/interoperability-services/e-land-register. (last visited Apr. 15, 2019).

42 E-Land Register, https://kinnistusraamat.rik.ee/ (last visited Apr. 15, 2019).

43 E-Land Register, *supra* note 42.

44 Centre of Registers and Information Systems, *E-Land Register,* https://www.rik.ee/sites/www.rik.ee/files/elfinder/article_files/e-land_register.pdf (last visited Dec. 30, 2018).

45 X-GIS, *Estonian Land Board,* https://xgis.maaamet.ee/xGIS/XGis (last visited Apr. 15, 2019).

other primary registers such as Land Cadastre, Commercial Register, Population Register and the e-Notary enabling paperless bureaucracy.[46]

The e-Land Register displays the registered owner of each property holding, shows the property boundaries and provides other information that potential buyers need to know, making it a critical tool for the real-estate market. The system, providing total transparency, has changed the way how real estate transactions are conducted in Estonia, removing the need to visit public offices and spend hours waiting for a government official to search records.[47] This paperless system has reduced the processing time for land transactions from up to three months to as little as eight days. Companies benefit from the security of having immediate access to land titles and the ability to validate ownership with a few clicks.[48]

As previously mentioned, selling real estate is one of the only three things one cannot carry out online in e-Estonia. If an owner wants to sell one's land or real property, he/she has to go to the public notary. The notary performs the necessary inquiries from the Land Register and prepares the contract (deed). The notary then sends a digitally signed contract and application electronically to the Land Register where it is automatically registered. The registrar receives the electronic application and prepares the electronic entry from a template (automatic). The assistant judge makes an entry to the Land Register. After that, the registrar sends the decision to the notary and an e-mail to the participants of the transaction (this is a semiautomatic electronic procedure).[49] There are no applications on paper between the notary and land register, and registrars do not have to retype information. Previously the information was typed, printed out, sent on paper and retyped.

III. e-Justice

Justice procedures—the cornerstones of democracy and the rule of law—should be fast and efficient. Estonia has developed fully automated court processes and electronic communication tools, providing it with one of the most efficient court systems in the world.

46 Centre of Registers and Information Systems, *supra* note 44.

47 E-Land Register, *supra* note 42.

48 E-Estonia, *supra* note 41.

49 Centre of Registers and Information Systems, *supra* note 44.

A. e-Law

The e-Law system is an online database for the Estonian Ministry of Justice that allows the public to read every draft law submitted since February 2003. Built using blockchain technology, it is formally known as the Electronic Coordination System for Draft Legislation.[50]

The Electronic State Gazette is the central database and official online publication for Estonian legislation. Access to the State Gazette and to all legal information services is free of charge and open to everyone. The most significant advantage of the electronic State Gazette over the paper version is the possibility to publish whole and up to date texts of legislation. Since 2010, all national legal acts are made public only in electronic form in Estonia.[51]

Users can see who submitted the legislation, its current status, and all the changes made to it as it passed through the parliamentary process.[52] Once an act becomes law, it is published in the online state gazette Riigi Teataja, another searchable database that acts as an open legal library.[53]

Projects such as these create an unprecedented level of transparency in the state, cut down on corruption, and encourage citizens to take an active interest in legislative affairs.

B. e-File

The e-File is the core of the Estonian judicial system. It is a central information system that provides data to the Court Information System as well as to the information systems of police, jails, prosecutors and criminal case management. It provides an overview of the different phases of civil, criminal, and administrative procedures, court adjudications, and procedural acts to all the parties involved. The development of e-File was initiated by the Government in 2005, acknowledging the need to break down information silos, that functioned independently from each other.[54] e-File supports simultaneous information exchange between different parties' information systems including police, prosecution offices, courts, prisons, probation supervision, bailiffs, tax and customs board, lawyers and citizens:

---

50 E-Estonia, *E-Law*, https://e-estonia.com/solutions/security-and-safety/e-law/ (last visited Dec. 30, 2018).

51 Centre of Registers and Information Systems, *State Gazette*, https://www.rik.ee/en/international/state-gazette (last visited Dec. 30, 2018).

52 Riigikantselei, *Eelnõude infosüsteem*, http://eelnoud.valitsus.ee/ (last visited Apr. 15, 2019).

53 State Gazette, https://www.riigiteataja.ee/en/ (last visited Apr. 15, 2019).

54 Centre of Registers and Information Systems, *E-File*, https://www.rik.ee/sites/www.rik.ee/files/elfinder/article_files/RIK%20eFile.pdf (last visited Dec. 30, 2018).

«e-File enables parties to proceedings and their representatives to submit proceedings' documents to the court electronically and monitor the progress of the related court proceedings. Citizens are allowed to dispute claims and decisions as well as make inquiries in the Criminal Records Database regarding themselves and other people. In the system, individuals can only see the proceedings in which they are involved in.»[55]

Using e-File saves time and money as data is only entered once and the communication between the parties can be carried out online. It enables an entirely digital workflow for all the parties in the proceeding process and provides precise statistics in the legal protection field.[56]

C. Public e-File

Public e-File is the part of e-File visible to everyone. The greatest challenge of Estonian courts was making sure that critical documents reached the tied parties.

The Public e-File portal opens a virtual door to the courts. The portal enables every party to start a case and access or send out documents. The portal is accepting the entrance of initial claims 24/7. The workflow engine delivers the necessary data to the portal for the allocated judge.[57] Public e-File portal enables citizens to initiate civil, administrative, judicial and misdemeanor proceedings and monitor these proceedings as well as submit documents to be processed.[58]

In Estonia, it is possible to submit digitally signed documents to court via e-mail or to use Public e-File. The portal allows using pre-filled petitions for submitting to courts and users can also improve and revise unfinished petitions initiated by themselves. Additionally, it is possible to challenge decisions of bodies conducting proceedings and to file appeals on court judgements. The portal also allows making inquiries to the Punishment Registry. The government favours the establishing of lower state fees for those initiating court proceedings via the Public e-File.[59]

---

55 E-File, *supra* note 54.

56 *Id.*

57 E-Estonia, *E-Justice*, https://e-estonia.com/wp-content/uploads/facts-a4-v04-e-justice.pdf (last visited Dec. 30, 2018).

58 Centre of Registers and Information Systems, *Public e-File*, https://www.rik.ee/sites/www.rik.ee/files/elfinder/article_files/RIK%20Public%20eFile.pdf (last visited Dec. 30, 2018).

59 Estonian Courts, *Public e-File Q&A*, https://www.kohus.ee/sites/www.kohus.ee/files/elfinder/dokumendid/the_public_e-file_questions_and_answers.pdf (last visited Dec. 30, 2018).

A user of the portal receives a notification about the court case via e-mail whenever the court has sent documents via the Public e-File portal. The court can also communicate by phone or social media network and inform the defendant about the documents in the Public e-File. The user can then receive and review the documents in the Public e-File portal. If the defendant is not a user of the portal, the court sends the documents via e-mail or post-service.[60]

Starting in 2014, it became mandatory to use the Public e-File for lawyers, notary, bailiff, trustee in bankruptcy, local self-government and public department.[61] The court prepares a judgment electronically and the judge who has made the judgment signs it with the digital signature. The court registers the judgment immediately in the information system of the courts.[62]

The main advantages of the Public e-File are that it is secure since an e-ID is needed to log in. It saves time since data can be viewed and proceedings initiated without having to go to the agency in person, and it reduces time spent waiting for a decision since the single data system hastens the officials' work. The majority of the data is accessed from online systems by using the X-Road. It has been decided in Estonia that by the year 2020, a criminal file may be digital.[63]

D. Court Information System

The Court Information System (KIS) is a state-of-the-art information management system for Estonian courts, bringing one information system portal for all types of court cases.[64] KIS enables the registration of court cases, hearings and judgments, automatic allocation of cases to judges, the creation of summons, publication of judgments on the official website and collection of metadata. KIS also has a search engine for court documents, judgements, hearings and cases. Confidential data and cases can only be seen by the judge of the case and court staff bound up with the case. If claims are sent using the Public E-File, all the necessary documents are automatically uploaded to KIS, and the clerk can start a new case with a click of a few buttons. If criminal cases are

60 *Id.*

61 *Id.*

62 *Id.*

63 Eneli Laurits, *Criminal procedure and digital evidence in Estonia*, Digital Evidence and Electronic Signature Law Review (2016), http://journals.sas.ac.uk/deeslr/article/download/2301/2254 (last visited Dec. 30, 2018).

64 E-Estonia, *E-Justice (2)*, https://e-estonia.com/solutions/security-and-safety/e-justice (last visited Dec. 30, 2018).

sent to the court from the prosecutor's office, all the necessary documents are also automatically uploaded to KIS.[65]

The latest version of KIS includes new classifications based on courts' needs, for example, types of cases, categories of cases, and subcategories.[66] As a tool for judges, the second generation KIS represents an important progression, with searches based on stages of proceedings, issuing of reminders, and monitoring of the length of time spent on each stage. When a court uploads a document to KIS, it is then sent via the X-Road to the e-File. The uploaded document is then automatically visible to the relevant addressees via the Public e-File, the web-based information system created for the public to exchange information with the courts. The addressee receives a notification to the e-mail. After the addressee accesses the Public e-File with his/her ID-card and opens the document, the document is considered as legally received. KIS then receives a notification that the document has been viewed by the addressee or his/her representative. If the document is not received in the Public e-File during the concrete time-period—court uses other methods of service. Authentication and signatures are enabled by e-ID including mobile ID.[67]

KIS makes court proceedings faster, allows judges to specialise and manage their workload, enables the automatic generation of documents and represents a single information system for the entire judiciary. According to OECD reports, there is a direct link between foreign investment volume and court transparency. The more transparent and effective the courts are, the more willingness there is to invest in the country.[68] KIS has enabled the average length of Estonian court civil proceedings to fall from 156 days to 99 days in just five years.[69] Today, 20,000 unique users log in to the Estonian court information system every month (country's population is 1.3 million).[70]

E. e-Notary

E-Notary is software for notaries that enables them to collect information from different databases for drawing up and formulating the phrasing of contracts, forward contracts to registers and monitor the implementation process of con-

---

65 E-Estonia, *supra* note 64.

66 *Id.*

67 Centre of Registers and Information Systems, *Court Information System*, https://www.rik.ee/sites/www.rik.ee/files/elfinder/article_files/RIK_e_Court_Information_System%2B3mm_bleed.pdf (last visited Dec. 30, 2018).

68 E-Estonia, *Courtal Net Group*, https://e-estoniax.com/solution/e-justice/ (last visited Dec. 30, 2018).

69 E-Estonia, *supra* note 57.

70 *Id.*

tracts. Since the e-Notary offers contract templates and all the necessary data can be requested from multiple registers with just a few mouse clicks, the formation of contracts is fast and easy. As a result, the e-Notary system has reduced paperwork, repeated data entries and printing, therefore, increased the efficiency of notaries' work. Notaries and notary office employees can access the e-Notary system.[71]

The software guides and assists the notaries when obtaining and entering necessary data for the drawing up of a contract. Once the contract has been digitally signed, the notary makes a digital copy of the signed contract and saves it in the digital archive. The contracts in the digital archive or specific related data are forwarded electronically by the e-Notary to other relevant registers. The e-Notary system allows notaries to submit queries to 17 different registries. All the information is received and sent to the registers electronically.[72]

IV. Concluding Remarks

The emergence of e-government initiatives all over the world is disrupting both the public and private sector and offers new business opportunities for a wide range of industries. For legal professionals, it is essential to understand the fundamental building blocks of a digital government to be able to get full use of the technology and solutions it enables.

For the public sector, it is necessary to include the best legal talent when designing digital public services to avoid situations where modern technology is in place but useless because the laws are not supporting it. The legislation, organisational change and IT systems are all equally quintessential factors behind seamless e-government services.

V. Bibliography

A. Online Sources

California Department of Technology, *eGovernment (eGov) Reference Architecture (RA)* (Jan. 2014), https://cdt.ca.gov/services/wp-content/uploads/sites/2/sites/2/2017/04/EA-eGovernment-eGov-V2.pdf (last visited Dec. 30, 2018).

71 Centre of Registers and Information Systems, *E-Notary*, https://www.rik.ee/en/international/e-notary (last visited Dec. 30, 2018).

72 Centre of Registers and Information Systems, *E-Notary Datasheet*, https://www.rik.ee/sites/www.rik.ee/files/elfinder/article_files/RIK%20eNotary.pdf (last visited Apr. 15, 2019).

Combe, Colin et al., *E-Government in Estonia: Development and Best Practice Background Paper*, World Bank (Aug. 2006), www.siteresources.worldbank.org/INTSLOVAKIA/Resources/eGovernmentEstonia.doc (last visited Dec. 30, 2018).

Centre of Registers and Information Systems, *Court Information System*, https://www.rik.ee/sites/www.rik.ee/files/elfinder/article_files/RIK_e_Court_Information_System%2B3mm_bleed.pdf (last visited Dec. 30, 2018).

Centre of Registers and Information Systems, *E-File*, https://www.rik.ee/sites/www.rik.ee/files/elfinder/article_files/RIK%20eFile.pdf (last visited Dec. 30, 2018).

Centre of Registers and Information Systems, E-Land Register, https://www.rik.ee/sites/www.rik.ee/files/elfinder/article_files/e-land_register.pdf (last visited Dec. 30, 2018).

Centre of Registers and Information Systems, *E-Notary*, https://www.rik.ee/en/international/e-notary (last visited Dec. 30, 2018).

Centre of Registers and Information Systems, *E-Notary* Datasheet, https://www.rik.ee/sites/www.rik.ee/files/elfinder/article_files/RIK%20eNotary.pdf (last visited Apr. 15, 2019).

Centre of Registers and Information Systems, *Public e-File*, https://www.rik.ee/sites/www.rik.ee/files/elfinder/article_files/RIK%20Public%20eFile.pdf (last visited Dec. 30, 2018).

Centre of Registers and Information Systems, *State Gazette*, https://www.rik.ee/en/international/state-gazette (last visited Dec. 30, 2018).

Daub, Matthias, Domeyer, Axel et al., *Digitizing the state: Five tasks for national governments*, McKinsey & Company (Nov. 2017), https://www.mckinsey.com/industries/public-sector/our-insights/digitizing-the-state-five-tasks-for-national-governments (last visited Dec. 30, 2018).

E-Estonia, *Courtal Net Group*, https://e-estoniax.com/solution/e-justice/ (last visited Dec. 30, 2018).

E-Estonia, *E-Justice*, https://e-estonia.com/wp-content/uploads/facts-a4-v04-e-justice.pdf (last visited Dec. 30, 2018).

E-Estonia *E-Justice (2)*, https://e-estonia.com/solutions/security-and-safety/e-justice (last visited Dec. 30, 2018).

E-Estonia, *E-Land Register*, https://e-estonia.com/solutions/interoperability-services/e-land-register (last visited Dec. 30, 2018).

E-Estonia, *E-Law*, https://e-estonia.com/solutions/security-and-safety/e-law/ (last visited Dec. 30, 2018).

E-Estonia, *Estonia and Finland to start sharing patient data. And that's just the start!*, https://e-estonia.com/estonia-and-finland-to-start-sharing-patient-data-and-thats-just-the-start/ (last visited Dec. 30, 2019).

E-Estonia, *Population Registry*, https://e-estonia.com/solutions/interoperability-services/population-registry/ (last visited Apr. 15, 2019).

E-Estonia, *smart ID*, https://e-estonia.com/solutions/e-identity/smart-id (last visited Dec. 30, 2018).

E-Estonia, *X-Road*, https://e-estonia.com/wp-content/uploads/facts-a4-v02-x-road.pdf (last visited Apr. 15, 2019).

E-Land Register, https://kinnistusraamat.rik.ee/. (last visited Apr. 15, 2019).

Estonian Courts, *Public e-File Q&A*, https://www.kohus.ee/sites/www.kohus.ee/files/elfinder/dokumendid/the_public_e-file_questions_and_answers.pdf (last visited Dec. 30, 2018).

Hammersley, Ben, *Concerned about Brexit? Why not become an e-resident of Estonia*, WIRED (Mar. 27, 2017), https://www.wired.co.uk/article/estonia-e-resident (last visited Dec. 30, 2018).

Information System Authority, X-Road, https://www.ria.ee/en/state-information-system/x-tee.html (last visited Dec. 30, 2018).

Information System Authority, *X-Road Factsheet*, https://www.x-tee.ee/factsheets/EE/#eng (last visited Apr. 15, 2019).

Invest in Estonia, *Banking & Financing*, https://investinestonia.com/business-in-estonia/financing/e-banking/. (last visited Apr. 15, 2019).

Kiškis, Mindaugas & Petrauskas, Rimantas, *e-Governance: Two Views on Legal Environment*, *in* Proceedings of the Second International Conference on Electronic Government (EGOV 2003) (Traunmüller, Roland ed,, Springer, 2003), https://doi.org/10.1007/10929179_73 (last visited Dec. 30, 2018).

Laurits, Eneli, *Criminal procedure and digital evidence in Estonia*, Digital Evidence and Electronic Signature Law Review (2016), http://journals.sas.ac.uk/deeslr/article/download/2301/2254 (last visited Dec. 30, 2018).

Ministry of the Interior, *Population Register*, https://www.siseministeerium.ee/en/population-register (last visited Dec. 30, 2018).

Raguseo, Elisabetta & Ferro, Enrico, *E-Government & Organizational Change: Towards and Extended Governance Model,* Researchgate (2011), https://www.researchgate.net/publication/256979622_E-Government_Organizational_Change_Towards_and_Extended_Governance_Model (last visited Dec. 30, 2018).

Riigikantselei, *Eelnõude infosüsteem*, http://eelnoud.valitsus.ee/ (last visited Apr. 15, 2019).

Sagan, Carl, *If you wish to make an apple pie from scratch, you must first invent the universe*, YouTube, https://www.youtube.com/watch?v=7s664NsLeFM (last visited Dec. 30, 2018).

SK ID Solutions, *Mobile ID*, https://www.sk.ee/en/services/digital-identity/mobile-id/ (last visited Apr. 15, 2019).

State Gazette, https://www.riigiteataja.ee/en/ (last visited Apr. 15, 2019).

Torres, Lourdes & Pina, Vicente et al., *E-government and the transformation of public administrations in EU countries: Beyond NPM or just a second wave of reforms?* (Jan. 2005), http://www.dteconz.unizar.es/DT2005-01.pdf (last visited Dec. 30, 2018).

X-GIS, *Estonian Land Board*, https://xgis.maaamet.ee/xGIS/XGis. (last visited Apr. 15, 2019).

Wiese Schartum, Dag, *Developing E-government Systems—Legal, Technological and Organizational Aspects*, Scandinavian Studies in Law (2015), http://www.scandinavianlaw.se/pdf/56-6.pdf (last visited Dec. 30, 2018).

Wolfgang, Ben, *Obama: «Should've called the Estonians» to help with Obamacare website*, The Washington Times (Sep. 3, 2014), https://www.washingtontimes.com/news/2014/sep/3/obama-shouldve-called-estonians-help-obamacare-web/ (last visited Dec. 28, 2018).

Vaata Maailma Sihtasutus, *Hansapanga pressiteade* (Jun. 2008), http://vaatamaailma.ee/uudised/hansapank-koostoos-vaata-maailmaga-jagab-sel-nadalal-paide-kontoris-tasuta-id-kaardilugejaid. (last visited Apr. 15, 2019).

Vassil, Kristjan, *Estonian e-Government Ecosystem: Foundation, Applications, Outcomes. Background Paper, Digital Dividends, World Development Report*, World Bank (Jun. 2015), http://pubdocs.worldbank.org/en/165711456838073531/WDR16-BP-Estonian-eGov-ecosystem-Vassil.pdf (last visited Dec. 30, 2018).

B. Legislative Material

Personal Data Protection Act, RT I 2007, 24, 127, https://www.riigiteataja.ee/en/eli/ee/512112013011/consolide/current (last visited Dec. 30, 2018).

Public Information Act, RT I 2000, 92, 597, https://www.riigiteataja.ee/en/eli/ee/514112013001/consolide/current (last visited Dec. 30, 2018).
Population Register Act, RT I 2000, 50, 317, https://www.riigiteataja.ee/en/eli/ee/516012014003/consolide/current (last visited Dec. 30, 2018).
Digital Signatures Act, RT I 2000, 26, 150, https://www.riigiteataja.ee/en/eli/530102013080/consolide (last visited Dec. 30, 2018).
Population Register Act, RT I 17.11.2017, https://www.riigiteataja.ee/en/eli/ee/Riigikogu/act/522032019005/consolide (last visited Apr. 15, 2019).
Electronic Communications Act, RT I 2004, 87, 593, https://www.riigiteataja.ee/en/eli/ee/Riigikogu/act/501042015003/consolide (last visited Dec. 30, 2018).

Dr Christian Öhner and Dr Silke Graf

Lawyer Bots

Rise of the Machines

TABLE OF CONTENTS

I. What's so special about Law anyway?

Digitization is a buzzword that has been playing a key role in the development and change of most industries for the last five to ten years. By now, almost every business person knows, that he or she has to cope with the new industry 4.0 that is changing the way things used to be in the centuries before. By now, almost every business person knows, that if their own business model does not fit to the new age of digitization, the chances to keep up with the competition do not look good.

The legal industry in general lags far behind in digitization and is reluctant to adopt a new delivery model, not to speak of an entirely new business model. Despite the fact that machines are already capable of replacing substantial parts of the daily legal business. Why is the legal industry happy to capitalize on digitization by making laws and advising businesses in this respect, but adamant in exploring its allure when it comes to legal operations?

A. Law consists of Rules

At first sight, the law does not seem very special regarding the characteristics a process would need if you want to automate it: Law, like mathematics, is a rule-based system. It consists of specific legal consequences that are linked to certain factual triggers. There are exceptions to those rules and also exceptions to those exceptions. Like in any spreadsheet calculation, the law is a collection of countless if-then-functions. As is any contract. Law and contracts are predestined to be digitized.

If it weren't for language: Written words are much more difficult for a computer to understand than numbers. Unlike calculations, where a 13 always means 13 and does not lend itself well for a fancy interpretation by a sleek lawyer, words usually have several meanings that are only revealed in their context. And also we humans often fail to grasp the meaning of a textual statement, as many spouses can readily attest.

Teaching a computer to detect a specific context and come up with the correct interpretation of a rather ambiguous term expressed as a word is one big challenge for scientists. It gets even harder when we talk about elaborate legal texts. Not only because lawyers, over time, have developed their own language that sometimes follows different rules than our colloquial language, but also because lawyers themselves often seem to be rather undecided as to what a particular sentence really means. Add to this the fact that there are roughly 7,000 languages in the world. Granted, many languages are not a major factor for business with sometimes as little as 1,000 or less humans speaking it. But the number of major languages is still significant, with 23 languages

accounting for roughly half of the world population. English, for example, is the mother tongue of less than 5% of humanity.[1]

But, as hard as it may be to teach computers to understand complex texts, it is only a matter of time when we will achieve this goal and machine learning is quickly altering the stakes of this once seemingly unconquerable challenge.[2] And there is no need to wait for that day. Machines are already capable of carrying out numerous tasks of the lawyer's daily work. And eventually they will. Following through on the ubiquitous mantra of industry 4.0: *«Everything that is repetitive can be digitized. And everything that can be digitized will be digitized.»*[3]

B. What is holding Lawyers back?

So, if the technical possibilities are not the limiting factor, what else is holding us back from digitizing legal affairs?

Like every other industry, lawyers too face the risk of becoming dispensable. Unemployment rates among academics are already on the rise. It is still hard for many of us to imagine that intellectual work is replaced by computer algorithms, just as manual labour on an assembly line is replaced by robots. Yet, a closer look at the usual work of an average lawyer reveals that lawyering has still much in common with manual labour: Both trace their origins back to the artisanal model of the Middle Ages. And, truth be told, not much has changed with respect to a lawyer's delivery model since then. After establishing the factual circumstances, he or she then looks for the rules that apply to those facts, which then yields the result of the legal analysis. Granted, nowadays the internet and databases support the subsumption process, but these tools seldom offer much beyond text search and, therefore, just a slightly more advanced approach to the written text. Which then serves as the basis for the production of more text, either in the form of an email to the client, a pleading to the court, an expert opinion or a publication in a law journal. Some of us may stand out by their eloquence in court, as Hollywood loves to portrait in numerous genre movies. But it mostly comes down to an individual lawyer working on one specific case at a time. Generally, we do not handle legal cases in a manner resembling a production line in industry 4.0.

---

1 Dylan Lyons, *How Many People Speak English, And Where Is It Spoken?*, Babbel (Jul. 26, 2017), https://www.babbel.com/en/magazine/how-many-people-speak-english-and-where-is-it-spoken/ (last visited Apr. 11, 2019).

2 Also *see* Marco Lagi, *Natural Language Processing—Business Applications*, Emerj (Feb. 21, 2019), https://emerj.com/ai-sector-overviews/natural-language-processing-business-applications/ (last visited Apr. 11, 2019).

3 Source unknown.

And we lawyers feel quite comfortable with the way things are. Probably because of an agency problem: We lawyers are not only the employees of the legal industry, we also own it.[4] This fact creates a disincentive to become more efficient, because other than the car manufacturer we do not only care about production metrics but also a lot about job security for our assembly workers aka lawyers.

But tradition and fear won't hold us back forever.

II. Why now?

Things are changing. Entirely new market players threaten the very domain of us lawyers. Universities start to emphasize legal technology education over technology law. New buzzwords are heard over lunch with attorneys all over the world.

The question is: Why now?

A. Technology as Barrier and Enabler

Much of the technical features that enable the digitization of law and legal operations has been available on the market for quite a long time. But due to limited language processing capabilities of computers[5] and the complexity of legal rules, the production of a meaningful algorithm to solve legal equations required a lot of effort and, thus, investment. In the market of law, which is not only fragmented by language but also specific local rules for essentially everything but basic human rights, the business case for industrialization was difficult.

While writing these words, machine learning and artificial intelligence (AI) are quickly changing the equation, however. Even in the absence of comprehensive language processing capabilities, machine learning and AI enable the transfer of technology from one specific domain to an adjacent area with limited human input and, thus, reasonable cost. The same applies for the conversion of a tool from one specific language to another.

One of the most prominent examples for lightning fast progress is *Google's AlphaZero*. *Yuval Hoah Harari*, a famous historian, philosopher and

---

4 Hedwig van Rossum, *Lawyers, law schools and social change–defining the challenges of academic legal education in the late modernity*, 25 International Journal of the Legal Profession 245–260 (2018).

5 George Seif, *An easy introduction to Natural Language Processing*, Towards Sciencs (Oct. 2, 2018), https://towardsdatascience.com/an-easy-introduction-to-natural-language-processing-b1e2801291c1 (last visited Apr. 11, 2019).

best-selling author of *«Sapiens»* and *«Homo Deus»*, uses the history of the game of chess to portrait the speed of advancement.[6] Chess computer technology culminated in 2016 in a program by the name of *Stockfish 8*, which had access to centuries of accumulated human experience in chess and mind-boggling computing power calculating 70 million chess positions per second. In December 2017, *Google's AlphaZero* defeated *Stockfish 8* in 28 out of 100 games and tied 72. Not one game was won by *Stockfish 8*. This is tremendous domination by the standards of chess. We should note here that the number of chess positions that *AlphaZero* calculated in every second was only 0.1% of the calculations performed by *Stockfish 8*. The question is, what did *Google* do to equip *AlphaZero* with the know-how to become the supreme ruler of the chess world? The answer is, nothing. No human taught *AlphaZero* anything about chess, it rather learned exclusively by playing against itself using cutting edge machine learning technology. How long did it take *AlphaZero* to self learn and become the best chess player ever to play on Earth? Four hours.[7]

If *AlphaZero* does not need any showcases or human coaching to, within four hours, arrive at the highest level of mastery ever attained in a game long considered the crowning of human intellect, it may eventually also come up with a somewhat decent draft sale and purchase agreement for an M&A transaction.

B. The New Culture of Lawyers

With competition from AlphaZero and its peers on the horizon and young lawyers now being inspired by *Yuval Hoah Harari's* books just as much as *John Grisham's*, the culture of the legal profession has started to change.

Young talents no longer want to work the same way their more experienced colleagues do and, much to the dismay of the legal establishment, they certainly do not want to work as much. The generations Y and Z want to work for their own personal fulfilment; and charging clients for endless hours of sifting through due diligence data and editing cross-references in a sale and purchase agreement of intimidating length does not provide the chance to make a difference in the world that they seek. The next generation of lawyers no longer fears change for the legal world; they fear the procrastination of reform of an outdated legal operating model. They also have a different attitude regarding automation; unlike their predecessors, they welcome the use of robotics and technology. They rather see it as an opportunity to free us from

---

6 Yuval Noah Harari, 21 Lessons for the 21 Century (Jonathan Cape, 2018).

7 Demis Hassabis & David Silver, *AlphaGoZero: Learning from Scratch*, DeepMind (Oct. 18, 2017), https://deepmind.com/blog/alphago-zero-learning-scratch/ (last visited Apr. 12, 2019); Harari, *supra* note 6.

monotonous and repetitive tasks in order to concentrate on the work that will most likely always be reserved for human beings, like creativity and philosophy. Most of the members of the generation Z say that if they had to decide between two similar employment offers, they would go for the employer with the better technology in his or her pocket.[8]

The change in minds is almost visible, as more and more lawyers are interested in software solutions and new business models. Software as a service (SaaS) is slowly becoming a factor for the legal industry, especially in the B2C area with SaaS and hybrid solutions on the rise.[9]

An example for this is *DoNotPay,[10]* an online robot lawyer that, *inter alia*, allows anyone to automatically claim asylum in the US, UK, and Canada. *DoNotPay* is the brainchild of *Joshua Browder,*[11] who initially created it to dispute the dozens of parking tickets he was racking up when he was 18. However, over time it has increased in complexity to offer legal advice in more states (all 50 states across the US are supported), for a greater variety of issues including volatile airline prices, data breaches, late package deliveries, and unfair bank fees. Although the service is currently free (and lets users keep 100 percent of the money they win in court), *Browder* said that he's considering charging for more specialized legal advice in the future.[12]

Another example is *Jobcenter-Schutzschild* in Germany.[13] Almost 50% of all Hartz 4 (the German social assistance for long-term unemployed) applications are incorrect. The consequences are too few payments and disadvantages for recipients. *Jobcenter-Schutzschild* runs an algorithm and then partners with lawyers to check whether the Jobcenter has calculated its services correctly. Other German services are a flight right portal that deals with delayed or canceled flights,[14] *MyRight* that focuses on the auto industry's emission scandals,[15] or a tool that provides analysis and appeal information for speeding tickets and other traffic offenses.[16]

---

8 Dell Technologies, *Gen Z is here. Are you ready?*, Dell Technologies (2019), https://www.delltechnologies.com/en-us/perspectives/gen-z.htm (last visited Apr. 11, 2019).

9 The Law Society, *Law Tech Adaption Research 2019*, (https://www.lawsociety.org.uk/support-services/research-trends/lawtech-adoption-report/ (last visited Apr. 11, 2019).

10 DoNotPay, https://www.donotpay.com/ (last visited Apr. 11, 2019).

11 Note: *Joshua Browder* was born in London in 1997, he is studying at Stanford University. Jon Porter, *Robot lawyer DoNotPay now lets you «sue everyone»*, The Verge (Oct. 10, 2018 12:13 PM), https://www.theverge.com/2018/10/10/17959874/donotpay-do-not-pay-robot-lawyer-ios-app-joshua-browder (last visited Apr. 11, 2019).

12 *Id.*

13 Casecheck GmbH/hartz4widerspruch, https://hartz4widerspruch.de/app (last visited Apr. 11, 2019).

14 Flugrecht, https://www.flugrecht.de/(last visited Apr. 11, 2019).

15 MyRight, https://www.myright.de/ (last visited Apr. 11, 2019).

16 Geblitzt.de, *So funtionierts*, https://www.geblitzt.de/so-funktionierts/ (last visited Apr. 11, 2019).

III. Is my Lawyer a Bot?

For both, lawyers and clients alike, the variety of software solutions for managing legal affairs is increasing. However, from our lawyer colleagues we often hear that the right tool has yet to be developed. While there is, of course, not one piece of software that solves all legal issues once and for all, there are already ample opportunities to approach the law and its application in a more technology oriented manner.

One category of solutions, which warrants a closer look already, can be designed and implemented with limited investment of time and resources and at surprisingly low level of technology skills: Meet your *Lawyer Bot*. Many flesh and blood lawyers, who already use Lawyer Bots for their work, do not even realize that they do. And those who do are often not aware of the whole range of possibilities that Lawyer Bots offer. Lawyer Bots can be considered the entry point into the realm of legal technology.

A. What is a (Lawyer) Bot?

When people hear the word «Bot», they often think of a chatbot. A chatbot, or in more scientific terms an Artificial Conversational Entity, is a computer program which conducts a conversation via auditory or textual methods and is often designed to convincingly simulate how a human would behave as a conversational partner.[17]

But a chatbot is only one type of bot, which is typically used in dialog systems and scans for keywords within the input, then pulls a reply with the most matching keywords or the most similar wording pattern, from a database.[18] While chatbots received some bad publicity, including those by famous tech giants like Microsoft, Twitter and Facebook[19], which swiftly were corrupted by the users' interactions or, putting it differently, efficiently acquired also the less desirable human traits from their experiential interaction with their mortal conversation partners. We should not dismiss the blessings that bots may bring about because they may also enable racist or other offensive behaviour, for which the developers did not account in their initial code. In its essence, a chatbot is simply a tool to facilitate the interaction between a human

---

17 Margaret Rouse, *IM Bot*, Tech Target (2019), https://searchdomino.techtarget.com/definition/IM-bot (last visited Apr. 11, 2019).

18 Margaret Rouse, *database (DB)*, Tech Target (2019), https://searchsqlserver.techtarget.com/definition/database (last visited Apr. 11, 2019).

19 Ingrid Angulo, *Facebook and YouTube should have learned from Microsoft's racist chatbot*, CNBC (Mar. 17, 2018 4:03 PM), https://www.cnbc.com/2018/03/17/facebook-and-youtube-should-learn-from-microsoft-tay-racist-chatbot.html (last visited Apr. 11, 2019).

and a computer, and there sometimes is room for improvement in connection with such interaction, as anyone who ever called a telephone company's complaint hotline can readily attest. And let's be honest: Not using bots would not ensure that such unwanted behaviour doesn't occur. In the end: To err is human.

Apple's Siri[20] and *Amazon's Alexa*[21] are all the rage as of the time of this writing, but there are also more traditional customer-service focussed examples like Ikea's Anna[22] or Alibaba's chatbot.[23] Some recognize colloquial language and others are limited to structured input into a text interface, but they all belong into the same category, even though their respective vision may fall anywhere on the spectrum from providing the answer to every question you may ever have to fixing your broken phone connection. What all chatbots have in common is that they tend to be rather visible, also to the casual observer of technology who has no interest in understanding the technology behind a user experience. The user experiences the human machine interaction, when she talks or writes something and expects the machine to provide the correct reply, and the result is either satisfying or annoying with little chance that the user does not form an opinion as to the quality.

In contrast, the vast majority of bots acts in the background without being noticed. In fact, by way of example roughly 52% of the internet traffic originates from bots.[24] So, obviously bots can do much more than just chat. A general definition of bot is a software that performs certain tasks automatically, it might do so only on command or because a specific task was carried out that triggers the bot. Thus, a bot might interact with users like a chatbot or it may interact with other systems like, for example, a bot screening through email text and automatically adding certain appointments to your calendar. Or the bots dominating the internet by helping, for example, to refresh your *Facebook* feed or figuring out how to rank search results. And usually, it is the bots that do not require human interaction which yield the greatest gains in efficiency. Notably, for tasks that have to be carried out multiple times, you may use a bot for such repetitive tasks.

Coming back to the legal industry, where substantial parts of the daily work tend to be repetitive, bots are destined to be in high demand. They even got their own buzzwords: Legal Bots, Lawyer Bots or Lawbots. Those Lawyer

---

20 Apple, *Siri*, https://www.apple.com/siri/ (last visited Apr. 11, 2019).

21 Amazon, *Alexa*, https://developer.amazon.com/alexa (last visited Apr. 11, 2019).

22 @IKEA_jp_Anna, https://twitter.com/IKEA_jp_Anna (last visited Apr. 11, 2019).

23 Susan Wang, *Merchants Deploy Alibaba's AI CustomerCustomer-Service Chatbo)*, Alizila (Apr. 3, 2017), https://www.alizila.com/online-merchants-deploy-alibabas-ai-customer-service-chatbot/ (last visited Apr. 11, 2019).

24 Adrienne Lafranc, *The Internet Is Mostly Bots*, The Alantic (Jan. 31, 2017), https://www.theatlantic.com/technology/archive/2017/01/bots-bots-bots/515043/ (last visited Apr. 11, 2019).

Bots are not limited to chatbot for the legal industry. While a chatbot may, of course, yield the results of legal research aimed at the correct case law for a certain set of facts or provide the most recognized attorney for a certain area of law in your region or help with the onboarding of a new client guiding you through the required know-your-customer rules; Lawyer Bots may also autonomously provide the solution to a legal case on the basis of predetermined facts or draft a legal document based on defined document standards.[25]

Therefore, a Lawyer Bot can be defined as a software that performs certain legal tasks automatically. The following categories are helpful to structure the analysis of possible areas of applications:

- Lawyer Bots aimed at providing a solution to a problem, from finding a suitable lawyer for a particular case to solving the case in the first place (thereby replacing the need for a lawyer).
- Lawyer Bots aimed at supporting the intellectual process of legal work, from assisting in legal research to drafting a contract or court plea, then to be used by a human lawyer or client.
- Lawyer Bots to facilitate the workflow between human or machine based systems, from simply filing a particular document into the proprietary court system to autonomously administer an entire court procedure.

B. Do Lawyer Bots know AI?

As lawyers like to say: it depends.

Before we go into details, let's take a closer look at the meaning of AI, which is a complex subject. AI is not a particular software, but rather a suite of systems within computer science, namely machine learning, natural language processing and neural network computing, geared towards the elements of learning (the acquisition of information and rules for using the information), reasoning (using rules to reach approximate or definite conclusions) and self-correction.[26]

Apart from the categories mentioned in the preceding paragraph, AI can also be categorized by its respective decision making approach,[27] into either purely reactive, limited memory, theory of mind or self-aware. To the day of this writing, all AI either falls into the category purely reactive or the category limited memory. This means that in the most basic form they have neither the

---

25 Jens Wagner, Legal Tech und Legal Robots (Springer Gabler, 2018) at 31.

26 *See* different definitions of AI and ML, e.g., Daniel Faggella, *What is Machine Learning*, Emerj (Feb. 19, 2019), https://emerj.com/ai-glossary-terms/what-is-machine-learning/ (last visited Apr. 11, 2019).

27 Futurism, *Types of AI: From reactive to self-aware*, https://futurism.com/images/types-of-ai-from-reactive-to-self-aware-infographic (last visited Apr. 11, 2019).

ability to form memories nor to use past experiences to inform current decisions (purely reactive) or in the next iteration they can include a look into the past, like for example self-driving cars that observe other cars' speed and direction (limited memory). We have yet to build machines that not only form representations about the world, but also about other agents or entities in it (theory of mind), understanding that people, creatures and objects in the world can have thoughts and emotions that affect their own behaviour and it requires one more step to create systems that can form representations about themselves (self-aware).[28]

Along another set of categories, we recognize weak AI or narrow AI, aimed at a particular task, like playing the game of chess, on the one hand and strong AI intending to think as complex as humans along various dimensions of tasks and environments on the other hand.

The above makes it evident that the subject of AI is quite broad, as are its applications. What makes AI so relevant for Lawyer Bots is its potential to not only autonomously respond to input from a user or another system but also learn from such interaction for the next transaction. We will use the example of a chatbot to illustrate this point: When you build a chatbot for internal compliance questions, you first determine possible questions users might have. You then feed these questions into your chatbot software, providing the respective answers along with the questions. Once completed, you can launch your chatbot and wait for people to actually use it. In the absence of AI, you have to anticipate the exact syntax of each question by the users or the chatbot cannot come up with a meaningful reply. Equipped with AI, however, the chatbot can detect the intended question even in the absence of the precise syntax that was fed into the software initially. And, over time, the ability to find meaning in the user's input improves based on the learning from past transactions, for example based on user feedback as to the accuracy of the chatbot and its level of proficiency to solve the user's problem.

This ability of AI to learn from user interaction has the potential to significantly lower the required investment of human time and know-how in the development process for a Lawyer Bot. Putting it differently, AI allows the deployment of Lawyer Bots into use cases that, in the past, could only be solved by a flesh and blood lawyer because of the high degree of individuality and the lack of substantial numbers of repetitive cases. Therefore, AI is not necessary for a Lawyer Bot, but it can substantially shift the threshold for its commercial viability.

28 Arend Hintze, *Understanding the four types of AI, from reactive robots to self-aware beings*, The Conversation (Nov. 14, 2016), http://theconversation.com/understanding-the-four-types-of-ai-from-reactive-robots-to-self-aware-beings-67616 (last visited Apr. 11, 2019).

C. The Risk of AI

This new possibilities AI brings do not come without a corresponding disadvantage, though. The benefits of AI learning from user interaction without crystal clear guidance from its creators from the beginning, bring along the risk that the judgement exercised by AI is not what its creators intended it to be. Already, AI advanced to a status where we cannot always comprehend the outcome of AI's computation. This phenomenon is aptly named *blackbox* and may turn out to be the crucial factor for the acceptance of AI into human's everyday life beyond the compilation of the next playlist on the home stereo.

It is natural for people to distrust what they do not understand—and there is a lot about AI that is not immediately clear. How does AI know what action to complete or decision to make? How can humans prevent AI from making a mistake? If AI turns down a mortgage application or singles out certain individuals for additional screening at the airport security, can somebody explain why? Does somebody have to? More importantly, if the human safety is at risk, how you can guarantee that the reasoning behind the AI system's decision-making is clear and accountable?

As an example, in 2017 a computer program used by a US court for risk assessment was reported to show biases against black prisoners. The program, named Correctional Offender Management Profiling for Alternative Sanctions (Compas), had a tendency to label black defendants as likely to reoffend at almost twice the rate as white people. The use of AI in the US justice system, aimed at the elimination of human prejudices, had—at least initially—backfired, as it turned out that the algorithm discriminated against African Americans too.[29]

But then, human judges aren't perfect, either. In his seminal book about human decision making, Nobel laureate *Daniel Kahneman* reports about a study of eight parole judges who spend their entire days reviewing applications for parole. The cases are presented in random order, and the judges spend little time on each one, an average of six minutes. In the study, the proportion of approved requests was plotted against the time since the last food break. The proportion spikes after each meal, when about 65% of requests are granted, while during the two hours or so until the judges' next feeding, the approval rate drops steadily to about zero just before the meal.[30] While the casual observer may be shocked by this, the fact that judges, too, are human beings is widely accepted among everyone who, at some point in their career, worked in the justice system.

---

29 Stephen Buranyi, *Rise of the racist robots—how AI is learning all our worst impulses*, The Guardian (Aug. 8, 2017), https://www.theguardian.com/inequality/2017/aug/08/rise-of-the-racist-robots-how-ai-is-learning-all-our-worst-impulses (last visited Apr. 11, 2019).

30 Daniel Kahneman, Thinking, Fast and Slow (Penguin, 2011) at 43.

From a philosophical and ethical perspective, the question therefore arises whether we want to continue accounting only for human imperfection in our laws and regulations. The general approach, until today, was to trace back the imperfection of artificial decision-making to some initial human flaw, for example in the coding of the software or the technical design. In the case of AI, this concept is severely limited, and allowing for the imperfection of AI in laws and regulations may yield far superior results. Let's look at self-driving cars as an example. Statistics can, eventually, proof beyond any doubt that the level of proficiency of self-driving cars is either superior or inferior to human driving. Assuming that at some point in time we will reach break-even and cars will drive far superior than their human pilots, it would make sense at that stage to also account for AI imperfection and not make the programmer who coded the AI in the first place responsible for an accident, which simply was beyond anything that could have been foreseen at the time of the initial development. If our law making does not make this, admittedly, huge step, we will at some day be stuck with a death toll in car traffic far greater than necessary, including incidents of drunk driving and even the use of cars and trucks as tactical weapons by terrorists, because the usage of self-driving cars will be severely limited by regulations despite a statistically far superior scenario.

IV. Rise of the Machines

As fascinating as this philosophical and ethical debate is, it would far exceed the volume of this writing to go into adequate depth. And, for the foreseeable future, it does not matter much.

We do not make a case for the replacement of human lawyers by Lawyer Bots. At least not now. However, Lawyer Bots can, and should, assist the human intellectual task of lawyering and inform decision making, thereby not replacing but augmenting legal work. There simply is no excuse not to do that, once the costs for investing into Lawyer Bots have come down to a point they are commercially viable. And, in many instances, we have reached the point of break-even.

If the, let's say, established legal industry will not embrace the possibilities that Lawyer Bots bring, that's fine. But then somebody else will. Take Google's mission statement, for example: *«To organize the world's information and make it universally accessible and useful. ... Google continues to focus on ensuring people's access to the information they need. ... The company organizes the information through its proprietary computer algorithms. ... Such organizing of information makes results useful to the individual user.»*[31]

31 Google, *About*, https://www.google.com/about/ (last visited Apr. 11, 2019).

You see that there is no carve out in that statement that implies that law is not part of the world's information, or that legal advice is not needed by the people. Taking the mission statement of Google and similar knowledge focused enterprises seriously, only regulations will shield the legal industry from disruptive change in the long run. This is neither a strong proposition for the incumbent legal industry, nor, of course, is it desirable to block progress merely on the grounds of ancestral protectionistic rules, assuming that there is real progress on the horizon. But looking at the example of the parole judges, there seems to be quite some room for improvement and true justice is still quite a long shot as of today.

We also advocate not philosophizing over content and perfection, while disregarding straightforward logistics and efficient access to justice. Lawyer Bots, like *DoNotPay*[32], bring the law to people, who heretofore lacked either the funding or the time it takes to exercise their right.

A. Are Lawyer Bots on the Rise?

Yes, they are. Legal tech fills big conference venues and are ubiquitous if you talk to in-house lawyers. And Lawyer Bots are among the most mature tools that already can yield a large return on investment, not only in the legal industry, but also helping enterprises with improved access to legal analysis for their employees. By lowering the stakes for those seeking justice, Lawyer Bots may also contribute substantially to a modern society and may be a more effective antidote to structural injustices than punitive damages and the occasional runaway jury in the rare trial.

Flightright[33] or *Fairplane*[34] are great examples. Both portals facilitate the enforcement of passengers' rights, notably compensation due to belated or cancelled flights. For a sole practitioner lawyer who is confronted by clients with such problem, working on the case usually does not pay off because of the limited dispute amounts at stake, often ranging from less than 100 Euros to some hundred Euros maximum. For the passenger, it is even worse going through the rules and, especially, airline bureaucracy that, one gets the impression, is targeted precisely at avoiding compensation payments through demoralization and raising the stakes in terms of time and effort required to make a claim. The founders of *Flightright* and *Fairplane* serve a market heretofore grossly neglected, not by the law itself but the justice system and its inadequate remedies for small stake cases, even if those small stake cases run into

---

32 DoNotPay, *supra* note 10.

33 FLIGHTRIGHT, https://www.flightright.com/ (last visited Apr. 11, 2019).

34 FAIRPLANE, https://www.fairplane.org/ (last visited Apr. 11, 2019).

the hundreds of thousands by number. *Flightright* and *Fairplane* captured this market by thinking out of the box and generating an online service, where the procedure for claiming the compensation is standardized and automated, costs for the clients are low while there is still a profitable outcome for the staff working the case.

But taking a look at the vast majority of lawyers, as of this writing the profession still has not progressed far over the last couple of years. Not that long ago the more innovative lawyers were those who sent out CD's with templates to clients. In fact, they still are, and one gets the impression that technology initiatives are driven more because clients no longer have access to CD ROM drives rather than the desire to serve clients in a more technology enabled manner.[35]

But at the same time, the number of legal tech start-ups increases substantially. The ideas are flowing. And while some entrepreneurs come up with the reinvention of the wheel time and again, there is a lot of innovation out there and great start-ups are bringing sophisticated and often already quite mature technology to the market.

B. What's to come?

It makes sense that we now observe a trend of Lawyer Bots making the press in mass disputes. But there are already many examples in other areas as well and, surely, a significant part of lawyer's daily work will be carried out by software and AI.

Apart from—from a technological perspective—straightforward knowledge management and document automation tools, as of the time of this writing we think that the next big wave of widely visible Lawyer Bots will facilitate legal analysis. By converting legal knowledge and subsumption workflows into an easily accessible digital user interface, many everyday cases can be dealt autonomously by the user. There is no more need to involve a lawyer, in-house or from an external law firm, to come to the correct result, save for more complex cases which are also duly flagged by the Lawyer Bot (with or without guiding the user to a specific flesh and blood lawyer who takes over where the algorithms identified its limits).

This kind of Lawyer Bot is, in its essence, just a more comprehensible form to present laws and regulations to the person seeking what is the law for a specific case. It does not replace the written text of the actual rule, but it packages it into a more understandable flow of if-then dialogues, including red flags where the facts are not sufficiently clear to come to an unambiguous re-

35 The CD ROM drive motive is a true story from the actual experience of the authors, no joke.

sult. The practical advantages are substantial, however, potentially dramatically improving the results of legal analysis that had to be conducted in the day-to-day business by the non-lawyer user without involving a lawyer. While helping this non-lawyer user in finding the answer to a legal problem, the Lawyer Bot can document the process and, thereby, further add to the reduction of compliance risks and increase accountability.

The authors recommend that the established legal industry becomes an integral part of this change and assists in the progress. We are still far from the level of maturity, where AI can also reliably establish the relevant facts that are the basis for legal analysis, in this Lawyer Bots do not bring about any change to the interaction between the user and its lawyer. If programmed by an experienced lawyer, who knows the language of the relevant industry and is able to anticipate common misunderstandings and can detect frequent misconceptions, a Lawyer Bot can be a powerful tool to improve the legal function in an enterprise as well as legal compliance and access to justice on an individual level. In the absence of high-quality algorithms and well formulated instructions to the user, Lawyer Bots may only add to the complexity of the law and represent yet another source where application mistakes may originate.

In high-stake scenarios, like M&A transactions or criminal law, experienced human lawyers will call the shots for a long time, before any significant decision-making authority is yielded to the machines, even if those machines augment the interaction between the lawyers and their clients. An algorithm can ask questions and may also recognize discrepancies or gaps in a set of fact. But, unless we develop reliable hard- and software that reads facial expressions and detects other non-verbal cues, substantial information that is conveyed by us humans cannot be considered by Lawyer Bots.

And even if we were to use science fiction technology for our client's problems one day in the future, would any client want to rely solely upon an algorithm in legal affairs? The law is, in its essence, a source of scholarly inquiry into legal history, philosophy, economic analysis and sociology and raises important and complex issues concerning equality, fairness, and justice. All those aspects do not lend themselves well to digital computing. The chances, therefore, lie in the automation of less complex analyses and the augmentation of complex human legal problem solving through Lawyer Bots and AI in general.

So, what will all this mean for the people who make up the legal profession? Legal technology will undoubtedly revolutionize the law, outdated business models will die, lawyers will have to adapt to keep up with disrupting innovations. Related areas, like publishers in the legal industry, deal with similar problems. To publish content, you no longer need knowhow or infrastructure. Everything you need to share your thoughts with the outside world is at the tip of your finger and within minutes a blog is built and social media will spread the word, provided it is good. We are convinced that Lawyer Bots will revolutionize many aspects of law and much of the legal industry. And if the established legal industry will not deploy them, sooner or later somebody else will. But these changes are, in the opinion of the authors, not to be dreaded. At least, not by those who are focussing on their creative potential. Lawyer Bots will help us getting rid of much of the mundane work, which is not desirable to do anyway, truth be told.

In this light, we do not see the legal profession entering the age of extinction. We are convinced it is the age of many possibilities, through the interaction of human with artificial intelligence and machines augmenting the human virtues, like prudence and justice.

V. Bibliography

A. Hard Copy Sources

HARARI, YUVAL NOAH, 21 LESSONS FOR THE 21 CENTURY (Jonathan Cape, 2018).

KAHNEMAN, DANIEL, THINKING, FAST AND SLOW (Penguin, 2011).

van Rossum, Hedwig, *Lawyers, law schools and social change–defining the challenges of academic legal education in the late modernity*, 25 INTERNATIONAL JOURNAL OF THE LEGAL PROFESSION 245–260 (2018).

WAGNER, JENS, LEGAL TECH UND LEGAL ROBOTS (Springer Gabler, 2018).

B. Online Sources

AMAZON, *Alexa*, https://developer.amazon.com/alexa (last visited Apr. 11, 2019).

Angulo, Ingrid, *Facebook and YouTube should have learned from Microsoft's racist chatbot*, CNBC (Mar. 17, 2018 4:03 PM), https://www.cnbc.com/2018/03/17/facebook-and-youtube-should-learn-from-microsoft-tay-racist-chatbot.html (last visited Apr. 11, 2019).

APPLE, *Siri*, https://www.apple.com/siri/ (last visited Apr. 11, 2019).

Buranyi, Stephen, *Rise of the racist robots—how AI is learning all our worst impulses*, THE GUARDIAN (Aug. 8, 2017), https://www.theguardian.com/inequality/2017/aug/08/rise-of-the-racist-robots-how-ai-is-learning-all-our-worst-impulses (last visited Apr. 11, 2019).

CASECHECK GMBH/HARTZ4WIDERSPRUCH, https://hartz4widerspruch.de/app (last visited Apr. 11, 2019).

Dell Technologies, *Gen Z is here. Are you ready?*, DELL TECHNOLOGIES (2019), https://www.delltechnologies.com/en-us/perspectives/gen-z.htm (last visited Apr. 11, 2019).

DoNotPay, https://www.donotpay.com/ (last visited Apr. 11, 2019).

Faggella, Daniel, *What is Machine Learning*, EMERJ (Feb. 19, 2019), https://emerj.com/ai-glossary-terms/what-is-machine-learning/ (last visited Apr. 11, 2019).

FAIRPLANE, https://www.fairplane.org/ (last visited Apr. 11, 2019).

FLIGHTRIGHT, https://www.flightright.com/ (last visited Apr. 11, 2019).

FLUGRECHT, https://www.flugrecht.de/(last visited Apr. 11, 2019).

FUTURISM, *Types of AI: From reactive to self-aware*, https://futurism.com/images/types-of-ai-from-reactive-to-self-aware-infographic (last visited Apr. 11, 2019).

GEBLITZT.DE, *So funtionierts*, https://www.geblitzt.de/so-funktionierts/ (last visited Apr. 11, 2019).

GOOGLE, *About*, https://www.google.com/about/ (last visited Apr. 11, 2019).

Hassabis, Demis & Silver, David, *AlphaGoZero: Learning from Scratch*, DEEPMIND (Oct. 18, 2017), https://deepmind.com/blog/alphago-zero-learning-scratch/ (last visited Apr. 12, 2019).

Hintze, Arend, *Understanding the four types of AI, from reactive robots to self-aware beings*, THE CONVERSATION (Nov. 14, 2016), http://theconversation.com/understanding-the-four-types-of-ai-from-reactive-robots-to-self-aware-beings-67616 (last visited Apr. 11, 2019).

@IKEA_JP_ANNA, https://twitter.com/IKEA_jp_Anna (last visited Apr. 11, 2019).

Lafranc, Adrienne, *The Internet Is Mostly Bots*, THE ALANTIC (Jan. 31, 2017), https://www.theatlantic.com/technology/archive/2017/01/bots-bots-bots/515043/ (last visited Apr. 11, 2019).

Lagi, Marco *Natural Language Processing—Business Applications*, EMERJ (Feb. 21, 2019), https://emerj.com/ai-sector-overviews/natural-language-processing-business-applications/ (last visited Apr. 11, 2019).

Lyons, Dylan, *How Many People Speak English, And Where Is It Spoken?*, BABBEL (Jul. 26, 2017), https://www.babbel.com/en/magazine/how-many-people-speak-english-and-where-is-it-spoken/ (last visited Apr. 11, 2019).

MYRIGHT, https://www.myright.de/ (last visited Apr. 11, 2019).

Porter, Jon, *Robot lawyer DoNotPay now lets you «sue everyone»*, THE VERGE (Oct. 10, 2018 12:13 PM), https://www.theverge.com/2018/10/10/17959874/donotpay-do-not-pay-robot-lawyer-ios-app-joshua-browder (last visited Apr. 11, 2019).

Rouse, Margaret, *database (DB)*, TECH TARGET (2019), https://searchsqlserver.techtarget.com/definition/database (last visited Apr. 11, 2019).

Rouse, Margaret, *IM Bot*, TECH TARGET (2019), https://searchdomino.techtarget.com/definition/IM-bot (last visited Apr. 11, 2019).

Seif, George, *An easy introduction to Natural Language Processing*, Towards Sciencs (Oct. 2, 2018), https://towardsdatascience.com/an-easy-introduction-to-natural-language-processing-b1e2801291c1 (last visited Apr. 11, 2019).

The Law Society, *Law Tech Adaption Research 2019*, (https://www.lawsociety.org.uk/support-services/research-trends/lawtech-adoption-report/ (last visited Apr. 11, 2019).

Wang, Susan, *Merchants Deploy Alibaba's AI CustomerCustomer-Service Chatbo)*, ALIZILA (Apr. 3, 2017), https://www.alizila.com/online-merchants-deploy-alibabas-ai-customer-service-chatbot/ (last visited Apr. 11, 2019).

PART 2:

WHAT NEW SUITS MIGHT LAWYERS NEED FOR THE FUTURE ?

Dr Guenther Dobrauz-Saldapenna and Corsin Derungs

Innovation, Disruption, or Evolution in the Legal World

Welcome to the Jungle[1]

TABLE OF CONTENTS

1 *Guns 'N' Roses* are the all-time favourite band of both authors of this chapter and their music has forever influenced and enriched our lives. As such it won't come as a surprise that we have chosen the title of the opening track of their seminal 1987 debut album «Appetite for Destruction» as the fitting subtitle for this chapter and «Get in the Ring» off their 1991 masterpiece «Use Your Illusion II» as the first headline in this chapter. Also the font used on the pages segmenting this book into its three parts was designed to echo and hence pay tribute to the cover of the Use Your Illusion I and II albums which itself was based on the fresco «La scuola di Atene» in the Stanze di Raffaello in the Vatican by Italian Renaissance artist *Raffaelo Sanzio da Urbino* (known as *Raphael)*. This entire chapter is dedicated to the memory of the late Professor *Richard John Artley* (1963–2013) who first inspired and tutored us on the fascinating subjects of innovation and disruption. The exciting journey continues and his legacy will live on.

I. Get in the Ring

Fuelled by accelerating digitization, increased global interconnectivity, and transparency (coupled with shifting overarching political agendas, altered user expectations, and technological advances), the legal industry faces unprecedented change across its entire value chain. Within this quadriga, the following two forces are the chief drivers of the chariot of change: The first driver is the **emergence of stable technological solution-ecosystems** which will string together the current impressive but isolated technological breakthroughs. These ecosystems offers both vertical, purpose-built applications and horizontal platform solutions. What initially had appeal only for an early-adopter niche audience will become acceptable for those commanding significant market share. The second driver is the manifestation of **future needs and expectations of the demand-side**[2] which as we have observed once before with the initial rise of General Counsels may lead to dramatic re-drawing of lines and re-shaping of the industry as outlined in other chapters in this book.[3]

But is it really disruption we will see or evolution? The importance of the advent of new technological solutions—especially as we enter the age of exponential technologies with their prospect of hyper-acceleration of change—supports the mantra that the legal industry will face disruption. This would eventually mean the passing on of dominance from established players to the successful promoters of new technology-based dominant designs as heralded by many LegalTech advocates. To try to determine the answer in an informed way, it is useful to first revisit the underlying key concepts of invention, innovation, diffusion, and disruption. Therefore, the first three sections in this chapter provide a summary of the essential research and theory by leaders in the field including *Joseph Schumpeter*, *James Utterback*, *Everett Rogers* and *Michael Porter*. Utilizing their theories on the trajectory of innovation, the last two sections then provide some predictions about how the law marketplace will have to adapt and evolve in the future. This chapter concludes on a positive note: Although legal professionals may need to put on «new suits», the future represents an enormous opportunity to reinvent what it means to be a lawyer and how we add value for our clients.

---

2 Guenther Dobrauz-Saldapenna, *Towards an agoge for tomorrow's legal professionals*, *in* MINUTES OF THE CONFERENCE ON THE FUTURE OF LEGAL SERVICES IN ST. GALLEN (Leo Staub ed., 2018) at 17.

3 *See* the excellent chapters by *Mari Sako* («The Changing Role of General Counsel») and *David Wilkins & María José Esteban Ferrer* («Taking the «Alternative» out of Alternative Legal Service Providers») in this book.

II. Invention, Innovation, Diffusion, and Creative Destruction

The starting point is to distinguish «invention»—the *generation* of ideas or concepts for new products or processes—from «innovation»—the *translation* of such new ideas into marketable products or processes—and from «diffusion»—the widespread *adoption* of these products or processes in the market as Austrian economist *Joseph Schumpeter* first conceptually established.[4] It is also essential to remember *Schumpeter's* seminal concept of «creative destruction»—the process of industrial transformation through radical innovation.[5] «creative destruction»—the introduction of revolutionary products and services by successful entrepreneurs—is the fundamental force driving sustained long-term, economic growth, but also destroys the power of established organisations in the short term.[6]

III. The Dynamics of Innovation

When it comes to innovation, it is by now well established that this usually arises and follows a certain lifecycle, which has been expertly summarized by *James Utterback* in his excellent book *«Mastering the Dynamics of Innovation»*.[7] He points out that the rate of innovation in a product class or an industry is usually highest during its initial, formative phase. During this «fluid phase», as he calls it, a great deal of experimentation with product design and operational characteristics takes place amongst competitors, and much less attention is given to the processes by which products are made. As a conse-

---

4 It should be noted that this taxonomy for which Schumpeter provided the conceptual basis in his 1939 book *«Business Cycles: A Theoretical, Historical and Statistical Analysis of the Capitalist Process»* and in later articles such as *«The Creative Response in Economic History»* (1947) and which is today often referred to as «Schumpeter Trilogy» did not specifically articulate the «Invention-Innovation-Diffusion» distinction and was largely elaborated by later writers based and expanding on his thinking. *See* for example Paul Stoneman, The Handbook of Economics of Innovation and Technology Change (Wiley-Blackwell, 1995) and Perihan Hazel Kaya, *Joseph A. Schumpeter's perspective on innovation*, 3 (8) International Journal of Econmocis, Commerce and Management 25–37 (2015).

5 Joseph Schumpeter, Capitalism, Socialism and Democracy (HarperCollins, 1942) and Joseph Schumpeter, Business Cycles: A Theoretical, Historical and Statistical Analysis of the Capitalist Process (McGraw Hill, 1939).

6 Schumpeter, *id.*

7 James M Utterback, Mastering the Dynamics of Innovation. How Companies Can Seize Opportunities in the Face of Technological Change (Harvard Business Review Press, 1994 [citing 1996 paperback edition]).

quence, the rate of process innovation is significantly less rapid at this stage.[8] During this formative period of a new product, the processes used to produce it are usually crude, inefficient, and based on a mixture of skilled labour and general-purpose machinery and tools.[9] At first, an innovation may be almost entirely a combination of design elements tried out in earlier uses or prototypes. Even disruptive innovations (more on that later), although typically originating from outside of the incumbent industry, usually arise in the context of and resembling the technology, products, or processes they will ultimately replace and hence, at first, are not easily distinguishable. For example, the first cars looked very much like the horse carriages which they shortly replaced.[10] According to *Utterback*, it is fairly common in new industries of particular assembled products that a pioneering firm gets the ball rolling with its initial product, a growing market begins to take shape around it, and new competitors are inspired to enter and either grow the market further or take a chunk of it with their own product versions.[11] No firm has a lock on the market at this early stage and no firm's product is really perfected. No single firm has yet mastered the process of manufacturing, or achieved unassailable control of the distribution channels. At this stage of the product's evolution, both producers and customers are experimenting. Within this rich mixture of experimentation and competition during the «fluid phase» and as the market grows, greater emphasis is usually placed on the development of components tailored especially for the product itself. Ultimately, these may be synthesized into a model that includes most features and meets most user requirements.[12] Eventually, some center of gravity forms in the shape of a *dominant design*—yet another term coined by *Utterback* together with *Abernathy*.[13]

A dominant design has the effect of enforcing or encouraging standardization so that production or other complementary economies can be sought.[14] Also, once the dominant design emerges, the basis of competition changes radically as the industry enters a «transitional phase» in which the major *product* innovation slows down and the rate of major *process* innovations speeds up.[15] A dominant design radically reduces the number of performance requirements to be met by a product by making many of those requirements implicit

---

8 Utterback, *supra* note 7, at xviii.

9 Utterback, *supra* note 7, at 82.

10 Appetite For Disruption, *Chapter 01 | The Dynamics of Innovation & Disruption,* YouTube (Oct. 14, 2018), https://www.youtube.com/watch?v=5BvmWcFHIW0 (last visited Feb. 4, 2019).

11 Utterback, *supra* note 7, at 23.

12 Utterback, *supra* note 7, at 30.

13 James M *Utterback & William J Abernathy, A Dynamic Model of Product and Process Innovation,* 3 (6) Omega, 639–656 (1975).

14 Utterback, *supra* note 7, at 32.

15 Utterback, *supra* note 7, at xviii.

in the design itself.[16] Hence, as the form of the product rapidly becomes settled, the pace of innovation in the way it is produced quickens. Competition begins to take place on the basis of cost and scale as well as of product performance. A firm in possession of collateral assets such as market channels, brand image, and customers switching costs will have some advantage over its competitors in terms of enforcing its product as the dominant design.[17] In the ensuing new era of competition, the linkage of product technologies with manufacturing process, corporate organization and strategy, and the structure and dynamics of an industry is essential. Interestingly, at least with respect to consumer products, narrowing the difference between the outward appearances of a new technology and those of the old and familiar can help in creating market success.[18] Before long, the competitive landscape changes from one characterized by many firms and many unique designs, to one of upwards consolidation with only a few firms with similar product designs surviving.[19] At this point, product variety begins to give way to standard designs that have either proven themselves in the marketplace as the best form for satisfying user needs, or designs that have been dictated by accepted standards, by legal or regulatory constraints.[20]

In the financial services world, or indeed in most regulated industries, the dominant design is chiefly created by regulation.[21] A good example for this is the Swiss investment funds market. Although Switzerland is one of the most important markets for the distribution of funds, it has not managed to become a significant domicile for retail or alternative funds. Indeed, even the Swiss domestic retail funds market is today dominated by funds imported from the EU. One key reason for this is that Swiss funds although more or less identical to their EU peers do not qualify as UCITS[22] or AIFMD[23] funds—the two regulatory dominant designs for retail and alternative investment funds in Europe respectively—and hence cannot be easily offered to the harmonized European market.[24]

Some industries then, according to *Utterback*, enter a «specific phase» in which the rate of major innovation dwindles for both product and process.[25]

---

16 Utterback, *supra* note 7, at 25.
17 Utterback, *supra* note 7, at 27.
18 Utterback, *supra* note 7, at 74.
19 Utterback, *supra* note 7, at 87 et seq.
20 Utterback, *supra* note 7, at 28.
21 Guenther Dobrauz-Saldapenna & Dieter Wirth, *Five propositions for future success of Switzerland as a Financial Centre*, Global Banking & Financial Policy Review 2015/16 173–179 (2016).
22 Undertakings for Collective Investment in Transferable Securities Directive.
23 Alternative Investment Fund Managers Directive.
24 Dobrauz & Wirth, *supra* note 21, at 173–179.
25 Utterback, *supra* note 7, at xviii.

These industries become extremely focused on cost, volume, and capacity. Product and process innovation only appears in small, incremental steps. The model also applies in the case of non-assembled products but in slightly altered form. When compared to process improvements, in the production of complex, assembled products, process innovations in non-assembled products have a more profound impact on productivity and costs. Also process innovations in this category are more likely to emerge from within an industry. Each new wave of innovation has its *fluid*, *transitional*, and *specific* phase.[26] Typically, the number of firms participating in later waves is lower.[27] The reason for this drop-off in the number of competing firms in later waves is no doubt related to the fact that markets are often well defined by the first wave of innovation. It is also related to the fact that the established firms develop the distribution channels and production facilities to serve these markets, limiting the number of possible firms that can reform the industry—even with superior technology. Thus, the number of firms participating in later waves is lower, unless the new wave of innovation substantially broadens or alters the market, or is indeed disruptive.[28]

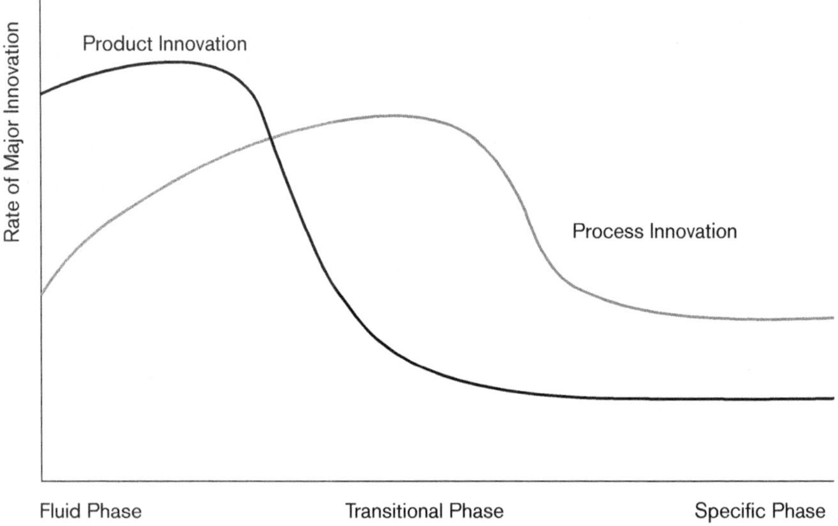

Exhibit 1: «The Dynamics of Innovation» [Source: Utterback xvii (1994)].

26 Utterback, *supra* note 7, at 99.
27 Utterback, *supra* note 7, at 100.
28 Utterback, *supra* note 7, at 101.

IV. Evolution vs Disruption

We have established that the dominant design is the one solution which wins the allegiance of the marketplace, the one that competitors and innovators must adhere to if they hope to command significant market following.[29] It embodies the requirements of many classes of users of a product, even though it may not meet the needs of a particular class to quite the same extent as a customized design would. It is a so-called satisfier of many in terms of the interplay of technological possibilities and market choices, instead of an optimizer for a few.[30] As such it is also the underlying trigger for the change in addressable customer base from earlier adopters to more mass markets.

But what happens beyond a specific consolidated wave? What about the sequence of such waves and the difference between evolution and disruption? This is probably best explained by looking at the unfolding dynamic from the perspective of diffusion or adoption of innovation. It was *Everett Rogers* who following earlier work by *Ryan and Gross*[31] stated in his book *«Diffusion of Innovations»*[32] that, based on bell-curve mathematics, adopters of any new innovation can be categorized as follows:

- **Innovators**: 2.5%;
- **Early adopters**:[33] 13.5%;
- **Early majority**: 34%;
- **Late majority**: 34%; and,
- **Laggards**:16%.

Rogers' approach was overly mathematical (and not 100% supported by his own or in fact any later data),[34] but he inspired uptake over time to be conventionally represented, quantitatively, by two types of graphs. The first, the «Sales Curve», which shows product sales over time, and secondly the «Market Penetration Curve», or «S-curve». The S-curve is the cumulative integral of the bell curve. It is slow at the start, more rapid as adoption increases, then levelling off until only a small percentage of laggards have not adopted. For the majority of products, this shows whether the product is still specialist—having typically not yet sold more than 15% of the total number it is expected

---

29 Utterback, *supra* note 7, at 24.

30 Utterback, *supra* note 7, at 25.

31 Bryce Ryan & Neal Gross, *Acceptance and diffusion of hybrid corn seed in two Iowa communities,* 1372) Researcht Bulletin 663–708 (1950).

32 Everett M Rogers, Diffusion of Innovations (The Free Press, 2003) at 5.

33 «Early adopters» is a term coined by *Rogers*.

34 Guenther Dobrauz-Saldapenna, Uptake Revisted (WVB, 2010) at 10.

to sell within its market—or whether it has become a mainstream product, having sold to typically more than 30% of potential purchasers.[35]

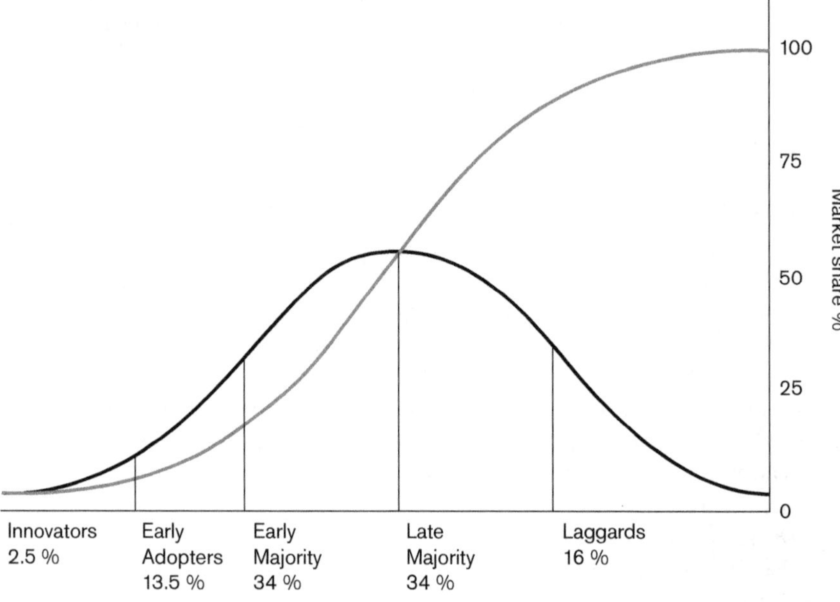

Exhibit 2: «Diffusion of Innovation» [Source: Wikipedia].

This distinction is also elaborated on by *Geoffrey Moore* who refers to the «chasm» between the early adopters of the product (the technology enthusiasts and visionaries) and the early majority (the pragmatists) and how to cross it.[36] Also *Clayton Christensen* has done great work looking at the primary uptake of new products, with an initial focus on the perspective of established companies trying to sustain themselves.[37] *Christensen* in particular distinguishes between «sustaining innovation» and «disruptive innovation». The former favours incumbents over new entrants as it essentially allows to serve (existing) high value customers or clients in a better way. Disruptive innovation often means that a new methodology and/or technology is used to create a new market or to provide low-cost alternatives to lower value customers or clients. This often allows entrants to overtake established players according to *Chris-*

---

35 Dobrauz, *Uptake Revisited*, *supra* note 34, at 12.

36 Geoffrey A Moore, Crossing the Chasm. Marketing and selling disruptive products to mainstream customers (HarperCollins Publishers, 1991 [citing 1999 paperback edition]).

37 Clayton M Christensen, The Innovator's Dilemma: When New Technologies Cause Great Firms To Fail (Harvard Business School Press, 1997).

tensen.[38] He also correctly identifies corporate structural change as a necessary precursor to new product innovation.[39] This is essential as quite often an unhappy by-product of success in one generation of technology is narrowing of focus and vulnerability to competitors championing the next technological generation.[40] Failing firms, at such stage, are often remarkably creative in defending their entrenched technologies, which often reach unimagined heights of elegance in design and technical performance only when their demise is clearly predictable: Horse carriages were never better or more beautiful than just before they were taken out by cars. Or as probably better put (paraphrasing similar statements to the same end):

> *«The stone age was not ended by lack of stones but the advent of new technology.»*
> *– Guenther Dobrauz-Saldapenna/Appetite For Disruption (2018)*[41]

It was again *Utterback* who showed that a second generation product, although initially functionally inferior to an established one, can and will overtake it if it raises the potential ceiling of functionality beyond the capabilities of the existing product.[42] This is because it raises customer expectations of satisfaction, leading to dissatisfaction with the existing product and hence a value gap. This opens up a window of opportunity for a new wave of innovation and restructuring of the given market.[43] This then gives rise to the question who—incumbents or newcomers—will be best placed to launch and capture value from such changes. This chiefly depends on whether the innovation is «evolutionary» or «revolutionary», i.e., «disruptive».

The one and only *Michael Porter* stated that most industry-shattering innovations do not spring from the established competitors in an industry but from new firms or from established firms entering a new arena.[44] This is true even though such radical innovations often are seen to be based on the synthesis of well-known technical information or components (what we would call orthodoxy elements of the original composite S-curve which become sparks of heresy igniting the fire of a new curve). They occur step by step and sometimes exist in embryonic form for many years before they become commercially

---

38 Christensen, *supra* note 37.

39 *Id.*

40 Utterback, *supra* note 7, at xxiv.

41 Appetite For Disruption, *Chapter 02 | Uptake Revisited—Evolution vs Disruption,* YouTube (Nov. 4, 2018), https://www.youtube.com/watch?v=Ad2hmsn9qP0&t=584s.

42 Utterback, *supra* note 7, at 101.

43 Utterback, *supra* note 7, at 159.

44 Michael E Porter, *Technology and Competitive Advantage*, 6 Journal of Business Strategy 60–78 (1985).

significant. One reason for the lethargy of well-established competitors in a product market undergoing potentially disruptive innovation is that the competitors face increasing constraints from the growing web of relationships that bind product and process change together.[45] At the start of production of a new product, general-purpose equipment, available components, and high skilled people may suffice to enter the market. As both product and market increase in sophistication, more specialisation is generally required in equipment, components, and skills. Thus change in one element, the product, requires changes throughout the whole system of materials, equipment, methods, and suppliers.[46] This may make changing much more onerous and costly for the established firm than for the new entrant. Often powerful competitors not only resist innovative threats, but also resist all efforts to understand them, preferring to further entrench their positions in the older products.[47] This results in a surge of productivity and performance that may take the older technology to unheard-of heights. But in most cases this is a sign of impending death.[48] What is also not helpful is the result of the typical upwards consolidation of an industry as it goes through the innovation cycle—sizeable and complex entities often run by operational experts who are quite distanced from the underlying technology (or the business of the business whatever that may be). These experts literally look down on new things coming up and at them out of a garage or off the end of lab bench.[49] At the time an invading or disruptive technology first appears, the established technology generally offers better performance or cost than does the challenger, which is still unperfected. Consider that the initial cars were inferior to horse carriages. The new technology may be viewed objectively as crude, leading to the belief that it will find only limited application.[50] The performance superiority of the established technology may prevail for quite some time, but if the new technology has real merit, it typically enters a period of rapid improvement—just as the established technology enters a stage of slow innovative improvements. Eventually, the newcomer improves its performance characteristics to the point where they match those of the established technology and rockets past it, still in the midst of a period of rapid improvement.[51] Purveyors of established technologies often respond to an invasion of their product market with redoubled creative efforts that may lead to substantial product improvements based on the same product architecture.[52] Here, the es-

45 Utterback, *supra* note 7, at xxvii.
46 Utterback, *supra* note 7, at 96.
47 Utterback, *supra* note 7, at 159.
48 Utterback, *supra* note 7, at xxvii.
49 Appetite For Disruption, *supra* note 41.
50 Utterback, *supra* note 7, at 158.
51 Utterback, *id.*
52 Utterback, *supra* note 7, at 159.

tablished product enjoys a brief period of performance improvement. However, the relentless pace of improvement in the new product technology allows the challenger to equal, and then surpass, the established product.[53]

V. Entering the Age of Hyper-Evolution

We strongly believe that all of the above models apply and are relevant to the legal realm, which obviously is predominantly a service rather than a product world with according stronger emphasis on other, softer factors than technology. It is also important to remember that today the focus of innovation is increasingly abstract as it transcends its previous areas such as technical capability, markets, brand, and processes. Furthermore, such elements are only some but by far not all relevant dimensions of the ever-expanding competitive spectrum. Also, in a globalised world where everything is hyper-connected and ideas are swiftly copied, the pace and cadence of innovation has significantly increased.[54] It has taken technological innovations such as the car, telephone, TV, and even the internet decades to reach (and eventually connect) millions of users in today's internet-based technology society. Compare that to a mobile phone app, building on many of these prior achievements, that can accomplish the same in a matter of days,[55] and the same will probably be true for other innovations as the exponential technologies age unfolds. Hence, what we increasingly face is so-called «Big-Bang Disruption» which has the potential to collapse the product life cycle we know (including *Everett Rogers'* classic bell curve of five distinct customer segments—innovators, early adopters, early majority, late majority, and laggards)[56] into only two segments: trial users, who often participate in product development, and everyone else. What this means is that where *Moore* (against the background of the industry dynamics of his time) focused on making the big leap from targeting early adopters to market-

---

53 Utterback, *id.*

54 Appetite For Disruption, *supra* note 39.

55 Although the popular internet meme that *«It Took the Telephone 75 Years To Do What Angry Birds Did in 35 Days»* is likely if not wrong but most certainly highly skewed—*see* Timothy Aeppel, *It Took the Telephone 75 Years To Do What Angry Birds Did in 35 Days. But what does it mean*, The Wall Street Journal (Mar. 13, 2015, 7:50 AM), https://blogs.wsj.com/economics/2015/03/13/it-took-the-telephone-75-years-to-do-what-angry-birds-did-in-35-days-but-what-does-that-mean/?mod=e2fb&fbclid=IwAR3Hj5dYTnBc53lGX9erpa9ISS6unXMo4rMF-4dP-f8NyMsFngyjb_Yp9jDc (last visited Feb. 3, 2019) and Timothy Aeppel, *50 Million Users: The Making of an «Angry Birds» Internet Meme*, The Wall Street Journal (Mar. 20, 2015, 1:00 PM), https://blogs.wsj.com/economics/2015/03/20/50-million-users-the-making-of-an-angry-birds- internet-meme/ (last visited Feb. 3, 2019) for an interesting background read on this—the basic idea is probably correct.

56 Moore, *supra* note 36, at 12.

ing to the early majority,[57] nowadays big-bang disruptions can be marketed to every segment simultaneously, right from the start. As such the adoption curve where these dynamics can apply has become something closer to a straight line that heads up and then falls rapidly when saturation is reached or a new disruption appears.[58]

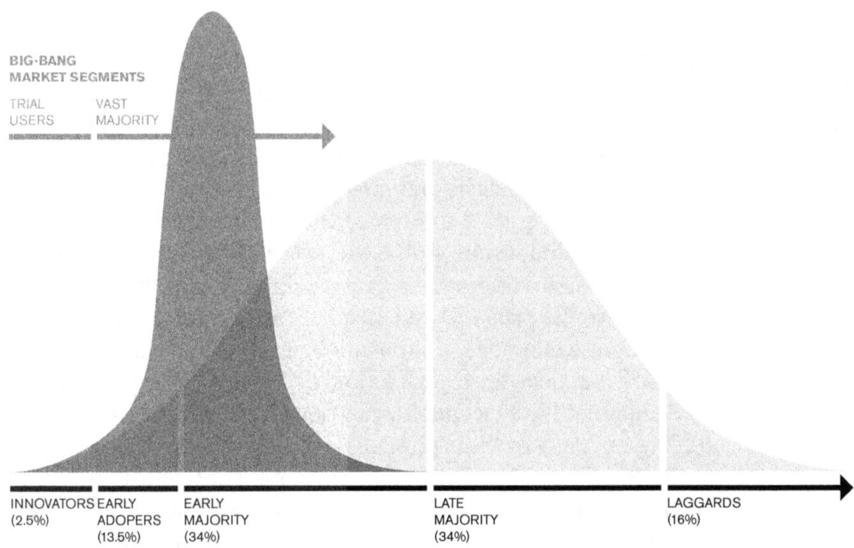

Exhibit 3: Big Bang Market Disruption [Source: Downes & Nunes (2014) at 47].

In the past years, the rate of adoption of innovations has accelerated at a dizzying speed across all sectors and industries.[59] This, depending on your perspective, leads either to a recurring identity crisis for existing products and services or an exciting opportunity to break up entrenched positions—which is particularly relevant for the legal world given its conservative structures which have been cultivated over decades, if not centuries.

Despite our fascination with the new technological opportunities and the potentially deicidal powers of innovation, when it comes to the legal world, we should expect to see hyper-evolution—an accelerated version of what *Ron*

---

57 Moore, *supra* note 36, at xiv.

58 Larry Downes & Paul Nunes, Big-Bang Disruption. Strategy in the Age of Devastating Innovation (Portfolio, 2014).

59 Susanne Durst, Serdal Temel and Helio Aisenberg Ferenhof (Eds.), Open Innovation and Knowledge Management in Small and Medium Enterprises (World Scientific Publishing Co., 2018) at 142.

Dolin and Thomas Buley refer to as «Adaptive Innovation»[60]—rather than disruption. The reason for this is that the legal industry, at present, is largely a regulated one. This may change over time given the arguments for improved access to justice and the increase in the number of advocates who have developed compelling arguments, evidence, and support for the view that many people would benefit more from what they call «just resolution» of legal problems.[61] They argue non-lawyer advocates and unrepresented lay people across a number of common justice problems have been observed to perform as well or better than lawyers. As such, they contend that if the goal is indeed to create access to justice, other services can be more effective and efficient than that provided by lawyers.[62] That being said, at present we do not have a strong indication of deregulation of the industry in the immediate future. In a regulated environment, as indicated above, delivery of the dominant design is also significantly determined by the ability to comply with regulation/enforced standards.[63] We strongly believe that **the dominant and most successful design in the legal industry will be a hybrid**. As a consequence, rather than disruption, we expect accelerated evolution to move the industry further up (and to prolong) the existing S-curve. We believe that such an environment typically favours incumbents with deeper investments pockets as long as they are able to: 1) recognise and swiftly integrate new, superior, and soon to be dominant technical solutions;[64] and, 2) leverage softer factors that are built around the ability to comply with required/prohibitive legal/regulatory requirements and industry champion parameters (such as bar admission, independence, talent pull, brand, reputation, and trust etc.). This, in turn, leads to upwards consolidation and the parallel rise of significant enabler-technology-platforms.[65]

---

60 Ron Dolin & Thomas Buley, *Adaptive Innovation: Innovator's Dilemma in Big Law*, 5 (2) Harvard Law School's The Practice (Jan.–Feb. 2019).

61 Christian Farias, *Everyone Needs Legal Help. That Doesn't Mean Everyone Needs a Lawyer,* The New York Times (Feb. 13, 2019), https://www.nytimes.com/2019/02/13/opinion/legal-issues.html (last visited Feb. 16, 2019).

62 Rebecca L Sandefur, *Access to What?* 148 (1) Daedalus 49–55 (2018) (published online Jan. 1, 2019), https://www.amacad.org/sites/default/files/publication/downloads/19_Winter_Daedalus_Sandefur.pdf) (last visited Feb. 16, 2019).

63 Dobrauz & Wirth, *supra* note 21, at 174.

64 On this note we should not forget that for example the ABA's Model Rules of Professional Conduct spell out a duty to maintain relevant technological knowledge and skills. Of course, as Robert Ambrogi notes the Model Rules are just that—a model. They provide guidance to the states in formulating their own rules of professional conduct. Each state is free to adopt, reject, ignore or modify the Model Rules. For the duty of technology competence to apply to the lawyers in any given state, that state's high court (or rule-setting body) would first have to adopt it. To date 35 states have adopted this *de facto* new standard. *See* Robert Ambrogi, *Tech Competence,* Law Sites (2019), https://www.lawsitesblog.com/tech-competence/ (last visited Feb. 5, 2019).

65 Dobrauz, *Towards an agoge for tomorrow's legal professionals, supra* note 2, at 19.

VI. Offerings and Organisations will be re-shaped by Changing Demand

As *Thompson Reuters* note:

> *«Since 2008, there has been a complete shift from a seller's to a buyer's market for legal services. In stark contrast to the traditional law firm model, clients are now in control of all key decisions impacting legal representation–from staffing and scheduling decisions to outsourcing requirements, from project management to pricing structures–and they are not likely to relinquish that control anytime soon.»*[66]

The big buyers of and significant providers of legal services themselves are in-house legal departments.[67] These are under significant pressure to continuously provide more for less and work against increasing complexity and shorter timelines. Therefore, legal departments are undergoing a structural evolution and their demand for support becomes significantly modified. At the same time, the mix of work required to deliver optimal output will change—essentially reducing the artisanal part to what truly requires skill and allowing key talent to focus on what really matters. In order to cater to this altered demand, law firms have to change. In a world where anything can be ordered with the click of a button, clients are now expecting professional services to be easily accessible, transparent, flexible, and fairly priced. But this goes far beyond simple digitization (which itself will go far beyond the J-curve of exponential growth of references to emojis in court opinions we have recently seen).[68] What we will see in the years to come is a fundamental transformation—«from pyramids to rockets» as aptly outlined by *BCG* in collaboration with *Bucerius CLP*.[69] Despite all their efforts, however, law firms will (in our view) have to accept alternative legal as well as technology and managed ser-

---

66 Thomson Reuters, *2019 Report on the State of the Legal Market,* (Jan. 14, 2019, 01:16 AM), http://images.ask.legalsolutions.thomsonreuters.com/Web/TRlegalUS/%7B7f73da9c-0789-4f63-b012-379d45d54cdf%7D_2019_Report_on_the_State_of_the_Legal_Market_NEW.pdf (last visited Feb. 11, 2019) at 13.

67 The Law Society of England and Wales, *The Future of Legal Services* (Jan. 28, 2016), https://www.lawsociety.org.uk/support-services/research-trends/the-future-of-legal-services/ (last visited Feb. 13, 2019) at 6.

68 Nate Robson, *Q&A: Getting Ready for the Emoji Law Revolution, in* LAW.COM (legaltech news), https://www.law.com/legaltechnews/2019/02/08/qa-getting-ready-for-the-emoji-law-revolution-397-16729/?kw=Q&A:%20Getting%20Ready%20for%20the%20Emoji%20Law%20Revolution (Feb. 8, 2019) (last visited Feb. 9, 2019).

69 Boston Consultig Group & Bucerius Law School, eds., *How Legal Technology Will Change the Business of Law*, at 10.

vices providers (and combinations thereof). This will likely not lead to one monolithic «enriched rocket» law firm design that caters to the reshaped in-house departments (and also to private clients via lawyer bots and automated legal documents supplied online). Instead, it will result in a new and more diverse composite, delivery ecosystem. It remains to be seen, however, which players will ultimately hold the reigns at which stage and in which segment.

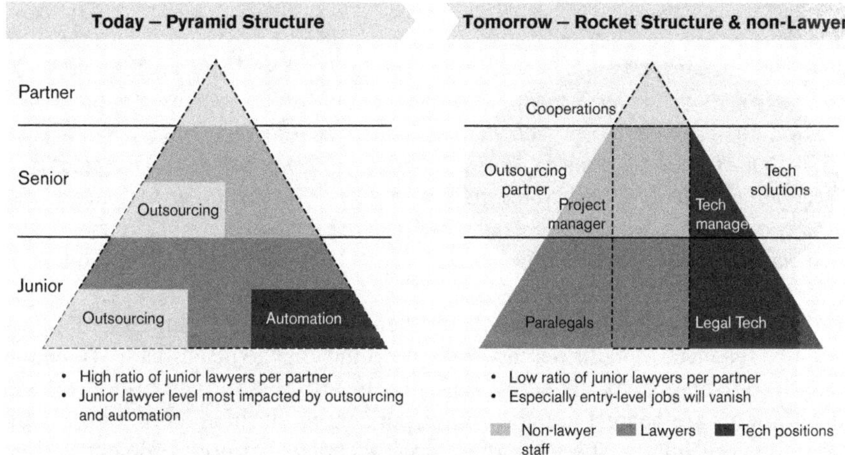

Exhibit 4: «From Pryamids to Rockets» [Source: BCG & Buccerius at 10].

It is obvious that the legal industry has yet to reach a point of real transformative change. So far, we have seen the introduction of a bit of tech-enabled efficiency and a slight change of the mix of service providers via the addition of alternative legal service providers. Otherwise, labour and paper still largely dominate.[70] In other words, the basic approach to practicing law has not changed much in the past 100+ years. It appears that this is not caused by a lack of tools or know-how, but instead by culture on both sides of the equation or, perhaps, by something which *Bon Jovi* once aptly singled out as «fear»:

> *«... but there's only one thing that's stopping us now, it's*
> *fear fear fear*
> *of a new thing...*
> *You ain't one for taking chances*
> *You work and you live and breathe that 9 to 5*

---

70 Ken Grady, *Stagnation And The Legal Industry. Real transformation has yet to arrive* (Jan. 2, 2019, 2:14 PM), https://medium.com/the-algorithmic-society/stagnation-and-the-legal-industry-bc801a8b4d38 (last visited Apr. 12, 2019).

Still that's what you call living
That's surviving to me
And surviving is living to die in
Fear.»[71]
– Bon Jovi, Fear (1992)

In a slightly more technical vein, *Ken Grady* summarized the situation as follows:

> *«The industry, and in particular the buyers of legal services, are not ready for real transformative change. They aren't ready for 60 minutes of work to be compressed into 60 seconds or 6 seconds. They aren't ready for the labor of 20 to be done by 1. Even though there are isolated examples of this happening, it hasn't become sustainable or wide spread. The buyers certainly aren't ready for a world filled with paper to be converted to a digital, computational world.»*[72]

But as the cost pressure on legal departments increases, the tipping point may soon be reached. In addition, law firms need the change just as badly (whether they like it or not) as the storm will shortly hit their shores. In-house legal departments are nearest to the earnings per share, return on investment calculations every quarter, because they were asked to be more efficient earlier. They are now starting to pass that request for enhanced efficiency on to their law firms.[73] According to the latest *Clio* research, lawyers today miss out on nearly 5.6 hours of billable work on each 8-hour work day as too much time is spent on other activities.[74] Although the top law firms reported a record year in 2018, this is only true for the uppermost echelons of the industry. In general, there is a growing segmentation in the marketplace between the top-performing firms and all the rest.[75] The top of the hourglass continue to win by focus-

---

71 Bon Jovi, Fear (PolyGram Records, 1992).

72 Grady, *supra* note 70.

73 Sue Reisinger, *Experts Disagree on Who Leads the Way on LegalTech—Law firms or In-House Counsel*, Law.com (Feb. 21, 2019, 2:33 PM), https://www.law.com/legaltechnews/2019/02/21/ex perts-disagree-on-who-leads-the-way-on-legal-tech-law-firms-or-in-house-counsel/?kw=Experts%20Disagree%20on%20Who%20Leads%20the%20Way%20on%20Legal%20Tech%26mdash%3BLaw%20Firms%20or%20In-House%20Counsel&utm_source=email&utm_medium=enl&utm_campaign=afternoonupdate&utm_content=20190222&utm_term=ltn (last visited Feb. 22, 2019).

74 Clio, *Legal Trends Report 2018*, Clio, *Legal Trends Report 2018* (Jan. 7, 2019, 10:09 AM), https://www.clio.com/wp-content/uploads/2018/10/Legal-Trends-Report-2018.pdf at 11 (last visited Apr. 11, 2019).

75 Dan Packel, *After a Record-Setting 2018 for Law Firms, Does a Reckoning Await?* Law.com (Dec. 17, 2018, 5:00 AM), https://www.law.com/americanlawyer/2018/12/17/after-a-record-setting-2018-for-law-firms-does-a-reckoning-await/ (last visited Feb. 2, 2019).

ing on talent management and high-value work. The bottom of the hourglass increasingly focus on building scale through the effective use of data, process management, and technology, and attempt to show client focus through productisation and partnering with other parts of the legal services supply chain.[76] In addition, mergers and consolidation dominate the agenda on an unprecedented scale.[77] For the middle and lower part of the spectrum, the pressure increases as the top law firms continue to branch out. For the past two decades, large law firms have been expanding into new markets at a tremendous pace. In particular, the United States' largest 250 law firms by attorney headcount, the so-called NLJ 250, have nearly doubled their geographic coverage by adding more than 1,400 new offices across the globe since 2001.[78]

> *«This process has fundamentally changed the legal market in two important ways. First, it has created a group of law firms with vast scale and geographic reach. Equally important is the impact that expansion has had on local law firms. Many regional legal markets have been transformed over the past decade. They have transitioned from localized markets, dominated by legacy firms, to highly competitive marketplaces, fully integrated into the global legal services market.»*[79]

Against this background, all law firms (irrespective of classification) want to and, indeed, need to increase revenues. Yet, the typical lawyer already works more than s/he plans to each week. Fundamental change is also needed on this side of the equation. This point is also highlighted in *Thomson Reuter's* latest industry research which concludes:

> *«While the number of worked hours has been reasonably stable in recent years, it is important to note that, compared to average billable hours in the pre-recession years (i.e., prior to 2008), there remains a significant difference. By way of illustration, in 2007, the billable hours worked averaged 134 per month. Through 2018, the average is now 122 per month, or a difference of 144 hours per year from the 2007 level. To see the economic impact of this reduction in productivity, one need only multiply this annual*

---

76 David Curle, *Legal tech adoption and the real drivers of change*, Thomson Reuters Blog (Feb. 8, 2019), https://blogs.thomsonreuters.com/legal-uk/2019/02/08/legal-tech-week/ (last visited Feb. 5, 2019).

77 Elizabeth Olson, *Law Firms Announced Record-Breaking 106 Mergers Last Year*, Big Law Business (Jan. 7, 2019), https://biglawbusiness.com/law-firms-announced-record-breaking-106-mergers-last-year (last visited Feb. 4, 2019).

78 AML, *The Invasion of Regional Legal Markets and How Mid-sized Firms Should Respond*, https://www.alm.com/intelligence/solutions-we-provide/business-of-law-solutions/analyst-reports/barbarians-gate-report/ (2018) (last visited Feb. 22, 2019)

79 AML, *id.*

difference by the average worked rate in 2018 of USD 489 per hour, to see that the decreased productivity over the last decade cost firms some USD 70,416 per lawyer per year in 2018. For a firm of 200 lawyers, that translates to a total cost of USD 14.1 million; for a firm of 400 to USD 28.2 million; and for a firm of 600 to USD 42.3 million.»[80]

Harvard Law School Professor *David Wilkins* sees the legal industry as one run on «elevator assets», stressing that law firms don't have to worry too much about locking their offices in the evening as their true assets leave the building in the evening via the elevator.[81] We agree with this view and don't believe that, despite the increasing importance of technology, this will completely change. Instead, we expect that particular, emerging disruptive, digital innovations will trigger a transition. Instead of using technology as a tool to increase efficiency and enable more sophisticated work in a people-leveraged business model, technology will be a core generator of the actual legal work product. Quite obviously this expected transition from core work being done by people assisted by machines to work being done by machines controlled by people will have a transformational impact on business models.[82] As *Paul Daugherty and H James Wilson* aptly presented in their model reproduced in Exhibit 5 below, a continuum exists from work that can only be done by humans (because of the degree of intellectual ambiguity and complexity, requiring a level of judgement or empathy of which machines are incapable) to work that can or should only be done by machines (because of the sheer volume of data involved, the complexity or the analysis to be performed, or because the machine can do the work as well or better than humans, far less expensively).[83] Within this continuum, we can (or rather we must) expect a steady shift in activities from left to right across the spectrum, with machines taking over more and more existing work, and humans, aided by those machines, taking on more sophisticated and entirely new kinds of work. Along with this, we would expect a middle ground existing between human and machine, where each depends on the other to deliver the best performance.[84]

---

80 Thomson Reuters, *supra* note 66, at 7.

81 Comment by Professor *David B Wilkins* during his joint lecture with *Ron Dolin* «Operationalizing Innovation in the Market for Legal Services» at the Harvard Law School Center on the Legal Profession on Feb. 13, 2019 as noted by Dr Guenther Dobrauz-Saldapenna.

82 Cambridge Strategy Group, *Thriving at the Edge of Chaos—AI, Blockchain and the Law Firm of the Future* (2018), https://mailchi.mp/c8a7253a01c3/thriving-at-the-edge-of-chaos-download (last visited Feb. 22, 2019) at 23.

83 Paul A Daugherty & H James Wilson, *What Are The New Jobs In A Human + Machine World?*, Forbes (Jul. 17, 2018 5:18 PM), https://www.forbes.com/sites/insights-intelai/2018/07/17/what-are-the-new-jobs-in-a-human--machine-world/#15f7830063e3 (last visited Feb. 7, 2019).

84 Paul R Daugherty & H James Wilson, Human + Machine: Reimagining Work in the Age of AI (Harvard Business School Press, 2018).

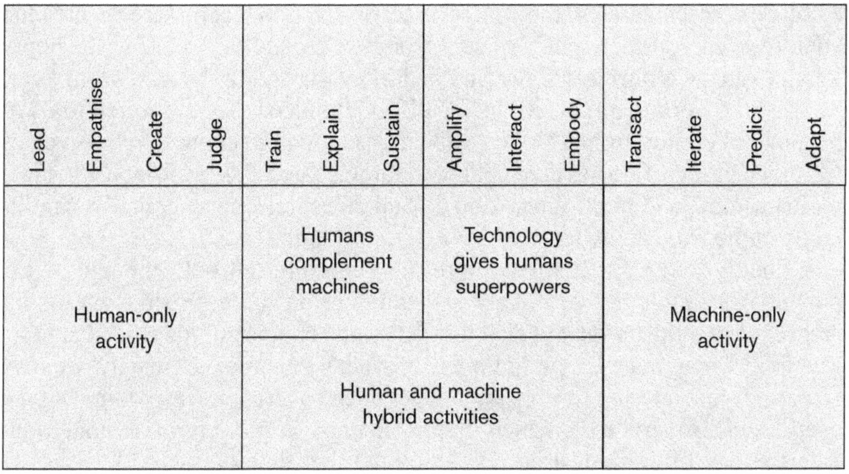

Lead, Empathise, Create, Judge	Train, Explain, Sustain	Amplify, Interact, Embody	Transact, Iterate, Predict, Adapt
Human-only activity	Humans complement machines	Technology gives humans superpowers	Machine-only activity
	Human and machine hybrid activities		

Exhibit 5: The Human/Machine Performance Continuum [Source: Daugherty & Wilson (2018)].

We are also convinced that smart people work best in a smart workplace which offers the prospect of not only a rewarding but also a meaningful journey with minimum precious time wasted on non-value adding tasks. So, let's take wasted hours out of an industry which has built a cult around the hour but where the last good day for the billable hour clearly was yesterday. If the move across the continuum (described above) is unavoidable, soon a point will be reached where charging for work on the basis of the human effort and investment by the firm alone becomes nonsensical. At that point, the «billable hour» will likely cease to have relevance, except in very rare circumstances.[85] Or as *Mark A Cohen* put it so pointedly: *«[...] just knowing the law and ‹bill baby bill› won't cut it any more».*[86]

With the right technology, it becomes possible to unlock untapped potential. The organizations that adopt the right technology coupled with a culture that values diversity of talent and a focus on the client at the center (over money)[87] will attract the brightest talent.[88] Now, with this in mind, it is time to

---

85 Cambridge Strategy Group, *supra* note 82, at 23.

86 Mark A Cohen, *Are Law Firms Becoming Obsolete?*, Forbes (Jun. 12, 2017, 5:36 AM), https://www.forbes.com/sites/markcohen1/2017/06/12/are-law-firms-becoming-obsolete/#5779f682264d (last visited Feb. 12, 2019).

87 Reena SenGupta, *The best law firm innovators alter their culture first*, Financial Times (Jun. 2, 2017), https://www.ft.com/content/4ed185c8-3bcc-11e7-ac89-b01cc67cfeec (last visited Feb. 5, 2019).

88 Note: This seems particularly important as young talent today is starting to consider pursuing careers in other sectors than the law where the career outlook is perceived as being less attractive. *See* for example Noam Schreiber, *An Expensive Law Degree, and No Place to Use It*, The New

embrace new technology, forge allegiances which previously were deemed too alien to even consider, and re-invent from the ground up. We tend to simply look towards California and the Silicon Valley to hand us the next set of keys. That won't work this time around. California, indeed, has pioneered tools of personal liberation from LSD to surfboards and mobile phones.[89] However, as we enter the world of exponential technologies and the legal industry faces multi-facetted and multi-dimensional challenges, relevant innovation can literally come from anywhere.[90]

Finally don't forget that we are now entering not only the age of exponential technologies but likely and building on these also the age of increased decentralization and disintermediation. The rise of the so-called «Gig Economy» may just be a first glimpse of what's to come. Ultimately, we may also move into an age of truly «liquid talent» and overcome the pyramidal (and even «rocket») structures which in our view are largely an increasingly outdated legacy of the industrial revolution. At that time the only blueprints to respond to the swiftly arising need to organize larger groups of people into a workforce were the army and the church. What was an efficient and effective delivery structure for almost two centuries now is increasingly challenged by the reality we face today and likely inadequate to fully unlock the potential of in particular diversity. Soon we may find ourselves effectively going back to a future where everyone will (again) become an entrepreneur around his or her specific skills and talents, forming constantly changing centers of gravity with other experts sourced globally and perfectly matched via networked platforms around rewarding and meaningful challenges. And once again technology could be a catalyst for this and new concepts such as pursued by for example *Catalant Technologies* out of Boston may change the narrative. And for the better.

So, it is time to embark on an unbiased journey of discovery! Although the future may require lawyers to put on «New Suits», it represents an enormous opportunity to reinvent ourselves for our own and our clients' benefit!

York Times (Jun. 17, 2016), https://www.nytimes.com/2016/06/19/business/dealbook/an-expensive-law-degree-and-no-place-to-use-it.html (last visited Feb. 16, 2019).

89 Appetite For Disruption, *Chapter 03 | Technology Bridge—Evaluating and Investing in Innovation,* YouTube (Nov. 18, 2018), https://www.youtube.com/watch?v=4qfeGuoWD_s&t=76s (last visited Feb. 8, 2019).

90 Remember: truly disruptive innovation typically comes from outside of the established industry! And as *Bruce Springsteen* once said:
«We learned more from a 3-minute record, baby,
Than we ever learned in school»
Bruce Springsteen, No Surrender (Columbia Records, 1984).

«Come on, come on, gotta trust in something strong
Gotta keep them wheels on turning
Or die with the rest and wrong
Hang on, hang on, gonna beat that wind for long
Yeah, eat that dust and savor the road less traveled on.»[91]
– Chuck Ragan, The Fire, The Steel, The Tread (2013)

VII. Bibliography

A. Hard Copy Sources

Artley, Richard John, Dobrauz, Guenther, et al., Making Money out of Technology, (Linde Verlag, 2003).

Christensen, Clayton M, The Innovator's Dilemma: When New Technologies Cause Great Firms To Fail, (Harvard Business School Press, 1997).

Daugherty, Paul R & Wilson, H James, Human + Machine: Reimagining Work in the Age of AI (Harvard Business School Press, 2018).

Dobrauz-Saldapenna, Guenther, *Towards an agoge for tomorrow's legal professionals, in* Minutes of the Conference on the Future of Legal Services in St. Gallen 17–21 (Leo Staub ed., Schulthess, 2018).

Dobrauz-Saldapenna, Guenther, Uptake Revisited. An Investigation into the Success & Failure Factors for Innovative Products in International Markets (WVB Wissenschaftlicher Verlag Berlin, 2010).

Dobrauz-Saldapenna, Guenther & Wirth, Dieter, *Five propositions for future success of Switzerland as a Financial Centre*, Global Banking & Financial Policy Review 2015/16 173–179 (2016).

Dolin, Ron & Buley, Thomas, *Adaptive Innovation: Innovator's Dilemma in Big Law*, 5 (2) Harvard Law School's The Practice (Jan.–Feb. 2019).

Downes, Larry & Nunes, Paul, Big-Bang Disruption. Strategy in the Age of Devastating Innovation (Portfolio, 2014).

Susanne Durst, Serdal Temel and Helio Aisenberg Ferenhof (Eds.), Open Innovation and Knowledge Management in Small and Medium Enterprises (World Scientific Publishing Co., 2018).

Kaya, Perihan Hazel, *Joseph A. Schumpeter's perspective on innovation*, 3 (8) International Journal of Econmocis, Commerce and Management 25–37 (2015).

Moore, Geoffrey A, Crossing the Chasm. Marketing and selling disruptive products to mainstream customers (HarperCollins Publishers, 1991 [1999 paperback version used for citations]).

Moore, Geoffrey A, Dealing with Darwin: How Great Companies Innovate at Every Phase of Their Evolution (Portfolio, 2005).

Porter, Michael E, *Technology and Competitive Advantage*, 6 Journal of Business Strategy 60–78 (1985).

Rogers, Everett M, Diffusion of Innovations (The Free Press (original 1962) 2003).

---

91 Chuck Ragan, The Fire, The Steel, The Tread (Ten Four Records, 2013).

Ryan, Bryce & Gross, Neal, *Acceptance and diffusion of hybrid corn seed in two Iowa communities,* 29 (372) Research Bulletin (Iowa Agriculture and Home Economics Experiment Station, 663–708 (1950).

Schumpeter, Joseph A, Business Cycles: A Theoretical, Historical and Statistical Analysis of the Capitalist Process (McGraw Hill, 1939).

Schumpeter, Joseph A, Capitalism, Socialism and Democracy (HarperCollins, 1942).

Schumpeter, Joseph, *The Creative Response in Economic History*, 7 (2) The Journal of Economic History 149–159 (1947).

Stoneman, Paul, The Handbook of Economics of Innovation and Technology Change (Wiley-Blackwell, 1995).

Utterback, James M, Mastering the Dynamics of Innovation. How Companies Can Seize Opportunities in the Face of Technological Change (Harvard Business School Press, 1994 [1996 paperback version used for citations]).

Utterback, James M and Abernathy, William J, *A Dynamic Model of Product and Process Innovation*, 3 (6) Omega 639–656 (1975).

B. Online Sources

Aeppel, Timothy, *It Took the Telephone 75 Years To Do What Angry Birds Did in 35 Days. But what does it mean*, The Wall Street Journal (Mar. 13, 2015, 7:50 AM), *https://blogs.wsj.com/economics/2015/03/13/it-took-the-telephone-75-years-to-do-what-angry-birds-did-in-35-days-but-what-does-that-mean/?mod=e2fb&fbclid=IwAR3Hj5dYTnBc53lGX9erpa9ISS6unXMo4rMF-4dP-f8NyMsFngyjb_Yp9jDc* (last visited Feb. 3, 2019).

Aeppel, Timothy, *50 Million Users: The Making of an «Angry Birds» Internet Meme*, The Wall Street Journal (Mar. 20, 2015 1:00 PM), https://blogs.wsj.com/economics/2015/03/20/50-million-users-the-making-of-an-angry-birds-internet-meme/ (last visited Feb. 3, 2019).

Ambrogi, Robert, *Tech Competence*, Law Sites (2019), https://www.lawsitesblog.com/tech-competence/ (last visited Feb. 5, 2019).

AML, The Invasion of Regional Legal Markets and How Mid-sized Firms Should Respond, https://www.alm.com/intelligence/solutions-we-provide/business-of-law-solutions/analyst-reports/barbarians-gate-report/ (2018) (last visisted Feb. 22, 2019).

Appetite For Disruption, *Chapter 01 | The Dynamics of Innovation & Disruption,* YouTube (Oct. 14, 2018), https://www.youtube.com/watch?v=5BvmWcFHIW0 (last visited Feb. 4, 2019).

Appetite For Disruption, *Chapter 02 | Uptake Revisited—Evolution vs Disruption,* YouTube (Nov. 4, 2018), https://www.youtube.com/watch?v=Ad2hmsn9qP0&t=584s (last visited Feb. 6, 2019).

Appetite For Disruption, *Chapter 03 | Technology Bridge—Evaluating and Investing in Innovation,* YouTube (Nov. 18, 2018), https://www.youtube.com/watch?v=4qfeGuoWD_s&t=76s (last visited Feb. 8, 2019).

Boston Consultig Group (BCG) & Bucerius Law School (ed.), *How Legal Technology Will Change the Business of Law* (Jan. 12, 2019, 8:36 AM), http://www.bucerius-education.de/fileadmin/content/pdf/studies_publications/Legal_Tech_Report_2016.pdf.

Cambridge Strategy Group, *Thriving at the Edge of Chaos—AI, Blockchain and the Law Firm of the Future* (2018), https://mailchi.mp/c8a7253a01c3/thriving-at-the-edge-of-chaos-download (last visited Feb. 22, 2019).

Clio, *Legal Trends Report 2018* (Jan. 7, 2019, 10:09 AM), https://www.clio.com/wp-content/uploads/2018/10/Legal-Trends-Report-2018.pdf.

Cohen, Mark A, *Are Law Firms Becoming Obsolete?*, Forbes (Jun. 12, 2017, 5:36 AM), https://www.forbes.com/sites/markcohen1/2017/06/12/are-law-firms-becoming-obsolete/#5779f682264d (last visited Feb. 12, 2019).

Curle, David, *Legal tech adoption and the real drivers of change*, Thomson Reuters Blog (Feb. 8, 2019), https://blogs.thomsonreuters.com/legal-uk/2019/02/08/legal-tech-week/ (last visited Feb. 5, 2019).

Daugherty, Paul A & Wilson, H James, *What Are The New Jobs In A Human + Machine World?*, Forbes (Jul. 17, 2018 5:18 PM), https://www.forbes.com/sites/insights-intelai/2018/07/17/what-are-the-new-jobs-in-a-human--machine-world/#15f7830063e3 (last visited Feb. 7, 2019).

Farias, Christian, *Everyone Needs Legal Help. That Doesn't Mean Everyone Needs a Lawyer*, The New York Times (Feb. 13, 2019), https://www.nytimes.com/2019/02/13/opinion/legal-issues.html (last visited Feb. 16, 2019).

Grady, Ken, *Stagnation And The Legal Industry. Real transformation has yet to arrive* (Jan. 2, 2019, 2:14 PM), https://medium.com/the-algorithmic-society/stagnation-and-the-legal-industry-bc801a8b4d38 (last visited Apr. 12, 2019).

Olson, Elizabeth, *Law Firms Announced Record-Breaking 106 Mergers Last Year*, Big Law Business (Jan. 7, 2019), https://biglawbusiness.com/law-firms-announced-record-breaking-106-mergers-last-year (last visited Feb. 4, 2019).

Packel, Dan, *After a Record-Setting 2018 for Law Firms, Does a Reckoning Await?* Law.com (Dec. 17, 2018, 5:00 AM), https://www.law.com/americanlawyer/2018/12/17/after-a-record-setting-2018-for-law-firms-does-a-reckoning-await/ (last visited Feb. 2, 2019).

Reisinger, Sue, *Experts Disagree on Who Leads the Way on LegalTech—Law firms or In-House Counsel*, law.com (Feb. 21, 2019, 2:33 PM), https://www.law.com/legaltechnews/2019/02/21/experts-disagree-on-who-leads-the-way-on-legal-tech-law-firms-or-in-house-counsel/?kw=Experts%20Disagree%20on%20Who%20Leads%20the%20Way%20on%20Legal%20Tech%26mdash%3BLaw%20Firms%20or%20In-House%20Counsel&utm_source=email&utm_medium=enl&utm_campaign=afternoonupdate&utm_content=20190222&utm_term=ltn (last visited Feb. 22, 2019).

Robson, Nate, *Q&A: Getting Ready for the Emoji Law Revolution*, law.com (legaltech news) (Feb. 8, 2019), https://www.law.com/legaltechnews/2019/02/08/qa-getting-ready-for-the-emoji-law-revolution-397-16729/?kw=Q&A:%20Getting%20Ready%20for%20the%20Emoji%20Law%20Revolution (last visited Feb. 9, 2019).

Sandefur, Rebecca L, *Access to What?* 148 (1) Daedalus 49–55 (2018) (published online Jan. 1, 2019), https://www.amacad.org/sites/default/files/publication/downloads/19_Winter_Daedalus_Sandefur.pdf) (last visited Feb. 16, 2019).

Schreiber, Noam, *An Expensive Law Degree, and No Place to Use It*, The New York Times (Jun. 17, 2016), https://www.nytimes.com/2016/06/19/business/dealbook/an-expensive-law-degree-and-no-place-to-use-it.html (last visited Feb. 16, 2019).

SenGupta, Reena, *The best law firm innovators alter their culture first*, Financial Times (Jun. 2, 2017), https://www.ft.com/content/4ed185c8-3bcc-11e7-ac89-b01cc67cfeec (last visited Feb. 5, 2019)

The Law Society of England and Wales, *The Future of Legal Services* (Jan. 28, 2016), https://www.lawsociety.org.uk/support-services/research-trends/the-future-of-legal-services/ (last visited Feb. 13, 2019).

Thomson Reuters, *2019 Report on the State of the Legal Market* (Jan. 14, 2019, 01:16 AM), http://images.ask.legalsolutions.thomsonreuters.com/Web/TRlegalUS/%7B7f73da9c-0789-4f63-b012-379d45d54cdf%7D_2019_Report_on_the_State_of_the_Legal_Market_NEW.pdf (last visited Feb. 11, 2019).

C. Other Sources

Bon Jovi, Fear (PolyGram Records 1992).
Bruce Springsteen, No Surrender (Columbia Records, 1984).
Chuck Ragan, The Fire, The Steel, The Tread (Ten Four Records, 2013).
Guns 'N' Roses, Get in the Ring (Geffen Records, 1991).
Guns 'N' Roses, Welcome to the Jungle (Geffen Records, 1987).

Dr Matthias Trummer, Dr Ulf Klebeck and Dr Guenther Dobrauz-Saldapenna

Strategic Mapping of the Legal Value Chain

There's A Light (Over at the Frankenstein Place)[1]

TABLE OF CONTENTS

---

1 Sometimes it feels like representatives of the legal establishment perceive those advocating change and in particular bringing technology to the legal world like folks straight out of «The Rocky Horror Picture Show»–hence our little tribute to this amazing rock musical by using one of its famous song titles as a subtitle.

I. Introduction

When thinking about the terms «legal technology», which is more a synonym for technologically optimizing (and automating) internal processes of legal practitioners, or «legal innovation», what is the real game changer for the whole legal industry, and their current rather extensive use by social media, press, and different legal practitioners, one might be tempted to go with *Mitchell Kowalski*, Visiting Professor in Legal Innovation at the University of Calgary Law School and his cunning re-interpretation of the world-famous David Bowie and Mick Jagger version of the song «Dancing in the Street»:[2]

> *«... It's an invitation for a revolution, a chance for tech to awe*
> *They'll be laughing and clowning, keyboards pounding,*
> *Hacking on the law,*
> *From Vancouver, BC,*
> *To Santiago, Chile now,*
> *Don' forget them in Nairobi,*
> *Or in the towers of KL,*
> *Back in the heat of Sevilla...»*[3]
> – *Mitchell Kowalski, The Great Legal Reformation* (2017) *Preface.*

Mitchell Kowalski is right that the professional legal services industry has gone through a «great reformation» caused and pushed forward by the technical evolution and digital transformation processes currently going on globally. Indeed, this necessarily comes along with an exponential growth of windows of opportunities and, thus, with an increase of players and, of course, of copycats striving to make use of them. A corresponding increase of media coverage of the term «LegalTech» seems, then, not surprising.[4]

Not only the so-called «megatrends», i.e., technological advances, demographic shifts, shifts in global economic power, resources scarcity, and climate

---

2 The song *«Dancing in the Street»* was written by *Marvin Gaye, William «Mickey» Stevenson* and *Ivy Jo Hunter*. It first became popular in 1964 when recorded by *Martha and the Vandellas* whose version reached No. 2 on the Billboard Hot 100 chart and peaked at No. 4 in the UK Singles Chart. It is one of Motown's signature songs and is the group's premier signature song. A 1966 cover by *The Mamas & the Papas* was a minor hit on the Hot 100 reaching No. 73. In 1982, the rock group *Van Halen* took their cover of «Dancing in the Street» to No. 38 on the Hot 100 chart and No. 15 in Canada on the RPM chart. A 1985 duet cover by *David Bowie and Mick Jagger* charted at No. 1 in the UK and reached No. 7 in the US. The song was also covered by *The Kinks, The Everly Brothers, Grateful Dead and Black Oak Arkansas* according to Wikipedia, Dancing in the Street.

3 Mitchell Kowalski, The Great Legal Reformation—Notes from the field i–iv (2017).

4 Jens Wagner, Legal Tech und Legal Robots – Der Wandel im Rechtsmarkt durch neue Technologien und künstliche Intelligenz (2018) at 4.

change, as well as urbanization but also the «Essential Eight»[5] (see Exhibit 1 below) contribute hereto as they are radically changing people's lives and also affect the law (as the agreed framework governing human coexistence). In addition, increasingly dense global, inter-connectivity and transparency, legal buy/sell dynamics, new delivery models, and altered client expectations are transforming the ways and methods of providing legal services, and, as a consequence, the entire legal value chain including its various legal market segments.

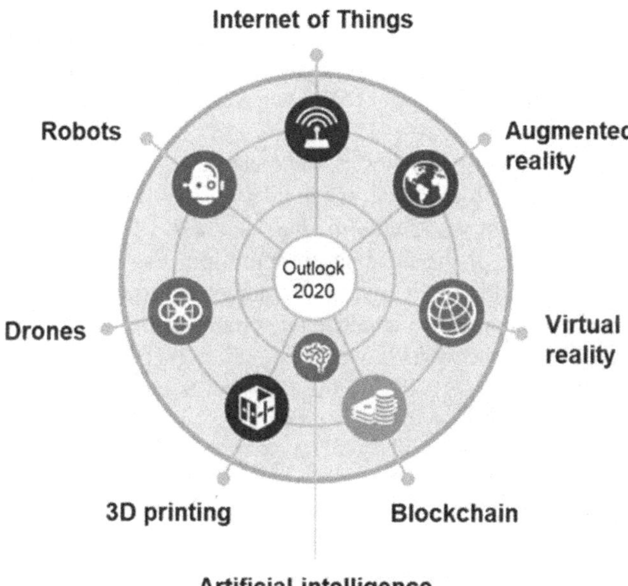

Exhibit 1: The Essential Eight [Source: PwC (2018)].

But what is the legal value chain and by which segments and elements is it characterized? We have all grown up with Prof *Michael Porter*'s mid-1980's value chain concept[6] and it has been a loyal friend and Swiss army knife-like tool on many consulting assignments. But to be quite frank, we have also more often than not struggled to successfully deploy it in the context of professional services strategy. We have found in our own experience from working at law firms and advising them on their set-up that most firms do not really have or

---

5 PwC, The Essential Eight—The Essential Eight technologies that matter for business today, https://www.pwc.com/gx/en/issues/technology/essential-eight-technologies.htm (last visited Apr. 12. 2019).

6 Michael Porter, Competitive Advantage: Creating and Sustaining Superior Performance (The Free Press, 1985).

depend too much on «Inbound and Outbound Logistics» nor do they consider them a primary activity. Also distinguishing between «Operations» and «Service» and the role of «Marketing & Sales», as promoted by *Porter*,[7] leaves much to be desired in a service business in general, but most definitely when it comes to the legal world. This is by no means meant to slander *Porter's* work which we hold in the highest regard and continues to be an important source of inspiration. However, we have, for our own purposes of trying to map the mechanics of the specialist legal realm, arrived at a different canvas made for the legal world.

We believe that the legal value chain, when mapped based on economic considerations, reveals many of the interdependencies and mechanics at play and, may as such, provide insight into effect (and potentially impact) changes to the individual parts may have.

At its very core is the eternal premises of someone facing a «legal problem», seeking a «legal solution» from «legal stakeholders» capable of providing solutions by applying methods of working with «legal sources». This is an admittedly rather simplified form of the legal subsumption process, which is at least known to every legal practitioner in civil law countries and considered as a fundamental legal principle according to which legal norms are applied to a fact in order to get a solution while observing the legal norms' specific hierarchy.[8]

Based on this understanding, we divide the legal value chain into three core phases:

Phase 1: Legal Problem
Phase 2: Legal Sources
Phase 3: Legal Solution

Each of these phases can again be split into three legal value chain sub-segments, which in turn consist of a varying number of legal value chain elements. This chapter proceeds as follows.

Section II, The Legal Value Chain, provides insights into these three phases. It illustrates the core segments, elements, and principles as we see them at present. Further, it attempts to predict how these phases might be affected or altered in the near future. It begins by addressing Phase 1, the «Legal Problem». It provides a high-level overview of the tools and methods by which legal stakeholders currently (and potentially in the near future) analyze a legal problem in order to eventually create a solution. It then addresses Phase 2: the «Legal Sources». It assesses how «regulatory framework», «legal education» and «research» will evolve further due to the ongoing digital transformation.

---

7 *Id.* at 11–15.

8 Stanley L Paulson, *Derogation, and Noncontradiction in «Legal Science» (reviewing Law and Legal Science by J.W. Harris)*, (48) 3/10 University of Chicago Law Review 806 (1981).

Next, this section focuses on Phase 3: the «Legal Solution». It analyzes how the governmental and non-governmental stakeholders apply legal sources to legal problems in order to lead to legal solutions. This section then provides an illustration of the legal value chain map at its current state and attempts to illustrate its expected (near-) future state. This section concludes by providing a short overview of the legal value chain's impact on various legal market segments, particularly on law firms, general counsels, legal departments/legal functions, alternative legal service providers, contingent workforce models in law, legal marketplaces, and platforms.

Finally in *Section III* we tackle the question of whether the current or near-future legal value chain following the current «legal problem-legal sources-legal solution-approach» is sustainable or whether it could be eroded entirely by emerging technologies such as Blockchain (and its smart contracts ledger systems) or lawyer-bots.

II. The Legal Value Chain—Now and Then

In our view, the process of solving legal problems, the essence of practicing law, and, thus, the legal value chain itself consists of three core phases, i.e., the Legal Problem Phase, the Legal Sources Phase, and the Legal Solution Phase.

In our understanding, each of these phases consists of three different segments (highlighted in «grey» in Exhibit 2 below) which each again is composed by a varying number of legal value chain elements (highlighted in «light grey» in Exhibit 2 below). The legal value chain map, at its current level, looks as follows:

The users and buyers of legal solutions are the cornerstones at the beginning and the end of the legal value chain. Their demands and expectations with regards to solving their legal problems through the application of various legal sources need to be observed by legal professionals and services providers understood as legal stakeholders in all three phases. Should these needs change, legal stakeholders are necessarily required to adapt as well in order to being capable to still provide valuable and sustainable legal solutions to them.

Some of the legal value chain elements of one legal value chain segment also overlap to legal value chain segments of other phases, e.g., most legal research and legal solution methods still follow a rather paper-driven approach (see the legal value chain element «paper-driven» in Exhibit 2, which is overlapping the legal value chain segments «Research» of the Legal Sources phase and «Methods» of the Legal Solution phase). In most cases this overlap is horizontal between two legal value chain segments of two different phases. Vertical overlap between legal value chain segments of one legal value chain phase occur implicitly.

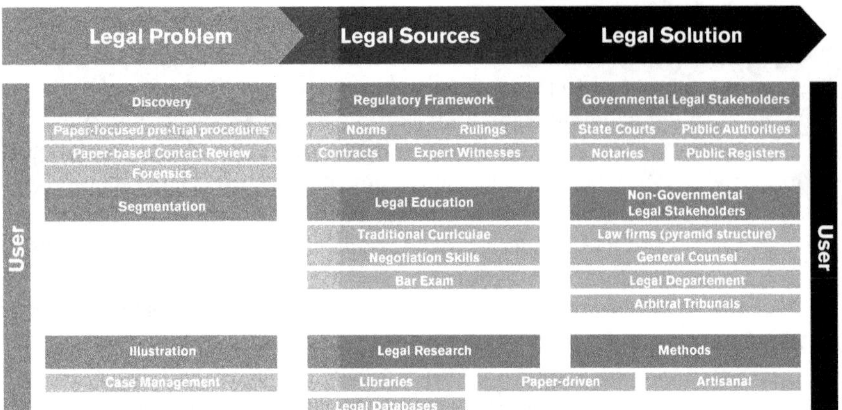

Exhibit 2: The Legal Value Chain [Source: Dobrauz-Saldapenna/Trummer, 2019].

A. The Legal Problem Phase

Almost all legal stakeholders are or should be problem-solvers, lawyers and general counsels in particular. Despite some exceptions, which we mention below, it does not really matter whether legal problem solving occurs in or outside of court. What really counts at the beginning of the «Legal Problem» Phase are «interpersonal skills» and, in particular, their use to understand and «dig into» a legal problem. *Carrie Menkel-Meadow*[9] described such skills like the capability to «*[...] listen heedfully*», in particular but not limited to lawyers, as essential in this regard.

We also rate technical abilities for discovering the legal essence of a legal problem, the skill to differentiate key issues of a legal problem from less important aspects and the ability to communicate them as equally essential.

1. Discovery

Discovering a legal problem in the sense of assessing its backgrounds and facts is the first key legal value chain segment of the Legal Problem Phase. This is very much in line with Design Thinking, which typically also has «discovery» as an initial phase or activity.[10]

---

9 Carrie Menkel-Meadow, *When Winning Isn 't Everything: The Lawyer As Problem Solver*, Georgetown University Law Center, https://scholarship.law.georgetown.edu/facpub/172/ (last visited Apr. 12, 2019).

10 *See* Norbert F Roozenburg & Johannes Eekels, Product Design: Fundamentals and Methods (Wiley, 1995).

It is essential, however, to distinguish in which legal system, common law or civil law, the legal problem is going to be solved beforehand as this effects the subsequent legal value chain segments, but also various elements of the legal value chain segment «discovery» itself. One example: The problem solving methods in common law countries are case law focused other than in civil law countries. Thus, the element «Rulings» respectively prejudiced court decisions relating to a specific case of the legal value chain segment «Regulatory Framework» of the Legal Sources Phase is potentially a lot more important for the actual legal solution process than «Norms» and their interpretation as they are in civil law countries.

As mentioned above, it also must be considered at this stage, whether the legal problem solving process involves courts or not. If so, some of the other legal value chain segments and elements will be less important as they then only require out-of-trial legal problem solving mechanism(s).

It also essential that civil law proceedings in common law countries are set up completely differently compared to those in civil law countries and foresee, for example, long-lasting pre-trial procedures requiring—somehow—much more sophisticated discovering mechanism. Regardless of the differentiation between in- and out-of-court «discovery» proceedings, most of the underlying processes and methods are—according to law—still paper-driven. They require going through huge paper trails which is a challenge in the age of digital transformation and exponentially growing electronic (big) data volumes which as a consequence then need to be printed.

Discovery methods will therefore fundamentally change in the upcoming years, particularly in common law countries, but also in civil law countries, as they are increasingly becoming subject to electronic approaches (i.e., e-discovery). By way of example:

- Pre-trial-procedures in the UK and Wales usually take place before the actual civil proceedings starts and serve as mechanism for exchanging all relevant data (i.e., «discovering» them) in order to achieve equality of arms between the parties of the trial. As already mentioned, these proceedings have been paperwork-driven over years and in big parts still are. The implementation of Part 31B in the UK's civil procedures rules (CPR) several years ago was a first move to implement rudimentary E-discovery mechanism as to the exchange electronic documents. However, these amendments have not met all needs of the legal practice though.
- The main reasons have been that the paper-based disclosure procedures have—regardless of Part 31.5 CPR[11] and its already existing electronic

11 Simmons & Simmons, *New draft rule on disclosure unveiled*, http://www.elexica.com/en/legal-topics/dispute-resolution-commercial/011117-new-draft-rule-on-disclosure-unveiled (last visited Apr. 12, 2019).

pre-trial discovery methods—and although not satisfying all needs of the legal practice in the «[…] the electronic age of emails, smart devices, and virtual data rooms»[12] been maintained as default options. The applicable legal framework has caused substantial lacks of efficiency in *a priori* time-consuming proceedings.

– Thus, the legislator has reacted and amended the underlying rules again. Since Jan. 1, 2019, an entirely new disclosure pilot scheme for Business and Property courts is in force.[13] These new mechanism shall accelerate and simplify the discovering processes.

What is crucial for this legal value chain segment, however, is that the various new e-discovering procedures cause that new service provides will likely play an essential role in the future. In other words, this legal value chain segment will not be dominated by professional legal service providers such as lawyers (or barristers in the UK) any more. New non-governmental legal stakeholders, particularly alternative legal service providers like the cloud-based e-discovery platform *Everlaw*,[14] which has recently raised USD 25 million from Silicon Valley based investors,[15] have entered the market and provide e-discovery platform solutions with an apparently smoother process-solution flow.

2. Segmentation

We strongly believe that methods of problem discovery are closely linked to those of segmenting essential legal problem data from less important. Depending on the jurisdiction, under which the respective legal problem is to be resolved, the relevant methods are still rather paper-driven and subject to artisanal working approaches. This will fundamentally change due to the progression of machine-learning and artificial intelligence-based predictive analytics tools coupled with legal data extraction solutions and their implementation into the workflow of law firms. Those tools not only enable the selection and differentiation of relevant data from less important one in tremendously high volume data sets (more or less big data sets), but also enable their categorization and

---

12 Taylor Wessing, *Newsflash: Disclosure pilot scheme for the Business and Property Courts* (Oct. 8, 2018), https://united-kingdom.taylorwessing.com/en/insights/brands-update/newsflash-disclosure-pilot-scheme-for-the-business-and-property-courts (last visited Feb. 3, 2019).

13 Simmons & Simmons, *Pilot Scheme for new disclosure rules approved by the Civil Procedure Rule Committee* (Jul. 31, 2018), http://www.simmons-simmons.com/en/news/2018/july/pilot-scheme-for-new-disclosure-rules-approved-by-the-civil-procedure-rule-committee (last visited Feb. 3, 2019).

14 Everlaw, https://www.everlaw.com (last visited Jan. 11, 2019).

15 Rachel Sandler, *This fast-growing startup just got $25 million from Silicon Valley investors to help lawyers everywhere save time and win more cases* (Jun. 28, 2018), Business Insider (Jan. 11, 2019, 9:14 AM), https://www.businessinsider.de/everlaw-legal-tech-aj-shankar-raises-25-million-2018-6?r=US&IR=T (last visited Feb. 3, 2019).

even a prediction of the potential outcome (e.g., of a lawsuit). Given that the legal value chain elements «Predictive Case Analytics» and «Legal Data Extraction» would then not only remain as elements of the «Legal Problem» phase, but would gradually merge via the «Legal Sources» phase even into the «Legal Solution» phase providing an all-in-one solution process flow. A most prominent tool of this category at present is *Lex Machina*,[16] which provides litigation data mining solutions to generate insights into big sized data sets.[17]

3. Illustration

The illustration of a legal problem, which basically implicates the visual processing of its key facts and corresponding case management, is essential for a time- and cost-efficient further legal solution process. Case and workflow management tools, like *Lexis Visualfiles*[18] or *Legal Trek*[19] are already in use in advanced law firms or legal departments for this purpose. Their implementation in the workflow of a law firm, will thus today no longer lead to first-mover-advantage but at least ensure fast follower status. More developed contract management tools—once evolved to contract lifecycle platforms—will, however, fundamentally change this, as they generate entirely new business models for professional legal services providers:

- After onboarding of clients onto these platforms, lawyers and other professional legal service providers will not only gain tremendously profound insights into the «contracts ecosystem» of their clients, but first and foremost also gain deep understanding of their and their contractual partners' needs, potentially way before they know themselves. It will hence not only be possible to set automatic reminders for observing (judicial or contractual) deadlines which *per se* is not exactly rocket science but also allow for automatic execution of (contractual) actions.
- On an even more sophisticated level it will be also possible to automatically amend contracts (provided this has been contractually agreed) following adjustments or change of applicable regulation, legislation and / or jurisprudence.[20]

Methods of illustrating and visualizing legal problems are in our experience also particularly important and potentially beneficial for the workflow of

---

16 Richard Susskind, Tomorrow's lawyers—An Introduction to Your Future 186 (Oxford University Press, 2nd ed. 2017).

17 *See* Lex Machina, *What We Do*, https://lexmachina.com/what-we-do/ (last visited Jan. 11, 2019).

18 *See* Lexis Nexis, *Lexis Visualfiles*, https://www.lexisnexis-es.co.uk/our-solutions/visualfiles/ (last visited Jan. 11, 2019).

19 LegalTrek, *What you get*, https://legaltrek.com/ (last visited Jan. 11, 2019).

20 Tilo Wendl & Klaus-Lorenz Gebhardt, *Vertragsgeneratoren und Vertragsmanagement*, *in* Rechtshandbuch Legal Tech 131 et. seqq. (Stephan Breidenbach & Florian Glatz, eds., C. H. Beck, 2018).

Mergers & Acquisition practice groups of law firms. The implementation and use of automated contract management tools (like *Exari*[21] or *smashdocs*[22]) or machine-learning respectively AI-based legal contract analysis tools in order to improve and accelerate legal due diligence processes seem to swiftly become state-of-the-art. Competitive advantages can, however, still be achieved by those moving fast on this opportunity—now.

These mostly cloud-based legal analysis applications such as *Kira*,[23] *Luminance*,[24] *eBrevia*[25] or *Leverton*[26] enable the extraction, legal review and, in particular, illustration of findings and anomalies (i.e., «legal problems») from and of huge virtual data room data sets for example in the course of legal due diligence processes—work usually performed by young professionals in law firms—in significantly less time than if done manually.

Increased cost-sensitivity of clients and expectations to deliver more accurate outcome in less time in a due diligence process, however, transform the workflow of legal due diligences and are the key drivers for the implementation of these tools.

As far as we see it, there is currently no accelerated market consolidation happening in the sill comparatively new AI-based legal analysis tools market. Based on our observations, both Kira and Luminance currently seem to have the largest market shares and are also rather well backed by venture capital.[27] As far as we see, strategic investors have obviously not gotten a taste for them yet. In the age of tremendously high valuations for software companies and market leaders like *Google, Facebook, Apple* and *Microsoft* always hungry for growth potential, this is quite a phenomenon. One reason might be that the

---

21 *See* Exari, https://www.exari.com/ (last visited Jan. 11, 2019).

22 *See* smashdocs, https://www.smashdocs.net/en/technology (last visited Jan. 11, 2019).

23 *See* Kira, *How it works*, https://www.kirasystems.com/how-it-works/ (last visited Jan. 11, 2019) *or* Jessica Galang, *Kira Systems uses machine learning to lead next generation of legal tech*, betakit (Mar. 25, 2016), https://betakit.com/kira-systems-uses-machine-learning-to-lead-next-generation-of-legal-tech/ (last visited Jan. 11, 2019).

24 *See* Luminance, https://www.luminance.com/index.html *or* Artificial Lawyer, *Interview: Emily Foges—CEO of AI Co. Luminance*, Artificial Lawyer (Apr. 7, 2017), https://www.artificiallawyer.com/2017/04/07/interview-emily-foges-ceo-of-ai-co-luminance/ (last visited Jan. 11, 2019).

25 *See* eBrevia, https://ebrevia.com/#overview (last visited Jan. 13, 2019).

26 *See* Leverton, *AI for Real Estate—Turning Myth into Reality* (Apr. 11, 2017), https://blog.leverton.ai/2017/04/11/ai-real-estate-myth-reality-0 (last visited Jan. 11, 2019).

27 *See* as to Kira: Jessica Galang, *Kira Systems receives §65 Million cad investment From New York'S Insigh Venture Partners*, Betakit (Sep. 5, 2018), https://betakit.com/kira-systems-receives-65-million-cad-investment-from-new-yorks-insight-venture-partners/ (last visited Apr. 22, 2019); and as to Luminance: Jeremy Kahn, *Mike Lynch-Backed Legal AI Startup Valued at $ 100 Million*, Bloomberg (Feb. 7, 2019), https://www.bloomberg.com/news/articles/2019-02-07/legal-ai-firm-luminance-valued-at-100-million-in-funding-round?utm_campaign=socialflow-organic&utm_source=twitter&utm_content=business&utm_medium=social&cmpid=socialflow-twitter-business (last visited Apr. 22, 2019).

aforementioned «giants» could be already one (or two) step(s) ahead in AI technology itself, but potentially not enough focused on the legal market at the same time. There are indications that this is changing as, for instance, *Microsoft* has recently brought the JFK files to its *Azure Cloud* where its data have been read out through cognitive search technology so that even handwriting has been understandable[28].

But what's for sure, law firms and other users can chose from a wide range of different solutions by a number of vendors. For the respective decision process in our view two factors seem particularly relevant:

- At first, it needs to be assessed, clarified and, of course, agreed with the respective vendor who will be the owner of further algorithms developed by and for these tools based on client input. Most of these tools come with a basic set of algorithms but currently the majority is developed in English with only limited availability or functionality of other languages requiring often significant input and/or co-creation of users to accelerate development which may lead to new intellectual property which then may give rise to the above question of ownership.
- Secondly, all machine-learning- respectively AI-based legal analysis tools require direct access to the data enabling not only reading the data but also processing it. The crucial thing for the use of these tools during a legal due diligence process is therefore the permission of the owner of the data (in case of an M&A transaction typically the sell-side) to have direct access to process it (and not only read it). This usually works via APIs implemented in the different virtual data rooms. In response to this most of today's data room providers have already set up interfaces enabling the use of AI-based legal contract analysis tools.[29]

The crucial thing is, however, that the unlocking of the APIs needs to be agreed with and confirmed by the sell-side before the actual kick-off of a legal due diligence of a transaction. In the age of strict data protection rules and due to the fact that sellers are usually cautious to grant buyers and therefore potential competitors (should a deal not close) direct access to their company data, this is often not a simple undertaking. In terms of moving a deal forward this might change, once the use of AI technology in due diligences processes is finally market-standard.

Law firms will have to evaluate carefully which AI-based legal contract analysis tool they are going to implement. They will potentially go for a tool enabling the greatest extent of flexibility when it comes to intellectual property

---

28 For more details on this *see* MICROSOFT, https://www.ailab.microsoft.com/experiments/jfk-files (last visited Apr. 22, 2019).

29 *See* KIRA, *Integrate with Intralinks*, https://kirasystems.com/how-it-works/intralinks/ (last visited Jan. 11, 2019).

issues of co-developed algorithms and support, and which can show the highest number of APIs interacting with virtual data room providers.

However it will still require more time until machine-learning- respectively AI-based legal contract analysis tools unfold their full potential, technologically and commercially.

B. The Legal Sources Phase

Once a «legal problem» is discovered respectively its underlying facts are assessed, the relevant data is segregated from the less important one, and in particular, visually processed, it is required to then find and further apply the right legal sources with respect to the actual solution of the legal problem. In this respect, the «Legal Sources» Phase is fed from the legal value chain segments «Regulatory Framework», «Legal Education» and «Legal Solution».

1. Regulatory Framework

When looking at the legal value chain, the regulatory framework required for solving legal problems itself does not only consist of legal norms and rulings (e.g., court decisions or notices and orders of public authorities). Contracts and expert witnesses etc. play an at least equally important role in our view.

Mapping all the different types of norms and contracts would not appear to be the right approach and is, of course, not possible given the huge amount of norms on for example communal, state, federal, supranational and international level. These legal and regulatory frameworks and their level of detail and complexity have grown exponentially over the last years triggering the overall growth of the legal industry and resulting in a vast amount of data that would have to be taken into account. Thus, the real challenge is not so much knowing each regulatory framework down to its last fragment or even neutron, but being capable of processing huge legal frameworks in a time-efficient manner and, of course, to identify the provision which are relevant for the matter at hand and its actual facts accurately. To achieve this access to all relevant legal norms and judicature as well as appropriate research tools are necessary.

In Austria, for instance, all (authentic) legal norms on federal and state level, all federal law gazettes and state law gazettes, high court decisions—e.g., of the Austrian constitutional court, supreme administrative court, the supreme court, various regional courts, the federal administrative courts, and the federal finance court etc.—as well as decisions of various Austrian public authorities and tribunals are accessible and also processable via the «Legal Information

System of the Republic of Austria».[30] It not only enables access to the aforementioned legal sources 24/7, but also provides for enhanced search functions.

Thus, global connectivity and an increasing need for more and more granular and specific data also have an impact on legislators and authorities and, in particular, on their interaction with individuals. E-Government solutions and e-Justice applications are not buzzwords any longer as they slowly become reality in many countries all around the world.[31] It would appear that Austria is also quite advanced in this respect as it also not only provides for a sophisticated electronic land register and companies' register, but is also constantly adding new tools to its actual e-government and e-justice applications platforms, such as most recently a case automation tool for the justice administration. This tool *inter alia* enables an online case administration, integrated text processing, access to social security online search masks and interfaces for exchange between all parties involved in administrative or court proceedings.[32] E-Justice solutions will also further blur the borders to the «Legal Solution Phase». In particular, online legal dispute platforms, which might also be run by non-governmental legal stakeholders, will become an integral alternative for the settlement of legal disputes. They might therefore directly compete with governmental e-Justice solutions.

2. Legal Education

Education is another important segment within the legal value chain and profoundly affects other segments and phases.

Traditional curriculae taught in law schools and the various paths leading to the bar exam to qualify as an attorney seem, however, not to meet all demands of an increasingly diverse ecosystem of legal professionals and service providers any longer. As far as we can see the vast majority of education and training methods employed and in the various jurisdictions still seem to be quite focused on what have historically been core legal areas and competences instead of evolving in step with the world around them. However, in the age of digital transformation and altered client needs, legal practitioners will have to acquire additional skill sets. This process started in the 20th century when lawyers embraced the use of basic IT infrastructure and started to learn foreign languages and to broaden their horizon by adding management know-how and

---

30 *See* RIS Rechtsinformationssystem des Bundes, https://www.ris.bka.gv.at/Englische-Rv/ (last visited Jan. 20, 2019).

31 For more details on this *see* the chapter on the E-Estonia example by *Karl Paadam & Priit Martinson* in this book.

32 Austrian Ministry of Constitutional Affairs, *Reforms, Deregulation and Justice, E-Justice Austria, IT applications in the Austrian justice system* (2017), https://www.justiz.gv.at/web2013/home/e-justice~8ab4ac8322985dd501229ce3fb1900b4.en.html (last visited Jan. 11, 2019).

other ancillary capabilities to their tool kit.[33] In our understanding, legal stakeholders of the future, irrespectively of whether they are lawyers or practicing as in-house counsel, will require skills in particular but not limited to

- design thinking
- project management, and
- change management.

Moreover, they will need to be familiar with innovative coding methods as applied during Legal Hackathons as well as with lean thinking methodologies (i.e., based on «start-define-learn-experiment-leap-test-measure-pivot (or persevere)-batch-grow-adapt-innovate» principles) as described by *Eric Ries.*[34] Should law schools not be able to teach the required knowledge and adapt their curriculae accordingly, the training for young professionals will need to be provided by the legal stakeholders (in particular by law firms and in-house departments) by themselves to a certain degree.

We cannot even begin to fathom the skills required in the future. That being said we believe that the skill set as mentioned above will clearly help legal stakeholders to meet altered needs of their clients instead of applying old-fashioned models which will eventually turn them into custodians of the legal past with no future.

3. Research

As the way we deliver legal education and the understanding of what it should comprise will need to change, also the methods of performing legal research will need to evolve. Consequently, this value chain segment is closely linked to the «Legal Education» piece.

In addition (and indeed in contrast) to libraries coupled with a largely paper-based research style, legal databases like the *Lexis Nexis 360 solution*[35] and others are currently the main sources for research. The approach to conduct legal research will, however, fundamentally change once the use of AI solutions like the *IBM Watson* and its legal offshoot *ROSS*[36] becomes market-standard.

This will again fundamentally change once computers are capable to actually «understand» words and interpret their context instead of only process-

---

33 Dirk Hartung, *Judex Calculat – Neue Berufsbilder und Technologie in der juristischen Ausbildung, in* Legal Tech – Die Digitalisierung des Rechtsmarkts 237 (Markus Hartung, Micha-Manuel Bues & Gernot Halbleib, eds., C. H. Beck, 2018).

34 Eric Ries, The Lean Startup—How Constant Innovation Creates Radically Successful Businesses (Crown Business, 2011).

35 *See* Lexis Nexis, *360*, https://360.lexisnexis.at/ (last visited Jan. 11, 2019).

36 *See* ROSS Intelligence, *AI Meets Legal Research*, https://rossintelligence.com/ (last visited Jan. 11, 2019).

ing information based on «0» and «1» combinations. In our understanding this will be the moment when the legal value chain will be truly disrupted, as then not only legal research methods will change (and become automated) in the age of a shorter shelf life of knowledge, but also access to legal sources and the creation of legal solutions will generally occur in a manner we cannot even fully imagine yet. That being said it is probably a fair assumption that the first generation of true digital natives will manage this as they are more capable of hitting the ground on this while other players who are not being capable to adapt will vanish.

C. The Legal Solution Phase

Following the discovery, the segmentation and illustration of a legal problem and after having identified the appropriate legal sources, the actual legal solution process takes place. This process is driven and dominated by governmental or non-governmental legal stakeholders and their various working methods to provide a legal solution for a specific legal problem.

1. Governmental Legal Stakeholders

In our understanding state courts, public authorities, notaries and various public registers, e.g., land registers or companies' registers etc., form the basic grid of governmental legal stakeholders.

Differences of the legal systems in common law and civil law countries are, however, not as important for describing them as they are for the legal value chain segment «Discovery» and its various different legal proceedings for instance.[37] The reason for that is rather simple: Both legal systems share—more or less—the same types and models of governmental legal stakeholders. As far as predictable, this basic grid of governmental legal stakeholders will also not «automatically» erode due to the ongoing digital transformation as this would require amendments of constitutional and regulatory frameworks in fact.

But what will happen, is that the working methods of governmental legal stakeholders will need to get technically optimized.

E-justice applications and the expansion of state-owned electronic legal communication resources and tools, in particular with respect to storing and processing of legal data within the interaction of state authorities, non-governmental legal stakeholders and users,[38] are first harbingers of that what might further occur in this legal value chain segment.

---

37 *See* Chapter 1.

38 Reinhard Gaier, *Justiz und Digitalisierung, in* Rechtshandbuch Legal Tech (Stephan Breidenbach & Florian Glatz, eds., C. H. Beck, 2018) at 196 et seq.

2. Non-governmental Legal Stakeholders

Unlike governmental legal stakeholders, which apparently seem not to be as endangered of getting disrupted by the ongoing digital transformation due protective constitutional and regulatory frameworks, non-governmental stakeholders and their industry will tremendously change.[39] New delivery models and legal/buy sell-dynamics due to altered client needs and expectations, technological advances, global interconnectivity and transparency are the cornerstones and key drivers of this new legal solution ecosystem.

This underlying evolutionary process will not only unveil and accentuate entirely new legal value chain elements. It will also give (further) rise to new players such as alternative legal service providers, legal marketplaces, and legal engineers or legal hackers. Robot Lawyers like LISA[40] enabling not only an automated creation but also an «automated negotiation» of non-disclosure agreements are first glimpses what might to come.

In sum this will require the current dominant legal value chain elements «legal departments», «general counsels» and, in particular, «law firms» to radically re-think their structural DNA. In particular, the following external factors influences that: In-house legal departments as big buyers of legal solutions provided by law firms are under tremendously high pressure to continuously provide more for less and work against increasing complexity of actual legal problems. Law firms as suppliers of legal solutions to in-house legal departments will have to share these challenges with their client.

At the same time, law firms as one of the centric suppliers of legal solutions will need to change as well in order to react on the technical shift coming along with the digital transformation. This will not only effect their working methods, but particularly their structure as well. Most traditional law firms currently follow a pyramid structure or bottle-neck-system having a high number of junior lawyers at the bottom, a lower number of senior staff in the middle and an even lower number of partners at the top.

As new ecosystems of delivering legal solutions will require far more diverse skill sets and let technology play a centric role within their services model, the structure of law firms will potentially evolve to a rocket form in future as outlined in the previous chapter. Lawyers will not only need to enter into co-operations with other non-governmental legal stakeholders, but will also have to outsource redundant legal services to LPO providers in order to free up their resources for rendering strategic high-stake legal services. In this regard, law firms will also need to employ non-lawyers (paralegals), project managers and legal engineers in order to further provide sustainable and value-

39 *See* Chapter «Innovation, Evolution, or Disruption in the Legal World» by *Dobrauz-Saldapenna & Derungs* as to the new dominant design in this respect.

40 Entrepreneur Lawyer, *AI App legal solutions for business people and consumers by ...*, http://entrepreneurlawyer.co.uk/RobotLawyerLISA (last visited Apr. 22, 2019).

adding legal solutions in future, and in particular to being capable to compete with alternative legal services providers.

3. Methods

As governmental and non-governmental legal stakeholders as deliverers of legal solutions will have to radically alter their structural composition, their working methods will also mutate.

Even now, most dominant working methods are still indicated from a high-level of artisanal or tailor-made legal work components and lower levels of industrial (or industrialized) and digital working methods. However, a progressing manifestation of altered client needs and expectations of users seeking for a legal solution will require an increased level of technology in use. Standard-work routines will not only be outsourced, but at least entirely industrialized and digitized. As mentioned above, this will then allow lawyers to focus on and spend more time for rendering strategic high-stake legal services.

General Counsels of in-house legal departments will also need to pursue new paths with respect to their working routines. *Erica Dhawan* recently described that successful Internet-era companies tend to increasingly employ legal generalists rather than specialists for their legal departments. The reason for this is the believe that sustainable innovation requires the involvement of legal experts from the beginning of the development process of a new product rather than approaching them occasionally; this approach, however, then requires a broader, more general legal skill set than specialists of specific area of law would have.[41] This conclusion is chiefly based on the report by *Eric Schmidt* and *Jonathan Rosenberg* of how the legal department at *Google* was built and is run where they state that the:

> *«[…] backward-looking, risk averse approach to the law, which is so common in corporate America, doesn't work in the Internet Century, when business evolves at a pace that is several orders of magnitude faster than the pace of legal change. A smart creative-fueled business that is trying to innovate will be lucky to be right 50 percent of the time, which can be a problem for a lawyer whose risk tolerance is in the single digits.*
>
> *Lawyers are, by training, backward looking. This makes sense, since so much of the law is determined by precedent: What happened before dictates what is OK going forward. They are also highly risk-averse. This also makes sense, because so many business lawyers practice in law firms and*

---

41 Erica Dhawan, *Why Your Innovation Team Needs a Lawyer*, Harvard Business Review (Jul. 21, 2016), https://hbr.org/2016/07/why-your-innovation-team-needs-a-lawyer (last visited Apr. 22, 2019).

the job of a corporate law firm is to keep its clients out of trouble. So when you ask most lawyers to access a situation, and if that situation is 99 percent good and 1 percent questionable, they will spend most of their time with you reviewing the questionable.

This is why, when they were building Google's legal department, David Drummond and his colleagues Kulpreet Rana and Miriam Rivera set out to create an environment where lawyers approached their jobs differently. Our general counsel, Kent Walker, likes to call this approach «horseback law». Take a look at any old Western movie... There is always the scene where a cowboy rides up on his horse and comes to a stop, surveying the situation and deciding what to do next. Kent advises his lawyers to do something similar: In certain situations, it's often enough to ride up on a horse (figuratively speaking, usually), make a quick assessment, then mosey on. While many decisions (e.g., major acquisition, a legal compliance question) may call for a detailed analysis, don't feel that you always have to dismount and spend weeks writing a fifty-page legal brief (ha!) of all the things that could possibly go wrong and what would happen if they did. In the early stages of a new project, the analysis won't be 100 percent correct anyway. In those situations, it isn't the lawyer's job to cover every possible angle in detail; it's his job to look into an unforeseeable future and provide educated, quick guidance to the business leaders making the decisions. Then saddle back up, pardner.

Horseback law works only if the lawyer is an integral part of the business and product teams, rather than just summoned occasionally. It works only with the right mixture of lawyers, which is why, in our early days, we tried to hire more generalists than specialists and spread our recruiting efforts across firms, businesses, and even nonprofits (but we rarely hired lawyers straight out of school). And since legal issues are bound to crop up when you are moving quickly and changing industries, it always helps to be doing the right thing by consumers and customers.[42]

D. Evolved Legal Value Chain Map

Considering the hypotheses outlined in the aforementioned chapters, the evolved legal value chain may then look like as follows (new legal value chain elements are highlighted in «grey» in Exhibit 3 below):

---

42 Eric Schmidt & Jonathan Rosenberg, How Google Works (John Murray, 2014).

Compared to the legal value chain map at its current level,[43] the evolved legal value chain map is much more diverse and provides for an increased number of different legal value chain elements which might not all be listed above. As already mentioned, lots of legal value chain elements merge via different legal value chain segments. We deem it as rather plausible that also most of the legal value chain segments will more and more mix up. For instance, lawyer-bots will provide legal solutions to legal problems in almost light speed so that legal value chain segments will not be kept separately any more.

New technologies like Blockchain and smart contracts ledger systems based on this technology will, however, lead to the question whether legal problems will occur in future at all? Contracts digitally transformed in Blockchain ledgers are basically safe from interventions and unwanted amendments.[44] Should they become state-of-the-art (it seems that this will still take some time), intermediaries like legal stakeholders providing legal solutions to legal problems will potentially lose their current function and definitely reinvent themselves.

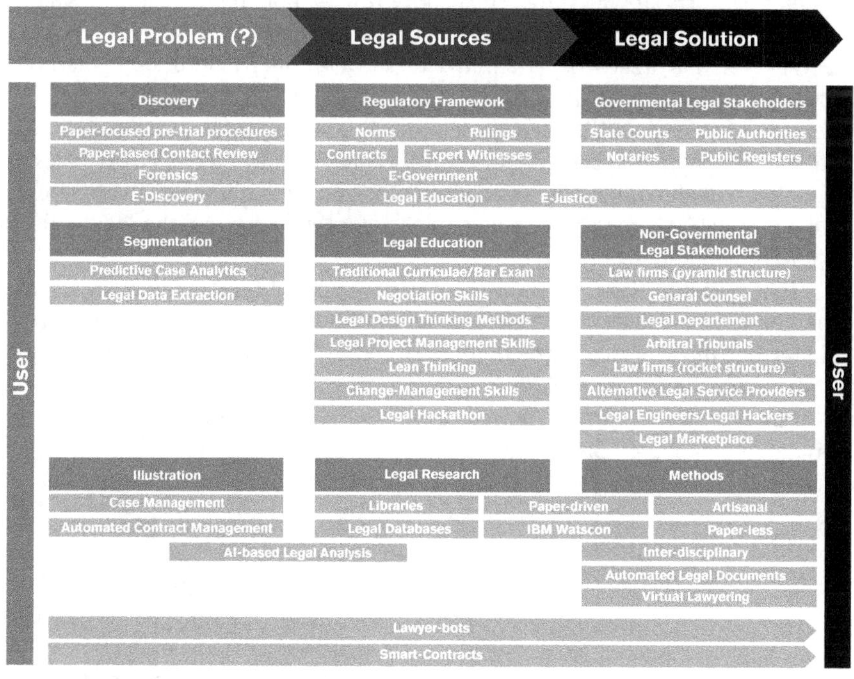

Exhibit 3: Legal Value Chain—Mark II [Source: Dobrauz-Saldapenna/Trummer, 2019].

---

43 *See* Chapter II.

44 For more information *see* Marco Iansiti & Karim R Lakhani, *The Truth About Blockchain* (2017), *in* HAVARD BUSINESS REVIEW 2017/Jan-Feb, https://hbr.org/2017/01/the-truth-about-blockchain (last visited Apr. 11, 2019).

III. Further Outlook

The digital transformation era will have major impacts on the legal value chain, their segments and different elements, if it is not already ending as recently mentioned by *Greg Satell* who sees quantum computing along with the usage of neuromorphic chips as the next much more radical big bang than digital computing is.[45]

What appears to be a threat for legal stakeholders, in particular for non-governmental ones, could turn, however, out to be their biggest opportunity to reinvent themselves for their own and their users' / clients' benefit—indeed it is a rather «*exciting time*».[46] Legal stakeholders have the opportunity to grow from «providers of answers» to certain legal problems to real «deliverers of solutions».[47] In order to reach this skill level of providing legal solutions, they must not be scared to death, but embrace the opportunities which come with the innovative power and technology of the digital transformation. They should not worry about being replaced by robots, but should see the changes of being freed up from repetitive and redundant work.

As *Mitchell Kowalski* attempted to show through overdubbing famous verses of «Dancing in the Street» while thinking about the changes going within the professional legal services industry, we expect an accelerated evolution rather than «Kodak»-disruption of the legal value chain. The experts of this book will show that when examining the current and future developments in the various key market segments of the legal industry and the legal values chain segments in general.

In any event, this evolution—in whatever direction it will might go and which opportunities it will create and offer in future—it will require a different mind-set of those who are practicing law and of those who are buying a legal solutions for their legal problem.

An original and untouched verse of the song «Dancing in the Street» as popularized by *David Bowie* and *Mick Jagger*'s version gets much more to the heart of the attitude legal stakeholders will need to have and, in particular, to the great time of opportunities we are living in:

---

45 Greg Satell, *The Industrial Era Ended, and So Will the Digital Era*, Harvard Business Review (Jul. 11, 2018), https://hbr.org/2018/07/the-industrial-era-ended-and-so-will-the-digital-era (last visited Apr. 22, 2019).

46 *See* Richard Susskind, Tomorrow's lawyers—An Introduction to Your Future 92 (2nd ed., Oxford University Press, 2017).

47 Guenther Dobrauz-Saldapenna, *Towards an agoge for tomorrow's legal professionals*, *in* Minutes of the Conference on the Future of Legal Services in St. Gallen 17–21 (Leo Staub ed., Schulthess, 2018) at 20.

«[…] Calling out around the world
Are you ready for a brand new beat
Summer's here and the time is right
For dancing in the streets […]»[48]

IV. Bibliography

A. Hard Copy Sources

BREIDENBACH, STEPHAN & GLATZ, FLORIAN, RECHTSHANDBUCH LEGAL TECH (C.H. Beck, 2018).

Dobrauz-Saldapenna, Guenther, *Towards an agoge for tomorrow's legal professionals*, *in* Minutes of the Conference on the Future of Legal Services in St. Gallen 17–21 (Leo Staub ed., Schulthess, 2018).

Gaier, Reinhard, *Justiz und Digitalisierung*, *in* Rechtshandbuch Legal Tech 196 et. seqq.

Hartung, Dirk, *Judex Calculat – Neue Berufsbilder und Technologie in der juristischen Ausbildung*, *in* LEGAL TECH – DIE DIGITALISIERUNG DES RECHTSMARKTS 237–244 (Hartung, Markus, Bues, Micha-Manuel & Halbleib, Gernot, eds., C. H. Beck, 2018).

KOWALSKI, MITCHELL, THE GREAT LEGAL REFORMATION—NOTES FROM THE FIELD (Iuniverse Inc, 2017).

Paulson, Stanley L, *Derogation, and Noncontradiction in «Legal Science» (reviewing Law and Legal Science by J.W. Harris)*, 48 (3) 10 University of Chicago Law Review, 806 (1981).

PORTER, MICHAEL, COMPETITIVE ADVANTAGE: CREATING AND SUSTAINING SUPERIOR PERFORMANCE (The Free Press, 1985).

RIES, ERIC, THE LEAN STARTUP—HOW CONSTANT INNOVATION CREATES RADICALLY SUCCESSFUL BUSINESSES (Crown Business, 2011).

SCHMIDT, ERIC & ROSENBERG, JONATHAN, HOW GOOGLE WORKS (John Murray, 2014).

SUSSKIND, RICHARD, TOMORROW'S LAWYERS—AN INTRODUCTION TO YOUR FUTURE (Oxford University Press, 2nd ed. 2017).

WAGNER, JENS, LEGAL TECH UND LEGAL ROBOTS – DER WANDEL IM RECHTSMARKT DURCH NEUE TECHNOLOGIEN UND KÜNSTLICHE INTELLIGENZ (Springer Gabler, 2018).

Wendl, Tilo & Gebhardt, Klaus-Lorenz, *Vertragsgeneratoren und Vertragsmanagement*, *in* RECHTSHANDBUCH LEGAL TECH (Breidenbach, Stephan & Glatz, Florian, eds., C. H. Beck, 2018).

ROOZENBURG, NORBERT F & EEKELS, JOHANNES, PRODUCT DESIGN: FUNDAMENTALS AND METHODS (Wiley, 1995)

B. Online Sources

Artificial Lawyer, *Interview: Emily Foges—CEO of AI Co. Luminance*, Artificial Lawyer (April 7, 2017), https://www.artificiallawyer.com/2017/04/07/interview-emily-foges-ceo-of-ai-co-luminance/ (last visited Jan. 11, 2019).

48 DAVID BOWIE & MICK JAGGER, DANCING IN THE STREET (1985).

Austrian Ministry of Constitutional Affairs, *Reforms, Deregulation and Justice, E-Justice Austria, IT applications in the Austrian justice system* (2017), https://www.justiz.gv.at/web2013/home/e-justice~8ab4ac8322985dd501229ce3fb1900b4.en.html (last visited Jan. 11, 2019).

betakit, https://betakit.com/kira-systems-uses-machine-learning-to-lead-next-generation-of-legaltech/ (last visited Jan. 11, 2019).

Dhawan, Erica, *Why Your Innovation Team Needs a Lawyer*, Harvard Business Review (Jul. 21, 2016), https://hbr.org/2016/07/why-your-innovation-team-needs-a-lawyer (last visited Jan. 17, 2019).

eBrevia, https://ebrevia.com/#overview (last visited Jan. 13, 2019).

Entrepreneur Lawyer, *AI App legal solutions for business people and consumers by ...*, http://entrepreneurlawyer.co.uk/RobotLawyerLISA (last visited Apr. 22, 2019).

Everlaw, https://www.everlaw.com (last visited Jan. 11, 2019).

Exari, https://www.exari.com/ (last visited Jan. 11, 2019).

Galang, Jessica, *Kira Systems receives §65 Million cad investment From New York'S Insigh Venture Partners*, betakit (Sep. 5, 2018), https://betakit.com/kira-systems-receives-65-million-cad-invest ment-from-new-yorks-insight-venture-partners/ (last visited Apr. 22, 2019).

Galang, Jessica, *Kira Systems uses machine learning to lead next generation of legal tech*, betakit (Mar. 25, 2016), https://betakit.com/kira-systems-uses-machine-learning-to-lead-next-generation-of-legal-tech/ (last visited Mar. 25, 2016).

Iansiti, Marco & Lakhani, Karim R, *The Truth About Blockchain* (2017), *in* Harvard Business Review 2017/Jan-Feb, https://hbr.org/2017/01/the-truth-about-blockchain (last visited Apr. 12, 2019).

Kahn Jeremy, *Mike Lynch-Backed Legal AI Startup Valued at $ 100 Million*, Bloomberg (Feb. 7, 2019), Https://www.bloomberg.com/news/articles/2019-02-07/legal-ai-firm-luminance-valued-at-100-million-in-funding-round?utm_campaign=socialflow-organic&utm_source=twitter&utm_content=business&utm_medium=social&cmpid=socialflow-twitter-business (last visited Apr. 22, 2019).

Kira, *How it works*, https://www.kirasystems.com/how-it-works/ (last visited Jan. 11, 2019).

Kira, *Integrate with Intralinks*, https://kirasystems.com/how-it-works/intralinks/ (last visited Jan. 11, 2019).

Lex Machina, *What We Do*, https://lexmachina.com/what-we-do/ (last visited Jan. 11, 2019).

LegalTrek, *What you get*, https://legaltrek.com/ (last visited Jan. 11, 2019).

Leverton, *AI for Real Estate—Turning Myth into Reality* (April 11, 2017), https://blog.leverton.ai/2017/04/11/ai-real-estate-myth-reality-0 (last visited Jan. 11, 2019).

Lexis Nexis, *360*, https://360.lexisnexis.at/ (last visited Jan. 11, 2019).

Lexis Nexis, *Lexis Visualfiles*, https://www.lexisnexis-es.co.uk/our-solutions/visualfiles/ (last visited Jan. 11, 2019).

Luminance, https://www.luminance.com/index.html (last visited Jan. 11, 2019).

Menkel-Meadow, Carrie, *When Winning Isn't Everything: The Lawyer As Problem Solver*, Georgetown University Law Center, 28 Hofstra L. Rev. 920 (2000), https://scholarship.law.georgetown.edu/facpub/172/ (last visited Apr. 12, 2019).

Microsoft, https://www.ailab.microsoft.com/experiments/jfk-files (last visited Apr. 22, 2019).

PwC, The Essential Eight—The Essential Eight technologies that matter for business today (Jan. 11, 2019, 4:26 PM), https://www.pwc.com/gx/en/issues/technology/essential-eight-technologies.html (last visited Apr. 11, 2019).

RIS Rechtsinformationssystem des Bundes, https://www.ris.bka.gv.at/Englische-Rv/ (last visited Jan. 20, 2019).

ROSS Intelligence, *AI Meets Legal Research*, https://rossintelligence.com/ (last visited Jan. 11, 2019).

Sandler, Rachel, *This fast-growing startup just got $25 million from Silicon Valley investors to help lawyers everywhere save time and win more cases* (Jun. 28, 2018), Business Insider (Jan. 11, 2019, 9:14 AM), https://www.businessinsider.de/everlaw-legal-tech-aj-shankar-raises-25-million-2018-6?r=US&IR=T (last visited Feb. 2, 2019).

Satell, Greg, *The Industrial Era Ended, and So Will the Digital Era*, Harvard Business Review (2018), https://hbr.org/2018/07/the-industrial-era-ended-and-so-will-the-digital-era (last visited Apr. 12, 2019).

Simmons & Simmons, *New draft rule on disclosure unveiled*, http://www.elexica.com/en/legal-topics/dispute-resolution-commercial/011117-new-draft-rule-on-disclosure-unveiled (last visited Apr. 12, 2019).

Simmons & Simmons, *Pilot Scheme for new disclosure rules approved by the Civil Procedure Rule Committee* (Jul. 31, 2018), http://www.simmons-simmons.com/en/news/2018/july/pilot-scheme-for-new-disclosure-rules-approved-by-the-civil-procedure-rule-committee (last visited Feb. 3, 2019).

SMASHDOCS, https://www.smashdocs.net/en/technology (last visited Jan. 11, 2019).

Taylor Wessing, *Newsflash: Disclosure pilot scheme for the Business and Property Courts* (Oct. 8, 2018), https://united-kingdom.taylorwessing.com/en/insights/brands-update/newsflash-disclosure-pilot-scheme-for-the-business-and-property-courts (last visited Apr. 12, 2019).

WIKIPEDIA, *Dancing in the Street*, https://en.wikipedia.org/wiki/Dancing_in_the_Street (last visited Apr. 12, 2019).

C. Other Sources

BOWIE, DAVID & JAGGER, MICK, DANCING IN THE STREET (EMI Records, 1985).

Simon Ahammer

Legal Publishers in Times of Digitization of the Legal Market

Risks, Challenges, and Opportunities arising from LegalTech for very Traditional Companies and Business Models

TABLE OF CONTENTS

I. Introduction[1]

For a long time, legal publishers (as well as law firms) were convinced that the consequences of the increasing digitization of the legal profession would not have any drastic effects on their current and future business models.

While the legal profession was of the opinion (and unfortunately still partly is) that a «people-centric business» such as legal advice could only be digitised to a very limited extent, most publishers until recently believed that the publication of legal content in the form of legal texts, judgments, articles, and commentaries in books or electronic form via research databases on the internet behind a paywall would also be sufficient in the future to achieve rising sales with consistently high returns.

This view is most certainly no longer true. The risks to the classic business model of legal publishers resulting from the increasing digitization of legal advice and the ecosystem around it are far greater and more drastic than previously assumed.

II. Business Models Risks of Specialized Publishers

Due to the digitalization of legal advice, law firms will find themselves amidst significantly intensified competition. This increased competitive pressure arises in legal advice to private individuals (business-to-consumers («B2C»)), the target market primarily of law firms with only a few professionals, which still represent the dominant organizational size in most European countries, and in questions of general civil law and tort law through even stronger competition between law firms, since for example the use of modern software solutions in case processing allows for significant competitive advantages to be achieved through higher efficiency (which lead to new remuneration models and thus to lower overall margins for legal services). Although the demand for legal advice is growing continuously every year and an end to this trend is not in sight,[2] the above mentioned factors will reduce both the amount of turnover per case as well as the number of cases requiring the involvement of a «real» human lawyer in many fields of law in the future. A «smaller cake» inevitably leads to increassed competition. The aforementioned changes in the market environment will lead, on the one hand, to a significant reduction in the number of law firms (some market observers already speak of a downright «anni-

1 Note: This chapter is a translation of a contribution originally penned in German.

2 Nicholas Bruch, *Law Firms Are More Profitable Than Ever. How are They Doing It?*, LAW.COM (Oct. 3, 2018 9:01 AM), https://www.law.com/2018/10/03/law-firms-are-more-profitable-than-ever-how-are-they-doing-it/ (last visited Apr. 12, 2019).

hilation» of small law firms)[3] and thus to a decline in the total number of legal professionals. On the other hand, the remaining units will make more intensive efforts than is customary today to significantly reduce both the costs per mandate and the general office costs in order to remain competitive in such changed market environment.

For specialist legal publishers, the aforementioned effects of digitization on the legal profession in the form of cost reductions and a decline in the number of law firms operating in the market have a direct negative impact on their sales and profit numbers. Since the aforementioned digitization effects in legal advice are not a rapid phenomenon, but rather a far-reaching, permanent change in the overall market environment,[4] the sales figures in the classic distribution model with legal content will decline significantly in the future. In addition, the previous business model of publishers with the (costly) publication of judgments is also coming under increasing pressure from various sides.[5] While in Germany the free publication of judgments, especially by courts of first instance, is progressing very slowly and so far it has mainly been possible to access decisions of the highest instance free of charge online, other European countries are already considerably further along in this respect.[6] However, the trend is clear: in the short to medium term, it will be very difficult for publishers to earn money by selling court decisions (and an analogous development to the «extinction» of the «loose-leaf collections» as a distribution format at the beginning of the 2000 years may be expected).

III. Digitization Opportunities

However, digitization also offers a variety of opportunities for legal publishers to expand their business areas and develop new sources of income. Publishers have two resources that will not lose any of their importance for the legal advice market, even with increasing digitization: 1) comprehensive, subject-specific content, some of which has been built up over decades; and, 2) an infrastructure that is based on a network of authors who, in interaction with editorial services provided by publishers, on the one hand «produce» high-quality new content and, on the other hand, reliably update existing con-

---

3 Carloyn Elefant, *Why Startups Fail Is Also Why Solo And Small Law Firms Fail*, Above the Law (Apr. 10, 2018 1:50 PM), https://abovethelaw.com/2018/04/why-startups-fail-is-also-why-solo-and-small-law-firms-fail/ (last visited Apr. 12, 2019).

4 Mark A Cohen, *Law Is Lagging Digital Transformation—Why It Matters*, Forbes (Dec. 20, 2018, 5:40 AM), https://www.forbes.com/sites/markcohen1/2018/12/20/law-is-lagging-digital-transformation-why-it-matters/#d520cc1515c5 (last visited Ar. 11, 2019).

5 *See* https://www.juraforum.de/urteile/.

6 *See* www.entscheidsuche.ch for a powerful disruptor example in Switzerland.

tent. Why are these resources now so important in the context of the digitisation of the legal sector?

The use of software technology in legal work should make it more efficient, easier to master and also cheaper and more transparent in the future. Today's knowledge domain of lawyers, the application of laws, and the judgments on facts (subsumption) is based (somewhat simplified) on the projection of facts of a particular case onto the correct sub-areas of the abstract body of rules of a legal system. In addition to the knowledge of the necessary examination schemes, this requires knowledge of the relevant decisions and the relevant secondary literature such as essays and commentaries in order to interpret applicable laws and ordinances in conformity with the law. Since the know-how necessary for this is usually not completely and readily «retrievable» solely from the memory of the professional, the legal activity, after a factual analysis of the legal aspects, always also includes the research and use of the search results obtained thereby.

Which of these activities will in future be taken over by machines, or rather software programs, in the context of digitisation? Do people still need legal advice at all? The prevailing opinion at present is that, even in the medium term, software will not be able to completely replace people in the legal activity explained above. The use of programs can therefore «only» support the work of legal professionals in certain areas.

IV. Applications for LegalTech in Publishing

So where can programs help? On the one hand, software solutions are suitable for making routine legal work more efficient, in particular for completing recurring tasks faster and more error-free.

A. Document Assembly Solutions

A good example of how software can perform recurring legal activities faster, easier, and more reliably than humans is the creation of standard documents from «text modules» by means of so-called document assembly solutions. Such applications have been around for almost 20 years, but so far these programs have been installed mostly locally in the firm.[7] Such systems were

7 Steve Kovalan, *Data & Analytics: Transforming Law Firms*, LAW.COM (Jan. 17, 2019 1:50 PM), https://www.law.com/2019/01/17/data-analytics-transforming-law-firms/ (last visited Apr. 11, 2019).

«filled» so far mainly by contents from the archives of the law firms or legal departments, which use this kind of software.

With the Internet and the resulting possibility of offering software solutions in the cloud centrally and without the need for local installation at law firms, interesting business opportunities are now opening up for publishers to become active in this area as software and content providers. For decades, legal publishers have been successfully publishing form manuals, which, in addition to sample texts, also contain additional information in the form of usage information, relevant citation of judgments and references to secondary literature.[8] These contents have so far (surprisingly) still been offered to a large extent in book form, but also online. The online versions are often simple, unaltered reproductions of the books, and to «giving» additional functionalities to these sample text collections online, which has only rarely been implemented to date.

The progress made in implementing complex software solutions in the «cloud» has now opened up the opportunity for publishers to offer the «smart» collections of formulations previously published as pure text collections in a document assembly solution. Through an «intelligent» integration of the sample texts in a modular manner into a corresponding online software offering, the usability of such collections of formulation suggestions on the part of the users could be considerably increased.

On the one hand, it would be possible to greatly simplify and optimize the selection of the desired text formulations by means of question-answer dialogues of the application, since the user of such an application does not have to get an overview of dozens of different variants of a certain model text type (e.g., employment contracts) manually and, therefore, in a very time-consuming manner as has been the case up to now. Rather, the program automatically compiles the necessary text components on the basis of the answers given by the user.

In addition, the integration of the contents of form manuals into a document assembly software opens up the possibility of only displaying necessary additional information and decision aids when certain formulation variants are selected if these are really relevant in processing. In the case of referenced decisions or comments in the secondary literature, a link can also be inserted so that the user, if desired, can directly call up the above-mentioned judgments or comments in the context of the current question.

Finally, when the sample texts are integrated into a cloud-based software solution from a publishing house, both the sample texts and the corresponding

---

8 Colin Lachance, *Why top law firms and publishers around the world are looking at Iceberg*, VLEX.COM (Apr. 17, 2018), https://blog.vlex.com/why-top-law-firms-and-publishers-around-the-world-are-looking-at-iceberg-fe0c0045b08c?gi=bd9f37bc02e8 (last visited Apr. 11, 2019).

additional information and query dialogs can be updated and supplemented quickly and in high quality by the authors and editors at any time. This in my view is a considerable advantage compared to document assembly solutions that are operated on site and «only» filled with in-house content and maintained in-house.

The aforementioned functionalities would already open up the possibility for publishers to successfully sell corresponding content in addition to the existing distribution channels in the form of «classic» sample collections via print media or online databases.

In addition, document assembly solutions for publishers have the potential to offer additional, completely new services on a subscriber basis in the form of update notifications.

A prerequisite for such a service is that the software solution offered by the publishing house has a powerful interface (API) which, in addition to transferring «composed» documents to connected software from third-party providers (for example, manufacturers of document management systems or office administration programs), also implements functionalities for sending information regarding updates of text elements contained in documents already transferred (push services). The software from other providers could use this data to inform their program users, for example, which cases in the law firm are affected by the updated text elements and which measures could therefore be taken by the law firm. Such a new service offering could considerably relieve users of the burden of monitoring already completed documents, in particular contracts.

B. Workflow Tools

In addition to the aforementioned document assembly solutions, increasing digitalization also opens up the possibility for publishers to integrate their content into programs in their actual mandate work, which, in addition to the creation of documents, support the work of lawyers directly.

In question are all legal activities, which are strongly formalized, but nevertheless often require legal considerations. Here, appropriate content-supported tools can considerably relieve the professional in the individual sections of mandate processing. Especially in consumer and private law (in particular road traffic law, tenancy law, family law, inheritance law, and labour law), such programs can provide valuable support.

Similar to the document assembly solutions mentioned above, the advantage of publishers over other providers is that they have the relevant legal content to support legal decisions. If this content is made available to the user at the right time during the individual sub-processes of his or her formalised mandate processing, a large part of the manual research work is no longer required and the manual data can be processed more quickly and cost-effectively. With this type of software solution, the benefit for the user could also be further increased by automatically entering content updates in addition to the current content, and automatically informing the users of the legal consequences for their daily work because of the content virtualisation carried out.

An example of such a workflow tool could be cloud-based software for the lawyer to advise on claims for damages in traffic accidents. In addition to providing support for a wide variety of damage calculations, including necessary legal assessments, the provision of tables for quantifying the individual damage items with automatic consideration of any judicially decided lump sums could considerably reduce the manual research activity during case processing and therefore speed up case processing overall. If one integrates with such a solution still (partly) an automated production of the necessary letters to the parties, then the average processing time per mandate would further decrease.

C. Computerized Data Analysis

In the analysis of documents, a basic distinction is made between two objectives, according to which the text is to be examined by programs. On the one hand, there are systems that specialize in data extraction, i.e., these solutions are used to determine the date of conclusion of the agreement, the names and addresses of the parties, the duration, etc. from archived contracts. On the other hand, software solutions try to evaluate texts semantically, that is, by means of analysis of the word positions, the used terms, frequencies etc., to «understand» text contents and to derive conclusions from them, for example the classification of submitted documents (e.g., recognition of documents as «rental agreements», even if the title says «lease agreement», but the text contains (only or predominantly) typical rental clauses).

In both directions, technologies such as Machine Learning (ML), Natural Language Processing (NLP) and Deep Learing (DL) are used.[9] All of these technologies are summarized under the term «artificial intelligence» (AI)—which must always be trained with reference texts before they are used in practice (and also during use). In the case of semantic text analysis, a usable «recognition rate» of the solution used requires particularly high quality training content in various variants from the «knowledge domain» of the docu-

9 Özgür Genc, *Notes on Artificial Intelligence, Machine Learning and Deep Learning for curious people*, Medium (Jan. 26, 2019), https://towardsdatascience.com/notes-on-artificial-intelligence-ai-machine-learning-ml-and-deep-learning-dl-for-56e51a2071c2 (last visited Apr. 12, 2019).

ments to be checked. It is also necessary that the training data is continuously updated so that the system can deliver consistently good results.[10]

1. AI Opportunities for Publishers

In the legal environment, it is exclusively the publishers who have such legal data at their disposal in the form of collections of judgements, legal texts, commentaries, essays, learning content etc., in the necessary quality and quantity. But it would be too simple to assume that one can simply «dump» all the publishers' collections of legal information into the software and the perfect analysis solution for the legal market is ready.

2. Learning Content Requirements for Text Analysis Solutions

a) Selections of Suitable Learning Information

Depending on the desired analysis capabilities of a software solution, a dedicated selection of legal content is required to carry out the learning processes. For example, extensive secondary literature (commentaries, essays) for applications that identify «legal weaknesses» either during the creation process of a document or subsequently in the form of missing regulatory facts or violations of applicable law, and suggest appropriate action and information to users and, if necessary, offer suitable text formulations, is fundamentally less suitable as learning material. The reason for this is that in my experience although these sources contain data on the question of the extent to which the document submitted would be legally incomplete or otherwise legally «incorrect», and the application could be learned accordingly, the concrete proposals for action to be derived by the legal advisors are rarely given in this type of secondary advice. Instead, in such a scenario the feeding of so-called «playbooks» into the AI system would be much more effective. To put it simply, playbooks are a kind of legal «cookbook» for the error-free production of certain types of documents, in particular contracts and terms and conditions, which consist of a «mix» of legal texts, relevant case law, examination schemes and supplementary instructions for action. These types of publications are often found in the Anglo-American legal system, whereas in Germany, for example, they are rarely found as in-house information in large law firms and legal departments.[11] This missing kind of learning information could, however, be created and updated by the publishers with the help of their extensive

---

10 Roland Yu, *Legal artificial intelligence: Can it stand up in a court of law*, Tech and Law Center (Feb. 22, 2017), http://techandlaw.net/legal-artificial-intelligence-can-stand-court-law/ (last visited Apr. 12, 2019).

11 Sterling Miller, *Ten Things: Creating a Good Contract Playbook* (Jul. 17, 2018), https://sterlingmiller2014.wordpress.com/2018/07/17/ten-things-creating-a-good-contract-playbook/ (last visited Apr. 9, 2019).

data collection of legal contents and by using their network of authors (who are supported technically and organisationally by proofreading) in the necessary design and quality especially for the learning phase of corresponding software solutions.

b) Processing of Legal Data

Furthermore, after the selection of suitable legal contents, a special preparation of data is always necessary before use in the corresponding software programs; in particular, the information for the learning process usually has to be manually categorized and marked («tagged»). In addition to a certain technical affinity, these activities also require an understanding of the subject matter, so that publishers have a clear advantage over traditional software providers in this respect as well, since the necessary technical expertise is undoubtedly available in their proofreading departments in the legal environment, where content is already indexed and enriched with additional—non-legal—information.

V. Future Positioning of Publishers in the Legal Market

Publishers should swiftly answer the question of which future role they would like to play in this LegalTech market segment given (as mentioned above) the expansion of business activities to areas of software-supported document analysis using AI functionality, automated-standardized text creation, and solutions supporting direct legal case processing. Further, additional know-how in the areas of programming, sales, and maintenance and expansion, restructuring, and adaptation of current structure and infrastructure will become necessary.

A. Possible Future Business Areas

Do publishers want to «limit» themselves in the future to the provision and maintenance of the legal content necessary for the operation of the software solutions or do they also want to provide applications and service platforms? If the latter, do they develop them themselves, buy them outright, or create them together with third-party providers? If a publishing house were to enter the market as a provider of software solutions and corresponding platform offerings, it would not only significantly expand its existing portfolio, but would also change its overall corporate orientation to that of a solution provider in which publishing activities would «only» represent a partial aspect alongside software development, consulting, and support of business activities.

1. Disadvantages of «Content Only» Providers

If publishers opt for the more obvious and potentially «easier» way of «limiting» themselves to the preparation, updating, and creation of new legal content for the above-mentioned third-party software solutions, their (brand) presence in the legal sector will likely decline sharply.

In contrast to the previous online portal solutions pursued by publishers which have still ensured a high level of brand awareness in the market based on continued direct interaction with the target group of professionals (in connection with the print offering), brand awareness will become weaker in the future as user numbers for such services will decrease as the market share of applications which will increasingly support and (partially) automate the legal activity, including research, will increase. As a result, the manual searches carried out by publishers with the help of search portals will become more and more superfluous.

If solutions in which publishing content (only) represents the invisible legal «fuel» were offered exclusively by third-party companies, the reference to the publisher behind them as a supplier of content information and thus an important component of branding might eventually be lost. (A «Powered by XYZ Publishing House» lettering on the user interface of a third party would not compensate for the consequences of this development.).

Such weakening of the brand would have considerable negative effects on the reputation of publishers with external authors, who usually carry out their activities for legal publishers less for monetary reasons than to increase their own reputation (personal branding) in the legal market.[12] A quantitative and qualitative reduction of their author network would inevitably lead to a deterioration in the content offered and thus further reduce economic success of a publishing house.

Although the print sector will continue to exist in the future—especially in the legal environment (albeit with ever decreasing significance)—it will become necessary for larger publishing houses to maintain and further develop their brand presence beyond books, magazines, and online research portals and, to that end, to act as providers of appropriate software solutions in addition to their function as suppliers of legal specialist information.

2. Publishers as Providers of Software Solutions

a) Status Quo

In my view the role as providers of software solutions and corresponding services is occupied by the established publishing houses. Although almost all providers have online offers for research, only a few companies from the pub-

12 Karl S Okamoto, *Reputation and the Value of Lawyers*, 74 (1) Or. L. Rev. (1995).

lishing sector offer further substantial software applications. The «cautious» attitude of many specialist publishers in the legal sector towards extending their portfolios to the sale of software products and corresponding online solutions, which has lasted for many years, means that very few publishers in this sector have built up significant know-how of their own, development capacities and sales structures.

There is not only a lack of the necessary knowledge regarding the creation and distribution of innovative software products. Due to the fact that the business model of print media has changed little over the years, it has (so far) not been necessary for publishers to rethink their aging enterprise architectures at a structural and organizational level—as is customary with software companies—or to establish new methods of cooperation and process control (e.g., agile project management). Publishers are not only internally that ill- positioned for the future; they are also externally hampered as they have gathered very little experience in integrating external partners in the development of new products. Why is this so?

Publishers are «used» to the fact that the intellectual creation process is firmly in their hands and under their control due to their history, which still characterizes many units today. For example, outsourcing of proofreading work, hardly ever takes place with specialist publishers.

b) Outsourcing of Software Projekts

This way of thinking should be (at least partly) urgently reconsidered in the area of software solutions. The high demand for qualified web developers, software architects, and data analysts for machine learning has already led to a situation in which the labour market in this area has virtually gone dry.[13] This will hardly change in the near future. In such environment, even large units are unlikely to be willing or able to afford to set up an effective and sufficiently large team for the complete in-house development of new LegalTech applications. However, complete outsourcing of the entire development, operation, and maintenance of publishing software solutions cannot be recommended either, as this would not lead to any build-up of know-how on the part of the publishing house. Further, it would also lead to a dangerous dependency on the producing software providers and to insufficient control of the service provider. How to solve this dilemma?

On the one hand, publishers need to realise that innovative, high-performance applications and platform services can only be designed, implemented and offered in cooperation with specialised external development companies. Complete in-house developments, on the other hand, have no future in publishing houses (any more), as the demands of the users have become too high

---

13 jf gagne, *Global AI Talent Pool Report 2018*, https://jfgagne.ai/talent/ (last visited Apr. 2, 2019).

and the creation process too complex—in addition to the aforementioned challenges of being able to attract critical mass of suitable talent.

c) Inhouse Competences and Developments

Nevertheless, publishers should acquire internal know-how in those aspects of the development process that are particularly closely related to the use and inclusion of legal content. Software technologies and development scenarios relating to the processing and preparation of legal content, the evaluation and (test) implementation of services in the context of artificial intelligence, the development of mechanisms to protect the publisher's information provided, the design and implementation of secure and powerful interfaces to the publisher's database systems are just a few examples of areas in which publishers should build their own development resources and competence. The results of modules developed in-house in these areas could then be combined with external components such as the implementation of user interfaces and user management to form a product. Although such approach also requires substantial investment on the part of the publishers, the teams required for this can be considerably smaller than in the case of departments for complete in-house developments. The knowledge gained and the development of reusable libraries of integrated program modules would enable publishers in the field of software solution development to implement appropriate projects economically, to implement software and expertise from external service providers and, in addition, to expand their unique selling proposition as «authors» of legal content through additional know-how for the use of this data in LegalTech applications. This domain of knowledge will probably have the same economic value in the future as the actual legal content itself.

d) Organisational Changes

In order to build and develop the internal development and competence teams described above, considerable changes are needed to the organisational structure of today's publishing houses in order to support and promote the dynamism and agility of such departments. In my personal view many publishers today are still managed by rigid, hierarchical structures and multiple management levels. Some of these «power structures» have been formed and consolidated over decades and are now being decisively defended; one could exaggerate to the point that some publishers carry with them more corporate structures than some listed companies. In such an environment, it is difficult to get and keep the desired software experts. In addition, the organizational structures mentioned above prohibit a creative, innovative, and agile way of working (for example: design thinking). Since consolidated organisational structures can usually only be changed and dissolved slowly in my experience, the development and competence teams mentioned should be set up separately from the existing publishing organisation in terms of both location and personnel.

This approach has already been used repeatedly in different industries in the past to develop or introduce new techniques, products and processes in an existing company. For example, Audi AG did not set up its entire development department for the new TT coupé model at its headquarters in Ingolstadt, but rather started it off in California and then completed it in Munich.[14]

According to former Chairman of the Board of Management Herbert Demel, at the time Chairman of the Board of Management of Audi AG, «… something like the TT would not have come out of normal factory routine. The normal setting produces a proper mainstream, but it is incredibly difficult to suddenly produce something completely different».[15]

B. Target Groups Expansion with LegalTech and Possible B2C Products

If, as described above, legal publishers will also be active in the legal market with software solutions in the future, the question arises whether these new offers will not also open up the possibility of addressing new groups of buyers in addition to the existing main target groups. So far, in my personal experience the publishing houses offer is mainly focused on professionals in law firms and legal departments. Although many publishing companies in the legal field also sell offers for «legal laymen», the main business field of the most important players in the market is the business-to-business (B2B) sector. By entering the market of content-supported applications and online services, publishers can also directly address the target group of private individuals (business-to-consumer (B2C) business)—provided that the relevant programming is implemented.

Some start-up online portals that are already on the market support private individuals, for example, in the legal enforcement of claims in the event of flight delays, rental defects, severance payments in the event of termination under employment law and the assertion of claims for social benefits.[16] Since the turnover per case of the services mentioned above is usually very low, these services must be highly scalable if they are to be operated profitably. This requires that the processes of the mandate processing are automated as far as possible, including a legal assessment of the individual facts. Therefore, almost all of these providers use technologies to evaluate data using artificial intelligence. In addition to case-specific data, the content of this evaluated in-

14 Auto Design Magazine, *Design History Audi TT 1998* (Jun. 30, 2017), http://autodesignmagazine.com/en/2017/06/audi-tt-tradition-and-technology-2/ (last visited Apr. 2, 2019).

15 Andreas Molitor, *Lasst uns Pferde stehlen*, 2017/1, Edition Brand Eins, at 29.

16 Examples explained in other chapters in this Book include www.flightright.de, https://hartz4widerspruch.de/app/, https://www.donotpay.com and others.

formation also includes judgements, laws, and comments, which are set in relation to the recorded case data.

Publishing house contents are thus an important component of such solutions in legal advice, so that a business activity of publishing houses also seems obvious in this market segment, in particular if these, as described above, change more and more to a solution provider. An expansion of the portfolio of legal publishers to include online services and platforms in the B2C sector could, in principle, take place either through the publication of their own services under the publishing brands or through strategic participation in (already existing) offers from third-party companies.

1. Proprietory Publications in the B2C Market

As already explained, workflow tools that support lawyers in their actual mandate work within the framework of factual analysis, legal assessment, research and also communication with the parties involved represent a promising future field of activity for legal publishers. The basic idea is that this type of software solution could also be adapted for use by «non-lawyers» in some legal areas (e.g., assertion of claims for damages in road traffic and tenancy law) in terms of user interface and user guidance. The involvement of «human» legal advice and representation would be necessary if such online services were used by private individuals, usually only when the claims are enforced in court. But even this could be mediated and «supported» by the offered software solution. Such a B2C offer could therefore be a «product variant» of a solution that would also be marketed for law firms and legal departments.

With its own offers, it would come naturally—apart from additional incomes from the enterprise of the solutions—to an enlargement of the awareness of the publishing house in the general public, which would ultimately benefit their brands and numbers. However, such solutions would make publishers direct competitors of law firms and indirectly jeopardize their business model. The result would probably be a weakening of the purchasing power of parts of the publishers' own main target group.

Even if the publication of the corresponding own publishing offers by the «relevant» law firms were not to initially lead to any negative financial effects, there would still be a danger that the reputation of the publishers (bringing the corresponding services online) would be damaged among the professionals. This could, as explained in above, lead to a decline in turnover and reputation in the legal market and to a weakening of publishing brands, the thinking being along the lines of «Who buys comments on employment law from publishers when these offer services online that focus on employment law mandates?».

2. Strategic B2C Offers and Participation

While the publication of software solutions and services under one's own name could lead to the risk of a deterioration in the market position in the B2B sector, above all, due to negative effects on the reputation of the publishing house, strategic participation in an (already existing) offering (with a focus on private individuals) represents an alternative way for publishers to gain a foothold in this market without having to fear a major uproar of the legal profession. Although such a participation would also indirectly create a competitive situation with lawyers whose activities include the same type of legal advice that is also covered by the service in question, possible negative effects on the reputation of the publishing house would most probably be considerably less, as the publishing house, in this constellation, is only active «in the background» and would, therefore, be perceived as a passive participant. A further advantage for publishers for this variant of market entry would be that the financial risks would be considerably lower with a participation than with its «own» products. If such an investment is made in companies that are already on the market, the publisher also has the opportunity to gain direct experience in a new market segment for (most) legal specialist publishers through this investment. The knowledge gained could then be used later as the basis for a strategic decision as to whether the publisher should gear its business model even more strongly to the B2C market in future.

VI. Summary

The increasing digitization of the legal market is also leading to far-reaching changes in the business models of legal publishers. Publishers do not have to completely «reinvent» themselves, but in order to remain successful in the future, they must develop from a «pure» content supplier to a provider of content-integrated software solutions (in addition to the existing content offerings in print and online).

In order to be able to cope with this expansion of their existing business model organizationally, the publisher must have the will of the management and the evidence to break down existing structures and tread new paths in the cooperation with external partners.

If publishers are prepared to change, more than in the past decades, they will continue to be very successful in the legal market in the future, as legal content (even if in other formats) will continue to play an important role in the «digital legal sector».

VII. Bibliography

A. Hard Copy Sources

Molitor, Andreas, *Lasst uns Pferde stehlen*, 2017/1, Edition Brand eins, at 29.

Okamoto, Karl S, *Reputation and the Value of Lawyers*, 74 (1) Or. L. Rev. (1995).

B. Online Sources

Auto Design Magazine, *Design History Audi TT 1998* (Jun. 30, 2017), http://autodesignmagazine.com/en/2017/06/audi-tt-tradition-and-technology-2/ (last visited Apr. 2, 2019).

Bruch, Nicholas, *Law Firms Are More Profitable Than Ever. How are They Doing It?*, law.com (Oct. 3, 2018 9:01 AM), https://www.law.com/2018/10/03/law-firms-are-more-profitable-than-ever-how-are-they-doing-it/ (last visited Apr. 12, 2019).

Cohen, Mark A, *Law Is Lagging Digital Transformation—Why It Matters*, Forbes (Dec. 20, 2018, 5:40 AM), https://www.forbes.com/sites/markcohen1/2018/12/20/law-is-lagging-digital-transformation-why-it-matters/#d520cc1515c5 (last visited Ar. 11, 2019).

Elefant, Carloyn *Why Startups Fail Is Also Why Solo And Small Law Firms Fail*, Above the Law (Apr. 10, 2018 1:50 PM), https://abovethelaw.com/2018/04/why-startups-fail-is-also-why-solo-and-small-law-firms-fail/ (last visited Apr. 12, 2019).

jf gagne, *Global AI Talent Pool Report 2018*, https://jfgagne.ai/talent/ (last visited Apr. 2, 2019).

Genc, Özgür, *Notes on Artificial Intelligence, Machine Learning and Deep Learning for curious people*, Medium (Jan. 26, 2019), https://towardsdatascience.com/notes-on-artificial-intelligence-ai-machine-learning-ml-and-deep-learning-dl-for-56e51a2071c2 (last visited Apr. 12, 2019).

Kovalan, Steve, *Data & Analytics: Transforming Law Firms*, law.com (Jan., 17 2019 1:50 PM), https://www.law.com/2019/01/17/data-analytics-transforming-law-firms/ (last visited Apr. 11, 2019).

Lachance, Colin, *Why top law firms and publishers around the world are looking at Iceberg*, vlex.com (Apr. 17, 2018), https://blog.vlex.com/why-top-law-firms-and-publishers-around-the-world-are-looking-at-iceberg-fe0c0045b08c?gi=bd9f37bc02e8 (last visited Apr. 11, 2019).

Sterling Miller, *Ten Things: Creating a Good Contract Playbook* (Jul. 17, 2018), https://sterlingmiller2014.wordpress.com/2018/07/17/ten-things-creating-a-good-contract-playbook/ (last visited Apr. 9, 2019).

Yu, Roland, *Legal artificial intelligence: Can it stand up in a court of law*, Tech and Law Center (Feb. 22, 2017), http://techandlaw.net/legal-artificial-intelligence-can-stand-court-law/ (last visited Apr. 12, 2019).

Professor Rolf H Weber

Smart Contracts and What the Blockchain Has Got to Do With It

TABLE OF CONTENTS

I. Playing field of technology and law

The term «smarts contract» encompassing the word «contract» must have a legal connotation, even if the ironical remark has been expressed two years ago that a smart contract is neither smart nor a contract.[1] In principle, a legal term does have a normative significance by way of a «legal order», implying the regularity and predictability of actions: «*those entering the market, or more specifically, a commercial transaction, know that their actions and the actions of others are governed by rules*».[2] Therefore, in order to assess what the blockchain has got to do with the smart contract, the relation between the two notions must be established.

Blockchain is a technological term describing a specific type of distributed ledger technology (DLT). So far, a commonly accepted definition has not been agreed upon; the International Organization of Securities Commissions (IOSCO) understands DLT as a «*consensus of replicated, shared, and synchronized digital data geographically spread across multiple sites, countries, and/or institutions*»;[3] therefore, the DLT is a combination of peer-to-peer networking, cryptography, and distributed data storage. Systematically, blockchain is a decentralized system in the form of a continuously growing list of records, that are linked and secured by use of cryptography.[4] Accordingly, the blocks hold badges of valid transactions that are hashed or encoded,[5] and the execution of transactions cannot rely on a centralized intermediary to support and coordinate its execution.[6]

The recent advent of smart contracts and blockchain shows the challenges caused by the fact that the regulatory growth is linear, while the technological growth is exponential. Often, until the normative environment has been established, the technological development already is much further advanced.[7] Technologies can cause a smooth transition of the environment or have a dis-

---

1 *See* David Adlerstein, *Are Smart Contracts Smart? A Critical Look at Basic Blockchain Questions*, Coindesk (Jun. 26, 2017), https://www.coindesk.com/when-is-a-smart-contract-actually-a-contract/ (last visited Feb. 2, 2019).

2 Marco Dell' Erba, *Demystifying Technology. Do Smart Contracts Require a New Legal Framework? Regulatory Fragmentation, Self-Regulation, Public Regulation*, SSRN (May 17, 2018), https://papers.ssrn.com/sol3/papers.cfm?abstract_id=3228445 (last visited Feb. 2, 2019) at 5.

3 IOSCO, *Research Report on Financial Technologies (Fintech)*, February 2017, https://www.iosco.org/library/pubdocs/pdf/IOSCOPD554.pdf (last visited Feb. 3, 2019) at 51.

4 *See* Aaron Wright & Primavera De Filippi, *Decentralized Blockchain Technology and the Rise of Lex Cryptographia*, SSRN (Mar. 10, 2015), https://ssrn.com/abstract=2580664 (last visited Feb. 1, 2019) at 4 et seq.

5 Dan Tapscott & Alex Tapscott, The Blockchain Revolution (Random House, 2016) at 75.

6 Primavera De Filippi & Aaron Wright, Blockchain and the Law. The Rule of Code (Harvard University Press, 2018) at 76.

7 Dell'Erba, *supra* note 2, at 4.

ruptive effect. Smart contracts are not only a creative innovation but a quite new instrument which might cause the emergence of different social and commercial conventions even if the changes are not really revolutionary.[8]

The blockchain is important for the execution of smart contracts since it is a distributed ledger that is able to efficiently record transactions in a permanent way, i.e., the technology is inherently resistant to modifications of data. As a consequence, once recorded data in a given block cannot be altered anymore retroactively without the alteration of all subsequent blocks. Such kind of process would require the (improbable) collusion of the peer-to-peer network community. Insofar, blockchain as a DLT does partly have disruptive effects, not at least due to the fact that in parallel to the cryptocurrencies, in particular Bitcoin, Ether, and Ripple, a large number of «second generation» blockchain applications have flourished.[9] The main examples are tokens transactions of whatever manner, often created by way of initial coin offerings (ICO) and smart contracts.

By storing data across its peer-to-peer network, the blockchain technology eliminates risks that could occur in the case of centrally stored data; as mentioned, decentralization is an important blockchain characteristic. This technical feature has an impact on the «life» of smart contracts: third party interventions in case of occurring problems are hardly possible. Ongoing technological developments tackle some basic characteristics of the present design of the blockchain technology since the rigidity of the computer routine makes it difficult to adapt coded smart contracts, i.e., a change of the parameters in the contractual environment can hardly be reflected in the program code. To what extent these developments lead to new forms of smart contracts remains to be seen.

II. Notion and elements of smart contracts

A. History of smart contracts

Often *Nick Szabo* is seen as the «inventor» of smart contracts. In 1994, he described a smart contract as being a «computerized transaction protocol that executes the terms of a contract».[10] Later, in 1997, Szabo used the description: «*The basic idea behind smart contracts is that many kinds of contractual*

---

8 For a general overview *see* Harold J Berman, Law and Revolution: The Formation of the Western Legal Tradition (Harvard University Press, 1983).

9 Sumit Kumar, *The battle among generations of blockchains is far from over,* Capgemini (Dec. 11, 2018), https://www.capgemini.com/2018/12/the-battle-among-generations-of-blockchain-is-far-from-over-yet/ (last visited Apr. 16, 2019).

10 *See* Nick Szabo, *Smart Contratcs* (1994), www.fon.hum.uva.nl/rob/Courses/InformationInSpeech/CDROM/Literature/LOTwinterschool2006/szabo.best.vwh.net/smart.contracts.html (last visited

clauses (such as collateral, bonding, delineation of property rights, etc.) can be embedded in the hardware and software we deal with, in such a way as to make breach of contract expensive (if desired, sometimes prohibitively so) for the breacher».[11]

Notwithstanding these descriptions from the nineties, a historical perspective allows a broader view of smart contracts than a concentration on the Szabo «invention»:

– A smart contract as described by Szabo is based on the vending machine; but the first such machine allowing automated payments was introduced in 1883 in a London subway.[12] In June 1948, when the Soviet Union cut off the road to Berlin, the United States and its Allies began the so-called Berlin Airlift sending huge volumes of food and other supplies to the divided city; in order to track the mountains of cargo, *Edward Guilbert* developed a «manifest system, that could be transmitted by telex, radio-teletype, or telephone».[13] Furthermore, Guilbert also invented a system of electronic data interchange (EDI) in 1965.[14]
– Smart contracts are definitely older than the DLT/blockchain technology, addressed for the first time in the so-called *Satoshi Nakamoto* research paper in 2008.[15]

As the aforementioned remarks show, smart contracts are not really an invention developed during this decade, but a technical measure having been known for quite some time. Nevertheless, the practical importance of smart contracts substantially increased since the blockchain as technical infrastructure is available.

B. Notion of smart contracts

Irrespective of the historical developments it can be said that the blockchain technology is facilitating the possibility of creating and executing contracts through DLT platforms. The smart contract basically describes a technology

---

Feb. 3, 2019) and *see* also Max Raskin, *The Law and Legality of Smart Contracts*, 1 Georgetown Law Technology Review (2017) 305, 336–37.

11 Nick Szabo, *Formalizing and Securing Relationships on Public Networks*, 2/9 First Monday Internet Journal (Sep. 1, 1997), firstmonday.org/ojs/index.php/fm/article/view/548/469 (last visited Feb. 1, 2019).

12 Dell'Erba, *supra* note 2, at 11.

13 De Filippi/Wright, *supra* note 6, at 73.

14 *See* Frank Hayes, *The Story So Far*, Computerworld (Jun. 17, 2002), http://www.computerworld.com/article/2576616/e-commerce/the-story-so-far.html (last visited Feb. 1, 2019).

15 Satoshi Nakamoto, *Bitcoin: A Peer-to-Peer Electronic Cash System*, https://bitcoin.org/bitcoin.pdf (Oct. 31, 2008) (last visited Feb. 1, 2019).

which (with legal effects) allows the exchange of digitally referenced goods and services based on computable contract terms.[16] However, it should not be overlooked that Szabo, when he conceptualized smart contracts, did not design any mechanism that could be a guarantee for the enforcement and the transfer of value. In contrast, he only identified the relationship between the smart contract implementation and the costs of a contractual breach. Smart contracts are used to memorize all parts of legal arrangements.

A working definition describes smart contracts as *«a consensual arrangement between at least two parties for an automated, independent commercial result from the satisfaction or non-satisfaction, determined objectively through code, of a specific factual condition»*.[17] In principle, in its pure form, a smart contract (expressed as bits of logic executed in a determined manner) is entirely embedded in a code; however, hybrid forms do exist, i.e., a smart contract can be based on a code with a separate natural language version.[18] Smart contracts reflect a concept of data-oriented contracts representing contractual obligations, thereby creating «computable» contract terms.[19]

Due to their technical determination, smart contracts are not really well suited to accommodate legal arrangements that cannot be fulfilled solely be referencing data stored or managed within a blockchain-based network (for example representations and warranties related to the compliance with applicable laws or a specific confidentiality undertaking); equally, problems occur if obligations are relational in nature since the parties need to precisely define their performance obligations.[20] Moreover, they are better usable to model predictable and objectively verifiable legal obligations. The parties need to precisely define the performance obligations and accurately memorize the parties' concrete «meeting of the minds». If elements of unpredictability are given or foreseeable and if, therefore, a certain flexibility to structure the ongoing contractual relationship is desirable, smart contracts are not able to comply with such a requirement.

Hereinafter, this contribution discusses the legal framework of smart contracts in various countries, but for demarcation reasons two preliminary remarks are noteworthy: (i) The determination of the applicable law and the competent courts (jurisdiction) is a major issue since parties usually act ano-

---

16 Rolf H Weber, *Smart Contracts: Do we need new legal rules?*, *in* DIGITAL REVOLUTION—NEW CHALLENGES FOR LAW Ch. II.1. (Alberto De Franceschi/Reiner Schulze/Michele Graziadei/Federica Riente/Salvatore Sica & Pietro Sirena, eds., Beck/Hart/Nomos, 2019 (forthcoming)).

17 Adlerstein, *supra* note 1.

18 Dell'Erba, *supra* note 2, at 13 and De Filippi & Wright, *supra* note 6, at 76–77.

19 De Filippi & Wright, *supra* note 6, at 74; Lukas Müller & Reto Seiler, *Smart Contracts aus der Sicht des Vertragsrechts*, ASP (2018) at 319; Harry Surden, *Computable Contracts*, 46 UNIVERSITY OF CALIFORNIA-DAVIS LAW REVIEW 629 et seq. (2012).

20 De Filippi & Wright, *supra* note 6, at 77 and 84.

nymously; these two aspects are not addressed hereinafter. (ii) Most legal statutes do not (yet) know legislative instruments particularly dealing with smart contracts, i.e., the following considerations are not based on stable legal jurisprudence and legal doctrine.

C. Characteristics and examples of smart contracts

A smart contract embraces the following typical characteristics:[21]

- *Self-execution*: The smart contract follows the chosen program logics, cryptographic protocols supplement the contractual terms and payment mechanisms.
- *Self-determination*: The execution of such contract is determined by the code (transactional logic); the counterparty is usually not known (anonymity is given in principle) and interventions by third parties are excluded.
- *Unchangeability*: Since transactions on the blockchain cannot be reversed, the adaptation of the terms of a smart contract is hardly possible.
- *Digital performance*: Smart contracts allow a «transfer» of digitally referenced goods and services, however, not a performance in the real world.

In view of the fact that a change of the contractual terms on the blockchain is hardly possible, the technological and legal security of the transactional execution is high. No personal trust or confidence in the counterparty is needed because the performance of the contract is reflected in the designed code. Authenticity is achieved by (i) keeping identical copies of the ledger on different computers, by (ii) allowing only a limited number of participants to update the list (and the proof), and by (iii) requiring validation of the executed updates by other participants.[22]

Since the scope of applicability of smart contracts is principally limited to digitally verifiable exchanges of goods and services, usually a simultaneous performance (digital execution against payment) takes place. Therefore smart contracts are not suitable if personable objectives or person-related aims should be realized. Furthermore, long-term contracts and contractual networks are not easily apt for the transactional logic of the predetermined code. Simi-

---

21 *See* for example Rolf H Weber, *Smart Contracts: Vertrags- und verfügungsrechtlicher Regelungsbedarf?* 6 SIC! (2018) at 291 et seq. and Hans Rudolf Trüeb, *Smart Contracts*, *in* FESTSCHRIFT FÜR ANTON K. SCHNYDER 723–734 (Pascal Grolimund et al., eds., Schulthess, 2018) at 723–24.

22 Weber, *supra* note 16, at Ch. II. 2 and Stefan Grundmann & Philipp Hacker, *Digital Technology as a Challenge to European Contract Law—From the Existing to the Future Architecture*, SRRN (July 17, 2017), https://ssrn.com/abstract=3003885 (last visited on Feb. 1, 2019) at 8.

larly, if understandings are of a relational in nature or if elements such as a discretionary decision or an appropriate result are of importance, smart contracts are not an appropriate instrument.[23]

So far, smart contracts are not very frequently applied in the real world; possible use cases encompass the following examples:[24]

- *Smart contracts for identity*: individuals can be granted the entitlement to own and control personal data; thereby, compliance, resiliency, and interoperability might be facilitated.
- *Smart contracts for securities and derivatives*: The paper-based registration and transfer processes of securities are time-consuming; the automated settlement particularly of derivatives increases the efficiency.
- *Smart contracts for trade finance*: The international transfers of goods is facilitated through faster compliance and monitoring of Letter of Credit conditions and trade payment processes; first projects are now developed by banks in practice, enabling the creation, modification, and validation of trade title, etc.
- *Smart contracts for supply chains*: The transparency in respect of products' origins is applied in practice in the agricultural and the precious metals areas; complex multiparty systems can be simplified.
- *Smart contracts for records and for financial data recording*: Automated processes improve transactional data transparency and identity; in relation to governments, partly the term RegTech is used (exchanges in the context of account information systems).
- *Smart contracts for land title and for mortgages recording*: Automated processes facilitate the statement of identity and increase confidence in the correctness of the register's contents.
- *Smart contracts for auto insurance and leasing*: The transactions are usually quite standardized and the existence of a repository for each policyholder facilitates the execution of the rights.

A major area of application of smart contracts is the insurance sector, in particular reinsurance contracts can be executed on the basis of smart contracts on a decentralized insurance market place. Furthermore, for consumer purposes, the company Etherisk offers an insurance protection for damages in case of delayed flights;[25] AXA has a similar services' offer (Fizzy).[26] In African countries, blockchain/smart contracts are partly used for banking services. Further-

---

23 Taken from Weber, *supra* note 16, at Ch. II. 2.

24 The following list of examples stems from Swiss LegalTech Association (SLTA), *Regulatory Task Force Report 2018* (Apr. 27, 2018), https://www.swisslegaltech.ch/think-tank/ (last visited Feb. 1, 2019) at 49–51.

25 Available at https://etherisk.de/.

26 Available at https://fizzy.axa/en-gb/.

more, financial derivatives and energy or emission certificates' derivatives can be traded on the basis of smart contracts.

D. Smart contracts as a matter of law

In principle, contractual and commercial rules have been designed to be applied to contractual negotiations generally involving two humans. This paradigm has gradually changed with the advent of the blockchain technology. The «legal order», beneficial for the development of the society and the market, is partly superseded by the technology. The «machine» is placed in a public space and the parties of the contract use the machine in order to achieve the desired transactional result.[27] Nevertheless, smart contracts are a matter of law as outlined hereinafter.

Smart contracts and blockchain are addressing issues that encompass (potentially disruptive) infrastructures and thereby go beyond specific concepts codified into the existing law, including the concept of enforcement.[28] The close link between code and law has been a discussion topic for the last 20 years, following Lessig's diagnose that code solutions, similarly to legal rules, principally reflect «information» that allocates and enforces entitlements.[29] The technical «regulator» (architecture) combines constraints of physics, nature, and technology; the architecture determines what the place of the online world will be in the life of individuals.[30]

Recently, the equation «code is law» has been inversed and became the new equation «law is code». Blockchain is the most prominent example for a technology that reinforces the approach of relying on code (rather than on law). The technically determined transactions are set ex ante, in contrast to the ex post enforceable rules.[31] The blockchain technology enabling the execution of smart contracts is a technical artefact inevitably having both social and political implications.[32] Due to the new technology, the enforcement of smart contracts is possible in an ex ante manner; correspondingly, legal remedies being imposed by courts in ex post judgements loose practical importance.

With the advent of the blockchain technology, law is progressively turning into code. In the past, legal rules have been drafted by humans and for humans. This «human» element can hardly be fulfilled by a technical code

---

27 Dell'Erba, *supra* note 2, at 39.

28 Dell'Erba, *supra* note 2, at 40.

29 Lawrence Lessig, Code and Other Laws of Cyberspace (Basic Books, 1999), at 3 and 87 et seq.

30 Lessig, *supra* note 29, at 89–90.

31 Rolf H Weber, *«Rose is a rose is a rose is a rose»—what about code and law?*, 34 Computer Law & Security Review (2018) at 701, 704.

32 Weber, *supra* note 31, at 704.

even if artificial intelligence and algorithms appear to support such a development. The notion «law is code» reflects the situation that legal obligations are expressed through «technological ledgers». Such a development questions human input into legal relations; thereby, law is at risk to lose a part of its democratic legitimacy and its guiding social functions.[33]

III. Regulatory framework for smart contracts

A. Glance on the law and economics perspective

Due to the finality of the technical code, smart contracts are likely to be certain and secure in relation to the specific performances. In other words, smart contracts have a high degree of clarity, precision, and modularity; in addition, the parties can design a smart contract in a way that no single person controls or is able to halt the program's execution.[34] Any encoded performance obligations will solely execute the designed program according to the terms and conditions expressly provided for in the underlying code (i.e., everything will happen as agreed).[35] From a broader societal perspective, this result appears to be desirable since people keeping their promises are morally good.[36]

Furthermore, smart contracts economize on contracting costs and enforcement costs. The preparation of a transaction, i.e., the making available of the technical infrastructure, can cause specific challenges, however, as soon as the smart contract is concluded, its execution runs without further human intervention at very low costs.[37] Since a smart contract is based on bits of logic executed in a deterministic manner, the possibility of misinterpretation of performance obligations is decreasing.

Generally looking, smart contracts reduce the role of trust in the conclusion of a contract; parties have to rely on the technical code and not on the trustworthiness of or the confidence in the (often unknown) counterparty. As a consequence, contract performance is not dependent on the individual commitment of the counterparty. Finally, since smart contracts are machine-read-

---

33 Weber *supra* note 31, at 705. *See* also Primavera de Filippi & Hassan Samer, *Blockchain Technology as a Regulatory Technology: From Code is Law to Law is Code*, 21 (12) First Monday (December 5, 2016), http://firstmonday.org/ojs/index.php/fm/article/view/7113/5657 (last visited Feb. 1, 2019) at 11–12.

34 De Filippi & Wright, *supra* note 6, at 80 and 81.

35 Weber, *supra* note 16, at Ch. IV. 1.

36 Dell'Erba, *supra* note 2, at 20.

37 Weber, *supra* note 21, at 292.

able, the chosen technology could also be used by autonomous devices and artificial intelligence (AI).[38]

Nevertheless, certain inconveniences must be kept in mind. As mentioned, smart contracts are not suitable for relational performances. Furthermore, a smart contract eventually executes a specific performance although, in view of given (and unenforceable) conditions that have not been coded, it does not make sense to execute it.[39] Even if a revocation and/or modification is technically possible, the technical change could become relatively complicated since the list of the blocks might have to be split by a so-called «hard fork» changing the protocol that makes previously invalid blocks/transactions valid (or vice versa).[40]

B. Civil (continental) law

1. Available legal instruments

Legal doctrine analyzing the specific challenges of smart contracts has principally acknowledged that most normative provisions contained in civil (continental) law are suitable to be applied to smart contracts. The problem of the (individual) «meeting of minds»[41] as precondition for the conclusion of a contract is existing, but can be overcome by the general assumption that the respective contract parties express their willingness to be bound by a smart contract when agreeing to the technical setting.[42] Without any doubt, the parties of a smart contract technically often do not fully understand the programming language having Java similarities or being Python or Solidity, an object-oriented syntax which is executed on the Ethereum Virtual Machine (EVM). In applying a wide interpretation of the criterion of «understandable language»[43] it is argued that persons who enter into a smart contract accept the binding force of the technical conditions even if they do not really understand all the

---

38 De Filippi & Wright, *supra* note 6, at 82.

39 Dell'Erba, *supra* note 2, at 21.

40 *See* the «Hard Fork» definition by Investopedia, *Hard Fork*, https://www.investopidia.com/terms/h/hardfork.asp#ixzz5DcrRKFhj (last visited Feb. 1, 2019).

41 *See* for example Weber *supra* note 16, at Ch. III. 1 and De Filippi & Wright *supra* note 6, at 74 and Stephen J Choi & G Mitu Golati, *Contract as Statute*, 104 Michigan Law Review 1129 et seq. (2006).

42 In short words it could be said that a «yes» to the smart contract is to be interpreted as a «yes» to the code design.

43 *See* also Andreas Furrer, *Die Einbettung von Smart Contracts in das schweizerische Privatrecht*, 3 Anwaltsrevue 103–115 (2018) at 107, Müller & Seiler, *supra* note 19, at 322; Gabriel O B Jaccard, *Smart Contracts and the Role of Law*, Jusletter IT (Nov. 23, 2017) at nos. 6 et seq.; De Filippi & Wright, *supra* note 6, at 74, state that the performance obligations of a smart contract are «not written in standard legal prose».

details of the technology. Expressed in an IT undertaking, language is code and code is language.

Reference can also be made to the concept of a matching system for express intent declarations in the sense of the term «parties' conduct» as used in some legal instruments. In particular, art. 2.1.1 of the Unidroit Principles of International Commercial Contracts in the version of 2016 provides for a contract conclusion by the «conduct of the parties»; the Commentary 3 thereto says that «automated contracting» falls under this term and meets this understanding.[44]

A specific problem concerns as General Business Condition (GBC). If the provider of digitally referenced goods or services is using GBC being likely the case in practice, it is difficult to acknowledge how the customer could read the respective provisions, as required by consumer protection legislation in the European Union (particularly the Consumer Rights Directive of 2011).[45] Possibly, the practical importance of this challenge might not be very substantial since smart contracts are mainly used in the context of relatively straightforward direct transactions in the B2B business with a simultaneous exchange of performances, based on highly standardized transactions parameters.[46]

2. Legal challenges in the contract conclusion context

Nevertheless, some legal changes in respect to the contract formation cannot be overlooked and should be considered by the legislators:

- The requirement that certain contracts (mainly consumer contracts) must be concluded in writing is impracticable since the procedures for electronic signatures do not fit the needs of the parties of smart contracts. But the problem of form requirements has also been recognized in other fields of law: for example the UNCITRAL Model Law on Electronic Transferable Records of 2017 (at least partly) accepts electronic «commercial

---

44 Unidroit, *Unidroit Principles of International Commercial Contracts (2016), Art. 2.1.1., Commentary 3 («conduct of the parties»),* https://www.unidroit.org/instruments/commercial-contracts/unidroit-principles-2016 (last visited Feb. 1, 2019) and Weber *supra* note 16, at Ch. III.1.

45 Consumer Rights Directive 2011/83, OJ 2011 L304/64 of November 22, 2011; Weber, *supra* note 21, at 294; Trüeb, *supra* note 21, at 731; Kristin B Cornelius, *Standards form contracts and a smart contract future*, 7 (2) Internet Policy Review (2018), https://policyreview.info/articles/analysis/standard-form-contracts-and-smart-contract-future (last visited Feb. 1, 2019) at 1 and 6.

46 Weber, *supra* note 16, at Ch. III. 2.; *see* also Markus Kaulartz & Jörn Heckmann, *Smart Contracts – Anwendung der Blockchain-Technologie*, 32 (9) Computer und Recht (2016) at 618 and 622 with further references.

papers».[47] A similar approach realizing the concept of functional equivalence could be chosen in the smart contract context.[48]

- The State has an interest that some fundamental legal principles are also observed even if the parties enter into a smart contract which cannot be reversed and does not allow third party interventions. The main example concerns the legal capacity for entering into valid contractual arrangements.[49] Precautions are to be introduced in order to avoid that minors are entering into burdensome smart contracts.
- Further, basic legal principles are the compliance with the public order or the morality undertaking or the compliance with principal personality rights as well as the contestability of a contract in case of an error or a threat during the negotiation process.[50] The enforcement of such fundamental principles can only be done if a technical possibility exists to intervene into the self-executing and self-determining nature of a smart contract. Technologically, an oracle can build the «bridge» to a respective dispute resolution mechanism.[51]

Furthermore, a need for a standardization of smart contract terms is obvious. This task could be assumed for example by the International Standardization Organization (ISO) which is already doing some work following a proposal submitted by its Australian branch. In addition, enterprises or groups like Ethereum Alliance, Mathereum, Open Law, Common Accord, Legalize and the R3 Consortium develop computational forms of legal conduct.[52]

---

47 *See* UNCTRAL, *UNCITRAL Model Law on Electronic Transferable Records* (2018), http://www.uncitral.org/pdf/english/texts/electcom/MLETR_ebook.pdf (last visited on Feb. 1, 2019).

48 Weber, *supra* note 16, at Ch. III.1.; Andreas Furrer & Luka Müller, *«Funktionale Äquivalenz» digitaler Rechtsgeschäfte,* Jusletter (Jun. 18, 2018), https://jusletter.weblaw.ch/services/login.html?targetPage=http://jusletter.weblaw.ch/juslissues/2018/940/-funktionale-aquival_b0cce8f-b0c.html__ONCE&handle=http://jusletter.weblaw.ch/juslissues/2018/940/-funktionale-aquival_b0cce8fb0c.html__ONCE (last visited Feb. 2, 2019).

49 Swiss LegalTech Association, *supra* note 24, at 44; Weber *supra* note 16, at Ch. III. 3.

50 Weber, *supra* note 24, at 294; Swiss LegalTech Association, *supra* note 49, at 44; regarding the oracle *see* Rolf H Weber, *Leistungsstörungen und Rechtsdurchsetzung bei Smart Contracts,* Jusletter (Dec. 4, 2017) at nos. 33–35; Rolf H Weber, *Contractual Duties and Allocation of Liability in Automated Digital Contracts, in* Digital Revolution: Challenges for Contract Law in Practice, 163–187 (Reiner Schulze & Dirk Staudenmayer, eds., Nomos, 2016) at 163, 167–68; Grundmann & Hacker *supra* note 22, at 21; De Filippi & Wright, *supra* note 6, at 75; *see* also below Chapter D.

51 *See* Weber, *supra* note 16, at Ch. III. 3; Trüeb, *supra* note 21, at 725; De Filippi & Wright, note 6, at 85–86.

52 Trüeb, *supra* note 21, at 725; De Filippi & Wright, *supra* note 6, at 85–86.

3. Contract performance

A smart contract clearly complies with the principle «*pacta sunt servanda*», i.e., the requirement to observe and fulfill with the terms of the contract.[53] In contrast, the law and economics approach allowing the parties to declare a so-called «efficient breach of contract» would not be possible in a smart contract scenario, but such a «restriction» strengthens the stability of the legal rules. The typical types of contractual non-performance scenarios such as the impossibility, the non-performance and the delay in delivery do not appear to play a relevant practical role in view of the automated execution of a smart contract as coded in the computer routine.[54]

In case of technology or program failures already developed legal concepts appear to be appropriate as guiding directives for the evaluation of existing problems (risks spheres concept, cheapest cost avoider concept).[55] Furthermore, basic principles of law such as the due diligence obligation in the contract performing activities can be appropriately applied by the courts in case of a smart contract.[56] The design of the program code and its decisions should also be done in a probability-based manner; new assessments in case of further developments based on algorithms appear to be possible.[57]

The most difficult issue in the contract execution concerns the digital performance, mainly if the written form requirement must be fulfilled. Eventually, a decentralized book entry regime for digital values should be made possible.[58]

C. Common law

As an example for the legal framework implemented in a common law country, the example of the United States is addressed hereinafter.

1. Uniform Commercial Code

Already in the past, under U.S. common law principles it was acknowledged that contracts can be expressed or implied; in many instances, no formal requirements had to be fulfilled in order for a court to find sufficient evidence of

53 Weber, *supra* note 50, at no. 18; Müller & Seiler, *supra* note 19, at 325 et seq.

54 For a more detailed overview *see* Weber, *supra* note 50, at nos. 19–21.

55 For further details *see* Weber, *supra* note 21, at 297–98; on the cheapest cost avoider approach *see* Emanuele Carbonara, Alice Guerra & Francesco Parisi, *Sharing Residual Liability: «The Cheapest Cost Avoider Revisited»*, 45/1 The Journal of Legal Studies, 173–201 (2016).

56 *See* Weber, *supra* note 16, at Ch. III. 2.

57 *See* also Weber, *supra* note 21, at 297.

58 For more details *see* Weber, *supra* note 21, at 299–300 with further references.

a binding contract.[59] As far back as 1893, the U.S. Supreme Court upheld in the judgment Bibb v. Allen an agreement communicated electronically using enciphered telegraph messages.[60]

The Restatement (Second) of Contracts defines a contract as «*a promise or a set of promises for the breach of which the law gives a remedy, or the performance of which the law in some way recognizes as a duty*».[61] According to legal doctrine, smart contracts create promises intended to be legally enforceable, even if a traditional contract and a smart contract are differently structured since the code-based promise is bypassing the traditional enforceability criteria.[62] Smart contracts constitute an exchange of concrete obligations and, therefore, a normative relation between the parties is existing. In addition, the computer routine (code) allows the execution of the transaction without further promises to perform.[63]

An analysis of Article 2 of the Uniform Commercial Code (UCC) leads to the result that the UCC typically covers transactions for the sale of goods, integrated from time to time with the common law principles. Article 2 of the UCC does not provide a definition of the different elements which lead to a mutual assent of the parties, i.e., the «meeting of the minds».[64] Moreover, the UCC (for example in sections 2-204, 2-205 and 2-206) adopts a flexible approach in respect of the conclusion of a «deal», even allowing informal negotiations. This fact is crucial for the acknowledgement of smart contracts as legally binding instruments.[65]

In view of the complexities of section 2-207 of the UCC, smart contracts could even be a useful tool in overcoming the battle of forms discussions by providing clarification to the negotiations, on the one hand, bypassing the informality of the negotiation deals and, on the other hand, bypassing the normative complexities.[66]

---

59 De Filippi & Wright, *supra* note 6, at 79.

60 Bibb v. Allen, 149 U.S. 481 (1893). The Supreme Court held that the agreement would be valid even if the way in which the arrangement was memorialized had been «expressed» unconventionally.

61 Restatement (Second) of Contracts (1981), § 1.

62 Kevin D Werbach & Nicolas Cornell, *Contracts ex Machina*, Duke Law Journal (2017) at 67 and 87.

63 Dell'Erba, *supra* note 2, at 24.

64 *See* also Stacy-Ann Elvy, *Contracting in the Age of the Internet of Things: Article 2 of the UCC and Beyond*, 44 Hofstra Law Review 839–31 (2015–2016) at 839, 872.

65 For further details *see* Dell'Erba, *supra* note 2, at 26–28; Donnie L Kidd & William H Daughtrey, *Adapting Contract Law to Accommodate Electronic Contracts: Overview and Suggestions*, 26 Rutgers Computer & Tech. L.J. 215 (2000), at 215 et seq.

66 Dell'Erba, *supra* note 2, at 28.

2. Other legal instruments

The interpretation of other legal instruments in the United States, in particular the Uniform Electronic Transaction Act (UETA), the Electronic Signature in Global and National Commerce Act (ESIGN) and the Uniform Computer Information Transaction Act (UCITA), does not lead to a different perception of the smart contracts as legally binding contractual undertakings between the parties.[67] According to the legal doctrine, broad definitions in both the ESIGN and the UETA accommodate blockchain technology and smart contracts if public-private key cryptography is used; for instance, under the UETA, a «record of signature» and «electronic record» may not be denied legal effect or enforceability if used as part of contract formation.[68]

The UETA also contemplates the use of automated software like smart contracts by referring to «*computer programs or ... other automated means used independently to initiate an action or respond to electronic records or performances in whole or in part, without review or action by an individual*».[69] The use of so-called «electronic agents» does not jeopardize the legal effect of an agreed transaction. Therefore, the mentioned legal instruments have been implemented in order to extend the validity for electronic records and signatures of transactions affecting interstate or foreign commerce. Consequently, smart contracts can be considered as valid instruments under these statutes.[70]

D. Enforcement challenges

Enforcement challenges mainly occur if the performance of the coded obligations should be adjusted. The technical device for such an adjustment is the so-called oracle to be designed by the programmers in the code.[71] An oracle makes it possible to determine or update specific performance obligations based on the subjective judgment of individuals; thereby, the contractual arrangement becomes more flexible and dynamic. The oracle usually refers to an arbitration library being in a position to feed back the relevant information which the computer routine puts into a position to execute the adjustment.[72] An oracle can also enable the contracting parties to start legal proceedings or engage in private dispute resolution. The details of the proceedings (arbitration

---

67 UETA, § 7; De Filippi & Wright, *supra* note 6, at 79.

68 UETA, § 2.

69 For an overview *see* De Filippi & Wright, *supra* note 6, at 79–80; Dell'Erba, *supra* note 2, at 29–33.

70 For an overview *see* De Filippi & Wright, *supra* note 6, at 80.

71 *See* the articles by Weber, *supra* note 50, Grundmann & Hacker, *supra* note 22 and De Filippi & Wright, *supra* note 6.

72 *See* also Raskin, *supra* note 10, at 321 and 333.

board, substantive law, procedural principles) and consequences of the envisaged «judgment» would equally have to be designed in the computer code.[73]

A special problem in the execution of smart contracts can occur if privacy concerns are prevailing. The degree of transparency on the blockchain may prove unappealing to contracting parties. Even when the transacting parties are not identified since pseudonymous accounts are used on most blockchains, identification techniques are often available to discern the identities of parties.[74] Without strong privacy protection (anonymity which does not allow a re-identification), smart contracts might prove unsuitable legal agreements if confidentiality is crucial.[75]

IV. Fragmentation issues and future conciliation of technology and law

Technological competition in the development of new infrastructures goes along with regulatory competition in the field of the legal environment of smart contracts. As mentioned, the standardization efforts have not advanced very far; regulatory competition, known for example from corporation law or tax law, may lead to regulatory fragmentation and regulatory uncertainty which could undermine the successful development of new commercial practices.[76]

In order to combat a potential fragmentation, legal research has tried to overcome the regulatory barriers of cross-border trade by advocating for harmonized rules. Subsequently to the well-known *lex mercatoria,* the new concept of a *lex cryptographica* has been developed,[77] possibly as an intermediate step of a redesigned *lex informatica.*[78] Common practices should avoid significant frictions and obstacles to the entrepreneurial initiatives in the area of digital business models.

Uniform principles could attempt to realize a legal environment in which regulation is not frustrating blockchain innovation and, nevertheless, is pro-

---

73 For further details *see* Weber, *supra* note 50, at nos. 37 et seq.; Jake Goldenfein & Andrea Leiter, *Legal Engineering on the Blockchain: «Smart Contracts» as Legal Conduct*, 29 Law and Critique (May 24, 2018), https://doi.org/10.1007/s10978-018-9224-0 (last visited Feb. 1, 2019) at 9 et seq.

74 De Filippi & Wright, *supra* note 6, at 83.

75 *Id.*

76 For a general overview *see* Rolf H Weber, *Regulatory Competition and Coordination as Policy Instruments*, 30/11 Journal of International Banking Law and Regulation 605–615 (2015).

77 *See* Wright & De Filippi, *supra* note 6.

78 To the origins of the Lex Informatica *see* Joel R Reidenberg, *Lex Informatica: The Formulation of Information Policy Rules through Technology*, 76 Texas Law Review 553–593 (1998); *see* also Rolf H Weber, Regulatory Models for the Online World (Schulthess, 2002) at 89–93.

tecting individuals by a «do no harm approach».[79] The concept of uniform principles is not a novelty, but has already been recognized in the Middle Ages with the creation of a transnational system of laws, commonly known as the *lex mercatoria*.[80] Similar developments also appear to be plausible in the new world driven by technologies.

The *lex cryptographica* or the *lex informatica* are referring to «architecture standards» allowing to acknowledge technology as a possible source of law and accept automated self-execution as an alternative enforcement to decisions of courts. The concept of a parallel private regulation coupled with the possibility of self-enforcement epitomizes the continuity of the *lex mercatoria* and the *lex informatica* in a new concept of blockchain regulation.[81] The *lex cryptographica* can be seen as a spontaneous corpus of rules emerging form the technical needs of the infrastructure and offering the advantage of being separated from any formalistic legislative process.

As already outlined, a certain movement from «code is law» to «law is code» appears to be obvious.[82] Good reasons to halt this movement do not exist. However, as mentioned, human interventions must remain possible in order to uphold human values. Referring to the title of this contribution, smart contracts have got a lot to do with blockchain technology; but the technology cannot fully supersede the law, therefore, to a certain extent smart contracts also remain a legal concept.

V. Bibliography

A. Hard Copy Sources

BERMAN, HAROLD J, LAW AND REVOLUTION: THE FORMATION OF THE WESTERN LEGAL TRADITION (Harvard University Press, 1983).

Carbonara, Emanuele, Guerra, Alice & Parisi, Francesco, *Sharing Residual Liability: «The Cheapest Cost Avoider Revisited»*, 45(1) THE JOURNAL OF LEGAL STUDIES 173–201 (2016).

Choi, Stephen J & Golati, G Mitu, *Contract as Statute*, 104 MICHIGAN LAW REVIEW 1129–1173 (2006).

DE FILIPPI, PRIMAVERA & WRIGHT, AARON, BLOCKCHAIN AND THE LAW. THE RULE OF CODE (Harvard University Press, 2018).

Elvy, Stacy-Ann, *Contracting in the Age of the Internet of Things: Article 2 of the UCC and Beyond*, 44 HOFSTRA LAW REVIEW 839–31 (2015–2016).

Furrer, Andreas, *Die Einbettung von Smart Contracts in das schweizerische Privatrecht*, 3 ANWALTSREVUE 103–115 (2018).

79 Dell'Erba, *supra* note 2, at 46.

80 Nikitas E Hatzimihail, *The Many Lives and Faces of Lex Mercatoria: History as Genealogy in International Business Law*, *in* 71 (3) LAW AND CONTEMPORARY PROBLEMS 169–180 (2008).

81 Dell'Erba, *supra* note 2, at 48.

82 *See* above Chapter D and Weber, *supra* note 31, at 704 et seq.

Jaccard, Gabriel O B, *Smart Contracts and the Role of Law*, Jusletter IT (Nov. 23, 2017).
Hatzimihail, Nikitas E, *The Many Lives and Faces of Lex Mercatoria: History as Genealogy in International Business Law*, 71 (3) Law and Contemporary Problems 169–190 (2008).
Kaulartz, Markus & Heckmann, Jörn, *Smart Contracts – Anwendung der Blockchain-Technologie*, 32 (9) Computer und Recht 618–624 (2016).
Kidd, Donnie L & Daughtrey, William H, *Adapting Contract Law to Accommodate Electronic Contracts: Overview and Suggestions*, 26 Rutgers Computer & Tech. L.J. 215–276 (2000).
Lessig, Lawrence, Code and Other Laws of Cyberspace (Basic Books, 1999).
Müller, Lukas & Seiler, Reto, *Smart Contracts aus der Sicht des Vertragsrechts*, 27 (3) AJP 317–328 (2019).
Raskin, Max, *The Law and Legality of Smart Contracts*, 1 Georgetown Law Technology Review 305–341 (2017).
Reidenberg, Joel R, *Lex Informatica: The Formulation of Information Policy Rules through Technology*, 76 Texas Law Review 553–593 (1998).
Surden, Harry, *Computable Contracts*, 46 University of California-Davis Law Review 629–700 (2012).
Tapscott, Dan & Tapscott, Alex, The Blockchain Revolution (Random House, 2016).
Trüeb, Hans Rudolf, *Smart Contracts*, *in* Festschrift für Anton K. Schnyder 723–734 (Grolimund, Pascal et al. eds., Schulthess, 2018).
Weber, Rolf H, *«Rose is a rose is a rose is a rose»—what about code and law?*, 34 Computer Law & Security Review 701–705 (2018).
Weber, Rolf H, *Smart Contracts: Do we need new legal rules?*, Ch. II.1. *in:* Digital Revolution—New Challenges for Law (De Franceschi, Alberto/Schulze, Reiner/Graziadei, Michele/Riente, Federica/Sica, Salvatore & Sirena, Pietro, eds., Beck/Hart/Nomos, 2019 (forthcoming)).
Weber, Rolf H, *Smart Contracts: Vertrags- und verfügungsrechtlicher Regelungsbedarf?*, 6 sic! 291–301 (2018).
Weber, Rolf H, *Contractual Duties and Allocation of Liability in Automated Digital Contracts*, Digital Revolution: Challenges for Contract Law in Practice 163–187 (Schulze, Reiner & Staudenmayer, Dirk, eds., Nomos, 2016).
Weber, Rolf H, *Regulatory Competition and Coordination as Policy Instruments*, 30/11 Journal of International Banking Law and Regulation 605–615 (2015).
Weber, Rolf H, Regulatory Models for the Online World (Schulthess, 2002).
Werbach, Kevin D & Cornell, Nicolas, *Contracts ex Machina*, Duke Law Journal 313–382 (2017).

B. Online Sources

Adlerstein, David, *Are Smart Contracts Smart? A Critical Look at Basic Blockchain Questions*, Coindesk (Jun. 26, 2017), https://www.coindesk.com/when-is-a-smart-contract-actually-a-contract/ (last visited Feb. 1, 2019).
Cornelius, Kristin B, *Standards form contracts and a smart contract future*, 7 (2) Internet Policy Review (2018), https://policyreview.info/articles/analysis/standard-form-contracts-and-smart-contract-future (last visited Feb. 1, 2019).
de Filippi, Primavera & Samer, Hassan, *Blockchain Technology as a Regulatory Technology: From Code is Law to Law is Code*, 21 (12) First Monday 11–12 (December 5, 2016), http://firstmonday.org/ojs/index.php/fm/article/view/7113/5657 (last visited Feb. 1, 2019).

Dell' Erba, Marco, *Demystifying Technology. Do Smart Contracts Require a New Legal Framework? Regulatory Fragmentation, Self-Regulation, Public Regulation*, SSRN (May 17, 2018), https://papers.ssrn.com/sol3/papers.cfm?abstract_id=3228445 (last visited Feb. 1, 2019).

Furrer, Andreas & Müller, Luka, *«Funktionale Äquivalenz» digitaler Rechtsgeschäfte*, JUSLETTER (Jun. 18, 2018), https://jusletter.weblaw.ch/services/login.html?targetPage=http://jusletter.weblaw.ch/juslis sues/2018/940/-funktionale-aquival_b0cce8fb0c.html__ONCE&handle=http://jusletter.weblaw.ch/juslissues/2018/940/-funktionale-aquival_b0cce8fb0c.html__ONCE (last visited Feb. 1, 2019).

Goldenfein, Jake & Leiter, Andrea, *Legal Engineering on the Blockchain: «Smart Contracts» as Legal Conduct*, 29 LAW AND CRITIQUE (May 24, 2018), https://doi.org/10.1007/s10978-018-9224-0 (last visited Feb. 1, 2019).

Grundmann, Stefan & Hacker, Philipp, *Digital Technology as a Challenge to European Contract Law—From the Existing to the Future Architecture*, SRRN (Jul. 17, 2017), https://ssrn.com/abstract=3003885 (last visited on Feb. 1, 2019).

Hayes, Frank, *The Story So Far*, COMPUTERWORLD (Jun. 17, 2002), http://www.computerworld.com/article/2576616/e-commerce/the-story-so-far.html (last visited Feb. 1, 2019).

Investopedia, *Hard Fork*, https://www.investopidia.com/terms/h/hardfork.asp#ixzz5DcrRKFhj (last visited Feb. 1, 2019).

IOSCO, *Research Report on Financial Technologies (Fintech)*, February 2017, https://www.iosco.org/library/pubdocs/pdf/IOSCOPD554.pdf (last visited Feb. 1, 2019).

Kumar, Sumit, *The battle among generations of blockchains is far from over*, CAPGEMINI (Dec. 11, 2018), https://www.capgemini.com/2018/12/the-battle-among-generations-of-blockchain-is-far-from-over-yet/ (last visited Apr. 16, 2019).

Nakamoto, Satoshi, *Bitcoin: A Peer-to-Peer Electronic Cash System*, https://bitcoin.org/bitcoin.pdf (Oct. 31, 2008) (last visited Feb. 1, 2019).

Swiss LegalTech Association (SLTA), *Regulatory Task Force Report 2018* (Apr. 27, 2018), https://www.swisslegaltech.ch/think-tank/ (last visited Feb. 3, 2019).

Szabo, Nick, *Smart Contratcs* (1994), www.fon.hum.uva.nl/rob/Courses/InformationInSpeech/CDROM/Literature/LOTwinterschool2006/szabo.best.vwh.net/smart.contracts.html (last visited Feb. 3, 2019).

Szabo, Nick, *Formalizing and Securing Relationships on Public Networks*, 2/9 FIRST MONDAY INTERNET JOURNAL (Sep. 1, 1997), firstmonday.org/ojs/index.php/fm/article/view/548/469 (last visited Feb. 3, 2019).

UNCTRAL, *UNCITRAL Model Law on Electronic Transferable Records* (2018), http://www.uncitral.org/pdf/english/texts/electcom/MLETR_ebook.pdf (last visited on Feb. 1, 2019).

Unidroit, *Unidroit Principles of International Commercial Contracts (2016), Art. 2.1.1., Commentary 3 («conduct of the parties»)* (2016), https://www.unidroit.org/instruments/commercial-contracts/unidroit-principles-2016 (last visited Feb. 1, 2019).

Weber, Rolf H, *Leistungsstörungen und Rechtsdurchsetzung bei Smart Contracts*, JUSLETTER (Dec. 4, 2017), https://jusletter.weblaw.ch/services/login.html?targetPage=http://jusletter.weblaw.ch/it/jus lissues/2017/917/leistungsstorungen-u_3e7a005a8f.html__ONCE&handle=http://jusletter.weblaw.ch/it/juslissues/2017/917/leistungsstorungen-u_3e7a005a8f.html__ONCE (last visited Feb. 1, 2019).

Wright, Aaron & De Filippi, Primavera, *Decentralized Blockchain Technology and the Rise of Lex Cryptographia,* SSRN (Mar. 10, 2015), https://ssrn.com/abstract=2580664 (last visited Feb. 1, 2019) at 4 et seq.

C. Case Law

Bibb v. Allen, 149 U.S. 481 (1893).

David Fisher and Pierson Grider

The Blockchain in Action in the Legal World

TABLE OF CONTENTS

I. Overview

Laws intermediate all aspects of society, setting the rules by which people interact with each other. As the professionals that help society to interpret and apply laws, lawyers are by their very nature the ultimate intermediaries. Indeed, the manner in which societies organize themselves highlights the critical importance of intermediaries in all aspects of life, from governments that provide services from birth 'til death, to banks that facilitate the transfer of money, to technology companies that store and process our data.

Recent years have seen the rise of something radically different, however. Blockchain technology, the foundational technology that makes cryptocurrencies such as Bitcoin possible, is based on peer-to-peer interactions, without intermediaries. What if you could transfer funds around the world without relying on the banking system? What if you could transact with a car service without relying on Uber in the middle? What if you could confirm your identity without relying on a government database to confirm the authenticity of your passport? And what if you could transfer shares of stock in a company to another owner without relying on a stock exchange or transfer agent? These are but a few examples of the dramatic evolution of business and society that blockchain technology may herald.

The legal industry has been heavily involved in blockchain technology, primarily via the provision of legal advice to clients, but blockchain technology is on track to alter the way the legal industry itself is organized. In fact, blockchain technology is likely to have a more rapid and pervasive impact on the legal industry then almost any other industry, for reasons that are unique to the industry.

II. Critical Intermediaries but without scale

Lawyers may be the ultimate intermediaries in society, but they fulfill that role without the economies of scale that we see in other industries such as banking, insurance, manufacturing, shipping, and technology. Imagine trying to ship a package around the country or around the world without Fedex. It would almost certainly be slower and more expensive. This is true of virtually all industries, where scale and concentration lead to greater efficiency and lower cost.

The structure of the legal industry is the reason why the legal industry isn't more concentrated, scaled, and efficient:

- There is a dizzying array of distinct jurisdictions, including local governments, state and provincial governments, and national governments.
- There are strong ethical requirements and regulations regarding how law firms are owned and how lawyers (and non-lawyers) are paid.

- There are strict requirements for maintaining privacy and privilege of client matters and information.
- The ownership model of most law firms is a partnership model, with compensation usually closely correlated with individual productivity (hours billed). Incentives—including incentives to invest in new technology—are not necessarily aligned.

Taken altogether, these complicating features (or are they bugs?) of the legal industry work against economies of scale and efficiency—a «Gordian knot» that resists untangling of any single element, regardless of a broad consensus within the legal industry that the it needs to become more efficient and productive.

III. Can blockchain technology untangle the knot?

While the greatest fascination with blockchain technology has been cryptocurrency, what may be more significant is what the cryptocurrency application of blockchain proved—that it is possible to share data in a highly trusted way between disparate parties, without a trusted intermediary such as an entity, person, or software application to facilitate the interchange. Applying this blockchain «technology of digital trust» to the legal industry thus holds the promise of bringing scale in trusted data interchange to an industry that otherwise is hopelessly locked in a myriad of silos that are too small and too many to be connected by other means.

Consider the example of a conventional contract between two commercial entities, both represented by an outside law firm. Multiple versions are emailed back and forth, as the contract is negotiated. Each law firm and each company stores copies of everything on their respective systems. Copies exist within each law firm's and each company's email system. By the time the contract reaches execution, there could be dozens of similar or identical copies of the contract existing on many software systems across four law firms and companies. And once the contract is executed, either physically or digitally, copies are stored separately at each law firm and company.

Absent the purposeful linking of software systems at multiple law firms and clients, there is no way to relate data across entity boundaries. Even if those links could be created, as they are with some very large clients, the ecosystem reality is that it's simply not possible to efficiently integrate the disparate technology systems of millions of different law firms and clients. Cloud-based software could be a partial solution, but it also ends up being a poor remedy because it creates as many problems with privacy, privilege, and security as it fixes with efficiency in data sharing and collaboration. So, the default technology interface between legal organizations usually ends up being email—the least collaborative and least secure technology available.

Taken as a whole, the legal industry has an extremely complex problem that is related to both the structure of the industry and the technical complexity of trying to relate data across a myriad of entities. Fortunately, blockchain technology is likely to solve this previously unsolvable problem.

Part of the foundational architecture of blockchain is the ability to confirm existence and authenticity of data across disparate entities. Per the contract example, above, adding blockchain technology to the software of the law firms and clients would create the ability to confirm the existence and authenticity of the many documents and versions circulating among multiple firms and clients, without the need to link systems.

Blockchain technology can be integrated into existing software, so it does not require significant new investments or changes in behavior. And because it can be implemented as part of existing systems with broad adoption in the legal market, it is possible to align the legal market around common technology standards for the use of blockchain by organizing a relatively small number of major software platforms such that they implement blockchain features according to an agreed standard.

IV. The Global Legal Blockchain Consortium rises

To realize a goal of a common standard for data interchange in the legal industry using blockchain technology, and to prevent the potential chaos of siloed blockchain technologies being adopted throughout the legal industry, an industry-led organization was needed to allow all parties to collaborate about blockchain standards, governance, and applications for the legal industry.

In August 2017, the Global Legal Blockchain Consortium[1] (GLBC) launched with a handful of major legal industry organizations. Now, the GLBC is the largest legal blockchain organization in the world. Members include some of the largest law firms, corporate legal departments, law schools and universities, software companies, and legal service providers. The GLBC hosts global events, members participate on committees, and organizations demonstrate blockchain integrations.

The GLBC is a nonprofit organization that focuses on creating governance and standards for the the use of blockchain technology in the legal industry. GLBC committees, such as the technical committee and policy committee, work to define standards so that all stakeholders in the legal industry may benefit from a blockchain technology enabled ecosystem. Ultimately, the GLBC seeks to align the world's legal industry around universal blockchain

1 Global Legal Blockchain Consortium (2018), https://legalconsortium.org/ (last visited Feb. 1, 2019).

standards that will improve legal services—more security, more integrity, and more productivity.

Because the GLBC involves a diverse group of legal organizations, the organization focuses on several areas where blockchain will immediately benefit all stakeholders. In particular, the consortium is focused on five areas where blockchain technology will improve the legal industry: 1) blockchain as a foundation for data integrity and authenticity for contracts, documents, and similar data; 2) blockchain technology to improve data privacy and security for contracts, documents, and communications; 3) blockchain used as a tool to improve the interoperability of data between large corporate legal departments, law firms, and other legal organizations; 4) productivity improvements and cost savings in the operation of legal departments and law firms; and, 5) use of blockchain to fortify and augment existing legal technology investments adding important functionality to legacy systems to extend their useful life.[2]

The GLBC was formed to align stakeholders in the world's legal industry around the adoption and use of blockchain technology in the business of law. To meet the objective of alignment and consensus, it was necessary to develop some guiding principles. First, a blockchain by its nature must be open source in order to be trusted by the community that uses it. The GLBC embraces open source software development as a way to reduce cost and increase speed to market of practical solutions. Second, members that host nodes of a blockchain have access to all of their data that they have written to it. This allows members to move their data to another database or blockchain without any impediment, if they so desire. Third, the GLBC recognizes that blockchain technology is not yet a mature technology, so the consortium is not restricted to any particular blockchain. The GLBC embraces the fact that members are investing in various blockchains, and it is the goal of GLBC members to harmonize the way the legal industry interacts with multiple blockchain technologies. Fourth, because the GLBC includes all stakeholders in the legal technology industry without bias or preferential treatment, conditions are ideal for collaborative development and cost sharing. This benefit is already being realized with the first proofs of concept that are emerging from GLBC members.

With regard to actual use of blockchain technology in the business of law, the GLBC developed a unique approach among the world's large blockchain consortia. Instead of asking members to make large financial contributions to the GLBC organization, the consortium has a requirement that members instead sponsor or support one or more blockchain business of law projects that are of interest to the members. In this way, the GLBC can accommodate a wide array of blockchain projects, without restriction, and it has had the effect

---

2 Global Legal Blockchain Consortium, *What is the GLBC?—Global Legal Blockchain Consortium* (2018), https://legalconsortium.org/what-is-the-glbc/ (last visited Feb. 1, 2019).

of making the GLBC the most vibrant blockchain development community in the world, with regard to the use of blockchain technology in legal industry software. It has had the effect to embracing the private interests of member organizations, while helping to make sure that private investments in development projects follow general standards that make will make the entire legal technology ecosystem more interoperable and efficient.

As the GLBC continues to grow, there will be many blockchain-based solutions created by members. Some of these will be brand new software and others will be integrations into existing legal software. Eventually, blockchain technology will provide the standard digital trust infrastructure underpinning the world's legal industry, and the Global Legal Blockchain Consortium is leading that effort.

V. The coming blockchain transformation of the legal technology

Almost everything we do has a legal context. For example, buying a cup of coffee is a consumer financial transaction. Visiting a website requires agreeing to terms and conditions. Cars record vehicle data when it is driven. If there is a dispute in anything we do, trusted data or evidence is needed to prove fault or responsibility. Recording data existence and authenticity on a blockchain accomplishes that objective in a manner that data can be trusted and verified by anyone. In this way, blockchain technology will provide critically needed trust in the data of virtually all legal software systems and platforms.

A. Document management systems

Law firms and legal corporate departments manage anywhere from thousands to millions of documents. These documents may have several versions exchanged by multiple parties. Document management systems (DMS) organize and authenticate these documents. However, these documents are eventually exchanged with other parties through email or other means exiting the environment of the DMS. When that happens, the identity of the document and authenticity might come into question. A party might not know if they have the correct version of the document or if this is the original document. If a document is generated in a DMS, and that DMS hashes the document to a blockchain, there is an immutable record of when that document was created, as well as a digital fingerprint of that document. Furthermore, document changes can be tracked and recorded to a blockchain. Even when that document leaves the DMS, that receiver and can check the version of the document on the

blockchain to confirm that they received the correct and most recent version. Blockchain technology thus creates a measure of universal document versioning that is not dependent on all parties using the same authoring software or document management system.

B. Contracts

Every stakeholder in the legal industry creates, negotiates, and executes contracts. Law firms and corporate legal departments often use software to create and modify these agreements. When a contract is negotiated and exchanged between parties, a party might not know if it is looking at the most current version of the contract. Furthermore, if a contract is created and amended at a later date, a party could dispute the version of the contract that is currently in force. If the identity, existence, and authenticity of the contract is recorded to a blockchain, however, there is an immutable record tracking the life of the contract creating an audit trail.

Going beyond proof of existence and authenticity, a blockchain record of a contract indicates that the data in the contract can be trusted—including things like financial terms, dates, and parties to the agreement. To the extent that those data objects have their own blockchain-based identity, such blockchain-recorded contracts can be made to be computable. Blockchain can make «dumb» contracts computable (as distinct from blockchain «smart contracts» which are self-executing stored procedures more akin to software programs than contracts). This capability to make ordinary contracts computable has already been demonstrated, and it may transform entire contracting ecosystems.

C. Billing systems

Billing systems and billing codes are chaotic between law firms and legal corporate departments. While there are some standards, they are not universal, and law firms and their clients experience significant data reconciliation costs and errors. Leveraging the same approach described for document management systems and contracts, the addition of blockchain identities for legal bills will make then instantly confirmable and reconcilable between law firms and client, dramatically reducing the friction involved in billing for legal services and getting paid for legal services. Blockchain technology will significantly streamline the financial side of the legal industry.

D. Calendaring systems

All attorneys and professionals involved in the provision of legal services use some type of calendaring system, and often they are required to use two or three calendaring systems to ensure redundancy. After all, a missed deadline can cost millions or result in sanctions for the attorney, as well as malpractice claims. It may appear that calendaring systems are all similar, but in reality, every law firm and every client maintains their own separate calendar, and though it may seem that the same event is recording in multiple calendars (for example, a court date), the reality is that there is no intrinsic integrity between calendar systems. Furthermore, there is no permanence to a calendar event that is recorded on an individual system and that could be created in retrospect from a missed deadline, or fabricated to hide something.

Recording the unique identity and existence of calendar events to a blockchain creates a unique, permanent record that can be referenced by both law firms and clients, allowing perfect data integrity and reconciliation. Appointments can be automatically created and updated and dynamically change if something happens, across entity boundaries, without the need to actually connect calendar systems. Additionally, recoding calendar entries to a blockchain creates an immutable record and audit trail of when that calendar event is created. No one can artificially go back and add/remove an event record to hide something. Blockchain is likely to transform the legal industry's approach to calendars.

E. E-mail security

A majority of all email exchanged is not encrypted between sender and recipient. This applies to sensitive and confidential information between clients and law firms. There are current solutions to encrypt email, but they is often clunky and not interoperable between systems. Because blockchain technology authenticates users using public-private key technology infrastructure, it is almost intuitive that this benefit would extend to the use of email. In other words, if the sender and recipient of an email both use the same blockchain, and therefore the same public key lookup, email encryption can be automatic. In this way, if the world's lawyers adopt blockchain technology in a standard way in their email ecosystem, the security of legal data and client data that is exchanged via email will be dramatically improved. This has already been demonstrated, and so blockchain technology may have the salutary effect of automatically improving email security for the world's lawyers.

F. Blockchain and Artificial Intelligence

Blockchain technology is likely to provide critical infrastructure for rapidly the advancing artificial intelligence software category of the legal industry. As legal AI begins to mimic the legal reasoning of lawyers, difficult questions arise as to the quality of the AI. To rely on AI, it is necessary to trust the AI. Blockchain provides the most trusted way to preserve an «audit trail» for artificial intelligence, ranging from proof of the data that is used to train the AI, proof of the state of important algorithms, and proof of the inputs and outputs. While it's not reasonable to be able to «explain» the AI, it is critical to have some trusted data so that outcomes and recommendations can be evaluated and tested. Without the data integrity that blockchain technology provides, advanced AI would increasingly suffer from concerns about trust in outcomes. Blockchain technology will enable the more rapid development, deployment, and use of advanced AI tools in the legal industry.

VI. The coming blockchain transformation of the legal industry

A. Law Firms

While most lawyers, up until now, have viewed blockchain through the lens of legal advice to clients—an incremental source of legal service revenue to law firms—the strategic consequence of blockchain technology embedded in the software systems of law firms will be the transformation of the way lawyers interact with clients, in terms of data and collaboration.[3] With greater security and data integrity, it will be easier for clients to work with outside counsel, due to less technology friction, and this may begin to reverse the trend of more legal work being taken in-house by clients.

To the extent that lower friction means lower costs for law firms in delivering legal service to clients, law firms will be able to deliver greater value to clients at the same price, without impacting law firm profitability. Lower cost of service and higher value per cost should lead to greater client demand and greater revenue and profitability for law firms. Said another way, reducing technology friction and cost removes some of the economic dead weight loss from the legal market.

---

3 John Licata, *For lawyers, it's time to rais the bar on blockchain*, Medium (Jul. 20, 2018), https://medium.com/mimir-blockchain/for-lawyers-its-time-to-raise-the-bar-on-blockchain-48031161613c (last vistited Apr. 12, 2019).

B. Corporate Legal Departments

For corporate legal departments, the introduction of blockchain technology into the legal software stack will reduce friction and cost while increasing interoperability with outside law firms and counterparty legal departments. At a minimum, the legal cost of operating companies may be reduced, but it's more likely that the demand for and consumption of legal services will rise, as the relative value of legal services will improve.

In terms of work with outside counsel engagements, corporate legal departments will enjoy much greater flexibility in selecting outside counsel based on capability and cost, as data interchange will be universal and secure, with radically improved data integrity. And in the context of internal business processes, the ability to interact with counterparty corporate legal departments will streamline the business processes of companies' business units. Legal review and negotiation will be fast, cheaper, and more secure.

C. Legal Software

The benefit of blockchain technology to the legal software market is that it holds the promise of universal data interchange standards. In plain language, this means that LegalTech companies can invent new applications, and those applications could be used by nearly any legal industry customer without regard to existing technology infrastructure. This would dramatically reduce the cost and complexity of implementation by the client, reducing a significant barrier to adoption.

There are major strategic and structural benefits to such an outcome related to scale and pace of innovation in the legal industry. If the first order effects are more data integrity and data security, the second order effects are more interoperability and lower implementation costs. With lower implementation and switching costs, purchasers of legal technology can focus more attention on the functionality of the technology itself, versus the impediments to adoption. This will be good for new entrants, and it will stimulate incumbents to be more innovative and competitive.

The third order effects, however, are when the next generation of LegalTech solutions take advantage of both the universal data interchange and interoperability, as well as the lower cost of adoption, to build a new generation of «ecosystem» applications in areas like collaboration, analytics, and AI that have all the benefits of premises-bases security and privacy and all of the benefits that people usually associate with cloud computing. This will be a new golden age of legal technology innovation, and it's just around the corner.

VII. A word about access to justice

It is no secret that there is a worldwide crisis regarding cost-effective legal services to the masses. Modern life becomes more complex by the day, and yet the legal industry has utterly failed to develop low-cost means to serve the needs of a majority of the population. While blockchain technology may not directly alter or improve upon this situation, the intrinsic security, data integrity, and universal data interoperability that a blockchain-enabled legal technology ecosystem can provide will hopefully give rise to a new generation of legal software and services that will begin to drive down the cost of legal service delivery, enabling far more citizens to access legal services that they need.

VIII. Summary

Lawyers are among the most trusted intermediaries in modern society, yet the technology that powers the industry is increasingly vulnerable. The current technology ecosystem of law poses a risk to the trust that is so central to lawyers' roles as intermediaries. It is ironic that a distributed ledger technology most closely associated with disintermediation, blockchain, is poised to bring much greater digital trust to the legal industry.

While data security may be the most urgent use of blockchain technology, the same digital trust that blockchain facilitates will have a profound impact on the efficiency and productivity of the legal industry, most likely in ways that are far more profound than most legal professionals expect. When you can trust data across entity boundaries, whether it is documents, contracts, calendar entries, legal bills, or any other type of legal data, almost everything changes. The coming years will see the steady integration of blockchain technology into all aspects of legal technology, and as adoption and use become more ubiquitous, a new generation of legal technology will emerge, including blockchain-backed artificial intelligence. The technology foundation of Bitcoin that first arose ten years ago to thwart and bypass intermediaries in modern life will usher in a new era of trust for some of the world's most important intermediaries—its lawyers.

IX. Bibliography

Online Sources

GLOBAL LEGAL BLOCKCHAIN CONSORTIUM (2018), https://legalconsortium.org/ (last visited Feb. 1, 2019).

GLOBAL LEGAL BLOCKCHAIN CONSORTIUM, *What is the GLBC?—Global Legal Blockchain Consortium* (2018), https://legalconsortium.org/what-is-the-glbc/ (last visited Feb. 1, 2019).

Licata, John, *For lawyers, it's time to rais the bar on blockchain*, MEDIUM (Jul. 20, 2018), https://medium.com/mimir-blockchain/for-lawyers-its-time-to-raise-the-bar-on-blockchain-48031161613c (last vistited Apr. 12, 2019).

Juan Crosby, Mike Rowden, Craig Mckeown and Sebastian Ahrens

eDiscovery

TABLE OF CONTENTS

I. Introduction

30 years ago, when two parties were involved in litigation, they were required to undertake a discovery process that typically involved collecting and reviewing hundreds or thousands of hard copy documents. Teams of lawyers and paralegals would work around the clock, tirelessly sifting through seemingly endless piles of letters, faxes, working papers, and telephone logs in order to uncover and review vital evidence. Consideration was given to legal privilege and relevance to the matter at hand and the resulting set of documents was furnished to the opposing party, typically by delivery of a number of binders containing reams and reams of paper.

Fast forward to today and the world has moved almost exclusively to electronic communications with the collection and reviewing process having to follow suit; the same process, known as eDiscovery, now involves the collection of large volumes of data containing emails, electronic documents, instant messages, text messages, voice recordings and many other forms of electronic data[1]. In addition, other data, known as metadata, can provide further details such as who created the document, when it was last modified and who had access to it.[2] In *Global Aerospace v Landow Aviation*[3] the defendants had an estimated 250 gigabytes (GB) of electronically stored information for review, equating to over two million documents. A traditional linear review would take roughly 20,000 hours, costing in excess of two million dollars with a likelihood of locating only a percentage of relevant documents.

It is also not just litigation that is causing eDiscovery processes to be undertaken. Regulation is now one of the main causes with new regulation and compliance activities required in industries such as Financial Services, and more widespread regulation being introduced such as the EU General Data Protection Regulation (GDPR).[4]

The combination of exponential growth in electronically stored information and new sources of demand for eDiscovery activities has meant that this type of work has already had to undergo a level of disruption and by necessity forced to respond to and adopt more widespread and advanced use of technology—which in many ways has driven real innovation and makes it a forerun-

---

1 Lee H Rosenthal, *A Few Thoughts on Electronic Discovery After December 1, 2006*, 116 Yale L.J. Pocket Part 167 (2006), http://yalelawjournal.org/forum/an-overview-of-the-e-discovery-rules-amendments (last visited Apr. 19, 2019).

2 Andrew Wilson, *How Much Is Enough: Metadata for Preserving Digital Data*, 10 (2–3) Journal of Library Metadata 205–217 (Mar. 2, 2010).

3 2012 WL 1431215, No. CL 61040 (Va. Cir. Ct., Apr. 23, 2012).

4 Lineal, *Data Subject Access Requests: Using eDiscovery Tools to Ensure Compliance and Save Costs* (2018), https://www.linealservices.com/data-subject-access-requests-using-ediscovery-tools-to-ensure-compliance-and-save-costs/ (last visited Apr. 19, 2019).

ner to the introduction of technology in other areas of legal activity.[5] But as this technology has advanced and the ability to search and review data gets faster and more accurate, what themes are developing? How are legal teams and technologists adapting? And what further disruption, challenges and opportunities are coming in the short, medium or and long term?

Throughout this chapter we will explore these questions in greater detail. When reviewing the current state of eDiscovery it will become apparent that data and people are driving change in this industry. This interplay between the growing volumes of complex data and the response from eDiscovery practitioners has led to many innovations in the industry. In examining these innovations, we will review where this data is found, how it is brought together for analysis and the advancement in technologies used to analyse this data. However it is important not to forget that people are at the heart of this change. We will examine how litigation teams have responded to innovation, providing some insights for other legal practitioners to consider as technology continues to impact their ways of working.

II. Does every cloud have a silver lining?

One challenge that is currently being looked at in some detail is the impact of cloud computing. Many organisations are now rapidly adopting and moving to cloud technologies to help support their core underlying technology needs and see significant business benefits from doing so.[6] Email, document management, finance, human resources and other core systems are being migrated to new cloud based platforms.

In parallel, the number of sources of data continues to increase. In addition to what might now be considered conventional electronic data such as email, more apps are being created, voice data now includes conversations with robots, video data includes dash cams and drone footage, photographic images contain geographical coordinates of where the image was taken and the adoption of the Internet of Things means that data is being created by devices in offices, vehicles and in homes. Some or all of this data could also be stored on cloud platforms.

---

5 JR Jenkins, *The Rise of Analytics in E-discovery: A Lifesaver When You're Drowning in Data* (2015), http://www.ftijournal.com/article/the-rise-of-analytics-in-e-discovery (last visited Apr. 19, 2019).

6 Kaite Costello & Sarah Hippold, *Gartner Forecasts Worldwide Public Cloud Revenue to Grow 17.3 Percent in 2019*, GARTNER (Sep. 12, 2018), https://www.gartner.com/en/newsroom/press-releases/2018-09-12-gartner-forecasts-worldwide-public-cloud-revenue-to-grow-17-percent-in-2019 (last visited Apr. 19, 2019).

But are organisations considering the impact all of this has on eDiscovery processes if they are involved in litigation or when subject to a regulatory review? How many sources of data do they have that may be relevant to the matter? Where does this data physically reside and who has access to it? Which country is it in? How will it be collected and can it be captured without collecting large volumes of other non-relevant data? Failure to consider some of these challenges can result in the efforts and costs of eDiscovery being much greater than is necessary.

That said, the introduction of regulation such as the EU GDPR and concerns over cyber security and the drive to reduce IT costs or indeed the costs of eDiscovery, have also led many to reconsider their data management strategy.[7] Effective Information Governance means that organisations know what data they have, where it resides, who has access to it and also that they have policies relating to how long each source of data needs to be kept.

Those organisations being more proactive have considered and planned for the need to perform eDiscovery which can lead to interesting decisions around data sources such as instant messaging, for example. Huge volumes of data can be generated by an organisation's instant messaging system and when employees use it there can often be a tendency to be less formal and potentially make comments and share information that they would typically not do through a more formal email communication. The costs of capturing and reviewing this data aligned to the possibility of information that is very damaging to your case being contained within it means that is can be of significant risk to the organisation. Therefore, in forming their Information Governance strategy organisations need to consider the impact eDiscovery will have on each data source and the need to retain this data.

As cloud platforms continue to disrupt the way many organisations operate, it is vital that those involved in performing eDiscovery are keeping pace and are prepared to work within this new environment. In addition to implementing effective Information Governance, legal teams also need to consider how cloud and other emerging technologies will help manage the increasing data volumes and complexity in modern eDiscovery matters.

---

7 Salvador Rodriguez, *Rise of the data protection officer, the hottest tech ticket in town*, Reuters (Feb. 14, 2018 1:12 PM), https://uk.reuters.com/article/us-cyber-gdpr-dpo/rise-of-the-data-protection-officer-the-hottest-tech-ticket-in-town-idUKKCN1FY1MY (last visited Apr. 19, 2019).

III. Can one platform meet all eDiscovery needs?

In a typical eDiscovery process, data is divided into two high-level categories: structured and unstructured data.[8] This delineation is largely to assist lawyers and technologists with determining the best methods for analysis. Structured information is data that is typically found in databases and has a meaning assigned. For example, a piece of structured information could be an employee's address stored within a HR system.

Conversely, unstructured information is typically data found in free form text, where meaning is not necessarily apparent before analysis. For example, a common unstructured data source is email communications. Before beginning any analysis, a legal practitioner knows very little about the meaning of an email, only that it was a message sent from one individual to another individual(s). Given the ambiguous nature of this data, previous discovery solutions tended to focus on how best to derive meaning effectively, through either keyword searching or natural language processing.[9]

In response to the increasing volume of data being held, the need to combine the analysis of structured and unstructured datasets and the need to integrate with emerging cloud solutions, the vendor landscape is evolving with some technology vendors seeing an opportunity to bring the entire eDiscovery process into one platform.[10]

These new Software as a Service (SaaS) solutions integrate with an organisation's email and document management systems so that right from the outset of a matter, searches can be quickly conducted across all of the relevant data (both structured and unstructured), legal holds can be issued to prevent data being modified or deleted and the data can be analysed, reviewed and redacted, all in one place to support an eDiscovery matter. This has also given legal teams the ability to spot correlations between datasets stored in multiple systems, an activity in the past that required teams to have a much greater level of technological expertise.

An example of this would be spotting changes to a finance system 5 minutes after a salesperson received an instant message from the CFO asking them to back date a sale into the previous quarter. Running searches on the text of the message alone may or may not have identified this, depending on the words used and the strength of the search terms. However, when correlated against an

---

8 Richard L Villars et al., *Big Data: What is it and Why Should You* Care (2011), http://www.tracemyflows.com/uploads/big_data/idc_amd_big_data_whitepaper.pdf (last visited Apr. 19, 2019).

9 Lewis Carroll, *The grossman-cormack glossary of technology-assisted review*, 7 (1) Federal Courts Law Review (2013).

10 *See* Relativity, https://www.relativity.com/ediscovery-software/relativityone/ (last visited Apr. 19, 2019).

analysis of unusual changes within the finance system the suspicious action can be more easily identified.

An advantage of these SaaS solutions is the ability for lawyers to interact with the data directly and perform a lot of the analysis without needing to have deep technology expertise. This is a significant development as lawyers can now view visual representations of the data, run searches, perform redactions, and cull large volumes of data, all with minimal support from technologists.

Does this mean the role of a technologist in eDiscovery is diminishing? Not at all, as lawyers become more technology savvy, technologist have shift their focus to emerging technology poised to further disrupt traditional eDiscovery method.

IV. The rise of the machines

With the growth of high quality data there has been an explosion in the growth of artificial intelligence (AI) offerings across all industries and markets, threatening to bring about large disruption. The legal industry is not immune to this trend.

Unlike many other areas of legal practice there is a relatively long history of leveraging the use of machine learning and broader artificial intelligence technologies in litigation, with articles in mainstream publications dating as far back as 2011.[11] This technology aims to help streamline legal processes, through applications such as predictive coding and document clustering. As data sets have continued to grow exponentially, there has been a big push to further increase the use of AI to assist in a discovery exercise. Through a variety of successful, and not so successful, applications of AI technology, it can be argued that litigation teams have shown the rest of the legal industry that disruption from technology can and should be embraced. However, like any new technology, early adopters were not immune to some initial growing pains.

11 Ben Kerschberg, *E-Discovery And The Rise of Predictive Coding* (2011), Forbes (Mar. 23, 2012 10:04 AM), https://www.forbes.com/sites/benkerschberg/2011/03/23/e-discovery-and-the-rise-of-predictive-coding/#2bc9d2d32d38 (last visited Apr. 19, 2019).

V. A promising start to the revolution...with some limitations

Predictive coding first gained mainstream attention last decade, where a promise of eliminating (or, at least, radically reducing) the need for humans to review large corpuses of potentially relevant evidence seemed like a very attractive proposition to any overworked or cost constrained legal team.[12] The concept was simple, rather than train inexperienced junior lawyers to find relevant information related to the matter, train a machine who, once trained, could in theory find information quicker and more accurately than any human. This process involved reviewing small, random sample sets of documents in order to train the machine on what is and is not relevant to the matter. In theory, after a few days of training you would have a machine perfectly calibrated to find and produce documents relevant to the matter.

Early adopters of the technology fell in love with this narrative but were surprised with the actual capabilities of a machine, especially when compared with alternative options on the market: outsourcers who offer armies of document reviewers often located in low cost jurisdictions.[13] Many lawyers were finding training the system to be cumbersome and time consuming, which also required a trainer with subject matter expertise (SME).[14] In the past these SMEs generally spent very little time reviewing documents during the process, so the thought of reverting back to document review was less than appealing. Furthermore, some lawyers found this technology produced more questions than answers in some case.[15] Other limitations included a rigid training process not suited for expanding document populations and the restriction on the number of topics the system could understand. What was positioned as a technology that could replace a junior lawyer, appeared to lack the basic cognitive abilities needed to perform a robust document review process.

This initial setback illustrated that perhaps disruption in the eDiscovery market would not be as quick as promised by some. However, as is often the case with disruptive technology, while the first iteration showed what might be possible, it is the second generation technologies and solutions that are much closer to delivering on the promise of disruption. Improvements in the technology, court acceptance and demystification led to wider spread adop-

---

12 *Id.*

13 The Law Society, *Legal process outsourcing: What you should know* (2011), https://www.lawsociety.org.uk/support-services/Advice/Practice-Notes/documents/Legal-process-outsourcing-guide/ (last visited Apr. 19, 2019).

14 Christina T Nasuti, *Shaping the Technology of the Future: Predictive Coding in Discovery Case Law and Regulatory Disclosure Requirements*, 93 North Carolina Law Review 26 (2014).

15 Dana A Remus, *The Uncertain Promise of Predictive Coding*, 99 Ioaw Law Review 1691 (2014).

tion and investment which was needed to further advance the uptake of this technology.[16]

VI. If at first you don't succeed, try, try, try again

Disruption in any industry will always be met with some resistance, in that people tend to default to the current processes due to familiarity and predictability of outcomes. In the past, a recommended discovery workflow would suggest keyword searching a corpus of documents and then manually reviewing the results. Legal teams were comfortable with this workflow as they have grown a custom too, dating all the way back their time in law school.[17] The first iteration of predictive technology radically changed this process, only suggesting a review of a random set of documents that may have no relevance to the matter.

New predictive coding technologies focus on continuous, active learning where system training is performed more regularly (as opposed to the previous generation, which relied on discrete training sessions), as first describe by *Cormack and Grossman.*[18] This new process mirrors standard discovery workflow, where facts impacting relevancy typically surface throughout the discovery process. This is a less radical change in the workflow, opting to use the technology to suggest documents that may be relevant in order to guide legal teams to the right answer. This is something lawyers and technologist should keep in mind when looking to deploy new technologies in other areas of legal practice: incremental advancements can sometimes have a larger impact than big bang transformations.

While improvement in the technology and approach of application has certainly helped to increase usage, one could argue the acceptance of the technology in various courts (which is naturally linked to its effectiveness too) has had a similar impact on uptake. In many jurisdictions we have started to see successful uses of the technology in litigation matters. The US led the way in 2012 with Judge *Andrew Peck*'s seminal endorsement of predictive coding in

---

16 Nicholas Barry, *Man versus Machine Review: The Showdown between Hordes of Discovery Lawyers and a Computer-Utilizing Predictive-Coding Technology*, 15 Vand. J. Ent. & Tech. L. 343 (2013).

17 Charles-Theodore Zerner, *Relying on keyword search for e-discovery? It may harm your case: important pitfalls and how to escape them* (2017), http://www.neworleansbar.org/news/committees/relying-on-keyword-search-for-e-discovery-it-may-harm-your-case#_ftn1 (last visited Apr. 19, 2019).

18 Gordon Cormack et al., *Evaluation of machine-learning protocols for technology-assisted review in electronic discovery*, in Proceedings of the 37th international ACM SIGIR conference on Research & development in information retrieval (SIGIR '14) 153–162 (2014).

Da Silva Moore.[19] More recently, we have seen similar landmark decisions in the UK (*Pyrrho Investments Ltd v MWB Property Ltd & Ors*[20]) and Australia (*McConnell Dowell Constructors (Aust) Pty Ltd v Santam Ltd & Ors (No 1)*[21] to use predictive coding for the management of large-scale litigation for the first time. While many courts have widely accepted that AI technology can bring improvements to the discovery process, legal teams should still approach this technology with cautious optimism.

With technology improvements and court acceptance, it is now incumbent on legal teams to ensure the technology is employed correctly. Failure to do so could result in additional discovery work, as well as loss in confidence in the technology by both the court and client. In these cases, any efficiency gains are certainly lost, not to mention the potential negative reputational impact. No legal team wants to be in the press for a mishandled discovery process. The key to avoiding these situations is to understand the capabilities of the technology and when specific limitations can impact the quality of the results. A joint legal and technology team is often needed to ensure the best results are achieved.

Both improvements in the technology and general acceptance within the industry has had a significant impact on the demystification of AI in the eDiscovery world. In the past, may have been the case that many practitioners may have avoided use of this technology largely based on the fears of the unknown. Legal practitioners traditionally are not trained on technology (although this is changing), so it is not surprising that claims that a computer can replace a highly educated litigator or reviewing lawyer may have been met with some scepticism.[22] Through various publications on the topic, speaking with peers and hands on use of the technology, many lawyers have moved beyond this scepticism, common with any disruptive technology, and have started to find practical areas for its application where it drives real benefits from a speed, insight and cost perspective.[23] With the growing collection of successful predictive coding use cases, legal teams have now started to look to AI technolo-

---

19 Monique Da Silva MOORE v. PUBLICIS GROUPE & MSL Group, 287 F.R.D. 182 (S.D.N.Y. 2012).

20 [2016] EWHC 256 (Ch).

21 [2016] VSC 734.

22 Mark A Cohen, *What Are Law Schools Training Students For?* (2018), Forbes (Nov. 19, 2018 5:56 AM), https://www.forbes.com/sites/markcohen1/2018/11/19/what-are-law-schools-training-students-for/#49c77ff964f2 (last visited Apr. 19, 2019).

23 Ari Kaplan, *Advice from Counsel—Can Predictive Coding Deliver on its Promise?*, FTI Technology (2014), https://www.ftitechnology.com/resources/white-papers/advice-from-counsel-can-predictive-coding-deliver-on-its-promise (last visited Apr. 19, 2019).

gies to see if there are other areas in the discovery process that could benefit from its application.[24]

VII. Success leads to further success

With the idea of training a machine to do legal work gaining traction in the industry, other technology vendors have started approaching this problem from a different angle. Technologists are utilising machine learning to augment lawyers, rather than replace them. In recent years, there have been impressive advancements in what machines are able to accomplish with little or no prior training, leveraging advancements in natural language processing in order to read and understand documents.[25] For example, some solutions are able to map the relationship between individuals referenced in a large corpus of documents, automatically creating a visual representation of the connections between various parties in matter.[26] This task, which would have taken weeks to complete, can now be accomplished in minutes.

These new technologies also pose interesting questions of how technology might further disrupt the legal industry. Unlike predictive coding, which aims to eliminate low complexity legal work, these technologies are focused on making lawyers more effective and efficient: augmentation opposed to automation. Lawyers who embrace these technologies will not see their jobs disappear, but rather their legal capabilities and the insights that they are able to provide enhanced, making them more competitive in the market. Moving beyond document review, legal teams have now started to explore other areas in the litigation process that may also benefit from the use of technology.[27]

VIII. Looking beyond the matter at hand

With the successful application of AI technology to streamline discovery activities, lawyers and technologists have also been examining whether similar technology can be applied to other parts of the litigation process to deliver new insights—such as, whether an algorithm can help predict the outcome of a le-

---

24 Jyoti Dabass & Bhupender Singh Dabass, *Scope of Artificial Intelligence in Law*, 10.20944/preprints201806.0474.v1.

25 Sotiris Kotsiantis & Panayiotis Pintelas, *Recent advances in clustering: A brief survey*, 1 (1) Wseas Transactions on Information Science and Applications 73–81 (2004).

26 Brainspace, https://www.brainspace.com/ (last visited Apr. 12, 2019).

27 Stephen Embry, *Litigation Predictive Analytics: Driving a Stake in the Heart of the Billable Heart?*, TechLaw Crossroads (Feb. 13, 2018), https://www.techlawcrossroads.com/2018/02/can-litigation-prediction-change-way-alternative-fees/ (last visited Jan. 14, 2019).

gal matter.[28] We have already discussed how these algorithms can help predict which documents will and will not be relevant to a matter, so the next logical step is to see if we can use data to predict a legal outcome. Unlike predictive coding, and related technologies, which are document focused, these new technologies consider other information sources, such as past outcomes of similar trials, the judge presiding over the matter and jurisdiction, among other impacting factors.

Legal outcome predictive technology is still very much in its infancy and there are many challenges that differ from those challenges found in the document review application of the technology. Currently the data sources available, such as the outcome of passed court cases, are not structured in a manner that is suitable for interrogation by AI technology.[29] While this limitation is expected to be addressed in the coming years through various data cleansing initiatives, researchers are still debating which method is best for determining future outcomes of a legal matter.[30] We expect to see more research on the topic in the coming years, which will help determine how the best way to utilise this technology. Technology, while certainly impressive, on its own will not solve the legal problems of today and tomorrow. Legal teams must consider how best to structure their teams in order to best leverage technology and ensure they benefit from innovation.

IX. Constructing a modern legal team

As we examine the proliferation of technology throughout the legal industry, it is clear that technology will play a key role in the future of legal practice. With so much discovery, technology now accessible to lawyers, it is no surprise that many lawyers are struggling to figure out which technologies to use and the structure of their team needed to manage all that these technologies can offer. This raises some important questions. Is a legal team only staffed with lawyers effective enough in today's disruptive environment? Should these teams outsource technology work or aim to bring it in house? Can a team

---

28 David Cowan, *Predictive analytics for lawyers: a five step process*, Raconteur (Nov. 30, 2018), https://www.raconteur.net/risk-management/predictive-analytics-lawyers (last visited Apr. 19, 2019).

29 Felix Steffek & Ludwig Bull, *Law and Autonomous Systems Series: Paving the Way for Legal Artificial Intelligence—A Common Dataset for Case Outcome Predictions*, Oxford Law Faculty (2018), https://www.law.ox.ac.uk/business-law-blog/blog/2018/05/law-and-autonomous-systems-series-paving-way-legal-artificial (last visited Jan. 14, 2019).

30 Stefanie Bruninghaus & Kevin D Ashley, *Predicting outcomes of case based legal arguments, in* Proceedings of the 9th international conference on Artificial intelligence and law—ICAIL 03 (2003).

of lawyers and technologists effectively work together to deliver a better outcome? Can a lawyer become a technologist or are they discrete skills sets?

Litigation teams have been at the forefront of these questions, largely due to necessity brought about by modern discovery disclosure requirements. The question on whether to build an in house capability versus outsource to a provider with specific expertise in the technology is something litigation teams have been considering over many years as the technology has become more accessible.

While discovery technology has made great strides in usability, specialised technical expertise is still required to run a discovery project effectively[31]. Modern technology is generally very good at dealing with standard use cases, such as processing email data, with little human intervention. It is the uncommon data sets and scenarios where expertise will be required. For example, while processing email might be considered a fairly straightforward task using discovery technology, different email archiving systems may lead to corrupt or incomplete document collections, which may not be apparent to an untrained lawyer or technologist. Having an expert in these scenarios can save time, money and countless headaches.

Clearly there are benefits in having this technical expertise on any discovery team, but where to source this expertise and at what cost is worth considering further. In general, technical positions are often difficult to staff due to short supply. Adding to this complication is the specialist nature of discovery work, which often takes at least two to three years of on the job training before an individual is sufficiently upskilled. Teams evaluating bringing this skill in house will have to consider whether their local market has available talent, usually found in a vendor or outsource provider, or whether they think they can provide training and wider career development to nurture this talent internally. The latter option also poses a further risk of attrition if there are any challenges keeping the team engaged.

In addition to organisations adding technical skills sets to their legal teams, either in-house or through an outsourcer, we are starting to see another trend within these same teams: the rise of the technology savvy lawyer. This lawyer understands both the legal and technology aspects of a discovery project. Many lawyers have developed this capability through on the job training, however we are beginning to see law course offerings that focus on technology and how it impacts the practice of law.

Should we expect to see lawyers of the future writing software code or complex data queries? Unlikely. We should, however, start to see more lawyers who are versed in the technology options in the market and how they can

---

31 Bennett B Borden & Jason R Baron, *Finding the Signal in the Noise: Information Governance, Analytics, and the Future of Legal Practice*, 20 Rich. J.L. & Tech 7 (2014).

be effectively utilised. These individuals will be capable of leading a team comprised of lawyers, technologists, and project managers, knowing when to utilise each skill set. In rarer cases, we will see lawyers who have deep technical knowledge where this makes sense for the portfolio of work that they look after. This interplay between technology and people will be a key driver for further innovation in eDiscovery. It is now useful to consider how key technologies will impact the discovery practitioners in the near and distant future.

X. The Future of eDiscovery

Rapid advancements in technology have certainly had a dramatic effect on how discovery matters are managed today. Exponential data growth combined with the increasing sophistication of artificial intelligence, have forced many legal teams to reconsider how best to service their clients. Looking forward, we see no reason not to believe that these trends will continue to force disruption in this area of legal practice.

We expect that case specific keyword searches and intelligent document classification will continue to be important tools for any legal practitioner. In the near future technology that leverages natural language processing (NLP) could prove to have similar or greater impact on the legal profession. While these technologies have become standard for most data scientists, strangely the legal profession struggled until recently to evaluate the use of this technology in discovery matters.

While traditional methods of statistical clustering of texts, used in most predictive coding technologies today, can help very much to bring down the costs of technology-assisted reviews, the recent developments in NLP promise much more. Modern cloud-based systems discussed previously bring impressive computational power that can leverage deep neural networks (DNN) to revolutionise the way machines process text based documents.

After Collobert et al. published their paper «Natural Language Processing (almost) from Scratch» in 2011,[32] deep learning has proven to be as valuable in NLP as it is in image classification and other typical AI disciplines. Before the application of deep neural networks, NLP software solutions were relying on ridged, task-dependent rules to allow the machine to «understand» the meaning of words and sentences. Conversely, DNN aims to mimic the way the human brain functions.

These new technologies are now able to understand language without the need for complex taxonomies or grammar rule sets. During the last five years,

32 Ronan Collobert et al., *Natural Language Processing (almost) from Scratch.* arXiv:1103.0398v1 [cs.LG] (Mar. 2, 2011).

DNN based computer systems have been able to autonomously deduce the meaning of linguistic input from copious amounts of text alone. These new technologies produced breakthrough results in various areas like classification, role labelling and machine translation. Even though there is still no machine that would be able to crack insider lingo and understand all aspects of human language, such as figurative meanings and word plays, we have now started seeing systems producing meaningful summaries of text and being able to read between the lines. These capabilities could disrupt the eDiscovery world like no other: Explorative analysis of unlimited amounts of text based on computer-aided processing as a means of finding the needle in the haystack means entire discovery expeditions could be completed in seconds.

In addition to more advance machine learning technology using NLP, we expect to see machine training to be shared across multiple matters, opposed to its discrete, matter based application today. Technology will learn and attempt to apply knowledge gained in one domain to a problem from another one, just as a human would do. In the past, the experienced human would bring his or her accumulated knowledge to every new task and would get more and more experienced over time. This helps humans to develop a sort of gut feeling and be able predict best strategies to address a problem. Going forward the expert can use the state and configuration of a DNN, representing all prior experience of the software, to solve new problems. Over time the software matures in the same way as the human would do.

Naturally, this introduces new challenges around data privacy and competition law and raises the question if society will want a few companies to own the accumulated knowledge of all AI in the cloud. Currently we see various attempts to build interoperable ecosystems that would allow for exchanging of AI models and domain knowledge. The technology companies from *Amazon* to *Facebook* to *Alibaba*, *Baidoo*, *IBM* and *Huawei* gathered to push their Open Neural Network Exchange (ONNX)[33] trying to secure the next big AI business for themselves. Other initiatives like *Bonseyes*[34] focus more on scenarios where the data must remain in the data provider's premises and aim at technology-stacks that are compliant with data privacy regulations like GDPR. More than the raw data, knowledge in the form of trained AI will become the oil equivalent of the data-driven economy in the next decades.

While the technology companies continue to build their business on access to massive computational resources and broad ranges of online data, they still lack access to specialist information and human experience one needs to train AI software for specific purposes like eDiscovery. That is where the law

33 Open Neural Network Exchange (ONNX), *see* https://onnx.ai/.

34 *Bonseyes*, an open platform for the development of systems of artificial intelligence from cloud to edge devices, *see* https://www.bonseyes.com/.

and professional service firms come into play. Going forward they will become vendors of digital knowledge leveraging the platforms that the cloud providers offer. The question remains if the legal profession and other professional service providers in this field are ready for such a drastic change in their business.

XI. Bibliography

A. Hard Copy Sources

Arulmurugan, R. et al., *Classification of sentence level sentiment analysis using cloud machine learning techniques*, Cluster Computing The Journal of Networks, Software Tools and Applications 1–11 (2017)

Barry, Nicholas, *Man versus Machine Review: The Showdown between Hordes of Discovery Lawyers and a Computer-Utilizing Predictive-Coding Technology*, 15 Vand. J. Ent. & Tech. L. 343 (2013)

Bonseyes, https://www.bonseyes.com/ (last visited Apr. 11, 2019).

Borden, Bennett B & Baron, Jason R, *Finding the Signal in the Noise: Information Governance, Analytics, and the Future of Legal Practice*, 20 Rich. J.L. & Tech 7 (2014).

Brainspace, https://www.brainspace.com/ (last visited Apr. 12, 2019).

Bruninghaus, Stefanie & Ashley, Kevin D, *Predicting outcomes of case based legal arguments*, *in* Proceedings of the 9th international conference on Artificial intelligence and law—ICAIL 03 (2003).

Carroll, Lewis, *The grossman-cormack glossary of technology-assisted review*, 7 (1) Federal Courts Law Review (2013).

Chowdhury, Aruni Roy et al., *Automatic adaptation of object detectors to new domains using self-training*, COMPUTER VISION AND PATTERN RECOGNITION (2019).

Cormack, Gordon, Maura R, *Evaluation of machine-learning protocols for technology-assisted review in electronic discovery*, *in* Proceedings of the 37th international ACM SIGIR conference on Research & development in information retrieval (SIGIR '14) 153–162 (2014).

Dabass, Jyoti & Dabass, Bhupender Singh, *Scope of Artificial Intelligence in Law*, 10.20944/preprints201806.0474.v1.

Kerikmäe, Tanel et al., *Legal Technology for Law Firms: Determining Roadmaps for Innovation*, 81 Croatian International Relations Review XXIV (2018).

Kotsiantis, Sotiris & Pintelas, Panayiotis, *Recent advances in clustering: A brief survey*. 1 (1) WSEAS Transactions on Information Science and Applications 73–81(2004).

Li, Kuan-Ching et al., Smart Data: State-of-the-Art Perspectives in Computing and Applications (Chapman & Hall, 2019).

Merchant, Kaiz & Yash Pande, *NLP Based Latent Semantic Analysis for Legal Text Summarization*, 2018 International Conference on Advances in Computing, Communications and Informatics (ICACCI) (2018).

Nadkarniet, Prakash M et al., *Natural language processing: an introduction*, (18) Journal of the American Medical Informatics Association, (2011).

Nasuti, Christina T, *Shaping the Technology of the Future: Predictive Coding in Discovery Case Law and Regulatory Disclosure Requirements*, 93 North Carolina Law Review 26 (2014).

Relativity, https://www.relativity.com/ (last visited Apr. 11, 2019). Remus, Dana A, *The Uncertain Promise of Predictive Coding*, 99 Ioaw Law Review 1691 (2014).

Thompson, Ken, *Regular Expression Search Algorithm*, 11 (6) Communications of the ACM (1968).

Wilson, Andrew, *How Much Is Enough: Metadata for Preserving Digital Data*, 10 (2–3) Journal of Library Metadata 205–217 (2010).

B. Online Sources

Cohen, Mark A, *What Are Law Schools Training Students For?* Forbes (Nov. 19, 2018 5:56 AM), https://www.forbes.com/sites/markcohen1/2018/11/19/what-are-law-schools-training-students-for/#49c77ff964f2 (last visited Apr. 19, 2019).

Collobert, Ronan et al., *Natural Language Processing (almost) from Scratch*, arXiv (Mar. 2, 2011), https://arxiv.org/pdf/1103.0398.pdf (last visited Feb. 2, 2019).

Cornell University Legal Information Institute, *Federal Rules of Civil Procedure, Title V. Disclosures and Discovery, Rule 34, Notes of Advisory Committee on Rules—1970 Amendment*, https://www.law.cornell.edu/rules/frcp/rule_34 (last visited Feb. 2, 2019).

Costello, Kaite & Hippold, Sarah, *Gartner Forecasts Worldwide Public Cloud Revenue to Grow 17.3 Percent in 2019*, Gartner (Sep. 12, 2018), https://www.gartner.com/en/newsroom/press-releases/2018-09-12-gartner-forecasts-worldwide-public-cloud-revenue-to-grow-17-percent-in-2019 (last visited Apr. 19, 2019).

Cowan, David, *Predictive analytics for lawyers: a five step process*, Raconteur (2018), https://www.raconteur.net/risk-management/predictive-analytics-lawyers (last visited Apr. 19, 2019).

Embry, Stephen, *Litigation Predictive Analytics: Driving a Stake in the Heart of the Billable Heart?*, TechLaw Crossroads (Feb. 13, 2018), https://www.techlawcrossroads.com/2018/02/can-litigation-prediction-change-way-alternative-fees/ (last visited Jan. 14, 2019).

Jenkins, JR, *The Rise of Analytics in E-discovery: A Lifesaver When You're Drowning in Data*, FTI Journal (2015), http://www.ftijournal.com/article/the-rise-of-analytics-in-e-discovery (last visited Apr. 19, 2019).

Kaplan, Ari, *Advice from Counsel—Can Predictive Coding Deliver on its Promise?* FTI Technology (2014), https://www.ftitechnology.com/resources/white-papers/advice-from-counsel-can-predictive-coding-deliver-on-its-promise (last visited Apr. 19, 2019).

Kerschberg, Ben, *E-Discovery And The Rise of Predictive Coding*, Forbes (Mar. 23, 2011 10:04 AM), https://www.forbes.com/sites/benkerschberg/2011/03/23/e-discovery-and-the-rise-of-predictive-coding/#2bc9d2d32d38 (last visited Apr. 19, 2019).

Lineal, Data *Subject Access Requests: Using eDiscovery Tools to Ensure Compliance and Save Costs* (2018), https://www.linealservices.com/data-subject-access-requests-using-ediscovery-tools-to-ensure-compliance-and-save-costs/ (last visited Apr. 19, 2019).

Rodriguez, Salvador, *Rise of the data protection officer, the hottest tech ticket in town*, Reuters (Feb. 14, 2018 1:12 PM), https://uk.reuters.com/article/us-cyber-gdpr-dpo/rise-of-the-data-protection-officer-the-hottest-tech-ticket-in-town-idUKKCN1FY1MY (last visited Apr. 19, 2019).

Rosenthal, Lee H, *A Few Thoughts on Electronic Discovery After December 1, 2006*, 116 Yale L.J. Pocket Part 167 (2006), http://yalelawjournal.org/forum/an-overview-of-the-e-discovery-rules-amendments (last visited Apr. 19, 2019).

The Law Society, *Legal process outsourcing: What you should know* (2011), https://www.lawsociety.org.uk/support-services/Advice/Practice-Notes/documents/Legal-process-outsourcing-guide/ (last visited Apr. 19, 2019).

Steffek, Felix & Bull, Ludwig, *Law and Autonomous Systems Series: Paving the Way for Legal Artificial Intelligence—A Common Dataset for Case Outcome Predictions*, Oxford Law Faculty (2018), https://www.law.ox.ac.uk/business-law-blog/blog/2018/05/law-and-autonomous-systems-series-paving-way-legal-artificial (last visited Jan. 14, 2019).

Villars, Richard L. et al., *Big Data: What is it and Why Should You Care* (2011), http://www.tracemyflows.com/uploads/big_data/idc_amd_big_data_whitepaper.pdf / (last visited Apr. 19, 2019).

Young, Tom et al., *Recent Trends in Deep Learning Based Natural Language Processing*, arXiv (Aug. 9, 2017, last revised Nov. 25, 2018), https://arxiv.org/pdf/1708.02709.pdf (last visited Apr. 14, 2019).

Zerner, Charles-Theodore, *Relying on keyword search for e-discovery? It may harm your case: important pitfalls and how to escape them.* (2017), http://www.neworleansbar.org/news/committees/relying-on-keyword-search-for-e-discovery-it-may-harm-your-case#_ftn1 (last visited Apr. 19, 2019).

C. Case Law

2012 WL 1431215, No. CL 61040 (Va. Cir. Ct., Apr. 23, 2012).

Monique Da Silva MOORE v. PUBLICIS GROUPE & MSL Group, 287 F.R.D. 182 (S.D.N.Y. 2012).

Pyrrho Investments Ltd v MWB Property Ltd & Ors [2016] EWHC 256 (Ch).

McConnell Dowell Constructors (Aust) Pty Ltd v Santam Ltd & Ors (No 1) [2016] VSC 734.

David Bundi

RegTech

A Mindset for Breakthroughs

TABLE OF CONTENTS

I. The Time is Now

A. Why People are Paramount

Regulatory Technologies, «RegTech», are information systems that enable compliance and business opportunities in a smart and efficient manner. Like any information system, a RegTech solution consists of people, processes, and an enabling technology. However, the people dimension is more often than not neglected, leading to all manner of challenges, which range from the development of the technology, to its adoption, implementation, and use.[1] Success in technology adoption and use has more to do with the emotions and mindset of the people participating in the processes, not in technology per se. For good and ill, people always are paramount. Technologies are here to enhance the professional and social lives of people, whether through automation or information.[2]

Hence, this chapter starts with the topic of people, to then look at the origins of RegTech, a new definition and several enabling technologies. The second part of the chapter elaborates a «Mindset for the Future» at financial institutions, regulators and RegTech providers to then conclude in the third part with a few innovative topics and technologies to fully enable breakthroughs in RegTech.

1. Love & Improvement

We know from *Kahneman and Tversky*[3] that emotional bias operates at all levels when making decisions. These are the qualities that make humans unique and are what will always separate people from machines. It is, however, where humans are often most fallible. In the light of today's progress in innovation and advanced technologies, there is, with a change of mindset, much improvement possible in the way financial institutions approach compliance and risk topics as shown in this chapter. First, «you've got to find what you love. If you haven't found it yet. Keep looking. Don't settle. As with all matters of the heart, you'll know when you find it», said Steve Jobs and I couldn't agree more with him. If you really love what you do, you will care about it and you will continuously improve the way you work. You will simply innovate and improve what you do and the things around you, because you love what you do. You need, however, to possess the resilience and courage to

---

1 Kalle Lyytinen & Rudy Hirschheim, *Information systems failures—a survey and classification of the empirical literature*, *in* 4 Oxford Surveys in IT 257–309 (1987).

2 Shoshana Zuboff, *Big other: surveillance capitalism and the prospects of an information civilization*, 30(1) JIT 75 (2015).

3 Daniel Kahneman & Amos Tversky, *Choices, Values, and Frames,* 39 American Psychologist 341 (1984).

follow it mindfully and admit bias to avoid the downside risks. Luck, as the saying goes, favors the prepared mind.[4]

2. Fixed & Growth Mindset

Mindsets exist along a continuum from the fixed to a growth orientation, according to *Dweck*.[5] Such observations are based on her research on motivation and success over several decades. A fixed mindset constrains optimal decision making, as it fails to learn and is biased. People have different fixed mindsets in different domains: such as, for example, capabilities in mathematics, languages or sports. The growth mindset enables a person to develop their knowledge and abilities over time, as people with such mindsets avail of every opportunity to learn. This ultimately brings more in the way of happiness, better health and a more fulfilled and successful life. Luckily, for the ones with a fixed mindset in some domains, mindsets can be changed.[6] Most often, people believe that the «gift» is the ability itself (e.g., what you see from outside looking at a person being good in a domain). «Yet what feeds it is that constant, endless curiosity and challenge seeking.»[7]

There is also a distinction between fixed and growth mindset with regard to risk-taking: People with a fixed mindset feel judged and evaluated all the time. If they do not do well on a test, they conclude they are not good in the domain at hand. This has repercussions on risk-taking as people operating from a fixed mindset have something to lose by trying and failing. In *Dweck's* book, «Mindset: The New Psychology of Success», she demonstrates that we can help underachievers become achievers by facilitating their discovery of how to approach things from a growth perspective. From a growth mindset, failures are perceived merely as learning opportunities, chances to see what we don't know yet or need to work on. In short, the fixed mindset leads to a fear of failure, and the growth mindset encourages risk-taking. This is obviously an important reason that the growth mindset is associated with higher academic and career achievement levels over time: «People in a growth mindset don't just seek challenge, they thrive on it.»[8]

3. Thinking & Doing

Several recommendations, based on the research cited above and my own experience, may be made at this point:

---

4 Louis Pasteuer, *Dans les champs de l'observation le hasard ne favorise que les esprits préparés*, https://en.wikiquote.org/wiki/Louis_Pasteur (last visited Jan. 2, 2019).

5 Carol S Dweck, Mindset: The New Psychology of Success (Ballantine Books, 2006) at 63.

6 Dona Matthews, *Book Review: Mindset: The New Psychology of Success (2006)*, Gifted Children, 2, 11 (2007).

7 Dweck, *supra* note 5, at 278.

8 Dona Matthews, *supra* note 6.

1. Think open, positive and big: An open and positive forward-looking mindset is what I personally live. Technology is there simply to scale your efforts. So, do not hesitate to think big.
2. Be passionate and never give up: The individual's passion and conviction may determine success and defeat of endeavors. «Passion beats intelligence. Burn for your ideas» said *Michael Sidler*,[9] investor and coach of startups recently at the Digital Health Day. Conviction is one more key ingredient to success, as explained by *Chris von Rohr*, founder of the legendary Swiss hard rock band Krokus, in his conversation with *Guenther Dobrauz-Saldapenna* in the «Appetite For Disruption» educational video series by the Disruption Disciples.[10]
3. Remember your roots: Even in a world of investors, rock stars, and cosmopolitans, it is crucial to remember your roots. Not in the sense to restrain you, or to push you, depending on your individual background, but as a source of strength and starting point of navigation through your life. Looking back, I have now spent 12+ years in Legal & Compliance in the financial industry internationally. My ancestors, however, were, on one side, mountaineers and, on the other side, hoteliers. This might be why I have always had a desire to guide people to undiscovered heights and bring them safely back as our longtime, loyal guests. Trust is the bond between all stakeholders and it needs to be earned, and that means earning it every day.
4. Assess and communicate: Assess, articulate and communicate problems and solutions, then realize these solutions.[11]
5. Collaborate: Collaborate in personal as well in professional life. There is no doubt that we achieve the best results when we work together.
6. Do it: Do not waste your time. Neither for yourself nor society. You only live once. The time is now.

---

9 Michael Sidler, *Most important success factors for strong and healthy startups at Digital Health Day Zurich, Switzerland* (Oct. 30, 2018).

10 Chris von Rohr, *A Critical Conversation with Chris von Rohr*, APPETITE FOR DISRUPTION (Jan. 2, 2019, 10:05 AM), https://www.youtube.com/c/appetitefordisruption (last visited Feb. 3, 2019).

11 Adolfo Pando Molina, *Digital Transformation Through Effective Culture Change (Part 2)*, LINKEDIN (Jan. 10, 2019; 5:10 PM), https://www.linkedin.com/pulse/digital-transformation-through-effective-culture-part-pando-molina-1e/ (last visited Apr. 11, 2019).

B. RegTech

1. Origin

The term RegTech is short for «Regulatory Technology» and was officially used for the first time on 15 March 2015 in a FinTech report by the UK Government Office of Science and a few days later in the HM Treasury's 2015 Budget Report by the British Finance Minister:[12] «FinTech has the potential to be applied to regulation and compliance to make financial regulation and reporting more transparent, efficient and effective—creating new mechanisms for regulatory technology, ‹RegTech›».[13]

In accordance with *Arner/Barberis/Buckley*, I understand RegTech not as a subcategory of FinTech, but as a separate phenomenon, which can be applied in many regulatory contexts and industry sectors, in contrast to FinTech's inherently financial focus.[14] From a horizontal perspective, RegTech is very broad in scope, because it affects all sectors of industry and creates holistic opportunities. The experiences gained with RegTech in the banking sector are helpful for the overall economy, and knowledge-oriented collaboration is the key for shared success. From a vertical perspective, RegTech can be differentiated between RegTech for companies, in other words in-house Compliance, and RegTech for government bodies, such as supervisory and regulatory authorities—this is also called SupTech.[15]

Certainly, «Regulatory Technologies» already existed before the term RegTech was created. The marriage of technology and regulation in the financial sector (and other industries) has been continuously evolving as illustrated by Arner/Barberis/Buckley in the multiple development stages of RegTech.[16]

2. Definition

To my knowledge, there is currently no universally accepted definition of RegTech. With reference to *Butler/O'Brien*[17] and by explicitly adding a fifth and sixth indent, I define RegTech as information technology (IT) that:

---

12 House of Commons, HM Treasury's 2015 Budget Report 53 Sec. 1.204, 98 Sec. 2.272 (Mar. 18, 2015).

13 Mark Walport, UK Government Chief Scientific Advisor, *FinTech Futures: The UK as a World Leader in Financial Technologies*, U.K. Government for Science 12 (Mar. 13, 2015).

14 Douglas W Artner, Janos Barberis & Ross P Buckley, *FinTech and RegTech in a Nutshell, and the Future in a Sandbox*, CFA Institute Foundation, 10 (2017), https://www.cfainstitute.org/-/media/documents/article/rf-brief/rfbr-v3-n4-1.ashx (last visited Apr. 11, 2019).

15 Swiss Bankers Association, *Interview with David Bundi, Chief Compliance Officer, RegTech: An enabler for established banks* insight #1.18, (Apr. 10, 2018), https://www.swissbanking.org/en/services/insight/insight-1.18/regtech-an-enabler-for-established-banks (last visited Apr. 3, 2019).

16 Douglas W Artner, Janos Barberis & Ross P Buckley, *supra* note 14.

17 Tom Butler & Leona O`Brien, *Understanding RegTech for Digital Regulatory Compliance, in* Disrupting Finance (Palgrave Macmillan, 2019), at 85, 86.

- Helps firms manage regulatory requirements and compliance imperatives by identifying the impacts of regulatory provisions on business models, products and services, functional activities, policies, operational procedures and controls;
- Helps control and manage regulatory, financial and non-financial risks;
- Performs regulatory compliance reporting;
- Enables compliant business systems and data;
- Enables based on its transformative potential, business opportunities, strategic and competitive advantages for firms; and, finally,
- Enables better health and transparency within specific industries and across industry sectors.

3. Technologies

There are several enabling technologies for RegTech. The following technologies are listed according to the amount of investment in their development and application; this ranking is based on multiple recent RegTech studies, and is presented in descending order. Also included are some applied examples.[18]

- Artificial Intelligence (AI) and Machine Learning (ML): Regulatory tracking and reporting, real-time fraud monitoring and reporting, reduction of false positives for Anti-Money-Laundering (AML) monitoring;
- Application Programming Interfaces (API): Integration of plug-and-play technology solutions to core banking systems, automated data reporting to regulators;
- Cloud Computing: Standardized and common data storage, enabling scaling-up operations in compliance functions in a timely and cost-effective manner, most future technologies have a Cloud-native option;
- Big Data Analytics: Reporting, data visualization, gathering insights from structured and unstructured data;
- Blockchain: Early ideas of shared ledgers for central AML and Know Your Customer (KYC) repository for regulators and financial intermediaries driving efficiency gains, immutable record of transactions enabling a traceable audit trail, compliance management, digital identity, cybersecurity;
- Robotic Process Automation (RPA) and Intelligent Process Automation (IPA): Enable productivity and efficiency gains by automating non-val-

---

18 SIA Partners & AEC FinTech, *RegTech Study: European Landscape* 18 (2018); 3 MEDICI, *MEDICI Signature Report: RegTech Report 2018—Executive Summary*, 7/8 (2018), http://sia-partners.com/sites/default/files/mag-reg-tech_finalvers2_1_0.pdf (last visited Apr. 11, 2019); Burnmark, Alvarez & Marsal, *RegTech 2.0* 15 (2018), https://www.burnmark.com/uploads/reports/Burnmark_Report_Jan18_RegTech.pdf (last visited Apr. 3, 2019); Dr. Ulf Klebeck & Dr. Günther Dobrauz-Saldapenna, *RegTech – eine digitale Chance für den europäischen Finanzmarkt*, Recht der Finanzinstrumente (2017), at 180, 181.

ue-added human activities. They reduce time to insight and free-up workforces for more productive purposes;

- Natural Language Processing (NLP): Enables productivity and efficiency gains with AML/KYC obligations, support of front and back office functions via chatbots;
- Biometrics and Visual Analytics: Enables productivity and efficiency gains for ID verification, facial recognition, fingerprints, IRIS scan;
- Cryptography: Enables secure, faster, efficient and more effective data sharing.

II. A Mindset for the Future

A. Financial Institutions

1. How to make decisions?

The reason why I have always been a strong advocate for diversity, concerning e.g., gender, age, nationalities, professional and cultural backgrounds, is pragmatic. It is well accepted that multiple perspectives increase the opportunities to find the best solution.[19] Discussions within a group of highly diverse individuals can, however, be challenging. Discussions need a leader to ensure that the debate stays on track; to keep to discussed topics as well as determining the next actions to be done by whom and by when. Collaboration requires that individuals express their views, and at the same time keep an open, positive, and curious mindset towards the inputs and views of others. Objectivity is paramount in this. Finally yet importantly, is the ability to listen: as the 14th *Dalai Lama* says in one of his famous quotes; «When you talk, you are only repeating what you already know. But if you listen, you may learn something new.» In summary, this is called inclusive decision-making, which is about «picking the brains of the people who are best positioned to evaluate alternatives, provide expert advice, and represent important stakeholders and viewpoints.»[20]

It is clear that RegTech can enhance human capabilities as they can make available heterogeneous data, and incorporate sophisticated data analytic tools into compliance, risk management, and reporting processes. Take, for example, «the incredible advances in predictive analytics, Artificial Intelligence, and data visualization enable decision-makers to actually see into the future (or multiple potential futures) before making a strategic decision. Companies

---

19 Jeff Loucks, James Macaulay, Andy Noronha & Michael Wade, Digital Vortex: How Today's Market Leaders can Beat Disruptive Competitors at Their Own Game (DBT Center Press, 2016) at 278.

20 Loucks et al., *supra* note 19, at 278.

can also mitigate human error and decision–by-fiat through the quantification of alternatives.»[21]

Financial institutions can thereby be properly equipped to make fast and consistently good decisions, particularly when decisions by management and other executive functions are «inclusive» and «augmented». In such cases, the right people can be involved and decisions will be based on the best available data and analysis.[22] This also means, however, that the functions providing information to the decision-makers need to be sufficiently equipped with resources to ensure, advance, and maintain good data quality, as well as advanced regulatory technologies.

2. How to increase innovation?

According to behavioral expert *Neville Gaunt*, CEO of Mind Fit, there are three foundational tenets of mind: The Can-Do attitude (powerful and in control); the Can't-Do attitude (helpless and in control); and the Won't-Do attitude (defensive and over control). This echoes the work of *Dweck*,[23] but in a business context. Furthermore, it breaks down a fixed mindset into Can't-Do and Won't-Do attitudes and behaviors, with Can-Do being the growth mindset. *Neville* and his team support young people, entrepreneurs, and executives of all levels with his «Mind Fit Map» to recognize the source of «unfit» attitudes that propel poor or bad behaviors. Can-Do people are eager to expand and deliver, which allows the organization to prosper and grow. Meanwhile, people with a Can't-Do mindset ignore and avoid, while employees with a Won't-Do mindset are the ones who resist every idea of change. The last ones are the most contagious and destructive, as saboteurs destroy engagement and act as a drag on organizational innovation and growth.

The solutions for a healthy organization is the support of leaders across all departments of the organization from Business to Compliance to IT etc. with a Can-Do behavior that brings out the best solutions and, also, the best in others, which together improves the entire organization. Leaders and employees displaying Can-Do behaviors put the team ahead of personal growth, but none-the-less volunteer at every opportunity. This process of innovation and growth is known as eliminating Behavioral Waste™ and requires new habits and thinking on personal, cultural and systemic levels. This of course means focus, hard work, and practice to keep a healthy company culture, like a body needs physical exercise and the right food to stay healthy.[24] As *Will Durant* opined

---

21 Loucks et al., *supra* note 20, at 137.

22 Loucks et al., *supra* note 20, at 138.

23 Dweck *supra* note 7, at 278.

24 David K Williams, *How To Increase Innovation By Eliminating «Behavioral Waste»* [Interview with Neville Gaunt], Forbes (Mar. 13, 2017 9:28 AM), https://www.forbes.com/sites/davidk-

«We are what we repeatedly do. Excellence is not an act, but a habit.»[25] Unlike most change programs, Mind Fit's approach is to develop a small percentage of the organization into Reality-Driven Leaders, as it is these leaders who are capable of driving and engaging an improved culture in the organization. For more information on the topic, I would like to recommend the publication «Recycling Behavioral Waste» by the authors *Graham Williams and Victor Newman*. The most important power to approach and enable new solutions in the RegTech context at financial institutions is «in your mind», as *Neville* explained to me recently in London at the occasion of a Meetup of our global Disruption Disciples movement.

3. How to help people to change?

Sometimes it is easy to see why some people do not like change: they may fear a shift of power, the need to learn new skills, or the stress of joining a new team. However, sometimes it is a little more complicated. There are employees who have the skills and are clever enough to make a change. They even genuinely support change in general. However, inexplicably, nothing changes. «Even as they hold a sincere commitment to change, many people are unwittingly applying productive energy toward a hidden competing commitment» according to *Kegan and Lahey*.[26] For example, when a manager uncovers an employee's competing commitment, behavior that has seemed irrational and ineffective suddenly becomes stunningly sensible and masterful, but unfortunately, on behalf of a goal that conflicts with what (the manager) and even the employee are trying to achieve.»[27] The processes described in the article «The Real Reason People Won't Change» of *Kegan and Lahey* help to overcome such alleged immunity to change of people and let's be frank: «helping people overcome their limitations to become more successful at work is at the very heart of effective management.»[28]

4. How to lead in times of change?

Although I am trained, through many years of international legal education, and from more than a decade of professional experience in Legal & Compliance, to always think first and then act, I have to admit that in the context of innovating, I have sometimes first acted and then learned through experience, and not analysis or introspection. Hence, I was particularly pleased to come

---

williams/2017/03/13/how-to-increase-innovation-and-growth-by-eliminating-behavioral-waste/ (last visited Feb., 3, 2019).

25 Will Durant, The Story of Philosophy (Outlook, 2012) at 87.

26 Robert Kegan & Lisa Lahey, *The Real Reason People Won't Change,* 11 Harvard Business Review (2001) at 118.

27 Kegan & Lahey, *id.*

28 Kegan & Lahey, *supra* note 26, at 118, 120.

across *Herminia Ibarra's* intelligent and thought-provoking book «Act like a leader, think like a leader.» Today's pace of change, multiple activities and non-stop availability and connectivity has an immense impact on leaders and their abilities to complete tasks. The challenge for leaders is that they are often so busy focusing on current issues and demands, they fail to realize that they remain stuck in outdated mindsets. Herminia's publication is a practical guide on how to change when you also need to lead. It offers advice on how to redefine your job in order to make strategic contributions, diversify your network, and become more playful with your self-concept. To use the words of *Paul Polman*, CEO of Unilever: «The book is for those who really want to make a difference—those willing to act their way into leadership situations they might previously have thought themselves out of.»[29]

5. How to build a Compliance function?

The starting point in building a Compliance function is to focus on the regulatory requirements that need to be met and related duties and responsibilities. The basic duties and responsibilities of the Compliance function at Swiss banks are, for example, published in the currently valid circular on Corporate Governance by the Swiss Financial Market Supervisory Authority.

To meet the regulatory requirements for run-the-bank and often also change-the-bank tasks, a bank is required to have professionals with a sound knowledge of compliance and the banking business. Teams with diverse and complementary skillsets are obviously the best option for organizations. The rise of financial regulation, the emergence of Big Data, processual complexity at banks, technology innovation and growth, the changing demands of customers, and the new business models that are now possible, have all led a significant evolution of the skills and capabilities required from Compliance Officers.

Depending on the specific type of bank, its business model, target markets and customers, I would argue for a Compliance function that is diverse in terms of group expertise in compliance and banking topics, as well as project management skills, an affinity for and basic understanding of technology, Big Data, Analytics, Machine Learning, and Artificial Intelligence. In addition, I would also expect an affinity for Gamification and Design, as well as, depending on the strategy of the bank, knowledge of Open Banking, Cloud, Voice-Technologies, Blockchain and last but not least Cybersecurity. This list might be challenging at first glance, however, this is the time we live in. Banking needs to transform in the coming years to remain profitable. Moreover, a transformation of banking without the inclusion of the Compliance function is not advisable.

---

29 Paul Polman, Act Like a Leader, Think Like a Leader (Harvard Business Review Press, 2015).

Innovation and RegTech solutions will not make Compliance Officers dispensable. They will however significantly change how the Compliance function performs its tasks. RegTech will lead to a much stronger focus on employees' tasks, where the human expertise is absolutely needed. The reason for this change is simple. It is the cost of compliance. Employees are, over the long-term, simply too expensive for performing routine tasks, which can now be performed automatically. RegTech enhances Compliance Officers abilities to perform their tasks, while also enhancing a broad spectrum of possibilities, as indicated in the definition of RegTech presented above. The change from manual tasks to automation, as well as the need to embrace enabling RegTech, will in the near future not be an option, but a necessity.

In the context of digital transformation and automation, one of the biggest challenges is the need to change education. This point was made by *Jack Ma*, Founder of *Alibaba*, China's largest e-commerce company, at the World Economic Forum in Davos, Switzerland:

> *«[O]nly by changing education can our children compete with machines. (The) way we teach is knowledge based. (...) We cannot teach our kids to compete with machines. We have to teach something unique, so a machine can never catch up with us. Machines will do things people will not want to (...) as well as tasks we are not capable of such as those involving too much data for a human to process. The Artificial Intelligence embedded in these machines will be augmenting human performance and freeing us to concentrate on activities where humans are better than machines...activities requiring creativity, strategic thinking, empathy and other soft skills.»*[30]

6. How to improve Compliance trainings?

Traditional classroom or web-based Compliance trainings do not always work sufficiently. Hence, the focus needs to be on behavioral change initially,[9] and then to capture and transfer the knowledge one requires to do the job at hand. Initially this change will focus on assessing what one does currently, and applying a different conscious action for change. If organizations regularly practice these new behaviors—in some cases potentially even with innovative Gamification approaches, Design Thinking, or Compliance-Customer-Journeys for relationship managers—employees will convert conscious actions to unconscious competence. «Imagine children learning to walk. Initially they are unsteady on their feet, and their concentration levels are focused on walking. However, through repetition and practice this conscious behavior converts to unconscious activity», as *Neville Gaunt* recently said to me in a private

---

30 Jack Ma, *Meet the Leader with Jack Ma at Word Economic Forum Davos, Switzerland*, YouTube (Jan. 24, 2018), https://www.youtube.com/watch?v=JW6YMNe52gU (last visited Feb. 3, 2019).

conversation. A process of implicit learning with the result of employees' automatic compliant behavior, without reference to policies, regulations or even a Compliance Officer would be ideal. Imagine how this would transform a bank, when managers and employees could put all their energies in the tasks they are hired to complete, without thinking about regulations?

B. Regulators

In the following sections, I have chosen a few examples of regulators and their amazing teams who are, in my personal view, in the context of RegTech true role models for their mindset and their actions. The enumeration is certainly non-exhaustive and there are other regulators, for example, the Monetary Authority of Singapore (MAS) doing great work in the RegTech space. The following mentioned regulators from the UK and Abu Dhabi stand out due to their innovative and collaborative thinking in the RegTech space and because they truly walk the talk with multiple initiatives.

1. UK Financial Conduct Authority

The most active player in RegTech within the international regulators currently probably is the UK Financial Conduct Authority (FCA).[31] The FCA's own RegTech subsection[32] on the website is the starting point to keep up to date with the latest initiatives of the regulator in the RegTech field. This measure by the FCA to provide an information platform dedicated to RegTech is mindset-wise a smart, simple, informative and visible action, which many other regulators have not yet done. From an FCA perspective, «RegTech applies to new technologies developed to help overcome regulatory challenges in financial services. (The FCA's) aim is to encourage the development of these technologies, as they could benefit consumers and the wider industry.»[33]

a) Calls for Input

In 2015, the FCA issued a Call for Input to find out more about how the regulator could support the adoption and development of RegTech. Through this Call for Input, demos and TechSprints, the FCA identified four important areas of focus:[34]

---

31 Rolf H Weber, *Regtech as a new legal challenge*, 46 Journal of Financial Transformation, (2017) at 10.

32 Financial Conduct Authority, RegTech, https://www.fca.org.uk/firms/regtech (last visited Jan. 2, 2019).

33 Financial Conduct Authority, *id.*

34 Financial Conduct Authority, *Our Work Programme,* https://www.fca.org.uk/firms/regtech/our-work-programme (last visited Jan. 2, 2019).

Efficiency and collaboration:

- Modernizing the Handbook: Using Semantics of Business Vocabulary and Business Rules (SBVR) and Natural Language Processing (NLP) to create machine-readable versions of the Handbook.
- Model Driven Regulation: Exploring the use of semantics in order to map and translate multiple internal and external data ontologies from different domains into a universal format.
- Digital Regulatory Reporting: Linking regulation, compliance procedures, databases and data standards together into a universal machine-readable format.
- Improving Employee Security: Working with behavioral modeling software with psychology and behavior change theory in order to measure and improve personnel security within financial services organizations.

Integration, standards and understanding:

- Standardized models for expressing data and processes with the aim of expressing transactions as collections of economic features and trade events.
- Creating a platform for intra-bank knowledge exchange on regulatory related matters. Adopting a Wiki-style approach to enable the sharing of best practices and knowledge to be crowd sourced.
- Exploring the possibility of a banking industry key global IT risk and controls framework assisting in resolving key challenges in leveraging new technology.

Predict, learn and simplify:

- Intelligent Regulatory Assistant: An intelligent assistant that acts as a regulatory lawyer, and interacts with a client to attempt to populate the authorization forms for regulatory approval.
- Intelligent Regulatory Advisor: An intelligent (Robo-advisor) front-end to a regulatory handbook that guides an applicant through the authorizations process by providing basic automated advice.
- Ascent Experiment: Working with various banks to test the possibilities of using NLP and Artificial Intelligence technologies to interpret the Markets in Financial Instruments Directive II (MiFID-II) regulations, and automatically build and manage a compliance program.

New directions:

- Blockchain Technology for Algorithmic Regulation and Compliance: Investigates the possibility of using Blockchain technology for automating regulation and compliance.

- SmartReg: TechSprint partners of a university and a bank are working on a project to use Smart Contracts and Distributed Ledger Technology to allow the FCA to verify compliance.
- Project Maison: Working with a distributed database technology company and global banks to explore the possibility of using Distributed Ledger Technology for regulatory reporting.

In February 2018, the FCA published a new Call for Input regarding Machine Executable Regulation. The regulator invited views on a PoC, which could potentially make it easier for firms to meet their regulatory reporting requirements. The feedback received and the positive industry participation in the pilot showed that the financial industry wants the FCA to further work on this topic.[35]

b) TechSprints

The FCA recognizes that there is an opportunity to bring market participants together to work collaboratively on shared challenges to assess and solve important issues in financial services via TechSprints since 2016. TechSprints are events that bring together participants from across and (!) outside of financial services to develop technology based ideas or PoCs to address specific industry challenges. These TechSprints are used as one of the FCA's regulatory tools to explore solutions to other challenges and act as a catalyst for change that helps to unlock the potential benefits of technology innovation. The FCA has hosted TechSprints on the following six topics so far: consumer access, unlocking regulatory reporting, financial services and mental health, model-driven machine executable regulatory reporting, AML & Financial Crime and pensions.[36]

In May 2018, the FCA invited me to participate as member of a cross-industry judging panel for the AML & Financial Crime TechSprint. At the largest TechSprint so far, with 260 participants from 100+ firms from 16 countries as well as regulators and law enforcement agencies from the United States, Europe, Middle East and Asia Pacific, we had the opportunity to evaluate solutions, which the teams had developed over three days. Some of the technologies and prototype solutions that were produced and showcased by the teams included:

35 Financial Conduct Authority, *Call for Input: Using Technology to achieve smarter regulatory reporting*, https://www.fca.org.uk/publications/feedback-statements/call-input-using-technology-achieve-smarter-regulatory-reporting (last visited Jan. 2, 2019).

36 Financial Conduct Authority, *Techsprints*, https://www.fca.org.uk/firms/regtech/techsprints (last visited Jan. 2, 2019).

- A shared database of «bad actors», secured and distributed using Distributed Ledger Technology. The database would allow a financial institution to query whether a new customer had been rejected by another financial institution due to financial crime activities or concerns.
- Natural Language Processing, topic modeling and text analytics to enhance financial crime-focused transaction monitoring solutions within financial institutions.
- Graph/network analytics to more readily identify relationships between entities to aid in due diligence and ongoing monitoring of potentially suspicious entities and activities.[37]

This AML & Financial Crime TechSprint has without a doubt been one of the very best events I have participated during my career. Highly committed, international, diverse, cross-industry teams met to work together and investigate how new technologies and greater international collaboration could help to improve prevention and detection rates in AML and Financial Crime. Notably, the United Nations (UN) estimated that yearly less than 1% of US$1.6 trillion of money laundered via the global financial system is intercepted globally. These are the proceeds of human, drug, arms and endangered wildlife trafficking, slavery, corruption, fraud and other crimes.[38]

Hence, the right mindset as shown during the TechSprint as well as in the keynote speech of *Christopher Woolard*, Executive Director of Strategy & Competition at the FCA, is the one of greater collaboration in fighting financial crime: What we need is a «network to beat a network. It is only by working together, pooling our resources and sharing our expertise, that we will achieve the real and tangible change we're all seeking. The truth is that without a harmonized approach, there can be no control. If we're truly going to cut the Gordian knot that is financial crime, we—both regulators and industry—have to collaborate. The potential when we collaborate is enormous.»[39]

Furthermore, *Woolard* advocated to embrace new technologies to combat money laundering. He explained that we need: «Machine Learning to improve the detection of suspicious activity, Artificial Intelligence driven anti-impersonation checks and Distributed Ledger Technology to improve the traceability of transactions are just some of the real, practicable solutions technology has gifted us. These benefits of such advances are obvious. Not only in reduc-

37 Financial Conduct Authority, *AML and Financial Crime International TechSprint*, https://www.fca.org.uk/events/techsprints/aml-financial-crime-international-techsprint (last visited Jan. 2, 2019).

38 Financial Conduct Authority, *id.*

39 Christopher Woolard, *Technology and global ties: turning the tide on financial crime*, Financial Crime & AML TechSprint in London (May 24, 2018), https://www.fca.org.uk/news/speeches/technology-and-global-ties-turning-tide-financial-crime (last visited Apr. 11, 2019).

ing the social cost of financial crime but in reducing the burden on firms of detecting it.»[40]

The follow-on AML & Financial Crime TechSprint is already planned to explore the potential for new technologies to enhance information sharing across jurisdictions.[41]

c) Global Sandbox Consultation[42]

In February 2019, the FCA launched the Global Sandbox Consultation. The FCA received 50 responses to this consultation. Overall, feedback to the consultation was positive. Key themes to emerge in the feedback were:

- Regulatory co-operation: Respondents were supportive of the idea of the initiative providing a setting for regulators to collaborate on common challenges or policy questions that firms face in different jurisdictions.
- Speed to market: Respondents cited one of the main advantages for the global sandbox could be reducing the time it takes to bring ideas to new international markets.
- Governance: Feedback highlighted the importance of the project being transparent and fair to those potential firms wishing to apply for cross-border testing.
- Emerging technologies/business models: A wide range of topics and subject matters were highlighted in the feedback, particularly those with notable cross-border application. Among issues highlighted were Artificial Intelligence, Distributed Ledger Technology, data protection, regulation of securities and Initial Coin Offerings (ICOs), KYC and AML.

d) Global Financial Innovation Network[43]

Based on the FCA's initial proposal to create a global sandbox, the following 12 financial regulators and related organizations launched the Global Financial Innovation Network (GFIN) in August 2018: Abu Dhabi Global Market (ADGM), Autorité des marchés financiers (AMF, Quebec), Australian Securities & Investments Commission (ASIC), Central Bank of Bahrain (CBB), Bureau of Consumer Financial Protection (BCFP, USA), Dubai Financial Services Authority (DFSA), Financial Conduct Authority (FCA, UK), Guernsey Financial Services Commission (GFSC), Hong Kong Monetary Authority (HKMA), Monetary Authority of Singapore (MAS), Ontario Securities Commission (OSC, Canada) and Consultative Group to Assist the Poor (CGAP).

---

40 Woolard, *Id.*

41 Financial Conduct Authority, *AML and Financial Crime International TechSprint*, *supra* note 37.

42 Financial Conduct Authority, *Global Financial Innovation Network*, https://www.fca.org.uk/publications/consultation-papers/global-financial-innovation-network (last visited Jan. 2, 2019).

43 Financial Conduct Authority, *Global Financial Innovation Network*, *supra* note 42.

While the group is in its infancy, it is keen to hear from other interested regulators or related organizations who wish to get involved. The network seeks to provide a more efficient way for innovative firms to interact with regulators, helping them navigate between countries as they look to scale new ideas. It will also create a new framework for co-operation between financial services regulators on innovation related topics, sharing different experiences and approaches. The consultation sets out the three main functions of the GFIN:

- Act as a network of regulators to collaborate and share experience of innovation in respective markets, including emerging technologies and business models;
- Provide a forum for joint policy work and discussions; and
- Provide firms with an environment in which to trial cross-border solutions.

2. Financial Services Regulatory Authority of the Abu Dhabi Global Market

a) A Technology-First Regulator

A financial regulator with an exemplary mindset who absolutely walks the talk is the Financial Services Regulatory Authority (FSRA) of the Abu Dhabi Global Market (AGDM). The international financial center of ADGM is located in the capital city of the United Arab Emirates and commenced operations on 21 October 2015. *Richard Teng*, CEO of the FSRA explains:

> *«Being a relatively new regulator established at a time when FinTech was a regulatory focal point and enabler of innovation globally, we had the opportunity to be a technology-first regulator, and reimagine the way we supervise and interact with financial markets and firms in the digital economy of the future. We were able to design and build our regulatory regime and structure from a clean slate taking in the latest best practices from over the world, including launching the first regulatory sandbox (the RegLab) in the MENA region in 2016.»*[44]

Having been a torchbearer and supporter of RegTech on countless international stages and workshops in my previous role as Compliance Officer and now as Head of RegTech, it is simply superb to listen to a technology-first regulator when *Teng* continues:

44 As noted by *Richard Teng*, CEO of Financial Services Regulatory Authority (FSRA) of Abu Dhabi Global Market (ADGM) in an E-mail to the author by *Wai Lum Kwok*, Capital Markets Executive Director, dated Dec. 17, 2018. On file with author.

«As a regulator, we are constantly seeking to achieve better regulatory outcomes in the industry. We see RegTech applications such as Artificial Intelligence, Machine Learning and advanced analytics offering enormous potential to improve on compliance outcomes and standards, while reducing complexity, costs and friction. With better tools, financial institutions can become more transparent and capable of good governance and decision-making. So accelerating and fostering the adoption of RegTech forms an important part of ADGM's wider objective to encourage best practices and raise industry standards.»[45]

b) e-Know-Your-Customer

The FSRA recently led an industry consortium of financial institutions in the UAE to develop a prototype of an electronic Know-Your-Customer (e-KYC) utility for the industry, where financial institutions and participants can share and validate basic customer identity information using Distributed Ledger Technology. The FSRA developed a PoC to test the operational and technological model of the e-KYC utility, as well as developed a governance framework and commercial model on which the e-KYC utility can operate on an inclusive, secure and sustainable basis. «By harnessing the power of RegTech, the e-KYC project demonstrates tangible benefits that may be offered by an e-KYC utility for financial institutions in the UAE. In addition to enhancing KYC checks across the industry, the utility can achieve significant cost efficiencies and financial inclusion driven by unified KYC standards and data protection regulations», said *Teng* on the successful conclusion of the first industry e-KYC utility project with UAE financial institutions.[46]

In another initiative, the FSRA showcased at the FinTech Summit in Abu Dhabi[47] in September 2018 their work on machine executable regulation as *Barry West*, Head of Emerging Technology at FSRA explained:

«By using Natural Language Processing, semantics and modeling techniques we were able to turn our AML rules into a digital ruleset. This was represented as a decision tree that enabled firms to map directly into their compliance procedures, their business processes and even their database designs. For demonstration purposes, we enacted a policy change and were able to see how this rippled all the way through to the onboarding app of the firm. The process of doing this not only highlighted the potential for

---

45 *Id.*

46 Richard Teng, *ADGM Successfully Concludes 1st Industry E-KYC Utility Project with UAE Financial Institutions* (Dec. 4, 2018), https://www.adgm.com/mediacentre/press-releases/adgm-successfully-concludes-1st-industry-e-kyc-utility-project-with-uae-financial-institutions (last visited Apr. 3, 2019).

47 FinTech Abu Dhabi, https://fintechabudhabi.com (last visited Jan. 2, 2019).

regulators to draft, implement, update and monitor regulation in completely new ways but also offered tangible proof in how we could move regulation from analog to digital.»[48]

c) Cloud-based Digital Sandbox

In 2019, the FSRA will be offering a Digital Sandbox, a Cloud-based platform for financial institutions to test with FinTechs regulatory engagements.[49] The Digital Sandbox will be API-enabled based on standards provided by the FSRA to ensure swift and safe connectivity and to promote easier collaboration among participants. This mechanism will enable firms to develop and test appropriate RegTech solutions and to better supervise new and emerging FinTech solutions with real-time monitoring capabilities. Last but not least, the FSRA works in its RegLab with RegTech firms to test solutions that embed regulatory requirements into tokens through smart contracts. Certainly, the achievements of the FSRA in such a short space of time, is underpinned by the immense importance they place on collaboration, as I learned from my interview with *Way Lum Kwok*, Capital Markets Executive Director at FSRA. Hence, there is no surprise that the FSRA is a founding member of the Global Financial Innovation Network.[50]

3. Swiss Financial Market Supervisory Authority

Mark Branson, CEO of the Swiss Financial Market Supervisory Authority (FINMA), positively mentioned RegTech in the context of FINMA's approach to market supervision at its annual media conference 2017:

> *«The tools and facilities available to our market supervision specialists have also improved enormously. Big data—some people refer to it as regulation technology or RegTech—has helped enormously, not least because it enables us to reconstruct complex cases. The data trail contains all the information we need.»*[51]

The theme of his next speech at the annual media conference in 2018 focused on technology:

---

48 FinTech Abu Dhabi, *id.*

49 Wai Lum Kwok, *supra* note 44.

50 Financial Conduct Authority, *Global Financial Innovation Network*, *supra* note 42.

51 Mark Branson, *Market Integrity: a Strategic Priority for FINMA*, FINMA Annual Media Conference (Apr. 4, 2017), https://www.finma.ch/en/~/media/finma/dokumente/dokumentencenter/myfinma/finma-publikationen/referate-und-artikel/20170404_jmk2017_rede_bnm.pdf?la=en (last visited Apr. 2, 2019).

«Innovation cannot be prescribed by the state—the industry itself has to step up and innovate. But we as a supervisory authority do have a role, in ensuring that the regulatory framework makes technological advancement possible. This does not mean orchestrating innovation. It means removing barriers to entry for the sake of healthy competition. (...) Our job is to identify and monitor the risks, and where required, to step in. (...) We recognize the potential that FinTech and Blockchain technology offer to the Swiss financial services industry. We have repeatedly demonstrated our commitment to innovation. FINMA regulations is technology-neutral. In other words, we make no distinction between digital and analog channels. (...) We want to see healthy competition through innovation, but not at the cost of the integrity of the Swiss financial sector. We are as passionately anti-crime as we are pro-innovation.»[52]

It is a good mindset, in my view, but there are more things the Swiss regulator can do in RegTech in future compared to other regulators like the FCA, MAS or FSRA.

RegTech is, however, neither new to the Swiss academic[53] world nor to other institutions and organization in Switzerland. In March 2016, a member of the House of Representatives filed a motion[54] with the title «Improvement of the Digitization in the Regulation (RegTech)» where the Federal Council was asked to analyze the possibilities for broadening the scope of the application of RegTech initiatives.[55] The Federal Council's Report on RegTech[56] on this motion stated that there is already good communication and collaboration between authorities, regulated entities and tech-providers in Switzerland, which need to be continued and strengthened. It is clear for all Swiss stakeholders, that technological innovation is key to preserving and even increasing the competitiveness of a strong financial center, as well as for all other industry sectors of the country.

---

52 Mark Branson, *Technology and the financial industry—opportunity or risk?*, FINMA ANNUAL MEDIA CONFERENCE (Mar. 27, 2018), https://www.finma.ch/en/~/media/finma/dokumente/dokumentencenter/myfinma/finma-publikationen/referate-und-artikel/20180327-rd-bnm-jmk-2018.pdf?la=en (last visited Apr. 2, 2019).

53 Franca Contratto, *«RegTech»: Digitale Wende für Aufsicht und Compliance*, 15 Jusletter, 1 (2016); Ulf Klebeck & Guenther Dobrauz-Saldapenna, *RegTech – eine digitale Chance für den europäischen Finanzmarkt*, Recht der Finanzinstrumente, 180, 181 (2017); Rolf H Weber, *Regtech as a new legal challenge*, 46 JOURNAL OF FINANCIAL TRANSFORMATION, 10 (2017).

54 Martin Landolt, *Postulat «Förderung der Digitalisierung in der Regulierung (RegTech)*, NATIONALRAT, 16.3256 (Mar. 18, 2016).

55 Rolf H Weber, *supra* note 53.

56 Swiss Federal Council, *RegTech Report of the Swiss Federal Council of 27 June 2018 to the motion of* Martin Landolt, *Postulat «Förderung der Digitalisierung in der Regulierung (RegTech)*, NATIONALRAT, 16.3256 (Mar. 18, 2016).

As a permanent member of RegTech working groups at economiesuisse and of the Swiss FinTech Innovations Association (SFTI),[57] and due to the participation in continuous RegTech initiatives with the Swiss Bankers Association (SBA), I can confirm that there is a positive spirit towards the use of RegTech in Switzerland.

Recently, *Erich Herzog*, Member of the Executive Board at economiesuisse sent to me the following statement for this book:

> *«It goes without saying that economiesuisse of course fully supports the private initiatives and the flabbergasting innovation of all the specialized companies that help tackling the increasing regulation by technological means and that we also fully support a digitized administration with respective interfaces that allow efficient interaction with companies and citizens. The latter is one of our most important current requests vis-à-vis the authorities.»*[58]

A positive commitment and mindset towards RegTech by the Swiss Bankers Association is continuously communicated in publications in various media[59] as well as on their own website: «RegTech solutions facilitate the efficient and effective implementation of regulatory requirements and therefore make a significant contribution to strengthening the competitiveness of the Swiss financial center.»[60]

To close the perspective on RegTech in Switzerland, I would like to share the following quote for this publication from *Urs Bigger*, Founder and Honorary Chairman of the Swiss Association of Compliance Officers (SACO)[61], founded in 1998 inter alia for the purpose of exchanging opinions and experiences: «Compliance Officers have not to be afraid of the RegTech evolution. It will not replace them, but rather ensure that all compliance risks are systematically and comprehensively identified to provide a robust tool for the assessment, management and reporting of those risks by the compliance function.»

---

57 Swiss FinTech Innovations, https://swissfintechinnovations.ch (last visited Apr. 2, 2019).

58 E-Mail to author dated Dec. 13, 2019. On file with author.

59 Swiss Bankers Association, *Interview with Andreas Barfuss, Head of Financial Market Law of the Swiss Bankers Association, RegTech: An enabler for established banks*, insight #1.18, (Apr. 10, 2018), https://www.swissbanking.org/en/services/insight/insight-1.18/regtech-an-enabler-for-established-banks (last visited Apr. 3, 2019); Richard Hess, *Regtech: Digitale Regulierung nützt dem Schweizer Finanzplatz*, Finews (Jul. 9, 2018), https://www.finews.ch/news/finanzplatz/32456-regtech-finanzplatz-schweiz-richard-hess-bankiervereinigung-sbvg (last visited Apr. 2, 2019).

60 Swiss Bankers Association, Position of the Swiss Bankers Association (SBA) on RegTech, https://www.swissbanking.org/en/topics/digitisation/regtech (last visited Jan. 2, 2019).

61 Swiss Association of Compliance Officers, https://www.complianceofficers.ch (last visited Apr. 2. 2019).

C. RegTech Providers

1. Team

According to research about how venture capitalists make investment decisions, the most important factor that contributes to successful as well as to failed investments is the team.[62] A passionate, let's-do-it-together team spirit is the starting point. Sufficient professional expertise to evaluate if there is a need for the offering the firm aims to provide, as well as the expertise to build the offering, and knowledge on how to sell it to the customer are crucial for a RegTech firm. The ultimate responsibility to build and lead a successful team lies with the CEO, independently of the size of the organization. Teams that are unbalanced with regard to the skills and professional experience at RegTech firms, as a result of employing almost exclusively tech- and sales-people without any regulatory or compliance professionals, or by hiring regulatory academics and professionals with a lack of people understanding technology and entrepreneurship, is not fruitful. At the same time, leading means taking the right and sometimes tough decisions, especially when friends are involved in the business, as superbly illustrated in the recorded interview «Tough Decisions. From a Garage to an Arena» by *Guenther Dobrauz-Saldapenna* with *Jon Schaffer*, which can be viewed on the Disruption Disciples website.[63]

One of the secrets to success lies in the perfect diversity of skills, knowing that true diversity leads to more challenging discussions but ultimately also to better results, if the leader manages to keep together the team. It is the mindset of the CEO or the tone of the top that gives the direction with regard to team spirit, passion, collaboration, diversity and a healthy culture of challenge and trust. At the same time, for a «bottom-up business approach (and) profound in its simplicity»[64] I would like to recommend *Guy Kawasaki's* book: «The Art of the Start: The Time-Tested, Battle-Hardened Guide for Anyone Starting Anything».

2. Product

According to my professional experience and interaction with startups for many years, it seems that many RegTech solutions provided by RegTech startups are not yet completed or ready to be sold to banks. Certainly, the challenge of startups to close deals by selling solutions in place to prove «the right to

---

62 Paul Gompers, William Gornall, Steven N Kaplan & Ilya A Strebulaev, *How do venture capitalists make decisions? Working Paper 22587*, National Bureau of Economic Research (Sep. 2016), http://www.nber.org/papers/w22587 (last visited Apr. 3, 2019).

63 Jon Schaffer, *Tough Decisions*, Appetite For Disruption (Nov. 11, 2018), https://www.appetitefordisruption.tv/conversations/jon-schaffer (last visited Jan. 2, 2019).

64 Pierre Omidyar, Guy Kawasaki's The Art of the Start: The Time-Tested, Battle-Hardened Guide for Anyone Starting Anything, (Portfolio, 2015) cover page.

exist» and to raise more capital to further develop the initial product is tough. Remember however, you never have a second chance to make a first impression. The ultimate aim for a RegTech startup cannot be a long list of PoCs and RegTech Awards. The provided RegTech solutions need, from a product point of view, to have a realistic chance to be implemented and used in day-to-day business life. RegTech is a new with regard to the latest technologies, which will transform the way we handle regulations. However, to a large extent, it is up to the RegTech providers to build trust in RegTech with what each RegTech firm does day by day. The reality is that financial institutions already have enough projects and issues to solve and are mostly short of time and resources with regard to the continuing workload. Hence, no bank is waiting for another PoC, unless there is a realistic chance that the product in scope works. In favor of the entire RegTech movement, the mindset of RegTech providers must always be to reach out to financial institutions with products that actually work.

3. Timing

Timing is everything, they say (in addition to many other things). A successful serial entrepreneur and CEO recently told me that his team had already completely developed a product some years ago and that they collectively decided not to go to market with the product because of the market conditions at the time, or in other words because the market was not yet ready for it. Now the time is right and they will go to market in 2019. There are situations where the technology is ready and the solution makes absolutely sense, but where the financial market is not yet ready to buy the product for reasons related to legacy core banking systems, alleged regulatory uncertainty, wrong incentivization of decisions makers, ignorance, etc.

The timeframe for the implementation of RegTech solutions in banks is far longer than most RegTech firms expect according to a survey report by Burnmark in 2018.[65] It discovered that most of the RegTech firms in the survey had only done PoCs with banks. *Burnmark*'s report shows the following findings from the survey: Many interviewed startups spoke about the time for internal go-ahead and «handling approvals from multiple areas within the same bank as the biggest challenge. In most cases, they will need to connect with internal IT and legacy systems and this could cause a significant resource drain as well. Operationally, the typical institution uses fragmented legacy technologies and equally fragmented data sources. The integration with the siloed data infrastructure of the banks also becomes a bottleneck in the onboarding process. This aside, it is notoriously tough for a RegTech startup to negotiate

---

65 Burnmark, Alvarez & Marsal, *RegTech 2.0* 15 (2018), https://www.burnmark.com/uploads/reports/Burnmark_Report_Jan18_RegTech.pdf (last visited Apr. 3, 2019).

with an entity whose IT, business and procurement departments are often individually influential and organizationally aloof.»[66]

4. Decision Maker

Finally, yet importantly, RegTech firms need to close deals. The questions is: «Who's the decision maker?» There is no single answer to this question. The person in charge of deciding about the go-ahead with a RegTech product can be very different, even for banks of the same size, market and location. The best way to approach this issue for RegTech startups is to listen to the potential customer and get to know the individual institution and its structures as well and as fast as possible. In fact, based on the complex organization of most banks, the CEO of a RegTech startup does well to hire employees with previous professional experience of the processes and structures of banks, or to collaborate with key players in the market who know the banks from previous and current projects, who build trust into the sales conversation based on their longtime relations with the customer and their strong brand. Firms must remember that their RegTech offer is first and foremost there to help the banks; and it helps to be likable when meeting the decision maker. These two aspects are questions of mindset too.

III. Enabling Breakthroughs

A. Enabling Digital Regulatory Compliance

«The technologies required to make Digital Regulatory Compliance and enhanced Risk Management a reality exist», said Professor *Tom Butler* at his keynote speech on Digital Regulatory Compliance[67] at the #RegTechtalks conference in Zug, Switzerland.[68] He participated in the recent UK RegTech Sprint and observed the Digital Regulatory Reporting (DRR) pilot, both of which were undertaken by the Bank of England and the FCA in conjunction with over 50 participants from across the financial industry in the UK. «These projects demonstrate the art of the possible», he stated. The RegTech Sprint took

---

66 *Id.*

67 Tom Butler, *Digital Regulatory Compliance: Necessary And Sufficient Conditions*, #REGTECHTALKS CONFERENCE, ZUG, SWITZERLAND, (Jun. 21, 2018) (Speech).

68 This first #RegTechtalks conference on 21 June 2018, which I had the opportunity to host, actually turned later out to be the most influential and biggest RegTech event in Switzerland so far with guests from most key financial institutions, all major banking associations in Switzerland, academia, lawyers, technology and regulatory specialists as well as guests from RegTech firms from across the world.

place during the last two weeks of November 2017, while the DRR pilot was executed from June through to December 2018.

Concurrent with these projects were the RegTech Council's New Initiatives Project, which Professor *Butler* also participated in, and two other RegTech pilots with global banks. He said that the latter pilot project used AI (not autonomous AI, it was ML and NLP trained by human lawyers) to demonstrate how a machine could read MiFID II and provide a list of obligations for supervised firms.

In the RegTech Sprint and RegTech Council's New Initiatives Project, Professor *Butler* and his researchers used a combination of AI (NLP) and human expertise to unpack regulations into a human and machine-readable format using standards-based semantic technologies. He stated that «this went one step beyond the pilot with the banks, in that the regulatory knowledge was captured in a knowledge base.» In this approach, the regulatory and related legal semantics were expressed as rules (obligations, prohibitions, and permissions) and vocabulary definitions on a web application. NLP assists the lawyer to do this. These are then stored in a knowledge base (organizational memory) so that regulatory, legal and business semantics and rules can be linked and queried. His experience in one of the FCA Sandbox's led him to conclude that if an organization captures its policies, standards and procedures and controls, and related information, in a knowledge base, then it is possible to map from a specific regulatory obligation straight through to a control or controls. He indicated that such an approach makes possible another type of AI-Knowledge Representation using regulatory and business compliance semantic models.

Professor *Butler* explained at the #RegTechtalks conference in Zug that a semantic model (i.e., an ontology) is simply a digital model of how information about the world is captured and expressed: «Think of a corporate WiKi sitting on top of a database, e.g., Wikipedia and DBpedia, and you get the idea. All this is working in practice». If financial institutions use such models, they can ensure compliance with BCBS239, as they can also be used as data meta-models to automate data gathering for regulatory reporting, compliance checking and risk management.

He related that the Bank of England and the FCA have demonstrated that an application may then be coded based on the logical models to permit organizations to determine compliance and to perform regulatory reporting using XBRL. The outcomes can then be stored on a Smart Contract Blockchain to enhance the integrity of supervision.

Put in the words of *Patrick Barnert*, visionary business leader and RegTech expert, at the same #RegTechtalks conference in Zug as mentioned before: «It's about disrupting the entire value chain by transforming the complete process from the beginning with machine-readable regulations until the very end with improved service offerings at lower cost for the clients.» In summary, less waste, less risks, less costs for all, with improved services and quality for all clients. I could not agree more.

B. Enabling Data Analytics Strategies and taking Banking to the Cloud

The current state of some core banking functions, coupled with the associated complexities and limitations of analytical technologies, are the source of major strategic challenges to banks, according to *Hans Kuhn*, Partner at the law firm Zulauf Partners and expert in Swiss and European banking and financial market law. Many banks are burdened by legacy IT architectures that are overly complex, inefficient, and extremely costly to run and maintain. *Kuhn* argues that this results from the fact that some banks have scores of transactions processing systems that each use different business logic structures and programming languages. Moreover, core banking and transactions systems are often siloed and separate from analytical systems used for accounting, risk management and regulatory reporting. Luckily, according to *Butler/O'Brien*, some financial institutions have started to address such core problems of data governance and data virtualization using semantic technologies that enable interoperability between systems.[69]

However, products and services in the financial services sector are still defined by complex bespoke agreements, according to *Kuhn*. Further, unlike real-world contracts (e.g., an agreement for the sale of machinery where money is exchanged against goods or services), financial contracts always involve, and only involve, (current or future) cash flows (i.e., money is exchanged against money). It is therefore relatively easy to describe these cash flows in a very precise, logic and machine-readable manner using a limited number of variables (amount, currency, time, payer, and payee). Importantly, common cash-flow patterns can be condensed into a limited number of standard contracts. For example, the Algorithmic Contract Types Unified Standards (ACTUS) capture nearly the complete universe of known financial instruments in less than 40 standardized contracts, ranging from simple debt or equity instrument to options and derivatives and secured or securitized instruments. According to *Kuhn* For each contract type, current and future cash-flow patterns can be fully described in formulas and their algorithmic representations, making financial contracts prime candidates to be digitized using smart contract technologies.

---

69 Tom Butler & Leona O`Brien, *Understanding RegTech for Digital Regulatory Compliance*, *in* DISRUPTING FINANCE (Palgrave Macmillan, 2019) at 85, 98.

An important first step regarding contract standardization has been made by the Legal Entity Identifier (LEI) initiative, which was a part of the derivatives market reform implemented after the financial crisis of 2008.[70] The LEI is a system for the unique identification of financial market participants to facilitate the management and control of risks by both the private sector and public authorities. So far, the LEI was limited to facilitate the reporting obligations for derivative transactions, but there is no reason why it should not be possible to extend the scope of this initiative to any company or legal entity which might become party to a financial contract.

For financial institutions starting out with the use of data and advanced analytic technologies, *Jim Marous*, Co-Publisher of The Financial Brand, advises—in his current resolutions for digital banking success—that banks should first develop a data analytics strategy that is big in long-term potential, but one that provides interim milestones based on the reality of available resources.[71] Entire banks cannot be changed at once, and each bank is different in its structure, strategy, and culture. Hence, it is important from an internal and cultural point of view to develop pilot projects that deliver small but impactful wins—early and consistently.[72]

RegTech offers the opportunity for more databased, integrated, and comprehensive compliance which increases a company's quality of work and transparency. Information gained via advanced data analytics will create benefits for risk functions and for the business. Think about the possibility of a single internal data highway with all customer information available to serve clients in an agile manner, while being in full control of all data, with no concerns for data governance, or any new regulations regarding data.[73]

For entirely new banks, or banks reconsidering the longtime impact of IT legacy systems to their business, new solutions like Cloud-native core banking systems are emerging. They promise banks the ability to fully realize the benefits of Cloud computing by providing the agility to quickly add new products with high scalability, accommodate shifts in banks' strategies or business models, or react to external changes in the market. The potential for such advances has been discussed for some time by commentators in IT communi-

---

70 European Securities and Markets Authority, *Briefing Legal Entity Identifier (LEI), ESMA70-145-238.*

71 Jim Marous, *5 Resolutions For Digital Banking,* The Financial Brand (Dec. 30, 2018, 6:05 PM), https://thefinancialbrand.com/78634/goals-resolutions-digital-banking/ (last visited Feb. 3, 2019).

72 *Id.*

73 Swiss Bankers Association, *Interview with David Bundi, Chief Compliance Officer, RegTech: An enabler for established banks,* insight #1.18, (Apr. 10, 2018), https://www.swissbanking.org/en/services/insight/insight-1.18/regtech-an-enabler-for-established-banks (last visited Apr. 3, 2019).

ties.[74] In a Swiss context, «Enabling the Cloud»[75] was the title of a recent article by *Martin Hess*, Chief Economist of the Swiss Bankers Association, in December 2018 and leading global consulting firms are currently providing offerings to take the Swiss private banking to the Cloud.[76] In this spirit the Swiss Bankers Association, on 26th of March 2019 published its Cloud Guidelines for the use of cloud services in banking.[77] The guidelines contain recommendations intended to help banks migrate their data to the cloud more easily and securely. Moreover, the upgrade to 5G in mobile communication in near future will also undoubtedly change the way we interact with technology in banking on a day-to-day basis, as has been repeatedly pointed out to me in recent discussions with my colleague and RegTech expert *Michael Werner*.

To conclude, as I have been saying for a long time on- and off- stage regarding the future of banking: many indications point to the Cloud.

C. Enabling Artificial Intelligence with a Human Mindset

The term Artificial Intelligence (AI) is increasingly used in publications and media using a variety of different meanings. For the purpose of this article, AI is defined as «the theory and development of computer systems able to perform tasks normally requiring human intelligence, such as visual perception, speech recognition, decision-making, and translation between languages» according to the Oxford Dictionary.[78]

AI is one of the most transformative forces of our time and the future, with the capability to generate tremendous benefits for customers, financial institutions, and the entire society.[79] However, AI also gives rise to risks, which need to be properly managed by humans. *Patrick Armstrong*, Senior Officer for Financial Innovation at the European Securities and Markets Authority

---

74 Bobby Hellard, *IBM chosen to push cloud-native banking platform: Thought Machine sees tech giant as the partner to accelerate its Vault platform*, IT Pro (Dec. 4, 2018, 5:32 PM), https://www.itpro.co.uk/cloud/32500/ibm-chosen-to-push-cloud-native-banking-platform (last visited Feb. 3, 2019).

75 Swiss Bankers Association, *Interview with Martin Hess, Chief Economist, Enabling the cloud*, insight #4.18 (Dec. 12, 2018), https://www.swissbanking.org/en/services/insight/insight-4.18/enabling-the-cloud (last visited Apr. 3, 2019).

76 Marcel Tschanz, *Taking Swiss private banking to the cloud*, PwC (Jan. 5, 2018, 6:50 PM), https://www.pwc.ch/en/insights/fs/swiss-private-banking-cloud.html (last visited Feb. 3, 2019).

77 Swiss Bankers Association, *Guidelines*, https://www.swissbanking.org/en/services/library/guidelines (last visited Apr. 15, 2019).

78 Larry D Hall, *Some financial regulatory implications of artificial intelligence*, 100 Journal of Economics and Business 55 (2017); Definition of Artificial Intelligence, Oxford Dictionaries, https://en.oxforddictionaries.com/definition/artificial_intelligence.

79 European Commission's High-Level Expert Group on Artificial Intelligence, DRAFT, Ethics Guidelines for Trustworthy AI, p. i (Dec. 18, 2018).

(ESMA), warned, «it is not without risks» when he spoke in 2017 about the many benefits for financial institutions to use regulatory technologies. Thus *Lucy McNulty* stated that «in collaborating with RegTech firms, financial institutions cannot delegate responsibilities for compliance and risk management activities. Instead the ultimate responsibility remains with the regulated financial institution.»[80]

A critical examination of the potential impact of AI concerning RegTech and other areas is crucial from a legal, compliance, and ethical perspective. These are topics I am currently working on and which I will address in upcoming publications and keynotes in near future.

The impact on AI needs at the same time also to be critically assessed from a business-orientated and customer-focused perspective. The area of intelligent virtual assistants, often powered by AI, is for example one of the customer-focused areas with most development in future according to the Business Innovation Review in 2018.[81] Speech Technology Expert *Carmina Jaro* holds that virtual voice assistants are an operational advantage to businesses using them «to complement human customer service»,[82] as long as there is a «seamless connection to a live agent in place»,[83] as there will always be unique customer queries that machines will not be able to handle.

The challenge for financial institutions aiming to use AI solutions starts however earlier. Firms need first to focus on data quality including data identification, enrichment, and integration. Then, to solve complex problems, today's algorithms need significant training by subject matter experts to deliver quality results. This means, AI hype aside, that human—and with that costly—intervention is still very much needed now. If we think about data as Machine Learning's strength according to *Lo Giudice*, then «knowledge engineering's strength is human wisdom. Used together, enterprises can dramatically accelerate the development of AI applications.»[84] We need more time and there is more time. For sure, the impact of AI to our lives and businesses in future will be substantial in my view.

---

80 Lucy McNulty, *Top regulator: City firms must bear responsibility for RegTech risks*, FINANCIAL NEWS (Dec. 20, 2019, 6:23 PM), https://www.fnlondon.com/articles/city-firms-must-bear-responsibility-for-regtech-risk-20170516 (last visited Apr. 2, 2019).

81 Denis Carter, *How real is the impact of artificial intelligence?*, 35(3) BUSINESS INFORMATION REVIEW (2018) at 99, 113.

82 Carmina Jaro, *How can chatbots increase your sales?*, LINKEDIN (Apr. 25, 2018), https://www.linkedin.com/pulse/how-can-chatbots-increase-your-sales-carmina-jaro/ (last visited Apr. 1, 2019).

83 Carmina Jaro, *Should I build my own chatbot?*, LINKEDIN (Feb. 6, 2018), https://www.linkedin.com/pulse/should-i-build-my-own-chatbot-carmina-jaro (last visited Apr. 1, 2019).

84 LO GIUDICE, D, GOETZ, M, PURCELL, B, LE CLAIR, C & GUALTIERI, M, PREDICTIONS 2019: ARTIFICIAL INTELLIGENCE NO PAIN, NO GAIN WITH ENTERPRISE AI. (Forrester Research, 2018).

Spiros Margaris, one of the leading global influencers in AI & FinTech argues, «not everything that is possible (with AI) should be done without thinking very carefully about the consequences to society and the world».[85] Firms focusing on using AI will need to have people with the right mindset in place. That is people with a sound judgment, who ask questions and who look at the broader context of machine recommendations and not just at its literal output.[86] Moreover, firms will need a new kind of empathetic «AI-Human-Translators» who are able to explain machine decisions in a way people understand how they originated and what the results actually mean.

In summary, «for the future of AI to be bright, the skills needed are human».[87]

IV. Conclusion

Financial institutions are groaning under the weight of regulations and the related growing costs of compliance. They are also challenged by the costs of maintaining complex IT legacy systems whose siloed data requires manual curation for risk data aggregation, compliance reporting and further important tasks. In my view, there is an imperative to change from business-as-usual scenarios and be open to change. As shown in this chapter, the Time is Now (Part A) to develop a Mindset for the Future (Part B) in order to Enable Breakthroughs (Part C) in RegTech.

Just as digital technologies are being used to underpin disruptive business models for new entrants, such as FinTechs, so too can technologies such as Data Analytics, Semantic Technologies, Cloud, Artificial Intelligence, Machine Learning, Natural Language Processing, and Blockchain underpin a paradigm change to Digital Regulatory Compliance that covers the entire «Regulatory Compliance Value Chain». «The technologies required to make Digital Regulatory Compliance and enhanced Risk Management a reality already exist»,[88] according to Professor *Tom Butler*. The concepts exist too, as I know

85 Analytics India Magazine, *Has the AI Train Left The Station? [Interview with Spiros Margaris]*, ANALYTICS INDIA MAGAZINE (Dec. 2018), https://www.analyticsindiamag.com/has-the-ai-train-left-the-station-an-interview-with-leading-ai-influencer-spiros-margaris/ (last visited Apr. 2, 2019).

86 Nish Bhutani, *For the future of AI to be bright, the skills needed are human*, LIVEMINT (Oct. 31, 2018: 6:45 PM), https://www.livemint.com/Leisure/ZoOp7dQaRaMnouBrMjUdaM/For-the-future-of-artificial-intelligence-to-be- bright-the.html.

87 Nish Bhutani, *For the future of AI to be bright, the skills needed are human*, LIVEMINT (Jan. 5, 2019: 6:45 PM), https://www.livemint.com/Leisure/ZoOp7dQaRaMnouBrMjUdaM/For-the-future-of-artificial-intelligence-to-be-bright-the.html.

88 Tom Butler, *Digital Regulatory Compliance: Necessary And Sufficient Condictions*, #REGTECHTALKS CONFERENCE, ZUG, SWITZERLAND, (Jun. 21, 2018) (Speech).

only too well. I'm convinced that a first ever enterprise-wide RegTech solution, that covers the entire «Regulatory Compliance Value Chain» can be built and fully implemented on a traditional core banking system and also on a new cloud-based one.

Digital innovations need to be carefully considered (Mindset) and developed (Technology) in an optimal manner from the outset for such breakthroughs to be both resilient and scalable. It all starts with a mindset, which recognizes that technologies are there to enhance human capabilities and which embraces open, diverse and solutions-driven collaboration. This is required if standards-based RegTech systems and concepts are to find purchase in the industry. It is, I believe, within our collective power as regulators, financial institutions and RegTech providers to demonstrate that #RegTechEnables!

V. Bibliography

A. Hard Copy Sources

Butler, Tom, *Digital Regulatory Compliance: Necessary And Sufficient Conditions*, #RegTechtalks conference, Zug, Switzerland, (Jun. 21, 2018) (Speech).

Butler, Tom & O`Brien, Leona, *Understanding RegTech for Digital Regulatory Compliance*, *in* Disrupting Finance, (Palgrave Macmillan, 2019).

Carter, Denis, *How real is the impact of artificial intelligence?* 35(3) Business Information Review 99–115 (2018).

Contratto, Franca, *«RegTech»: Digitale Wende für Aufsicht und Compliance*, 15 Jusletter, 1 (2016).

Dweck, Carol S, Mindset: The New Psychology of Success, (Ballantine Books, 2006).

Durant, Will, The Story of Philosophy (Outlook, 2012).

European Commission's High-Level Expert Group on Artificial Intelligence, DRAFT, Ethics Guidlines for Trustworthy AI, p. i (Dec. 18, 2018).

European Securities and Markets Authority, *Briefing Legal Entity Identifier (LEI), ESMA70-145-238.*

Hall, Larry D, *Some financial regulatory implications of artificial intelligence*, 100 Journal of Economics and Business 55 (2017).

House of Commons, HM Treasury's 2015 Budget Report 53 Sec. 1.204, 98 Sec. 2.272 (Mar. 18, 2015).

Kahneman, Daniel & Tversky, Amos, *Choices, Values, and Frames,* 39 American Psychologist 341 (1984).

Kegan, Robert & Lahey, Lisa, *The Real Reason People Won't Change,* 11 Harvard Business Review 118 (2001).

Klebeck, Ulf & Dobrauz-Saldapenna, Guenther, *RegTech – eine digitale Chance für den europäischen Finanzmarkt*, Recht der Finanzinstrumente, 180 (2017).

Landolt, Martin, *Postulat «Förderung der Digitalisierung in der Regulierung (RegTech),* Nationalrat, 16.3256 (Mar. 18, 2016).

Lo Giudice, D., Goetz, M., Purcell, B., Le Clair, C. & Gualtieri, M., Predictions 2019: Artificial Intelligence No Pain, No Gain With Enterprise AI (Forrester Research, 2018).

Loucks, Jeff, Macaulay, James, Noronha, Andy & Wade, Michael, Digital Vortex: How Today's Market Leaders can Beat Disruptive Competitors at Their Own Game 137, IMD (2016).

Lyytinen, Kalle & Hirschheim, Rudy, *Information systems failures—a survey and classification of the empirical literature*, *in* 4 Oxford Surveys in IT 257–309 (1987).

Matthews, Dona, *Book Review: Mindset: The New Psychology of Success (2006),* 2 Gifted Children 12 (2007) (book review).

MEDICI, *MEDICI Signature Report: RegTech Report 2018—Executive Summary*, 7/8 (2018).

Omidyar, Pierre, *Guy Kawasaki's The Art of the Start: The Time-Tested, Battle-Hardened Guide for Anyone Starting Anything*, cover page, (Portfolio, 2015).

Oxford Dictionaries, https://en.oxforddictionaries.com/definition/artificial_intelligence.

Pasteuer, Louis, Dans les champs de l'observation le hasard ne favorise que les esprits préparés.

Polman, Paul, Act Like a Leader, Think Like a Leader (Harvard Business Review Press, 2015).

Sidler, Slider, *Most important success factors for strong and healthy startups at Digital Health Day Zurich, Switzerland* (Oct. 30, 2018).

Swiss Bankers Association, Position of the Swiss Bankers Association (SBA) on RegTech.

Swiss Federal Council, *RegTech Report of the Swiss Federal Council of 27 June 2018 to the motion of* Martin Landolt, *Postulat «Förderung der Digitalisierung in der Regulierung (RegTech),* Nationalrat, 16.3256 (Mar. 18, 2016).

Walport, Mark, UK Government Chief Scientific Advisor, *FinTech Futures: The UK as a World Leader in Financial Technologies*, U.K. Government for Science 12 (Mar. 13, 2015).

Weber, Rolf H, *Regtech as a new legal challenge*, 46 Journal of Financial Transformation 10 (2017).

Zuboff, Shoshana, *Big other: surveillance capitalism and the prospects of an information civilization,* 30(1), JIT 75 (2015).

B. Online Sources

Analytics India Magazine, *Has the AI Train Left The Station? [Interview with Spiros Margaris],* Analytics India Magazine (Dec. 2018), https://www.analyticsindiamag.com/has-the-ai-train-left-the-station-an-interview-with-leading-ai-influencer-spiros-margaris/ (last visited Apr. 2, 2019).

Artner Douglas W, Barberis, Janos & Buckley, Ross P, *FinTech and RegTech in a Nutshell, and the Future in a Sandbox*, CFA Institute Foundation, 10 (2017), https://www.cfainstitute.org/-/media/documents/article/rf-brief/rfbr-v3-n4-1.ashx (last visited Apr. 11, 2019).

Bhutani, Nish, *For the future of AI to be bright, the skills needed are human*, livemint (Oct. 31, 2018: 6:45 PM), https://www.livemint.com/Leisure/ZoOp7dQaRaMnouBrMjUdaM/For-the-future-of-artificial-intelligence-to-be-bright-the.html (last visited Feb. 2, 2019).

Mark Branson, *Technology and the financial industry—opportunity or risk?*, FINMA Annual Media Conference (Mar. 27, 2018), https://www.finma.ch/en/~/media/finma/dokumente/dokumentencenter/myfinma/finma-publikationen/referate-und-artikel/20180327-rd-bnm-jmk-2018.pdf?la=en (last visited Apr. 2, 2019).

Branson, Mark, *Market Integrity: a Strategic Priority for FINMA*, FINMA Annual Media Conference (Apr. 4, 2017), https://www.finma.ch/en/~/media/finma/dokumente/dokumentencenter/myfinma/finma-publikationen/referate-und-artikel/20170404_jmk2017_rede_bnm.pdf?la=en (last visited Apr. 2, 2019).

Burnmark, Alvarez & Marsal, *RegTech 2.0* 15 (2018), https://www.burnmark.com/uploads/reports/Burnmark_Report_Jan18_RegTech.pdf (last visited Apr. 3, 2019).

Financial Conduct Authority, *AML and Financial Crime International TechSprint,* https://www.fca.org.uk/events/techsprints/aml-financial-crime-international-techsprint (last visited Jan. 2, 2019).

Financial Conduct Authority, *Call for Input: Using Technology to achieve smarter regulatory reporting,* https://www.fca.org.uk/publications/feedback-statements/call-input-using-technology-achieve-smarter-regulatory-reporting (last visited Jan. 2, 2019).

Financial Conduct Authority, *Global Financial Innovation Network,* https://www.fca.org.uk/publications/consultation-papers/global-financial-innovation-network (last visited Jan. 2, 2019).

Financial Conduct Authority, *Techsprints,* https://www.fca.org.uk/firms/regtech/techsprints (last visited Jan. 2, 2019).

Financial Conduct Authority, *Our Work Programme,* https://www.fca.org.uk/firms/regtech/our-work-programme (last visited Jan. 2, 2019).

FinTech Abu Dhabi, https://fintechabudhabi.com (last visited Jan. 2, 2019).

Gaunt, Neville, *How To Increase Innovation By Eliminating «Behavioral Waste,* Forbes (Mar. 13, 2017), https://www.forbes.com/sites/davidkwilliams/2017/03/13/how-to-increase-innovation-and-growth-by-eliminating-behavioral-waste/#681e0cb98b9d (last visited Feb. 2, 2019).

Gompers, Paul, Gornall, William, Kaplan, Steven N & Strebulaev, Ilya A, *How do venture capitalists make decisions? Working Paper 22587*, National Bureau of Economic Research (Sep. 2016), http://www.nber.org/papers/w22587 (last visited Apr. 3, 2019).

Hellard, Bobby, *IBM chosen to push cloud-native banking platform*: *Thought Machine sees tech giant as the partner to accelerate its Vault platform*, IT Pro (Dec. 4, 2018, 5:32 PM), https://www.itpro.co.uk/cloud/32500/ibm-chosen-to-push-cloud-native-banking-platform (last visited Feb. 3, 2019)

Hess, Richard, *Regtech: Digitale Regulierung nützt dem Schweizer Finanzplatz*, Finews (Jul. 9, 2018), https://www.finews.ch/news/finanzplatz/32456-regtech-finanzplatz-schweiz-richard-hess-bankiervereinigung-sbvg (last visited Apr. 2, 2019).

Jaro, Carmina *How can chatbots increase your sales?*, LinkedIn (Apr. 25, 2018), https://www.linkedin.com/pulse/how-can-chatbots-increase-your-sales-carmina-jaro/ (last visited Apr. 1, 2019).

Jaro, Carmina *Should I build my own chatbot?*, LinkedIn (Feb. 6, 2018), https://www.linkedin.com/pulse/should-i-build-my-own-chatbot-carmina-jaro/ (last visited Feb. 2, 2019).

Ma, Jack, *Meet the Leader with Jack Ma at Word Economic Forum Davos, Switzerland,* YouTube (Jan. 24, 2018), https://www.youtube.com/watch?v=4zzVjonyHcQ (last visited Feb. 3, 2019).

Marous, Jim *5 Resolutions For Digital Banking,* The Financial Brand (Dec. 30, 2018, 6:05 PM), https://the financialbrand.com/78634/goals-resolutions-digital-banking/ (last visited Feb. 3, 2019).

McNulty, Lucy, *Top regulator: City firms must bear responsibility for RegTech risks*, Financial News (Dec. 20, 2019, 6:23 PM), https://www.fnlondon.com/articles/city-firms-must-bear-responsibility-for-regtech-risk-20170516 (last visited Apr. 2, 2019)Schaffer, Jon, *Tough Decisions*, Appetite For Disruption (Nov. 11, 2018), https://www.appetitefordisruption.tv/conversations/jon-schaffer (last visited Jan. 2, 2019).

Pando Molina, Adolfo, *Digital Transformation Through Effective Culture Change (Part 2),* LinkedIn (Jan. 10, 2019; 5:10 PM), https://www.linkedin.com/pulse/digital-transformation-through-effective-culture-part-pando-molina-1e/ (last visited Apr. 11, 2019).

SIA Partners & AEC FinTech, *RegTech Study: European Landscape* 18 (2018); 3 MEDICI, *MEDICI Signature Report: RegTech Report 2018—Executive Summary*, 7/8 (2018), http://sia-partners.com/sites/default/files/mag-reg-tech_finalvers2_1_0.pdf (last visited Apr. 11, 2019); Burnmark, Alvarez & Marsal, *RegTech 2.0* 15 (2018), https://www.burnmark.com/uploads/reports/Burnmark_Report_Jan18_RegTech.pdf (last visited Apr. 3, 2019); Dr. Ulf Klebeck & Dr. Günther Dobrauz-Saldapenna, *RegTech – eine digitale Chance für den europäischen Finanzmarkt*, Recht der Finanzinstrumente (2017), at 180, 181.

Swiss Association of Compliance Officers, https://www.complianceofficers.ch (last visited Apr. 2. 2019).

Swiss Bankers Association, *Interview with David Bundi, Chief Compliance Officer, RegTech: An enabler for established banks,* insight #1.18, (Apr. 10, 2018), https://www.swissbanking.org/en/services/insight/insight-1.18/regtech-an-enabler-for-established-banks (last visited Apr. 3, 2019).

Swiss Bankers Association, *Interview with Martin Hess, Chief Economist, Enabling the cloud,* insight #4.18 (Dec. 12, 2018), https://www.swissbanking.org/en/services/insight/insight-4.18/enabling-the-cloud (last visited Apr. 3, 2019).

Swiss Bankers Association, *Interview with Andreas Barfuss, Head of Financial Market Law of the Swiss Bankers Association, RegTech: An enabler for established banks,* insight #1.18, (Apr. 10, 2018), https://www.swissbanking.org/en/services/insight/insight-1.18/regtech-an-enabler-for-established-banks (last visited Apr. 3, 2019).

Swiss Bankers Association, *Guidelines,* https://www.swissbanking.org/en/services/library/guidelines (last visited Apr. 15, 2019).

Swiss FinTech Innovations, https://swissfintechinnovations.ch (last visited Apr. 2, 2019).

Teng, Richard, *ADGM Successfully Concludes 1st Industry E-KYC Utility Project with UAE Financial Institutions* (Dec. 4, 2018), https://www.adgm.com/mediacentre/press-releases/adgm-successfully-concludes-1st-industry-e-kyc-utility-project-with-uae-financial-institutions (last visited Apr. 3, 2019).

Tschanz, Marcel, *Taking Swiss private banking to the cloud,* PwC (Jan. 5, 2018, 6:50 PM), https://www.pwc.ch/en/insights/fs/swiss-private-banking-cloud.html (last visited Feb. 3, 2019).

von Rohr, Chris, *A Critical Conversation with Chris von Rohr,* Appetite for Disruption (Nov. 25, 2018), http://www.appetitefordisruption.tv/conversations/chris-von-rohr/ (last visited Jan. 2, 2019).

Williams, David K, *How To Increase Innovation By Eliminating «Behavioral Waste»*[Interview with Neville Gaunt], Forbes (Mar. 13, 2017 9:28 AM), https://www.forbes.com/sites/davidkwilliams/2017/03/13/how-to-increase-innovation-and-growth-by-eliminating-behavioral-waste/ (last visited Feb., 3, 2019).

Woolard, Christopher, *Technology and global ties: turning the tide on financial crime,* Financial Crime & AML TechSprint in London (May 24, 2018), https://www.fca.org.uk/news/speeches/technology-and-global-ties-turning-tide-financial-crime (last visited Apr. 11, 2019).

Dr Marcel Lötscher[1]

SupTech

Challenges posed by supervisory transformation

TABLE OF CONTENTS

---

1 The essay reflects the personal opinion of the author. The statements do not claim to correspond to the position of the Financial Market Authority (FMA) Liechtenstein. Please also note the following restriction: In accordance with the nature of the topic and the author's resumé, with respect to the regulatory influence, this paragraph refers solely to European regulation of securities and the markets. This focus includes collective investments and their management companies, the asset management companies, financial instruments as well as further topics related to the capital markets. SupTech is also tangibly represented via the transaction data delivery of MiFIR and EMIR as well as the fundamental principles of the GDPR, MiFID II and PSD2.

I. Prologue

The following essay aims to illustrate the extent to which SupTech can play a role in ensuring that supervisory authorities are not subject to information bias and can instead integrate the findings from *Bonini's* paradox[2] in the management of big data. The goal of all this is to be able to achieve efficient and effective data management with due regard to prudent use of the fees and levies provided by the intermediaries.

But first a look at the history of literature: The novel *Sylvie and Bruno Concluded*[3] by *Lewis Carroll*, a British author from the Victorian era, was published in 1893. It tells the story of a one-to-one scale map: a map as a reproduction of reality, but without any form of simplification or (risk-based) focus on important cartographic events.[4] In the novel, the map was produced on the orders of the Emperor. In today's European regulatory environment, a (rule-based) directly applicable regulation[5] would be chosen. Although it was extremely expensive to produce the map, it was in fact never used. This was because whenever the map was unfolded, the farmers fought vociferously against the blocking of their fields. The insights gained from the one-to-one scale map could therefore only be exploited if the productivity of the working population suffered. This would be considered a case of overregulation today. Over time, the country itself was used as the map for the sake of simplicity, and it was determined that not only was this just as good as using the one-to-one scale map, it also enabled them to avoid the negative side effects described above.

A map on a scale of one-to-one is therefore impractical as a collection of all representable and geographically accessible information about a country. It is also a cumbersome process to have to record all details of reality down to the micro level. A map on a scale of one-to-one becomes an end in itself and the technical measurement effort, amount of data and production costs increase disproportionately each time the scale comes closer to the ever-changing reality.[6]

---

2 *See* Charles P Bonini, Simulation of information and decision systems in the firm (Literary Licensing, 1963).

3 *See* Lewis Caroll, Sylvie and Bruno Concluded (Ray Dyer ed., 2015) (1893).

4 *See* Margherita Barile, *Bijective*, MathWorld (Dec. 18, 2018 10:00 AM), http://mathworld.wolfram.com/Bijective.html (last visited Feb. 1, 2019).

5 *See* University of Portsmouth European Studies, *Direct applicability and direct effect*, http://hum.port.ac.uk/europeanstudieshub/learning/module-3-governance-in-a-multi-level-europe/direct-effect-and-direct-applicability (last visited Dec. 18, 2018).

6 Anyone who has ever searched for a street using *Google Earth* knows what the above-mentioned authors are talking about. But none of them would have ever thought that today you can use a one-to-one scale map in electronic format on a smartphone. With *Google Earth* for instance you can overlay satellite and aerial images of different resolutions with existing geodata. The infor-

We become subject to information bias,[7] on the one hand, and on the other to *Bonini's* paradox. Information bias states that people often take better decisions when they have less information but assess this conversely. It is generally the case that information is instead collated for the decision, even though the information collated is irrelevant for the decision itself. *Bonini's* paradox reveals that the more comprehensive models of complex systems become, the more incomprehensible these are in actual use. This is because the more realistic a model is, the more difficult it is to understand the real underlying process that the model is actually intended to reproduce (simply). We suffer from information overload and have too much information to be able to process this, or can't see the forest for the trees, as the saying goes. We will return to the image of the map once again in the appraisal at the end of these considerations.

II. SupTech as a Cross-Disciplinary Approach

A. Concept and Meaning

SupTech is a cross-disciplinary and portmanteau term at the same time. It consists first of all of the financial market authority as a supervisor (with Sup as an abbreviation for supervision) of a country's financial market. With its supervisory activity the financial market authority ensures stability for financial institutions and the financial market and provides protection for customers. The financial market authority takes the necessary actions aimed at protecting customers and the reputation of the financial center in the event of breaches of the supervisory regulations. As part of efforts to combat malpractices, the financial market authority also persecutes cases in which activities requiring licensing are executed without the respective license. Secondly it consists of the concept of the latest technologies (with Tech as an abbreviation for technology), which primarily including electronic data processing (EDP).

As a cross-disciplinary approach, SupTech ensures a balancing act between the traditional activity of the financial market authority combined with the technological developments of the modern era. As a portmanteau term, SupTech aims to represent this connection in the same way as the related concepts FinTech and RegTech. However, SupTech refers to the originary activities of the financial market authority.

---

mation offered is enormous, but does it also serve the purpose of a location determination and smart orientation? Often only the simplification of the view (i.e., the enlargement of the scale) helps to be able to gain the overview again.

7 *See* Michael Vaughan, The Thinking Effect: Rethinking Thinking to Create Great Leaders and the New Value Worker (Nicholas Brealey Publishing, 2012).

According to my research, the term was mentioned for the first time in a *Toronto Centre* publication dated August 2017[8] and then coined for a wider audience by *Ravi Menon* from the *Monetary Authority of Singapore (MAS)* at the occasion of the *FinTech Festival* November 2017[9]. Both of SupTech's definitions largely focus on strengthening supervision and reducing compliance costs. It does so by using innovative technology to support supervision. In essence, SupTech is the term that describes the paradigm shift in financial supervision as a result of the financial crisis and the emerging FinTech industry. SupTech helps authorities in their digitalization projects to make reporting and regulatory processes more efficient and agile. With digitalization, financial supervision is moving away from the current (over)reliance on reports of past data, extensive on-site inspections and delayed supervisory actions towards a pro-active, intrusive, forward-looking and intensive financial supervision. This requires more frequent and more granular data, sophisticated analytics, and sound data processing capabilities.[10]

Currently, SupTech initiatives can be observed at a number of financial market authorities around the globe. They predominantly focus on data collection, data analytics, and also data exchange.[11]

B. Boundaries

SupTech is not RegTech is not FinTech. Despite all the necessary delimitations, there are also plenty of overlaps. FinTech is examined from various sides in this anthology and I will refrain from making further comments on this.

As another portmanteau term, RegTech is a fusion of the words Regulatory and Technology. The latest technologies should be used to support regulatory management from an efficient and effective IT perspective within the financial market architecture and at the level of financial market intermediaries. The idea is that RegTech should automate the management of the flood of regulation (regulatory tsunami) with the aid of electronic data processing so that scalability can also be achieved in the regulatory area. As such, RegTech

---

8 *See* Toronto Centre, *FinTech, RegTech and SupTech: What They Mean for Financial Supervision* (2017), https://res.torontocentre.org/guidedocs/FinTech%20RegTech%20and%20SupTech%20-%20What%20They%20Mean%20for%20Financial%20Supervision.pdf (last visited Feb. 3, 2019).

9 The author was a participant in this event and followed the presentation of the referenced person.

10 *See* Toronto Centre, *supra* note 8, at 10.

11 *See* Dirk Broeders & Jermy Prenio, *Innovative technology in financial supervision (suptech)—the experience of early users*, Bank for International Settlements—FS Insights on Policy Implementation No. 9 (2018), https://www.bis.org/fsi/publ/insights9.pdf (last visited Feb. 3, 2019).

represents the counterpart of SupTech, or in other words: SupTech is RegTech for supervisory authorities. FinTech on the other hand refers to the use of electronic data processing across the financial service provider's entire value chain.

III. Economic and Social Sciences Influence

A. General

According to *Richard A Posner,* application of the economic analysis of law is neither new nor is it controversial. He believes that the only thing that is controversial is the diverse nature of problems in the world of law that should now be examined in more detail using economic analysis of law, and in particular the so-called Financial Market Authority Act.[12] If jurisprudence limits itself to the interpretation of existing norms and the recording of ambiguities, then it deprives itself of any role in the process of continuing to develop the law.[13]

Thus, calling upon economics as a social science to examine and assess legal issues ensures legal progress as opposed to simply ensuring the extraction of direct judgements within the scope of legal doctrine. The supervisory regulations are now examined more closely against the background of new institutional economics and behavioral finance. The financial market supervisory authorities are also prone to the following cognitive biases. The supervisory authorities do not know all of the information any more than the *homo economicus*[14] (although they frequently already have plenty of information); and they can not always act—detached from practical constraints effectively and rationally as they are bound inter alia by administrative regulations.[15]

---

12 *See* Richard A Posner, *Recht und* Ökonomie*: Eine Einführung (Law and economics: an introduction)* 90 *in* Ökonomische Analyse des Rechts (Economic analysis of law) (Heinz-Dieter Assmann et al., 1993).

13 *See* Jan C Schuhr, Rechtsdogmatik als Wissenschaft: rechtliche Theorien und Modelle (Duncker & Humblot, 2006) at 35.

14 The model of the homo economicus is an abstraction of human behavior and is used as a basis for analyzing economic correlations in neoclassical economics. The principal characteristic of the homo economicus is their ability to engage in perfectly rational behavior and their attempts to maximize utility. Complete information that is available without restriction is a further characteristic assumption. The homo economicus knows all options for action and their consequences.

15 *See* instead of many with further notes Marcel Lötscher, Die vermögende Privatperson als qualifizierter Anleger (Tectum Verlag, 2014) at 143–173.

B. New Institutional Economics

1. Introduction

New institutional economics is a more recent theory in economics that examines the effect of institutions on economic units (private households, companies). A distinction needs to be made between new institutional economics and (so called old) institutional economics.

New institutional economics is an established global field of research today that has its origins in the 1970s. It is concerned with the development and impact of the institutional framework of exchange processes. As such, new institutional economics can be viewed as a further development of neoclassical economics that specifically requires this institutional framework with the assumption of the *homo economicus* as a given. New institutional economics advises choosing the institution or organization that sees honesty as more rewarding than dishonesty and thereby possesses an inherent self-assertive power.[16]

The property rights approach, transaction cost approach, and principal-agent theory form the general core of new institutional economics. This is because every actual economic interaction affects property rights and involves transaction costs and at least two contracting partners who represent their own interests in each case.[17]

According to new institutional economics, the limited capacity for information processing is the greatest flaw of the neoclassical assumption of perfect information.[18] The neoclassical assumption is subject to the fact that all stakeholders on the market are fully informed on time and free of charge. However, stakeholders on the market in particular take decisions without having complete information available. Market failures then occur as a result of information deficits if the information is distributed asymmetrically among the market stakeholders and the functioning of the financial market is impaired as a result.[19]

---

16 *See* GABLER WIRTSCHAFTSLEXIKON, *Neue Institutionenöknomik*, https://wirtschaftslexikon.gabler.de/definition/neue-institutionenoekonomik-38077 (last visited Apr. 15, 2019).

17 *See* ELISABETH GÖBEL, NEUE INSTITUTIONENÖKONOMIK: KONZEPTION UND BETRIEBSWIRTSCHAFTLICHE ANWENDUNGEN 60 (UTB, 2002).

18 *See* BIRGER P PRIDDAT, STRUKTURIERTER INDIVIDUALISMUS: INSTITUTIONEN ALS ÖKONOMISCHE THEORIE 250 (Metropolis Verlag, 2005).

19 *See* MICHAEL FRITSCH, MARKTVERSAGEN UND WIRTSCHAFTSPOLITIK: MIKROÖKONOMISCHE GRUNDLAGEN STAATLICHEN HANDELNS 247 (8th ed., Vahlen, 2011).

2. Principal-agent theory

The principal-agent theory covers cases where information is distributed asymmetrically between the principal[20] and agent.[21] The principal knows less or is able to observe less than the agent. The information asymmetry may exist before and/or after the conclusion of the contract or in both instances. Accordingly, the agent has an incentive to behave opportunistically before and/or after the conclusion of the contract or in both cases.[22] However, the principal expects a fair return service from the agent to whom he assigns specific tasks as part of the order. Measuring this performance is difficult, however, as there is no complete or free market transparency. This makes the risk of the principal being deceived by the agent a significant one.[23]

The agent has an informational advantage over the principal and is therefore better able to assess its opportunities. The principal's ability to monitor and evaluate the agent's actions on the other hand is not satisfactory. As a utility maximizer the agent will also use this informational advantage for its own needs and not act solely in the principal's best interests. The three most significant problem areas with the principal-agent theory are hidden characteristics, hidden action, and hidden information, which are outlined briefly below. Hidden characteristics involve the problem that the principal is unable to learn the agent's characteristics before conclusion of the contract, either with respect to the agent's character or to the products and services provided by the agent. These characteristics frequently remain hidden and there is a risk of an adverse selection. The problem of hidden action only arises after the contract has been concluded, describing the fact that the principal is unable to monitor the agent's activities continuously. Hidden information refers to the problem that although the principal is able to monitor the agent's activities, he does not have the specific knowledge required to assess these activities. The greater the agent's special knowledge the more likely it is that there will be hidden information as a result of the prevailing information asymmetry. As utility maximizer, the agent will then select the action that involves the greatest benefit for him personally.[24]

This information asymmetry between the principal and agent, the parties' conflicting goals, and the self-serving behavior of the homo economicus as a utility maximizer form the premises of the principal-agent theory.

The asymmetric distribution of information means that consumers will only base their willingness to pay on the average quality to be expected. Ser-

---

20 The principal is e.g., the financial market supervisory authority.

21 The agent is e.g., the financial service provider.

22 *See* RUDOLF RICHTER & EIRIK G FURUBOTN, NEUE INSTITUTIONENÖKONOMIK: EINE EINFÜHRUNG UND KRITISCHE WÜRDIGUNG 596 (4th ed., Mohr Siebeck, 2010).

23 *See* Göbel, *supra* note 17, at 62.

24 *See* Göbel, *supra* note 17, at 100–103.

vice providers offering above-average quality will, therefore, generate comparatively lower profits as they are required to cover higher costs. Providers are thereby forced to produce goods of average quality at the maximum. However, if consumers becomes aware of the reduction in average quality, they will adapt their willingness to pay accordingly. This negative spiral only ceases once the worst possible quality of goods can be offered, and the price settles at the lowest level. This negative spiral is termed adverse selection.[25] There is uncertainty regarding quality as the parties are unable to monitor certain characteristics (hidden characteristics) or information (hidden information) prior to conclusion of the contract.[26]

A moral hazard refers to those problem situations that arise from hidden actions and hidden information.[27] The agent either has more information available than the principal after concluding the contract or the possibility for hidden action presents itself to him. *Richter and Furubotn* speak here of opportunism after conclusion of the contract (ex post opportunism).[28] This results in behavioral uncertainty among the stakeholders.

Information asymmetry can frequently be reduced with the relatively poorly informed market participant, i.e., the principal, attempting to acquire additional information (screening) and/or the relatively well-informed market participant, i.e., the agent, distributing information that is as credible as possible about the good quality offered by them (signaling). In summary, the uninformed party should improve his/her level of information and the better-informed party should provide more information.[29]

Information asymmetry can also be reduced by attempting to lessen the imbalance through controls, and the objectives can be harmonized through skilled design of tangible incentive schemes. A trusting relationship can be established between the principal and agent to complement both these solutions and mitigate the parties' opportunistic behavior. The principal draws more trust as the agent strives to reduce the information asymmetry and provides evidence of trustworthiness before and after conclusion of the contract.[30]

The supervisory authority can require service providers to provide information proactively about important product characteristics or contractual amendments of material content in each case. This can occur e.g., through mandatory publication obligations or further specific responsibilities to provide information. However, information asymmetry will not be rectified completely as a result of any transparency ordered by lawmakers. The information

---

25 *See* Fritsch, *supra* note 19, at 250.

26 *See* Jens Winter, Leasing aus institutionenökonomischer Sicht (Gabler, 2011) at 8.

27 *See* Göbel, *supra* note 17, at 103.

28 *See* Richter & Furubotn, *supra* note 22, at 592.

29 *See* Fritsch, *supra* note 19, at 262–263.

30 *See* Göbel, *supra* note 17, at 118.

not only needs to be available, it also needs to be understandable to the recipient. This is a problem in particular when the recipients do not have the corresponding educational background. In the absence of any initiative or suitability with respect to the provision of information by the service provider (agent), then the state can also assume this task.[31]

Both sets of circumstances involving adverse selection based on asymmetrical distribution of information and moral hazard are problem areas confronting a financial market supervisory authority, particularly at times of information overload based on the problem of big data. There is an inherent risk that the supervisory authorities will no longer be able to see the forest through the trees and that the main task of investor protection, at least in the transformation phase, will only be able to be fulfilled to a limited extent.

C. Behavioral Finance

Behavioral economics is a sub-area of economic science. It is concerned with human behavior in economic situations. It involves examination of sets of circumstances in which people act contrary to the model assumption of homo economicus, i.e., the rational utility maximizer. Such questions also continue to be examined by game theory.[32]

With the model of the homo economicus, the neoclassical theory takes into account investor behavior almost completely based on the abstraction of human behavior. However, if we observe the actual operations on the financial markets, then barely any market participant meets its requirements of strict rationality: investors have an information deficit, make mistakes in forming expectations and also at times allow themselves to be guided by irrational motives in their decisions.[33]

The homo economicus is thereby simply an ideal and not a realistic reflection of actual human behavior. According to the neoclassical doctrine, the psychological factors cancel each other out and are irrelevant for market examination purposes.[34] Pursuant to the idea of adverse selection, irrational in-

---

31 *See* Fritsch, *supra* note 19, at 278.

32 *See* Vienne Behavioral Economics Network, *Was ist Behavioral Economics?*, https://vben.at/was-ist-behavioral-economics/ (last visited Apr. 15, 2019).

33 *See* Rainer Ellenrieder, Synergetische Kapitalmarktmodelle: Erklärung der Wertpapierkursentwicklung durch Integration des menschlichen Anlegerverhaltens in ein Kapitalmarktmodell (Uhlenbruch Verlag, 2001) at 93.

34 *See* Stefan Wendt, Die Auswirkungen von Corporate Governance auf die Fremdfinanzierungskosten von Unternehmen: Eine empirische Analyse der Folgen von Aktientransaktionen durch Insider (Springer Gabler, 2011) at 36; Esther Merey, Industrie- und Kapitalmarktdynamik: Eine modelltheoretische Wirkungsanalyse auf der Basis von künstlichen neuronalen Netzen (Kovač, 2011).

vestors are eliminated from the market over the long term as a result of the financial losses suffered. According to the neoclassical opinion, professional investors act consistently more or less rationally and can compensate for any errors in price determination via arbitrage. However, systemic distortions have been ascertained in investor behavior using observations from behavioral science.[35]

Building on new institutional economics the neoclassical financial theory approaches are expanded to include behavioral, psychological, and sociological aspects. Behavioral finance now looks for the reasons behind limited rationality and the consequences arising from this for behavior.[36] SupTech can now be an instrument for the financial market supervisory authorities to break through these shortcomings, which have been explained on the basis of behavioral science in this chapter.

IV. Legal and Regulatory Influence

A. General

The hierarchical structure of the legal and regulatory influence on a national supervisory authority is diverse and extensive. Not only are different target groups involved at the global, European, and national levels, the regulations are also partly principle-based and partly rule-based, and there are obviously also hybrid forms.

Principle-based law is characterized by the fact that the regulations require interpretation and are not conclusive. Although the aim of the regulation is stipulated as mandatory, different ways or means of achieving the relevant objective are left to the addressee's discretion. Rule-based law, on the other hand, is strict and limited in its flexibility. As such rule-based law satisfies the maxim: lawmakers' rule, and the supervisory authority applies and executes the law. Rule-based law corresponds with the traditional image of state monitoring and intervention, as the authority's actions should be measured against the statutory regulations in all cases and must be subject to unrestricted judicial control.[37]

SupTech, like all government action, must be embedded in the legal framework of each nation state. Therefore, the different levels of legal influence and their similarities and differences will be briefly explained.

35 *See id.* 93–94.

36 *See* Wendt, *supra* note 34, at 36 et seq.

37 *See* Manfred Wandt, Prinzipienbasiertes Recht und Verhältnissmässigkeitsgrundsatz im Rahmen von Solvency II, (VVW, 2012) at 8–11.

B. International IOSCO Standards

Since 2011, the Financial Market Authority (FMA) Liechtenstein has been a full member of the International Organization of Securities Commissions (IOSCO[38]) founded in 1983. The organization has around 200 members worldwide.[39]

IOSCO plays the leading role in establishing international standards in the area of securities supervision. It also promotes cooperation between securities supervision authorities. The member authorities exchange information and develop standards aimed at improving supervision over securities trading and market participants both nationally and internationally. The aim is to achieve fair and efficient securities trading that accounts for investors' interests. IOSCO recommendations also frequently shape the law and market structures at the national and EU levels. Active collaboration in all important bodies of IOSCO and asserting the national interests is thus of particular importance. IOSCO recommendations are predominantly principle-based. The reports, standards, and resolutions of IOSCO apply consistently to all IOSCO members. They are enacted by the Presidents Committee, IOSCO's central decision-making body. Reports and recommendations from the Technical Committee or the Emerging Markets Committee are only addressed to those members represented on these committees. These bodies are responsible for actually working on the standards and recommendations.[40]

The IOSCO Objectives and Principles for Securities Regulation are the guiding principles by which the quality of a country's securities commission is measured as part of international assessments. The IOSCO Multilateral Memorandum (MMoU) also represents the international standard for cooperation and exchange of information in the area of securities supervision. Fulfilling these standards is a prerequisite for becoming a member of IOSCO.

IOSCO published a final report in 2009 on risk-based supervision entitled Guidelines to Emerging Market Regulators Regarding Requirements for Minimum Entry and Continuous Risk-Based Supervision of Market Intermediaries[41]. The objectives of supervision of the market intermediaries in the securities area are as follows:

---

38 *See* International Organization of Securities Commissions (IOSCO), https://www.iosco.org/ (last visited Apr. 15, 2019).

39 *See* Financial Market Authority (FMA) Liechtenstein, https://www.fma-li.li/de/internationales/global/internationale-organisationen.html (last visited Apr. 15, 2019).

40 *See* Federal Financial Supervisory Authoriy (BaFin) Germany, https://www.bafin.de/DE/Internationales/GlobaleZusammenarbeit/IOSCO/iosco_node.html (last visited Apr. 15, 2019).

41 *See* Emerging Markets Committee of the International Organization of Securities Commissions (IOSCO), *Guidelines to Emerging Market Regulators Regarding Requirements for Minimum Entry and Continuous Risk-Based Supervision of Market Intermediariew* (2009), http://www.iosco.org/library/pubdocs/pdf/IOSCOPD314.pdf (last visited Feb. 3, 2019).

> *«The supervision of market intermediaries has three broad objectives: to protect client assets from insolvency of the intermediary or appropriation by the intermediary or its employees; guard against defaults and sudden disruptions to the market, either through sudden insolvency or settlement failure; and, to ensure that intermediaries are fair and diligent in dealing with their clients. Regulation, therefore, sets licensing standards (limiting the market place to those with sufficient resources and qualification), prudential standards (protecting against sudden financial failure), internal controls and risk management standards (reducing the possibility of default or to appropriate client assets), and business conduct rules (ensuring proper handling of client accounts)»*[42]

The challenge in terms of risk-based supervision is primarily the fact that the data volume has increased continuously over time. In other words, the maps for overview of intermediaries, products and markets are becoming more and more detailed and with higher granularity.

C. European Directives and Directly Applicable Regulations

Multiple bodies work together to create legislation within the European Union: the European Commission, the Council of the European Union and the European Parliament. The Economic and Social Committee and the Committee of the Regions are also consulted in developing legislative acts.[43]

European legislation differs significantly from legislation in the Member States. It is characterized by very lengthy proceedings and many actors. Although the procedures take a very long time, the time frames for influencing the design process are often very short. The lack of development of a European public view has led to a very informal procedure which forces individual interest groups to remain very close to events at all times and pursue their issues very closely. There is therefore an inherent information asymmetry here.

The directives and directly applicable regulations take on an important role in the European Union's legislative procedure, which is why these should be briefly explained further: Directives stipulate an objective and a time frame for its implementation. They must be transposed into national law by the Member States. The Member States are free to determine the means used to do this. If a Directive is not transposed into national law or its adoption is not complete or not within the time frame, European citizens can under certain

---

42 *See id.*, at 3.

43 *See* European Union, *Institutions and bodies*, https://europa.eu/european-union/about-eu/institutions-bodies_en (last visited Apr. 15, 2019).

conditions invoke it directly before the national courts.[44] (Directly-applicable) Regulations, on the other hand, apply directly in all European Member States once they have been enacted. They are directly binding for Member States, their authorities and bodies. If a Regulation conflicts with a national law then the Regulation takes precedence. Decisions are addressed to a particular addressee and are directly binding on the latter with respect to all their parts.[45] The stipulations arising from the European directives and directly binding regulations are often rule-based.

In other words, the rules are becoming more and more detailed and concrete. There is a growing lack of discretion for national supervisors. Risk-based and target-group-oriented action is made more difficult because not every size is suitable for everyone and therefore size compatibility suffers.

D. ESMA Guidelines and Recommendations

The European Securities and Markets Authority (ESMA) headquartered in Paris was founded in early 2011. ESMA is generally seen as a successor to the Committee of European Securities Regulators (CESR) but its responsibilities and powers go well beyond those of the CESR. The ESMA is part of the European System of Financial Supervision (ESFS) and is the key institution for the supervision of securities and markets in Europe.[46]

The ESMA's primary objectives include improving investor protection and ensuring the integrity, transparency and efficient functioning of the securities market. Additional important areas of activity include promoting supervisory convergence, creating a Single Rulebook and ensuring direct supervision[47].

The ESMA is authorized to issue guidelines and recommendations[48] on the application of EU law in those areas not covered by the technical regulatory or implementation standards. The Authority should be able to publish the reasons for non-compliance with the guidelines and recommendations by the supervisory authorities in order to guarantee transparency and increased com-

---

44 *See* EUR-Lex, *The direct effect of European law,* https://eur-lex.europa.eu/legal-content/EN/TXT/?uri=LEGISSUM%3Al14547 (last visited Apr. 15, 2019).

45 *See* EU-Info, *Gesetzgebung,* http://www.eu-info.de/europa/eu-richtlinien-verordnungen/ (last visited Dec. 7, 2018).

46 *See* European Securities and Markets Authority (ESMA), *Who we are,* https://www.esma.europa.eu/about-esma/who-we-are (last visited Apr. 15, 2019).

47 *See* European Securities and Markets Authority (ESMA), *Interactive Single Rulebook* (ISRB), https://www.esma.europa.eu/rules-databases-library/interactive-single-rulebook-isrb (last visited Apr. 15, 2019).

48 *See* European Union, *EU Regulations, Directives and other acts,* https://europa.eu/european-union/eu-law/legal-acts_en (last visited Dec. 18, 2018).

pliance with these guidelines and recommendations by the national supervisory authorities. The guidelines and recommendations often involve a hybrid form of principle-based and rule-based regulations. In other words, the need for a level playing field results in the fact that overly detailed requirements and rules can sometimes contradict each other and (smart) supervision becomes increasingly difficult.

V. Application Areas and Risks of SupTech

A. Introduction and Risk Assessment

The application areas for SupTech can be divided into data collection, data analysis, and data exchange. In addition to the application areas described below, the risks of SupTech should not be ignored. Specifically, the huge data retention harbors risks related both to cyber security and to the fact that the flood of information itself means that the supervisory authorities have a major responsibility in terms of analysis and assessment. As long as the relevant information was not available, the supervisory authority could denounce this behavior as being the responsibility of the intermediary to provide.

However, supervisory authorities now have large amounts of data (big data) and have a responsibility within the framework of supervision (see for a better understanding the above sections III/IV) to implement risk-based data assessments and to sanction in case of breaches of supervisory rules within the scope of enforcement in order to achieve the supervisory authority objectives of: guaranteeing the stability of the financial market, protecting customers, avoiding abuses and implementing and complying with recognized international standards. Yet, risk-based also means assuming responsibility for the selection decision, a decision that must be supported as part of the supervisory strategy—not by the executive management, but also by the supervisory board as the supreme body.

B. Data collection

New data collection mechanisms are at the core of the emerging paradigm shift in financial supervision. Technology fuels the development of sophisticated and data-intensive approaches to supervision[49]. SupTech applications support the data management (registration and monitoring) as well as the reporting processes (reporting) at the authority. In the field of reporting, applica-

49 *See* Toronto Centre, *supra* note 8, at 10–12; Bank for International Settlements, *supra* note 11.

tions include forms of automated reporting as well as real-time monitoring. SupTech will likely lead to an upsurge in reporting utilities, i.e., specialized companies set up to collect and process raw data from institutes for the purpose of supplying the data to the financial market authority. Closely related to this push-approach is the pull-approach. In the latter, the authority obtains data directly from the IT-systems of institutions with the frequency that suits the needs of the supervisor. Direct data exchange will make templated reports obsolete and increase efficiency throughout the process by reducing manual data handling, human error and validation iterations. Real-time monitoring is the closest form of monitoring. By linking directly to the market places the financial market authority is able to collect data at its root. Real-time systems provide alerts about anomalies observed in the markets which trigger subsequent investigations.

All forms of data collection have in common that their reporting is automated and covers all relevant data without having a negative impact on the financial intermediaries' day-to-day business. Reporting includes event-related reporting as well as regular reporting and reports on financial and supervisory information.

C. Data analytics

SupTech will enable real-time supervision thanks to smart supervision. The collection of (almost) real-time data that is not constrained by formatted templates gives supervisors additional flexibility to extract those pieces of information that are most relevant from a risk-based perspective and to generate customized indicators and reports at any time.[50] The data is analyzed on a continuous basis and presented in the supervisory authorities' Supervision Cockpit using a Risk Map (analyzing and monitoring). A data analysis using self-learning artificial intelligence ensures that the supervision can also be completed using objective criteria and that subjective artificial distortions do not result in unequal treatment. Smart supervision can also—building on aggregate data—enable the system to propose core areas for ongoing supervision, linking reporting data with current market and company data. Furthermore, SupTech will enable supervisory authorities to shift increasingly from continuous monitoring to exception-based supervision, in which automated analyses identify outliers or abnormal situations either on institute-level or on sector level.

The ultimate goal of SupTech will be the paradigm shift towards a predictive data-driven supervision that uses the available information not only to

---

50 *See* Toronto Centre, *supra* note 5, at 7–10; Bank for International Settlements, *supra* note 11.

identify breaches in the past but to predict behavior or risky situations in the future and thus put the supervisory authority in a position to act ahead of time in a preemptive manner.

D. Data exchange

Transaction data, either based on transactions in financial instruments in accordance with MiFIR or OTC transactions in accordance with EMIR are made available directly to the financial market supervisory authorities. This data must of course be linked with the aggregated data from the past and included in the assessment. It is not only the national supervisory authorities that should have access to this data but also the supervisory authorities of the counterparty included via memorandum of understanding if more information is required in the context of enforcement measures. Additional supervisory data can be provided as part of consolidated supervision or within the framework of a review of a higher-level supervisory authority (e.g., ESMA). The tax law data and exchange of this must naturally be kept strictly separate from the national, European and international data exchange (IOSCO Multilateral Memorandum of Understanding).

VI. Appraisal and Epilogue

SupTech is a buzzword today that needs to be brought to life in daily supervisory practice. Several supervisory authorities are currently, *literally,* trying the find a needle in a haystack with their risk-based supervision.

SupTech will change the job description of the traditional supervisor in the financial market area. *Richard* and *Daniel Susskind* have summarized these effects, that the supervisory authorities will equally be unable to avoid, as follows:

> *«Our personal and working lives will continue to be overhauled by technology, including even more powerful processing power; artificial intelligence that can discern patterns, identify trends and make accurate predictions once reserved to humans; a cloud that offers seemingly limitless cheap storage capacity; lightning quick communications; ever greater miniaturization; and rapid decline in the cost of components.*
>
> *New capabilities are emerging on an apparently daily basis, and what is striking about most of these systems is that they could not have been delivered 5 years ago because we did not have the technological wherewithal: the mobile platforms, the bandwidth, the software and more.*

There are 6 billion mobile subscribers around the world, of which 2 billion are smart phone users, and this number is expected to double by 2020. When 3 billion people are connected, they communicate and research very differently; they also socialize, share, build communities, cooperate, crowd-source, compete and trade in ways and on a scale that has no analogous in the analogue world.»[51]

In the prologue, we introduced the problem of a one-to-one scale map. At the initial stages of cartography world maps were drawn with unknown regions simply omitted. The maps had no white spots and gave the impression that they included all information. Big data gives the impression that all data is available and that we know the reality. It was only in the 15th and 16th centuries that people had the courage to provide white spots on world maps. Things for which it was known that nothing was known. People consciously accepted the gaps they had and focused on what they knew and also needed.[52] People de facto took a risk-based approach.

Not only smart regulation, but also a subsequent smart supervision is therefore a necessary consequence of SupTech that is only feasible using the latter. Only risk-based supervision, the acceptance of gaps, and assumption of responsibility in this regard brings us closer to the objectives and responsibilities imposed upon us as (therefore smart) supervisory authorities. And in the same way as the white spots aroused the scientific curiosity and encouraged expeditions and the risk of black swans occurs,[53] only continuous (re)evaluation of risk-based supervision will bring supervisory authorities closer to achieving their objectives, whether at the national, European or international levels. Otherwise supervisory authorities will be subject to the erroneous belief and the fallacy that only more information automatically results in better decisions.[54]

The supervisory authority's aim is not to achieve the perfect one-to-one scale map as a depiction of reality, but rather to achieve a hazard and risk map that ensures that it is properly armed for the situation and can draw the right conclusions and implement the appropriate actions. Knowledge is power, as the saying goes, but too much knowledge always leads to powerlessness. All efforts will fail in the event of information overload as the supervisory authorities are subject to information bias and *Bonini's* paradox. This are the reasons

---

51 Richard Susskind & Daniel Susskind, The Future of the Professions (Oxford University Press, 2017) at 6.

52 *See* also Yuval Noah Harari, Eine kurze Geschichte der Menschheit (Dva, 2013) at 349–365.

53 *See* Nassim Nicholas Taleb, The Black Swan (2nd ed. Penguin, 2012) at 105–107; Dobelli, Rolf, Die Kunst des klugen Handelns (15th ed., Hanser, 2017) at 105–107; Bank for International Settlements, *supra* note 11.

54 *See* Dobelli, *supra* note 33, at 33–35.

why only accurate and specific information in the sense of smart (and better) regulation[55] also results in effective and efficient actions on the part of a supervisory authority (so called smart supervision). One thing is clear; SupTech's influence will change the approach of financial market regulators and transform it in the sense of positive destruction.[56]

VII. Bibliography

A. Hard Copy Sources

BONINI, CHARLES P, SIMULATION OF INFORMATION AND DECISION SYSTEMS IN THE FIRM (Literary Licensing, 1963).

CAROLL, LEWIS, SYLVIE AND BRUNO CONCLUDED (Ray Dyer Ed., 2015) (1893).

DOBELLI, ROLF, DIE KUNST DES KLUGEN HANDELNS [THE ART OF SMART ACTION] (15th ed., Hanser, 2017).

ELLENRIEDER, RAINER, SYNERGETISCHE KAPITALMARKTMODELLE: ERKLÄRUNG DER WERTPAPIERKURSENTWICKLUNG DURCH INTEGRATION DES MENSCHLICHEN ANLEGERVERHALTENS IN EIN KAPITALMARKTMODELL [SYNERGETIC CAPITAL MARKET MODELS: EXPLANATION OF SECURITY PRICE DEVELOPMENT THROUGH INTEGRATION OF HUMAN INVESTOR BEHAVIOR IN A CAPITAL MARKET MODEL] (Uhlenbruch Verlag, 2001).

MICHAEL FRITSCH, MARKTVERSAGEN UND WIRTSCHAFTSPOLITIK: MIKROÖKONOMISCHE GRUNDLAGEN STAATLICHEN HANDELNS [MARKET FAILURE AND ECONOMIC POLICY: MICROECONOMIC PRINCIPLES OF STATE ACTION] (8th ed., Vahlen, 2011).

GÖBEL, ELISABETH, NEUE INSTITUTIONENÖKONOMIK: KONZEPTION UND BETRIEBSWIRTSCHAFTLICHE ANWENDUNGEN [NEW INSTITUTIONAL ECONOMICS: CONCEPT AND ECONOMIC APPLICATIONS] (UTB, 2002).

HARARI, YUVAL NOAH, EINE KURZE GESCHICHTE DER MENSCHHEIT [A BRIEF HISTORY OF HUMANKIND] (Dva, 2013).

LÖTSCHER, MARCEL, DIE VERMÖGENDE PRIVATPERSON ALS QUALIFIZIERTER ANLEGER [THE WEALTHY PRIVATE INDIVIDUAL AS A QUALIFIED INVESTOR] (Tectum Verlag, 2014).

MEREY, ESTHER, INDUSTRIE- UND KAPITALMARKTDYNAMIK: EINE MODELLTHEORETISCHE WIRKUNGSANALYSE AUF DER BASIS VON KÜNSTLICHEN NEURONALEN NETZEN [INDUSTRIA AND CAPITAL MARKET DYNAMIC: A MORAL THEORETICAL IMPACT ANALYSIS ON THE BASIS OF ARTIFICIAL NEURAL NETWORKS] (Kovač, 2011).

Posner, Richard A, *Recht und Ökonomie: Eine Einführung (Law and economics: an introduction)* 90 *in* ÖKONOMISCHE ANALYSE DES RECHTS [ECONOMIC ANALYSIS OF LAW] (Heinz-Dieter Assmann et al., 1993).

PRIDDAT, BIRGER P, STRUKTURIERTER INDIVIDUALISMUS: INSTITUTIONEN ALS ÖKONOMISCHE THEORIE [STRUCTURED INDIVIDUALISM: INSTITUTIONS AS ECONOMIC THEORY] (Metropolis Verlag, 2005).

RICHTER, RUDOLF & FURUBOTN, EIRIK G, NEUE INSTITUTIONENÖKONOMIK: EINE EINFÜHRUNG UND KRITISCHE WÜRDIGUNG [NEW INSTITUTIONAL ECONOMICS: AN INTRODUCTION AND CRITICAL ASSESSMENT] (4th ed., Mohr Siebeck, 2010).

---

55 *See* EUROPEAN COMMISSION, *Better Regulation Toolbox based on the Better Regulation Guidelines* (2015), http://ec.europa.eu/smart-regulation/guidelines/docs/swd_br_guidelines_en.pdf (last visited Dec. 23, 2018).

56 *See* JOSEPH A SCHUMPETER, KAPITALISMUS, SOZIALISMUS UND DEMOKRATIE (UTB, 1993) at 132–142.

SCHUHR, JAN C, RECHTSDOGMATIK ALS WISSENSCHAFT: RECHTLICHE THEORIEN UND MODELLE [LEGAL DOCTRINE AS SCIENCE: LEGAL THEORIES AND MODELS] (Duncker & Humblot, 2006).

SCHUMPETER, JOSEPH A, KAPITALISMUS, SOZIALISMUS UND DEMOKRATIE [CAPITALISM, SOCIALISM AND DEMOCRACY] (UTB, 1993).

SUSSKIND, RICHARD & SUSSKIND, DANIEL, THE FUTURE OF THE PROFESSIONS (Oxford University Press, 2017).

TALEB, NASSIM NICHOLAS, THE BLACK SWAN (2nd ed. Penguin, 2012) at 105–107.

VAUGHAN, MICHAEL, THE THINKING EFFECT: RETHINKING THINKING TO CREATE GREAT LEADERS AND THE NEW VALUE WORKER (Nicholas Brealey Publishing, 2012).

WANDT, MANFRED, PRINZIPIENBASIERTES RECHT UND VERHÄLTNISSMÄSSIGKEITSGRUNDSATZ IM RAHMEN VON SOLVENCY II [PRINCIPLE-BASED LAW AND PROPORTIONALITY WITHIN THE SCOPE OF SOLVENCY II] (VVW, 2012).

WENDT, STEFAN, DIE AUSWIRKUNGEN VON CORPORATE GOVERNANCE AUF DIE FREMDFINANZIERUNGSKOSTEN VON UNTERNEHMEN: EINE EMPIRISCHE ANALYSE DER FOLGEN VON AKTIENTRANSAKTIONEN DURCH INSIDER [THE IMPACT OF CORPORATE GOVERNANCE ON COMPANY BORROWING COSTS: AN EMPIRICAL ANALYSIS OF THE CONSEQUENCES OF SHARE TRANSACTIONS BY INSIDERS] (Springer Gabler, 2011).

WINTER, JENS, LEASING AUS INSTITUTIONENÖKONOMISCHER SICHT [LEASING FROM AN INSTITUTION ECONOMIC PERSPECTIVE] (Gabler, 2011).

B. Online Sources

Barile, Margherita, *Bijective*, MATHWORLD (Dec. 18, 2018 10:00 AM), http://mathworld.wolfram.com/Bijective.html (last visited Feb. 1, 2019).

Broeders, Dirk & Prenio, Jermy, *Innovative technology in financial supervision (suptech)—the experience of early users,* BANK FOR INTERNATIONAL SETTLEMENTS—FS INSIGHTS ON POLICY IMPLEMENTATION No. 9 (2018), https://www.bis.org/fsi/publ/insights9.pdf (last visited Feb. 3, 2019).

EMERGING MARKETS COMMITTEE OF THE INTERNATIONAL ORGANIZATION OF SECURITIES COMMISSIONS (IOSCO), *Guidelines to Emerging Market Regulators Regarding Requirements for Minimum Entry and Continuous Risk-Based Supervision of Market Intermediaries* (2009), http://www.iosco.org/library/pubdocs/pdf/IOSCOPD314.pdf (last visited Feb. 3, 2019).

EU-INFO, *Gesetzgebung*, http://www.eu-info.de/europa/eu-richtlinien-verordnungen/ (last visited Dec. 7, 2018).

EUR-LEX, *The direct effect of European law,* https://eur-lex.europa.eu/legal-content/EN/TXT/?uri=LEGISSUM%3Al14547 (last visited Apr. 15, 2019).

EUROPEAN COMMISSION, *Better Regulation Toolbox based on the Better Regulation Guidelines* (2015), http://ec.europa.eu/smart-regulation/guidelines/docs/swd_br_guidelines_en.pdf (last visited Dec. 23, 2018).

EUROPEAN SECURITIES AND MARKETS AUTHORITY (ESMA); *Interactive Single Rulebook* (ISRB), https://www.esma.europa.eu/rules-databases-library/interactive-single-rulebook-isrb (last visited Apr. 15, 2019).

EUROPEAN SECURITIES AND MARKETS AUTHORITY (ESMA); *Who we are,* https://www.esma.europa.eu/about-esma/who-we-are (last visited Apr. 15, 2019).

EUROPEAN UNION, EU *Regulations, Directives and other acts,* https://europa.eu/european-union/eu-law/legal-acts_en (last visited Dec. 18, 2018).

European Union, *Institutions and bodies,* https://europa.eu/european-union/about-eu/institutions-bodies_en (last visited Apr. 15, 2019).

Federal Financial Supervisory Authoriy (BaFin), https://www.bafin.de/DE/Internationales/GlobaleZusammenarbeit/IOSCO/iosco_node.html (last visited Apr. 15, 2019).

Financial Market Authority (FMA) Liechtenstein, https://www.fma-li.li/de/internationales/global/internationale-organisationen.html (last visited Apr. 15, 2019).

Gabler Wirtschaftslexikon, *Neue Institutionenökonomik,* https://wirtschaftslexikon.gabler.de/definition/neue-institutionenoekonomik-38077 (last visited Apr. 15, 2019).

International Organization of Securities Commissions (IOSCO), https://www.iosco.org/ (last visited Apr. 15, 2019).

Toronto Centre, *FinTech, RegTech and SupTech: What They Mean for Financial Supervision* (2017), https://res.torontocentre.org/guidedocs/FinTech%20RegTech%20and%20SupTech%20-%20What%20They%20Mean%20for%20Financial%20Supervision.pdf (last visited Feb. 3, 2019).

University of Portsmouth European Studies, *Direct applicability and direct effect,* http://hum.port.ac.uk/europeanstudieshub/learning/module-3-governance-in-a-multi-level-europe/direct-effect-and-direct-applicability (last visited Dec. 18, 2018).

Vienne Behavioral Economics Network, *Was ist Behavioral Economics?*, https://vben.at/was-ist-behavioral-economics/ (last visited Apr. 15, 2019).

Dr Antonios Koumbarakis

Legal Research in the Second Machine Age

TABLE OF CONTENTS

I. Introduction

Over the last two centuries, developed countries moved from the technological age to the digital age. As part of this transformative process, technology now provides us with a variety of opportunities. Given that fact, the question arises: What should the future of legal research look like. To answer that question, this chapter focuses on the future of legal research. It examines the main changes and concerns regarding how legal research can improve as well as the changes in how lawyers will work. It also provides an overview of the main legal research tools available while shedding light on the uncertainties and transitions in that area.

II. Technology, Legal, and Regulatory Work

Technology has had a massive impact on most areas of human activity. As such, it is not surprising that technological developments significantly challenge the nature of legal research.[1] Electronic legal research will, inter alia, affect the way the law develops as well as the way lawyers understand and argue their cases, right down their choice of precedent in litigation. Lawyers therefore need to be aware of the challenges and opportunities in the legal research field. For example, in a digital work environment, lawyers need to excel at sifting through large amounts of unindexed text. Judges require sources in order to adeptly deliver effective judgments. Search algorithms, Big Data[2] and Artificial Intelligence (AI)[3] play a pivotal role in improving the quality of the legal profession. In other words, with free legal sources and analytical tools, researchers and lawyers depend on algorithms rather than expert human editing, and it is important that lawyers understand the limits of the various layers

---

1 Eugene Clark, *Future Trends in Legal Research and Scholarship: Implications of the Establishment of a Cyberinfrastructure for E-Research*, 16 J.L. INF. & SCI. 114 (2005).

2 Understanding and defining the concept of Big Data is no easy task because there is no single accepted definition. The phenomenon of Big Data and the term itself shall remain flexible to accommodate inevitable adjustments. Nevertheless, Big Data consists of the use of highly developed IT tools to create a very large flow of different types of data (e.g., consumer data from websites, data generated from payment transactions) (*see* Guenther Dobrauz-Saldapenna, Michael Taschner & Antonios Koumbarakis, *Big Data Regulation—Quo Vadis?* (Mar. 15, 2018), https://www.pwc.ch/en/publications/2018/big-data-regulation-quo-vadis.pdf (last visited Feb. 6, 2019).

3 Artificial intelligence is the process of simulating human intelligence through machine processes (*see* Michael Copeland, *The Difference Between Artificial Intelligence, Machine Learning and Deep Learning*, NVIVDA, https://blogs. nvidia.com/blog/2016/07/29/whats-difference-artificial-intelligence-machine-learning-deep-learning-ai/ (last visited Feb. 6, 2019).

of the available information.[4] Against this complex backdrop, law review and regulatory platforms will play an important role in how lawyers and regulatory supervisors work.

A. Law Review Platforms

Prior to the digital revolution, the most important legal resources needed for professional practice were commercial in nature, but times have changed and today the whole range of valuable legal information is outside the paywalls of law firms.[5] Courts and regulatory authorities have moved to online databases, and lawyers regularly use computers for their daily work.[6] Law reviews have launched online versions such as Westlaw Edge, Lexis and SSRN. Similarly, governmental and intergovernmental agencies have adapted and offer relevant research databases. The European Union (EU), for instance, offers one of the most comprehensive legal databases, translated in 23 languages, to be found on the internet.

As regards private companies, with Big Data and Artificial Intelligence, the next generation will be legal research platforms such as ROSS Intelligence,[7] Lexis Analytics, LawGeex, Beagle, CARA, Fastcase, Casemaker and Harvard Law's Caselaw Access Project, which completed the digitization of all US case law.[8] Given these tools, here is an initial overview of the main online versions and legal / regulatory platforms (see Exhibit 1 and Exhibit 2). Considering the startling developments, it is hardly surprising that already in 2015, the commercial market on legal research was estimated at $8 billion.[9]

---

4 Terry Hutchinson, *Legal Research in the Fourth Industrial Revolution*, 43 Monash U. L. Rev. 567 (2017).

5 Clark, *supra* note 1.

6 *Id.*

7 ROSS is a legal research platform powered by AI for U.S. law.

8 Bob Ambrogi, *Legal Research Gets Smarter and More Comprehensive in 2018*, Lawsites (Jan. 1, 2018), http://www.adrtoolbox.com/2019/01/44629/ (last visited Feb. 6, 2019).

9 Erik Eckholm, *Harvard Law Library Readies Trove of Decisions for Digital Age*, NY Times (2015), https://www.nytimes.com/2015/10/29/us/harvard-law-library-sacrifices-a-trove-for-the-sake-of-a-free-database.html (last visited Apr. 8, 2019).

Year of launch	Legal product	Preexisting challenge	Available at
2019	PwC Legal Regulatory Radar	Keeping track of regulatory initiatives at all levels and offering in-depth analysis of relevant legislation	https://www.pwc.ch/en/industry-sectors/financial-services/fs-regulations/regulatoryradar.html
2018	EVA	More efficient access to case law	https://eva.rossintelligence.com/#/login
2018	Westlaw Edge	Avoiding lengthy research by means of word or case suggestions	https://legal.thomsonreuters.com/en/products/westlaw/edge
2018	Lexis Analytics	Integrated tool for litigation, regulation and transaction	https://www.lexisnexis.com/en-us/products/lexis-analytics.page
2015	Beagle	Helps navigate contracts	http://beagle.ai/
2015	Casemaker	Finding all federal and state court cases and statutes	https://public.casemakerlegal.net/products/casemaker/
2015	Ross Intelligence	Finding all federal and state court cases and statutes	http://rossintelligence.com/
2014	LawGeex	Contract review automation	https://www.lawgeex.com/
2013	Casetext / CARA	Helping to find all federal and state court cases but also independently making proposals for relevant cases	https://casetext.com/product

Solution
A platform ensuring oversight of all relevant regulatory initiatives (e.g., sustainability regulation, EBA outsourcing standards or securitization regulation). This is particularly relevant given the increase in number and scope of financial market regulations on a global scale. It offers: – A very high degree of customization (e.g., geographic scope, regulatory authorities, regulations and regulatory sources) – Tailor-made solutions that cover specific organizational structures – Regulatory repositories of all relevant regulations – High-level impact analysis for all jurisdictions, client types, product types, etc. – Generic analysis of relevant regulatory initiatives
EVA is mainly a tool for analyzing briefs but it is also useful for checking the subsequent history of cited cases and determining if they are still good law. It can be used to find cases that are similar to a given case or to find cases that have similar language or that contain the same quotes.
Noticeable features of Westlaw Edge include: – An enhanced, AI-powered version of the KeyCite citator providing warnings when cases may no longer be good law in circumstances that traditional citators could not identify. – WestSearch Plus, an AI-driven legal research tool that quickly guides lawyers to answers on specific legal questions. – Integrated litigation and detailed docket analytics covering judges, courts, attorneys and law firms for both federal and state courts. – Statutes Compare, a tool that allows researchers to compare changes to statutes. Westlaw Edge will be offered as a subscription upgrade to Westlaw subscribers. Thomson Reuters will continue to operate Westlaw in its current form until 2024, but going forward it will focus most of its development effort on the new Westlaw Edge platform.
Products within the Lexis Analytics suite are organized into three categories: – Litigation analytics: analytics products under the litigation umbrella include Lex Machina and a new offering, Context, which identifies the language a judge most often cites in opinions. – Regulatory analytics: allows attorneys to better manage compliance, helping them track regulatory developments, predict which laws will pass, and understand what to disclose and how to disclose it. – Transactional analytics: empowers attorneys with the latest precedents and clauses to manage transactions more efficiently and effectively. The tools analyze, compare and benchmark the frequency and content of other industry disclosures to help strengthen negotiations and build better deals.
It automatically scans contracts, identifies some of the most important parts and categorizes everything to make it searchable.
Casemaker is a lower-cost legal research tool with a large database of state and federal case law and statutes. It is also a citator tool. Casemaker has added the decisions of the United States Patent and Trademark Office to the federal library.
Ross Intelligence delivers a plethora of on-point case law, regulatory and statutory information. It offers a platform optimized for natural language searches, which tends to provide search results that better address a customer's intent and the context of their query, leading to more efficient legal research.
LawGeex combines machine-learning algorithms, text analytics and the knowledge of expert lawyers to deliver in-depth contract reviews using the legal team's predefined criteria. Contract review becomes quicker and more efficient.
Casetext is a full-service legal research platform. It has all federal cases and statutes, and all state cases and statutes above the trial court level. It also puts red flags on cases that are no longer good law, provides links to cases that cite the case currently being read, and has a Black Letter Law database containing points of law that have been well settled, among many other useful features. Casetext's database coverage is extensive, including a long list of primary source law at the state and federal level. Casetext's Case Analysis Research Assistant (CARA) is its AI-backed legal research tool that helps to discover relevant cases and briefs based on complaints, briefs and memos that are uploaded into CARA. After uploading a brief, CARA will analyze the brief, making all subsequent research more intelligent and instantly returning relevant cases regarding the same facts, legal issues, jurisdiction and motion at issue.

Year of launch	Legal product	Preexisting challenge	Available at
2009	Free Law Project	Finding all federal and state court cases in one location	https://free.law/archives.html
2008	Mendeley	Managing large quantities of literature and documents	https://www.mendeley.com/?interaction_required=true
2006	Zotero	Managing large quantities of literature and documents	https://www.zotero.org/
2005	Caselaw Access Project	Finding all federal and state court cases in one location	https://case.law/
1999	Fastcase	Finding all federal and state court cases in one location	https://www.fastcase.com/
1994	SSRN	Providing free access to academic works	https://www.ssrn.com/en/

Exhibit 1: Genesis of Law Review Platforms.

Solution
Collects and freely distributes online all United States court opinions, both state and federal, and historical and current. It also provides data and research services to support academic researchers and journalists in their efforts to study and report on the legal world. Furthermore, the Project hosts the RECAP Project including the RECAP Archive and the extensions for Chrome and Firefox. This project frees millions of dockets, docket entries and documents from PACER, making them searchable on CourtListener and uploading them to the Internet Archive for permanent backup. In Addition, the Project develops technologies for use in legal research, such as opinion and PACER notification services, advanced search capabilities and a citator. These tools are deployed in CourtListener.
Mendeley is a freely available literature management program. The software helps keep track of references as well as: – Save references directly from the browser with the Web Importer – Manage and organize references – Directly read PDFs with the integrated PDF viewer – Quote in Word with the Citation plug-in – Synchronize the Mendeley library to different devices
Zotero is an open-source citation management tool that is designed to store, manage and cite bibliographic references such as books and articles. In Zotero, each of these references constitutes an item. Items can be anything from books, articles and documents to web pages, artwork, films, sound recordings, bills, cases or statutes, among many other things.
The Caselaw Access Project is making all U.S. case law freely accessible online. With the Caselaw Access Project, 40 million pages of published U.S. court cases as well as 6.4 million other cases, some going back as far as 1658, are made available. There are two ways to access the data: API (programmatically accessing metadata, full-text search or individual cases) or bulk downloads (for large collections of cases).
Fastcase offers access to a variety of state and federal materials including all federal case law and state cases going back to at least 1950 in all jurisdictions. Through a recent partnership with HeinOnline, Fastcase now provides access to both law reviews and historical matters from HeinOnline. Docket Alarm, a tool integrated into Fastcase, makes available more than 250 million legal documents.
Formerly known as the Social Science Research Network, SSRN is a repository devoted to the rapid dissemination of scholarly research in the social sciences and humanities. It has also been expanding into the life, physical, health and applied sciences since 2017. It is the largest open-access repository in the world according to Ranking Web of Repositories. Academic papers in PDF format can be uploaded directly to the SSRN site by authors and are then available as free downloads worldwide.

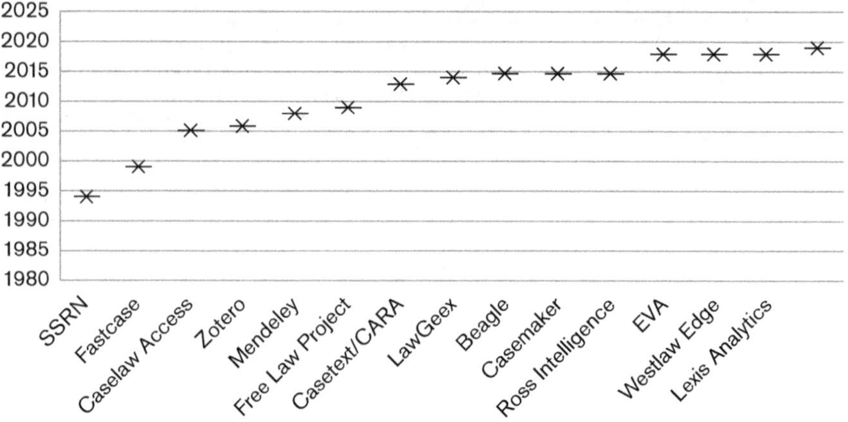

Exhibit 2: Mapping of Law Review Platform Launches.

Exhibit 2 shows that many of the available legal research tools have gone live just in the last four years. This confirms our observation that technology-driven solutions already play, and will continue to play, an important role in the future of legal research.

B. Legal Research in Switzerland

Availability of legal information online differs by type, jurisdiction and subject matter. There is a clear correlation between the way legal research is conducted and other factors such as a country's technological development, people's trust in technology and the quantity of digitized legal information. In Switzerland, a developed country with general trust in technology, a lawyer still spends on average up to 30% of his or her time on legal research.[10] On the one hand, this is owed to inaccurate search algorithms unable to cope with the amount of data in a comprehensive but straightforward way[11] or a phenomenon called «link or reference rot».[12] On the other hand, tools which are able to generate the desired search results in our experience still quite often only cover

10 Achim Kohli, *What legal research could look like in Switzerland in the future*, *in* Minutes of the Conference on the Future of Legal Services in St. Gallen 44–47 (Leo Staub ed., Schulthess, 2018).

11 *Id.*

12 This means that according to some sources over 50 % of cited links in Supreme Court opinions no longer point to the intended page. Roughly 70 % of cited links in academic legal journals

limited and specialists legal sources or areas.[13] A good example for specialist online research tools in Switzerland is www.entscheidsuche.ch for court decisions. Thus, the Swiss example clearly demonstrates one of the shortcomings of digitalized legal research: inaccuracy and difficulties with the vast quantities of information.

At the same time, the ambitions to address exactly these shortcomings are obvious. Matryx, a Swiss LegalTech Startup, and the Swiss Data Science Center (SDSC developed a conceptual approach towards legal research in the future.[14] According to their findings, future legal research rests on four pillars:[15]

i) Precise research hits: limiting the amount of suggestions is key in order to receive more targeted and precise results. Therefore, machine-learning and natural language processing algorithms require constant improvement.
ii) Application of the latest technology: in order to improve search results, Matryx and the SDSC will develop a self-learning algorithmic system capable of discerning legal texts.
iii) Research and publication platforms will be blended: there is an increasing trend towards online platforms where both research and publication are possible.
iv) Proactive search: content of different platforms is merging. This will lead to inter-system communication and tools automatically updating one another.

C. Example: PwC Legal's Regulatory Radar

Since the global financial crisis, regulatory reform has topped the agenda for financial institutions (e.g., sustainable finance regulation, EBA outsourcing guidelines, securitization regulation or Basel IV).[16] Regulations continue to dramatically change the financial industry landscape in order to rebuild the credibility of financial markets. As such, PwC Legal Switzerland has developed a regulatory «radar» platform that will be used by financial institutions to identify regulatory initiatives. The platform will also provide financial institutions with regulatory updates that draw their attention to potential actions and help satisfy regulatory consolidation requirements. Furthermore, compliance

---

and 20% of all science, technology and medicine articles suffer from the same problem. First solutions like perma.cc seek to address and resolve this.

13 *Id.*

14 *Id.*

15 *Id.*

16 Guenther Dobrauz-Saldapenna & Dieter Wirth, *Navigating to Tomorrow. Swiss Banking 2013: Challenges and Opportunities*, 2013/2014 Global Banking and Financial Policy Review 192–195 (2013), https://papers.ssrn.com/sol3/papers.cfm?abstract_id=3186063 (last visited Feb. 9, 2019).

officers and lawyers will be able to assign tasks and responsibilities, which in turn helps improve efficiency in their analysis of regulatory topics. The benefits, including an early warning system and increased business success through early identification and generic impact analysis, are described below:

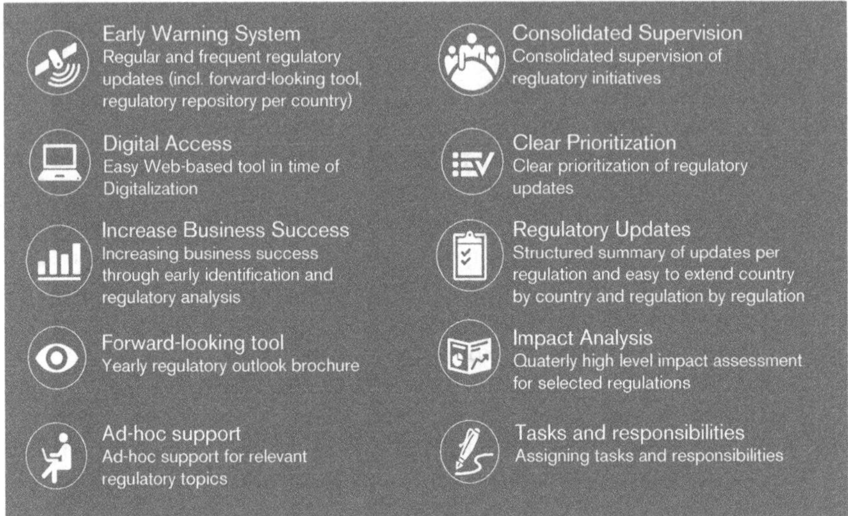

Exhibit 3: Benefits of a tech-powered research platform example [Source: PwC Legal Switzerland (2019)].

The PwC Legal Regulatory Radar figure above shows the opportunities for users. It also illustrates that the fear of lawyers being replaced by emerging legal or regulatory technologies is based on a misunderstanding. Like all tools, they not only require an operator, but they require one who knows how to best use the tool for its intended purpose. Regulatory technology research tools ultimately require a human to monitor them, to tell them what they are looking for and to sift through that research to make sure that all of the relevant regulatory information is there.[17]

Although there is abundant talk about technology replacing humans and leading to increasing unemployment, also in the legal sector, developments point in a different direction. In contrast to common belief, technology is increasingly deployed for repetitive tasks whereas humans can focus on work that computers cannot do and bringing to the table what computers for the time being still do not have: a sense of strategy, creativity, judgement and empa-

17 Sean Semmler & Rose Zeeve, *Artificial Intelligence: Application Today and Implications Tomorrow*, Duke Law & Technology Review 16 (2018).

thy.[18] Similarly, humans have a level of understanding of processes as well as legislative developments and judicial decisions which apparently cannot be matched my machines at present. Furthermore, it would appear that currently only humans can adequately assess the impact and repercussions of certain legal information. In essence: The quality of legal analysis still crucially depends on human skills. Hence, it can be argued that for the time being and presumably for some more time legal research is chiefly assisting human work rather than replacing it.[19] Admittedly, however, there is a likelihood that certain jobs in the legal research field will be carried out by technology in the very near future. In particular, jobs that can be standardized are prone to loss. As such it is our belief that on the one hand, repetitive tasks will be outsourced to technology. On the other hand, tasks requiring a highly skilled labour force and particular human skills will retained and potentially even become more important.

D. The Rise of Interdisciplinarity

Technology has presented us with new research methods based on content and discourse analysis of social media. Because of law's practice-oriented foundations, there has been limited reflection on the nature of legal research.[20] Academics are increasingly working in interdisciplinary teams and combining them with empirical methods used by economists. In other words, they are mixing the perspectives of a trained legal professional who is examining the law with the external perspectives used in other disciplines.[21] All of these developments are pointing to a need for enhanced training in legal research and analytic skills. In other words, there is an implication that the lawyer of the future will need to be well versed in interdisciplinary analytical toolkits.

---

18 Steve Lohr, *A.I. Is Doing Legal Work. But It Won't Replace Lawyers, Yet.*, NY Times (Mar. 19, 2017), https://www.nytimes.com/2017/03/19/technology/lawyers-artificial-intelligence.html (last visited Apr. 8, 2019).

19 *Id.*

20 Terry Hutchinson, *Legal Research in the Fourth Industrial Revolution*, 43 Monash U. L. Rev. 567 (2017).

21 *Id.*

III. The Implication for «Digital» Scholarship

Many lawyers still find it easier to read paper than to read a screen.[22] This may change with younger generations, but it remains a potential problem today. The real question for legal education is when to jump on the bandwagon—now, or later when someone else has already worked out all the kinks.[23]

A survey shows that new associates in law firms spend almost three quarters of their time on a digital device or computer, legal research being one of their main digital activities at work.[24] However, the same survey indicates that more than half of the respondents had never received any kind of formal research training covering these new tools.[25] Thus, there is a need for the reform of legal education in order for law students to be prepared to the meet the challenges of a digitalized working environment. It clearly is not enough to know the law but also to find it.

Clearly, technology is changing the way in which legal research is conducted. Whether this is good or bad is left to personal judgement. At the same time, there are views that the law itself will change with changing research approaches. For instance, it could be argued that the law will be considered more critically by the public as it becomes more widely accessible in shorter time. In this process, politics, institutions, academia and eventually all of society would be impacted.[26] More readily available legal information will open discussions to broader classes of population. This will require a rethink of established approaches, not only in teaching.

Equally, lawyers will need to adapt their problem-solving techniques as well as their conceptual analysis of the texts required for quality doctrinal scholarship. Furthermore, legal educators will have to play an important role in this transition period. Modern lawyers not only need to be highly skilled researchers, but also must possess excellent critical faculties in order to sort through the mass of materials that the new systems are providing.[27] Consequently, the need will arise for a new form of «digital» scholarship that compiles information and creates new knowledge, interpretations and understanding.

IV. The Benefits and Drawbacks of Computer-assisted

---

22 Andrea Charlow, *The Future of Law Review Platforms*, 32 Touro Law Review 6 (2016).

23 *Id.*

24 Steven Lastres, *Rebooting Legal Research in a Digital Age*, Insights Paper (2012).

25 *Id.*

26 Paul Hellyer, *Assessing the Influence of Computer-Assisted Legal Research: A Study of California Supreme Court Opinions*, Library Staff Publications 5 (2005).

27 Hutchinson, *supra* note 4.

Legal Research

The traditional approach of conducting search for legal information by browsing books and scanning through hardcover journals is becoming less and less relevant nowadays in our own experience. Instead as we see in our daily practise most researcher at least uses a mixed approach. This mix will continue to be altered towards digital research in the not too distant future as sources will increasingly if not exclusively become available electronically.

Generally, online databases have the advantage of not having to restrict themselves to certain information. Theoretically, they have no physical limitations and can hold more information than any library or storage could ever hold. Case reports are an example of where digitalized legal research can offer a technical solution. Given the physical constraints, more than half of the cases in the United Kingdom (UK) have gone unreported since 1999.[28] Exhibit 4 presents a broad overview of pros and cons of using technology to facilitate legal research.

Pros

- **Efficiency**: administrative tasks such as filing or searching of sources can be reduced – saves time and costs
- **Speed**: considering constantly changing legal provisions, online tools ensure up-to-date information compared to hardcopies
- **No limits**: online tools do not have physical limits – they can contain unlimited amounts of information (e.g. all cases can be reported)
- **Document Organization**: specialized document software can enhance the organization of documents, including all internal cross-references
- **More 'work satisfaction'**: automated document review, proofreading, and legal research saves time and energy for higher-level work and enhances creativity
- **Litigation analytics**: intelligent legal research software enables attorneys to test out variations in fact patterns or legal analyses to identify the most advantageous strategy
- **Paper-free (however, they require a lot of energy)**
- **Lower research costs, more flexibility and increased transparency for clients**: e.g. case management and/or information systems with a degree of client access enables progress view and can reduce inputting time and errors
- **Flexible Research**: Legal research becomes possible 24/7

Cons 

- **Loss of certain jobs**: certain professions are replaced; (however, jobs in other sectors (particularly the IT sector) are created)
- **Legal research tools lack analytical depth**: they lack the creativity to search in other spots for similar sources
- **Loss of 'human emotion'**: danger of relying on big data too much - legal strategies require emotions and a certain 'human' feeling
- **Overconfidence in technology and danger of compiling mountains of 'useless' information:** technology doesn't replace knowledge of the law
- **Complexity:** technical tools, devices and machines that we interact with on a daily basis but don't fully understand - minor glitches can cost time and expense
- **Over-reliance on Gadgets and risk of power failure**: reliance on mobile phones, computers, and other digital gadgets causes problems when they are lost, break or run out of power
- **Lack of laws and regulatory dilemma**: what, when and how should regulators regulate? The speed of product innovation makes it possible to bring a new product to market while formal rulemaking is still dealing with the last product launch

Exhibit 4: Pros and Cons of technology-based legal research.

---

28 Masoud Gerami & Aidan Hawes, *Justis: at the Forefront of the Evolution of Legal Technology in the UK*, 18 Legal Information Management (2018).

V. Conclusion

Society has largely moved into the digital age in which technology is playing an increasingly important role. The legal research landscape has changed and today has a clear focus on tools allowing for flexible but comprehensive access to legal information. Easy entry to the law is the order of the day. It is probably still too early to arrive at a final conclusion on whether the advantages of relying on technology in legal research will outweigh the disadvantages to a degree that will lead to a complete shift or replacement. Even though some of the benefits are obvious, there are also other aspects such as data security which will become increasingly important and must be considered. Ultimately and as with all LegalTech also in research is a tool meant to help lawyers to become more efficient.

VI. Bibliography

A. Hard Copy Sources

Charlow, Andrea, *The Future of Law Review Platforms*, 32 TOURO LAW REVIEW 6 (2016).

Clark, Eugene, *Future Trends in Legal Research and Scholarship: Implications of the Establishment of a Cyberinfrastructure for E-Research*, 16 J.L. INF. & SCI. 114 (2005).

Gerami, Masoud & Hawes, Aidan, *Justis: at the Forefront of the Evolution of Legal Technology in the UK*, 18, LEGAL INFORMATION MANAGEMENT (2018).

Hellyer, Paul, *Assessing the Influence of Computer-Assisted Legal Research: A Study of California Supreme Court Opinions*, LIBRARY STAFF PUBLICATIONS 5 (2005).

Hutchinson, Terry, *Legal Research in the Fourth Industrial Revolution*, 43 MONASH U. L. REV., 567 (2017).

Kohli, Achim, *What legal research could look like in Switzerland in the future*, *in* MINUTES OF THE CONFERENCE ON THE FUTURE OF LEGAL SERVICES IN ST. GALLEN 44–47 (Leo Staub ed., Schulthess, 2018).

Semmler, Sean & Rose, Zeeve, *Artificial Intelligence: Application Today and Implications Tomorrow*, DUKE LAW & TECHNOLOGY REVIEW 16 (2018).

B. Online Sources

Ambrogi, Bob, *Legal Research Gets Smarter and More Comprehensive in 2018*, LAWSITES (Jan. 1, 2018), http://www.adrtoolbox.com/2019/01/44629/ (last visited Feb. 6, 2019).

Copeland, Michael, *Difference Between Artificial Intelligence, Machine Learning and Deep Learning*, NVIVDA (Jul. 29, 2016), https://blogs.nvidia.com/blog/2016/07/29/whats-difference-artificial-intelligence-machine-learning-deep-learning-ai/ (last visited Feb. 6, 2019).

Dobrauz-Saldapenna, Guenther, Taschner, Michael & Koumbarakis, Antonios, *Big Data Regulation—Quo Vadis?* (Mar. 15, 2018), https://www.pwc.ch/en/publications/2018/big-data-regulation-quo-vadis.pdf (last visited Feb. 6, 2019).

Dobrauz-Saldapenna, Guenther & Wirth, Dieter, *Navigating to Tomorrow. Swiss Banking 2013: Challenges and Opportunities*, 2013/2014 GLOBAL BANKING AND FINANCIAL POLICY REVIEW 192–195 (2013), https://papers.ssrn.com/sol3/papers.cfm?abstract_id=3186063 (last visited Feb. 9, 2019).

Eckholm, Erik, *Harvard Law Library Readies Trove of Decisions for Digital Age*, NY TIMES (Oct. 28, 2015), https://www.nytimes.com/2015/10/29/us/harvard-law-library-sacrifices-a-trove-for-the-sake-of-a-free-database.html (last visited Apr. 8, 2019).

Lastres, Steven, *Rebooting Legal Research in a Digital Age*, INSIGHTS PAPER (2012).

Lohr, Steve, *A.I. Is Doing Legal Work. But It Won't Replace Lawyers, Yet.*, NY TIMES (Mar. 19, 2017), https://www.nytimes.com/2017/03/19/technology/lawyers-artificial-intelligence.html (last visited Apr. 8, 2019).

PwC Legal Switzerland, *Regulatory Radar*, https://www.pwc.ch/en/industry-sectors/financial-services/fs-regulations/regulatoryradar.html (last visited Mar. 6, 2019).

Luis Ackermann

Artificial Intelligence and Advanced Legal Systems

TABLE OF CONTENTS

I. Introduction

When *Deep Blue,* the famous chess computer from *IBM,* defeated the then world champion *Gary Kasparov* in 1997, the victory was publicly perceived as a triumph of the machines that caused worldwide headlines and heralded the beginning of a new era of artificial intelligence.

It soon became clear that *Deep Blue*'s ability was mainly driven by brute force and a lot of manual fine- tuning. The machine was, admittedly, quite good at chess (its performance was indeed so incredibly strong that Kasparov was initially convinced that trickery was involved), but beating the champion was a matter of speed and meticulousness, not intelligence. Decisive for the outcome was the machines ability to analyse 200 million board positions per second. Genius, it turned out, was only one way to succeed in chess.

Significant advances in computer science and an exponential growth of computing power have enabled machines to outperform people in gameslike *Jeopardy* in 2011, *Go* in 2015 and *poker* in 2017.[1] Today, everyone can download a free app to their smartphone that is significantly more performant than *Deep Blue* and flexible enough to beat any chess style. Needless to say, the impact of artificial intelligence and machine learning is not limited to playing games. It will play a major role in the future of most service industries, including the legal profession. But like the inaccurate public perception of *Deep Blue*'s achievements, the potential of today's AI boom is misestimated by many, which leads to a misallocation of resources and hinders technological progress.

The time has come to clear up any misunderstandings, demystify the underlying technology, and give non-technical stakeholders a sense of what is feasible today i.e., to disclose where the technical limits lie and what is expected to come. This chapter is intended to provide a brief technical introduction, followed by our vision of the future world of legal work and the introduction of a framework to help build it.

II. Artificial Intelligence and Machine Learning

Arthur Samuel defined Machine Learning (ML) as the *«field of study that gives computers the ability to learn without being explicitly programmed»*.[2] This distinction between explicitly programming a machine—prescribing a strict set of rules to follow blindly (i.e., an algorithm)—and enabling it to find its

1 Noam Brown & Tuomas Sandholm, *Superhuman AI for heads-up no-limit poker: Libratus beats top professionals*, 359 SCIENCE (2018).

2 Arthur L Samuel, *Some Studies in Machine Learning Using the Game of Checkers*, 3 IBM JOURNAL OF RESEARCH AND DEVELOPMENT (1959).

own algorithm for a given problem is 60 years later still the most spot-on way to explain the fundamental characteristic of ML.

ML is a subfield of the overarching concept of Artificial Intelligence (AI), which is the study of intelligent agents or, more specifically, machines that are not only able to learn but alo mimic *all* cognitive functions commonly associated with the human mind.

There are several competing definitions for ML and AI, but a broad consensus exists that ML is the branch of AI that provides technology which can be applied in practice today. AI, on the other hand, is more of an umbrella concept that will remain in the academic realm until it will emerge as an actual technology in form of Artificial General Intelligence (AGI) that can perform any intellectual task that a human being can.

While there is a lot more to intelligence than learning facts and recognising patterns, Machine Learning provides a vast array of tools to make machines considerably more flexible and allow for applications that have not been attainable just a few years ago.

ML techniques can be subdivided into three types of learning, which are outlined in the following overview.

A. Supervised Learning

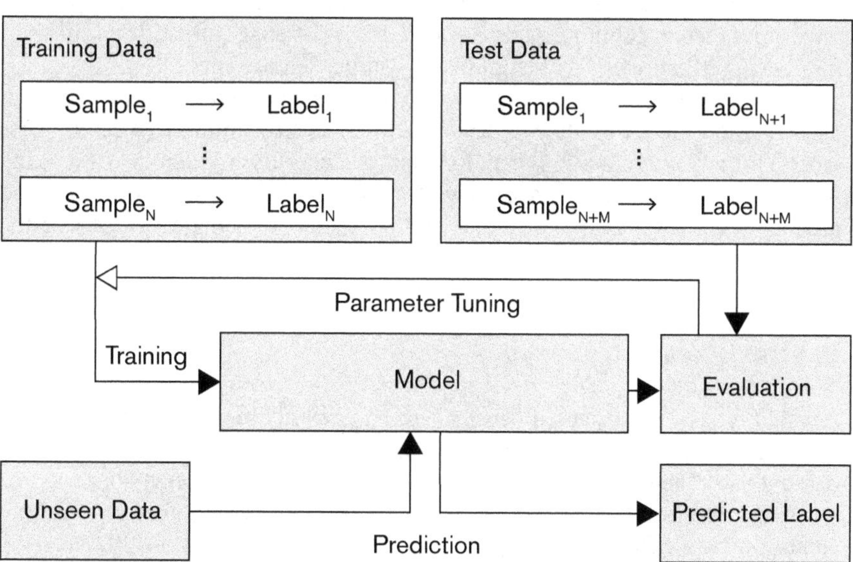

Exhibit 1: Supervised Learning.

The most common type of ML is called *Supervised Learning* and is, essentially, a form of automated function approximation. The goal is to find a function $X \rightarrow y$ that most closely describes the given problem, i.e., a function that will return the best estimation y for any given X. As the name suggests, a function approximation will not generally produce the *true* y but, given enough data, the functions accuracy can be reliably quantified to assess its usability for practical applications.

To train a machine in a supervised way, it is supplied with a set of observations (the *ground truth*), split into a *training* and a *test set*. Employing one of many available supervised learning algorithms, the machine then tries to generalize the *structure* of the training set and adjusts its parameters until it finds a combination that predicts the correct answer for the highest (or a high enough) percentage of records in the test set (i.e., the closest approximation to the solution). A balanced distribution of samples in the training and test set is necessary to prevent the model from overfitting to the training set—after all, the objective of the trained model is to infer information from previously unseen data, not to specialise on the samples.

The sample set must be sufficiently big to be representative of the domain the model should learn. Size requirements depend on multiple factors such as feature complexity, sample heterogeneity or target accuracy and must be evaluated for each individual use case. With traditional algorithms, a few hundred samples are sometimes enough to reliably train and test a model, but particularly more recent techniques like *Deep Learning* often require millions of samples because they work with significantly larger feature spaces.

Supervised learning can solve *classification* and *regression* problems. A classification model predicts a *discrete* class label (or multiple discrete class labels) for any given input. It can, for example, classify a document by tagging it with the appropriate field of law. A regression model on the other hand predicts a *continuous* quantity and can be used to calculate values like the percentage chance of winning a case, for instance.

B. Unsupervised Learning

Another type of ML is called *Unsupervised Learning*. In contrast to supervised learning, it does not rely on a labelled data set for training as it is not used to compute a predetermined value but to detect hidden structures in data.

Unsupervised methods correlate data features to find patterns and are commonly used for dimensionality reduction and clustering tasks. Assessing and interpreting their output usually requires manual labour but they still offer large efficiency gains and allow for the exploration of huge data sets.

In practice, labelled data is often not available in large enough quantities for supervised learning. Depending on the data set, manually labelling the data

can be prohibitively costly and time-consuming, and for some applications (e.g., online training on real-time data) even technically infeasible. With a *semi-supervised* approach, a small labelled set can be augmented with unsupervised learning and the resulting labelled data set is subsequently used to train a supervised model.

C. Reinforcement Learning

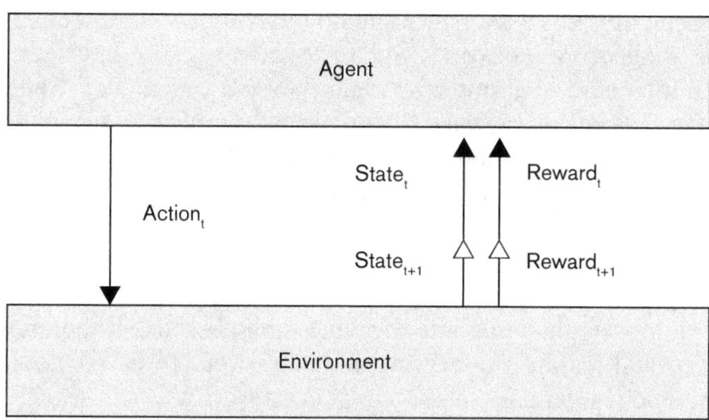

Exhibit 2: Reinforcement Learning.

Unlike supervised and unsupervised learning, *Reinforcement Learning* (RL) does not rely on a static data set for training. Instead, the learning agent is put in an environment and given the only objective of maximising reward. The agents' actions are iteratively observed and rewarded (or punished) so it can get an increasingly complete idea of its surroundings and learn an optimised policy to autonomously act on after training.

This *trial and error* approach of learning is very similar to the way humans learn in the early stages of development. It is particularly useful for problems with large state spaces and the need for real-time decisions.

While Reinforcement Learning does not require a static data set to learn from, the agent must be able to quantify all relevant variables the environment describes to make an informed decision. Additionally, the agent must be allowed to make mistakes (even «fatal» ones) without being subjected to irreversible consequences. Lastly, it must be possible to define concrete functions to compute the reward for taking an action.

Because these requirements are only met in extremely controlled environments or simulations, Reinforcement Learning is currently almost exclusively applied to simulatable problems, that range from robotics and autonomous driving to gaming and stock trading. But given enough increase in computing power and advances in monitoring and measuring methods, it is reasonable to expect a continuous expansion of RL to more and more applications.

D. Deep Learning

Deep Learning (DL) is a variation of the aforementioned types that has recently received a lot of attention and enabled a whole range of new ML applications. Explaining the detailed mechanisms of DL would go beyond the scope of this chapter. Essentially, it is a statistical method that allows computers to recognise patterns using neural networks. Such networks contain inputs and outputs, not unlike the neurons in our brain, and they are called *deep* when they consist of a cascade of layers, each dealing with a particular aspect of feature extraction and transformation. An algorithm called *back-propagation* is employed to adjust the mathematical weight of the connections between the neurons based on the quality of the computed result, similar to how relevant synapses are strengthened during the learning process in a human brain.

The key benefit of Deep Learning is that it works on problems with significantly larger feature sets than previously manageable, because it requires considerably less manual feature engineering and extraction. To do so, however, it depends on much larger data sets.

The continuous increase in available data and computing resources (notably, advances in the development of graphics processing units) is primarily responsible for the recent upswing in the field of DL, which for decades has been mainly dormant. These developments eventually led to ground-breaking scientific achievements at the beginning of the 2010s (notably *Krizhevsky*'s use of a neural network in the ImageNet challenge[3] which beat the other participating models by a huge margin of 10.8%) that sparked the interest of investors and other researchers and gave rise to the current AI boom.

Although DL algorithms are inspired by patterns of communication and information processing in biological nervous systems, they differ in various aspects from the structure and function of the human brain. Unless and until these gaps are bridged, it is unwise to expect human-like problem solving from Deep Learning. While the technique works well for close-ended classification tasks, it has thus far not shown very promising results in applications with limited amounts of training data or wide ranges of sample diversity.

3 Alex Krizhevsky, et al., *ImageNet Classification with Deep Convolutional Neural Networks*, 60 Communications of the ACM (2017).

III. State of the Art

«Any sufficiently advanced technology is indistinguishable from magic.»
– Arthur C Clarke, Profiles of the Future (1973)

The more complex ML algorithms become, the more magical their output may initially appear. But as the preceding introduction has shown, ML is not magic, just cleverly applied statistics and stochastic, supported by a lot of other branches of mathematics—magic *tricks*, if you will.

Magic or not, with ML we are now able solve a number of problems that until recently were unattainable for machines. Models trained by ML enhance security systems with anomaly detection, improve ranking in search applications, provide speech recognition and natural language generation for virtual assistants, support medicine with image recognition and diagnostics, make predictions no one wants (advertising)—and those that save lives (earthquakes), optimise supply chains and drive cars.

According to the 2018 AI Index,[4] 61'098 AI papers were published in 2017, 13.3% more than the year before. This activity is also reflected in an improvement in accuracy scores that measure the overall quality of ML algorithms: The highest BLEU score achieved in 2018 for machine translation between German and English was 48.4% (compared to 35.1% in 2017), the syntactic structure of sentences has been parsed with an accuracy of 95.3% (2017: 94.2%), and machines can now recognise (albeit not yet adequately understand) the spoken language as well as humans and even surpass them in certain tasks like object detection.

In short, ML as the driving force behind the Information Age excels at finding hidden correlations in huge amounts of data and solves a growing number of problems that require data transformation and translation. Given continued trends in research and computing power, ML performance can be expected to steadily improve at those tasks.

Correlation is a very useful tool, but many domains require basic cognitive abilities that machines haven't developed yet, such as causal inference or common-sense reasoning.

---

4 The AI Index, 2018 Annual Report (2018).

IV. Lack of Common Sense

Levesque concisely describes today's ML applications: *«products we now call ‹smart› are far from intelligent in the way we apply the term to people».*[5]

In the absence of common sense, machines are little more than hard-working simpletons. Assigning them laborious and intellectually undemanding tasks is perfectly fine, but beyond that their employment can quickly become dangerous. They are, for instance, extremely susceptible to *biases* (face recognition misclassifies dark-skinned females with an error rate of up to 34.7% compared to 0.8% for lighter-skinned males[6]), can be easily manipulated by *adversarial attacks* (reading comprehension accuracy drops from 75% to 36% when an adversarially constructed sentence is introduced[7]) and are incapable of sensibly reacting to completely unexpected (i.e., untrained for) situations[8].

Intellectual limitations are not the only obstacle to overcome. Most ML methods are rather inflexible and need application-specific training and customisation—which requires a lot of data and technical expertise and as a result becomes unattainable for many companies. But these are teething troubles that can be overcome by training skilled personnel, increasing computing capacity and new methods like transfer learning. In comparison to these, the lack of common sense is a serious problem of adolescence without an obvious solution in sight.

V. The Future of AI

Notable industry leaders seem convinced of the impending arrival of AGI. Facebooks CEO *Mark Zuckerberg* stated in 2015 that his company's AI will *«get better than human level at all of the primary human senses: vision, hearing, language, general cognition»* within *«the next five to 10 years».*[9] *Shane Legg*, co-founder and chief scientist at *Google*'s *DeepMind* expects to *«see an*

5 Hector J. Levesque, Common sense, the Turing Test, and the quest for real AI (The MIT Press. 2017).

6 Joy Buolamwini & Timnit Gebru, *Gender Shades: Intersectional Accuracy Disparities in Commercial Gender Classification* § 81 (A Friedler Sorelle & Wilson Christo eds., PMLR 2018).

7 Robin Jia & Percy Liang, *Adversarial Examples for Evaluating Reading Comprehension Systems*, abs/1707.07328 CoRR (2017).

8 In a best-case scenario, the algorithm can at least evaluate a low confidence score and conclude that no decision should be made—but a lot of techniques still don't provide reliable self-assess ment for outliers outside the training phase.

9 Harry McCraken, *Inside Mark Zuckerberg's Bold Plan For The Future Of Facebook*, Fast Company, (Nov. 16, 2015).

impressive proto-AGI» by 2020 and the arrival of *«human level AGI»* by 2028.[10]

Considering the previously discussed shortcomings of ML and the relatively young age of the field, it seems rather unlikely that AGI or human-level AI is indeed about to be introduced. *Melanie Mitchell* aptly summarized the reliability of predictions about AI in a recent New York Times article:[11]

> *«As someone who has worked in A.I. for decades, I've witnessed the failure of similar predictions of imminent human-level A.I., and I'm certain these latest forecasts will fall short as well.»*

Leading researchers like *Brooks*[12] and *Marcus*[13] agree that the mere refinement of current methods is unlikely to lead to AGI and that entirely new ideas are needed instead. Others like *LeCun*[14] have more confidence in Deep Learning's potential but also see a lot of hurdles to overcome. What they all share though is *Mitchell*'s assessment that an AGI breakthrough more likely lies in the distant future.

Prediction is, as the Danish proverb goes, difficult, especially when dealing with the future. Fortunately, we don't have to rely on predictions anyway. Quoting the statistician and uncertainty expert *Nassim Nicholas Taleb*, *«we just need to be prepared for all relevant eventualities»*.

These are the three conceivable future scenarios for which we should be prepared: (a) AGI will indeed emerge in the next 10 years, (b) it will take significantly longer, or (c) for technical or practical reasons we will never be able to develop or use AGI.

The good news is that we can prepare for all these scenarios with a single strategy. After all, the preconditions for an AGI—complete digitization and data availability, advanced interfaces, technical training, regulatory compliance and security measures, to name a few—are congruent with the requirements for the effective employment of ML today. Once these common building blocks are laid, we are prepared for eventual breakthroughs and can benefit the most of technological advances in the meantime.

---

10 Shane Legg, *Goodbye 2011, hello 2012* (2011), http://www.webcitation.org/73x4BluZc (last visited Apr. 10, 2019).

11 Melanie Mitchell, *Artificial Intelligence Hits the Barrier of Meaning*, The New York Times (Nov. 5, 2018) (last visited Apr. 11, 2019).

12 Rodney Brooks, *The Origins of «Artificial Intelligence»* (2018), http://www.webcitation.org/74i9WUkhM (last visited Apr. 11, 2019).

13 Gary Marcus, *Deep Learning: A Critical Appraisal*, abs/1801.00631 CoRR (2018).

14 Yann LeCun, *Open Plenary* (2017).

VI. AI: Ad Interim

After *Kasparov* eventually accepted that no foul play was involved and that he was actually beaten by a machine, he embraced the new technology as a tool that could be used to his advantage and began developing what he would introduce a year later under the name *Advanced Chess*. This variation of the game is played by two teams, each consisting of a human and a machine. In a collaborative effort, the human player can focus on strategic thinking and creative planning and delegate intricate and computation-intensive tasks like strategy analysis and blunder prevention to the machine. To succeed in *Advanced Chess,* you still had to be a good chess player; but soon no human could win an *Advanced Chess* match without the help of a computer.

Initially, at least, it will not be robot lawyers to disrupt the industry, but human-machine teams that combine the human expertise, intuition, diligence and creativity with the rigorous precision, vast memory, speed and tirelessness of machines.

It's time to play *Advanced Law.*

Imagine all your colleagues, current and former, looking over your shoulder while you are, for instance, drawing up a contract, using their experience to advise you on tricky clauses, point to relevant reference material and prevent you from making mistakes. Minus the snarky comments and other interpersonal issues, of course, but with the ability to precisely analyse the context and cross-reference it to every single document in the corpus in real-time. Such virtual assistants make lawyers radically more efficient and resilient to negligence.

The idea of humans and machines collaborating on legal work[15] is not new, of course, but has so far not been realized. This is because the technological capabilities required for a practical and sufficiently effective solution simply did not exist or where considered uneconomical, but also due to the extensive structural changes necessitated by such a form of collaboration. For virtual assistants to effectively learn from their human co-workers and be able to intervene at precisely the right time, the collaboration must occur in a very close manner and cover the entire workflow. Algorithms need to analyse and react to every user action and depend on access to all potentially relevant data.

Although not all technical challenges have been overcome so far, recent advances in natural language processing, information retrieval, data analysis and a whole host of other technologies have paved the way to finally develop the first generation of virtual assistants that are working well enough to justify the implementation costs. Because these are non-autonomous systems that do not replace the work of lawyers but augment it, their decision-making abilities,

15 *See*, e.g., Kevin D. Ashley, Artificial intelligence and legal analytics: new tools for law practice in the digital age (Cambridge University Press, 2017).

for instance, must not be perfect—they contribute by taking on the grunt work and leave the more complicated tasks to their human co-workers, observe their approach and steadily improve their skills until they feel confident enough to participate in similar scenarios.

Remus and *Levy* propose a classification of legal tasks into those with a *light*, *moderate* and *heavy* impact of automation on lawyer employment[16] is based on their classifications but slightly adjusted to reflect the impact on *all* legal work[17] and, more importantly, taking into account the effect of virtual assistants on tasks that are thus far difficult (or impossible) to automate but can be augmented relatively easily (particularly *Document Drafting*, *Legal Writing*, *Research* and *Communication* tasks).

Task	Tier One Firms	Tier Two-Five Firms
Heavy Impact	25.10%	32.00%
Document Review	4.10%	3.60%
Document Drafting	5.00%	4.00%
Case Administration and Management	3.70%	5.60%
Legal Research	0.50%	0.40%
Document Management	0.40%	0.70%
Legal Writing	11.40%	17.70%
Moderate Impact	39.30%	35.40%
Due Diligence	2.00%	3.40%
Legal Analysis and Strategy	28.50%	27.00%
Other Communications/Interactions	8.80%	5.00%
Light Impact	35.40%	32.30%
Fact Investigation	9.20%	9.60%
Advising Clients	9.30%	3.20%
Court Appearances and Preparation	13.90%	14.50%
Negotiation	3.00%	5.00%
Totals	99.80%	99.70%

Exhibit 3: Percent of invoiced hours spent on various tasks, grouped by estimated extent of computer penetration. Based on data from Remus & Levy (2017) with adjusted estimates (clarified in footnote 17). Percentages do not sum up to 100% due to rounding.

---

16 Dana Remus & Frank Levy, *Can Robots Be Lawyers: Computers, Lawyers, and the Practice of Law*, 30 Geo. J. Legal Ethics (2017).

17 Remus and Levy's analysis is very thorough and well worth reading. It investigates the impact of automation on the employment of lawyers, not legal workers in general, and therefore estimates lower impacts on tasks which are predominantly performed by paralegals and clerical staff. This chapter, on the other hand, addresses the potential effect of IT systems on the legal market as a whole and the assessment of some tasks has been adjusted accordingly. Other tasks have been re-evaluated due to Remus and Levy's decision to ignore the full potential of existing technology. It is this authors opinion that most of the currently deployed solutions still leave a lot of room to improve in regard to their efficiency and that this potential should be factored in.

With a moderate to heavy impact of computer penetration on up to 67.4% of tasks performed by humans today, the economic viability of technological investments is apparent. Given the technical feasibility and the cost effectiveness of deploying the technology, only one challenge remains: implementation complexity.

Upgrading legacy systems step-by-step will hardly lead to a sustained solution that meets the requirements mentioned above. On the contrary, the move to *Advanced Legal Systems (ALS)* requires disruptive changes to the way of work, the processes and the IT infrastructure of legal professionals. In rather conservative environments such changes are often met with fear and hostility and require a clear vision with a concrete action plan to be seriously considered. The following overview of a prototypical *Advanced Legal System* should give you an idea about the kind of questions that must be addressed. It is by no means exhaustive but intended as a framework that gives you food for thought and guides you through the first steps of planning.

VII. Advanced Legal Systems

Advanced Legal Systems are not specific software products but holistic IT environments for legal professionals, designed to facilitate task augmentation and automation in a maximally extendable way.

The most crucial concept of ALS is based on the recognition that complex IT systems cannot be completely planned in advance. They must be designed to dynamically evolve so they can adapt to new technology and business requirements as quickly as possible. Naturally, this evolution must still be controlled, just not with a five-year plan. This agile approach demands a continuous commitment to the subject, which may seem intimidating at first glance. But embracing the opportunity and acquiring in-house IT competence will pay off soon and protect you from new competitors from the tech market.

Whether you decide to become a natively digital law firm and develop parts of your system in-house or prefer to concentrate on your core business and out-source your infrastructure, your IT system should be in constant motion. The current approach of major upgrade projects every five or ten years will (a) soon be too expensive (as the complexity of and the dependency on these systems increase, so does the cost of abruptly changing them at once) and (b) become a competitive disadvantage when the competition is able to deploy emerging technology years in advance.

A. Architecture

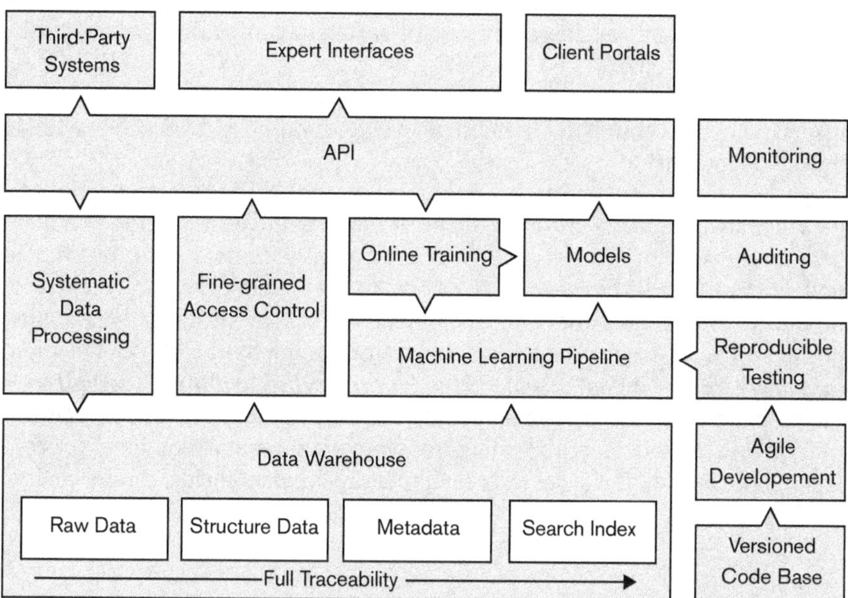

Exhibit 4: Overview of all components of a prototypical Advanced Legal System.

Exhibit 4 provides an overview of the key components of an ALS and the data flow between them.

A central *Application Programing Interface* (API) is responsible for the communication between all components and represents the core of the system. It connects end user applications, third party systems and self-service portals with the underlying data and ML services.

The development environment should be closely connected to the production system (or a shadow version thereof) to give developers direct access to training and feedback data and allow them to quickly release new features or bug fixes. To maintain high auditability, all source code should be versioned and signed and tests should be written in a reproducible manner. New releases are automatically tested and deployed to the production system to reduce development cycle times.

Every component has a well-defined and exclusive responsibility for certain functions or processes. This *separation of concerns* allows for the continuous improvement or replacement of individual components and increases the transparency of the systems inner workings. The possibility to replace components and move to different vendors is of paramount importance for three reasons: (a) the quality of a vendor's service (in absolute or relative terms) can decrease rapidly for a multitude of reasons (acquisition being a common one), (b) a vendor may suddenly fail to deliver its services or (c) try to exploit your dependency on them (artificially increasing moving costs is a notoriously popular business strategy of software companies that should be actively combatted).

Some components may assume data ownership that needs to be strictly respected by others in order to maintain a *single source of truth* and guarantee the data's integrity.

All data flowing into the system through the API is systematically processed and structured. The original and all its derivatives are stored in a database and linked for full traceability. It is then pushed into the ML pipeline to update pre-trained ML models. The effort to digitize information received or produced in analogue form ranges from low (e.g., systematically scanning postal correspondence or automatically transcribing phone calls) and medium (e.g., digitizing archived cases) to high (e.g., convincing affiliates and government agencies to adopt open standards—or even accept digital communication) and infeasible (e.g., recording non-verbal communication in direct contacts), but since digital systems are completely blind to analogue information, the importance of a high degree of digitisation cannot be stressed enough.

B. Security

Regulatory requirements for digital security are expected to become increasingly stringent in the coming years—and rightly so. In a fully digitized environment, the attack surfaces become larger and the impact of an exploit can be devastating. Security can no longer be an afterthought, but must be the foundation of a systems design.

The core information security objectives—Confidentiality, Integrity and Availability—demand that information can only be accessed by authorized parties (confidentiality), is not modified in an unauthorized or covert way (integrity) and is accessible at all times (availability).

To ensure confidentiality, all outgoing data must be subjected to a fine-grained access control system that is able to grant or deny access based on the context of the request. Data used for Machine Learning must be anonymised—before or after training, but necessarily in a way that prevents identity leaks from the model. Likewise, incoming information must be carefully screened and all versions and derivatives must be securely stored to maintain data integrity. Additionally, all data must be encrypted in transfer and at rest.

Availability is an obvious objective from a business perspective but equally vital for security reasons. Systems should be geographically redundant and run on dedicated hardware in physically controlled environments or multi-cloud setups in order to stay resilient to provider outages and avoid vendor lock-in.

The health of the entire system must be systematically monitored and auditing systems must be put in place that record all transactions and report on suspicious activity. These passive measures must be backed up by regular manual audits and robustness tests to improve and establish trust in the automated processes.

Legal systems face a number of domain specific challenges beyond these basic requirements, notably taking proper account of lawyers' professional secrecy and client confidentiality and ensuring due diligence. Firms serving clients in multiple geographical regions or with varying confidentiality levels will require *segmentation capabilities* to stay in compliance with conflicting regulations. In some cases, *model quarantines* might be needed to prevent data contamination between business units.

While technical measures are designed and implemented by technicians, identifying the regulatory requirements and ensuring compliance will remain the responsibility of the systems operator. A comprehensive and enforceable security policy should be drafted early and consequently followed when making further design decisions to assume this responsibility.

C. Expert Interfaces

As the complexity of a system increases, so does the importance of user-centric design—because no system, however powerful, can unfold its power if its users can't operate it. In order to develop maximally efficient applications, users must be involved in the design process right from the outset, and their feedback must be actively sought (and considered) during the development process. The *User Interfaces (UI)* provided by ALS should adapt to the user whenever possible, not vice versa.

Expert Interfaces (EI) are a subclass of UIs designed for experienced users that require more control over the underlying data and processes. They are the primary work tools for professionals in ALS and as such are allowed to require a higher degree of training than consumer-grade UIs. Nevertheless, designing them requires the same (if not a higher) degree of attention to detail and usability because these factors contribute disproportionately to user adaptation and efficiency.

1. Virtual Agents

A seamless interaction between human experts and virtual agents is a fundamental goal of ALS. To facilitate this cooperation, EIs must be designed with the following objectives in mind:

– *Learning effect:* Each aspect of the interaction should be designed to increase the learning effect for both parties. When training the agent, special care must be taken to ensure that no incorrect conclusions are inferred and that each reaction can be directly linked to the triggering action.

- *Transparency*: For experts to understand why an agent makes a suggestion, they must be able to examine its decision-making process, the underlying data and all involved models. This establishes trust and helps identifying areas with potential for improvement.
- *Control* of the agent: Experts must be able to intervene correctively in an agent's decision and
- such interventions must be embedded in the agent's model with special priority.
- *Unobtrusiveness:* Dialogs and suggestions must be designed as unobtrusively as possible and interruptions are prohibited without sufficient confidence of their value.
- *Personalisation*: Each expert's agent must be trained individually to adapt to their way of working and custom preferences while keeping the ability to collectively learn from other agents' insights.
- *Responsiveness:* Immediate feedback to a user interaction is important for a streamlined workflow. Information that cannot be provided fast enough should be held back and presented ex post in accumulated form.

2. Structured Data Interfaces

Structured Data Interfaces (SDI) enable experts to work directly with abstract data references. This data-driven approach reduces or eliminates a considerable amount of routine work from information aggregation and research to document generation and validation. As further discussed below, structured data exempts machines (and humans) from having to interpret information, which reduces ambiguity and improves accuracy. Interfaces that integrate *Structured Query Languages*, for instance, can provide instant answers to precise questions (as opposed to natural language questioning, which is better suited for broader search applications) and aggregate huge amounts of data. Another example of SDIs are *Structured Templating* applications that allow for the semi-automated generation and updating of «programmed» documents.

D. Expandability

The only thing that is constant is change. Designing an expandable and pluggable system allows for fast adaption of new technology and—combined with an agile development approach—continuous improvement.

1. Modern Development Environments

To keep up with the latest technology and stay competitive, it is advisable to have at least part of the software development is done in-house. ALS should

provide modern development environments based on version control systems with cryptographically signed releases, automated testing and deployment and an agile development life cycle. This facilitates rapid prototyping of new ideas and the development of internal products and new services.

2. Open Source and Open Standards

Unlike proprietary software, *Open Source Software* (OSS) is distributed with its source code, which allows IT professionals to alter, improve and fix it without dependency on the vendor. It is advisable to use OSS whenever possible to avoid vendor lock-in and being dependent on third-party support to operate your core business.

The use of open standards facilitates communication with third-party systems and the replacement of individual components. *Open Government Data* is an important data source for ALS because it provides up-to-date direct access to laws, regulations, statutes and judicial decisions.

3. Structured Data

Structured data is extremely important for the accuracy of ML processes. The more structured a document is, the less an algorithm has to interpret its content—which naturally has a positive effect on accuracy. More structure also means increased transparency—tagged entities in a document, for instance, are not only unambiguously usable by a machine but also allow a human to quickly scan the document with the view of the machine.

Information must not be changed or lost when exchanging data between two systems. For structured data, this requires the use of standardized formats that all connected systems understand.

Incoming data must be structured as soon as it enters the system. This process can and should be automated but might initially need some manual assistance. However, systems that already create structured data at the source should be preferred.

VIII. A Call for Boldness

During the rise of chess computers, a whole generation of chess grand masters went into early retirement because they did not want (or were not able) to adapt to the new technology. Shortly thereafter, the introduction of Advanced Chess culminated in the creation of a whole new league of chess—there are now separate tournaments for humans only and those for human-machine teams.

The situation in the legal world will be similar—professionals who refuse to adapt to technological progress will continue to have a job in the foreseeable future, but they will soon be playing in a different league than their digitally augmented competitors.

The shift to *Advanced Legal Systems* is going to require quite some time and resources, but the competitive advantage will pay off quickly—especially for early adopters (and the rest will inevitably have to follow). Our advice to all those hungry for disruption: Act now, from a position of strength, rethink your IT strategy, free from preconceptions, and be bold enough to not only consider radical change but actually realize it.

IX. Bibliography

A. Hard Copy Sources

ARTHUR C CLARKE, PROFILES OF THE FUTURE (revised edition 1973).

Brown, Noam & Sandholm, Tuomas, *Superhuman AI for heads-up no-limit poker: Libratus beats top professionals*, 359 SCIENCE (2018).

Buolamwini, Joy & Gebru, Timnit, *§81, in* GENDER SHADES: INTERSECTIONAL ACCURACY DISPARITIES IN COMMERCIAL GENDER CLASSIFICATION (A Friedler Sorelle & Wilson Christo eds., PMLR 2018).

Jia, Robin & Liang, Percy, *Adversarial Examples for Evaluating Reading Comprehension Systems*, abs/1707.07328 CoRR (2017).

KEVIN D ASHLEY, ARTIFICIAL INTELLIGENCE AND LEGAL ANALYTICS. NEW TOOLS FOR LAW PRACTICE IN THE DIGITAL AGE (Cambridge University Press, 2017).

Krizhevsky, Alex et al., *ImageNet Classification with Deep Convolutional Neural Networks*, 60 COMMUNICATIONS OF THE ACM (2017).

LEVESQUE, HECTOR J, COMMON SENSE, THE TURING TEST, AND THE QUEST FOR REAL AI (The MIT Press, 2017).

Markus, Gary, *Deep Learning: A Critical Appraisal*, abs/1801.00631 CoRR (2018).

McCraken, Harry, *Inside Mark Zuckerberg's Bold Plan For The Future Of Facebook*, FAST COMPANY, Nov. 16, 2015.

Melanie Mitchell, Artificial Intelligence Hits the Barrier of Meaning, THE NEW YORK TIMES, Nov. 5. 2018.

Remus, Dana & Levy, Frank, *Can Robots Be Lawyers: Computers, Lawyers, and the Practice of Law*, 30 GEO. J. LEGAL ETHICS (2017).

Samuel, Arthur L, *Some Studies in Machine Learning Using the Game of Checkers*, 3 IBM JOURNAL OF RESEARCH AND DEVELOPMENT (1959).

THE AI INDEX, 2018 ANNUAL REPORT (2018).

B. Online Sources

Legg, Shane, *Goodbye 2011, hello 2012*, http://www.webcitation.org/73x4BluZc. (2011) (last visited Apr. 11, 2019)

Rodney Brooks, The Origins of «Artificial Intelligence» (2018), http://www.webcitation.org/74i-9WUkhM (last visited Apr. 11, 2019).

Rus, Daniela & LeCun Yann, *AI and Future of Work: Opening Remarks and Open Plenary* (2017), https://www.artificial-intelligence.video/ai-and-future-of-work-opening-remarks-and-open-plenary-daniela-rus-and-yann-lecun (last visited Apr. 11, 2019).

Dr Christian Öhner and Dr Silke Graf

Automated Legal Documents

TABLE OF CONTENTS

I. Introduction

In this book, many topics are covered, from artificial intelligence (AI) to blockchain technology. Those are all fascinating topics and show the potential for legal technology, which will certainly lead to substantial disruption of the law and the legal industry. This article focuses on document automation, a subject, which the authors believe, has particularly high practical implications and, therefore, should receive proper attention by the technology-minded legal industry despite the fact that it does not necessarily require highly sophisticated technology.

II. What is Document Automation?

In essence, document automation is just templates on steroids. Lawyers have used templates for ages. Rarely, a brief or a contract is written on a blank sheet of paper. Usually, there are at least some parts of any document already prepared in some knowledge management system and the lawyer only has to check them for any update requirements and specifics that are not yet built into the template. A 2017 survey by the *American Bar Association* among US lawyers showed that document assembly software, which automatically creates the most-used legal documents, such as precedent wills, contracts, and letters, are available at 42% for solo practitioners and rise to 63% for law firms.[1]

Document automation takes the idea a step further, aiming at the creation of a final document that is already tailored to the specific case at hand. On the way, the user is guided by questions and, in a sophisticated document, the answers not only serve as input for the creation of the document but also determine the subsequent questions that will be presented to the user. Thereby, the number of inputs a user has to make in order to finalize a document are limited to the specific requirements of the user for the individual case at hand, further enhancing efficiency.

In the consumer space, document automation is already widespread and numerous providers capture a share of the legal market from flesh and blood attorneys. Examples range from divorce forms, last wills and child custody to sales agreements and bills of sale. There are websites where you can get all these forms, sometimes free of charge. *USLegalForms.com*[2] offers a stunning 85,000 forms online and boasts more than three million customers. A prominent example of cutting-edge technology is *Robot Lawyer LISA*'s property

1 ABA, *Techreport 2017*, https://www.americanbar.org/groups/law_practice/publications/techreport/2017/ (last visited Feb. 3, 2019).

2 U.S. LegalForms, https://www.uslegalforms.com/ (last visited Feb. 3, 2019).

contract tool,[3] which promises a fast, efficient, effective, fair, and convenient way to create legally binding agreements in the B2C real estate realm. Business in a Box,[4] in contrast, offers all templates you need to start, run, and grow your business and aims at start-up entrepreneurs, thereby shifting into the B2B space. And recently competition comes even from sovereign nations, like Austria, where the government itself offers an automated solution[5] to register a standard limited liability company with automated documentation (and even without a notary, which was absolutely unthinkable in German speaking jurisdictions—until it wasn't and the Austrian legislator just butchered one of the holiest cows in German language corporate laws in 2018).

But in the B2B economy, document automation is surprisingly slow. One pioneering provider is *PartnerVine*[6] that has created a market platform for law firms to sell their automated legal documents online to clients. Their vision is to provide high quality legal documents to inhouse legal departments, potentially in the future with a customer rating for specific products that guide the buyer to the most advanced documents.

III. How mature is Document Automation?

A. Limiting Factors

If there are high practical implications and the technology is readily available, why then is document automation not already more widely used by law firms and especially inhouse legal functions?

We think that the reason why document automation is taking off at a rather leisurely pace is related to the culture of the legal profession and its dogmatic belief that no standardization can do justice to all the individual aspects of a particular case: It would be irresponsible to unleash standard documents on the legal affairs of individual persons or businesses. Not only would this entail the risk to miss important individual features, which are relevant for the case at hand, but it would also lead to highly trained lawyers being left out of the equation by laymen handling their legal affairs on their own because of cost reasons.

---

3 Robot Lawyer LISA, *Property Contracts*, http://robotlawyerlisa.com/property/ (last visited Feb. 3, 2019).

4 Business in a Box, https://www.business-in-a-box.com/ (last visited Feb. 3, 2019).

5 Unternehmensserviceportal, https://www.usp.gv.at/Portal.Node/usp/public/content/gruendung/egruendung/269403.html (last visited Feb. 3, 2019).

6 PartnerVine, https://www.partnervine.com (last visited Feb. 3, 2019).

B. Advantages of Document Automation

Of course, these arguments have some merit. But tested against reality, it is hard to argue against the virtues of document automation. First and foremost, document automation of course does not require that highly trained lawyers are left out. Rather, document automation can augment the process of how legal affairs are handled and add quality as well as efficiency to human lawyering.

Document automation has the potential to substantially enhance the quality of legal products. If used by a trained professional lawyer, the product based on automated documents offers a higher level of consistency and, of supreme relevance, offers a reliable basis for the lawyer to focus on the specifics of a case that require very individual provisions. If distracted by getting the standard provisions right, the lawyer does not only incur a risk to make a mistake in the bread and butter part of the document, but also of less cognitive capacity, to direct to the cutting edge provisions where the added value lies. If an automated document is used by a layperson, the product is still much more likely to suffice for the standards set by the user than an alternative product, either authored by the untrained user to be the best of her abilities or copied from some precedent that may fit the case at hand now, or more likely be rather unsuitable because of the precedent's individual features. In any case, the automated document based on the highly sophisticated creation of an experienced lawyer and paired with the prerequisite legal technology know-how, offers a far superior result than a traditional product. The traditional approach is usually to look for a more or less fitting precedent, which then first has to be re-standardized by way of manual user input before it can again be tailored to the specifics of the case at hand. In contrast, when setting up a template for automation, the legal architect usually combines several templates, does research in sample books and endeavours to create a document that fits to the most common use cases. This document then will be maintained regularly, so the user can be sure that the template is always up-to-date and ready-to-use.

Apart from the improvement in quality, automated documents offer one big advantage the regularly created text document does not: data. By structuring the template into answers to specific questions, the final document is equipped with a whole bunch of information about the content. Nowadays, when we want to retrieve one specific piece of information, we have to reread the paper probably several times to find what we are looking for. And even then, we might fail, even though we created the paper by ourselves. By using automated templates, we have the whole content not only as text that is (even for lawyers) often hard to overlook, but also structured in a data base. At a time where we finally start to realize the importance of data and the capabilities it enables, this factor should play a key role in the decision to change our old-fashioned working process. Think of the effectiveness of the contract management system when feeding it with automatically generated documents or of the impact this would have on the due diligence. Provocatively put, a due diligence as we know it would no longer be needed since we could retrieve all the data we want to by pushing a button. Now, we have to use special AI software that scans our texts and does the structuring in data for us. This produces extra costs, requires extra time and resources, and demands from us to simply trust the software to find what we need, which still is a problem.[7] And the benefits do not stop there: Providing the content as a data set gives us the opportunity to improve many other workflows. We could, for example, define that an email will be drafted automatically depending on the answer to a specific question. Once having our content available as data set, we will probably have uncountable ideas of how we could use it.

Of course, all of the above leads also to gains in efficiency. The time, and thereby the cost, to produce a given legal product is substantially reduced by using an automated document. Because the upfront investment requires to develop a balanced standard that already takes all common requirements into account and a highly structured string of queries to capture the relevant user input, the initial drafting steps can be reduced to answering a manageable number of questions and the machine produces a meaningful, often ready-to-send, draft in seconds.

Document automation has significant implications for traditional legal business models. First, the time savings realized with document automation facilitate flat fee or value billing models and, thereby, serve the trend away from hourly billing with a viable alternative. Uncertainty regarding the time necessary for document generation is reduced, which makes legal spending more predictable. Fewer resources yield better documents and, in a market that in general no longer offers unusually high margins, a profitability boost should be welcome in the legal industry.

C. What is already possible?

The technology for document automation is already widely available. The differences in the various technologies are rather experienced in terms of their user friendliness, a factor not to be underestimated given the cultural leap of faith required on the side of traditional lawyers to embark upon the legal technology journey.

As of this writing and as far as we can see it—at least in the business law sector—document automation is not yet a factor. In our opinion, this is due to three major reasons.

---

7 *See* our other chapter «Lawyer Bots. Rise of the Machines» in this book for more details on this.

For one thing, the established legal industry is delaying the widespread adoption of document automation. The reason is that it does not fit established business models, where lawyers usually are still paid on the basis of time spent rather than value created. From an incentive point of view, in a billable hour environment, a lawyer is not directly incentivized to work swiftly. Of course, there are competitive factors and a general pressure on legal spending, which act as some balance, but those create only indirect incentives for lawyers who bill by the hour.

Another factor is that lawyers are very sensitive when it comes to sharing their knowledge. By providing automated documents to clients, or by using them internally in their law firm, lawyers make part of their expertise available to clients and colleagues. Depending on the quality of a lawyer's know-how, the knowledge shared may account for a significant part of such lawyer's assets. And again, as long as clients pay for junior associates doing the bread and butter drafting from (almost) scratch, there is not much pressure to overcome the reluctance felt when it comes to generous knowledge sharing.

The third factor is that lawyers are usually not well educated in process and design thinking. It requires a different mindset to structure and draft an automated document. And the more design minded software specialists lack the required legal know-how. Combining these two areas of specialization takes effort, and there is a lot of cultural difference to be bridged. Even the legal publishing industry, so far, has failed entirely to enhance their book template publications, which have been available for many decades and offer precedents for basically anything, from a divorce filing to a sophisticated sale and purchase agreement with complexity easily passing one hundred content pages.

IV. Will Document Automation disrupt the Legal Industry?

With *PartnerVine* and other new market entrants the equation may change quickly, however. A separation of the procurement of bread and butter legal work from more sophisticated legal products is intriguing.

An inhouse lawyer could, for example, buy the non-disclosure agreement for a potential transaction online. The transaction moves forward and s/he shops the web for data room rules and a process letter describing the terms for the intended divestiture. Traditionally, the inhouse legal department either had to do this work on its own, on the basis of templates and precedents usually inferior to what law firms have in their knowledge management repository. In practice, often the lawyer—inhouse or in a law firm—tasked with drafting a document searches her/his inbox for a document with some resemblance to the

desired outcome and takes if from there. The alternative is to hire an external law firm for this work, which involves additional cost for which a budget may or may not have been created at a stage when the eventual closing of the deal is all but certain. Once the transaction moves forward, however, also in the automated document world the external lawyers are brought in, eventually, but now they can focus on the specific high value work and are not side-tracked by mundane standard documentation at the beginning of a transaction, nor do they have to charge the client for it.

Once the offering is available, and there is no doubt that eventually—and also that in the long run the quality of automated legal documents will be beyond doubt—businesses will adopt their processes to it. Potentially, this will set resources in the inhouse legal departments free for more important tasks. Likely, it will reduce external law firms to sophisticated and highly individualized lawyering.

V. Bibliography

Online Sources

ABA, *Techreport 2017,* https://www.americanbar.org/groups/law_practice/publications/techreport/2017/ (last visited Feb. 3, 2019).

Business in a Box, https://www.business-in-a-box.com/ (last visited Feb. 3, 2019).

PartnerVine, https://www.partnervine.com (last visited Feb. 3, 2019).

Robot Lawyer LISA, *Property Contracts*, http://robotlawyerlisa.com/property/ (last visited Feb. 3, 2019).

Unternehmensserviceportal, https://www.usp.gv.at/Portal.Node/usp/public/content/gruendung/egruendung/269403.html (last visited Feb. 3, 2019).

U.S. LegalForms, https://www.uslegalforms.com/ (last visited Feb. 3, 2019).

PART 3:

HOW WILL LAWYERS FIT INTO THE NEW SUITS OF THE FUTURE?

Maurus Schreyvogel

Fix What Ain't Broken (Yet)

Embracing Operational Excellence for creating the Legal Function of the Future

TABLE OF CONTENTS

I. Introduction

Many legal functions focus primarily on output quality. This can be a costly proposition, especially when the legal function mostly provide services in a bespoke manner.

In times of shrinking margins, senior management expect their functions to increase efficiency and provide services at lower cost. For many years legal functions were able to defend their cost base and only had to make symbolic contributions to these cost cutting exercises.

More recently this changed and legal departments, like all the other functions, faced difficulties in accomplishing budget cuts. Given that legal functions were able to defend their budgets for so long, many were not ready and able to respond to the *more for less challenge* in a sustainable manner. Instead, calls for cost containment were responded to primarily by reducing headcount. And requests to decrease response time made the remaining legal resources work even harder.

This isn't exactly the environment to kick-off fundamental reform programs, therefore the suggestion to all in-house legal resources is to *fix what ain't broken (yet)* as early as possible. Transformation programs work best if a function is still *in control* of its destiny and can formulate an intrinsic and purpose-driven reason for change.

If your function has not considered operational excellence much and your legal service delivery model is mostly based on personal relationships, bespoke work products, and if you get the feeling that the legal function falls behind other functions in terms of automation, it might be a good time to challenge your function's way of working.

The good news is that you can likely still harvest *low hanging fruits* and, therefore, progress quickly on your functional maturity journey. Also, you can learn and benefit from the achievements and failures of other corporate functions. For instance, you might not yet have exhausted all available service delivery models, sourcing strategies, or footprint considerations that optimally fit the wide variety of legal verticals such as litigation (regulatory or commercial). Trust that your finance, procurement, or HR function have considered these things already and are likely to be more than happy to share their learnings from their own transformation programs with you.

I will start by sharing my personal view on key events and milestones of the Novartis journey towards operational excellence. We certainly have not reached our target operating model yet—as a matter of fact, at this point in time, we are entering a next phase of fundamental change. Still, we have been on our journey long enough to develop a methodology—or way of working—that helps us be more effective in driving improvements compared to when we started.

I will share this methodology in the third part and leave you with practical insights, which we collected from the numerous improvement programs which

we ran in the last decade. In between, I will briefly share my take on three events, each of which had an important impact on our journey and maybe even on the legal industry overall.

I will not cover specific technological advances from which in-house legal functions benefit despite the fact that those can be considered productivity boosters that improve quality at the same time. The key reason for that approach is the belief that in order to maximize the use of technology, a function needs to achieve a certain level of functional majority, which this chapter is focusing on. Nevertheless, in part four I will share a simple matrix, which targets supporting a high level evaluation of a technology offering.

II. The Novartis journey towards operational excellence

A. Early successes

I joined the trademarks department of Novartis in 2004. My responsibilities included oversight and management of a trademark portfolio of approximately 30,000 trademarks. Email was available but it was still common to communicate with outside counsel via paper mail or fax. Therefore, one way to measure my workload was in centimeters. I am referring to the height of the pile of paper mail that I received on a daily basis in conjunction to the before mentioned trademark portfolio.

Today our trademark attorneys communicate with their agents and trademark offices through an electronic docketing platform. Furthermore, and thanks to a sophisticated electronic law engine many prosecution tasks no longer need human intervention but are executed based on digitized playbooks. This reduces attorney time spent on prosecution tasks to a minimum and enables them to focus on activities of higher strategic relevance.

Our patent attorneys leverage similar digital helpers to support their operations. Furthermore, there is some level of standardization and automation within other legal verticals such as litigation support services and data privacy. The impact of these improvements to the organization are of great value:

- We managed to free-up resources to focus on activities of high strategic relevance as mentioned above. This does not only have a positive cost impact, but it more importantly creates more attractive role profiles, which helps us to *attract and retain talent.*
- Whereas it is hard to measure cost savings within the organization if improvement programs do not target to cut jobs—which is true for the above described programs—it is easy to measure external cost savings: Over a period of only five years, our programs resulted in a *reduction of the IP portfolio cost by 25%.*

- Finally, it served us well to embark on these optimization initiatives before there were pressures to do so. This enabled us to run these programs within the function and according to timelines that were appropriate given that we needed associates to change the way they worked. Since we were able to improve service delivery times and coverage through these programs, we managed to improve functional service satisfaction scores.

B. Stagnation

After the above described initial successes engaging in operational excellence our expansion to additional legal verticals stagnated. For a long time, we struggled to grasp the harmonization potential of work done within the general legal groups.

Importantly, pharmaceutical companies do not have mass transactions since we operate in a highly regulated business to business environment. There are few partnerships per country, and there is a high level of differences as we have to adhere to country specific healthcare regulations and systems.

Still, there are the usual domains where we expect some level of repetition. For example, in the legal support to the procurement function, HR work, or in the area of development. In retrospect, the following two aspects seem to be most relevant to why our journey towards operational excellence stagnated:

- There was no obvious reason for our associates to change. We scored high service satisfaction and the collaboration with other functions worked and still does work well. Therefore, most legal associates felt valued and appreciated the freedom in their service delivery that came with the high level of autonomy that all legal associates enjoyed. Only within the last two years, other functions started to challenge our service delivery speed and wondered whether it was possible to simplify our service delivery. The comments suggesting simplifications targeted more predictability from our services which was a clear call for more harmonized and less bespoke services.
- The improvement journey with the trademark and patent teams were unique from the perspective that the legal function owned the end-to-end process. This means that once we achieved a decision to file a trademark, patent, or industrial design, we owned the entire portfolio of work thereafter, up to the point where we had to make renewal or annuity decisions. This is quite different from most other transactions where legal is collaborating with other functions to achieve certain goals. An attempt to improve, for example, the procurement process within a company requires a strong collaboration of multiple functions in order to succeed. Whether the legal function is an obvious choice to be taking the lead in improving an end-to-end process is different in every company. In

some (mostly smaller and younger) companies, contract management is owned by the legal function and, therefore, it is the legal department that serves as process owner and also provides the technology to support the process landscape. Based on my observation, larger and more established companies keep buy side contract management with the procurement function and sell side contract management with the commercial function. The same is true for Novartis, we own such a small portion of the contracting process that we are not an obvious owner to transform the end-to-end process.

C. Acceleration

There are two developments that helped unlock the stagnation of our journey towards operational excellence. As you will note, both drivers fall outside of our function.

- In 2014, Novartis created a service division, Novartis Business Services (NBS), to centralize procurement, IT, HR services, accounting and real estate and facilities management. Whereas previously, these functions were part of a commercial division, they now provide their services to the company in a harmonized manner. As part of this centralization, we started to design and organize our processes with an enterprise end-to-end perspective. This means that aspects from multiple functions will be organized in a single project to create a new way of working. Legal participates in most of those initiatives where, as a global line function, it is challenged to come up with as harmonized and streamlined approaches as possible.
- Over the next five years, we expect an unprecedented number of launches that will require a lot of attention of the legal function; and it will not be possible to deliver our contribution in a timely fashion if we do not let go of other activities or become more efficient in how we do things.

With these two in parallel ongoing events, we recently launched an initiative to reimagine how we work. The goal of the initiative is to *create capacity* to support the launches and adapt to the *more standardized ways* of working that other function embraced earlier on.

The tag line of the initiative is to *give back two hours* to legal associates every day by removing tasks of low strategic value and with a minimal risk exposure to centralized service delivery or automation.

To obtain an informed baseline we launched an activity survey where we asked our associates to tell us how they distribute their activities across the legal verticals and sub-verticals. The fact that we had a 95% response rate on this survey shows a high level of commitment towards operational excellence and a willingness to reimagine how we work and potentially let go of tasks that could be taken-on elsewhere or even be automated.

Since this initiative is still ongoing, I cannot report on final outcomes, but I can share that the energy of engagement of our associates to this initiative will accomplish change that for a long time was taboo and hence will bring us closer to our operational excellence goals.

III. Recent significant news

Following news on developments in the legal market—especially the development of in-house legal departments—I spotted the following three events, which can help predict the direction in which the legal sector might be heading and serve as a compass for the journey towards operational excellence of the Novartis legal team.

A. JPMorgan Chase & Co.[1]

In summer of 2017, JPMorgan Chase & Co. announced the introduction of a learning machine that parses financial deals that once kept legal teams busy for thousands of hours. The program, called *Coin*, for Contract Intelligence, does the mind-numbing job of interpreting commercial-loan agreements that, until the project went online in June, consumed 360,000 hours of work each year by lawyers and loan officers.

What I found interesting about the news was not the achievement as such—which, granted, deserves a lot of recognition—but the way this achievement was presented. The Forbes titles reads «JPMorgan Software Does in Seconds What Took Lawyers 360,000 Hours» which very publicly suggests that there was a waste of time and resources and that there are activities within legal departments or with outside counsel that can be considered a commodity. This bursts the mystic bubble within which our industry operated for far too long and which slowed progress significantly for a long period of time.

1 Hugh Son, *JPMorgan Software Does in Seconds What Took Lawyers 360,000 Hours*, Bloomberg (Feb. 28, 2017, 1:24 PM), https://www.bloomberg.com/news/articles/2017-02-28/jpmorgan-marshals-an-army-of-developers-to-automate-high-finance (last visited Apr. 2, 2019).

B. LawGeex[2]

In a study published by LawGeex in February of 2018, *20* US-trained lawyers, with decades of legal experience ranging from law firms to corporations, were asked to issue-spot legal issues in five standard NDAs. They competed against a LawGeex AI system that had been developed for three years and trained on tens of thousands of contracts.

The research was conducted with input from academics, data scientists, and legal and machine-learning experts, and was overseen by an independent consultant and lawyer. Following extensive testing, the LawGeex Artificial Intelligence achieved an average 94% accuracy rate, ahead of the lawyers who achieved an average rate of 85%.

As with the news on JPMorgan I find the report very instructive. What I found most relevant about this report was that many reputable lawyers participated in this exercise and that there was a lot of attention and great discussion about this experiment in many channels, which to me indicates that there are more and more curious legal professionals who seriously consider changing the way we work.

C. Welcome to Legal 2.0[3]

DXC Technology is a newly created Fortune 200 company resulting from the merger of CSC and a large division of Hewlett-Packard. Bill Deckelman, the general counsel of DXC took the event of the merger as an opportunity to rethink the service delivery model of his newly created legal department. He wanted to create a legal department that was more nimble and less constrained by fixed costs. He introduced a performance-based counsel selection network and he turned to a managed services company to reduce the size of the rather large, combined legal department.

I find this move very refreshing as Deckelman did not settle for trying to do *more with less*. Instead he tried to do *different*. It will be very interesting to observe the further journey of DXC legal and to learn from the experiences of the DXC legal associates and all the legal professionals that contribute to DXCs mission (be it representatives from law firms or managed services partners)

---

2 LawGeekx, *AI vs. Lawyers. The Ultimate Showdown*, Law Geekx, https://www.lawgeex.com/AIvsLawyer/ (2018) (last visited Apr. 2, 2019).

3 Frannie Sprouls, *Welcome to Legal 2.0*, Modern Counsel (Dec, 13, 2017), https://modern-counsel.com/2017/dxc-technology/ (last visited Apr. 2, 2019).

D. Conclusion

My ultimate take-away from these three events is proof that change is happening. It is no longer promises from consultants or legal technology providers. It is reality. After so many years of stagnation, we finally seem to be moving towards a more service-oriented delivery model. And we are considering resources from a wide variety of options, including technology, to optimally and jointly shape and support the goals of the companies that we serve.

IV. Three Questions–and your answers will guide your journey towards operational excellence

The Novartis journey towards operational excellence did not follow a master plan because, quite frankly, we did not have one. Neither did we have a legal operations department nor a person focused on service delivery or operational excellence at the outset.

The starting point of our journey was a burning platform: namely the uneasiness of our IP professionals concerning whether they were on top of their respective portfolio. The IP function then took matters in their own hands and reimaged how they procured and maintained IP rights. The improvement process was not very systematic but followed a trial and error approach.

The introduction of legal operations followed similar principles but change was harder to achieve because the pain points on the general legal side were smaller, distributed, and hidden in the detail of the function.

In retrospect, and based on the learning of our operational excellence journey, we developed a methodology to guide future initiatives. Developed probably is a too big of a word since the methodology is based on common sense and many other companies and consultants came to a similar conclusion.

The methodology is a logical order of three questions. Answering each of them will help define the purpose, activities, delivery options and resources model of a function.

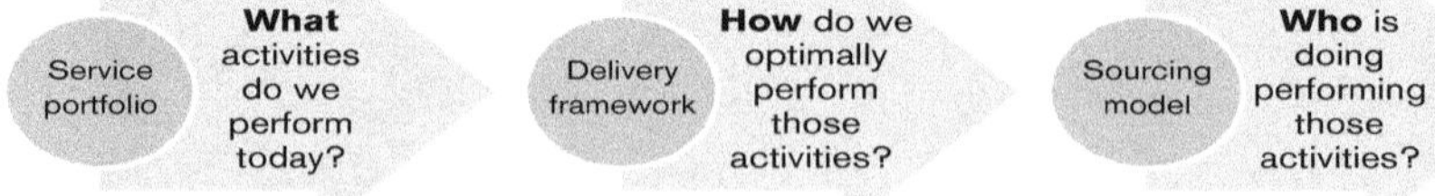

Exhibit 1: The Three Questions.

A. Service Portfolio

The initial step consists primarily of an information gathering exercise. If your function performs timekeeping or records activity in a matter management system you likely already have a dataset that you can leverage for this exercise. Otherwise, you can gather the data points through a function survey or introduce timekeeping for a limited period of time.

Before launching your fact-finding initiative make sure to explain to your associates *why* you are undertaking this analysis and what it will help to accomplish. This will provide buy-in and prevent low engagement or even anxiety. Also develop a communication strategy—your associates will want to learn about the outcome of the survey and potential next steps. Since considerations on delivery frameworks and sourcing models will take time, it is important to manage expectations.

If you choose to run an activity survey, ensure that the survey is as simple as it can be. Depending on the size of your department and urgency in completing the fact gathering, consider interviews, which will open a dialogue with your associates. This will likely provide you with more nuances and insights compared to running an online survey.

If you choose to run an activity survey, ensure that the survey is as simple as it can be. Depending on the size of your department and urgency to completing the fact gathering consider interviews, which will open a dialogue with

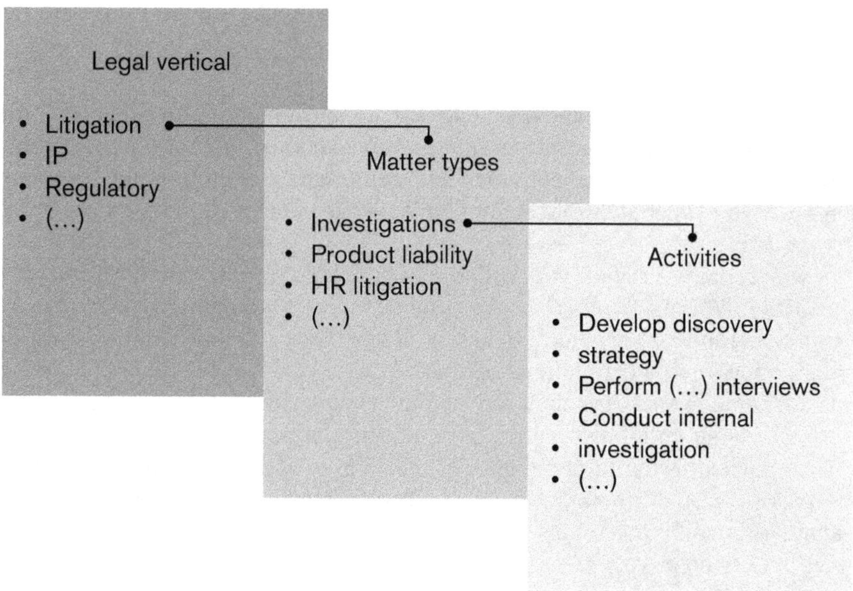

Exhibit 2: Legal Verticals & Activities.

your associate. This will likely provide you with more nuances and insights compared to running an online survey.

One way to keep the survey concise is to structure it along your legal verticals and ask your associates to estimate percentage of time spent by vertical. Your associates will only need to respond to the more detailed questions of a vertical if they selected it on the initial screen. This will shorten the survey for the majority of your associates.

B. Delivery Framework

Once you have the results from your activity survey or the time statements of your associates, the analysis can begin. The simplest and possibly most effective way is to place your activities in three buckets:

Stop doing	Do more of	Start doing
• Activity 1 • Activity 2 • (...)	• Activity 1 • Activity 2 • (...)	• Activity 1 • Activity 2 • (...)

Exhibit 3: Action Mapping.

In order to keep things simple start by focusing on the legal function only. This means that *stop doing* certain activities does not necessarily mean an activity will no longer be done, it just means that the legal function should no longer perform a given activity in the way it is done today.

You might want to consider soliciting input from associates that perform activities that you are uncertain in which buckets they fall. Then you might consider reviewing these activities with representatives from other functions in order to collect additional data points on the value add and importance of those activities.

In certain verticals you will likely collaborate with external resources such as law firms or other service providers. Try to obtain their activities as well to complete the picture. In case you have an electronic billing system in place you will find the required data there, otherwise you can easily gather the data from the vendors as they rely on time statements for their billing.

Once the initial distribution is done consider *how* these activities should be conducted in the future. Consider whether an activity should be *bespoke*, *ready-made* or even *automated*. Also consider whether you want to enable another function to be more self-sufficient and whether legal should be directive or collaborative.

In order to help your assessment look at the risk exposure and strategic relevance of a given activity and it might help to determine how an activity

should be measured. Is it for example important that the activity is enabling speed/agility or is service delivery time not that relevant. If service delivery time is of essence it might be worthwhile to consider automating activities. If a given activity leads to a bet-the-company decision you will likely want well informed judgment embedded in the process, which might warrant a bespoke approach.

If possible, assess end to end processes. In mostly automated environments such as high-volume low complexity contracting, legal has the opportunity to move away from supporting at a transactional level to developing generally applicable templates and standardized escalation paths. The consequence might be that the involvement of the legal function will only marginally be on legal review but rather be focused on:

- Template creation and maintenance
- Training and accreditation of contract owners on contractual standards
- Serving as an escalation body

This move away from daily transactions will free up time for the legal function to further improve end-to-end processes and test and introduce smart contracts that bring automation to the next level.

There is a great paper by *Jason Heinrich, Michael Heric, Neal Goldman and Paul Cichocki* titled *«A higher Bar»*[4] which provides many additional considerations to determine the optimal service delivery framework, which I highly recommend if you want to go deeper into this topic.

C. Sourcing Model

We established what we want do and how we want to go about doing it. The next step is about finding the optimal resources to perform these activities. The last step of our journey is sensitive because we are discussing people: our colleagues and business partners. Therefore, I recommend not to consider the current organization but develop the sourcing model on the basis of the data collected in the two prior steps. This makes this last and crucial step more objective. Given that there is likely to be more work than the legal function can take-on, this exercise will enable appropriate work allocation rather than the legal function being a target to reduce resources.

There is a wide variety of resources and engagement models that we should consider. In my opinion, there is enormous opportunity to improve

4 Jason Heinrich, Michael Heric, Neal Goldman & Paul Cichocki, *A higher bar*, Bain & Company (2014), https://www.bain.com/contentassets/f42f67a8ab8b4c20b2603953ce25ab7e/bain_brief_a_higher_bar.pdf (last visited Apr. 2, 2019).

output quality, service delivery speed, and cost if we are open to consider alternative sourcing options.

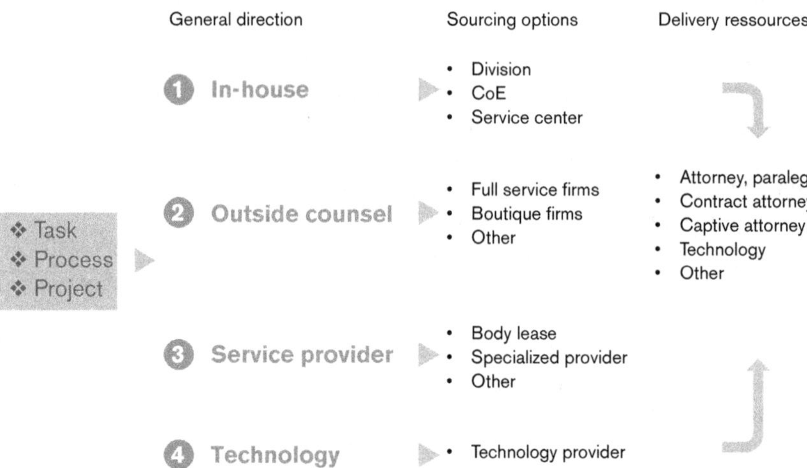

Exhibit 4: Alternative Sourcing Options.

To assign specific activities to resources I suggest leveraging the value matrix (see below). The process on how to do this is explained in detail in the *ACC guide to value based staffing.*[5]

In short, activities should be placed on the matrix considering risk potential and competitive advantage. The ACC describes risk potential as the extent to which it is possible for an activity to negatively impact the company—financially, with respect to regulatory compliance or by damaging the company's reputation. The impact on competitive advantage is described as the degree to which the activity drives competitive advantage and supports the company strategy.

The value matrix using these two variables as axes is a useful means of identifying the relative value placed on the work done by the legal function.

As can be seen in the matrix, work with both high-risk potential and high impact on competitive advantage is perceived as having the highest value, while the lowest value work has lower risk potential and strategic impact.

---

5 Association of Corporate Counsel (ACC), *ACC guide to value based staffing,* https://www.acc.com/vl/membersonly/SampleFormPolicy/loader.cfm?csModule=security/getfile&pageid=1487891&page=/legalresources/resource.cfm&qstring=show=1487891&fromLibrary=1&title=Guide%20to%20Value%20Based%20Staffing%20Curated&recorded=1 (last visited Apr. 2, 2019).

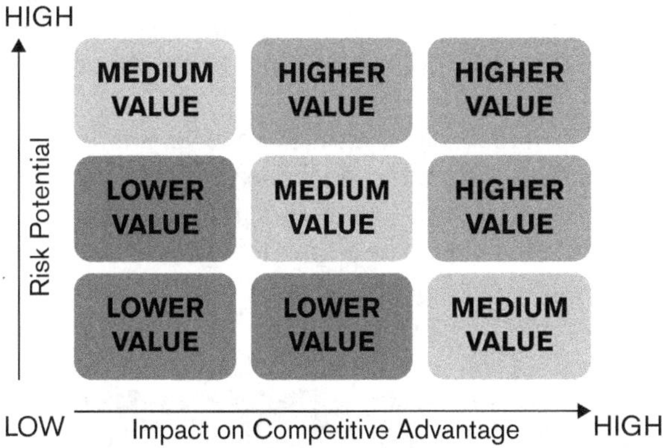

Exhibit 5: Value Based Staffing [Source: ACC[6]].

Since the allocation of activities is likely to be done differently by various resources the authors of the value guide suggest running calibration sessions to ensure considering multiple angles before making a final allocation.

The execution of the sourcing model will require close collaboration with other functions and a new engagement model for outside counsels and legal service providers.

V. Technology

Technology is becoming an increasingly important component of legal service delivery. As mentioned in the introduction, technology requires a solid operational foundation and a clearly defined use case to be at its best. If the preconditions are not present or the associates are not ready to embrace technology, implementations will likely fail.

Whilst the legal technology offering has for a long time been modest, it is encouraging to see how much focus and investment is finally targeting the legal industry.

Whereas there are mature technologies available for many use-cases—especially to support legal operations (for example electronic billing or matter management systems)—technologies to support substantive legal work (for example patent drafting), are not yet developed for seamless implementation. By that I mean that these systems will work well in conjunction with technol-

6 ACC, *supra* note 5.

ogy savvy legal professionals who are willing and able to experiment but are not yet ready to be implemented more broadly. Therefore, it is crucial to develop a technology strategy that not only focuses on need but also considers the technology readiness of the legal function and the maturity of the market offering.

Buying decisions, especially in the area of substantive legal solutions are still a little tricky. Whilst it is hard to determine which idea and company will control a given field, it is definitely worthwhile experimenting based on concrete needs and well defined requirements. The below tool provides general guidance on the complexity of implementing technology based on four buckets of applications that I see most relevant to the in-house legal functions.

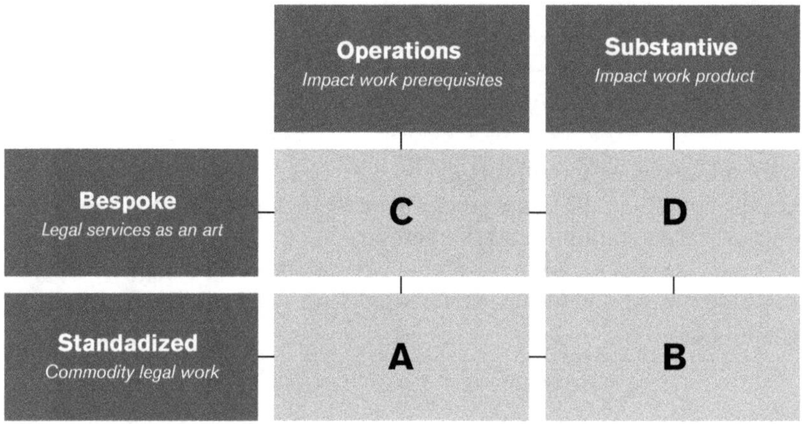

Exhibit 6: Implementation Complexity.

A. Standardized | operations

This is likely to be the most common area to leverage technology in the legal field. Legal hold management, self-service portals, and electronic billing solution serve as examples. These technologies are similar to tools used by other functions and should not be too hard to establish. Granted, an effective implementation of an electronic billing system will require interfaces to accounts payable systems, which isn't trivial, but corporate IT in conjunction with finance should be in a position to support. Change management will be relatively easy within the legal function as core processes of the function remain untouched.

B. Standardized | substantive

There have been great developments in this field over the last 18 to 24 months. Examples include document / contract review systems, online dispute resolution tools and document assembly tools for instance in the area of patent prosecution. The tools are simple to implement but a little bit hard to leverage their full potential—especially if these tools have to work with unstructured data. Legal associates will have to change their way of working in order to fully leverage these technologies, which will take some time.

C. Bespoke | operations

Tools in this group have been around for quite some time. It will be interesting to see how these tools further develop given the technological advances and the increased interest and hence availability of development dollars in the legal technology sector. I would place specialized procurement platforms that help structure legal cases in this group and the group of tools that target digitizing legal education. As these are rather look-up or sign-on technologies, these are easy to implement and most of them are fairly easy to be used. Therefore, this certainly presents a group to be considered early on in the process.

D. Bespoke | substantive

Tools in this group have in common that they suggest or at least support judgement. I would place tools that help to predict outcomes or help model scenarios in this bucket. Smart contract creation and audit tools might fall in this category as well. This tools are fairly simple to implement, but it will be important to invest sufficient time to learn how to use these tools effectively.

E. Technology Market Overview

Finally, and because the market is developing rapidly, I do not want to share a technology market overview in a printed book but refer you to a couple of dynamic resources that I turn to on regular basis for that matter:

- Collection of many blogs on legal innovation and technology: https://prismlegal.com/keeping-up-with-km-ai-and-legal-tech-recommended-sources/?utm_source=Lexoo+In-House+Roundup&utm_campaign=1539974d44-EMAIL_CAMPAIGN_2018_07_06_09_51&utm_medium=email&utm_term=0_ba31f8b27a-1539974d44-531833473
- A categorized list of legal technology: https://techindex.law.stanford.edu/

– A curated startup map: https://www.legalgeek.co/startup-map/
– A buying support tool for contract management systems: https://software.iaccm.com/#results

VI. Concluding Remarks

I am very excited to be working in an in-house legal function because I believe there has not been a better time to do so, and it is likely that there will be more change and improvement in this next decade than in the last century. Despite the fact that we have been developing slowly and that there is quite some change resistance in our industry, we are now learning about relevant and successful transformation of legal functions around the globe on a weekly basis. I believe that change will continue to happen and that the change impact will widen dramatically: the journey towards operational excellence of in-house legal departments will impact the vendor landscape and their service offering which likely will shake-up the entire industry. Therefore, once again my recommendation to take charge and fix what will soon need fixing.

VII. Bibliography

Online Sources

Association of Corporate Counsel, *ACC guide to value based staffing*, https://www.acc.com/vl/membersonly/SampleFormPolicy/loader.cfm?csModule=security/getfile&pageid=1487891&page=/legalresources/resource.cfm&qstring=show=1487891&fromLibrary=1&title=Guide%20to%20Value%20Based%20Staffing%20Curated&recorded=1 (last visited Oct. 4, 2018).

Heinrich, Jason, Heric, Michael, Goldman, Neal & Cichocki, Paul, *A higher bar*, Bain & Company (2014), https://www.bain.com/contentassets/f42f67a8ab8b4c20b2603953ce25ab7e/bain_brief_a_higher_bar.pdf (last visited Apr. 2, 2019).

Son, Hugh, *JPMorgan Software Does in Seconds What Took Lawyers 360,000 Hours*, Bloomberg (Feb. 28, 2017, 1:24 PM), https://www.bloomberg.com/news/articles/2017-02-28/jpmorgan-marshals-an-army-of-developers-to-automate-high-finance (last visited Apr. 2, 2019).

Sprouls, Frannie, *Welcome to Legal 2.0*, Modern Counsel (Dec. 13, 2017), https://modern-counsel.com/2017/dxc-technology/ (last visited Oct. 4, 2018).

Law Geekx, *AI vs. Lawyers. The Ultimate Showdown*, Law Geekx (2018), https://www.lawgeex.com/AIvsLawyer/ (last visited Apr. 2, 2019).

Jordan Urstadt

Law Firm Strategy for Legal Products

The gating items for law firms pursuing legal products

TABLE OF CONTENTS

I. Introduction

Products substitute for services. As the scope of legal products increases, the demand for legal services declines. Particularly for law firms in the middle market, the future is one where clients don't contact lawyers directly, but referrals come from software. The margins on products can be excellent, but you need to sell at volume to get there. Since law firms don't sell products, clients don't ask for them. The rapidly growing market for legal products is still tiny compared to the market for traditional legal services. You could pick up *Clayton Christensen*'s «Innovator's Dilemma» and use the chapters as a checklist.[1]

There are a few differences with Christensen's model that are unique to professional services though. Those differences go a long way to explaining the slow rate of technological change in the legal industry. There are two fundamental reasons for those differences:

- the privileged position of lawyers and law firms as underwriters of legal risk, and
- the fact that Christensen's model is based on products replacing other products, while in the legal industry, products are replacing services.

Both of those reasons mean that products will not entirely substitute for services. They also mean that the practices of top tier lawyers will remain focused on service and resistant to fundamental disruption. Legal services will not only continue at the top end, but will remain highly profitable. Those law firms that are able to continue to focus on bet-the-company work, top tier legal advice, and the syndication of legal risk will not be fundamentally disrupted by technology. Based on the revenue trends of law firms over the last decade or so, there are about 25 law firms in the global 100 that are successfully focusing on that bet-the-company work.

We call work outside that top tier of bet-the-company work the «middle market», and it is being disrupted by legal products. Any law firm that does not want to gamble on its future needs to have a responsible strategy for legal products, whether that means understanding why bet-the-company work is likely to continue to be sold as a service, or why the middle market is likely to be sold as a product, with the sale of services arising from it. In this article, I have identified the gating items for a law firm pursuing a tech strategy for legal products. This article is separated into discussions of pricing, distribution, and incentives.

---

1 Clayton M Christensen, The innovator's dilemma: when new technologies cause great firms to fail (Harvard Business School Press, 1997).

II. Pricing[2]

For those law firms that have built products, the fundamental gating item for every firm is pricing. Without a sensible pricing and branding strategy, law firms will either end up giving their tech away, or not competing. In this section, I will discuss the current pricing strategies and the way forward for law firms.

A. Current Pricing

With the exception of *PartnerVine*, today there are pricing strategies for the business-to-consumer (B2C) space, vertically-integrated platforms like Thomson Reuters Practical Law, emerging companies' practices, and high-volume clients.

1. B2C Pricing

Before *PartnerVine* launched, the only price points for legal products were from B2C companies like *LegalZoom* and *Rocket Lawyer*. The B2C companies did not have to pay for a law firm's expertise, professional requirements, or liability. Also, as new entrants to the market, they got to cherry pick high-volume products like wills and incorporation documents. The pricing in the B2C space was based solely on volume, and, although they should certainly be taken into account when setting a pricing strategy for a law firm, those price points don't reflect the expertise, professional requirements, or ability to syndicate risk that are the distinguishing factors of a law firm. Those factors are important reasons why a law firm's pricing strategy should be different than that of a B2C legal tech company, and those factors should help establish a positive price/quality relationship between a law firm's products and its services.

2. Vertically-integrated Platforms

One of the greatest transfers of value from law firms to technology companies was the content law firms provided to Practical Law, which created a tremendously successful exit for the owners of *Practical Law* when they sold their company to *Thomson Reuters* in 2013.[3] Today, vertically-integrated platforms are mainly subscription-based, and the increase in revenues of the top performers like Thomson Reuters Practical Law is a testament to the fact that they

---

2 *PartnerVine* does not discuss pricing for individual products here.

3 Today, a similar transfer of value is happening in the transfer of data from law firms to their tech partners in relation to machine learning/AI, which will lead to a similar fortune earned by the shareholders of legal publishers or newer tech companies at the expense of law firm revenues.

are growing at the expense of middle market work. The subscription pricing of *Thomson Reuters Practical Law* is a better benchmark for pricing for law firm products as the offer is clearly targeted to the B2B space. Unbundling those subscriptions for pricing at the product level is not particularly hard to do.

3. Emerging Companies Practices

Law firms have given away software in the emerging companies space for many years. With the first comprehensive offers put together by *Goodwin* and *Orrick* and joined by many other firms like Cooley, the model is to maximize the funnel of potential clients to pick up services work. Some of those automated document platforms have reached downloads that would create USD 6.5 million in revenue if they were priced at USD 50 each, but there is not much new investment going into those platforms in markets like the US. From my discussions with firms, their teams are moving toward *PartnerVine*'s revenue-generating model or are focusing on consulting on legal tech for high volume clients. The emerging companies space is a good example of law firm tech used in support of services that does not lead to the virtuous circle of volume sales and corresponding investment that helps both law firms and their clients. Law firms giving away software for free doesn't solve the Innovator's Dilemma for law firms, it just avoids it. A law firm's legal products need to be sold separately from their services to create a virtuous circle of sales and investment.

4. High Volume Clients

The final model for pricing for legal tech from law firms is sales of tech to high volume clients. In that instance, both the legal tech and the price points are custom and the margins can be healthy. The key take home for firms that are building great businesses for high volume clients is not that software should not be sold at volume, but that the relative advantage of standardized and custom software needs to be clearly articulated. Corporate purchasers of custom software are not in the market for standardized software, and in my experience would not consider it. As a result, the markets are not incompatible, but are an important part of a law firm's pricing strategy, with custom work at one end and standardized work at the other. Importantly though, a custom practice can't compete in the long term with software that has more users and the virtuous circle of feedback and investment that the software creates.

One important upside for a law firm that clearly prices legal products is to provide a separate market for a law firm's discussions with clients that is not in reference to the deep cost-cutting on services being pursued by major companies with automated RFPs and reverse auctions. For large companies, legal spend is either now or will be completely transparent in short order. With that transparency, a firm that competes on price for middle market work is increasingly rendered ineligible for more profitable top tier work. If you take that trend to its logical conclusion, there will be law firms doing bet-the-company work and law firms doing middle market work, and the firms doing middle market work will need to consolidate to reduce the depth of discounting. Selling products and services separately provides a separate frame of reference for clients in middle market work that does not disqualify a law firm from bet-the-company work. A further upside from the investment in tech is that it will make the law firm's lawyers more productive and more valuable to clients and the firm.

B. Pricing for Law Firm Legal Products

A sensible pricing strategy for a law firm's legal products needs to take into account the current pricing strategies for the tech described above, and the pricing for a law firm's services, which will be distinguished from legal products as services are by their nature custom and require expensive expertise with professional obligations and associated liability. For new and innovative products, law firms have pricing power, and most of the products I discuss with law firms fall into this category. With any pricing strategy, there is a balance between pricing and volume, tempered by the discussions of innovation adoption and distribution in the next sections, which serve to increase the use of legal products generally.

To look further at the balance between pricing and volume, there are usually two strategies for product companies to take with new products: the skimming strategy and the penetration strategy. The skimming strategy sells less product at higher margins, while the penetration strategy seeks to deter new entrants into the market by aggressively pricing products for higher volume. See exhibit 1 on the next page.

The Skimming Strategy may make sense for law firms concerned with protecting the price/quality ratio of their services. It also makes sense to test out the market and build experience. Even with a Skimming Strategy, law firms increase their return on investment with every sale and market their technology expertise. Given the importance of protecting the price/quality relationship between products and services, the Skimming Strategy makes sense particularly as the market for legal products develops.

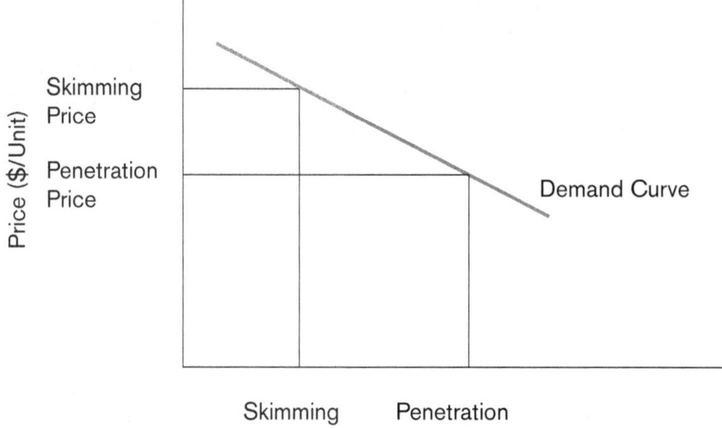

Skimming generates a higher profit margin while penetration generates greater volume

Exhibit 1: «Skimming vs Penetration» [Source: Babu John Mariadoss[4]].

C. Branding

Branding presents several options for a pricing strategy, but also the risk of diminishing the upside of a smart pricing strategy. Setting up a separate brand for legal products allows law firms to build expertise in products without diluting the premier brand for bet-the-company work. It also leaves the product team with no branding advantage over the long list of tech companies that are not affiliated with law firms. A second option is a recognizable sub-brand, which will communicate that the products benefit from the reputation and skills of the premier brand. That recognizable sub-brand could be used not just for products but also middle-market services, so that the premier brand will not be linked to discounted services as pricing becomes increasingly transparent for high volume clients.

4 Babu John Mariadoss, Core Principles of Marketing (2015), https://opentext.wsu.edu/marketing/ (licensed under Creative Commons Attribution-NonCommercial-ShareAlike 4.0 International) (last visited Apr. 11, 2019).

D. The Innovation Adoption Curve

Unlike a traditional product pricing strategy, legal products also need to consider the innovation adoption curve, which means that any business model will have less volume than it would in a mature market.[5] *Everett Rogers'* «Diffusion of Innovations» theory as explained in the previous chapter by *Guenther Dobrauz-Saldapenna* and *Corsin Derungs* is based on the adoption of innovative crops in the 1950s,[6] and it has been applied successfully to many fields including legal technology, with Bill Henderson setting the standard for LegalTech.[7]

Importantly for law firms, Rogers identified five factors that account for 49 to 87 percent of the rate of adoption of an innovation, which are as follows:

- Relative Advantage
- Compatibility
- Complexity
- Trialability
- Observability

The factors are described from the perspective of a potential user, and are important parts of selling LegalTech. *PartnerVine* has consulted with many law firms for how to meet these requirements, and one aspect of that discussion is the impact of those five factors on a firm's pricing strategy. Some of those five factors contribute to a lower entry price for using a new product to spur adoption, and because that discussion lends itself to the size of the market rather than a pricing strategy within it, that discussion takes place alongside the pricing strategy above.

E. Ethical Obligations and not Pricing Tech

Bar associations, particularly in the US, have been moving forward with the adoption of a duty to be competent in technology. In 2012, the American Bar Association approved a change to the Model Rules of Professional Conduct to include a duty to be competent in technology. That rule has been moving through state bar associations in the US. Almost all major law firms have adopted technical proficiency as a goal, and the investment in tech to enhance productivity for lawyers has been booming as a result.

---

5 That doesn't mean that a law firm shouldn't invest in technology, just that the investment should be right-sized for the market. *See* discussion of incentives below.

6 Everett M. Rogers, Diffusion of innovations (Free Press, 2003).

7 Bill Henderson, *What is the Rogers Diffusion Curve (004)*, Legal Evolution (May 8, 2017), https://www.legalevolution.org/2017/05/rogers-diffusion-curve-004/ (last visited Feb. 3, 2019).

With the duty of competence, a law firm strategy that does not require productivity gains from technology is no longer tenable. As the cost of investment in technology grows, the question is how to value the investment, which has only been done on *PartnerVine*. Apart from the firms that are using technology to market their practices, the practice of a majority of firms has been to use tech internally, but obscure the time savings to protect the logic of a law firm's hourly billing rate (which only makes sense after automated work has been done). In some cases, that situation has led to a padded bill. As the duty to be competent in technology turns into an increasingly large expense that is not recoverable with the billable hour, a law firm would be foolish not to price the product of technology separately from traditional services.

III. Distribution

If a law firm figures out how to price its products, the next gating item is not how to build those products, but how to sell them. Building products is supported by a strong ecosystem of tech companies, and it generally makes sense to partner with the best-in-class provider at the time a law firm needs the tech. Distribution, however, is a special case because the platform model is such a powerful one and trumps other models for distribution online. The company I founded, *PartnerVine*, has been laser-focused on this issue since we started in 2015, and we've dedicated ourselves to a model that is complementary to law firms. As a result, the discussion of this gating item is intimately connected to *PartnerVine*'s model, which is the pioneer in the space.

Distribution includes several issues that are extremely important to law firms, including:

- The right distribution for services and products;
- Potential disintermediation of law firms and their clients; and,
- Liquidity for specialized products.

Those issues address the innovator's dilemma for law firms in ways that do not arise for the vast majority of productivity tech that is sold today, and are the reasons why distribution is a critical gating item for law firms.

A. The Right Distribution for Services and Products

Distribution demonstrates the fundamental difference between services and products. Products are meant to be sold at volume, while the optimal pricing strategy for services will find itself with higher pricing and less volume. When it comes to how law firms sell legal tech today, the problem is acute.

1. The Last Mile Problem

The Last Mile Problem describes the difficulty a law firm faces in earning revenue from LegalTech. First described by *Bill Henderson* in his article *The Legal Profession's Last Mile Problem*,[8] he makes the case that lawyers are failing to adopt legal tech because there are not «business models that will reliably reward lawyers and their organizations for quantum leaps in legal productivity». Henderson's Last Mile Problem describes three solutions for a lawyer that has built a «box» that can double productivity:

1. The lawyer can pass on the benefit to the customer at no extra charge;
2. The lawyer can double her rates because the lawyer is twice as productive; or,
3. The lawyer and the client negotiate a deal where the client shares in the productivity gains.

In the hypothetical, the lawyer passes on selling the 20-in-10 box because the lawyer won't get the client to double the law firm's rates. For that lawyer, increasing productivity by investing in tech is bad for the bottom line. It's a fundamental insight that defines the workflow framing a law firm's innovator's dilemma. As described below, this problem is solved by a law firm's tech-first delivery of legal services on *PartnerVine*.

2. Software Should be Sold at Volume

The Last Mile Problem as described by *Bill Henderson* assumes a bilateral negotiation between a client and a law firm. The negotiation is for services, and the technology that automates repeatable processes does not get valued properly because the client only needs it once. The answer to the Last Mile Problem is to sell a law firm's technology as a product, for a price that reflects the volume of its use. Legal products are software, and software should be sold at volume. Separating the sale of services and products breaks out the business case for products and allows for investments in legal products independent of a law firm's services business.

Importantly, establishing a separate business case for legal products allows for an appropriate allocation of resources to the development of legal products. The market for legal products today is small relative to the traditional legal industry, although it is growing quickly. As discussed below, a law firm needs to protect its core services business and create a virtuous circle of volume sales and investment for its products.

---

8 Bill Henderson, *The Legal Profession's «Last Mile Problem»*, Bill Henderson (May 26, 2017), https://www.billhenderson.com/articles/2017/5/26/the-legal-professions-last-mile-problem (last visited Feb. 3, 2019).

B. Potential Disintermediation of Law Firms and Their Clients

Products can be used without personal contact, which brings up the possibility that a law firm will no longer own the relationship with its clients. The concern is a real one and requires consideration of the opportunities and alternatives. For starters, the sale of products by law firms or their partners is not without precedent—books and articles are the closest kin. The publisher in that instance managed distribution, and the lawyer and law firm earned business through referrals. For books, authors traditionally earned a pittance of the proceeds of a sales—around 5%. In *PartnerVine*'s model, the vast majority of the proceeds go to the law firm. Secondly, if it is agreed that a product needs to be sold at volume to succeed, the idea that a direct connection between the law firm and the user should accompany every sale should be replaced with a concern for control over the product and capturing leads coming from that product. *PartnerVine*'s model is built to promote both. Law firms can partner with tech companies in the production of products (and may want to do so to focus on services), but the choice is theirs. The key is not to look at products like services. The alternative is having a tech company own the product and set the pricing for services—as *LegalZoom* is doing with great success.

C. Liquidity for Specialized Products

As long as a law firm's primary asset is partners that practice law, a law firm's competitive advantage will be specialized expertise. In contrast, technology companies, which have no revenue from specialized legal services, are incentivized to minimize spending on expertise until they can find a product that sells at volume. Law firms can succeed at high volume products, but their competitive advantage compared to technology companies lies in specialized areas of the law.

There is a good argument to be made that specialized areas of the law will be turned into products in the same way that more high-volume areas of the law will be—and that is a great opportunity for law firms. In *Bill Henderson*'s post, *Two types of legal innovation: Type 0 substantive law, Type 1 service delivery,*[9] *Henderson* makes the case that a major source of profits for law firms come from innovations in the practice of law. Such innovations in substantive law are independent of technology, and are often profit centers for a

---

9 Bill Henderson, *Two types of legal innovation: Type 0 substantive law, Type 1 service delivery*, Legal Evolution (Oct. 28, 2018), https://www.legalevolution.org/2018/10/two-types-legal-innovation-type-0-type-1-071/ (last visited Feb. 3, 2019).

given practice area. As time goes by, however, the expertise to capture that innovation spreads to other law firms, and profits generally decrease. *Henderson*'s second point is that innovations in service delivery are often tech-oriented and unrelated to innovations in substantive law. The next logical step from the article is that, should law firms pursue innovative delivery for their innovations in substantive law, they could capture more of the profits of those substantive law innovations and consolidate the market for those specialties. That leads to a tech-first delivery of legal services like *PartnerVine*.

IV. Incentives

The third gating item for law firms pursuing a responsible tech strategy is to get the incentives right. Without the right incentives, a law firm's tech strategy will, over time, suffer from poor execution. In particular, a law firm should be able to make the right decisions regardless of changes in key decision-makers, which is a critical problem for law firms as they are incentivized to maximize the sale of services on an annual basis.

As discussed in more detail in my earlier article *The Right Incentives for Legal Tech*, there are at least three conflicts of interest that make it difficult to successfully execute a law firm's tech strategy:[10]

- The investment period required for tech means that one set of partners in a law firm makes the investment in technology but another set of partners gets the revenue. That's a fundamental mismatch of benefits and burdens, particularly if you ask for an investment from partners that are uncertain if their billing pyramid will be as big in the future as it is today.
- If technology is successful, it shifts the value drivers of the business from services to products. For a partner, that means value moves away from that partner's provision of services towards the partnership as the owner of the product. As a result, that partner has less control over his or her share of the value of the business.
- Finally, the core of any law firm partnership is the incentive to maximize annual revenue, and that does not match the investment period required for Legal Tech. Law firms have endless versions of how they put together that incentive to maximize annual revenue, but the key element of a partner's share of profits is the annual review of the partner's billing pyramid. When you're investing in disruptive technology that slims that pyramid, the incentive is wrong.

---

10 Jordan Urstadt, *The Right Incentives for Legal Tech*, PartnerVine (Apr. 12, 2018), https://www.partnervine.com/blog/the-right-incentives-for-legal-tech (last visited Feb. 2, 2019).

The solution is well-known to corporate partners and involves a spin-out of the Products business. The spin-out will not only match the benefits to the burdens, it will go a long way to right-sizing the products business to its market, which as mentioned before is small today but growing quickly. It will allow for a separate P&L where small wins can make a big impact, which reflects Christensen's recommendation for products companies facing the emergence of a disruptive product.[11] Such a spin-out will allow for ownership and control to be localized for the products business so the right stakeholders are making decisions for the business. It will also provide elegant terms of engagement between the law firm and the products business, with agreements for the law firm's intellectual property and provision of services.

The reason why incentives are listed as the third gating item for law firms here is not because it isn't fundamental to execution of a law firm's tech strategy, but because most law firms today are far from addressing the issue. Although there have been notable setbacks recently, the law firms that are pushing ahead with tech usually do it in a skunkworks or by force of personality.

For law firms in the top tier, their services are more resistant to disruption, as described in more detail above. In addition, their cost of capital is higher because lateral hires remain important for both expanding and defending a firm's revenue and profitability. Given those issues, top tier law firms should not ignore a tech strategy, but (preferably with a recognizable sub-brand as described above), instead, invest in legal tech in proportion to the market, with the understanding that the size of their revenue base will likely make them an important player. Top tier firms have the additional advantage of applying their skills and reputation to new products, which is a classic growth-in-adjacent-markets story, with the adjacent market in this case being the legal market served by less profitable competitors. Finally, a top-tier law firm's investments in legal tech act as a hedge in case its services prove more subject to disruption.

V. Conclusion

Law firms should protect their core business, which is services. How that plays out in practice depends on the market:

– For firms that can win bet-the-company business, the core portion of their business is that which is not likely to be disrupted. For firms that are solely dedicated to bet-the-company business, the development of legal

---

11 Clayton M Christensen, The innovator's dilemma: when new technologies cause great firms to fail (Harvard Business School Press, 1997).

products is a growth-in-adjacent-markets opportunity. There are very few firms globally that are dedicated to bet-the-company work.

- For firms that earn revenue outside of bet-the-company work, a strategy for legal products is required. For these firms, partners with more than a six to seven-year time horizon should consider the development of legal products as an important part of their law firm's competitive positioning. As discussed in the section on incentives above, a spin-out dedicated to legal products is a smart option, although some firms will make the leap to products based on culture alone.

Once a law firm has started producing legal products, the next gating items are pricing and distribution. In terms of a pricing strategy for legal products, price skimming is a sensible first step, although the upshot of that is that volume (and adoption) will be lower. At the very least though, every sale will create a revenue stream for what would otherwise be an expense. In terms of distribution, the logic for the distribution of products is fundamentally different from services, with products hitting their optimum price point at far more volume than services. That should change a law firm's conclusion on sensitive issues like the potential disintermediation of a law firm from its clients, and focus concern on the control of those products rather than the means of distribution.

It is always good to look at the hardest questions first, and these gating items attempt to do that for law firms considering legal products. Without addressing those hard questions, a law firm is more likely to sit on the sidelines, and to watch middle market work disappear without further notice.

VI. Bibliography

A. Hard Copy Sources

Christensen, Clayton M, The innovator's dilemma: when new technologies cause great firms to fail (Harvard Business School Press, 1997).

Mariadoss, Babu John, Core Principles of Marketing (2015), https://opentext.wsu.edu/marketing/.

Everett M Rogers, Diffusion of innovations (Free Press, 2003).

B. Online Sources

Henderson, Bill, *The Legal Profession's «Last Mile Problem»*, Bill Henderson (May 26, 2017), https://www.billhenderson.com/articles/2017/5/26/the-legal-professions-last-mile-problem (last visited Feb. 3, 2019).

Henderson, Bill, *Two types of legal innovation: Type 0 substantive law, Type 1 service delivery,* Legal Evolution (Oct. 28, 2018), https://www.legalevolution.org/2018/10/two-types-legal-innovation-type-0-type-1-071/ (last visited Feb. 3, 2019).

Henderson, Bill, *What is the Rogers Diffusion Curve (004)*, LEGAL EVOLUTION (May 8, 2017), https://www.legalevolution.org/2017/05/rogers-diffusion-curve-004/ (last visited Feb. 3, 2019).

Urstadt, Jordan, *The Right Incentives for Legal Tech*, PARTNERVINE (Apr. 12, 2018), https://www.partnervine.com/blog/the-right-incentives-for-legal-tech (last visited Feb. 2, 2019).

Dr Silvia Hodges Silverstein and Dr Lena Campagna

Legal Procurement

A Catalyst for Change in the Legal Industry

TABLE OF CONTENTS

I. Introduction

The legal landscape is rapidly changing: consolidating firms, the growth and expansion of non-traditional legal services providers as well as of legal technology used for both the practice and business side of the law, clients with more skills and knowledge about the process of legal services delivery. One of the catalysts for much of the change is the emergence of legal procurement. This chapter describes how advanced legal procurement capability can serve your organization, key benchmarks for legal procurement, tools and tactics legal procurement employs, the benefits you can derive from employing legal procurement professionals, and future directions for legal procurement.

Since the last recession, general counsel and legal departments are no longer the only buyers of corporate legal services, particularly for very large organizations. Legal procurement, the department or corporate function responsible for acquiring goods and services, has been gaining traction. Procurement is defined as the «overarching function that describes the activities and processes to acquire goods and services. Importantly, and distinct from «purchasing», procurement involves the activities involved in establishing fundamental requirements, sourcing activities such as market research and vendor evaluation and negotiation of contracts.»[1]

The involvement of procurement is said to be one of the side effects of a «power shift» to the client.[2] Procurement compares and contrasts, uses data and develops evidence-based rationale for major reductions in legal spending.

Companies with significant legal spending started to involve procurement in the evaluation and selection of legal services providers in the early-to-mid 2000s, with the earliest legal procurement activities dating back to the mid-to-late 1990s.[3] Among the first industries to embrace legal procurement were highly regulated (and often highly litigious) industries such as pharmaceutical

---

1 Purchasing insights.com, *Definition of Procurement—Procurement vs Purchasing*, http://purchasinginsight.com/resources/what-is/definition-of-procurement-procurement-vs-purchasing/ (last visited Sept. 26, 2015). Purchasing is defined as «[t]he process of ordering and receiving goods and services. It is a subset of the wider procurement process. Generally, purchasing refers to the process involved in ordering goods such as request, approval, creation of a purchase order record (a Purchase Order or P.O.) and the receipting of goods.» *Id.*

2 Silvia Hodges Silverstein, *Buyers, Influencers and Gatekeepers: Firms Must Learn the Ins and Outs of Legal Service Procurement*, N.Y. L.J., May 12, 2014, at S6 [hereinafter *Buyers, Influencers and Gatekeepers*].

3 *See*, e.g., DuPont Legal Model, *About the DuPont Legal Model*, https://www.dupontlegalmodel.com/initiatives/about-the-dupont-legal-model (last visited Sept. 28, 2018) (procurement activities dating back to 1992); Heidi K Gardner & Silvia Hodges Silverstein, *GlaxoSmithKline: Sourcing Complex Professional Services* 2, 4 (Harv. Bus. Sch. Case No. 414–003, rev. 2014) (finding that the legal industry has undergone great transformation in the past two decades prompting greater incorporation of legal procurement in the early 2000s).

companies and financial services institutions, as well as energy companies and utilities.[4]

In many corporations, legal services used to be largely exempt from the intense cost scrutiny other business units and functions have been facing for years.[5] The recent financial crisis sparked and accelerated the process for the adoption of legal procurement, particularly in large corporations.[6] Publicity about billing practices, big ticket spending, and profit pressure is at the root of this seismic shift.[7]

Legal departments have been using some procurement tools for over two decades.[8] DuPont spearheaded the convergence trend in legal services in 1992.[9] Many legal departments have since adopted the «DuPont Model»'[10] It is based on the ideas of reducing the number of suppliers to facilitate management of outside counsel and increasing purchasing power to obtain lower rates from outside counsel.[11] Current approaches are built on this pioneering model.

---

4 *See,* e.g., Silvia Hodges, *Power of the Purse: How Corporate Procurement is Influencing Law Firm*, Law Practice Today (Jan. 2012), http://www.americanbar.org/publications/law_practice_today_home/law_practice_today_archive/january12/power-of-the-purse-how-corporate-procurement-is-influencing-law-firm.html [hereinafter *Power of the Purse*] (finding that «[C] orporate purchasing departments started sourcing engineering and architectural services in the late 1980s, marketing, public relations and advertising services in the mid-late 1990s, accounting and tax services in the mid 2000s ...»).

5 *See id.* («*Until recently, the legal department was excluded f*rom company-wide cost cuttings. This is no longer the case.»).

6 Anthony Licata, *A CFO's Perspective*, 14 Strategies 10 (2012) (finding that the market crash spurred CFOs of large companies to adopt legal procurement).

7 *See,* e.g., Chris Provines, *Rep-Less Medical Sales Model: Wake up—It's Just Part of a Bigger Procurement Trend*, Chris Provines (Mar. 28, 2015), http://chrisprovines.com/2015/03/28/rep-less-medical-sales-model-wake-up-its-just-a-part-of-a-bigger-procurement-trend (finding bundled billing practices, cost pressure, and new disruptive service providers accelerated the shift to procurement).

8 *See,* e.g., *About the Dupont Legal Model*, *supra* note 3 (finding that the DuPont Legal Model has been in use since 1992).

9 Symposium, *Evolving Role of the Corporate Counsel: How Information Technology Is Reinventing Legal Practice*, 36 Campbell L. Rev. 383, 438 (2013).

10 Maurice S Byrd, Esq., Exec. Legal Consultant, Lexis Nexis, The Effective Utilization of Paralegals in corporate legal Departments, Presentation for ACC LA Roundtable 30 (Oct. 2, 2014).

11 According to the website http://www.dupontlegalmodel.com, the «DuPont Legal Model has provided a solid, dynamic, integrated approach to providing services to the DuPont Company since 1992. The Legal Model's competitive edge has been derived by applying business discipline to the practice of law.» *About the Dupont Legal Model*, *supra* note 3.

II. What is Legal Procurement?

Legal procurement departments are both tactical and strategic in nature and are often a culmination of professionals with expertise spanning a wide array of disciplines outside the legal field. Many departments have employees with expertise ranging from data analysis and sourcing technology to manage spending and increasing efficiency in hiring outside counsel.[12] This diversity in expertise is critical as professional procurement and spend management is an area where most general counsel and in-house lawyers have had limited education and professional experience. Procurement can have a significant impact on their organization's bottom-line. It is hence unsurprising that the number of Fortune 500 companies and major international organizations with dedicated legal procurement personnel is quickly increasing.[13]

The sophistication and effectiveness of legal procurement is influenced by the maturity and experience of the procurement professionals involved, «their awareness and understanding of the distinction of legal services and of the quality of the legal work product».[14] It is also influenced by the way procurement professionals are being measured and rewarded and by the level of collaboration between the company's procurement professionals and in-house lawyers.[15]

III. Who Wants to Involve Legal Procurement?

Procurement's involvement is typically a mandate by the organization's top management, its CEO or CFO.[16] The main reasons are their desire to improve cost management, reducing supplier spending, ensuring that the organization buys goods and services in compliance with organizational policies, and making sure the organization gets good products and services from reputable suppliers. Other drivers include the intention to achieve more objective comparisons of legal service providers through measuring and benchmarking outside counsel's value and the desire to streamline operations, improve efficiencies, find better ways to structure both fee arrangements and budgeting, and increase predictability and transparency.[17] These areas fall into procurement's

---

12 *See id.*

13 *See id.* («More and more FTSE 350, Fortune 500, and multinational corporations now involve business people in the sourcing of legal services and the management of legal service providers.»).

14 *Buyers, Influencers and Gatekeepers*, *supra* note 2, at S6.

15 *Id.*

16 *See id.*

17 *See*, e.g., *id.*

core competencies and are examples of where procurement can make value-added contributions for their employers.

IV. Procurement's Key Benchmarks

While price may not always be the decisive argument for legal services, procurement's ability to reduce spending remains an integral benchmark to measure its success. The *2018 Buying Legal Services Survey* findings suggest that legal procurement is very successful in reducing spend and saves employers significant amounts of money.[18] These reductions or cost avoidances translate into significant savings per share. According to the Survey, legal procurement professionals were able to save their employers 14.6 percent of the total legal spend on average. For 2018, procurement forecasted a 16.9 percent reduction in legal costs, which means savings are up six percent in the last two years.[19] The most successful legal procurement professionals saved their employers 20.8 percent on average. The highest reported savings achieved were 57 percent. The least successful groups («below average success» and «not successful») were only able to achieve 4.8 percent and 5.3 percent of savings in 2018.

According to the Survey, the biggest factor for determining savings is the legal procurement professional's tenure in the legal category. It has significant effects on what procurement can achieve. The Survey found that procurement professionals with 10 or more years in legal procurement on average achieved 19 percent in savings. Those with five to nine years in the legal category saved 15 percent on average, while those with two to four years achieved 13 percent on average. Interestingly, those with one year or less in legal procurement were able to save 15 percent. It may suggest that some significant quick wins are achievable through applying procurement tools. Once the «low hanging fruit» have been picked, a deeper understanding of the category may be necessary to continue to achieve large savings.[20]

Big savings are also more likely when in-house counsel and procurement have a good working relationship, as a it was a clear indicator for savings: procurement professionals describing the relationship with their colleagues in the law department as «partners» were able to achieve 21 percent in savings on average. Those describing the relationship with in-house counsel as «collegial» saved 15 percent on average, while those with «reluctant» or «non-existing» relationships saved only 7 and 9 percent on average.[21]

---

18 *See* Buying Legal Council 2018 Buying Legal Services Survey-Insights into Legal Procurement (https://www.buyinglegal.com).

19 *See id.*

20 *See id.*

21 *See id.*

Alignment with their colleagues in legal operations («legal ops») is similarly important for legal procurement professionals to guarantee success for their employer. Those describing the relationship with legal ops as «partners» were able to achieve 17 percent in savings on average, those with «collegial» relationships with legal ops saved 14 percent on average, while those with «reluctant» relationships still managed to save 10 percent on average.[22]

It takes time to build relationships between the internal departments, to build trust, and to know what is working for their organization. Legal procurement in the largest companies (with $25B in revenue or more, so-called «Fortune 100» companies and international equivalents), saved on average 15.6 percent of spend, which translates into $16M of savings annually. They were outdone only by companies with less than $500M in revenues: here, procurement was able to save 19 percent on average, which translated into $800K of savings annually. Companies with $4.1B-$25B in revenue (size-wise classified as «Fortune 500» companies and international equivalents) on average saved 14.3 percent of legal spend, translating into $13M of savings annually.[23]

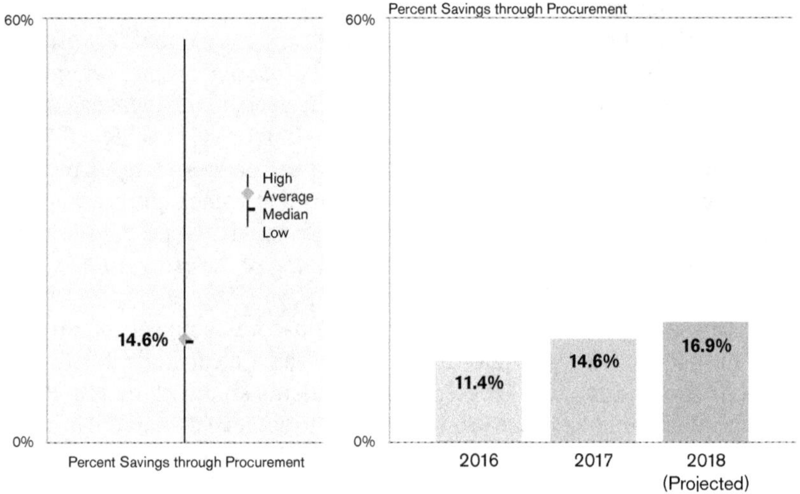

Exhibit 1: Average Savings Through Procurement [Source: 2018 Buying Legal Services Survey at 7].

22 *See id.*
23 *See id.*

V. Procurement Tools and Tactics

Even though procurement's involvement may result in lowering spending on outside counsel, this does not mean that procurement professionals are only interested in cost savings and that in-house lawyers are only interested in the quality of the service, regardless of spending. More and more procurement and legal departments together—often supported by a legal operations function—use a range of metrics and benchmarks in addition to price when selecting and evaluating the offerings of different law firms. In fact, the vast majority of clients negotiate discounts—and legal procurement professionals are typically in charge of it: in the before mentioned Survey, 88 percent of respondents negotiate discounts with legal services providers on behalf of their employer. An additional eight percent plan to use this tactic.[24] Also very common, legal procurement activities include issuing requests for proposal (RFPs), developing sourcing and purchasing strategies for legal services, as well as issuing and enforcing outside counsel billing guidelines. 76 percent of survey respondents already issue RFPs; another 17 percent plan to do so. This suggests that RFPs have become the standard way to choose legal services providers. Clients increasingly use web-based legal RFP platforms. 75 percent of survey respondents develop sourcing and purchasing strategies for legal services, and 18 percent plan to do it.[25] Again, this suggests that fewer and fewer (large) clients leave legal services unmanaged.

74 percent issue and enforce outside counsel billing guidelines, and an additional 18 percent plan to issue and enforce them. This suggests that legal procurement has started to become a more mature and increasingly professionally managed, category. The establishment of panels or a preferred list of vendors is also quickly becoming a common tool. 72 percent of organizations are currently using panels/preferred provider lists and 25 percent are planning to use them in the future. This leaves few clients without established panels/lists, and more firms risking the possibility of losing long-standing clients in the next round of panel formations.

eBilling is on the rise as well; 69 percent are currently using it, and another 22 percent are planning to use it in the future. Similarly, the negotiating of alternative fee arrangements (AFAs) is currently being done by 65 percent of survey respondents and another 31 percent are planning to do so. 63 percent presently conduct data analytics, and 33 percent are planning to use it in the future. Those longer in procurement (for five or more years) are more likely to use eAuctions, require eBilling, use legal project management, and conduct

24 *See id.*

25 *See id.*

data analytics than those newer to the legal category.[26] As argued before, time appears to drive success. Going through the stages, procurement professionals learn what works well and what does not.

We expect to see the most growth in the areas of legal project management: while only 27 percent are currently using legal project management, 50 percent are planning to use it in the future. Likewise, pre-matter scoping of work is currently used by less than half of survey respondents (46 percent), but 41 percent are planning to employ it in the future. Also, in an up-trend is conducting invoice audits—44 percent currently audit invoices, but 36 percent plan to do so. 60 percent freeze their firms' rates, and another 21 percent are planning to do so. Running eAuctions was the least commonly used legal procurement activity, although their popularity is increasing: 18 percent of survey respondents currently use eAuctions, and an additional 26 percent are planning to use them in the future.[27]

It is clear that with the help of legal procurement the sourcing of legal, alternative, and ancillary legal services is quickly moving from largely unmanaged or «passively» managed to an actively managed category of spend. Legal procurement is doing its job and earning its seat at the table.

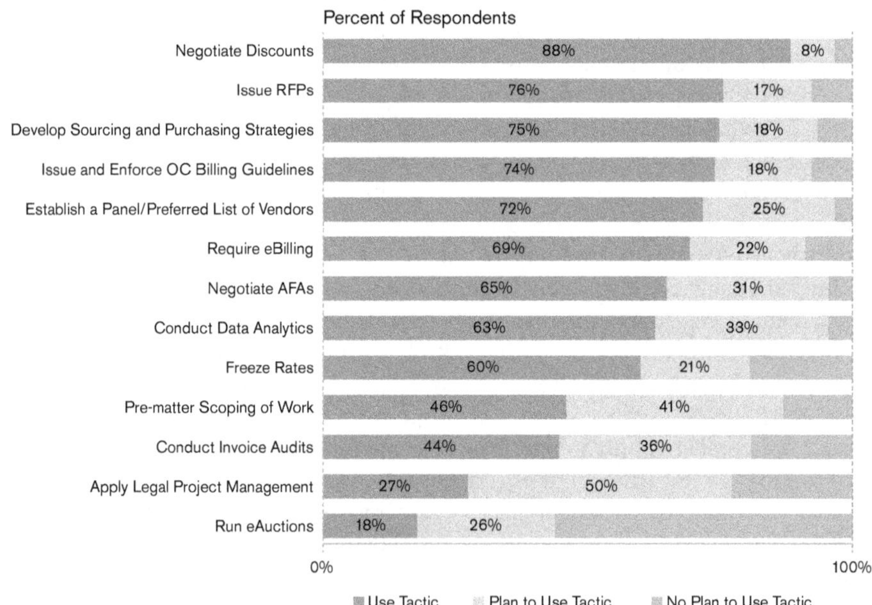

Exhibit 2: Procurement Tools & Tactics [Source: 2018 Buying Legal Services Survey at 15].

26 *See id.*
27 *See id.*

VI. Concluding Remarks

Legal procurement is quickly gaining traction and growing, particularly among the companies with significant legal spending. Few today believe that companies will return to sourcing legal services by the legal department alone, without procurement's involvement.[28] Looking at other professional services beyond legal, it is clear that procurement changed the way these services are bought during the last 25 years.[29] This has occurred in a time sequence: engineering and architectural services since the late 1980s, marketing, public relations and advertising services since the mid-late 1990s, accounting, auditing, and tax services since the early-mid 2000s, and legal services in the last five-plus years.[30]

For law firms, the involvement of procurement in the sourcing of legal services means that new management approaches for the delivery of legal services are called for along with the introduction of business thought and project management, more flexibility in regards to fee arrangements as well as stricter cost management.[31] Law firms are advised to get acquainted with the changes that procurement's involvement brings and make the necessary adjustments sooner rather than later. This means focus on expertise, process re-engineering, cost management, and use of lower cost labor.

The change is also significant for in-house legal departments, as they no longer can mandate law firms selection based on existing relationships, but are expected to adhere to corporate sourcing principles (including regular competitive bidding) and to share budget responsibility.[32] While there is perceived overlap with legal operations' role, it has to be noted that legal procurement applies procurement processes to the legal functions through both purchasing and sourcing, while legal operations is a multi-disciplinary function focused on better managing the legal department and optimizing legal services delivery within the organization, which includes areas such as litigation support and eDiscovery, IP management, data governance and records management, knowledge management as well as financial planning. Legal ops professionals typically have a legal background and report to the general counsel, while legal procurement professionals usually come from a quantitative background (such as finance, accounting, business and report to the head of procurement and the chief financial officer (CFO)). Their skillset, focus, breadth, and depth are hence very different from legal operations. It makes sense that legal oper-

---

28 Symposium, *supra* note 9, at 441.

29 Silvia Hodges, *You Better Know Their Names and Understand Their Metrics: Corporate Procurement Influences the Law Firm Selection, 14 Strategies,* (2012) at 4–5.

30 *Id.*

31 *Id.* at 5.

32 *Id.* at 6.

ations collaborates with legal procurement and utilizes procurement's expertise and capacity to focus on buying legal services and managing supplier relationships.

In the future, legal procurement's involvement is likely to go further than streamlining the sourcing process or reducing the cost for legal services. Procurement may look at the cost and benefits of long-term relationships/partnering with legal services suppliers as well as the cost to retender.

Procurement may also focus more on unbundling services and matching specific tasks with the most appropriate suppliers, such as using «top tier» providers for some tasks and «low cost» providers for other tasks. Procurement has learned this in working with other professional services. Standardization and automation have also provided significant gains in other professional services categories and managing «peaks, troughs, and scope risk across portfolios of work has brought real efficiencies» to many other corporate services.[33]

Another potential area for procurement's involvement is the assessment and qualification of information security capabilities of outside counsel firms. How legal procurement will be viewed by its colleagues in the legal department and in the legal industry at large, what it will buy, the influence it will have, and how it will assist the legal department in getting better value and being good stewards of their employer's money, will continue to change.

It is likely that instead of measuring hours, clients will focus on measuring output, results, service levels, overall cost, and time to resolution. The future holds the prospect of «more for less» and advantage to the sophisticated, procurement-enabled client. Law firms are advised to be ready for their new counterparts in procurement.

VII. Bibliography

A. Hard Copy Sources

Gardner, Heidi K & Hodges Silverstein, Silvia, *GlaxoSmithKline: Sourcing Complex Professional Services* (Harv. Bus. Sch. Case No. 414–003, rev. 2014).

Hodges Silverstein, Silvia, *Buyers, Influencers and Gatekeepers: Firms Must Learn the Ins and Outs of Legal Service Procurement*, N.Y. L.J., May 12, 2014, at S6.

Licata, Anthony, *A CFO's Perspective*, 14 Strategies 10 (2012).

Symposium, *Evolving Role of the Corporate Counsel: How Information Technology Is Reinventing Legal Practice*, 36 Campbell L. Rev. 383, 438 (2013).

33 *Id.*

B. Online Sources

BUYING LEGAL COUNCIL, *2018 Buying Legal Services Survey-Insights into Legal Procurement*, https://www.buyinglegal.com (last visited Oct. 5, 2018).

DUPONT LEGAL MODEL, *About the DuPont Legal Model*, https://www.dupontlegalmodel.com/initiatives/about-the-dupont-legal-model (last visited Sept. 28, 2018).

Hodges, Silvia, *Power of the Purse: How Corporate Procurement is Influencing Law Firm*, LAW PRACTICE TODAY (Jan. 2012), http://www.americanbar.org/publications/law_practice_today_home/law_practice_today_archive/january12/power-of-the-purse-how-corporate-procurement-is-influencing-law-firm.html (last visited Oct. 3, 2018).

Provines, Chris, *Rep-Less Medical Sales Model: Wake up—It's Just Part of a Bigger Procurement Trend*, CHRIS PROVINES (Mar. 28, 2015), http://chrisprovines.com/2015/03/28/rep-less-medical-sales-model-wake-up-its-just-a-part-of-a-bigger-procurement-trend (last visited Oct. 4, 2019).

PURCHASING INSIGHT, *Definition of Procurement—Procurement vs Purchasing*, http://purchasinginsight.com/resources/what-is/definition-of-procurement-procurement-vs-purchasing/ (last visited Sept. 26, 2015).

C. Other Sources

Maurice S. Byrd, Esq., Exec. Legal Consultant, Lexis Nexis, *The Effective Utilization of Paralegals in corporate legal Departments*, Presentation for ACC LA Roundtable 30 (Oct. 2, 2014).

Tom Braegelmann[1]

Restructuring Law and Technology

Challenges of Technology and Digitization for the Fast-paced Legal Areas of Corporate Restructuring, Bankruptcy and Insolvency

TABLE OF CONTENTS

---

1 This article is written with a general scope in mind, but unavoidably from the perspective of a restructuring lawyer with U.S. and EU/German experiences.

I. Introduction

Restructuring[2] law is beautiful, but also a lot of work.[3] The ideal is to save distressed but essentially viable companies in order to create economic value and preserve jobs. The reason for the heavy workload and fast pace: if a financial or operative crisis of a company conjures up the need for a corporate debt restructuring, a reorganization of the company, or even a filing for bankruptcy or insolvency, then the relevant data, especially contractual, accounting and business data, tends to be both massive, woolly, and at the same time incomplete. In fact, a company on the brink of bankruptcy or insolvency is often riddled with fragmentary and contradictory data about its dire financial circumstances and its major contractual relationships. This is sometimes precisely why the company's crisis was ignored and not caught earlier in the first place, when it maybe could have been prevented with a simple refinancing or gradual adjustment of its business model. Can technology make this data complete and help recognize financial distress quicker and earlier? This begs the question: of course it can, but when, and what are the obstacles, and are those obstacles of a kind that can be overcome?

---

2 The European Parliament recently adopted the following legal definition of restructuring: «‹restructuring› means measures aimed at restructuring the debtor›s business that include changing the composition, conditions or structure of a debtor›s assets and liabilities or any other part of the debtor›s capital structure, such as sales of assets or parts of the business and, where so provided under national law, the sale of the business as a going concern, as well as any necessary operational changes, or a combination of those elements;» in Art. 2. 1. (2) of the European Parliaments version of the «Proposal for a Directive of the European Parliament and of the Council on preventive restructuring frameworks, second chance and measures to increase the efficiency of restructuring, insolvency and discharge procedures and amending Directive 2012/30» The European Parliament voted in favour of this Directive on March 28, 2019. *See* for the official version of the text in all official EU languages: https://eur-lex.europa.eu/legal-content/EN/TXT/?uri=EP:P8_TA(2019)0321. The English Version is also available at www.europarl.europa.eu/RegData/seance_pleniere/textes_adoptes/provisoire/2019/03-28/0321/P8_TA-PROV(2019)0321_EN.pdf.

3 … for often handsomely paid lawyers.

II. Restructuring Law as Essential and Fundamental Part of Legal Systems

The digitization of the legal systems of the world and thus also of their respective bankruptcy/insolvency resolution procedures is inexorably and inevitably progressing. Why should this digital condition as the new basis for all legal interactions even worry restructuring lawyers? Isn't it still true that «*[a] lawyer's time and advice are his [or her] stock in trade*»? (A quote often attributed to *Abraham Lincoln*)[4] Yes, but that is no longer sufficient. Today, Lincoln would have to add: legal technology gadgets based on AI, big data, and distributed ledger technology; general legal analytics tools; document management software; deep online legal research databases; empowered marketing and business intelligence departments; etc. Moreover, while traditionally, bankruptcy and insolvency law is concerned a lot with traditional collateral/security (like real state, machinery, receivables and share pledges), the new reality of restructurings is also learning to deal with new digital assets like cryptocurrencies, tokens and smart contracts.[5] The real world is establishing new and fast digital and automatic asset transactions and enforcement mechanisms,[6] to which traditional restructuring law needs to react as this challenges the traditional bankruptcy/insolvency court case tools like the automatic stay or the forced disposal of assets. Restructuring law as a cornerstone of commercial law is thus also in the grip of the factual and legislative digitization of law that takes place in so many legal areas. It can be expected that there will soon be new and better software solutions and online platforms that will enable more, better and earlier opportunities for reorganizations, restructurings and swift bankruptcy/insolvency proceedings, with better outcomes for creditors, employees, the economy and the companies themselves.

---

4 It is however unconfirmed.

5 *See* the recent case in Russia which was brought in front of Moscow courts in the summer of 2018, where a debtor's estate showed a value of about 15 million US dollars. The catch, however, was that the funds were invested in Bitcoins, which this led to the question of whether Bitcoins could be legally part of the debtor's estate. Initially the Russian courts denied this by pointing out that the Russian Civil Code did not contain any allocation rules for this type of property or assets. This formalistic consideration was overruled upon appeal. *See* Sergey Treshchev & Elena Malevich, *Russia: cryptocurrency and bankruptcy estate,* 12 (2) Insolvency and Restructuring International, 30 et seq. (2018). The appellate court decision is available (in Russian) at http://kad.arbitr.ru/PdfDocument/3e155cd1-6bce-478a-bb76-1146d2e61a4a/58af451a-bfa3-4723-ab0d-d149aafecd88/A40-124668-2017_20180515_Postanovlenie_apelljacionnoj_instancii.pdf (last visited Apr. 14, 2019).

6 *See* in general Kevin Werbach, The Blockchain and the New Architecture of Trust (The MIT Press, 2018), and Primavera De Filippi & Aaron Wright, Blockchain and the Law (Harvard University Press, 2018).

So, let's take stock of where the legal field of corporate restructurings stands in face of the challenges of modern technology.

In this chapter, the term «restructuring» is used as an umbrella term for different legal processes involving the crisis (and the solution) of midsize to large companies/corporations, including all pre-court and court stages, i.e., (i) the stage of worsening financial distress, e.g., before a company is insolvent or in a bankruptcy proceeding which is why it still has a chance to go through a pre-insolvency restructuring/reorganization without court involvement; (ii) the stage where a company is not insolvent but nonetheless in a bankruptcy proceeding, e.g., in a strategic restructuring scenario, for instance in order to effectuate a debt-to-equity swap or to remove shareholders that are unwilling or unable to financially contribute to the rescue of the company; and, (iii) the stage where the company is insolvent and/or over-indebted and in a—usually mandatory—insolvency proceedings.[7]

Restructuring law has developed into a significant economic factor because when parties enter into a contract, it is of major importance in such commercial law transactions how quickly—in the event of default or crisis—a judicial or out-of-court/pre-court restructuring solution is possible, and whose assets, collateral/security and money are then in danger. Essentially, the question is: Who has to bear the restructuring/insolvency risk? This question is inherently asked whenever a contract is concluded. So, if contractual clauses and their risk allocations are always informed and influenced by the question who has to bear this risk, then the digitization and transformation of restructuring law will as a reflex have a fundamental impact on general commercial contractual law in practice. In addition, the ongoing digitization of company law also enables new and rapid restructuring options. So, arguably, what happens in restructuring law, does not stay in restructuring law but rather spills over in all of commercial law.

III. Big but Bad Data: The traditional challenge remains the new challenge to be tackled

Once a corporate crisis is in full swing, the management and its advisors have so many things to juggle at the same time (from making sure that your employees are paid and stay on; and that your customers and vendors do not lose trust and do not leave you; to seeking and ensuring new financing opportunities; to attending bankruptcy/insolvency court hearings and negotiations with major

7 The distinctions between and elements of these stages differ from country to country and may not all be available everywhere.

creditors). Therefore, getting a good grip and overview over the contractual relationships and financial data of a company is a daunting (but necessary) task, especially if a lot of that data is partly irrelevant, missing, entombed in paper records or in fragments of partially signed PDFs that are dispersed over multiple email-inboxes or several incompatible cloud-based document management systems. How to make sense of this? As long as there is no crisis, people and companies ignore a lot of data messiness, as they can always deal with it on an ad-hoc-basis. Not so in a crisis.

Anybody who works in restructuring has seen this and wondered why large swaths of the business world finds corporate housekeeping and proper document management so hard. How can modern legal technology (Legal/Law Tech) help restructurings? Legal software innovation could help speed up and reduce the cost of legal advice and document discovery. Moreover, a corporate crisis is often accompanied by legal violations, like missed filing deadlines, breached contractual obligations—something that LegalTech intends to prevent and cut back. But, let's face it: if a company cannot pay its debts as they come due, no ordinary software can do something about it anymore at that point.[8]

So, let's assume that modern legal technology will soon make it possible that transactions are documented in a much better and much more accessible and also processed more quickly. The hope is then that unwieldy facts and fragmentary mountains of documents, which until now could hardly be grasped at all because of their enormous size and fragmented state, can be mastered again without consuming the lifetime of very many lawyers or clerks for a cumbersome and tedious legal due diligence done by hand. But, and there lies the rub, at the same time more software and technology in general, and LegalTech in particular, may actually increase the flood of data as well: think of all the emails and slack channels and WhatsApp groups and online contracting platforms even small companies use and populate with their business data, and you realize that the massively increasing data volume that every business nowadays creates and which may become relevant and needs to be searchable cross-platform in a crisis, can irritate and paralyse the current legal systems, so that they may be crushed under the data mountain that are growing. How is a single bankruptcy judge going to review Terabytes of data? She cannot during her lifetime, if not helped by software.

But how do you tackle the usual corporate mess of a debtor in distress when you do not have much time and need the information now? Engaging a big international law firm or auditing firm is often not possible because (i) of the prohibitive costs, or (ii) it even may not have enough lawyers/accountants

8 Except for cryptocurrency mining of course, which however included the exchange rate risks and mining costs and will thus usually not help in a short time frame.

readily available to handle the job, or both. So, due to these financial and factual constraints, for a long time, a lot of data was simply not thoroughly examined and not contextualized in restructuring scenarios.[9] It turns out that restructuring law is still an often laborious and repetitive mixture of experience, legal knowledge, research into the puzzling facts of a case, including the repetitive use of some carefully guarded (and kept secret) templates and forms.[10] This is quite expensive for the client (often the debtor) and costs time. This become downright annoying when you know how well other areas of life and law are already enjoying the fruits of digitization: why can't the application of restructuring law not be faster if you can already find your new favorite film at Netflix within 60 to 90 seconds? Why can't you find within the same timeframe in your digital corporate vault the one and only decisive PDF piece of evidence, instead of heaving to review oodles of irrelevant PDFs before you get to the right one? A legal data base should not give you tons of results to be briefly read but immediately the single court case (if it exists) that you need to cite in your court brief (a so-called *Schmeckendorf* case, as my former New York boss, *Paul Silverman*, called such court cases that fit exactly to one's own case and fact pattern and help to win your day in court)? If on Amazon, the recommendations of other books are always pretty good and help, why can a document management system not automatically collect and show the incoming restructuring professionals all relevant emails and PDFs of a contentious financing, and why can a legal database not yet pre-formulate parts of court briefs? This would all be helpful but still is in its infancy.

And at the same time, speed is such a decisive factor in restructuring cases. Much better and much more comprehensive automated and AI-powered solutions are therefore desperately needed to accelerate the processes. Within a very short time, bankruptcy professionals must decide whether, for example, a company can continue at all or must be shut down immediately, whether employees are entitled to continue to be paid, and much more. In these cases, automatic computer-powered analysis tools would offer an advantage. They do partly exist already, especially in countries where the tax authorities mandate that companies process certain business data in standardized data formats.[11] These are then analyzed by applicable software tools for crisis indicators and payment patterns. They are a great help when it comes to making valid decisions quickly. But so far, what is on offer in the legal technology

---

9 *See* for instance concerning the backwardness of German restructuring law: Tom Braegelmann, *The Digital Judiciary*, LR 10, 11 (2018), https://legal-revolution.com/images/pdf/The_Digital_Judiciary.pdf (last visited Apr. 12, 2019).

10 Tom Braegelmann, *Datenmangel, Jura und XAI*, 1 RETHINKING LAW 22–23 (2019).

11 Michael Hermanns & Valerie Wachter, *Gutachterliche Ermittlung von Insolvenzgründen zur retrograden Feststellung des Zeitpunkts der Zahlungsunfähigkeit anhand von elektronischen Buchungsdaten*, 21 (29) ZINSO 1589–1595 (2018).

market is nice, but mostly niche-products and not the killer-app that would transform or at least accelerate restructuring law completely. Yes, AI data-extraction from thousands of similar employment agreements and the comparison of thousands of contractual clauses against a market standard is available, works reasonably well, is cost-efficient and this nice and almost as must-have, but not enough. Must lawyers thus continue to rely on the chance and coincidence of their individual research skills, the composition of their teams, and their respective individual and historically frozen state of their legal education and further training? How long will the legal market have to accept this spotty human element that still guides most lawyering? When it comes to restructuring law, the answer is: for a long, long time because, while there are certainly some powerful LegalTech tools available to help, from AI-based document review and machine-learning-powered data extraction to semantic analytics from the third wave of AI.[12] it is currently still state of the art to let human minds review, synthesize and give legal meaning to anything an AI engine or other LegalTech tool has produced.[13] Why you ask? Here is why: there is usually a lot of data in corporate restructurings available, which creates a heavy workload, while it is often at the same time obviously not complete, which creates another heavy workload i.e., making sense of the heaps of data from a legal perspective.

Apart from whether one does or does not—for reasons of legal policy—want to use powerful software tools (especially AI solutions that give useful results but for unexplained reasons), at the core of a legal system, and in restructuring in particular, there is a fundamental problem with law and AI: up to now, the development of powerful AI tools requires considerable amounts of data.[14] That is still the state of the art, even though there is talk of and research into a third wave of AI that would need less data.[15] And there is a twist:

---

12 *See* the announcement by the Defense Advanced Research Projects Agency («DARPA») on September 7, 2018, «DARPA Announces $2 Billion Campaign to Develop Next Wave of AI Technologies», stating: «To address the limitations of these first and second wave AI technologies, DARPA seeks to explore new theories and applications that could make it possible for machines to adapt to changing situations. DARPA sees this next generation of AI as a third wave of technological advance, one of contextual adaptation.» Available at: https://www.darpa.mil/news-events/2018-09-07; *see* also the introduction to Explainable Artificial Intelligence (XAI) by *David Gunning* from DARPA, available at: https://www.darpa.mil/program/explainable-artificial-intelligence.

13 Regular and legal tech hackathons, while fun, will also hardly improve this as long as they are not used to scrub and improve databases.

14 Michael Grupp, *25 facts about AI & Law you always wanted to know (but were afraid to ask)*, MEDIUM (Apr. 7, 2019), https://medium.com/@Grupp/25-facts-about-ai-law-you-always-wanted-to-know-but-were-afraid-to-ask-a43fd9568d6d (last visited Apr. 12, 2019).

15 *See* Nico Kuhlmann, *Die Dritte Welle von Künstlicher Intelligenz*, LEGAL TECH BLOG (May 29, 2018), https://legal-tech-blog.de/die-dritte-welle-von-kuenstlicher-intelligenz-interview-mit-dr-sven-koerner-thingsthinking (last visited Apr. 12, 2019).

most legal systems and legal cultures do not provide enough data (case law, contracts, business information) for the current standard of AI development.[16] In other areas, sufficient amounts of data are for sure available, for example for speech recognition (notably: for dictation, not so much for actually understanding texts), online shopping, self-driving cars and for sorting cat photos.[17] But sufficient data is not available for the law. Apart from the U.S., case law is world-wide in most countries, not published completely, and the amounts of case law are arguably too small.[18] Moreover, outside of the U.S., many nation-wide insolvency case online platforms require a lot of operational effort to handle, are finicky, and still do not provide reliable and user-friendly access to bankruptcy/insolvency courts.[19] Case in point: in the EU, where (apart from the ECJ) the member state courts issue their decisions, even when they apply directly applicable EU law, they do so only in their local language. So there is no EU-wide public case law database for all EU member state courts decisions on EU law. And even if there was enough data, the issue would be how to curate it in order to decide, by legal standards, what part of such data is authoritative and not contradicted by other parts. That is to say: even if there was enough data in principle available, you would have to make judgements about its veracity, accuracy, completeness, and the weight of its authority. In essence, you would need to make a legal judgment. Software may become able to do such judgments, but the question would be, whether the judgment is of sufficient quality and acceptable for humans.

The conundrum of a lack of powerful software tools for comprehensive and all-purpose and all-document-type data recognition and, crucially, understanding (apart from the basic data extraction tools that are already out there) irks restructuring professionals to a great extent because they see of course how other areas of law and technology are quickly developing and improving and becoming faster. So, obviously, there is a lot of dissatisfaction with the currents market standard of restructuring procedures as far as they concern the legal and technological tools for achieving a good overview and legal understanding of a company in crisis. Moreover, the current court systems and trustee/insolvency administrator solutions and online web-services offered by the traditional legal systems are often perceived as inefficient, lengthy and cumbersome or worse, misleading, thereby destroying the remaining value a struggling company may have for its creditors, employees and shareholders.[20]

16 Grupp, *supra* note 14.

17 *Id.*

18 Braegelmann, *Datenmangel, Jura und XAI*, *supra* note 10, at 22.

19 Braegelmann, *The Digital Judiciary*, *supra* note 9, at 10, 11, marginal number 5.

20 *See* for instance recital 5 of the new EU Restructuring Directive: «In many Member States it takes more than three years for entrepreneurs who are insolvent but honest to be discharged from their debts and make a fresh start. Inefficient discharge of debt and disqualification frame-

Now, it can be expected that all over the world restructuring, bankruptcy, and insolvency procedures will become faster over the course of their inevitable digitization. Because, in any case, the question is no longer whether legal procedures and the application of laws will be digitized, but rather to what extent and whether this digitization will happen. There is a risk that the digitization of restructuring law (because it is so difficult due to the problem of big bad messy data that is insufficient for AI applications) will only be a copy of traditional paper-based processes and not a transformation of restructuring, bankruptcy, and insolvency procedures into a kind of (for better or worse) new restructuring justice. Currently, the outlook may still be that restructuring will morph into a mere digitized copy of the old offline restructuring world. Let's hope not. As everyone knows, computing power is accelerating everywhere, and thus the digital tools that lawyers use are also improving all the time in speed, scope, competence, and, crucially, user experience.

However, if it turns out that only certain legal areas will improve via technology because this is only financially viable in such areas (think of the settlement of late-flight airline damages claims, online dispute resolution in e-commerce), then the advancing digitization of legal systems may lead to a «digital justice gap». Some legal areas (family law, immigration law etc.) where fees are not high may not improve technologically. Others, like restructuring, may not improve technologically because of the steep factual hurdles and lack of data. But, there should not be a technological separation of economically attractive areas of law, where rapid modernization is taking place, from the other areas of law forgotten by technical innovation impulses. So, it is worth discussing legal policy proposals to make sure that effective legal protection is increasingly provided by software in all legal areas: equal LegalTech for all. Where there are no private solutions for LegalTech, since no one finances them, but such solutions are objectively necessary, the government should see whether and how equivalent solutions can be created. One crucial thing is to ensure open and free government data to enable private actors to create smart LegalTech software solutions. As described, lack of good and sufficient data is an obstacle for new restructuring solutions. Before government steps in and tries to create those itself, it may want to increase the

---

works result in entrepreneurs having to relocate to other jurisdictions in order to benefit from a fresh start in a reasonable period of time, at considerable additional cost to both their creditors and the entrepreneurs themselves. Long disqualification orders, which often accompany a procedure leading to discharge of debt, create obstacles to the freedom to take up and pursue a self-employed, entrepreneurial activity.»—that directive was recently adopted by the European Parliament on March 28, 2019 concerning the «Proposal for a Directive of the European Parliament and of the Council on preventive restructuring frameworks, second chance and measures to increase the efficiency of restructuring, insolvency and discharge procedures and amending Directive 2012/30»—available at: http://www.europarl.europa.eu/RegData/seance_pleniere/textes_adoptes/provisoire/2019/03-28/0321/P8_TA-PROV(2019)0321_EN.pdf.

publicly available data on which others can then build competing solutions. For instance, in a corporate crisis, you usually inspect the accounting systems and software immediately. Tax files and tax data bases, both for authorities and the tax advisors, are usually kept relatively neatly and contain a wealth of information about the history of a company's financial health. As far as there is a internal tax accounting databases at companies (which is pretty much standard worldwide), those can be read out automatically to get an initial overview. But still many Bankruptcy/Insolvency/Restructuring firms would like to see more innovation in this area because the analysis of documentation and data is so important to them.[21] At present, however, when it comes to bankruptcy/insolvency/restructuring, digitization is still an issue and a hurdle. Companies are still allowed to use and keep dead, paper databases. Much of what is already being automated in certain other legal fields (like online banking) has to be done manually still in general corporate law: visits to the notary, keeping books and records in paper files. Because of this, even more valuable time is lost. Hence, the wish list of restructuring professions for processes that they believe should be automated is long. At present, many paper-based formalities slow things down, for instance, in Germany you have to go to a notary in order to effectively execute certain share pledges or changes in the shareholder composition and capital structure.[22] Too many days may pass before new shareholders are legally allowed to act and inject fresh money in a company. You often do not have this time in times of crisis. Hence, apart from changes in restructuring law, restructuring professionals will also gain a lot of help if the digitization of company law is finally implemented in the EU and the US and elsewhere. Then, you could carry out many corporate changes immediately and online and possibly without the help of a notary. As such, new shareholders would be able to act immediately after the closing of a deal. The acceptance rates for creditors' meetings could also be achieved much more easily if the meetings could be held online. You can think of many things to improve in the area of corporate law which would, as a reflex, also improve restructuring law and increase the success rate of restructurings because much less time is wasted.

Certain areas of restructuring are even less suitable for an AI/big data approach of analytics: the trading of non-performing loans («NPL», e.g., loans in default, where payments are missed, but where the debtor and the granted collateral are nonetheless financially attractive to certain investors) are for instance very difficult to categorize and analyze in an automated fashion and streamline because the underlying documentation concerning the collateral

---

21 *See* Sabine Reifenberger, *Automatisierung: Die lange Wunschliste der Restrukturierer*, Finance Magazine (Mar. 8, 2018), https://www.finance-magazin.de/banking-berater/kanzleien/automatisierung-die-lange-wunschliste-der-restrukturierer-2009651/ (last visited Apr. 12, 2019).

22 *Id.*

and the history of the defaults and the collateral is very individual concerning its history, lengthy, and not easily compared with any market standard. When you look at the often non-standard and sometimes exasperatingly creative rescue documentation that was added to many NPL's in the aftermath of the financial crisis from 2008 on, you wonder whether an AI could ever spot any patterns there. You also wonder whether you would want any precious legal AI to learn anything from it except the lesson to avoid messy and fast contractual fixes (that were, all things considered, often fine at the particular moment, but keep adding to a coral shelf of contractual fixes which smothers many large NPL's portfolios). But it is these messy and fast contractual fixes that pop up when a loan or a company is inching closer to a crisis, that land later on the table or tablet of a restructuring lawyer.

Automated analysis works best with standardized contracts. For example, the fact that employment contracts can nowadays be analyzed well in an automated way and scrutinized for essential clauses is a boon to HR departments and M&A deals. This could also help restructurings, if, for example, a software company in crisis is about to be sold in a fire sale and the last thing holding the deal back is a review of the employment contracts of software developers, to be checked for proper IP/Work for hire clauses. Or, in the event of the insolvency of a labor intensive company, one could pre-scan the workforce's in-house documentation in order to avoid unsocial and unfair dismissals of the most vulnerable employees.

But if it is the case that the data is just missing and that the data that is available is not necessarily enough and not that useful (both from the scientific perspective of AI as science and legal science) for smart applications, then why do we want anything to do with AI, LegalTech, software, data science on the one had and good old restructuring law and practice on the other? Well, one should not deny that with AI one can improve the search in databases and document management systems and the like. However, you would then still need humans to draw conclusions from the research and the automatic summaries. As of now, you cannot let AI or any software draw legal conclusions because how can one be sure that the software products—even if they deliver results—actually deliver legally correct results? Legal decisions need a written justification. Could AI, for example, draft bankruptcy petitions, insolvency filings, court briefs including legal citations, or properly and exhaustively research a legal question in case law and literature databases oe (pre-)subsume cases and create perfect contract samples according to the respective market standard? No, under today's standard of AI and data analysis, all you get is statistical correlations, and it is often no longer comprehensible why a certain decision has been suggested, even if the result of the decision is convincing. In jurisprudence, AI would therefore have to learn to justify itself in human-readable form, i.e., for legal purposes in proper legal lease or at least legal jargon to be acceptable for lawyers. This is a completely new field of research, called

XAI, i.e., explainable AI, which is still in its infancy.[23] Only when XAI is technically possible can AI be used to 1) support deep legal evaluations of companies and, 2) come up with reasons as to why a company's status and financial is dire or not form such a broad data analysis. Until then, human legal judgement of the facts and the law will rule supreme in restructuring law. Otherwise, at some point, we won't know why an AI-based tool gives us a certain overview of a company in crisis (but people may nonetheless adopt the AI's conclusions unexamined and misunderstood, but that is another subject).

IV. Help is on its way: The Legislative Promise of the EU's new pre-insolvency restructuring framework

Some governments, and namely the EU with its new Restructuring Directive, are aware of the fact that restructuring law, as a basis of commercial and contract law, is having difficulty to be more digital, to use better software tools, to come to grips with fragmentary and unstructured data dumps, and thus to preserve more value and achieve its statutory and societal goals.[24] So, government is here to help—for better or worse, but I would think mostly for the better. Because in light of the obvious diagnosis above that restructuring law is hampered by sketchy and bad data, and because this is not the fault of restructuring law but rather of corporate law and bad corporate housekeeping, the recent proposal by the EU for a pre-insolvency restructuring procedure—with major consequences for insolvency, corporate and banking law[25]—may be the requisite statutory push that lifts restructuring law's data quality to a better quality level and a major part of the world economy.

Not only will the new EU restructuring framework (i) allow a 75% majority of creditors to restructure a company's debt, mostly out-of-court, and way earlier than at an acute insolvency stage; while (ii) at the same time, stopping all enforcement actions for 4–12 months («*stay*»): and, (iii) leaving the management in charge («*debtor in possession*»). That is alone is groundbreaking for many EU member states, including Germany. But crucially, and in line with the diagnosis above, the EU's preventive approach comes with the proposal to make sure a company is warned early on that it is steering toward a

---

23 Gunning, *supra* note 12.

24 *See* for instance the new Art. 3 para 1 and 4 of the new EU Restructuring Directive that mandates the introduction of new and digital early warning tools in order to prevent bankruptcies.

25 The agreement in the *EU Council* took place on December 17, 2018. This «*final compromise*» is now before the EU Parliament, which will adopt it in early 2019. Far-reaching changes are no longer to be expected. The compromise wording of the entire directive is already available at: https://data.consilium.europa.eu/doc/document/ST-15556-2018-INIT/en/pdf

crisis. In detail: The EU is now proposing the introduction of early warning tools, via the harnessing of IT technology and online environments. See Art. 3 of the upcoming EU restructuring directive, as adopted by the EU Parliament on March 28, 2019 (emphasis added):[26]

> **Article 3**
>
> Early warning and access to information
>
> 1. Member States shall ensure that debtors have access to one or more clear and transparent early warning tools which can detect circumstances that could give rise to a likelihood of insolvency and can signal to the debtor the need to act without delay.
>
> For the purposes of the first subparagraph, **Member States may make use of up-to-date IT technologies for notifications and for communication**.
>
> 2. Early warning tools may include the following:
>
> (a) alert mechanisms when the debtor has not made certain types of payments;
>
> (b) advisory services by public or private organisations;
>
> *(c) incentives under national law for third parties with relevant information about the debtor, such as accountants, tax and social security authorities to flag to the debtor a negative development.*
>
> *3. Member States shall ensure that debtors and employees' representatives have access to relevant and up-to-date information about the availability of early warning tools as well as the procedures and measures concerning restructuring and discharge of debt.*
>
> ***4. Member States shall ensure that information on access to early warning tools is publicly available online and that, in particular for SMEs****, it is easily accessible and presented in a user-friendly manner.*
>
> *5. Member States may provide support to employees' representatives for the assessment of the economic situation of the debtor.*

Obviously, such warning tools can only work if the available data has a sufficient quality. Hence, this proposal makes sense only if the member states implement it with additional measures forcing or convincing companies to create and keep better data about themselves in a structured and complete and machine-readable way, and if that happens, all of restructuring will work better. You could enact laws to ensure that corporations (from their founding) on must structure their internal data and processes and their legal relationships (with shareholders, customers, vendors, employees, management and regulatory authorities) in a clear and complete structured unitary database that is by

26 Concerning the «Proposal for a Directive of the European Parliament and of the Council on preventive restructuring frameworks, second chance and measures to increase the efficiency of restructuring, insolvency and discharge procedures and amending Directive 2012/30»—the text adopted by the European Parliament is available at: http://www.europarl.europa.eu/RegData/seance_pleniere/textes_adoptes/provisoire/2019/03-28/0321/P8_TA-PROV(2019)0321_EN.pdf.

itself machine-readable and does not require post-fact data extraction and data creation. Soon all corporations could be forced to create an electronic digital twin of themselves in coded and machine-readable form. As cloud data services become cheaper and more reliable, this should be feasible for most companies.

According to the EU's official legislative reasoning provided with the initial legislative proposal,[27] these early warning systems should lead to more successful restructurings as they will be initiated at a much early stage than now. Thankfully, and conspicuously, the provision is formulated in a technologically neutral way. However, it is clear that such a financial early warning system can currently only function digitally, if it is supposed to be fast and efficient. However, this can only succeed if the corresponding financial data and corporate documentation is available electronically, in a structured way and in high quality, and if the companies' financial software has corresponding interfaces. It would then be conceivable, for example, to have systems that automatically issue warnings to management (for instance as a pop-up in the morning when they open their laptops) when a liquidity crisis or shortfall is imminent or when an insolvency is more likely than not. What might also be introduced could be that breaches of important conditions in loan agreements (like covenants, minimum revenues, liquidity reserves, dismissal of managing directors, etc.) would be automatically determined and communicated the respective creditors, other stakeholders and, if necessary, the managing directors e.g., via a *«computable contract» or even a «smart contract»*. Looking at this, the question arises whether artificial intelligence (AI) could be applied in order to—in the parlance of the EU's restructuring directive—*«detect circumstances that may give rise to the likelihood of insolvency and signal to the debtor the need to act without delay.»* Even then, it would still be a long way to the utopia (or dystopia, depending on how one sees it) in which companies would be subject to a computer-controlled automatic filing of a bankruptcy petition or a motion for the opening of insolvency proceedings, including the automatic selection of an insolvency administrator or trustee by an algorithm. That will need to be reserved to the courts and human judges and human restructuring professionals working in the judicial system.

---

27 *See* for instance recital 22 of the new EU Restructuring Directive: «The earlier a debtor can detect its financial difficulties and can take appropriate action, the higher the probability of avoiding an impending insolvency or, in the case of a business the viability of which is permanently impaired, the more orderly and efficient the liquidation process would be. Clear, up-to-date, concise and userfriendly information on the available preventive restructuring procedures as well as one or more early warning tools should therefore be put in place to incentivise debtors that start to experience financial difficulties to take early action.»

V. Incomplete Contracts as stubborn long-term issue unsolvable by technology?

But even if major and fundamental legislative reforms like the EU's restructuring framework are introduced and all companies would provide a clean digital twin of themselves for a quick analysis of their financial and operative ailments, there remain major gaps that technology cannot fill at this point: Consider in addition to the specific messiness of data in restructuring scenarios, the general legal problem and riddle of «incomplete contracts», which exacerbates the technological hurdles of the legal field of restructuring law.[28]

Contracts are often nebulous, «fuzzy», sometimes on purpose and sometimes not, even if they were not (due to time constraints)—formulated and negotiated in a hurry. Contractual texts are frozen in time and even when they were mostly complete at the time they were entered into, they become fragmentary again over time as facts, economics, people, interests, intentions, statutory and case law change and mutate, as they always do, thereby «creating» new gaps in contractual relations and requiring recurrent contractual updates. The reason is simply that a contract of a few (or even thousands of) pages cannot predict all eventualities of business life or how reality and statutory and case law will develop. Contractual parties also do not have the option of repeatedly balancing out their contractual relationships in ongoing negotiations and via constant amendments of their contractual documentation as they have to attend to their business and cannot preoccupy themselves with contractual language perpetually.

This is the problem of «contractual incompleteness«»», which has been identified and studied in depth by *Oliver Hart*, winner of the 2016 Nobel Prize in Economics as such:

> *«[C]omplete contracts (...) are contracts where everything that can ever happen is written into the contract. There may be some incentive constraints arising from moral hazard or asymmetric information but there are no unanticipated contingencies. Actual contracts are not like this, as lawyers have realized for a long time. They are poorly worded, ambiguous, and leave out important things. They are incomplete. (...) [A] critical question that arises with an incomplete contract is, who has the right to decide about the missing things? We called this right the residual control or decision right. The question is, who has it? (...) Economists are drawn to areas with simple, elegant, and uncontroversial models. The area of incomplete con-*

---

28 Tom Braegelmann, *Incomplete Contracts: Eine Sisyphusaufgabe für Legal Tech-Fans*, 1 RETHINKING LAW 26 (2018).

tracts is not like that; it is messy. But contracts are incomplete in reality and contractual incompleteness underlies numerous significant phenomena, some of which have great policy relevance.»[29]

LegalTech and especially AI can help here, but the problem will never go away, and here is why: LegalTech applications, whether they use AI, machine learning or smart contracts or the like, will find it to be hardly possible to automatically complete contracts. You would to know and evaluate the new unique facts that challenge an old contract. Especially, it is not possible for software to try to actually implement and enforce general (and tedious) severability clauses in living contractual relationships or to find out through machine learning and big data how in—the living practice of—contractual execution these contractual gaps are taken care of without testing them in court. The reason: people and companies most often settle their legal cases out of court—and in secret and shrouded in NDAs (which is why no AI will probably ever know or learn from the vast majority of contractual settlements, even though those are a major tool of commerce).

In any case, Oliver Hart recognized the signs of the times and got hired as a consultant for a blockchain startup that wants to build better smart contracts in order to at least whittle down the problem of incomplete contracts.[30] Now it will be exciting to see whether the promises of blockchain technology/ideology make less incomplete contracts possible. Hart said in this context: «Blockchain can be very helpful in automating certain things (...) Incentives are at the heart of all this. But also governance, how these things are organized. (...) Almost all legal disputes have to do with contract incompleteness (...) I don't know how to quantify the costs of all that, but I think just casual empiricism suggests that those costs are pretty big, and if people could write better contracts or get themselves on the same page so *they can agree on what was meant to happen, those costs will be reduced.»*[31] Good luck to those endeavors, when in light of the diversity of the legal world we live in, incomplete contracts, as long as they are written in plain and thus inherently ambiguous language, will probably stay with us forever. And, as discussed, if incomplete contracts already pose a challenge in regular transactions and legal conflicts,

---

29 Oliver Hart, *Incomplete Contracts and Control*, 107(7) American Economic Review 1731–1752 (2017), https://scholar.harvard.edu/files/hart/files/incomplete_contracts_and_control.pdf (last visited Feb. 3, 2019) at 1732, 1749.

30 Michael del Castillo, *Nobel Prize Winner Joins Blockchain Startup To Fix Smart Contracts*, Forbes (Aug. 1, 2018), https://www.forbes.com/sites/michaeldelcastillo/2018/08/01/nobel-prize-winner-joins-blockchain-startup-to-fix-smart-contracts/#4dd34917cc7f (last visited Feb. 3, 2019).

31 Michael del Castillo, *Nobel Prize Winner Joins Blockchain Startup To Fix Smart Contracts*, Forbes (Aug. 1, 2018), https://www.forbes.com/sites/michaeldelcastillo/2018/08/01/nobel-prize-winner-joins-blockchain-startup-to-fix-smart-contracts/#4dd34917cc7f (last visited Feb. 3, 2019).

then this is even more so the case in a restructuring situation, as in such situations new facts crop up everywhere that may challenge contractual terms and assumptions. So, as long as technology cannot effectively tackle the puzzle of permanently incomplete contracts, the issue of incomplete contracts will add to the restructuring burden of the debtor.

VI. Specific Challenge: Smart Contracts and Digital Assets vs. the Automatic Stay and other traditional Restructuring Tools.

The section above mentioned smart contracts as part of the vision to tackle contract incompleteness. And indeed, digital and self-executing contracts challenge what you can actually do with the traditional set of legal tools that many restructuring laws provide. Whether what follows is convincing to the reader may depend on his or her view what a smart contract actually is (e.g., an independent software agent or a boring script), as the legal and technological discussion is still ongoing.[32]

However, it is already clear that more and more contracts will be digital and run by or via software within online environments. So, one could say: «The charm of the idea and concept of smart contracts is that anyone (...) can now much easier than ever automatize the performance and enforcement of many of their legal obligations, thereby ensuring much better compliance with contracts and laws, while remaining in control. (...) The tools of digital rights management and of digitally operating and deploying contracts will be available to all, big and small, filling the digital justice gap and improv[ing] *access to justice for everyone. This is the vision of what smart contracts should be able to do.*»[33]

If that vision comes true, and depending how indepent from any legal system smart contracts may operate and modify digital assets, it may challenge restructuring law at it core: Because, in a corporate crisis, it is of tangible importance who actually holds or effectively controls the debtor's assets in question, either in direct possession or under direct control, by legal means or via a *de facto* position of possession or power; for example: who has the keys

---

32 *See* the chapter on smart contracts in this book. Notably, the charismatic leader of the Ethereum Project recently stated: «To be clear, at this point I quite regret adopting the term ‹smart contracts›. I should have called them something more boring and technical, perhaps something like 'persistent scripts'.», Vitalik Buterin (@VitalikButerin), TWITTER (Oct. 13, 2018 10:21 AM), https://twitter.com/VitalikButerin/status/1051160932699770882 (last visited Apr. 11, 2019).

33 Tom Braegelmann, *in* LEGAL TECH—HOW TECHNOLOGY IS CHANGING THE LEGAL WORLD. A PRACTITIONER'S GUIDE (Hartung et al., eds., 2018) at 283.

to the company's truck (that was pledged as a an asset to secure a loan) and drives it of the company's premises); who has the login data for the Company's online (and pledge) bank account and empties it completely? There is an old, anglo-american, legal adage according to which «*possession is nine-tenths of the law.*»[34] That may be so. The inventor of the term «Smart Contract», computer scientist and lawyer Nick Szabo, recently succinctly rewrote this as a motto for the digital era: «*If ‹possession is 90% of the law›, then a good smart [contract] may be ‹99% of the law›»*.[35]

Hence, if under traditional legal rules factual possession of a thing makes up 90% of the law, then smart contracts (or any other strong digital contracts for that matter) could amount to 99% of the law. In the era of digital law, this would mean that up to now (whether in 90% of cases or less) the one who factually is holding a thing in his or her hands or is controlling it will in the end actually prevail in a dispute over such thing (in fact/reality, i.e., even if contrary to the law); but in the the future, the digital environment of digital contracts and digital assets may inexorably determine most rights and control/ownership of digital assets and initially enforce them as programmed, whether this is legal or not. Whether that specific vision of smart contracts should (disturbingly) come true is debatable. You may want to inquire: what about the rule of law? Where will it indeed remain, if soon not only possession/control creates a position of power, in a in the crisis, no matter what the legal situation is, but also the automated, insurmountable digital control of transactions via smart contracts? And here one goal of restructuring law comes in and is at issue: equal treatment of all creditors. In order to treat them equally, you need to collect and preserve the debtor's estate. What if new digital environments for (smart) contracts and digital assets make this factually impossible or at least hard and burdensome for the debtor?

A special feature of statutory crisis management mechanisms (bankruptcy/insolvency proceedings, pre-insolvency preventive proceedings, schemes) is the potential or mandatory suspension of further legal acts affecting the debtor's assets in the form of a moratorium or *automatic stay*. Enforcement or other acts of access are legally prevented by such a moratorium, a violation of which is regularly subject to financial sanctions. Similarly, these instruments, be it bankruptcy/insolvency proceedings, a restructuring plan, a *scheme of arrangement* or something comparable, regulate the distribution of the debtor's assets or his reorganization. These tried and tested (and, by their very nature, in each country differently accentuated and applied) instruments for the preservation of the debtor's estate and, where appropriate, the legally

---

34 *See* LAW.COM, *possession*, https://dictionary.law.com/Default.aspx?selected=1555 (last visited Apr. 12, 2019).

35 Nick Szabo (@NickSzabo4), TWITTER (Oct. 14, 2018 3:51 PM), https://twitter.com/NickSzabo4/status/1051606530108190720 (last visited Apr. 12, 2019).

controlled distribution or reorganizations of assets reach their limits when it is no longer people who are acting but technology, machines or software that carry out the relevant legal acts. To the extent that the advantage of automated processes is seen precisely in their immunization against external influence, problems of a legal nature must arise if the law requires that these processes be changed, influenced or even discontinued or immediately interrupted in fact. Insolvency law, in particular, offers rather strict means to intervene in property rights and transactions, for example, and to trim down vested interests and acquired rights. These legal means can be counteracted and neutralized in their immediate legal effect if the software reality can no longer be changed by these mere legal tools.

If one continues to think of the technical possibilities, it would also be conceivable that lenders/bank automate the enforcement or realization/disposal of collateral that so far is difficult to realize (e.g., pledged shares or IP/software licenses) by means of Smart Contracts (possibly by softening/ignoring notarization obligations). Whether this is a utopia or dystopia of financing law is a question of legal policy. In some cases there will be such possibilities without the legislator having to allow them. If a financing contract built in this way now independently determines (via so-called oracles, e.g., commercial registers or trusted third party information providers) that contractual conditions for the realization of collateral have been fulfilled (e.g., through the breach of covenants, non-payment of instalments), the collateral would be realized (without title, clause and delivery) by itself, i.e., the financier as collateral taker would thus immediately become a new shareholder, license holder or account holder, and as owner would then have the opportunity to transfer these collateral immediately, without an auction, bailiff or cumbersome delivery requirements. Instead of an inefficient *«race to the courthouse»,* which is currently pretty much prevented by bankruptcy/insolvency law, and for good reasons of efficiency, there would be a *«race of the fastest smart contract»,* where bankruptcy/insolvency law would be left behind, unnoticed, in the dustbin of legal history (because the potential insolvent assets, driven by smart-contract, might disappear in seconds before the insolvency administrator logs into the company's IT-systems at all). This example alone proves that restructuring needs to deal now and intensively with modern technology and to adapt its instruments for an adequate handling of it.

Questions to be asked are, for instance, how do you as, an insolvency administrator, take possession of a digital environment and its smart contracts, and manage it? In addition, are insolvency administrators or other publicly appointed liquidators of companies allowed to participate at all in transactions with crypto currencies and other blockchain-based digital assets for the purpose of maintaining or liquidating a company's assets, even if it is only for the purpose of liquidating a company that had performed an ICO or holds other digital assets, as part of a bankruptcy/liquidation estate? May an insolvency administrator who finds, for example, several valuable Bitcoins or smart contracts in the debtor's estate sell or assign them? These case are already cropping up in many countries[36] and will become more and more relevant.

A collision between good old restructuring law and our new digital reality will occur in particular if a relevant smart contract that is running on a public and generally accessible, e.g., permissionless blockchain; because then this Smart Contract, without the support or influence of a legal system, can have its own kind of inexorable and unstoppable power of self-enforcement within the framework of the respective blockchain, at least as far as the payments and digital assets that are manipulated by the particular smart contract, are also blockchain-based. In this respect, a smart contract is de facto binding and cannot be broken up or stopped with the traditional restructuring tools like an automatic stay or a court order, since its digital causality chain (within its digital environment) cannot actually be stopped. Like the water-hauling brooms of the sorcerer's apprentice in *Goethe*'s poem *«Der Zauberlehrling»,* they will continue to function by moving independently after starting, no matter if the result is disastrous.

In addition, modern digital assets so far escape a precise determination of their status under restructuring law, bankruptcy/insolvency courts are still catching up with the question as to what Bitcoins or Crypto-Tokens are—a right *in rem*, a mere unsecured claim, a legal, valuable but intangible «object» that is not an intellectual property right as its creation only requires «sweat of the brow» (or rather «sweat of the miner») and no creativity? Bitcoins and Crypto-Tokens can be understood as an asset of the debtor's estate in the legal sense,[37] and in the future this will may also apply to many other digital assets and tokens as well as correspondingly tokenized assets (e.g., company shares, real estate)—especially if these can be digitally and unambiguously, uniquely, unalterably and easily be transferred and pledged by means of a digital register with a complete chain of title in a manner accepted by commerce and (sometimes necessarily) only after permitted by statute. This will make it possible to create new types of financial collateral for granting loans if the debtor's assets are recognized as such transferable digital assets. This is where blockchain-based digital assets become interesting for restructuring professionals,

---

36 In addition to the case from Russia, the author knows several current cases in Germany that are however not in the public domain yet. Other prominent cases are Mt.Gox from Japan (https://en.wikipedia.org/wiki/Mt._Gox), Envion from Switzerland/Germany (https://de.wikipedia.org/wiki/Envion. *See* Nathaniel Popper, *In the World of Cryptocurrency, Even Good Projects Can Go Bad*, NY Times (May 31, 2018), https://www.nytimes.com/2018/05/31/technology/envion-initial-coin-offering.html (last visited Apr. 12, 2019).

37 Christoph Paulus & Tom Braegelmann, *Smart Contracts im Krisenfall*, in Rechtshandbuch Smart Contracts (Tom Braegelmann & Markus Kaulartz, eds., C. H. Beck, forthcoming 2019) at 239.

as securities/collateral and their treatment in a corporate crisis are always a core topic of restructuring law. For example, if a debtor does not pay, a Smart Contract may be able to collect and realize the collateral/security itself. The contract therefore executes itself, within a blockchain ecosystem this is possible without a bankruptcy court, bailiff or other actor.

It is to be expected that business and legislation will be resourceful in creating more and more new digital assets as these can be highly liquid and their transaction chains are automatically documented. These digital assets can then be used as new collateral for lending through smart contracts. Many banks are also experimenting with digital assets and smart contracts to handle complex financial transactions that require collateral.[38] In the event of a crisis, this also raises the question for restructuring lawyers of how to deal with such collateral/securities in bankruptcy/court proceedings, who is entitled to them, how and whether they can be encumbered and collected, and so on. (several practical cases are already pending and known, for instance in Germany).

The mechanism of restructuring proceedings to suspend enforcements and transactions means that at least in principle, from a certain point in time on (the court filing, the actual insolvency, etc.), any subsequent payments by the debtor to a third party or any acquisition of objects of the debtor's assets of any kind whatsoever is invalid and can be contested/avoided via a preference action in court. As a rule, this means that what has been acquired by a third party, even if lawfully and via contract, must be returned to the debtor in order to treat all creditors equally and to avoid a race to the courthouse. This legal consequence of bankruptcy/insolvency contestation/avoidance/preference actions does not change if the contested transaction not triggered by a human but by an unstoppable smart contract. The insolvency administrator will have to contact the third party at the other end of such contract and demand repayment, in and out of court.

The automatism regularly inherent in Smart Contracts leads straight into legal problems even before the initiation of insolvency proceedings in court. The reason is that many legal systems prohibit managing directors from making any payment to third parties as a matter of principle in case the managing directors' company is insolvent or trading while insolvent. If the managing directors nonetheless permit and execute such payments anyhow, they may be personally liable. This legal principle is part and parcel of restructuring law, meant to protect the debtor's estate. Managing directors must thus permanently monitor the financial circumstances of the company. What follows from this legal principle is that part of this permanent self-monitoring must now be

---

38 *See* Finextra, *Commerzbank and Deutsche Bourse settle repo transaction on blockchain*, Finextra (Mar. 6, 2019), https://www.finextra.com/newsarticle/33486/commerzbank-and-deutsche-bourse-settle-repo-transaction-on-blockchain (last visited Apr. 12, 2019).

that any smart contract that a company deploys which either merely provides a service or which initiates the conclusion of a contract for a service must contain a provision by which management is able to switch it off in the event of insolvency. Or, the smart contract is given to opportunity to review the company's financial situation periodically in order to determine by itself whether it better shut down in order to save the management from personal liability. The factual problem in this context is however the technical approach that blockchain-based smart contracts are basically «immutable» and «unstoppable» (unless they are openly programmed for subsequent intervention by third parties). So what can management do if an immutable and unstoppable smart contract continues to mercilessly make payments to the detriment of the company even after the company has become insolvent (just as the broom in Goethe's sorcerer's apprentice is still dragging buckets of water in when everything is already flooded) and inevitably drives the management into personal liability? This is not a theoretical case: insurance companies already operate systems that calculate the passenger's damages compensation for flight delays immediately after landing in accordance with the EU regulation on passenger rights and pay it out automatically.[39] This works because the flight delay data is always up-to-date and can be retrieved online in clean and trusted formats. But such a set-up, while maybe desirable from the standpoint of the passengers and consumer protection legislation, can be extremely detrimental to an airline's liquidity, as all passengers on a specific flight would receive the compensation at precisely the same time a few seconds after a delayed landing. Accordingly, in a financial crisis, an airline must consider twice whether it wants to be subject to such an automated system, which can impair its liquidity at any time and which cannot simply be switched off during the crisis. The same applies in general: a management must be aware of the special risks if it allows the use of immutable and unstoppable Smart Contracts. This discussion will continue.

VII. Conclusion: The human element of restructuring law

The legal policy question that you need to ask when technology is introduced into legal relations is always: «what about the rule of law?» Make sure to ask it and do not presume that technology will, by default, protect the rule of law; this is never a default but always a choice. Case in point: if everyone is in agreement—or threatened into agreement with economic pressure—then a

39 One major example is the tool offered by the insurer Axa. *See* Axa, *AXA goes blockchain with fizzy* (Sep. 13, 2017), https://www.axa.com/en/newsroom/news/axa-goes-blockchain-with-fizzy (last visited Apr. 11, 2019).

corporate restructuring can also be settled in other ways than by applying restructuring law or without explicit reference to law. If legal technology tools make this easier, so much the better for successful restructurings but maybe not so much better for the rule of law. It thus remains to be seen whether the expansion of legal technology will improve justice (and if so, for whom, because the same thing or solution may seem just for some and unjust to others). Unfortunately, there are many lawyers who have little affinity with technology and thus may not be aware that technology may either boost the protection of the rule of law or endanger it.

And to look at the more mundane issues of legal technology on restructuring practice: Currently, many lawyers still find it difficult, for example, to correctly use the algorithms that automatically evaluate contracts when dealing with LegalTech software tools such as *Luminance*, *Kira* or *Leverton*. Why do they even bother, if they do not like it? Some restructuring professionals are still treating advanced software tools as a foreign language that they do not understand and do not have time to learn. They may throw them at their new and young associates but then lack the competence to assess whether the associates did a good job. Moreover, do the actual lawyers on the ground, the seasoned senior associates, counsels and local partners, e.g., those who do the lion share of actual legal work and factual analysis in most larger law firms, use any of the digital analysis tools that the law firm partners already bought for them? Strong anecdotal evidence would appear to show that these lawyers, who are supposed to use these tools, often do not use them, because they are still quicker at doing the legal work by hand, and they still have trouble using these tools, as these tools often do not have the greatest user experience, or take a while to learn and are boring. As many lawyers are currently overworked anyhow, imagine how likely it is that they stay long at the office at night in order to learn a couple of new software tools or to train document recognition for incremental improvement of the AI that will only show itself in a couple of years. That is not very likely. Hence, currently, at this stage of the digitization of the law, there is a rising and innocent passive resistance of the employed lawyers against using these digital tools, as they sometimes distract them from doing the actual work and make them stay longer in the office or stay longer awake in their home office. However, in the long run this will not persist as the younger lawyers will from the beginning on be using these digital tools and will not know anything else. Moreover, the greatest the pressure to innovate restructuring practice with technology comes from outside. Many clients have automated their own processes and built up pristine data centers and now expect the same from their restructuring lawyers, in order to be able feed the results of the restructuring lawyers into their own systems without glitches and loss of information. Moreover, the lack of junior lawyers in the legal industry in general (young people are more and more choosing less traditional professions) means that LegalTech solutions are in demand for more and more legal areas in order to replace the lacking human lawyers. Add to that there are even less young applicants in the restructuring law sector. This all increases the pressure to find automated solutions for routine tasks so that the human colleagues can devote themselves to value-creating topics such as actual legal thinking and arguing and such as legal assessments of facts and legal risks.

The challenge is to preserve the enormous opportunities offered of the enhanced and accelerated digitization of the law, legal proceedings, and legal services via LegalTech without the legal system developing major blind spots. With digitization, there is fundamental change in the system of the application of law and law enforcement afoot, in line with the current Digital Zeitgeist: «Software is eating the world» it is said,[40] and hence many think that software must also be eating the legal world, and indeed it has been chewing it out for some time now. But, as it may have become clear in this chapter, not only in the legal profession in general, but in restructuring in particular, the human element will remain an essential condiment and spice to the legal world, even more so if this human element is enhanced and supercharged with more and more powerful software tools, AI and smart contracts, and better data than ever. One should also not forget the importance of direct human contact in restructuring law, face to face. As an example, during my time as a bankruptcy lawyer in New York, I witnessed live and *on the record* in the courtroom of the U.S. Bankruptcy Court for the Southern District of New York in lower Manhattan how the Bankruptcy Judge *Martin Glenn* cut considerable fees of the lawyers of the debtor, the bookselling chain Borders, at a hearing, because they apparently had plagiarized a large part of their pleadings from another prominent law firm.[41] That this copying was even possible is an effect of the robust and reliable data structure of the U.S. Federal Court System. But to be able to swiftly slap such embarrassing sanctions for reasons of equity onto human actors in the legal system, and then, after they wholeheartedly apolo-

---

40 Marc Andreessen, *Why Software Is Eating The World*, The Wall Street Journal (Aug. 20, 2011), https://www.wsj.com/articles/SB10001424053111903480904576512250915629460 (last visited Feb. 3, 2019).

41 Tiffany Kary, *Borders Wins Approval of $505 Million Bankruptcy Loan*, Bloomberg (Mar. 15, 2011 6:04 PM), https://www.bloomberg.com/news/articles/2011-03-15/borders-wins-approval-of-505-million-bankruptcy-loan-from-geec-led-group%20- (last visited Feb. 2, 2019) «imitation is the sincerest form of flattery, Glenn said, telling Borders lawyer Jeffrey Gleit that the motion is «taken almost verbatim» from Weil Gotshal›s request to pay utilities in Blockbuster and didn›t cite Weil. Glenn said Kasowitz is barred from submitting a fee request for its work on the motion, including those for inserting the Borders case caption on a Weil pleading. «I understand your honor›s point, and it›s well taken,» Gleit said, apologizing. » *See* also Will Hooper & Mary Katherine Rawls, *Borders Group, Inc.'s Final Chapter: How A Bookstore Giant Failed In The Digital Age. Chapter 11 Bankruptcy Case Studies* (2014), https://trace.tennessee.edu/utk_studlawbankruptcy/38 (last visited Feb. 3, 2019).

gize in public and on the record, in turn to simply move on with the more important restructuring efforts, shows as *pars pro toto* that the human element will remain useful in calming and streamlining procedures as powerful as restructuring/bankruptcy/insolvency cases in order to encourage that all parties concentrate—while faced with time and data constraints—on the reorganization objective. Hence, restructuring law, while in need of much better technology and data (which will eventually arrive—here is hoping—to speed things up), will probably always suffer sometimes from worse than usual fragmentary and messy data and the need to make swift decisions on an incomplete information basis. In those critical cases, you will still need human judgment and decision making in order to focus and achieve the goals of restructuring law, in order to preserve value for the creditors, save employees' jobs, and grant a fresh start to the debtor.

VIII. Bibliography

A. Hard Copy Sources

Tom Braegelmann, *Datenmangel, Jura und XAI*, 1 REthinking Law 22–23 (2019).

Tom Braegelmann, *Incomplete Contracts: Eine Sisyphusaufgabe für Legal Tech-Fans*, 1 REthinking Law 26 (2018).

De Filippi, Primavera & Wright, Aaron, Blockchain and the Law (Harvard University Press, 2018).

Michael Hermanns & Valerie Wachter, *Gutachterliche Ermittlung von Insolvenzgründen zur retrograden Feststellung des Zeitpunkts der Zahlungsunfähigkeit anhand von elektronischen Buchungsdaten*, 21 (29) ZInsO 1589–1595 (2018).

Treshchev, Sergey & Malevich, Elena, *Russia: cryptocurrency and bankruptcy estate*, 12 (2) Insolvency and Restructuring International 30 et seq. (2018).

Werbach, Kevin, The Blockchain and the New Architecture of Trust (The MIT Press, 2018).

B. Online Sources

Andreessen, Marc, *Why Software Is Eating The World*, The Wall Street Journal (Aug. 20, 2011), https://www.wsj.com/articles/SB10001424053111903480904576512250915629460 (last visited Feb. 3, 2019).

Axa, *AXA goes blockchain with fizzy* (Sep. 13, 2017), https://www.axa.com/en/newsroom/news/axa-goes-blockchain-with-fizzy (last visited Apr. 11, 2019).

Braegelmann, Tom, *The Digital Judiciary*, LR 10, 11 (2018), https://legal-revolution.com/images/pdf/The_Digital_Judiciary.pdf (last visited Apr. 12, 2019).

Buterin, Vitalik (@VitalikButerin), Twitter (Oct. 13, 2018 10:21 AM), https://twitter.com/VitalikButerin/status/1051160932699770882 (last visited Apr. 11, 2019).

Defense Advanced Research Projects Agency, *DARPA Announces $2 Billion Campaign to Develop Next Wave of AI Technologies* (Sep. 7, 2018), https://www.darpa.mil/news-events/2018-09-07 (last visited Apr. 12. 2019).

del Castillo, Michael, *Nobel Prize Winner Joins Blockchain Startup To Fix Smart Contracts*, Forbes (Aug. 1, 2018), https://www.forbes.com/sites/michaeldelcastillo/2018/08/01/nobel-prize-winner-joins-blockchain-startup-to-fix-smart-contracts/#4dd34917cc7f (last visited Feb. 3, 2019).

Finextra, *Commerzbank and Deutsche Bourse settle repo transaction on blockchain*, Finextra Mar. 6, 2019), https://www.finextra.com/newsarticle/33486/commerzbank-and-deutsche-bourse-settle-repo-transaction-on-blockchain (last visited Apr. 12, 2019).

Grupp, Michael, *25 facts about AI & Law you always wanted to know (but were afraid to ask)*, Medium (Apr. 7, 2019), https://medium.com/@Grupp/25-facts-about-ai-law-you-always-wanted-to-know-but-were-afraid-to-ask-a43fd9568d6d (last visited Apr. 12, 2019).

Gunning, David, *Explainable Artificial Intelligence (XAI)*, https://www.darpa.mil/program/explainable-artificial-intelligence (last visited Apr. 12, 2019).

Hart, Oliver, *Incomplete Contracts and Control*, 107(7) American Economic Review 1731–1752 (2017), https://scholar.harvard.edu/files/hart/files/incomplete_contracts_and_control.pdf (last visited Feb. 3, 2019).

Hooper, Will & Rawls, Mary Katherine, *Borders Group, Inc.'s Final Chapter: How A Bookstore Giant Failed In The Digital Age. Chapter 11 Bankruptcy Case Studies* (2014), https://trace.tennessee.edu/utk_studlawbankruptcy/38 (last visited Feb. 3, 2019).

Kary, Tiffany, *Borders Wins Approval of $505 Million Bankruptcy Loan*, Bloomberg (Mar. 15, 2011 6:04 PM), https://www.bloomberg.com/news/articles/2011-03-15/borders-wins-approval-of-505-million-bankruptcy-loan-from-geec-led-group%20- (last visited Feb. 2, 2019).

Kuhlmann, Nico, *Die Dritte Welle von Künstlicher Intelligenz*, Legal Tech Blog (May 29, 2018), https://legal-tech-blog.de/die-dritte-welle-von-kuenstlicher-intelligenz-interview-mit-dr-sven-koerner-thingsthinking (last visited Apr. 12, 2019)

law.com, *possession*, https://dictionary.law.com/Default.aspx?selected=1555 (last visited Apr. 12, 2019).

Paulus, Christoph & Braegelmann, Tom, *Smart Contracts im Krisenfall*, Rechtshandbuch Smart Contracts (Tom Braegelmann & Markus Kaulartz, eds., C. H. Beck, forthcoming 2019).

Popper, Nathaniel, *In the World of Cryptocurrency, Even Good Projects Can Go Bad*, NY Times (May 31, 2018), https://www.nytimes.com/2018/05/31/technology/envion-initial-coin-offering.html (last visited Apr. 12, 2019).

Sabine Reifenberger, *Automatisierung: Die lange Wunschliste der Restrukturierer*, Finance Magazine (Mar. 8, 2018), https://www.finance-magazin.de/banking-berater/kanzleien/automatisierung-die-lange-wunschliste-der-restrukturierer-2009651/ (last visited Apr. 12, 2019).

Szabo, Nick (@NickSzabo4), Twitter (October 14, 2018 3:51 PM), https://twitter.com/NickSzabo4/status/1051606530108190720 (last visited Apr. 12, 2019).

C. Legislative Material

European Parliament legislative resolution of 28 March 2019 on the proposal for a directive of the European Parliament and of the Council on preventive restructuring frameworks, second chance and measures to increase the efficiency of restructuring, insolvency and discharge procedures and amending Directive 2012/30/EU (COM(2016)0723 – C8-0475/2016 – 2016/0359(COD)), available at: https://eur-lex.europa.eu/legal-content/EN/TXT/?uri=EP:P8_TA(2019)0321 (last visited Apr. 11, 2019).

Philipp Rosenauer and Steve Hafner

From Legal Process and Project Management to Managed Legal Services (MLS)

Delivering the Goods

TABLE OF CONTENTS

I. Introduction

With the evolution of the internet, social media, and mobile communication, technology continues to make a significant impact on legal practice around the world. The change on the forefront of every attorney and general counsel's mind (as well it should be) is the direct impact information technology has on legal consulting and attorney services. Anyone with an internet connection and basic research skills can get the information necessary to make decisions that would have required legal counsel or hiring an attorney in the pre-internet era. The growing trend of online, no-fee legal advice has also led to many traditional firms and legal practices to reorganize their pricing structure, alter long held policies regarding what services cost and which ones require an attorney versus a certified paralegal or other paraprofessional.[1] For many law practices, technology may seem like the enemy disrupting their revenue stream by making it difficult to compete when charging fees for over the phone or in person consultation.

However, it is not only technology that is changing the way legal services are delivered. Two other aspects that need to be considered (and which are often overlooked) are legal process and project management as well as managing legal services with the support of an outsourcing provider. The following chapter describes these two topics in more detail and encourages everybody, to be open to these new developments in the legal marketplace.

II. Legal Process and Project Management

A. Background and problem statement

Have you ever wondered what drives clients of typical law firms crazy? Well, in most cases it includes one of the following reasons: poor responsiveness and communication, unnecessary costs or billing surprises, lack of innovation, inconsistent and confusing billing, as well as overstaffing.[2] It comes as no surprise why this is the case. Under the traditional approach, an attorney would

---

1 A good example for this trend is the launch of PwC Legal's Flexible Legal Ressources offering (initially in the UK and Switzerland) which extends the classical workbench of attorneys and lawyers to be able to offer a more diverse talent pool and indeed at different price levels and following delivery models. Other firms such as Swiss law firm Schellenberg Widmer have followed suite.

2 American Bar Association, *Legal Project Management 101: Integrating Legal Project Management into your practice*, American Bar Association (May 18, 2018, 12:30 PM), https://www.americanbar.org/content/dam/aba/multimedia/cle/materials/2016/05/ce1605lpm.pdf (last visited Feb. 1, 2019).

receive a phone call from a client reporting for example that a business deal has been stuck, providing the lawyer only a skeleton outline of the terms. Together with such fragmented information, the lawyer would be asked how quickly he can produce the required documents to make the deal proceed. An important, but uncomfortable question would also include costs. With this classic approach, there was little discussion regarding business objectives, priorities, allocation of responsibilities, optimum resources, deal and operational risks, budgeting, etc.

Law firms and attorneys have for too long tried to preserve a service delivery model that is based on billing by the hour. The more hours, the higher the revenues. There was actually no real need to work efficiently because as long as the entire industry follows the same approach, nobody is facing a significant competitive disadvantage. Such a modus operandi might have been a prevailing and accepted practice in the last millennium. However, in an age of deal lawyering, such an approach can place a lawyer at a significant competitive disadvantage, make the work unprofitable, and even risk the loss of the client relationship.[3] Moreover, not only with new legal technologies but also with a shift of power from the law firm to the client we are seeing a change in this area. Only those law firms that follow a process of legal project management will be competitive in the future, which means delivering legal services on time and on budget.

Legal project management enables lawyers and those who manage legal work (either in law firms, law departments or alternative legal service providers) to define, demonstrate, and deliver greater value by balancing the scope of work, time and resources for optimal efficiency, and outcomes and client experience. Still many distinguish the business of law from the practice of law. However, innovators in legal project management take an integrated approach.[4] Practicing law is not an academic exercise, nor an end in itself. Providing effective legal services means addressing a client's business need, opportunities, and risk profile; and it may also implicate public policy and legal precedent. A client experience is always personal as well as professional. Legal project management was designed to meet all these challenges.[5]

Although some might perceive legal project management as complex, it is actually, what successful lawyers already do. Nevertheless, a more system-

---

3 Byron S Kalogerou, *How Practicioners can apply legal project maangement to M&A: New Tools for new Times*, Business Law Today (Aug. 12, 2014) at 1, https://businesslawtoday.org/2014/08/how-practitioners-can-apply-legal-project-management-to-ma-new-tools-for-new-times/ (last visited Apr. 11, 2019).

4 Aileen Leventon, *Innovations in Legal Project Management*, Ark Group (Dec. 28, 2018, 10:45 AM), https://www.ark-group.com/sites/default/files/product-pdf-download/Innovations-LPM.PDF (last visited Feb. 1, 2019).

5 Leventon, *id.*

atic approach is often needed. In essence, effective project management is about sound communication at critical points with the right people. So legal project management is both: a mindset and an inclusion of peers, subordinates, leadership and clients.[6]

For clients and legal service providers, legal project management offers the following benefits:[7]

- **Linking Cost to Value:** establishing a clearer link between the cost of legal services and the value those services add to the client's business
- **Clarifying expectations**: allowing clients to define the successful outcome before work begins and enabling the lawyer to design a more reliable estimate of the costs to achieve success
- **Clarifying Roles and Responsibilities**: fostersing greater clarity among members of legal teams, within the law firm and in-house across the many organizations involved in doing a deal.

B. Legal Project Management Definition

In general, project management is the application of knowledge, skills, tools and technique to project activities to meet project requirements. Besides that, the following project management process plays an integral role: initiation, planning, execution, monitoring and control, and closure.[8] For legal departments and law firms, having a matter management software established is not enough. Project management requires an integration of planning, budgeting, and communication.[9]

Legal project management in essence always follows 4 phases as described below[10]:

- **Scope**: what are the goals and deliverables of the project?
- **Schedule/People/Budget:** what are the parameters within which the project must be accomplished?

---

6 Leventon, *supra* note 4.

7 American Bar Association, *LPM Advanced: Using Legal Project Management in M&A and other Transactions*, American Bar Association (Dec. 29, 2016, 10:25 AM), https://www.americanbar.org/content/dam/aba/multimedia/cle/materials/2016/06/ce1606lpm.pdf (last visited on Feb. 2, 2019).

8 Project Management Institute, A Guide to the Project Management Body of Knowledge: PMBOK Guide 5 (3rd ed., Project Management Institute, 2004).

9 Association of Corporate Counsel, *Guide to Project Management*, Association of Corporate Counsel (Dec. 29, 2018, 11:23 AM), https://www.acc.com/advocacy/valuechallenge/toolkit/loader.cfm?csModule=security/getfile&pageid=1293786&recorded=1 (last visited Feb. 1, 2019).

10 Association of Corporate Counsel, *id.*

- **Conduct of Legal Matter:** how can we carry out the project within the established parameters?
- **Closing Review:** to constantly improve, what are the project results and lessons learned after the project completion?

C. Defining the Scope of the project

A scope will identify what the project is about and what needs to be accomplished. The scope should consider the following elements: it should be specific, realistic and divisible into concrete tasks because it will be the basis for all further planning and execution within the project. It needs to be clarified why the project is important, what success will look like, what is needed and what will finally be provided. Timeline, staffing and budget will be easier to determine if the scope is clearly defined. A project charter is key in this phase.

Besides that, it needs to be determined how, to whom and how often the progress of the project will be communicated. Such a plan for communication needs to be developed and the start of the project to ensure that all stakeholders are informed and aware of developments. The essential elements of each communication plan are: identify goal of each communication, target audience and means of communication (e.g., meeting, e-mail, report or other).[11]

D. Schedule, People and Budget

In this stage, tasks and activities need to be identified to achieve the specified outcome. The major divisions are project phases and milestones.[12] Milestones are specific events demonstrating progress or completion of a phase. In an investigation, this could include initial case assessment, document review, case and document preparation, interviews, court appearances, discovery, negotiation, and settlement.

After having identified major phases and milestones, specific tasks and activities must be defined as well as their sequence to actually achieve a milestone. For example, certain tasks in the document review phase could include developing a protocol for reviewers, training reviewers, and the conducting the actual review of the documents by reviewers. Essential questions to ask include: What is the necessary timing for completion? Who will perform which tasks? How much will the various components as well as the entire project cost? Answering all of these questions results in a project plan—a doc-

---

11 Association of Corporate Counsel, *supra* note 9.

12 *Id.*

ument which includes the project scope, milestones, schedule, responsibilities and estimated costs. This project plan is the central document for managing the project.[13]

Within a project plan, also role and responsibilities of the project members must be clarified. Often a so called RACI matrix is used for this task. It describes the roles of people in delivering the project and provides structure and clarity. Tasks are splitted into 4 key responsibilities and assigned to different people in the project[14]:

- **Responsible**: those people who execute the work to achieve the task. It is possible to have multiple responsible people.
- **Accountable**: this role is answerable for the correct completion of the task. Only one accountable person should be specified for each task.
- **Consulted:** people whose opinion is sought.
- **Informed:** people who are kept up to date on the progress of the project and the activities.

E. Conduct of Legal Matter

The most important element in managing a legal project is proper communication. This can be achieved by a variety of different meetings[15]:

Kick-Off Meeting: a formal project initiation meeting ensures that all relevant parties know that the project is off and running. Such a meeting at the outset of the project helps to clarify expectations of all team members. Everybody needs a clear understanding what is in scope and what is out of scope of the project. Besides that, the role and responsibilities of each project member must be clearly articulated.

Regular Team Meetings: the frequency of team meeting very much depends on the length of the project and how fast it is progressing. This might be daily, weekly or monthly. The main goal of this meeting is to communication to every project member the progress of the project and any potential changes in parameters (e.g., scope, time or budget cannot be satisfied as originally planned).

Reporting and Management: the project plan (including phases, milestones and tasks) and the budget plan must be regularly updated and presented to project stakeholders. The project plan shows the progress of the tasks in terms of timing and completion rate. Budget reports demonstrate the use of financial resources. In essence, a project status report should include informa-

---

13 Association of Corporate Counsel, *supra* note 9.

14 *Id.*

15 *Id.*

tion on tasks completed since the last update, upcoming meetings and tasks, questions, timeline and budget updates as well as risks and dependencies.

As mentioned, all these meetings and reports serve one purpose: proper communication and transparency. Developing a communication plan is a key part of the planning process for the project. Communications need to be available according to the plan so that all stakeholders stay in the loop.

F. Closing and Review

Before formally closing a legal project, the outcome as well as the deliverables should be reviewed together with the client. Such review has several advantages: (a) the client is aware of and addressing their needs; (b) the client can provide feedback regarding the project and (c) educate the client regarding issues that will improve communication and expectations for similar projects.

Especially with team members, a wrap-up meeting should be conducted to take a look at the following questions:

- What went well?
- Where there unexpected elements?
- Was the original planning accurate?
- What are the learnings for future projects?

A summary of the lessons learned should be communicated to team members or others who will be managing and performing similar projects.[16]

G. Avoiding Common Pitfalls and Resistance

Once you have set-up your legal project management process, there are a number of common pitfalls that need to be avoided. In order to make legal project management a success, it is important to know the pitfalls involved and mitigate them at an early stage. These pitfalls include[17]:

- Inadequately trained or inexperienced project managers
- Failure to set and manage expectation
- Poor leadership at any and all levels
- Failure to adequately identify, document and track requirements
- Poor plans and planning processes
- Poor effort estimateion
- Cultural and ethical misalignment

---

16 Association of Corporate Counsel, *supra* note 9.

17 Association of Corporate Counsels, *The World of Project Management for Lawyers Annual Meeting* (2013).

- Misalignment between the project team and the business it serves
- Inadequate or misused methods
- Inadequate communication, including progress tracking and reporting

Besides all of this, we often also see that even the best-defined processes for legal project management are subject to great resistance. The reason is mainly that people (and also many lawyers) resist the mindset change required for legal project management. The below table lists the most common objections including questions and statements that can be used to overcome this resistance:[18]

Objection	Mitigating Questions and Statements
Clients don't know what their objectives are.	Do you have a list of typical questions you ask to help a client define their objectives? Do you and your client draft a written statement of objectives for discussion and mutual agreement? Do you seek to determine whether other decision makers or stakeholders in the client's organization share those objectives once defined?
Planning is waste of time. Cases evolve so quickly and have so many surprises that things never work out the expected way.	Does the fee incurred ever exceed the quoted budget estimate? How do you tell if you are ahead or behind in work on the matter? What would suffer if you spent 30 minutes planning your next matter immediately upon accepting a legal mandate?
Clients don't require budgets.	Do they pay in full whatever is billed to them or is there sometimes pushback on fees? Have there every been conversations with clients that included fee discussions? How is it determined what fee and/or timing to tell the client in the engagement letter? Have initial fee estimates ever proved to be wrong?
This kind of work has been done for many years. We know how to provide services.	Have there ever been tasks that are completely different from what was expected? Do clients every push back on feeds or require write-offs to keep them happy?
There is just more work to do that can be handled.	Is it possible to delegate more of the tasks that are done now that don't require your level of skill, knowledge and training?
Becoming more efficient will results in a drop of hourly revenue.	Is it possible that competitors could take the work away by offering the same quality of lower fees, due to greater efficiency? Is it really good business practice to have the client pay for a lack of efficiency? If the time it takes to deliver quality services to a client is reduced, can that found time be invested in new business or other activities?

18 Gary Richards, *Overcoming Resistance to Legal Project Management*, LegalBizDev (Dec. 29, 2018, 12:43 PM), https://www.acc.com/valuechallenge/resources/loader.cfm?csModule=security/getfile&pageid=1406772&fromLibrary=1&recorded=1 (last visited Feb. 3, 2019).

H. Summary

Ultimately, it's up to you to decide whether you want to deliver legal services to your client in the old-fashioned way that is increasingly coming under pressure or if you decide to go for new delivery models that help you to stay competitive also in the future. In order to facilitate this decision, first of all the status quo of the organization with respect to legal project management needs amalyzing. The below table shows three different stages (Early—Intermediate—Advanced) for an organisation in terms of legal project maturity.[19] It is your task to determine where you currently stand and where you want to go to in the future:

Early	Intermediate	Advanced
- No or ad hoc project oversight.	- Formal project management is applied in some cases. - People are familiar with the process.	- Formal legal project management is applied in all cases. - People are very familiar with the process.
- No standardized processes or process evaluations.	- Process reviews and improvement initiatives are conducted in extreme situations; - Only some processes are systematic.	- Sponsorship is visible. - Process improvement is methodically and continuously conducted in all appropriate situations and driven from within affected groups. - Most work processes are systematic and documented.
- Organized teamwork only takes place on an ad hoc basis.	- Staff is fostering best practices - Staff have had some good experience with project management and process improvement and know to suggest or accept them in certain circumstances	- Continuous improvement review - Project and process management have become an integral part of the culture - Staff are highly motivated to evaluate and improve individual and department practices
- Little or no executive sponsorship.	- Skilled resources have been identified - Dedicated time is allocated	- Project Management Professionals are part of the staff
- Ignorance about the benefits of project and process management.	- Project and process management principles are endorsed by Leadership	- Good visibility into project, processes and metrics documenting ongoing impact

19 ACC Maturity Model Webcast Series, *Project & Process Management*, Association of Corporate Counsel (Apr. 28, 2018, 12:00 PM), https://acc.inreachce.com/Details/Information/E4C61AE9-BC57-4957-8C02-68042C3DFC52 (last visited Feb. 1, 2019).

III. Managed Legal Services to enrich legal services

A. Legally related activities with repetitive, standardized nature and economies of scale

One of the first questions to ask in connection with Managed Legal Services (MLS) is whether one has a clear understanding of taxonomy. So: what does MLS actually mean? Managed Legal Services are legal services that are provided by using business management methods and tools.[20] The aim is to increase quality and processing speed while at the same time reducing costs. It is important to understand that MLS is not a second-class legal service, but an enrichment of legal services with additional elements from various areas such as IT, project and process management and so on.

To ensure the interaction of such different disciplines, a great deal of competence and knowledge is required, and this, ideally from a single source. The potential of MLS, both for the supplier and for the customer, can only be fully exploited when a certain volume is reached. Then the economies of scale begin to play a decisive role. In order to achieve these economies of scale, however, a clear prior analysis of those tasks and work steps that entail a repetitive and standardized form of working. Once these have been determined, the next step is to define which of these steps can be processed more cost-efficiently and quickly.

A classic example of such repetitive tasks, which will be explained later in this chapter, is the revision of contract documents.

B. The interaction of different types of service providers as an opportunity

So far so good. MLS can be understood as interaction of the core elements processes, technology and people[21]. MLS works in such a way, that different types of service providers work together to perform work activities. It is important to understand that not only people with a purely legal background are capable of carrying out such activities. It can even be the other way around: wherever it makes sense, other professional groups such as project managers, IT experts, (data) analysts, and process experts are involved in addition to lawyers. The interaction of these different service providers paired with spe-

---

20 David Morley, *A revolution in legal services*, Thomson Reuters (Dec. 27, 2018, 9:10 AM), https://blogs.thomsonreuters.com/answerson/revolution-legal-services/#survey (last visited Feb. 3, 2019).

21 Mark A Cohen, *The new Legal Career,* Forbes (Dec. 27, 2018, 3:08 PM), https://www.forbes.com/sites/markcohen1/2017/06/05/the-new-legal-career/ (last visited Feb. 3, 2019).

cific working methods and the use of new, intelligent techniques leads to the fact that different activities can be carried out very economically.

Possible (working) methods and examples of tools to be used:

- Definition and introduction of clearly defined processes and workflows
- Use of playbooks and templates
- Automation and digitalization of processes
- Use of management tools such as dashboards and dedicated Key Performance Indicators (KPIs)
- Use of different software for the analysis and further use of data
- Service Level Agreements
- Process analytics, process design, workflow control
- Division of work into segments
- Use of flexible resources on an hourly basis

C. Development to date and market potential

If you go back a few years, it can be said that there have been two waves of alternative legal service providers (ALSPs) appearing in the market. One in the period from 1999 to 2007, where companies such as Axiom, Consilio, Exibent or Lawyers on Demand came onto the market.[22] A second wave could be observed between 2010 and 2015, where companies with a strong technological focus entered the market. Some of these companies were Kira Systems, Ravel Law or ROSS Intel.[23]

The market has evolved enormously as recent reports, such as the Thomson Reuters 2017 Alternative Legal Service Study, indicate that the provision of alternative legal services is an 8.4 billion dollar industry worldwide.[24] Moreover, this figure does not include those companies that produce legal technology to perform legal activities. This market alone will be worth billions more. Looking at the enormous development of this sector, which has generated many billions of dollars in the last decades, the potential is still enormous. Currently, only 1% of the total Corporate Legal expenditure is used for services such as MLS.[25]

---

22 Jordan Furlong, *Where next for alternative legal service providers,* Infolaw Limited (Dec. 27, 2018, 5:10 PM), http://www.infolaw.co.uk/newsletter/2018/03/next-alternative-legal-services-providers/ (last visited Feb. 3, 2019).

23 Jordan Furlong, *id.*

24 Maniti Barot, *2017 ALSP Study: Understanding the growth and benefits of these new legal providers,* Thomson Reuters (Dec. 28, 2018, 9:30 AM), https://blogs.thomsonreuters.com/legal-uk/2017/02/06/2017-alsp-study-new-legal-providers/ (last visited Feb. 2, 2019).

25 Lisa Hart Shepherd & Carly Toward, *2018 State of Corporate Law Departments,* Legal Executive Institute (Dec. 28, 2018, 11:30 AM), http://www.legalexecutiveinstitute.com/wp-content/uploads/2018/02/2018-State-of-Corporate-Law-Departments-Report.pdf (last visited Feb. 2, 1019).

The steady increase of such alternative service providers has led to a reduction in routine work in the million range of working hours and simple legal work from the desk of the attorneys of law firms. This work can be carried out more efficiently, more cost-effectively and often with a higher degree of quality and planning security by the alternative service providers. The potential cost savings should not be underestimated. According to Ray Bayley, the greener of Novus Law, the ratio is as follows: For every dollar his company earns, law firms save four dollars.[26] Not only is it important that these routine tasks have left the law firms, but it is important to understand that they have been better or redefined, structured and simplified as part of the transition to the alternative service provider.

These findings clearly show that law firms have inefficiently handled a very large amount of (mostly simple, repetitive) work. It can also be concluded, that for a long time there was a willingness (or even uncertainty) to tolerate and pay for these inefficiencies. Moreover, such work was or is more and more no longer part of the relevant work repertoire of a law firm. There has been a disintermediation of routine work from law firms. And this with such success in recent years, that alternative service providers no longer have to prove themselves with MLS. In future, the legal market can thus be divided into two segments on the supply side: routine legal work and complex legal work:[27]

1. Routine legal work:

This segment is staffed by alternative legal service providers, which primarily use technology and specifically defined processes to handle basic legal tasks. They thus disintermediate the tasks of law firms whose lawyers should not perform the tasks anyway because they are too expensive.

Currently we are still in the process of this disintermediation. The sector of alternative service providers continues to develop, consolidation will begin and major industry specialists will emerge. This will entail a strong correction of the market and be an important step forward for legal consumers in terms of obtaining legal services.

2. Complex legal work:

This segment is focused on complex, higher-value tasks. These tasks require good lawyers who primarily work in traditional law firms. This segment de-

---

26 Rachel Zahorsky & William D Henderson, *Who's eating law firms' lunch*, American Bar Assocoiation (Dec. 28, 2018, 1:30 PM), http://www.abajournal.com/magazine/article/whos_eating_law_firms_lunch (last visited Feb. 3, 2019).

27 Mike Heuer, *How Law Firms Can Compete with Alternative Legal Service Providers*, Bigger Law Firm (Jan. 8, 2019, 4.10 pm), https://www.biggerlawfirm.com/how-law-firms-can-compete-with-alternative-legal-service-providers/ (last visited Apr. 12, 2019).

pends on the subdivision on the supply side. The inventory of this segment will increasingly reduce and the future will show what the law firms will focus on. What will be decisive is how they deal with it and how they manage to maintain all important and demanding legal services.

D. Why should a company consider purchasing Managed Legal Services?

Looking at the current market development, it can be seen that there are two main reasons why it can be interesting for a company with certain organizational structures and processes to consider Managed Legal Services. First, relevance of legal operations and legal COOs has increased enormously:[28] The requirements and expectations of internal legal departments have changed enormously in recent years. Until around 2008, for example, the departments were not specifically focused on managing the teams and related work processes according to the company's business principles.[29] Of course, certain standards and processes were defined, but in the subsequent practical implementation in day-to-day life, these requirements were not given too much attention. This has begun to change since 2008, with the onset of the last major financial crisis.[30] As a consequence, the first legal operations units with dedicated chief operating officers (legal COOs) were set up in the Anglo-American legal area. Looking at Europe, it can also be seen that the importance and relevance of such legal operations units is also increasing there.[31]

This is where Managed Legal Services comes into play. Because the language of alternative legal service providers, who offer MLS as a service, is the same as the one of legal operations units, both parties can benefit from each other and intensify their interactions in order to ultimately achieve the desired result of business optimization.[32]

---

28 Catherine J Moynihan & Rachel M Zahorsky, *Legal Ops Can Transform the Practice of Law, but Only if Everyone Embraces It*, ACC Association of Corporate Counsel (Mar. 13, 2019, 4:15 PM), https://www.accdocket.com/articles/legal-ops-can-transform-the-practice-of-law.cfm (last visited Apr. 12, 2019).

29 Mark A Cohen & Bruno Mascello, *Why should anybody invest in a law firm or a legal services provider*, University of St. Gallen (Dec. 29, 2018, 08:30 AM), https://lam.unisg.ch/knowhow/why-should-anybody-invest-in-a-law-firm-or-a-legal-services-provider?id= (last visited Feb. 2, 2019).

30 Hart Shepherd & Toward, *supra* note 25.

31 Helen Burness, *The In-House Experience: What Makes A Legal COO*, Halebury Ventures Limited (Dec. 29, 2018, 10:15 AM), https://halebury.com/the-in-house-experience-what-makes-a-legal-coo/ (last visited Feb. 3, 2019).

32 Hart Shepherd & Toward, *supra* note 25.

Second, there is the development of the professionalization of the purchase of legal services (Legal Procurement). For some years now, the strong development of transparency has generally expanded in the market. Due to globalization and the comprehensive information available on the Internet, a comparison can now be made with every service. This trend has also not stopped at the legal sector and, therefore, it is normal in the course of the purchasing process of legal services nowadays, that comparisons are made. This transparency has led to an enormous professionalization of the purchasing of legal services and will contribute to the trend especially in moderate or bad economic times.[33]

In the context of this development trend in legal procurement, it can be seen that, in addition to traditional legal providers such as law firms, other legal service providers with service offerings in the MLS area are increasingly being examined in detail during negotiations on the award of mandates and are also receiving mandate surcharges.[34] An important reason for this is, above all, the use of modern technology, which enables alternative legal service providers to analyze the existing value chain more comprehensively in the context of mandate award negotiations. Based on the analysis, processes can be optimized, automated or outsourced. In addition, with the help of clearly defined KPIs and overview platforms such as dashboards, the processing statuses can point out more transparency in ongoing operations.[35]

E. The revision of contract documents as an example

So now, we understand how which services can be considered for MLS, how the interaction of different types of (alternative) service providers can be seen as an opportunity, what the past development has been and where the market can move. However, in order to make the theory a bit more tangible, this section briefly shows how a Managed Legal Services service can be implemented on the basis of a practical example.

---

33 David J Parnell, *Buying Legal Council's 2018 Legal Procurement Survey: Insights Into The Buying Of Legal Services*, Forbes (Dec. 29, 2018, 10:30 AM), https://www.forbes.com/sites/davidparnell/2018/04/11/buying-legal-council-2018-legal-procurement-survey/#8bdf245601cd (last visited Feb. 3, 2019).

34 Thomson Reuters Legal Executive Institute, *Alternative Legal Service Providers 2019*, Thomson Reuters, (Jan. 28, 2019, 4:20 PM), https://legal.thomsonreuters.com/content/dam/ewp-m/documents/legal/en/pdf/reports/alsp-report-final.pdf?cid=9008178&sfdccampaignid=7011B000002OF6AQAW&chl=pr (last visited Apr. 12, 2019).

35 Sterling Miller, *Ten things. Setting goals for the legal department*, Wordpress (Dec. 29, 2018, 11:30 AM), https://sterlingmiller2014.wordpress.com/tag/kpi-legal-department/ (last visited Feb. 3, 2019).

As an example, we take an everyday situation of a medium-sized company with almost 500 employees. The company is active in the service sector and has a large number of comprehensive framework agreements, non-disclosure agreements or even complex IT contracts.

The legal department, which manages these various contracts, usually files the contracts physically, but also electronically at different locations. There is no concrete overview in the sense of an inventory of the contracts and the clauses defined therein (e.g., deadlines). If adjustments or additions have to be made to such contracts, this often entails risks, which should be analysed in detail, recognised and taken into account. In addition, it is often the case that the legal department has too little time and resources to carry out such activities. The result is inefficiencies and unnecessary risks that can arise. Inefficiencies because, due to the lack of an overview, the companies creates very similar contract documents over and over again. In addition, risks arise due to the different types of filing systems and the lack of an overview of the maturities contained in the contracts.

Such challenges can be tackled with the support of MLS. These risks and inefficiencies can be optimized. Ideally, an MLS team will be assigned to the internal legal department in such a case. The team shall be quickly onboarded and integrated to the internal organization and work processes. By means of an appropriate analysis of the existing processes, the processes are then scrutinized and optimization possibilities are worked out.

The results of these analyses can be, for example, so-called playbooks. In order to check and adapt documents as efficiently as possible and nevertheless in detail for (risk) aspects to be considered, so-called playbooks are very often used for the implementation in the MLS area. These manuscripts contain (in detail) the activities to be performed and, in this context, the dependencies to be checked. Based on predefined relapse scenarios, the risks are adequately classified and, if necessary, the corresponding legal / technical specialists of the company's internal department are involved. In combination with these procedures, clear overview documents are prepared and regular status updates are made available to the relevant stakeholders.

With the introduction of such organizational measures, an optimization of the internal process flows with regard to efficiency and error susceptibility can be brought about. Thanks to the overview documents in the form of dashboards, dependencies and deadlines can be identified at an early stage and adequately regulated. Furthermore, the internal legal specialists are relieved of repetitive, but mostly simple tasks and can focus on more demanding tasks.

IV. Concluding Remarks

After the demanding years following the financial crisis, a significant change in the legal market development can be recognized. Young, well-trained people are filling the legal market with alternative service providers and consolidating their raison d'être in the segment of routine legal work. Older, classically established law firms are anxious to maintain the high-quality work, but have difficulties finding out how they can carry it out sustainably and profitably with their existing structures and systems. The consequence will be that various companies will be merged, resulting in large industry players. However, these companies do not necessarily have to do this as their main activities. Large audit and management consulting companies have also recognized the market potential and are increasingly entering the market as alternative service providers for routine legal activities. This can be done either by building up internal knowledge or by cooperating with an existing alternative service provider. It therefore remains exciting to observe how this market will continue to develop and how the distribution of the tasks mentioned in this chapter will be divided between alternative service providers and traditional law firms. Can alternative service providers further increase their footprint in the legal market? Can the classically organized law firms assert themselves for complex legal work and offer their services economically adapted to the market? The future will show!

V. Bibliography

A. Hard Copy Sources

PROJECT MANAGEMENT INSTITUTE, A GUIDE TO THE PROJECT MANAGEMENT BODY OF KNOWLEDGE: PMBOK GUIDE 5 (3d ed., Project Management Institute, 2004).

B. Online Sources

American Bar Association, *LPM Advanced: Using Legal Project Management in M&A and other Transactions*, AMERICAN BAR ASSOCIATION (Dec. 29, 2016, 10:25 AM), https://www.americanbar.org/content/dam/aba/multimedia/cle/materials/2016/06/ce1606lpm.pdf (last visited Feb. 2, 2019).

American Bar Association, *Legal Project Management 101: Integrating Legal Project Management into your practice*, AMERICAN BAR ASSOCIATION (May 18, 2018, 12:30 PM), https://www.americanbar.org/content/dam/aba/multimedia/cle/materials/2016/05/ce1605lpm.pdf (last visited Feb. 1, 2019).

ACC Maturity Model Webcast Series, *Project & Process Management*, ASSOCIATION OF CORPORATE COUNSEL (Apr. 28, 2018, 12:00 PM), https://acc.inreachce.com/Details/Information/E4C61AE9-BC57-4957-8C02-68042C3DFC52 (last visited Feb. 3, 2019).

Association of Corporate Counsel, *Guide to Project Management*, ASSOCIATION OF CORPORATE COUNSEL (Dec. 29, 2018, 11:23 AM), https://www.acc.com/advocacy/valuechallenge/toolkit/loader.cfm?csModule=security/getfile&pageid=1293786&recorded=1 (last visited Feb. 1, 2019).

Association of Corporate Counsels, *The World of Project Management for Lawyers Annual Meeting* ASSOCIATION OF CORPORATE COUNSEL (2013).

Barot, Maniti, *2017 ALSP Study: Understanding the growth and benefits of these new legal providers,* Thomson Reuters (Dec. 28, 2018, 9:30 AM), https://blogs.thomsonreuters.com/legal-uk/2017/02/06/2017-alsp-study-new-legal-providers/ (last visited Feb. 2, 2019).

Burness, Helen, *The In-House Experience: What Makes A Legal COO,* Halebury Ventures Limited (Dec. 29, 2018, 10:15 AM), https://halebury.com/the-in-house-experience-what-makes-a-legal-coo/ (last visited Feb. 3, 2019).

Cohen, Mark A, *The new Legal Career,* FORBES (Dec. 27, 2018, 3:08 PM), https://www.forbes.com/sites/markcohen1/2017/06/05/the-new-legal-career/ (last visited Feb. 3, 2019).

Cohen, Mark A & Mascello, Bruno, *Why should anybody invest in a law firm or a legal services provider,* UNIVERSITY OF ST. GALLEN (Dec. 29, 2018, 08:30 AM), https://lam.unisg.ch/knowhow/why-should-anybody-invest-in-a-law-firm-or-a-legal-services-provider?id= (last visited Feb. 2, 2019).

Furlong, Jordan, *Where next for alternative legal service providers,* INFOLAW LIMITED (Dec. 27, 2018, 5:10 PM), http://www.infolaw.co.uk/newsletter/2018/03/next-alternative-legal-services-providers/ (last visited Feb. 3, 2019).

Hart Shepherd, Lisa & Toward, Carly, *2018 State of Corporate Law Departments,* Legal Executive Institute (Dec. 28, 2018, 11:30 AM), http://www.legalexecutiveinstitute.com/wp-content/uploads/2018/02/2018-State-of-Corporate-Law-Departments-Report.pdf (last visited Feb. 2, 1019).

Heuer, Mike, *How Law Firms Can Compete with Alternative Legal Service Providers,* BIGGER LAW FIRM (Jan. 8, 2019, 4.10 pm), https://www.biggerlawfirm.com/how-law-firms-can-compete-with-alternative-legal-service-providers/ (last visited Apr. 12, 2019).

Kalogerou, Byron S, *How Practicioners can apply legal project maangement to M&A: New Tools for new Times*, BUSINESS LAW TODAY (Aug. 12, 2014), https://businesslawtoday.org/2014/08/how-practitioners-can-apply-legal-project-management-to-ma-new-tools-for-new-times/ (last visited Apr. 11, 2019).

Leventon, Aileen, *Innovations in Legal Project Management,* ARK GROUP (Dec. 28, 2018, 10:45 AM), https://www.ark-group.com/sites/default/files/product-pdf-download/Innovations-LPM.PDF (last visited Feb. 1, 2019).

Miller, Sterling, *Ten things. Setting goals for the legal department,* WORDPRESS (Dec. 29, 2018, 11:30 AM), https://sterlingmiller2014.wordpress.com/tag/kpi-legal-department/ (last visited Feb. 3, 2019).

Moynihan, Catherine J & Zahorsky, Rachel M, *Legal Ops Can Transform the Practice of Law, but Only if Everyone Embraces It,* ACC ASSOCIATION OF CORPORATE COUNSEL, (Mar. 13, 2019, 4:15 PM), https://www.accdocket.com/articles/legal-ops-can-transform-the-practice-of-law.cfm (last visited Apr. 12, 2019).

Morley, David, *A revolution in legal services,* THOMSON REUTERS (Dec. 27, 2018, 9:10 AM), https://blogs.thomsonreuters.com/answerson/revolution-legal-services/#survey (last visited Feb. 3, 2019).

Parnell, David J, *Buying Legal Council's 2018 Legal Procurement Survey: Insights Into The Buying Of Legal Services,* FORBES (Dec. 29, 2018, 10:30 AM), https://www.forbes.com/sites/davidparnell/2018/04/11/buying-legal-council-2018-legal-procurement-survey/#8bdf245601cd (last visited Feb. 3, 2019).

Richards, Gary, *Overcoming Resistance to Legal Project Management*, LegalBizDev (Dec. 29, 2018, 12:43 PM), https://www.acc.com/valuechallenge/resources/loader.cfm?csModule=security/getfile&pageid=1406772&fromLibrary=1&recorded=1 (last visited Feb. 3, 2019).

Thomson Reuters Legal Executive Institute, *Alternative Legal Service Providers 2019,* Thomson Reuters, (Jan. 28, 2019, 4:20 PM), https://legal.thomsonreuters.com/content/dam/ewp-m/documents/legal/en/pdf/reports/alsp-report-final.pdf?cid=9008178&sfdccampaignid=7011B000002OF6AQAW&chl=pr (last visited Apr. 12, 2019).

Zahorsky, Rachel & Henderson, William D, *Who's eating law firms' lunch*, American Bar Assocoiation (Dec. 28, 2018, 01:30 PM), http://www.abajournal.com/magazine/article/whos_eating_law_firms_lunch (last visited Feb. 3, 2019).

Jameson Dempsey, Lauren Mack, & Phil Weiss

Legal Hackers

Grassroots Legal Innovation on a Global Scale

TABLE OF CONTENTS

This chapter is about Legal Hackers, currently the largest grassroots legal innovation community in the world. Legal Hackers is a community that seeks to foster creative problem-solving at the intersection of law and technology. Since 2012, the Legal Hackers community has come together in independent, self-organized chapters around the world to co-create the future of law and policy through free educational sessions, prototyping workshops, and policy discussions. By embracing the open, collaborative ethos and the do-it-yourself spirit of hacker culture, Legal Hackers seeks to break down silos in the legal industry and facilitate the rapid dissemination of legal innovation throughout the world.[1] This short chapter will describe the history, mission, and impact of Legal Hackers.

I. Hacker Culture

Legal Hackers organizers are inspired by the «Hacker Ethic,» which originated at the Massachusetts Institute of Technology (MIT) in the late-1950s and 1960s and has been an important force in global technology innovation ever since. The original hackers, as described in *Steven Levy*'s 1984 book *Hackers: Heroes of the Computer Revolution*, were precocious and obsessively creative students and local computer enthusiasts in the greater Boston area who gathered, often late into the night, exploring the inner working of computer hardware, creating games (like *Spacewar!*, an influential early video game), and writing programs to bend computers to their will.[2] A second wave of hackers, including Apple co-founder *Steve Wozniak*, convened through meetups like the Homebrew Computer Club in Silicon Valley, sharing pieces of hardware and advancing the personal computer movement and video game industry.[3]

These early hackers embraced a shared ethos—the «hacker ethic»—built around six central tenets. First, that «essential lessons can be learned about … the world … from taking things apart, seeing how they work, and using this knowledge to create new and even more interesting things.»[4] Second, that *«[a] free exchange of information ... allowed for greater overall creativity.»[5] Third, that «[t]he best way to promote th[e] free exchange of information is to have an open [decentralized] system, something that presents no boundaries between a hacker and a piece of information or an item of equipment that he needs in his quest for knowledge, improvement, and time online.»*[6] Fourth, that

1 *See* Legal Hackers, *Our Story*, www.legalhackers.org/our-story (last visited Jan. 12, 2019).
2 Steven Levy, Hackers: Heroes of the Computer Revolution 3–147 (1984).
3 *Id.* at 151–312.
4 *Id.* at 28.
5 *Id.* at 28–29.
6 *Id.* at 29–31.

«[h]ackers should be judged by their hacking, not bogus criteria such as degrees, age, race, or position.»[7] Fifth, that *«[y]ou can create art and beauty on a computer.»*[8] Sixth and finally, that *«[c]omputers can change your life for the better.»*[9]

Together, these principles—which were largely unwritten until the publication of *Levy's* book—served as the cultural foundation of several disruptive innovations in the last half-century. Hackers (and those inspired by the hacker ethic) helped to spur the personal computer revolution, the free and open-source software movement, the open knowledge movement, the free culture movement, and the open education movement.[10] And while there is still much work to be done in each of those areas, their pervasiveness highlights the fundamental success of hacker culture in creating fertile soil for innovation.

While some hackers define «hacking» with specific reference to computers, early hackers saw hacking as something broader. In his article *«On Hacking»,* influential MIT hacker *Richard Stallman* discussed how the original hackers viewed their activities:

> *«Hacking included a wide range of activities, from writing software, to practical jokes, to exploring the roofs and tunnels of the MIT campus. Other activities, performed far from MIT and far from computers, also fit hackers' idea of what hacking means: for instance, I think the controversial 1950s «musical piece» by John Cage, 4'33", is more of a hack than a musical composition. The palindromic three-part piece written by Guillaume de Machaut in the 1300s, «Ma Fin Est Mon Commencement», was also a good hack, even better because it also sounds good as music. Puck appreciated hack value.*
>
> *It is hard to write a simple definition of something as varied as hacking, but I think what these activities have in common is playfulness, cleverness, and exploration. Thus, hacking means exploring the limits of what is possible, in a spirit of playful cleverness. Activities that display playful cleverness have «hack value.»*[11]

---

7 *Id.* at 31.

8 *Id.* at 31–34.

9 *Id.* at 34–38.

10 *See id.* at 212–13; Christopher Tozzi, For Fun and Profit: A History of the Free and Open Source Software Revolution (The MIT Press, 2017) at 265–68; Hans Põldoja, The Structure and Components for the Open Education Ecosystem (Aalto University, 2016) at 26–28; Eric S Raymond, *Origins and History of Hackers, 1961–1995* (2003), http://www.catb.org/~esr/writings/taoup/html/hackers.html (last visited Apr. 28, 2019).

11 Richard Stallman, *On Hacking,* https://stallman.org/articles/on-hacking.html (last visited January 12, 2019).

Legal hacking falls within the hacking paradigm. Indeed, *Stallman* himself is the author of the GNU General Public License (GPL), a self-perpetuating free software license that leverages legal tools–copyright licenses to advance hacker values, including the requirement that anyone who uses the licensed work must license their own resulting software under the same license.[12] Since then, free and open-source software communities have developed a myriad of governance models, licensing structures, and quasi-legal cultural norms, all of which we would consider «legal hacks». In the 1990s, hackers such as *Nick Szabo* explored the concept of «smart contracts» which were agreements implemented using computer code or other digital technologies.[13] Drafting clever smart contracts may also be considered legal hacking, although in the not-so-far away future, drafting smart legal contracts may evolve into a daily task for legal professionals.

Law schools have also acted as central convening points for lawyer hackers and open culture advocates. For example, Harvard Law School's Berkman Klein Center for Internet & Society and Stanford Law School's CodeX Center for Legal Informatics have advanced an open ethos to address law and technology issues. The legal informatics research community, including the International Association for Artificial Intelligence and Law has spent decades exploring ways that technology can make the legal system more efficient, effective, and just.[14] And programs around the world, such as LawWithoutWalls, have embraced cross-disciplinary, project-based learning to further legal innovation.

There have been several hacker-inspired movements that have explored issues at the intersection of law and technology, including Creative Commons, Wikimedia, and the Internet Society.[15] The free law movement, in particular, has embraced the values of hacker culture as applied to law, with individuals such as *Thomas R Bruce* and *Peter W Martin* of the Legal Information Institute at Cornell University; *Carl Malamud* of Public.Resource.org; the late *Aaron Swartz* and *Mike Lissner* of the Free Law Project serving as standard-bearers in freeing legislation, standards, regulatory codes, and case law from copyright licenses and expensive, proprietary legal technology databases. The «gov 2.0» movement, including Code for America and similar communities, have also brought together lawyers and technologists («civic hackers») to improve

---

12 *See* The GNU General Public License, https://www.gnu.org/licenses/gpl-3.0.en.html (last visited January 12, 2019).

13 *See,* e.g., Nick Szabo, «*The Idea of Smart Contracts*» (1997), https://web.archive.org/web/20160831070942/http://szabo.best.vwh.net/smart_contracts_idea.html (last visited Apr. 11, 2019).

14 *See,* e.g., Trevor Bench-Capon et al., *A history of AI and Law in 50 papers: 25 years of the International Conference on AI and Law*, Artificial Intelligence and Law 20.3 (2012).

15 *See* Creative Commons, www.creativecommons.org; Wikimedia Foundation, www.wikimediafoundation.org; Internet Society, https://www.internetsociety.org/.

government transparency and service delivery.[16] Many gov 2.0 advocates are also active in Legal Hackers.

II. The Origin of Legal Hackers

The terms «legal hacking» and «legal hackers» predate the Legal Hackers organization, and appear to have been coined and first explored by *Tim Hwang*, who opened a legal startup, *Robot Robot & Hwang*, with the aim of *«open[ing] broad new opportunities for experimentation and fashion the emergence of a kind of legal hacking as a field of endeavor.»*[17] Predicting a *«big, bad, rootin'-tootin' High Noon style shootout on a global scale»* between large incumbent firms and new upstarts, *Hwang* noted that *«[f]or legal hackers and supporters of legal hacking, there's both ideological and pragmatic reasons to get into this fight. Not on any one side, but on creating applications and services that aid both sides.»*[18] Noting that *«neither side of this fight has it quite where the legal hacker wants it yet,» Hwang* lamented that the new upstarts *«largely want to just replicate the same old services and activities, but just cheaper, faster, and more efficiently,»* but that *«the conflict itself fuels a demand for the kind of research and development that legal hackers want ... so it's worth finding ways to grease the wheels of collision.»*[19] *Hwang* later launched a «legal hacking» conference, the New and Emerging Legal Infrastructure Conference (NELIC) on April 15, 2011, organized the first FutureLaw Conference in 2013, and was active in the nascent legal design movement.[20]

While the concept of legal hacking predates the Legal Hackers organization, the global Legal Hackers community began in 2012 as a project of the Brooklyn Law Incubator & Policy (BLIP) Clinic at Brooklyn Law School in Brooklyn, New York.[21] Founded in 2008 by Professor *Jonathan Askin*, BLIP

---

16 *See* Joshua Tauberer, Civic Hacking, Open Government Data: The Book (2nd ed., 2014), https://opengovdata.io/2014/civic-hacking/ (last visited Apr. 29, 2019); *see id.* at «History of the Movement», https://opengovdata.io/2014/history-the-movement/; *see* also Alex Howard, *Defining Gov 2.0 and Open Government* (Jan. 5, 2011), http://gov20.govfresh.com/social-media-fastfwd-defining-gov-2-0-and-open-government-in-2011/ (last visited Apr. 29, 2019).

17 Robot Robot & Hwang, About, https://www.robotandhwang.com/about/ (last visited Jan. 12, 2019).

18 Tim Hwang, *On Legal Arms Dealing*, Robot Robot & Hwang, Sept. 26, 2010, https://www.robotandhwang.com/2010/09/on-legal-arms-dealing/ (last visited Apr. 11, 2019).

19 *Id.*

20 Tim Hwang, *Three Updates*, Robot Robot & Hwang (Oct. 2, 2016), http://www.robotandhwang.com/2013/10/three-updates/ (last visited Apr. 29, 2019); Tim Hwang, *NELIC Registration is Open!*, Robot Robot & Hwang (Mar. 9, 2011), https://www.robotandhwang.com/2011/03/nelic-registration-is-open/ (last visited Apr. 29, 2019); Tim Hwang, *Some Design Notes on FutureLaw 2013*, Robot Robot & Hwang (Mar. 4, 2013), http://www.robotandhwang.com/2013/03/some-design-notes-on-futurelaw-2013/#more-484 (last visited Apr. 29, 2019).

21 *See* Legal Hackers, *supra* note 1.

provides *pro bono* legal support to pre-seed technology startups in New York City. Central to BLIP is the concept of the Lawyer 2.0: the tech-savvy lawyer who can effectively advocate up and down the legal stack—from commercial contracts to tectonic policy shifts–all while leveraging the tools and methods of the technology community to effectively and efficiently represent clients. *Askin* developed this vision after years working as a telecommunications and technology attorney and lobbyist in Washington, DC, where, in his view, *«every D.C. lawyer advocating for tech entrepreneurs thought they were full-blown tech lawyers,»* but were instead mere «policy advocates.»[22]

The period of late 2011 to 2012 was an important moment in technology activism in the United States. In late 2011, the U.S. Congress introduced two bills: the Stop Online Piracy Act (SOPA) and the PROTECT IP Act (PIPA) (companion bills in the United States House of Representatives and Senate, respectively).[23] Both would have given the United States government stronger enforcement mechanisms against websites that were allegedly hosting content without the appropriate licenses from the copyright holders.[24] Because content platforms in the Web 2.0 era relied heavily on user-generated content—including countless remixes, covers, reinterpretations, and clips—and existing law incentivized platforms to not actively police their platforms (instead relying on the notice-and-takedown framework enshrined in the Digital Millennium Copyright Act (DMCA)), the SOPA/PIPA bills would have forced platforms to heavily regulate user-generated content or face the prospect of judicially-imposed shutdowns of their websites. In response, technology activists, entrepreneurs, and platform companies mobilized in opposition to the bills.[25] They focused on lobbying Congress, rallying users, and otherwise making their views known. Most notably, several platforms blacked out their sites in protest.[26] By mobilizing their user bases to call their representatives in Congress and participate in protests, the platforms were ultimately able to successfully block the passage of SOPA and PIPA.

---

22 Jonathan Askin, *A Remedy to Clueless Tech Lawyers*, VentureBeat (Nov. 13, 2013), https://venturebeat.com/2013/11/13/a-remedy-to-clueless-tech-lawyers/ (last visited Apr. 29, 2019).

23 Stop Online Piracy Act, H.R. 3261, 112th Cong.§ 103(a)(1)(B) (1st Sess. 2011), available at http://www.gpo.gov/fdsys/pkg/BILLS-112hr3261ih/pdf/BILLS-112hr3261ih.pdf; Preventing Real Online Threats to Economic Creativity and Theft of Intellectual Property Act of 2011 (PROTECT IP), S. 968, 112th Cong. § 3(a)(1)(B)(1st Sess. 2011), available at http://www.gpo.gov/fdsys/pkg/BILLS-112s968rs/pdf/BILLS-112s968rs.pdf.

24 David Kravets, *A SOPA/PIPA Blackout Explainer*, Wired (Jan. 18, 2012), https://www.wired.com/2012/01/websites-dark-in-revolt/ (last visited Apr. 29, 2019).

25 *See* Vlad Savov, *The SOPA blackout: Wikipedia, Reddit, Mozilla, Google, and many others protest proposed law*, The Verge (Jan. 18, 2012), https://www.theverge.com/2012/1/18/2715300/sopa-blackout-wikipedia-reddit-mozilla-google-protest (last visited Apr. 29, 2019).

26 SOPA Strike, http://sopastrike.com/ (last visited Apr. 29, 2019).

Professor *Askin's* students—including *Phil Weiss*, *Warren Allen*, *John Randall*, and others—wanted to get involved in the ongoing SOPA/PIPA debate. *Askin* thought that a «legal hackathon» could be the answer, but there wasn't much precedent for it. Traditionally, the goal of a hackathon was to build a functioning piece of software or hardware over the course of a day or two, sometimes tied to a specific operating system, API, or theme. At that time, there had been several «law hackathons» focused on computable legislation, but none focused on using the hackathon model for collaborative policymaking—a «legal hackathon». BLIP's legal hackathon took place on April 15, 2012 in the Moot Court Room of Brooklyn Law School. Speakers included *Tim Wu*, a law professor who coined the term «network neutrality»; *Andrew Rasiej*, founder of the New York Tech Meetup and Personal Democracy Forum; *Tim Hwang*; and *Nina Paley* of Question Copyright. During the afternoon, teams broke out to prototype ideas for improving U.S. federal intellectual property policy. The hashtags used for the event were #legalhack and #hacktheact, the former of which has since become the primary hashtag of the global Legal Hackers movement.

With the BLIP Legal Hackathon behind them, the law students (many of whom were graduating 3Ls) returned to their studies and upcoming bar exam preparation. But for a few of the hackathon organizers, the success of the hackathon demanded further action. That September, Weiss and Allen, with the help of Randall, formed a Meetup group named *New York Legal Hackers*.[27] The idea of New York Legal Hackers was to create an open, collaborative forum for lawyers, technologists, entrepreneurs, and academics to meet and «legal hack» (a verb) issues at the intersection of law and technology. *Tariq Badat*, another Brooklyn Law School classmate, and *Lauren Mack*, a recent graduate from Benjamin N Cardozo School of Law who had attended the BLIP Legal Hackathon, quickly joined as co-organizers of the group.

New York Legal Hackers grew rapidly, reaching 500 members in its first year. Early events focused on data privacy, user-generated content, alternative dispute resolution for startups, immigration policy, fashion design, encryption, public wifi, and legal technology startups.[28] Unlike traditional law and policy events, Legal Hackers hosted their events in startup coworking spaces like General Assembly, Projective Space, and eBay NYC. Speakers included law professors, general counsels, startup founders, and information security researchers. But the early ambitions of Legal Hackers were local, focusing on serving the New York City community based on local interests. That would soon change.

---

27 New York Legal Hackers, https://www.meetup.com/legalhackers/ (last visited January 12, 2019).

28 *Id.*

III. Building a Chapter-Based Community

While Legal Hackers originally formed to serve the New York City technology and startup community, the movement soon spread to other cities, which formed their own «chapters» of Legal Hackers. In 2012, two original New York Legal Hackers members—open data advocate *Rebecca Williams* and telecommunications attorney *Jameson Dempsey*—moved from New York City to Washington, DC for new employment options. *Williams* and *Dempsey* had been active in the New York Legal Hackers community through attending and organizing events. *Dempsey* had also worked closely with Professor *Askin* during his time at Brooklyn Law as a student, research assistant, BLIP clinical student, and BLIP fellow, and had attended the first legal hackathon.

When *Williams* and *Dempsey* arrived in DC, they thought there was a great opportunity to open a second chapter of Legal Hackers. The chapter model was inspired by other decentralized, chapter-based, technology-focused communities, including the Internet Society, Wikimedia, Code for America, and Sandbox. The newly formed DC Legal Hackers added a third organizer, *Alan deLevie,* then a law student at American University Washington College of Law and now a developer at Casetext, began to organize events. One member of DC Legal Hackers, *Amy Wan*, later moved to Los Angeles, where she founded the third chapter: LA Legal Hackers. In 2013, *Dan Lear*, a Seattle-based technology transactions attorney and legal technology evangelist, wrote an article, «Hacking the Law» for the American Bar Association Journal, highlighting the nascent Legal Hackers movement, and began his own legal innovation meetup.[29] Other Legal Hackers chapters formed in the U.S. cities of Boston, Chicago, Detroit, and Miami, embracing the open, collaborative mission of Legal Hackers. The first European chapter of Legal Hackers launched in Stockholm, followed soon thereafter by chapters in Barcelona, Bogotá, Costa Rica, and Seoul.

As more chapters formed, the original New York Legal Hackers team took on a new role: international community organizers. They updated their branding, adopted a motto («We are explorers. We are doers. We are Legal Hackers.»), formalized the chapter onboarding process, prepared a chapter handbook with best practices, and thought about ways to bring together chapter organizers to meet and share.

Beginning in 2014, a new, global organization called Legal Hackers began gathering local chapter organizers to share experiences, collaborate, and plan the future. Seeking to improve upon the first legal hackathon—which revolved more around discussion rather than actual building of tech solu-

---

29 *See* Dan Lear, *Hacking the Law,* American Bar Association Law Practice Today Newsletter (Jan. 14, 2014).

tions—the New York Legal Hackers organized a Data Privacy Legal Hackathon, which combined the principals behind the first legal hackathon (discussion around innovation at the intersection of law and technology) with the objectives of a more traditional hackathon (building a working prototype over the course of a weekend with a panel of judges awarding prizes). The New York team, along with Legal Hackers in London, England and the Bay Area, California (USA), challenged participants to create a technology-enabled tool that addresses a common legal problem in the field of data privacy in a 24-hour period. Organizers and participants in the three cities connected through virtual means to discuss data privacy issues and how their hackathon teams were attempting to solve them. This type of multi-chapter collaboration on hackathons and the growing Legal Hackers community inspired the annual Legal Hackers Summit, which first took place in 2015, and brought Legal Hackers organizers from all over the world together in a single location (either physically or virtually).

Today, the Legal Hackers community spans the globe, with chapters in most major global cities. Several countries have multiple chapters, including Australia, Brazil, Canada, Colombia, Croatia, France, Germany, Italy, Nigeria, Portugal, Spain, Switzerland, the United Kingdom, and the United States. These chapters are independent, self-organized, and self-governed, catering first and foremost to the interests of the local community where the chapter is located. As a result, each Legal Hackers chapter is different, both in terms of governance, membership composition, funding (if any), and event topics. Active chapters are actively encouraged to maintain a diverse organizing team, a social media presence, and regular free, public events for the entire local community. Together, these characteristics create robust building blocks for a sustainable and engaged community. At the same time, chapters are encouraged to experiment with different forms of convening and connecting that advance the Legal Hackers mission.

IV. The Legal Hackers Mission

Legal Hackers chapters around the world are bound by a common mission to foster creative problem-solving at the intersection of law and technology. By «fostering» creative problem-solving, the aim of Legal Hackers is not to direct innovation (like an incubator, accelerator, or venture capitalist would), but to facilitate it by connecting and inspiring community members to learn from one another, build together, and to discuss important issues in an open, collaborative, and welcoming environment—creating an «open culture» for law with a common ethos. Importantly, when Legal Hackers chapters discuss the intersection of law and technology, both terms are meant broadly: law means law, legal practice, policymaking, and norms, while technology means any tools, systems, or services. As a result, Legal Hackers explore ways that technology can improve law, legal practice, and policymaking, while also exploring ways that law and policy can address rapidly changing technologies (e.g., artificial intelligence, blockchain technologies, and the sharing economy).

Legal Hackers has adopted several safeguards to mitigate against any potential co-optation of the community. First, Legal Hackers is not a commercial enterprise. Legal Hackers is 100% volunteers and not controlled by any commercial entity. Second, Legal Hackers is not a trade association or business network. Unlike trade associations, members do not need to pay dues to join the community and do not need to be a part of a certain profession or hold a special degree. In this way, Legal Hackers remains open to all who wish to participate. Third, Legal Hackers is not a political advocacy group. Specifically, while Legal Hackers chapters around the world host events to discuss technology policy issues and members may have opinions about policy issues, Legal Hackers (as chapters or a global movement) does not take positions on specific issues (e.g., there is no official Legal Hackers position on data protection regulation). Finally, Legal Hackers emphasizes that it does not engage in, support, or condone illegal activities or «black hat» computer hacking.

V. Who are Legal Hackers' Members?

Legal Hackers includes in its membership anyone who is passionate about creative problem-solving at the intersection of law and technology and embraces the Legal Hackers' open, collaborative ethos. Legal Hackers membership includes lawyers, policy professionals, technologists, entrepreneurs, academics, and other professionals and enthusiasts. Legal Hackers includes students and retired law firm partners, first-time entrepreneurs and serial entrepreneurs, private practitioners and government officials.

By embracing a system of values, a Legal Hackers member is more than the combination of the lawyer, her tools, and her approach toward the law. Legal hacking also includes a belief about the way that the legal system should operate and those who should be able to help shape it. Specifically, that there is value in multidisciplinarity (or, better yet, antidisciplinarity[30]), that legal information should be accessible, that legal processes should be human-centered, and that technology, responsibly deployed, can improve access to justice.

---

30 *See* Joi Ito, *Antidisciplinary* (Oct. 2, 2014), https://joi.ito.com/weblog/2014/10/02/antidisciplinar.html (last visited Apr. 29, 2019).

VI. What Does Legal Hackers Do?

To advance the Legal Hackers mission, local chapters host regular, typically free, public events for their community. Legal Hackers chapters are independent and self-organized, and each chapter determines the number, format, and content of its events. As a general matter, Legal Hackers chapter events fall into three categories: education, prototyping, and discussion.

First, Legal Hackers offers educational and informational events, bringing individuals of different backgrounds and interests together to share their skills and expertise. Educational activities may include workshops teaching lawyers coding, data science, or design thinking, or workshops teaching developers, designers, and entrepreneurs about the basics of open source licensing or venture capital fundraising.

Second, Legal Hackers brings together community members for hands-on activities and challenges such as hackathons, design thinking exercises, and prototype jams. The purpose of these events is to embrace the «hands-on imperative,» working to build tools and projects that advance legal innovation. For example, Legal Hackers chapters have hosted hackathons and prototyping events on issues including access to justice, disabilities accessibility, and blockchain-for-law applications.

Third, Legal Hackers brings together local stakeholders to discuss potential solutions to pressing technology policy challenges, such as network neutrality, data protection, the sharing economy, and blockchain regulation. Our goal is not to direct or shape policy, or to lobby for specific proposals, but to create an open forum for discussion that involves a variety of stakeholders who themselves can identify challenges and formulate solutions. In this way, we hope to serve as a trusted third party for these types of discussions. Participants can then take these new ideas and perspectives and implement them in their professional capacity or personal projects.

Through these events, Legal Hackers' aim is to create a *lingua franca*—a common language—and common identity between individuals of different disciplines, including lawyers, technologists, entrepreneurs, designers, and academics. In so doing, Legal Hackers hopes to train a new generation of tech-enabled lawyers, break down silos in the legal industry, build tools to increase access to justice, serve as a neutral forum for policy discussions, and ultimately facilitate rapid dissemination of legal innovation around the world.

VII. Global Community, Global Opportunity

As the Legal Hackers community has grown, the possibility for collaboration among chapters throughout the world has grown with it. Global collaboration between Legal Hackers chapters has included global and regional summits designed for chapter organizers, as well as multi-chapter festivals and workshops.

Since 2015, Legal Hackers has hosted its annual summit, bringing together chapter organizers from around the world to meet in person and share their experience and expertise. These organizers-only summits are the highlight of the Legal Hackers' year, and feature inspiring keynotes, lightning talks, hands-on workshops, social activity, and group planning.

Starting in 2018, Legal Hackers chapters also began to organize regional summits for other chapters in the region. Kyiv Legal Hackers hosted the first European Legal Hackers Summit in Odessa, Ukraine in May 2018; Singapore Legal Hackers hosted the first Asia-Pacific (APAC) Legal Hackers Summit in November 2018; and São Paulo Legal Hackers hosted the first Latin American (LATAM) Legal Hackers Summit in April 2019. These summits combined a closed-door day for organizers to meet and share activities, opportunities, and challenges, and an open day for the broader community to learn about Legal Hackers and issues at the intersection of law and technology.

In addition to organizer-focused summits, Legal Hackers also began to host multi-chapter conference and workshops focused on a specific topic or theme. In March 2018, Legal Hackers invited the global community to participate in a Computational Law & Blockchain Festival (CL+B Fest), a «decentralized conference» that took place in thirty-seven self-organized «nodes» around the world over a single weekend (with several nodes run by groups outside the Legal Hackers chapter network).[31] The event flipped the traditional conference model on its head: rather than ask individuals from around the world to fly to a central location, Legal Hackers and its event partners prepared a template that any organizer around the world could adopt or adapt for their local community, relying on local speakers, sponsors, and participants to provide a free and open forum for education, prototyping, and policy discussion. Nodes were encouraged to stream their proceedings for free and to make any output freely accessible. Nodes were also encouraged to submit reports for possible inclusion in the first issue of Stanford University's Journal of Blockchain Law & Policy. Reports from five nodes were ultimately accepted for inclusion in the journal.

Since the CL+B Fest (which hosted its second edition from March–May 2019), there have been additional multi-chapter decentralized events on issues including open media licensing and access to justice. Just as Legal Hackers' first legal hackathon inspired similar events around the legal industry, we ex-

31 Jameson J Dempsey, *Overview: A Decentralized Approach to Developing Technology Law and Policy on a Global Scale*, 1 Stanford J. Blockchain Law & P. 64 (2018), *available at* https://stanford-jblp.pubpub.org/pub/clb-fest-overview (last visited Apr. 11, 2019).

pect that the decentralized conference model will similarly encourage global law and policy activities.

VIII. What's Next?

Over the last seven years, Legal Hackers has grown from a legal hackathon in Brooklyn to a global movement with 140 chapters, over 430 volunteer organizers, and a community of tens of thousands worldwide. Legal hackathons have become commonplace in the legal innovation ecosystem, including the Global Legal Hackathon, which was the brainchild of an organizer of the Toronto Legal Hackers chapter. Legal innovation communities have sprouted around the world, some in the open spirit of Legal Hackers and others with more commercial aims (including events designed for marketing and business development).

Legal Hackers aim is to remain at the forefront of legal innovation, in a constant state of experimentation, finding new ways to connect and inspire within local communities and around the world. And just as technology evolves, so too will the issues that Legal Hackers addresses. Over time, our goal is build an «open culture» for law that will facilitate rapid response to pressing issues in a manner that respects local values and legal structures while providing opportunities for cross-border and cross-industry collaboration. We hope you will join us.

IX. Bibliography

A. Hard Copy Sources

Bench-Capon, Trevor, et al., *A history of AI and Law in 50 papers: 25 years of the International Conference on AI and Law*, Artificial Intelligence and Law 20.3 (2012).

Lear, Dan, *Hacking the Law,* American Bar Association Law Practice Today Newsletter (Jan. 14, 2014).

Levy, Steven, Hackers: Heroes of the Computer Revolution (Doubleday, 1984).

Põldoja, Hans, The Structure and Components for the Open Education Ecosystem (Aalto University, 2016).

Tozzi, Christopher, For Fun and Profit: A History of the Free and Open Source Software Revolution (The MIT Press, 2017).

B. Online Sources

Askin, Jonathan, *A Remedy to Clueless Tech Lawyers*, VentureBeat (Nov. 13, 2013 5:00 AM), https://venturebeat.com/2013/11/13/a-remedy-to-clueless-tech-lawyers/ (last visited Apr. 29, 2019).

Dempsey, Jameson J, *Overview: A Decentralized Approach to Developing Technology Law and Policy on a Global Scale*, 1 Stanford J. Blockchain Law & P. 64 (2018), *available at* https://stanford-jblp.pubpub.org/pub/clb-fest-overview.

Howard, Alex, *Defining Gov 2.0 and Open Government* (Jan. 5, 2011), http://gov20.govfresh.com/social-media-fastfwd-defining-gov-2-0-and-open-government-in-2011/ (last visited Apr. 29, 2019).

Hwang, Tim, *Three Updates*, Robot Robot & Hwang (Oct. 2, 2016), http://www.robotandhwang.com/2013/10/three-updates/ (last visited Apr. 29, 2019).

Hwang, Tim, *Some Design Notes on FutureLaw 2013*, Robot Robot & Hwang (Mar. 4, 2013), http://www.robotandhwang.com/2013/03/some-design-notes-on-futurelaw-2013/#more-484 (last visited Apr. 29, 2019).

Hwang, Tim, *NELIC Registration is Open!*, Robot Robot & Hwang (Mar. 9, 2011), https://www.robotandhwang.com/2011/03/nelic-registration-is-open/ (last visited Apr. 29, 2019).

Hwang, Tim, *On Legal Arms Dealing*, Robot Robot & Hwang, Sept. 26, 2010, https://www.robotandhwang.com/2010/09/on-legal-arms-dealing/ (last visited Jan. 12, 2019).

Ito, Joi, *Antidisciplinary* (Oct. 2, 2014), https://joi.ito.com/weblog/2014/10/02/antidisciplinar.html (last visited Apr. 29, 2019).

Kravets, David, *A SOPA/PIPA Blackout Explainer*, Wired (Jan. 18, 2012), https://www.wired.com/2012/01/websites-dark-in-revolt/ (last visited Apr. 29, 2019)

Legal Hackers, *Our Story*, www.legalhackers.org/our-story (last visited Jan. 12, 2019).

New York Legal Hackers, https://www.meetup.com/legalhackers/ (last visited January 12, 2019).

New York Legal Hackers, https://www.meetup.com/legalhackers/events/past/ (last visited April 11, 2019).

Raymond, Eric S, *Origins and History of Hackers, 1961–1995* (2003), http://www.catb.org/~esr/writings/taoup/html/hackers.html (last visited Apr. 28, 2019).

Robot Robot & Hwang, *About*, https://www.robotandhwang.com/about/ (last visited Jan. 12, 2019).

Savov, Vlad, *The SOPA blackout: Wikipedia, Reddit, Mozilla, Google, and many others protest proposed law*, The Verge (Jan. 18, 2012), https://www.theverge.com/2012/1/18/2715300/sopa-blackout-wikipedia-reddit-mozilla-google-protest (last visited Apr. 29, 2019).

SOPA Strike, http://sopastrike.com/ (last visited Apr. 29, 2019).

Stallman, Richard, *On Hacking*, https://stallman.org/articles/on-hacking.html (last visited Jan. 12, 2019).

Szabo, Nick, *«The Idea of Smart Contracts»* (1997), https://web.archive.org/web/20160831070942/http://szabo.best.vwh.net/smart_contracts_idea.html (last visited Apr. 11, 2019).

Tauberer, Joshua, Civic Hacking, Open Government Data: The Book (2nd ed., 2014), https://opengovdata.io/2014/civic-hacking/ (last visited Apr. 29, 2019).

The GNU General Public License, https://www.gnu.org/licenses/gpl-3.0.en.html (last visited Jan. 12, 2019).

Noah Waisberg and Will Pangborn

New Jobs in an Old Profession

Profiles of Workers in New Legal Jobs

TABLE OF CONTENTS

The legal job market is changing. You don't need us to tell you that. More use of standardized processes, outsourcing, and technology (including AI) are creating, destroying, and changing legal jobs. There is much opportunity for more change to come.[1]

As software automates work traditionally done manually by lawyers, new legal jobs are being created. What are these new jobs? What do people in them do? What are their backgrounds? To better understand the new legal roles that exist today, the article provides profiles of a number of *Kira Systems* employees with traditional legal backgrounds who are now in non-traditional legal roles. Even within this one contract-analysis-AI-focused software company, and even within roles with identical titles, you will notice that these Kirans (what Kira Systems calls employees) have different backgrounds and different roles today. Of course, Kira Systems is one legal technology company among many, so it is likely that the spread of new legal roles (including the backgrounds and tasks of people in these jobs) is extensive.

Without further ado, here are the profiles!

I. Modern Legal Jobs Highlight: Co-Founder and CEO of a Legal AI Software Company

In 2010, *Noah Waisberg* left the New York City corporate practice of law firm Weil, Gotshal & Manges LLP as a fourth year associate. After leaving Weil, he helped create and launch a new legal AI software called Kira (originally known as DiligenceEngine). Eight years later, Kira is used in over 40 countries by many of the world's leading firms to help their lawyers review contracts faster and more accurately. As Kira Systems' Chief Executive Officer, Noah oversees the business side of the organization and works closely with Co-Founder and Chief Technology Officer, *Dr. Alexander Hudek*, to spearhead the overarching direction and strategy of the company. Kira Systems has grown from Noah and Alex in 2011, to over 130 team members today, and the software is used by thousands of lawyers, auditors, consultants, and others. The following is a description of Noah's role, in interview format.

Describe your job—what do you do day to day?

***Noah**: Although each day is different, I really have three different focus areas as CEO. (1) The first is stepping up as the team leader to help support my team members anyway I can. I work on monitoring and supporting the performance of the employees and helping them in company initiatives. As a leader, I am constantly trying to not only add great talent into the company but*

---

1 Noah Waisberg, *Automating Law*, Kira Systems Blog (July 12, 2011), https://info.kirasystems.com/blog/automating-law (last visited Apr. 2, 2019).

retain the amazing employees we currently have. (2) Second, I act as a face for the organization and work on speaking with customers, prospects, media, and the public about the market at large and Kira Systems' own offerings. (3) Third, I help set, communicate, and monitor implementation of our company's strategy, including working with stakeholders like our investors, team, and customers.

What traditional legal skills come in handy in your new role, and what new skills have you gained on the job?

***Noah**: My past legal expertise has been an essential part of the Kira journey. I can empathise with our customers and keep the business on the right customer-focused path. I know what it means to go through a contract review process and understand the pain points our customers may be experiencing. Being able to review contracts from a legal perspective has also been essential in the development in our software. When Kira was first created, I spent years just training our artificial intelligence software on how to find key provisions, meaning I spent a lot of time looking for and highlighting contract provisions for it to learn from. The software could not have been trained without that legal expertise. Finally, I have a high level of attention from my legal training, specifically from my time on a law journal, and from working in Biglaw.*

I am still constantly learning new skills in my role, especially as our team continue to grow. Some skills I have picked up are the general management of people, how to run a startup company, and the intricacies of overseeing an organisation.

What do you wish you could tell a new junior lawyer about legal career paths and how they are changing?

***Noah**: Relationships matter. Remember to be kind to people in law school, your law firm, other peer businesses, and anywhere beyond. Even though I am now 12 years out of law school, I still keep in contact with many people from over the years. A bunch now hold interesting, senior roles. Many have become Kira supporters. And others are shaping the legal industry at large in exciting ways. Stay in touch with people, even if your career path takes you in a different direction.*

II. Modern Legal Jobs Highlight: Chief Product Officer

Steve Obenski has taken an interesting and veering path since becoming a lawyer. His passion for technology policy has taken him from working as an associate at Wilmer Hale and another law firm, to joining an early stage tech startup to learn how businesses grow and function, to working at Thomson Reuters to focus on product and general management. And now he works at Kira Systems, where, after holding a marketing/sales leadership role, he is now the company's Chief Product Officer. The following is a description of Steve's role, in interview format:

Describe your job—what do you do day to day?

Steve: *Over the course of my time at Kira Systems, I have had the privilege of doing many different roles to help grow the business side of the organization. I have managed sales and marketing, negotiated customer contracts, and worked closely with the founders on business decisions—all in the way of service, of improving the lives of lawyers. Now that Kira Systems has grown into a much bigger company, I've shifted my focus fully onto product management. As the Chief Product Officer, my goal is to understand where the market for machine learning contract analysis is currently, and where it's going in the short to long run. I manage an extremely talented product team that keeps their ears to the ground in order to test product improvement hypotheses, generate data, and paint the roadmap of what we need to build to take our software to the right places. It is all very data-driven and process-oriented.*

What traditional legal skills come in handy in your new role, and what new skills have you gained on the job?

Steve: *The critical thinking you learn as a lawyer is seriously helpful wherever you go; it forces you to think in a structured way. Advocacy is another major skill that has carried forward. Whether it's negotiating deals or working on briefs or motions in court, you are constantly learning to make your argument persuasive. In business, it is extremely helpful to have that skill, and it can become an extremely powerful business tool if you combine it with emotional intelligence and how to deal with people.*

What do you wish you could tell a new junior lawyer about legal career paths and how they are changing?

Steve: *In my first year as an associate I received a good piece of advice from my mentor: «Remember that you have a brain, and you can use it.» Junior lawyers take too long to learn how to speak truth to power. Although it was hard to see at the start of my career, I would tell myself to speak up and be less timid. Take some chances and recognize that partners at law firms appreciate when you do have an idea or attitude. Especially in the world of artificial intelligence and LegalTech, don't be afraid to suggest a new and improved way of doing things (such as using software for better due diligence) internally and provide solid reasoning. It is your career, and it is an opportunistic time to take charge of it.*

III. Modern Legal Jobs Highlight: AI Practice Consultant, Legal Markets

The role of «AI Practice Consultant» is a customer-facing role with the overarching goal of helping law firms adopt and be successful with Kira's artificial intelligence. Each AI Practice Consultant is a lawyer by trade and combines his/her practice area specialties with Kira's machine learning capabilities to provide best-in-class recommendations for legal clients. *Sondra Rebenchuk* is an AI Practice Consultant at Kira Systems. She was formerly a law firm associate at Goodmans LLP, and now manages relationships with a number of Kira Systems' legal customers, including top-tier Canadian and US law firms such as Osler, Hoskin & Harcourt LLP, Fasken, and Torys LLP. The following is a description of Sondra's role, in interview format:

Describe your job—what do you do day to day?

Sondra*: I work with our law firm partners to help them understand Kira as a tool. I provide them with an understanding of why Kira is good to for their business, and ultimately empower them to talk to their clients about the benefits for them and working with technology. I also work very closely with the legal in-house Knowledge Management / IT teams to ensure a smooth implementation of the new technology across the firm. I also love getting to train the junior lawyers who are practicing for the first time and are very open minded for the benefits of LegalTech. This next generation of lawyers are really those who have great ideas and are excited at the new legal possibilities with AI software in the mix.*

What traditional legal skills come in handy in your new role, and what new skills have you gained on the job?

Sondra*: In my years as an associate, I really learnt the importance of having empathy for the type of work that my clients do. I understand the amount of pressure they are under (from clients, time constraints, etc.), and the world they live in. Using this knowledge, I can best speak to how new technology can really help them day to day. Furthermore, working as a practitioner develops key skills such as critical thinking and prioritization. I can deliver the same high level of client service that they would in turn want to deliver to their clients.*

A new skill, that was not remotely on my radar as an associate, is knowledge of change management. Learning how to approach situations where you take away the way an entire organization does something and teach them to do it differently. There's a lot of skepticism with LegalTech, so change is especially challenging for legal firms. Having the opportunity to facilitate the process, put together new programs, and train individuals on technology for legal firms is a brand-new skill set that I can take forward with me through my career.

What do you wish you could tell a new junior lawyer about legal career paths and how they are changing?

***Sondra**: During law school, I saw a legal career path in an extremely linear way. I put a lot of pressure on myself to stay on the partner path, but in retrospect, I would not have dealt with the same amount of stress if I had known my options and learnt early that it's okay to deviate from that linear path and be more open to new and exciting opportunities.*

IV. Modern Legal Jobs Highlight: AI Practice Consultant, Corporate Markets

Kira is used by more than just law firms. So, Kira Systems also offers dedicated AI practice consultant support focused on corporate customers. *Robin McNamara* joined Kira Systems upon finishing his articling experience at a major law firm in Toronto, and quickly learnt how to contribute to the business side of a legal AI company. Today, Robin manages corporate accounts as Kira's customer success manager, including consulting with some of Kira Systems' key accounts. The following is a description of Robin's role, in interview format:

Describe your job—what do you do day to day?

***Robin**: What my job boils down to is being an external advisor to guide our corporate customers in using the software in the best way possible for them. I work to align Kira's resources to solve whatever problems they may have along the way. I build solid relationships with our corporate customers, set them up with the software, and shepherd them through their use to deliver the best value possible.*

What traditional legal skills come in handy in your new role, and what new skills have you gained on the job?

***Robin**: There are many skills that all lawyers learn, even in my short time of articling: detailed writing, polished client-facing skills, relevant legal subject matter expertise, etc. However, I have definitely learnt a lot more of my business skills during my time at Kira Systems. Working across departments and learning how they relate to one another has been a skill that will stick with me for many years to come. I didn't realize how little to no concept I had of how a business functions before jumping into my role now and working with so many teams to develop one strong product.*

What do you wish you could tell a new junior lawyer about legal career paths and how they are changing?

***Robin**: The opportunities within traditional firms are still there, and will continue to be there, but there is lots of opportunity for brand new business models to be successful in this modern legal market. It's up to you to go find them.*

V. Modern Legal Jobs Highlight: Legal Knowledge Engineering Manager, M&A and General Commercial

AI software learns how to work from the people who train it. Given that it's garbage in, garbage out, it is key that the people who are training the software do high quality work.[2] At Kira Systems, these team members are called Legal Knowledge Engineering Associates. This team of associates use their legal industry expertise to review and analyze contracts in Kira to teach the machine-learning software to find and extract key provisions such as Change of Control, Term, Renewal, Assignment, and many more. *Resa Jacob* is a former five-year associate who now works as a Legal Knowledge Engineering Manager at Kira Systems, specializing in training Kira's software to find M&A and general commercial agreement provisions. The following is a description of Resa's role, in interview format:

Describe your job—what do you do day to day?

Resa: *My primary responsibility is to procure and upload existing contracts into Kira in order to build machine-learning (ML) models on the software that can find and extract key M&A provisions. Aside from using my legal knowledge to train the AI behind software, as a manager, I provide oversight to the members of the annotation team who are also working on building out my ML models. With my role being at the intersection of legal and software expertise, I also leverage my knowledge to help other teams (such as sales, customer success, and marketing), in addition to customers to provide a deeper understanding of Kira's machine-learning models and their legal implications.*

What traditional legal skills come in handy in your new role, and what new skills have you gained on the job?

Resa: *It was very important to me to find a job where I can apply all of my general legal knowledge I learnt through my education and time as an associate, and this job allows me to leverage that knowledge daily. Being able to read, understand, and appreciate contract terms, as well as know where to find provisions, allows me to best determine which ML models are best suited to be trained on the software.*

---

2 Noah Waisberg, *Garbage In, Garbage Out: Why Who Instructs An Automated Contract Provision Extraction System Matters—Contract Review Software Buyer's Guide Part X*, Kira Systems Blog (May 5, 2014), https://info.kirasystems.com/blog/2014/05/05/garbage-in-garbage-out-why-who-instructs-an-automated-contract-provision-extraction-system-matters-contract-review-software-buyers-guide-part-x (last visited Apr. 2, 2019); Noah Waisberg, *Further Information on Why Who Instructs An Automated Contract Provision Extraction System Matters—Contract Review Software Buyer's Guide Part XI*, Kira Systems Blog (Jun. 1, 2014), https://info.kirasystems.com/blog/2014/06/01/further-information-on-why-who-instructs-an-automated-contract-provision-extraction-system-matters-contract-review-software-buyers-guide-part-xi (last visited Apr. 2, 2019).

Ultimately, what I've really learnt is how to balance wearing different hats, with different roles, while dealing with different teams. When you're at a law firm you are working on designated files and can be very isolated. My position now allows me to get exposure to other teams and work cross-collaboratively on our software.

What do you wish you could tell a new junior lawyer about legal career paths and how they are changing?

Resa*: I knew early that being a partner wasn't for me, and always knew I wanted to try something else, but I never realized just how much things were changing. Discovering legal tech as an option was very exciting, and I continue to learn how there are so many more jobs out there that value lawyers with experience but where you do more than providing legal advice. That said, I am extremely grateful for beginning my career at a law firm. Working through that that type of environment allowed me to build a strong work-ethic and appreciation for law at the start of my career.*

VI. Modern Legal Jobs Highlight: Director, Legal Knowledge Engineering

Leading the Legal Knowledge Engineering team, *Anne McNulty* is at the forefront of training legal AI software, Kira, to find and extract key provisions from contracts. Having spent several years as an associate, she has since help build this entire new department in a LegalTech startup, managing a team of lawyers doing jobs that did not exist a decade before. The following is a description of Anne's role, in interview format:

Describe your job—what do you do day to day?

Anne*: What my job is at its core is that I manage the team that teaches Kira to find information. I have a team of legal knowledge engineering managers, associates, and part-time annotators that all help train the software to improve the lives of our users. Within that, I constantly have to think strategically of what contracts I need to find to train the system, what use cases we need to serve, how well we currently fit those use cases, and ultimately piecing that all together to determine the overall next steps of the team and the processes to follow.*

What traditional legal skills come in handy in your new role, and what new skills have you gained on the job?

Anne*: A big traditional skill that is important to my function is having integral legal subject matter knowledge from my time as a lawyer. My team builds a product that lawyers use so it's always been helpful to have lived in that world and understand the type of work and contracts they deal with. Beyond that, my time as a lawyer really pushed me to live up to a high client service level and client expectations. Law firms push you to work hard and* *push you to work at a higher caliber that stays with you throughout your career. It really changed my belief in what I'm capable of delivering at work, what's possible.*

What has been interesting is that I realized how I was never totally happy at my law firm jobs because they only required me to use a subset of my skills. Working in LegalTech, I am much happier because I am constantly being pushed to use every skill I possess and learn new things. I enjoy that challenge and feel much more engaged now than I ever have before.

What do you wish you could tell a new junior lawyer about legal career paths and how they are changing?

***Anne**: It's worth putting in the time to look into the other options. I was always focused on becoming a law firm partner, but I've since realized that I would not have been happy with that career path. I stumbled into my career, but junior lawyers now have so much opportunity to plan out new career paths that once didn't exist. Keep an open mind, do your research, and find out what you don't know. And remember that in the end, it'll all work out.*

VII. Modern Legal Jobs Highlight: Legal Knowledge Engineering Manager, Accounting & Audit

After spending nearly a decade working internationally from Japan to the Caribbean, *Patrick Shaunessy* left the finance industry to return to Canada and pursue a J.D. and Business Degree. Patrick left his job as an associate at a leading Canadian law firm after four years and joined Kira Systems as a member of the Legal Knowledge Engineering team; however, he is leveraging both his international business and finance experience with his legal knowledge to train the Kira software on an emerging corporate market: accounting & audit. The following is a description of Patrick's role, in interview format:

Describe your job—what do you do day to day?

***Patrick**: The main area of my focus falls onto building models to support accounting and business functions. As it stands today, we have room to grow our foothold in those markets, so my goal is to really look at expanding into these areas by speaking with existing clients, determining what AI models they require for success, and develop a strategy to meet their needs. I approach my role much differently than the Legal Knowledge Associates who focus on M&A because accountants take a much different approach to their work; they are more pragmatic. Rather than building out a large quantity of AI-models, I have to focus on building fewer strategic models for accountants. By working with our amazing existing clients, we are really able to determine the best strategies for building a product that matches the needs of accountants in addition to lawyers.*

What traditional legal skills come in handy in your new role, and what new skills have you gained on the job?

***Patrick**: In a law firm, you are very much grounded to the country or location you work, however I have been lucky enough to work internationally (whether physically or at a global company). Of course working across the globe was an enriching personal experience, but beyond that it also allowed me to be more in tune to the sensitivity required while working internationally and across cultures. Professionally, it has helped me explore different ways of doing business, especially while working on a software like Kira that is used in so many different countries globally.*

What do you wish you could tell a new junior lawyer about legal career paths and how they are changing?

***Patrick**: When you're in law school there's a focus on the traditional career-route, but that's not for everyone. It results in many that decide to leave law altogether. I would say if you're unsure if that traditional route is for you, explore the many interesting opportunities that are available to you now, and follow your interests.*

I didn't start off with a specific plan. I initially followed my passions and let my career develop naturally. Looking back, those interests are exactly what led me to where I am today.

VIII. Concluding Remarks

In a changing world, having data is helpful. Ideally, these profiles of a subset of the employees with legal backgrounds at one legal technology company (amidst a rapidly-growing world of new legal jobs), help you better understand some roles that hardly existed a decade ago, as well as others (like CEO or Chief Product Officer) that have been around for some time. Some takeaways you could get from these profiles are:

- ***Different* Jobs**. Even within one legal AI company, there are lots of different roles occupied by people with legal backgrounds. Even within the same roles, there are people with fairly different jobs at different companies. There are many more legal technology companies out there, and there are likely to be even more differences in jobs across them.
- **Traditional Foundations**. The profiled Kirans all worked in Biglaw (most for several years) prior to entering Newlaw jobs. (Note that there are also lawyer-background Kirans who did not work in Biglaw prior to joining Kira Systems. Their experience prior to Kira Systems was sometimes in-house or at smaller firms. Plus, there are a couple who exited law for sales right after law school.) The Kirans who are profiled generally found their traditional legal experience a good background for their current work, teaching them attention to detail, how to create high-quality

output, strong work ethic, as well as how law firms operate and what lawyers do. This trend of lawyer-background Kirans tending to have traditional legal experience may be because of how heavily Kira Systems focuses on enhancing traditional lawyer work. Or, perhaps it's a self-sustaining bias towards traditional legal backgrounds on the part of people who do the hiring for these roles! Either way, it's a relatively common characteristic for certain roles at Kira Systems. While there are a number of roles in Kira Systems that are heavily populated by people with a legal background, the vast majority of Kirans have no prior legal experience whatsoever. Groups including sales, marketing, software development, design, systems, support, administration are filled with people who never went to law school or worked as lawyers, and they have been critical to Kira Systems' success.

– **It's A Wide World.** Several profiled Kirans noted that they entered their legal career thinking that there was one linear track to follow, and were surprised to find jobs like the ones they are now in. Pay attention to what is available out there, and be open minded!

This is a wonderful time in the legal profession. There is lots of opportunity to work differently and better, and an increased receptivity to new legal solutions. Seize the moment to create a legal career that excites you!

IX. Bibliography

A. Online Sources

Noah Waisberg, *Automating Law*, Kira Systems Blog July 12, 2011 (Jan. 21, 2019, 4:19 PM), https://info.kirasystems.com/blog/automating-law (last visited Apr. 2, 2019).

Noah Waisberg, *Garbage In, Garbage Out: Why Who Instructs An Automated Contract Provision Extraction System Matters—Contract Review Software Buyer's Guide Part X*, Kira Systems Blog May 5, 2014 (Jan. 21, 2019, 4:32 PM), https://info.kirasystems.com/blog/2014/05/05/garbage-in-garbage-out-why-who-instructs-an-automated-contract-provision-extraction-system-matters-contract-review-software-buyers-guide-part-x (last visited Apr. 2, 2019).

Noah Waisberg, *Further Information on Why Who Instructs An Automated Contract Provision Extraction System Matters—Contract Review Software Buyer's Guide Part XI*, Kira Systems Blog Jun. 1, 2014 (Jan. 21, 2019, 4:42P M), https://info.kirasystems.com/blog/2014/06/01/further-information-on-why-who-instructs-an-automated-contract-provision-extraction-system-matters-contract-review-software-buyers-guide-part-xi (last visited Apr. 2, 2019).

B. Other Sources

Interview by Will Pangborn with Noah Waisberg, CEO, Kira Systems, in Toronto, ON, Canada. (Jan. 15, 2019).

Interview by Will Pangborn with Steve Obenski, Chief Product Officer, Kira Systems, in Toronto, ON, Canada. (Jan. 15, 2019).

Interview by Will Pangborn with Sondra Rebenchuk, AI Practice Consultant (legal), Kira Systems, in Toronto, ON, Canada. (Jan. 11, 2019).

Interview by Will Pangborn with Robin McNamara, AI Practice Consultant (corporate), Kira Systems, in Toronto, ON, Canada. (Jan. 21, 2019).

Interview by Will Pangborn with Resa Jacob, Legal Knowledge Engineering Manager, Kira Systems, in Toronto, ON, Canada. (Jan. 11, 2019).

Interview by Will Pangborn with Anne McNulty, Director, Legal Knowledge Engineering, Kira Systems, in Toronto, ON, Canada. (Jan. 15, 2019).

Interview by Will Pangborn with Patrick Shaunessy, Legal Knowledge Engineering Manager, Kira Systems, in Toronto, ON, Canada. (Jan. 21, 2019).

Salvatore Iacangelo

The Law Firm of the Future

(Keep on) Rockin' in the Free World[1]

TABLE OF CONTENTS

1 Neil Young, Rockin' in the Free World (Reprise Records, 1989).

I. Legal Services Today

A. The Business Model Challenge

Today`s large law firms pursue a business model that has been (and continues to be) very successful since the last decades. This business model is based on the law firm´s ability to blend the talents of experienced legal practitioners and partners with those of motivated junior qualified lawyers who are driven by a strong and powerful incentive—the opportunity to become a partner of the law firm, i.e., to win «the promotion-to-partner tournament».[2] On the other hand, the large law firms` evolution has showed how the very same drivers of growth will likely lead to the business model's undoing: As more and more associates become partners, more and more junior associates need to be hired to maintain the leverage and more and more business needs to be acquired and generated in order to maintain the food chain in place.[3]

To summarize, today's larger law firms` business model is characterized by:[4]

- Attraction, training, and development of top legal talents;
- Leverage of employed lawyers to perform more routine work when serving clients, resulting in a pyramidal firm structure, with a restricted number of equity partners owning the firm and deciding upon any matter;
- Creation of a competitive environment, motivating junior lawyers to strive for equity partnership;
- Partnership structure and related culture;
- Pricing predominantly driven by hourly-based rates;
- Emphasis on technical perfection and allocating any type of risk to the client typically neglecting any risk-based advisory approach.

The combination of these characteristics has led to great challenges in governance and business strategy. Partner-owners typically operate as largely autonomous individuals (with teams) and are involved in most, if not all, decisions. Further, only little profits are retained within the firm, making it difficult to execute on strategies that involve «one firm» approaches and mid-/long term, larger investments in future projects. This combination of characteristics has

---

2 Marc Galanter & Thomas Palay, Tournament of Lawyers: the Transformation of the Big Law Firm (University of Chicago Press, 1991).

3 Cambridge Strategy Group, *Thriving at the Edge of Chaos—AI, Blockchain and the Law Firm of the Future* (2018), https://mailchi.mp/c8a7253a01c3/thriving-at-the-edge-of-chaos-download (last visited Feb. 22, 2019).

4 George Beaton & Imme Kaschner, Remaking Law Firms—Why & How (American Bar Association, 2016).

also proven to be very challenging to drive change in a group of self-assured, high-earning individuals that neither see nor feel any need to act, given the background of the revenues and, more specifically, the margins being generated. In addition, remuneration linked to personal performance measured on time-based outcomes considerably restricts the incentive to manage profitability by increasing efficiency and improving existing time-consuming (and, hence, profitable) processes.[5]

In his theory of competitive advantage, *Michael Porter* (1980) teaches that there are three and only three ways of achieving sustainable competitive advantage and these three ways are largely mutually exclusive because the business models required to exploit each do not co-exist well with each other. Porter's sources of competitive advantage are to find unique ways, valued by clients and other stakeholders, to:

- be cheapest in the market;
- be differentiated—i.e., better (in the eyes of clients) than competitors;
- exploit a market niche where demand exceeds the supply capacity of competitors in that space.

At its core, law firm strategy involves making choices about the above and then about the mix of clients, services, and markets in which the firm chooses to compete as a result. It is as much about what a law firm decides not to do, as what it decides to do. Multiple businesses with the very same value proposition will not be able to co-exist because clients and others upon whom the business depends for its success will tend to value one of the businesses over the others.

It is very difficult for law firms offering the same services and strategies as each other to present at the same time, different value propositions to clients. Although law firms may perceive themselves to be very different, clients frequently disagree. In a hypercompetitive market, this is a very serious matter. Differentiation is widely recognized to be important, but very seldom convincing to clients. Further, clients are more discerning and seek value beyond mere price reductions; drivers of client behavior are not always intuitive.[6]

The current law firms` business model is, allegedly, less well suited to successfully perform in an industry which has been changing and is now characterized by buyer power (given the myriad of law firms competing for mandates), cost-down pressures imposed by large corporate clients, increasing use of technology and digitalization as well as of substitute services. Driven by clients´ demand, alternatives to time-based remuneration, flexible working models and services, increasing digitalization, and decreasing information

---

5 Beaton & Kaschner, *supra* note 3, chapter 13.

6 Cambridge Strategy Group, *supra* note 2, at 60.

asymmetry between lawyers and non-lawyers make the traditional law firm business model more and more questionable.[7]

B. The Service Offering Challenge

The industry is experiencing several change driving trends at the same time:

- Demand to «do more for less»;
- Need for risk-based approaches with respect to the application of law and the provision of legal services and advice;
- Continuous shift of the provision of legal services from law firms to in-house legal departments;
- Growing role of information technology and digitalization in the entire legal practice;
- Commoditization of repetitive legal services.

Certainly, the business pressure applied on in-house legal departments to either directly provide or source more cost-efficient legal and compliance services articulates clear client demand and forces law firms to consider alternatives to their conventional provision of legal services to allow them to continue to win work. Certainly, the cost pressure supports the trend to bring more and more legal work in-house. Consequently, the structure of the legal services industry is changing because of in-house legal departments´ increasing ability to replace law firms for work that they used to outsource. Further, legal services procurement of big corporate clients has developed and become more sophisticated. More and more often, legal services are better and more suitably provided by multidisciplinary professional services firms, especially where large scale, repetitive services are provided with the capabilities and support of information technology solutions. Many law firms face these price-down pressures with discounts. Many others adapt the way they produce and sell legal services by analyzing carefully the value chain and allocate technical and human resources appropriately. As a matter of fact, only the latter is sustainable in the long run[8].

Information technology and digitalization affect law firms in relation to (i) how they perform their work, enabling them more efficient provision of legal services in more client-focused/client-centric processes; and, (ii) the spaces they practice in. Certainly, the impact of digitalization on business activities, in general, affects law firms greatly, given that clients expect more and more smarter delivery as well as less duplicative and non-value adding pro-

7 Beaton & Kaschner, *supra* note 3, chapter 2.

8 Beaton & Kaschner, *supra* note 3, chapter 2.

cesses. It forces law firms to be much more cognizant of the business goals and strategies of their individual clients and to provide much more of a plug and play service in a broader ecosystem. In a digital driven world, clients do not want to pay for the learning of the firm e.g., training, creating a contract template, or designing a proposal of an offering. Thanks to transparency of price and costs in combination with decreasing asymmetry of information, law firms, like other professional services firms, are finding it increasingly difficult to charge for the services and efforts that they used to charge for. These developments are forcing the legal industry to become more client-centric (more focused on providing clients with a convenient service experience) and more data- and technology-driven in terms of research, document preparation, and report compilation. Technology will continue to help individual lawyers to work, but it will also enable the commoditization of more and more legal services and more direct and efficient collaboration among legal teams beyond the law firm and/or the client's organization. Technology advancements will also make disintermediation possible and accelerate it accordingly.[9]

Within law firms today, technological solutions are used to support the delivery of bespoke legal advice. Metrics applied to measure the productivity of information technology often focus on user time. This is because revenues are driven by billable hours and information technology is interpreted as an operational cost center, a necessary means to deliver the work while the value lies in the advice, in the content. However, information technology is becoming more and more a strategic asset, with project cycles becoming shorter and shorter, requiring not only technology to be agile, but also decision processes and deployment loops. This is too often in contradiction with the prevailing incentivization in law firm partnerships to extract the profits today rather than tomorrow, in addition to the limited willingness to adopt new technology solutions. With the advancement of immersive technologies and their consolidation and commoditization, in a few years, virtual work environments will be the reality. These virtual work spaces have the potential to enable collaboration even further and to reduce the need for physical office space, one of the highest cost items for top tier law firms. It will become even easier to aggregate lawyer networks at much lower costs than law firms have been doing so far. Barriers of entry for the high-end legal market will be dramatically reduced creating an opening for smaller firms with well-established brands to expand.[10]

---

9 International Legal Technology Association, Legal Technology Future Horizons (2014) at 102 and Beaton & Kaschner, *supra* note 3, chapter 2.

10 Beaton & Kaschner, *supra* note 3, chapter 2.

C. The Talent Challenge

In addition to the difficulty of hiring legal talent willing to engage in a demanding career, law firms increasingly face the difficulty of hiring professionals with expertise at the intersection of legal services with information technology, business development, project management, process (re-)design, and/or operational excellence. Given the drive for efficiency, there is also the need to define more specifically what work is best done by qualified lawyers as opposed to resources with other law- (or non-law-) related qualifications. The regulatory framework that reserved the provision of legal services to qualified and licensed lawyers is being softened. These developments will likely influence how law firms recruit and retain their talent pool, how they structure remuneration and fringe benefits, and how they shape their leadership structure.[11]

Beyond flexible, task-appropriate work arrangements, new ways of doing legal work often rely on a reduction in fixed costs. When paying for work on an as-needed basis, changes in life and financial planning for (freelance) legal professionals is required. Increasing lateral mobility and hiring, a typical and proven growth strategy for mature markets, pose significant economic and cultural challenges for law firms, often eroding the long-term focus and the partners` willingness to invest in a firm, thereby limiting resources that are available for strategic innovation initiatives. In a service profession where, despite increasing commoditization, the most significant asset is still the individual's intellectual capital, recruiting, developing, and leveraging that asset will continue to be a very significant revenue lever.

II. Digital Disruptions

Along with the geo-economic, socio-political, demographic and environmental trends[12] that are going to change human beings in the near future, we are at the verge of a wave of disruptive transformation, induced by dynamically interconnected effects of several digital technological trends, which, in their combination, will likely transform our lives and, hence, also our clients' legal needs over the coming decade on an unprecedented scale.[13] These digital technological change agents include:

- Artificial Intelligence and Machine Learning;
- Distributed Ledger Technology (DLT);

---

11 Beaton & Kaschner, *supra* note 3, chapter 2.

12 International Legal Technology Association, Legal Technology Future Horizons (2014) at 23.

13 Cambridge Strategy Group, *supra* note 2, at 23.

- Big Data Analysis;
- Internet of Things;
- Advanced Wireless Networks;
- Quantum Computing.

The change in the strategic and technological environment will drive a need for a new business model that aligns. That said, a successful law firm today—understandably—may not yet see the urgency to radically adapt if its financial results continue to support and reinforce its existing business model. This is likely because digital transformation tends to focus on maximizing automatization of existing processes—it is often not driven by a comprehensive and thorough strategic plan. However, digital transformation inevitably creates culture and service delivery change, which requires adjustment to the business model as the way that the firm engages with its clients and other stakeholders adapts.

To best understand how and to what extent the current people-leveraged business law firm model must be transformed to a digitally leveraged model, one must first understand how digital disruption is changing client legal needs. To yield innovative insights, this exploration must take place in collaboration with clients, in a structured and systematic way, e.g., analyzing the impact on specific client business and legal needs down the vertical of client, industry, area of law, and particular issue. In the near future, the only sustainable source of competitive advantage for a large law firm will be its ability to out-compete others in anticipating new client business and legal needs and adapting to meet these in a faster and more profitable way than competitors. To be truly sustainable, though, these capabilities need to be deeply embedded into the law firm's business model. The innovation and creativity involved cannot be relegated to a fraction of the law firm leadership`s attention.[14]

III. Future Client Needs

There are several commentators that have emerged since the global financial crisis (2008), predicting the imminent demise of traditional law firms. *Richard Susskind's* books «The End of Lawyers?» (2010) and «The Future of Professions» (2015, together with *Daniel Susskind*) are predominantly quoted as «the» source highlighting and outlining the imminent doom of large law firms, but there are plenty thereof. Most do comprehensively point out the problems and reasons why things need to change, but often, workable and pragmatic solutions are missing.

---

14 Cambridge Strategy Group, *supra* note 2, at 7 and 8.

Will today's leading law firms still be leading tomorrow? Most of the current discussion seems to conclude that many of the existing leading law firms will have to transform or will be replaced by new forms of legal service providers. In «The Innovator's Dilemma», *Clayton Christensen* describes why it is so difficult for market leaders, when an industry is disrupted, to defend their positions against new competitors with technologies and business models that clients prefer. Consequently, one very plausible scenario that can be constructed is where the future global legal services market is dominated by the «Big 4» global advisory firms (and, by then, their technology platforms), alternative or virtual service providers like Axiom and Elevate and other new legal service providers with new business models proven to be successful and will have emerged thanks to clients' preference. However, an equally plausible scenario can be conceived where a significant number of existing law firms successfully transform their business models and continue to thrive in this new, digitally driven world.[15]

Sophisticated, premium, bespoke legal advice is very different to the technology products that underpin most of *Christensen's* thinking. A customer deciding to purchase music does not, when choosing between buying and downloading a track from Apple Music or Amazon, consider the importance of his/her relationship with the musician or record label. The customer knows that the same quality of music will be delivered by both. Buying a track from Apple Music, though, means the customer pays only for the hit single wanted, and the single is delivered directly to the customer's app and available on any of the customer's device. Even more radically by comparison, subscribing to Spotify or Apple Music enables the customer to receive a stream of music personalized to his/her taste, for one single subscription fee. If we compare buying music to buying legal services, clients still perceive the latter to be more complex, bespoke and of crucial importance for their businesses or interests. The depth of skills, know-how, and judgement involved in some types of legal services will most probably always be heavily dependent on skilled, experienced lawyers and their interaction with clients.

Consider that law firms are not hampered by massive legacy investments in factories, manufacturing equipment, business systems and suppliers in the value chains of their products and services. Law firm balance sheets are very thin, at least as far as tangible assets are concerned, very similar to the balance sheets of modern tech companies. The key to transforming a law firm business model is gaining consensus across the business owners (i.e., the partners) and getting the law firm employees to change the way that they think and are used to work. This is not a trivial matter, but certainly easier than it would be, were it to occur along with difficult decisions about writing off expensive assets and

15 Cambridge Strategy Group, *supra* note 2, at 46.

financing new ones. Most obstacles in law firms (and other professional services firms) are rather self-inflicted and not induced or imposed by the industry or the business nature. It should be far easier for law firms to transform their business models than it is for many of their clients[16].

We all are already seeing great progress and digital transformation taking place in due diligence reviews, contract drafting, legal research, eDiscovery, prediction technology (which helps forecast litigation outcomes), and document automation. More sophistication and accuracy will further improve the results of these activities being performed with the help of advanced technology solutions, such as client portals and intranet-based collaborative platforms. These technological solutions are applying continuous pressure on law firms' models to evolve. One only must look back over how much change has occurred in the past decade to see that evolution is indeed taking place at a notable speed. New literature about business model transformation and digital transformation across industry sectors is beginning to provide useful guidance. The same drivers of change in the legal sector are also driving change in client industry sectors in general. Law firms are «*predominantly responsive institutions rather than proactive institutions, as they react to clients' demands instead of supplying their own initiatives to clients.*[17]» Hence, the best source of market intelligence is the law firm's own client base which law firms should utilize and interview much more proactively.

Most client executives and in-house lawyers themselves have not yet sufficient clarity about how their legal needs are likely to change over the next three to five to seven years, in response to the impact of the emerging digital technologies. At a workshop on «AI, Blockchain and the Future of Legal Services» held at the MIT Media Lab in Boston in October 2017, one speaker is reported to have commented that helping clients to understand their own emerging legal needs may be the best business development opportunity to emerge in decades. It is also probably the best opportunity that exists for law firms to find and elaborate the insights that they require to correctly calibrate their strategy development and business transformation efforts. The discovery trip into the client needs of tomorrow is something that needs to be tackled in an iterative and collaborative way, by clients and their external legal advisors jointly. The benefit for clients is the opportunity for proactive input into their own strategic planning and risk management processes. The benefit for law firms is the indication of how they need to allocate their investments in technologies, train their people, and develop new competencies. These types of exploratory exercises must be pursued in a structured, properly planned pro-

---

16 Cambridge Strategy Group, *supra* note 2, at 47.

17 John Flood, What Do Lawyers Do? An Ethnography of a Corporate Law Firm (Quid Pro Books, 2013).

cess that is designed in collaboration with the clients to systematically gather their feedback and input, including their constructive criticism—unlike the debriefs that occur over lunch (between client and law firm partner) after having (successfully) completed a very large project (and only after the success of other large projects!). Several approaches might be adopted for these inquiries, including design thinking workshops or agile sprints. Each law firm is different and operates in a different business environment. Hence, a good approach that meets most situations is a combination of scenario planning followed by more focused examination of the issues that the scenario planning yields.[18]

IV. The Law Firm of the Future

A. Preface

The law firm of the future will react to client demands, put client needs at the center of its activity and efforts, and anticipate the changes that will eventually occur in an increasingly mature market like the legal services market. The law firm of the future will adapt aspects of how work is won and how work is done. Competing legal services providers will be compared in terms of how they win work, how they produce work, and how they are led and governed. In the future, legal services providers will be closer to the business model of client companies than traditional law firm partnerships.

The pace and nature of the change in the legal services industry calls for transformational rather than incremental changes in law firms. Change at an organizational level happens in the stages described by Kurt Lewin—unfreeze, transform, refreeze[19]. Lawyers tend to be conservative and risk averse in their personality, and their inherent aim for perfection is in contradiction with an experimental approach that foresees failure as a necessary part of development and change. Innovation must become an integral part of the future law firm's strategy, starting in small steps and including the assessment of the risks involved in building a manageable portfolio of innovation initiatives. This requires resources, leadership, and incentivization, which will create a shared understanding and experience, and facilitate the process emotionally and rationally.

---

18 Cambridge Strategy Group *supra* note, 2, at 47.

19 Kurt Lewin, *Frontiers of Group Dynamics Concept, Method and Reality in Social Science; Social Equilibria and Social Change*, 1 Human Relations (1947).

B. Client Needs

In five to seven years, it is reasonable to assume that the digital tools emerging in legal practice will have advanced to the point where all legal services involving the standard application of legal knowledge will be delivered by technology. Large pieces of work that have traditionally been performed by qualified lawyers by hand will be inefficient to be delivered in that way, let aside the willingness of in-house departments to pay expensive hourly fees for it. Information technology solutions will be fundamentally faster AND better at doing that very same work. Many of the new «digitally native» client legal needs that emerge will be better delivered with the support of information technology solutions rather than by lawyers alone. In such a business world, the logic consequence indicates that the only services requiring personal (human) lawyers` coverage will be: (a) developing, controlling and providing oversight to the information technology solutions; and, (b) premium bespoke legal services that require uniquely human skills, know-how, expertise and judgment, beyond the capabilities of the information technology solutions. Human excellence will not only be a differentiator, but a prerequisite for survival. In such a business world, it is difficult to imagine a large law firm operating with mediocre lawyers.[20]

In-house counsels will play a pivotal role in the development of the law firm of the future and in the evolution of the legal services offering provided by traditional external law firms and legal services providers. The transformation of the legal services practice by information technology solutions and the questioning of value by in-house counsels and corporate clients in general will drive external legal advisors to fundamentally revisit their roles and service offering. This will very likely unfold within in-house departments evolving needs for corporate lawyers to orientate their focus more and more on helping (internal) clients achieve (financial) performance goals, as well as ensure that the company acts with integrity, in a sound risk-based approach.[21]

In-house counsel will not only focus on ensuring compliance with the spirit as well as the letter of the laws of the jurisdictions in which the company does business, but also actively foster constructive relations with internal and external stakeholders against the background of maximizing the profits and indirectly the value of the company. As such, they will be both solution and goal oriented and require to work efficiently and effectively by forming collaborations with other companies to promote public policies that mitigate the harmful externalities of corporate conduct. The in-house counsel and—by ex-

20 Cambridge Strategy Group, *supra* note 2, at 51.

21 Benjamin Heineman, The Inside Counsel Revolution: Resolving the Partner-guardian tension (American Bar Association, 2016).

tension—also the external legal counsel advising the company, will act in equal measure as trusted (and experienced) business advisors responsible for risk mitigation, compliance, and protection of the company's legal interests as well as for contributing to the achievement of the company's (financial) performance goals. As such, they will have an increasingly trans-jurisdictional and multi-disciplinary focus.[22]

Growth of in-house departments parallels a reduction in external legal expenditure with the allocation of the remaining spend depending on the nature of the work and on internal and market data analytics that identify opportunities to decrease external spend, but also to monitor and improve efficiency of their own processes. While it is not a core competence of corporations to run large legal departments, strategic, regulatory and risk factors will make it sensical to in-source and closer control certain legal service activities. Spending will be even more consolidated through panels and other means to maximize clients' buying power and the benefits of long-term cooperation between clients and their external providers. Procurement professionals will be increasingly involved (even more than they are now) in selecting outside counsel and comparing service level agreements.[23]

In this context, law firms frequently argue that given the size and risks of large-scale transactions, legal costs charged are relatively small in relation to the potential gains, and that they are considered a necessary cost of doing business. This may hold true for some very special matters, but from the perspective of in-house counsels, these high-risk transactions are the exception and they have developed a clear understanding of the different tiers of work based on the risk and importance of the matter, as very well explained by Mike Roster[24]:

> *«In-house counsels apply the 85/15 rule: For 15 percent of their legal spend, the price does not matter. It is the kind of matter litigation, corporate transaction or something similar–where the general counsel does not care about cost. And the CEO and the board do not care. It is a very important matter and cost is not the issue. But for the remaining 85 percent of their legal spend, cost is determinative. There are typically 10, 20 or more law firms and practice groups who can handle the work superbly, not just okay,*

---

22 Heineman, *supra* note 20.

23 Beaton & Kaschner, *supra* note 3, chapter 4.

24 Michael Roster, *Association of Corporate Counsel Value Challenge: Facing Up to the Challenge—The Transition*, Association of Corporate Counsel (2013), https://www.acc.com/advocacy/valuechallenge/loader.cfm?csModule=security/getfile&pageid=1365193&page=/valuechallenge/index.cfm&qstring=&title=ACC%20Value%20Challenge:%20Facing%20Up%20to%20the%20Challenge%20-%20Law%20Firm%20Metrics&recorded=1 (last visited Feb. 21, 2019) at 19.

but superbly. In light of this market reality, the legal work is going to go whoever is most competitive on cost. That does not mean the work will always go to the absolutely cheapest firm. Corporate Counsel typically know if a firm has underbid or does not understand the matter, and if that is the case, the firm will not be mandated. But the firms that have the right expertise and clearly understand what is at stake are going to be in the running and will be selected on the basis of costs.»

An external legal advisory firm that delivers services and coverage in support of such an internal function will likely have a different, extended mix of services and delivery channels, than the more either transactional or litigation-oriented suite of services that has characterized most large law firms in the past few decades. In-house teams will play more and more an important role in shaping their company's strategy in the future, well beyond the simple assessment of the company's compliance with the word of law. This requires the ability to very quickly and thoroughly assess the legal implications of different strategic scenarios and options, as to enable the company to see the law as an element to enhance competitive advantage. The future in-house counsels will not only be able to comment on compliance or risk matters, but far beyond, they will serve as active shapers of the opportunities that will arise from the law and its application in the business context and against the background of sound and extensive business expertise and judgement. The boundaries between legal advice and other forms of business advice (i.e., strategy, technology, processes) are likely to blur further in coming years. If these developments take place, the law firms that thrive will demonstrate value as deeply competent trusted advisors in such an interdisciplinary environment, moving them away from the procurement driven «vendor» approach that has emerged in recent years.[25]

C. The Business Model

One of the most interesting debates is whether the partnership business model has run its course and whether successful law firms in the future will not rather have to adapt their business structure. Indeed, the law firm partnership might be «a poor institutional choice for the delivery of legal services in today's legal market», as «its structure fails to serve virtually all of its stakeholders».[26]

---

25 Cambridge Strategy Group, *supra* note 2, at 52.

26 Jonathan Molot, *What's Wrong with Law Firms? A Corporate Finance Solution to Law Firm Short-Termism*, SOUTHERN CALIFORNIA LAW REVIEW 88–1 (2014).

However, change without careful thought can also make things unnecessarily complicated and create new issues. More lawyers and business units mean changes to the way the firm is governed and how people communicate and collaborate. Systems and processes can become misaligned, making it more difficult to get things done. As new clients, services, service delivery channels, and markets are added to the law firm's strategic portfolio, greater complexity in the organization will be inevitable, irrespective of whether the law firm maintains its partnership structure or not. Although almost all modern business theory is founded on the premise of control, and thinking holds, that people might misbehave and harm the interests of the business if there is no clear set of rules established and enforced, in today's organizations, this thinking has basically led to complicated rules, performance-incentivized remuneration and reward systems, as well as to mistrust between hierarchical levels of an organization. At the same time, this is exactly the thinking that intelligent, independent, and high-performing professionals try to reduce to the minimum when organizing themselves in partnerships. In an environment where the underlying drivers of the business are evolving quickly, in ways that are frequently not predictable, and the best strategic responses are unclear beforehand, control that is too constraining of people's ability to find solutions and implement them can be very harmful.[27]

Another criticism of the law firm partnerships model is that it places too much emphasis on current revenue generation, i.e., «profits-per-partner», and not enough focus on building long term value. However, the very same pattern also keeps listed companies focusing on quarterly earnings instead of more sustainable indicators of economic growth[28]. Generally, irrespective of the company structure, both law firm partners and corporate executives tend to sacrifice long-term value creation for short-term performance. A corporate structure with shares (and options) creates an opportunity to broaden the equity ownership but other options exist that do not reduce high performance professionals to the level of mere employees. The role ambiguities between shareholder, manager/leader, and producer that plague partnerships also afflict business structures of other professional service firms where significant equity is owned by members of the firm, and other kinds of business that are closely held by the company's employees. Instead of debating the merits of partnerships per se, a more constructive debate is around the behavior and mentality needed to help partnerships function more effectively as governance structures.[29]

There are further reasons for questioning the partnership model, e.g., the need to fund technology and other investments in the future in ways that law

27 Cambridge Strategy Group, *supra* note 2, at 57, 58.
28 Cambridge Strategy Group, *supra* note 2, at 53.
29 Beaton & Kaschner, *supra* note 3, chapter 5.

firms in some jurisdictions currently are not in a position to sustain. Today, arguably, partners have too much discretion and, as such, it is difficult to gain consensus and ensure that everybody implements agreed-to plans. Instead, for the benefit of a stronger firm offering, producer partners should be allowed less autonomy, and there should be greater separation between the roles of shareholder vs. manager/leader. Further, I am personally convinced that the alignment of shareholder, manager/leader AND producer roles is one of the differentiating strengths of a professional services law firm—therefore, partnerships will remain the best governance model for premium law firms in the future, given that groups of high performance professionals do best when they have not only an equity stake in the businesses in which they practice, but also significantly contribute to how the business is managed. It is likely, though, that better results would be obtained by enhancing collaboration and the free flow of resources (especially information) between partners and encouraging entrepreneurial behavior, rather than imposing too much «corporate» structures, governance and controls.[30]

D. More Digital

If artificial intelligence and other technology solutions are, in practice, digital enablers which will extend and augment human capabilities rather than replacing humans, the question is: Why wouldn't a law firm seek to use these types of sophisticated technology solutions (not only AI, but also others) as much as possible, to deliver better and more efficient legal services to clients? Using these technology solutions will be the new legal research and reading work, the new base for legal services and legal advice. Besides the work for which humans are inherently better suited, a large amount of joint work and joint learning between humans and the information technology tools is required to get the most out of the machines. Consequently, it will be pivotal for law firms to extend their network into a web of skilled collaborators and suppliers who provide them with digital tools to enhance their legal services offering. A limited permanent workforce will focus on the law firm`s core competencies, combined with a proven, but large ecosystem of specialists and consulting firms to draw on when specific expertise is required to complement the core legal services offering. Eventually, one law firm will also enter into collaboration relationships with other law firms renowned and active in areas with are not at the firm's core. Therefore, it is likely that law firms will not position themselves as full-service law firms—given the breath of skillset required to

30 Cambridge Strategy Group, *supra* note 2, at 53.

provide clients, especially in-house counsels, with legal services in the form and quality and within the channel desired.[31]

At the same time, given the significant spend on IT, law firms should aim to get maximum value from this capability they have been continuously expanding and developing over the last years, by putting in place an appropriate operating model that positions and establishes technology solutions as part of the service provision and not only as a means. To that end, they should structure IT governance to have senior management accountability and oversight and create seamless IT integration across the operations of the law firm on a platform that integrates tools and applications for customer relationship management, enterprise resource planning/billing, knowledge management, analytics, business information, finance, accounting, communication, and collaboration, in a way that allows, from a data management point of view, to change the tools at any point in time as to allow the law firm to quickly react to future technical developments. It is worth highlighting that knowledge management, especially, is further enabled and enhanced through technology and, with the appropriate search and retrieval tools, can be optimized in terms of quality and time (i.e., margins), enabling expertise to be leveraged beyond custom-made individual advice, unlocking the access to the (documented) know-how of the firm in an unprecedented way and short time. In addition, increasingly, analytics will replace the old-fashioned legal research and legal study work and will enable law firms to provide more quantitative information relating to legal risk management, laying the foundation for risk-based advisory approach. With increasing computer power and improved methods of data analysis, even high-volume data can be analyzed to reveal actionable patterns (systematically, and not only in due diligence or investigation situations). Legal advice will embrace visualizations and the use of graphs and charts to illustrate data and concepts. Law firms will become proficient in this area: they will use results of external analytics to quantify and assess specific legal risks relating to outcomes such as costs and awards as well as the assessment of repetitive legal process to optimize result to be aligned with clients` business goals.[32]

E. The Workplace

Apart from the addition of desktop computers, the disappearance of paper libraries, and a sharp reduction in the number of secretary work stations, the layout of most traditional law offices has not changed since decades. It still emphasizes boundaries between «lawyers» and «non-lawyers» and individu-

---

31 Cambridge Strategy Group, *supra* note 2, at 53.

32 Beaton & Kaschner, *supra* note 3, chapter 12.

als rather than openness and teamwork[33]. However, digital tools that allow people to work remotely are impacting the world of work and accelerating the change to a more flexible, location independent and permeable working environment. The law market is not immune. Today, the most modern approaches to law office design create work spaces to enhance informal collaboration that sparks innovation and creativity, resulting in new forms of collaboration with freelance pools of «lawyers» and «non-lawyers». Unfortunately, these changes have been triggered more by a drive for efficiency and cost reduction than a genuine search for ways to improve collaboration.

F. Insourcing, Outsourcing and Co-Sourcing Processes

The rise of technology solutions that enhance the provision and performance of legal services will not only disintermediate the value chain even further and force law firms to provide their legal services in combination with these solutions, but also require them to confront questions around insourcing, co-sourcing, or outsourcing some of the services (e.g., virtual data room infrastructure, eDiscovery tools, etc.) that until now were not considered an inherent part of the legal services offering. Options for sourcing will include on-demand workers, captive entities (both in relation to legal services provision and technology solutions), and near- and off-shoring tactics (as well as third-party outsourcing as parts of the legal services ecosystem). Clients' needs, especially those of in-house counsels, will be the driving force, leading law firms to regularly explore alternative sourcing options. A clear understanding of how legal work is produced, at what cost, and how it relates to risk, will be necessary to identify appropriate outsourcing targets. Quality and confidentiality may lead to issues in an outsourcing setup, but also force law firms to think more along the value chain, have more focus on a process-oriented workflow view of the provision of services, and adopt concepts of key performance and key risk indicators when providing services and advice, especially to in-house counsel functions. Consequently, price-sensitive work will qualify more and more for alternative sourcing or be performed by flexible, freelance staff. The need for this type of service provision is evidenced by the rise of specialized legal process outsourcing firms that, besides providing legal services in this manner, are also in a better position than law firms to quickly acquire and leverage disruptive technological innovations because of strong technological and process expertise, clear governance structures, and access to (and willingness to leverage) significant capital. Even in the absence of clear technological game changers, legal process outsourcing providers are expected to move their of-

33 Beaton & Kaschner, *supra* note 3, chapter 58.

ferings up the value chain as both their expertise and competition in the legal process outsourcing market increase.[34]

G. Legal Project Management

Legal project management or, in other words, the structured approach to the management of legal matters in order to meet the clients` and the law firm`s expectations in respect of quality, time and budget, will become increasingly important and it will call for experts who are specialized in this discipline. More and more, clients (especially in-house counsels) expect that their internal lawyers as well as external law firms shall apply judgment to optimize processes to achieve sound balance between quality, cycle time, efficiency, risk, and service. Technology solutions enable effective and efficient project management and process improvements but relying only on technology in implementing legal project management and neglecting the change management challenge in motivating lawyers to work differently than they are used to, will not lead to successful implementation. Lawyers, working on any large project, will have to consciously select a specific approach to legal project management, the related tools that are suited to the clients` needs, as well as the key metrics to monitor during and after the implementation, in order to capitalize on the greatest possible benefits.[35]

In the past, due to the unpredictability of the decisions and actions of clients, parties, courts, and regulators, it was difficult and a welcome excuse to not be able to deliver outcomes within preset time frames and budgets. Law firms typically allocated risks and uncertainties to clients and the related remuneration was based on the time spent rendering the very comprehensive service. Today, there is a strong and growing demand from clients to change the way fee risk is allocated. Law firms are expected to take on (at least) some of the risk through alternative fee arrangements based on the prediction of costs and resources. Legal project management and, more specifically, the experience with it, is expected to bring a certain degree of predictability (irrespective of the complexity of the matter) and, transparency. Clients want law firms to provide for each of the constituent parts of a legal matter to be reliably estimated in a standardized manner, and for possible alternative courses of action to be anticipated, resourced, and executed as needed, in line with agile project management methodology.[36]

---

34 Beaton & Kaschner, *supra* note 3, chapter 10.
35 Beaton & Kaschner, *supra* note 3, chapter 11.
36 Beaton & Kaschner, *supra* note 3, chapter 11.

H. Scale

Scale, as such, is largely discredited in business literature as a source of competitive advantage, except where lack of scale causes problems due to insufficient critical mass in areas of core competence. Many recent law firm mergers referred to «increased scale» as the key reason for the merger, but typically, mergers occur in industries that are under pressure and where at least one of the merging firms is under pressure. Another key reason mentioned in connection with law firm mergers is the formation of a «full service law firm». While this notion might have been appealing to some in-house counsel clients in the past, the successful positioning of niche players serving big corporate clients with a very limited, but deep specialization and focus on few if not only one area of expertise such as tax or labor law has eventually proven to be appealing. As such, it is likely that the leading law firms of the future will be as large as they need to be to deliver their core suite of legal services and not the full suite thereof. Generally, in a digitally-leveraged world where excellence is the defining requirement for all the humans in the business, quality will always trump scale.[37]

I. Collaboration with Other Professionals

The progress of technology solutions will eventually restrict the domain of human lawyers practicing in law firms to legal work that cannot be better done:

a. by machines; and
b. in multidisciplinary teams.

Against this background, and given the growth of the «Big 4» with respect to the provision of legal services, it is likely that a significant amount of work currently done by traditional law firms will transfer to the «Big 4»'s multi-disciplinary teams. Inevitably, law firms will create multi-disciplinary teams as well, including lawyers, digital technologists, project managers, process specialists and other professionals, to meet client needs, preferences and requests. Therefore, new forms of multi-disciplinary practices will be formed around legal cores[38]. Ultimately, the business models with the most successful delivery of services will prevail. Whether or not one agrees with this new model, the views of clients will prevail.

---

37 Cambridge Strategy Group, *supra* note 2, chapter 4.

38 Cambridge Strategy Group, *supra* note 3, at 54.

V. Bibliography

A. Hard Copy Sources

Beaton, George & Kaschner, Imme, Remaking Law Firms—Why & How (American Bar Association, 2016).

Christensen, Clayton M, The Innovator`s Dilemma—When New Technologies Cause Great Firms to Fail (Harvard Business Review Press, 1997).

Flood, John, What Do Lawyers Do? An Ethnography of a Corporate Law Firm (Quid Pro Books, 2013).

Galanter, Marc & Palay, Thomas, Tournament of Lawyers: the Transformation of the Big Law Firm (University of Chicago Press, 1991).

Heineman, Benjamin, The Inside Counsel Revolution: Resolving the Partner-guardian tension (American Bar Association, 2016).

International Legal Technology Association, Legal Technology Future Horizons (2014).

Lewin, Kurt, *Frontiers of Group Dynamics Concept, Method and Reality in Social Science; Social Equilibria and Social Change*, 1 Human Relations (1947).

Molot, Jonathan, *What's Wrong with Law Firms? A Corporate Finance Solution to Law Firm Short-Termism*, Southern California Law Review 88–1 (2014).

Porter, Michael E, Competitive Strategy: Techniques for Analyzing Industries and Competitors (Free Press, 1980).

Susskind, Richard, The End of Lawyers? (Oxford University Press, 2010).

Susskind, Richard & Susskind, Daniel, The Future of Professions (Oxford University Press, 2015).

Weill, Peter & Vitale, Michael R, Place to Space, Migrating to eBusiness Models (Harvard Business Review Press, 2001).

B. Online Sources

Cambridge Strategy Group, *Thriving at the Edge of Chaos—AI, Blockchain and the Law Firm of the Future* (2018), https://mailchi.mp/c8a7253a01c3/thriving-at-the-edge-of-chaos-download (last visited Feb. 22, 2019).

Roster, Michael, *Association of Corporate Counsel Value Challenge: Facing Up to the Challenge—The Transition*, Association of Corporate Counsel (2013), https://www.acc.com/advocacy/valuechallenge/loader.cfm?csModule=security/getfile&pageid=1365193&page=/valuechallenge/index.cfm&qstring=&title=ACC%20Value%20Challenge:%20Facing%20Up%20to%20the%20Challenge%20-%20Law%20Firm%20Metrics&recorded=1 (last visited Feb. 21, 2019).

Professor Michele DeStefano

The Secret Sauce to Teaching Collaboration and Leadership to Lawyers

The 3-4-5 Method of Innovation utilized in LawWithoutWalls

TABLE OF CONTENTS

I. The Easy Sell: In the Process of Learning How to Innovate, Lawyers Hone Leadership and Collaboration Skills[1]

It is a hard sell to convince lawyers that they need to learn how to innovate. However, when we consider the skillset and mindset that is honed in the process of learning how to innovate, this decision should be a no-brainer. This is because, as discussed in my earlier chapter in this book, the call for innovation by clients is also a call for service transformation. When clients ask their lawyers to innovate, they are asking for their lawyers to co-collaborate more proactively and with a different mindset and skillset.[2]

The easy sell is that, in the process of learning how to innovate, lawyers learn to do just that: they learn to co-collaborate and hone the mindset and skillset that clients desire. An additional and under-emphasized benefit to learning how to innovate and honing the innovator's DNA is that we also hone the DNA of leaders. When you compare the key qualities of an inclusive, adaptive leader with the key qualities of an innovator, they overlap.[3] Research demonstrates that innovators, like leaders, have high emotional intelligence and communication skills; they are empathetic, open- and growth-minded, self-aware, associative, and audacious.[4]

This is why I believe that all lawyers should try their hand at innovation, even if their business model is not broken. This is also why I believe that inno-

---

1 The material and text included in this chapter includes excerpts from a forthcoming book: Michele DeStefano, The 3-4-5 Method of Innovation for Lawyers: A Handbook of Exercises and Best Practices (forthcoming).

2 For a more thorough discussion of the skillset and mindset that lawyers need, *see* Michele DeStefano, Legal Upheaval: A Guide to Creativity, Collaboration, and Innovation in Law (Ankerwycke, 2018) at 28–55 (describing the Lawyer Skills Delta).

3 Ronald Heifetz, Marty Linsky & Alexander Groshow, The Practice of Adaptive Leadership (Harvard Business School Press, 2009).

4 Bernadette Dillon & Juliet Bourke, *The Six Signature Traits of Inclusive Leadership*, Deloitte (Apr. 14, 2016), https://www2.deloitte.com/insights/us/en/topics/talent/six-signature-traits-of-inclusive-leadership.html (last visited Apr. 14, 2019) (identifying the six essential traits of inclusive leaders as courage, cognizance, commitment, curiosity, cultural intelligence, and collaboration); Daniel Goleman, *What Makes a Leader?* Harvard Business Review (Jan. 2004), https://hbr.org/2004/01/what-makes-a-leader (last visited Apr. 12, 2019); Sunnie Giles, *The Most Important Leadership Competencies According to Leaders Around the World,* Harvard Business Review (Mar. 15, 2016), https://hbr.org/2016/03/the-most-important-leadership-competencies-according-to-leaders-around-the-world (last visited Apr. 12, 2019); Katherine Graham-Leviss, *The 5 Skills That Innovative Leaders Have in Common*, Harvard Business Review (Dec. 20, 2016), https://hbr.org/2016/12/the-5-skills-that-innovative-leaders-have-in-common (last visited Apr. 11, 2019); Bill McBean, *The 5 Characteristics of Great Leaders*, Fast Company (Jan. 24, 2013), https://www.fastcompany.com/3004914/5-characteristics-great-leaders (last visited Apr. 12, 2019); *see generally* Travis Bradberry & Jean Greaves, Leadership 2.0 (TalentSmart, 2012).

vation should be the new, key discipline in legal education for practicing and aspiring lawyers. By teaching practicing and aspiring lawyers how to innovate, we are, in turn teaching collaboration and leadership—and the lawyers don't even know it. It's like getting away with putting broccoli in someone's ice cream—it's the secret sauce.

But it's not an easy sauce to whip together. That is, although these benefits may make the need for teaching innovation an easy sell, teaching lawyers how to innovate is not an easy task. This chapter begins by explaining why this is so and why we need to utilize a method of innovation designed specifically for lawyers. It then describes the method of teaching innovation that I designed, re-designed, and tested over the past 10 years on over 200 multidisciplinary teams that included lawyers, business professionals, and law and business students: The 3-4-5 Method of Innovation for Lawyers. It then explains the secret sauce, why this new method works. Finally, this chapter concludes with a call to action.

II. Why Lawyers Need Their Own Method of Innovation

As my prior chapter explains in more detail, teaching lawyers to innovate, collaborate, and be leaders is a barrier-filled journey. Here, I will only highlight a few, starting with the hurdles associated with leadership and collaboration (leaving aside innovation, because my prior chapter describes in detail the reasons why lawyers have trouble honing the DNA of innovators).

The reality is that all lawyers need to be good leaders, whether they work in a corporate legal department, at a law firm, a government agency, a non-profit, or as a solo attorney. No matter the type, lawyers, even if they don't have a team, even if they don't *actually* practice, they lead; they lead clients, they lead social transformation, they lead regulatory efforts, they lead companies, and sometimes, they lead nations. And, when they lead, they have a lot of power and sway. As the many, many articles on leadership make clear, there are right and wrong ways to lead. In her book, *Lawyers as Leaders*, *Deborah Rhode*, Professor at Stanford Law School, makes the point that there are many lawyers in the legal profession who have the *potential* to be leaders, but because training does not focus on some of the core essential attributes to be leaders, they are not equipped with the right skills to lead *right*.[5] And she's

5 Deborah L Rhode, Lawyers as Leaders (Oxford University Press, 2013) («Although leadership development is now a forty-five-billion-dollar industry, and an Amazon search reveals close to 88,000 leadership books in print, the topic is largely missed in legal education.»). *See also* John Dean, *Teaching Lawyers, and Others, To Be Leaders*, (1) Verdict (2013), https://verdict.justia.com/2013/11/01/teaching-lawyers-others-leaders (last visited Apr. 12, 2019) (explaining that lawyers are the dominant profession of the United States Congress and Presidency); *cf.* Nick

right: Very few courses attempt to train aspiring lawyers to be successful leaders in law school. Instead, the culture and curricula at many law schools do the opposite; they discourage the attributes of adaptive leadership.[6] This appears to also be true within many law firms, as very few directly reward lawyers for being adaptive leaders (i.e., inclusive and collaborative). Thus, lawyers may be set up for failure given that we live in a changing world that demands inclusive, adaptive leadership capability from its lawyers.[7]

Worse yet, lawyers and aspiring lawyers themselves agree that lawyers lack the attributes of leaders. Recently, *Susan Sturm*, a professor at Columbia Law School, did a study on how lawyers view themselves. She provided a list of attributes and asked participants to categorize the attributes under the label «lawyer» or «leader» (explaining that any of the attributes could be used to describe both). She found the following:[8]

LAWYER	LEADER
Problem solving	Problem solving
Strategic	Strategic
Combative	Creative
Critical	Empathetic
Adversarial	Collaborative
Rule-Oriented	Risk-Taking

This research supports the conclusion that lawyers, as professionals, do not identify themselves as having the same same skillset and attributes as leaders.

Similar problems exist related to innovation and collaboration. In law school, very few courses teach collaboration or even involve collaboration. In January 2011, when I started teaching design thinking and innovation to lawyers through LawWithoutWalls («LWOW»), there was no other law school or lawyer executive education program attempting to do this. Today, there are many. I am proud to say that some of my students have now created programs in design thinking and innovation at their schools after participating as student

Robinson, *The Decline of the Lawyer Politician*, 65 (4) Buffalo L. R. 657 (Aug. 2017) (showing that there is a slow, gradual decline of lawyers in Congress and the U.S. Presidency since the 1960s).

6 Susan Sturm, *Reaction: Law Schools, Leadership, and Change*, 127 Harv. L. Rev. F. 49, 50 (2013), https://harvardlawreview.org/2013/12/law-schools-leadership-and-change/ (last visited Apr. 11, 2019).

7 *See generally*, Heifetz et al., *supra* note 3.

8 This chart comes from a paper that Susan Sturm presented at the AALS meeting in New Orleans in 2018 that has not been published yet. It is called *Lawyer Leadership: Embracing the Paradoxes*. The abstract can be found here: https://sectiononleadership.org/2019/03/08/lawyer-leadership-embracing-the-paradoxes/.

hackers in LawWithoutWalls, including *Margaret Hagan* (now director of Stanford's Design Legal Design Lab) and *Anna Pope Donovan* (now the Vice Dean of Innovation at University College London).

That said, even with these developments, many students graduate law school without being taught how to innovate or collaborate. Further, the way law school students are assessed in law school is generally on an individual basis. As *Sturm* points out, «[l]aw school cultures and curriculum tend to be highly individualistic and competitive, to encourage conformity, and to discourage risk-taking.»[9] This is also true of the cultures of law firms. Lawyers are often assessed solely on their individual contributions; i.e., the billings, origination, billable hours, etc. When lawyers are put in situations where they are supposed to collaborate (e.g., on committees or an RFP team), they often divvy up the work and end up coordinating and cooperating, but not collaborating—and even when they try to collaborate *for real*, they may not do it very well, for all the reasons discussed in my other chapter in this book.

Hundreds of interviews I've conducted of both in-house and law firm lawyers around the world support my contention that lawyers don't collaborate well. So too does my experience teaching 1000s of current and future lawyers. In addition to the lack of training and extrinsic motivation (described above), there are other inhibitors to lawyers collaborating well:

First, lawyers often don't know what we mean by *collaboration*. Recently, I was talking to a managing partner about her firm's recent re-organization by industry group and her dismay with the results thus far. She said: «You know, we learned that we are not supposed to use the word ‹cross-sell.› That's a no-no. Instead, we are supposed to use the word ‹collaborate.› But, I don't think we know what that means.»

Second, lawyers often don't know *why* they are collaborating, and without the «why», there is little incentive (intrinsic motivation) to collaborate at all, let alone collaborate *right*. (Note: My earlier chapter touts the importance of intrinsic motivation).

Third, lawyers often don't identify which parts of a project are ripe for collaboration and which should be done individually. When they are put on a team to collaborate, the default (dreaded) conclusion is that this means everyone will have to collaborate together on *everything*—which would be impossible and terribly inefficient—so they give up collaborating altogether, often before the process even begins.

Fourth, lawyers often don't recognize that «teamwork is an individual skill».[10] As a result, they don't put the effort into honing their own *individual*

---

9 *See* Sturm, *Reaction: Law Schools, Leadership, and Change*, *supra* note 6, at 50.

10 Christopher M Avery, Teamwork is an Individual Skill: Getting Your Work Done When Sharing Responsibility (Berret-Koehler Publishers, 2001).

abilities to team, nor do they attempt to identify what skills they are good at and can bring to the team to help the team collaborate better.

Lastly, the way courses on innovation, collaboration, and design thinking are described may not resonate with lawyers. While it is true that innovation is iterative, messy, unpredictable, and prone to failure, the emphasis that many design thinking methods place on these aspects can be off-putting to lawyers who (as described in my book, *Legal Upheaval*) are often risk-averse, analytical, and methodical.[11] Many methods do not identify *how* or *when* to move from one stage to another in the ideation process or *who* should be doing *what*. Many methods also do not delineate timeframes and role identification nor do they differentiate competent from incompetent failure. These are all parameters that are part of standard operating procedure for lawyers and, when removed, make us feel like we are operating too far outside of our comfort zone. Further, lawyers sometimes discount the value of design thinking methods, mistakenly believing that they are focused on designing products, instead of designing products and services.

I created the 3-4-5 Method of Innovation for Lawyers with all of these gaps in mind. The 3-4-5 Method is an innovation process grounded in design thinking principles and constructed especially for lawyers based on lawyers' temperament, training, and work preferences. It emphasizes the *how* and *who*; further, it makes the *what* and *when* super, super clear so that collaboration comes easier (and perhaps with more certainty in the process) than it might otherwise. And it does this in three phases, over four months, in five steps: hence the 3-4-5 title. Although the steps are iterative, this method details specific instructions and exercises for each step, along with deliverables, role identification, time commitment, and, importantly a timeline: the series of meetings that must occur among the team and with external advisers along the innovation journey. This method focuses on purpose, goals, accountability, and transparency. It also focuses on *service* innovation. Armed with this level of information and predictability, lawyers are willing to put in the time to get the results: new skills, new mindsets, and new behaviors—not to mention an innovation at the intersection of law, technology, and business.

III. The 3-4-5 Method of Innovation: How it Works

The 3-4-5 Method of Innovation for Lawyers teaches lawyers how to innovate by dividing the innovation journey into 3 phrases over 4 months and 5 Steps. It is designed to do three things: 1) create innovations at the intersections of

---

11 DeStefano, *Legal Upheaval, supra* note 2, at 56–70 (describing lawyers' crutches, their temperament and training, as the source of the gap in skills, behavior, and mindset).

law, business, and technology; 2) hone 21st century professional service skills desired by clients (including innovation, cultural competency, creative problem finding and solving, business planning, communication, leadership, and collaboration); and, 3) transform relationships between lawyers and clients. The ultimate vision is to develop cross-competent business leaders with excellent creative, collaborative problem finding and solving skills who delight clients by approaching service with the mindset, skillset, and behaviors of innovators.

A. Teaming: 5 Steps to a Project of Worth[12]

The 3-4-5 Method of Innovation is a team-based experiential method of learning. Each team is assigned a challenge by its employer (or its client). The challenge represents a pain point or opportunity for the assigning entity. (Generally, the person or committee of people that picks the challenge is very senior). The challenge can focus on anything that is of importance to the entity; e.g., increasing business («How can a payment provider, like Visa, collaborate with FinTech startups to navigate regulations and drive industry transformation?»); improving efficiency of the legal department («How can in-house lawyers use legal tech to enhance their value without having invest a huge amount of money in the tech?»); or enhancing corporate responsibility («How can advances in technology further a reduction in food waste?»).

After narrowing down the challenge to a manageable-sized problem, the team's charge is to create a solution to the problem (along with a prototype, business case, and commercial) and then present that solution to the relevant stakeholders. Teams accomplish all of this by following the 5 Steps to a Project of Worth (explained in further detail in my book, *Legal Upheaval*):[13]

- Step 1: Explore and Investigate the Challenge, Background, and Big Picture
- Step 2: Find and Refine the Problem or Opportunity
- Step 3: Define, Understand, and Empathize with the Target Audience
- Step 4: Solve the Problem: Ideate the Solution and Create a Prototype
- Step 5: Plan, Assess, and Test: Build a Business Case and Pitch Your Idea

The most difficult steps to progress through are Steps 2 and 3. As mentioned in my other chapter in this book, research shows the best problem solvers are the best problem finders.[14] Lawyers, trained to complex problem solve, can

12 For a more detailed explanation *see* DeStefano, *Legal Upheaval, supra* note 2, at 155–76.

13 DeStefano, *Legal Upheaval, supra* note 2, at 173–6.

14 Tina Seelig, What I Wish I Knew When I Was 20: A Crash Course on Making Your Place in the World (Harper One, 2009) at 20; Daniel H Pink, To Sell Is Human: The Surprising Truth About Moving Others (Riverhead Books, 2012) at 5; 88–9.

often prefer to jump directly to Step 4. But the challenges that the teams are assigned need to be refined and whittled down, and a consumer story needs to be uncovered and understood. And the team needs to really empathize with the target audience to ensure that the team understands *why* this problem or opportunity matters, and to ensure that they are solving a real problem (and not a symptom of the problem) for a real target audience. The 3-4-5 Method of Innovation is rigorously defined, yet we still have to repeat—and go back and forth between—steps. Sometimes, we take huge steps back and only baby steps forward. Sometimes progress feels chaotic before it feels integrative. There is no certainty that progress is made from moving from Step 1 to Step 2, or from Step 2 to Step 3, because what we find in Step 3 can send us back to Step 2. Further, we often have to go through more than one of the Seven Essential Experiences (described in more detail below) to move forward within one step.[15] However messy, the results can often be sublime.

The members of the teams are intentionally diverse in every way possible: culture, discipline, age, expertise, talents, and backgrounds. The entire team is made up of approximately 7–9 people with varying, yet very clear delineation, of roles as follows:

THE MULTI-DISCIPLINARY TEAM

CORE TEAM
- Hackers
- Team Leaders and Topic Expert

3 SUB TEAMS
- Hackers
- Team Leaders and Topic Experts
- Mentors

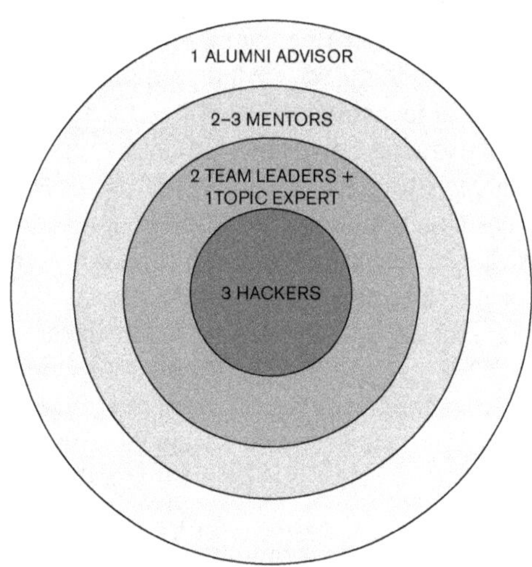

Exhibit 1, The Multidisciplinary Team.

---

15 DeStefano, *Legal Upheaval, supra* note 2, at 138–52 (describing the Seven Essential Experiences that all lawyers must go through to achieve innovation).

- Hackers: The Hackers are the doers who drive the development of the project, the problem fine-tuning, investigative research, idea generation, target audience identification, business case development, and concept creation. Although they are the drivers, and have autonomy, they work within the culture and expectations set by the Team Leaders; (think of Team Leaders as bosses/clients/primary mentors). The hackers also incorporate guidance, feedback, and expertise of Topic Experts and Mentors throughout the LWOW process.
- Team Leaders: Team Leaders are the guiders. They guide the Hackers' research methodology and outreach, oversee project development and management, aid the team in developing creative, practical solutions, and provide critical feedback on the Hackers' work (from communication style to substantive content).
- Topic Experts: The Topic Experts are substance providers. They are experts on the challenge assigned to the team. They lead and mentor by enhancing the team's understanding of the nuances of the problem and providing feedback as needed. They help identify resources that can help the team gain the necessary industry knowledge. They also advise the team about the proposed solution to ensure that it solves the business challenge in a valuable and viable way.
- Mentors: The Mentors are the supporters. They provide mentoring and advice related to problem solving, research, and professional growth and generally use their experience and connections to support the team on their journey.
- Alumni Advisors: The Alumni Advisors are the navigators. They have prior experience in the 3-4-5 Method of Innovation as a Hacker. They help the teams navigate the journey by serving as a resource to the Team Leaders in project management. They monitor the team's progress to ensure their team is on track towards meeting their deliverables.

Note: This team structure can be modulated to any organization's needs as long as there are multiple layers of sub-teams with clear identified roles and expectations.

The team is supported by a group of external coaches and boosters who help the teams to refine their solutions, identify branding, develop their business case, deal with teaming issues, and bring their Projects of Worth to life.

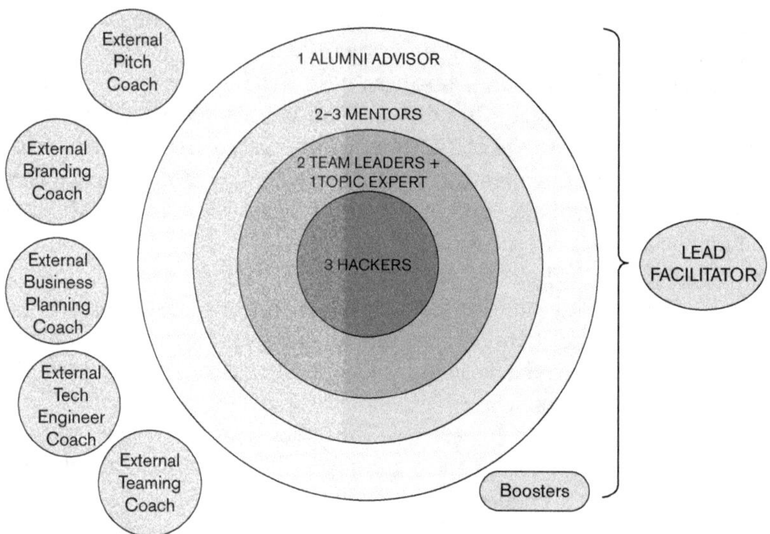

Exhibit 2, Supporting Roles.

- <u>External Coaches</u>: The External Coaches serve as coachers who are not part of any one team; they serve to help the team by providing an external perspective based on their area of expertise.
  - <u>External Pitch Coaches</u> watch and critique teams' mock pitches before the final event in order to help improve the team's substance, viability, creativity, and presentation style.
  - <u>External Branding, Business Planning, and Tech-Engineer Coaches</u> serve as specialists and help teams based on their specialty in branding, business planning, or technology.
  - <u>External Teaming Coach</u>: This person serves in the role of team saver. They work with all teams to promote individual emotional intelligence and a collective, cohesive, healthy group working dynamic. They serve as a resource and cultural compass for teams, especially those who suffer from dysfunction or conflict.
  - <u>Boosters</u> give an additional boost to teams by providing guidance and mentoring based on their own expertise. This is the smallest of all time commitments to the team, and often, Boosters are involved on an ad hoc basis.
- <u>Lead Facilitator</u>: Because the structure of the teams are fairly flat in that decision making, and accountability is pushed to all participants including the Hackers, the Lead Facilitator role requires strong leadership and close attention to each team and each project. This person must lay out big-picture vision while also being intensely focused on each team's 5 Step progress on a technical, design, and substantive level (while also be-

ing empathetic). While the leader should help instill a community culture that is fun, open, collaborative, and creative, the Lead Facilitator must be very transparent about the difficulty and hard work involved in the innovation journey and the expectations of each member to live up to their role responsibilities.[16] (Note: The number of lead facilitators required depends on the number of teams.)

B. Timing: 3 Phased Journey Over 4 Months

This method of innovation is divided into 3 phases over the course of 4 months.

Phase 1 is the KickOff, where all participants come together (in person) for two to three days filled with teaming, idea generation, and problem finding and solving exercises, along with participating in a mini-hackathon that includes an ignite presentation by the team at the end of the KickOff.[17] Importantly, the KickOff is designed to be a mini-version of the entire 3-4-5 Method. To that end, participants are trained in and practice the 5 Steps to a Project of Worth that they will have to go through *for real* after the KickOff and how they will progress successfully through the steps; i.e., by following the 3 Rules of Engagement and going through Seven Essential Experiences. The KickOff is the most essential ingredient to team success. It creates the community culture, psychological safety, and sets the protocols and expectations and, importantly, creates commitment and accountability at the community, team, and individual level. It is designed to meet three goals: 1) build an esprit de corps within and across teams; 2) knit together engaged and committed teams of individuals; and 3) prepare and get buy-in and commitment from participants for the personal and professional work ahead.

Phase 2 begins after the KickOff, during which teams work virtually for the next few months, participating in virtual team meetings with the other members on the team and also with the External Coaches and Lead Facilitator as they progress through the 5 Steps. Through these meetings, teams receive feedback to improve the viability, financial structure, and overall positioning and creativity of the project. This is part of the prototyping, testing, reassessing, and improving process. The entire community of teams also meets periodically to attend interactive virtual webinars that provide substantive training to help teams reach their goals: Topics include consumer storytelling, proto-

---

16 Gary P Pisano, *The Hard Truth About Innovative Cultures*, Harvard Business Review 62–71 (Jan.–Feb. 2019), at 70 (explaining the importance of having a balance between flatness and strong leadership and transparency «about the harder realities of innovative cultures» and the «tough responsibilities» of the participants).

17 Since 2013, The 3-4-5 Method of Innovation has also been used successfully without any in-person meetings between the teams. Instead, the KickOff and ConPosium are held entirely online.

typing, branding, and business planning, and more. The live chat during these webinars and the ability to see each other via video enable us to share our experiences and serve to keep the community engaged and connected.

Phase 2 is when the hard work gets done and lots of battles are not won. It is when the teams have to actually adopt what I describe in my book as the Three Rules of Engagement.[18] It is also when the teams have to live up to the intentions and protocols that they set at KickOff. And, at times, it is when teams face personal, professional, and cultural divides. When this happens (and it happens!), teams meet with the External Teaming Coach. The *virtual* teaming part of Phase 2 is likely the most important life-skill learned in the four-month journey. This is because the future of working (if it isn't here already) is on global teams, and virtual teaming, especially globally, is so hard. It is hard enough to get the time zones right, let alone the technology, not to mention the even harder hurdle of cultural differences and preferences as they relate to virtual interaction (and interaction in general). With this method, we learn the right ways to team virtually.

Phase 3 is the last week of the four-month journey. It is when the teams reconvene in person to present their Projects of Worth (dynamic pitch, prototype, business case, commercial, tagline, and more). We call this ending event The ConPosium. There, the teams present in front of an audience of 200 people and a multidisciplinary panel of judges including a lawyer, business professional, and venture capitalist. First and foremost, the ConPosium is a community celebration to reunite the community as one. We create that celebratory atmosphere in various ways: We include the audience with a live stream, a live private Skype chat, live public twitter, and the ability to vote on the projects, backed by tons of music. In this way, it is a bit like *American Idol* meets *Dragon's Den*. It is purposefully designed to feel nothing like a traditional conference or symposium, hence the made-up name: The ConPosium. Instead, like the KickOff, it is a transport to an alter-world. It is big and bold and *all that*. We celebrate our successes and our failures and we reunite in person after all the hard, virtual work we have done together. The ConPosium is not only about celebration. It is also a form of reflection (of monitoring and testing). Although it feels like the end of the innovation journey, it is not. As part of the 5 Steps to a Project of Worth, the ConPosium is a time for feedback, for testing our prototypes, and for analyzing our business cases. The ConPosium is an opportunity to present the problem, solution, and prototype in front of 200 people and receive critique from learned experts and from each other via the live Skype chat.

18 DeStefano, *Legal Upheaval, supra* note 2, at 85–132.

IV. The Secret Sauce: Why the 3-4-5 Method of Innovation Works[19]

The 3-4-5 Method of Innovation has been used successfully with over 200 multidisciplinary teams made up of lawyers, law and business school students, business professionals, and entrepreneurs from all over the world, and from all sorts of organizations and companies including law firms (*White & Case*, *Eversheds Sutherland*, *Pinsent Masons*, and *Cozen O'Connor*), corporate legal departments (*HSBC*, *Microsoft*, *Spotify*, *LATAM*, and *Asset Services*), consulting firms (*Accenture*, *Leah Cooper Consulting,* and *Legal Mosaic*), law companies/alternative legal service providers (*Legal Zoom*, *Elevate Services*, and *iManage*), and non-profits (*probono.net* and *the Ethics and Compliance Initiative*).

Based on our survey research over the past nine years, we know that it works. Although there are many reasons it works, we know that two contributing factors to its success are: First, there is clarity around and commitment to the roles, (filling in the) holes, and goals for the participants on each team. Second, both extrinsic and intrinsic motivation is cultivated to incent participants to learn how to collaborate towards innovation.

A. Roles, Holes, and Goals; and a P.A.C.T.

Although the KickOff is designed to create a culture of creativity, collaboration, openness and fun, the work that is done by the teams as they go through the 3-4-5 Method is difficult in unimaginable ways. In order to successfully meet the challenge of collaboration towards innovation on a multidisciplinary global team of diverse participants, we need a clear delineation of roles, responsibilities, and time commitments. What is true in our personal relationships is also true in our work relationships among teams: The expectations that aren't set are the expectations that aren't met. This is why we focus on our roles and accountability to play them.

Therefore, as explained above, the 3-4-5 Method of Innovation for Lawyers details specific instructions and exercises for each of the 5 Steps to a Project of Worth, along with role identification, and time commitment.

With respect to holes, although there is no «i» in team, we've already established that teamwork has a significant individual component.[20] In fact, individual performance issues related to teaming can create *holes* that prevent the

19 For a more detailed explanation, see DeStefano, *Legal Upheaval, supra* note 2, at 135–76.

20 Avery, *supra* note 10.

team to progress. This has happened many times over the years. The External Teaming Coach works with individuals and teams who have an individual who is a performance problem. But each person has to commit to working individually on honing the skill of teaming. Further, as individuals, we need to take individual responsibility for the success of the team. Therefore, focus on the individual is essential. Indeed, we start with the individual (as opposed to the team) and we emphasize it.

We first look to the Lawyer Skills Delta and identify our weaknesses and our strengths. We ask which three skills/attributes each participant wants to hone during this four-month journey, and which three skills/attributes they can bring to the team to help the team with their dynamics and in their quest to reach their ultimate goal.

Every participant also takes a personal work style assessment (DISC) that, generally, identifies people as dominant doers, persuasive influencers, steady cooperators, or conscientious planners. It is only by understanding our own working styles (and building a common language around them) that we can learn to work with others whose work styles are different from our own. Therefore, we create a team DISC map of each team members working styles to understand our individual and combined working styles, and to identify strengths, weaknesses, holes, and opportunities for growth. We also do this to build a common language on the team that proves useful when giving and receiving feedback.

Further, as part of the 3-4-5 Method, we teach The Three Rules of Engagement: Open Mind, Open Heart, and Open Door.[21] These rules, although they may sound corny, are essential and serve as reminders and tools to hone the individual skills and mindset along the way, as well as help us keep an eye on the «i's» in innovation (discussed in my prior chapter) so that our identity as lawyers and our individual work preferences and motivations do not get in our way. These rules are part of the community agreement we make. We ask all individuals to agree and commit to 4 Teaming Tenets:

1. <u>Collaborate with the Three Rules of Engagement: Open Mind; Open Heart; Open Door</u>: When we do this, the value we add as a collective is greater than the individual parts. A commitment to the Three Rules of Engagement, however, does not mean that we will not experience conflict; instead, it ensures that we can have healthy debate, which is essential for progress towards the solution.[22]

---

21 DeStefano, *Legal Upheaval, supra* note 2, at 85–132.

22 Pisano, *supra* note 16, at 68 («If people are afraid to criticize, openly challenge superior's views, debate the ideas of others, and raise counterperspectives, innovation can be crushed»); *see also* Patrick Lencioni, *The Five Dysfunctions of a Team: A Leadership Fable* (Jossey-Bass: November 2011) 202–04 (describing that absence of trust leads to fear of conflict which leads to artificial harmony instead of healthy conflict and constructive debate).

2. Forgive Fast and Often: Remember, research shows «collaboration is second or third nature for a large majority of us and this predisposes us to consistently revert to our more selfish ways.»[23] Forgiving others is a favor to ourselves because in forgiving we are able to let go of the negativity that came when the action triggered us.
3. Give the Gift of Candid Feedback Often: Research shows that teaming problems are often related to a performance problem of one individual as opposed to the entire team.[24] Therefore, it is important to give feedback to any individual quickly, candidly, and with empathy. This is why we say candid feedback is a gift (and an essential one). Yes, we have a culture of collaboration and psychological safety, yet research supports our focus on candid feedback. It is critical to ensure progression and, ultimately, innovation. Open, regular feedback ensures the only type of failure we experience as a team or as individuals is what Gary A. Pisano, Professor at Harvard Business School, calls «productive failure» (as opposed to «unproductive failure», which is a waste of everyone's time).[25]
4. Connect + Connect to Connect (Tech and Meeting Accountability): There are two types of connecting that all of us need to commit to for an effective virtual teaming journey. First, we need to actually be able to connect from a technological standpoint. True, sometimes the *tech gods* do not enable us to have a strong connection with video and audio. In those moments, we need to «forgive fast and often», because our teammates are as upset as we are. Other times, however, we have not done what we should to ensure that our tech works so that we are physically *present*. The second type of connecting is the the kind that is hard virtually, and that is connecting with focus and staying mentally *present* (which is why we always keep our videos on during all virtual meetings).

We then turn to team goals. Clear team goals are the key to teaming. Just as there are right and wrong ways to lead, there are right and wrong ways to team. The right way begins by establishing purpose not only for the community and the teams but also for the sub-teams and individuals on the team. This has been a key component of the 3-4-5 Method of Innovation for years and recently has been substantiated. *Carlos Valdes-Dapena*, in his book, *Lessons from Mars*, discusses the importance of «crystallizing intent» for individuals, sub-groups, and the total team.[26] At a LWOW KickOff, each individual, sub-team, and team makes a P.A.C.T. that sets out why we are going on this four-month jour-

---

23 Carlos Valdes-Dapena, Lessons from Mars: How One Global Company Cracked the Code on High Performance Collaboration and Teamwork, (Change Makers Books, 2018) at 20.

24 Valdes-Dapena, *supra* note 23, at 179–206.

25 Pisano, *supra* note 16, at 65–6.

26 Valdes-Dapena, *supra* note 23, at 179–206.

ney, what we hope to achieve as individuals and a team, and a commitment to the community culture and the culture and creative cadence of our individual teams based on open discussion about preferences and work styles:

- (P for purpose) We identify and distinguish between group, sub-group, and individual purpose; i.e., why we are working on this project, and why we care about this project.
- (A for agreements) We set expectations around roles, responsibility, and accountability and, importantly, we decide what we will collaborate on versus delegate, divide, and be responsible for individually. We also memorialize, in writing, our community, individual, and team agreements.
- (C for creative cadence) We work together to identify our work style preferences and how we want to work together as a team, including communication style, technology, and response time.
- (T for Timing) Teams map their own timing for when they will meet. We also map out the process and timing for progress as a community. We also get really specific on the timeline, meeting schedule, and deliverables, because working on a multidisciplinary, virtual team is complex and the journey through the 3-4-5 Method of Innovation is filled with virtual meetings of different types and challenges. We review the series of what we call «milestone» meetings that must occur among the team and with external advisers along the innovation journey. We provide this information in two different formats. First, we provide a chart that gives a week-by-week view of what meetings/webinars happen and when (indicating date, time, type, and who needs to attend). Second, we provide an outline that describes the purpose, format, preparation, and expected deliverables for each of these official/milestone meetups, including information on who should attend, who should be responsible for sending meeting recaps and takeaways to the entire team, and immediate next steps following each meeting.

This P.A.C.T. helps the team understand how they will *team* on a go-forward, creates accountability at all different levels, and in so doing, it enhances collaboration.[27]

27 Pisano, *supra* note 16, at 69 («There is nothing inherently inconsistent about a culture that is both collaborative and accountability-focused … Accountability and collaboration can be complementary and accountability can drive collaboration.»).

B. Extrinsic and Intrinsic Motivation

As discussed in my prior chapter, research demonstrates that we need both extrinsic and intrinsic (inner commitment) motivation to change behavior.[28] With the 3-4-5 Method of Innovation for Lawyers, we get both.

Extrinsic motivators (external rewards) are baked into the method. First, volunteering or being selected to be a part of a team that is going to go on a four-month innovation journey to solve a problem identified by a senior leader at one's organization (or client) is an honor. Also, the fact that the company is paying for the participation; i.e., that innovation is being made a compensated part of one's job is extrinsic motivation as well. Second, an extrinsic motivator is the opportunity to grow and shine; given the importance of the challenge, the time and money the company has invested, and the ending presentation in front of key stakeholders and peers, the stakes are high—not to mention the innovation that may save thousands of dollars or generate revenue.

The 3-4-5 Method of Innovation also contains the three key ingredients that, according to research, cultivate intrinsic motivation among professionals including lawyers: 1) autonomy (sense of control and having a choice); 2) competence (i.e., mastery); and, 3) relatedness (i.e., connection or sense of purpose).[29] I will discuss each in turn.

1. Control/Autonomy

According to organizational psychology research, the key to making sure that people feel a sense of control/autonomy is to involve them in the goal-setting process and implementation plan.[30] This is one of the reasons why we have the teams make their own P.A.C.T.s. Additionally, no matter what role a participant plays, the team has choice over their work and final Project of Worth. Research shows that when people have a choice, they feel a great sense of autonomy.[31] True, teams get a lot of feedback, advice, mentoring, and coach-

---

28 *See generally* Daniel H Pink, Drive: The Surprising Truth About What Motivates Us (reprt. ed. 2011); *see generally* Nik Kinley & Shlomo Ben-Hur, Changing Employee Behavior: A Practical Guide for Managers (Palgrave MacMillan, 2015), Kindle Edition, location 810–28 of 4884.

29 Kinley & Ben-Hur, *supra* note 28, at 817–33; *cf.* David Rock, *SCARF: A Brain-Based Model for Collaborating with and Influencing Others*, NeuroLeadership Journal, https://www. epa.gov/sites/production/files/2015-09/documents/thurs_georgia_9_10_915_ovello.pdf (last visited Dec. 12, 2018) (explaining the five domains of human social experience that can activate our brain and trigger people into threat mode as an acronym SCARF: S for status, C for certainty, A for autonomy, R for relatedness, and F for Fairness). Research on lawyers also shows that these three ingredients are critical for lawyers to experience high well-being. *See,* e.g., Lawrence S Krieger & Kennon M Sheldon, *What Makes Lawyers Happy? A Data-Driven Prescription to Redefine Professional Services?*, 83 George Washington Law Review 579–588 (Feb. 2015).

30 Kinley & Ben-Hur, *supra* note 28, at 843.

31 *Id.* at 883.

ing, but the teams (as a whole and as individuals) have a lot of options and opportunity to make decisions. Consider that the challenge that the team is originally assigned is always broader than the problem the team ends of solving. This gives teams lots of options during the problem finding and narrowing process that happens in Steps 2 and 3 in the 5 Steps to a Project of Worth. The teams decide how to narrow in on a manageable-sized problem for a discreet target audience. Importantly, they do so with some guidance. As mentioned above, the 3-4-5 Method is rigorously planned out on purpose to help teams navigate key decisions which, given the science of how people make choices, is essential.[32] As Pisano points out, the better culture for innovation is one that inspires experimentation but with strict discipline.[33]

2. Competence

Research demonstrates that people are more motivated to change their behavior when they feel competent to do so.[34] This does not mean that people do not want to be challenged or that the goals cannot be tough. Quite the contrary. Studies have shown that regardless of role or level, people who view their job as challenging experience greater job satisfaction and feelings of success.[35] In fact, psychological theory suggests that positioning behavior-change as a challenge inspires people to change—especially if you emphasize the person's abilities (strengths) that will enable them to meet the challenge, give praise for progress, and instill a sense of pride in the work that they are engaging in.[36] At a LWOW KickOff, we have all individuals identify the skills that they want to focus on honing (that are challenging to them) and we also have them identify the skills that they excel at and can bring to the team to help the team; i.e., we position the skills-building as a challenge and also focus on the strengths of each individual.

We also give the teams a lot of tools to measure progress and to receive praise for that progress. First, as mentioned above, we practice the Three Rules of Engagement, which become second nature over time. Second, we train the teams that there are Seven Essential Experiences that all teams must go through to get from their large problem to their narrower problem and solution. These experiences are tools for how to progress from problem to solution. For example, *falling in love* is an analogy for how to approach the problem-finding

---

32 *Id.* at 895.

33 Pisano, *supra* note 16, at 67.

34 Kinley & Ben-Hur, *supra* note 28, at 922.

35 Andrew J Elliot, & Judith M Harackiewicz, *Goal setting, achievement orientation, and intrinsic motivation: a mediational analysis,* 66 (5) Journal of Personality and Social Psychology 968 (1994); Gary P Latham & Edwin A Locke, *Enhancing the benefits and overcoming the pitfalls of goal setting,* 35 (4) Organizational Dynamics 332–40 (2006).

36 Kinley & Ben-Hur, *supra* note 28, at 970–73.

process. We tell the teams that they need to fall in love with their problem and the consumer (the target audience experiencing the problem). We urge them to try to recall how it felt when they first fell in love with someone. Back then (when they were in love), they were likely filled with curiosity. They wanted to know everything about their love interest: their background, past loves, what makes them happy and sad, etc.. They maybe even found interesting the mundane; e.g., how that person got ready for bed at night, or held the steering wheel while driving. Back then, they asked questions about everything. Similarly, now, we want them to ask question upon question, dig deeper and deeper until they know every in—and—out about the problem and the target audience. So, by and large, the Seven Essential Experiences serve as emotional measures so that people feel competent that what they are feeling is normal; further, they are reminders to ensure each person is putting effort into teaming. Lastly, they also serve as tools to help the team understand the problem, refine the problem, build a consumer story, and create a solution, business case, and prototype.

The 3-4-5 Method is purposefully segmented into 5 Steps so that teams can see their progression, and realize that even if steps are done out of sequence or repeated, each meeting is a measurable milestone for the team. Lastly, the reason we call our end results *Projects of Worth* is because in only four months, we can't guarantee that each team will actually create an innovation; i.e., a viable solution that can be brought to life to solve the problem. What we can guarantee is the change in mindset, skillset, and behaviors talked about above. As long as each person individually commits to the Three Rules of Engagement, Seven Essential Experiences, and 5 Steps to a Project of Worth, there is no way to fail, even if the innovation fails, because we have failed with competence and we have grown as leaders and collaborators.

3. Connectedness/Relatedness

The three phases in the 3-4-5 Method are designed purposefully to create community and connection i.e., relatedness. The KickOff is a bonding experience above all else that sets teams up to team with empathy and a feeling of connectedness. The virtual teaming phases includes webinars in which the entire community re-groups together as one to learn and engage. This keeps us connected not only to our teams and sub-teams, but the community at large. Further, each team is deeply connected to the goals of the project because their charge is to solve a real challenge that a client or their organization is facing; furthermore, the team has selected the narrower problem with which they fell in love.[37] In the process of going through the 5 Steps, most teams have to start over at some point. When they do, as long as the starting over was not due to

37 *Id.* at 991 («It is about how connected people feel to both goals and other people.»).

incompetence or irresponsibility, we celebrate the death of the killed idea and go back to find a different problem or solution with which to fall in love, and to which we will commit. So by the end, there isn't a team still teaming that isn't completely connected to its project and its purpose. Plus, the team goes through this journey together and builds a level of connection beyond that which was built at KickOff.

In sum, people know why they are teaming, they are personally connected to the problem they are solving and to each other, and they have a *practical* method to get there.[38] Further, everyone on the team is focused not only on solving the problem but also on honing a new skillset and mindset. The innovation at the end? That's just the icing. The cake is that change in behavior that results. The cake is honing the DNA of an innovator who is a leader and can collaborate with others the way clients desire.

V. Conclusion: A Call to Action for Law Schools, Law Firms, and Legal Departments

Teaching innovation to lawyers, therefore, answers three calls: the call for innovation, the call for collaboration, and and the call for leadership from lawyers. However, there is one call that has not been answered, and that is the call to law schools, law firms, and legal departments to provide a culture that inspires lawyers and aspiring lawyers to learn how to innovate (intrinsic motivation) and that provides external rewards to those that do. The 3-4-5 Method of Innovation can be used in any organization on any multidisciplinary team. Currently, it is being practiced via LawWithoutWalls by over 35 law and business schools and 16 organizations in the law marketplace. Over the past decade, hundreds of teams have embarked upon the 3-4-5 Method-guided journey. Our global LWOW community totals more than 2500 professionals who stay involved to nurture their new skillsets, mindsets, and supportive community—to keep that innovator's DNA pulsing, and keep the intrinsic motivation alive. So I end with a call to you, the reader, to find a way to get your organization to put on a new suit by giving the 3-4-5 Method of Innovation for Lawyers a try.

38 *Id.* at 1003–27.

VI. Bibliography

A. Hard Copy Sources

AVERY, CHRISTOPHER M, TEAMWORK IS AN INDIVIDUAL SKILL: GETTING YOUR WORK DONE WHEN SHARING RESPONSIBILITY (Berret-Koehler Publishers, 2001)

BRADBERRY, TRAVIS & GREAVES, JEAN, LEADERSHIP 2.0 (TalentSmart, 2012).

DESTEFANO, MICHELE, THE 3-4-5 METHOD OF INNOVATION FOR LAWYERS: A HANDBOOK OF EXERCISES AND BEST PRACTICES (forthcoming).

DESTEFANO, MICHELE, LEGAL UPHEAVAL: A GUIDE TO CREATIVITY, COLLABORATION, AND INNOVATION IN LAW (Ankerwycke, 2018).

Elliot, Andrew J, & Harackiewicz, Judith M, *Goal setting, achievement orientation, and intrinsic motivation: a mediational analysis,* 66 (5) JOURNAL OF PERSONALITY AND SOCIAL PSYCHOLOGY 968–980 (1994).

HEIFETZ, RONALD, LINSKY, MARTY & GROSHOW, ALEXANDER, THE PRACTICE OF ADAPTIVE LEADERSHIP (Harvard Business School Press, 2009).

KINLEY, NIK & BEN-HUR, SHLOMO, CHANGING EMPLOYEE BEHAVIOR: A PRACTICAL GUIDE FOR MANAGERS (Palgrave MacMillan, 2015).

Krieger, Lawrence S & Sheldon, Kennon M, *What Makes Lawyers Happy? A Data-Driven Prescription to Redefine Professional Services?*, 83 GEORGE WASHINGTON LAW REVIEW 579–588 (Feb. 2015).

Gary P Latham & Edwin A Locke, *Enhancing the benefits and overcoming the pitfalls of goal setting,* 35 (4) ORGANIZATIONAL DYNAMICS 332–40 (2006).

PINK, DANIEL H, TO SELL IS HUMAN: THE SURPRISING TRUTH ABOUT MOVING OTHERS (Riverhead Books, 2012).

PINK, DANIEL H, DRIVE: THE SURPRISING TRUTH ABOUT WHAT MOTIVATES US (reprt. ed., Riverhead Books, 2011).

Pisano, Gary P, *The Hard Truth About Innovative Cultures*, HARVARD BUSINESS REVIEW 62–71 (Jan.–Feb. 2019).

RHODE, DEBORAH L, LAWYERS AS LEADERS (Oxford University Press, 2013).

Robinson, Nick, *The Decline of the Lawyer Politician*, 65 (4) BUFFALO L. R. 657 (Aug. 2017).

SEELIG, TINA, WHAT I WISH I KNEW WHEN I WAS 20: A CRASH COURSE ON MAKING YOUR PLACE IN THE WORLD (Harper One, 2009).

VALDES-DAPENA, CARLOS, LESSONS FROM MARS: HOW ONE GLOBAL COMPANY CRACKED THE CODE ON HIGH PERFORMANCE COLLABORATION AND TEAMWORK, (Change Makers Books, 2018)

B. Online Sources

Dean, John, *Teaching Lawyers, and Others, To Be Leaders*, (1) VERDICT (2013), https://verdict.justia.com/2013/11/01/teaching-lawyers-others-leaders (last visited Apr. 12, 2019).

Dillon, Bernadette & Bourke, Juliet, *The Six Signature Traits of Inclusive Leadership*, DELOITTE (Apr. 14, 2016), https://www2.deloitte.com/insights/us/en/topics/talent/six-signature-traits-of-inclusive-leadership.html (last visited Apr. 14, 2019).

Giles, Sunnie, *The Most Important Leadership Competencies According to Leaders Around the World,* HARVARD BUSINESS REVIEW (Mar. 15, 2016), https://hbr.org/2016/03/the-most-important-leadership-competencies-according-to-leaders-around-the-world (last visited Apr. 12, 2019).

Goleman, Daniel, *What Makes a Leader?* Harvard Business Review (Jan. 2004), https://hbr.org/ 2004/ 01/what-makes-a-leader (last visited Apr. 12, 2019).

Graham-Leviss, Katherine, *The 5 Skills That Innovative Leaders Have in Common*, Harvard Business Review (Dec. 20, 2016), https://hbr.org/2016/12/the-5-skills-that-innovative-leaders-have-in-common (last visited Apr. 11, 2019).

McBean, Bill, *The 5 Characteristics of Great Leaders*, Fast Company (Jan. 24, 2013), https://www.fastcompany.com/3004914/5-characteristics-great-leaders (last visited Apr. 12, 2019).

Rock, David, *SCARF: A Brain-Based Model for Collaborating with and Influencing Others*, NeuroLeadership Journal, https://www.epa.gov/sites/production/files/2015-09/documents/thurs_georgia_9_10_915_ovello.pdf (last visited Dec. 12, 2018).

Sturm, Susan, *Reaction: Law Schools, Leadership, and Change*, 127 Harv. L. Rev. F. 49, 50 (2013), https://harvardlawreview.org/2013/12/law-schools-leadership-and-change/ (last visited Apr. 11, 2019).

Maria Leistner[1]

The Importance of Diversity

And how it will change the practice of Law forever and for the better (with help from Technology)

TABLE OF CONTENTS

1 The essay reflects the personal opinion of the author and although there might be research supporting the views in this essay, it is written as a thought-piece based entirely on the author's personal experience. The statements do not claim to correspond to the position of UBS.

I. Introduction

Not long ago, I was attending a conference in Europe organised by a big law firm, with the participation of top partners from various major law firms, predominantly European but also American and Asian. A diverse forum, one may argue, as to multi–cultural representation, but certainly not as to gender (there were six women in the total of over hundred participants) or race (two Asian faces only) or age, for that matter. The typical participant was male, middle aged, and Caucasian, in the «senior partners of law firms» mould (dress code included). As the conference went on, my agitation levels went higher too. The first two panels, dedicated to technology, innovation, and changing law firms were all male only. I was invited to speak on the third panel on «talent development», with four female partners and one male participant. That sudden shift of the majority of the female participants to the speakers' podium resulted in only two female colleagues remaining in the auditorium. I was fuming by then and made my frustration clear at the outset of the panel discussions—why is it that women were invited to the talent discussion topic but not to the innovation or technology related ones, I asked? We know the answer: «women» equals «soft skills» and «emotional intelligence», all these characteristics often underlined as strengths, but actually left to the female management constituency as something that others are «not as strong at», ergo should not be / do not want to be bothered with. I have, at least, as much to contribute on the «hard topics» as I have on the soft ones, I stated clearly. Possibly, even more than many of the contributors on those panels. Indeed, I thought that there were very few meaningful remarks on innovation and technology, and few meaningful thoughts on how the law firms should and will embrace the exponential changes that these will bring to the legal profession. Well, no surprise there—the lack of diversity of the forum and panels was only the external side of the lack of desire to embrace change and transform into a «law firm of the future» and, consequently, lack of substance when discussing the «topics of the future». And, before someone accuses me of a biased client's law firm bashing intent, let me be clear—this is the status currently of the legal industry overall, not only limited to the law firms, but in-house departments too.

Indeed, the composition of the senior echelons of the in-house legal departments is perhaps only slightly better than that of the law firms in terms of diversity (any type of diversity in terms of make-up or behaviours). The lack of diversity there reflects the state of the in-house departments overall and is, in my view, one of the main reasons for lack of major changes within the general counsel functions too. I have spent a significant part of my time whilst in in-house positions in the past several years trying to persuade my in-house colleagues that we need to change, to modernise ourselves, to innovate, in order to find the relevance that our people need to feel so that they stay in the profession and, for many, in the financial industry.

The legal industry, I argue in this paper, overall, is still one of the most conservative ones, with changes happening much more slowly than in other industries. Old models of legal service of both law firms and in-house departments, lack of diversity at a senior level in particular, lack of strategic thinking and innovation, insufficient advancement of technology usage, lack of understanding that being a trusted adviser doesn't mean reactive advice through long legal memoranda, the rise of compliance and regulatory specialists and industries chipping big chunks off the traditional domains of the traditional legal advisory services, lack of (desire to get a better) understanding of the operational and other risks of the companies and how legal risk fits in the overall risk profile of the firms, this list can go on for a while. All these are factors that have contributed to the decrease of prestige of the legal profession, of the interest in legal studies as well as of the desire of legal professionals to stay longer in the more traditional models of the profession and the profession overall. Technological advancements are, however, changing the legal profession and we need to embrace them in order to keep transforming the legal services industry, as others have argued in this book, but, most importantly—to keep attracting and retaining the best talent. And, whilst my observations are based on my experience with big law firms and multinational financial players, creating an environment that allows our people to thrive is a must for everyone—and it will need to happen in different ways going forward.

II. Current Status–Seriously Suboptimal

Long hours (not necessarily always fully spent in the most efficient and productive way), old models of selling time as value, work product consisting of memoranda (heavily disclaimed), advice without often understanding the business / project / transaction well and without ability to be really impactful, analytical skills often underused by clients who think they «know best», being dismissed as mere scribes and often left with work that is outside the legal advice or legal risk management area, but of administrative or execution character and often avoided by others, baulked at when it comes to how expensive they are. I can go on for a while in that spirit.

In the past, the counterargument for becoming a lawyer has been the relative prestige of the job and, in particular should one be able to make it to the higher echelons of the profession, the pay. Nowadays, with the changing of the job profiles throughout different industries, elimination of jobs, new roles cropping up all over, being a lawyer does not seem to be as attractive as it was only a decade ago. The financial crisis in 2008 had a number of effects on the legal industry, starting with the decreased interest in applications for law schools and less opportunities for the law school graduates.[2] The tendency continued for a while and, whilst there seems to be somewhat of a rebound in 2018 in particular, the interest in legal studies is far from what it used to be before the crisis.[3] The most prestigious law schools seem to still be able to attract candidates, not near the previous numbers, but enough to keep them going strong, however, the less prominent schools are less capable of attracting candidates.[4] Different explanations are given for this decrease, a lot to do with the change in the financial industry post crisis, the emergence of different,

---

2 **Theme:** Poor state of the legal job market is affecting graduate recruitment
See Andrew Soergel, *Hiring Outlook Bleak for New Law Grads* (Aug. 18, 2016, 4:19 PM), USNews, https://www.usnews.com/news/articles/2016-08-18/hiring-outlook-bleak-for-new-law-grads (last visited Feb. 3, 2019):
The article outlines the fact that 2008 had a major impact on the legal industry, even going as far as describing the bubble bursting. This resulting decrease in opportunity for potential law graduates has pushed applicants into other fields of studies that are safer bets.
«Newly minted law graduates from the class of 2015 locked down fewer private practice jobs than any graduating class in nearly two decades, according to a new report from the National Association for Law Placement.
Fewer than 34,000 2015 alums had landed jobs as of March 15—about 10 months after the typical May graduation, leaving adequate time to study for and take the local bar exam—according to the report published Wednesday. Less than 23,000 found a job in the private sector, where wages are typically higher.
The last time employment metrics were that low was 1996, when the country held more than 25 million fewer workers than it does today.»

3 **Theme:** Application levels being low is an opportunity for applicants
See Ilana Kowarski, *Less Competitive Law School Admissions a Boon for Applicants* (Aug. 8, 2017, 8:30 AM) USNews, https://www.usnews.com/education/best-graduate-schools/top-law-schools/articles/2017-08-08/law-school-admissions-less-competitive-than-2008 (last visited Feb. 3, 2019):
«Turmoil in the legal job market and pessimism about the future of the legal profession have deterred some people from applying to law school». A clear distinction seems to be made between top ranked universities (i.e., the top 14 in this specific article) and the rest of the universities. A graphic demonstrates the different levels of applications and the effect across the downward trend since 2008. The average of the total law school in the US was impacted much more heavily (applications halved during this period) compared to the average of the top 14 universities in the US (decreasing by a little over 20% during the period 2008–2016).»

4 **Theme: 2018 applications on the rise**
See Ilana Kowarski, *Law School Applications Increased This Year* (Jan. 29, 2018, 8:00 AM), USNews, https://www.usnews.com/education/best-graduate-schools/top-law-schools/articles/2018-01-29/law-school-applications-increased-during-president-trumps-first-year (last visited Feb. 3, 2019):
This USNews article reports an upward trend in law school applications in 2018 (approx. 11 per cent on the previous year), arguing that this is driven by economic growth, political news cycle and steep tuition discounts. The last paragraph of the article indicates that the increase in applications is not spread evenly among all schools. The surge is more pronounced in top schools or where there is already a high application rate compared to other schools:
«Parrish, of the Maurer School of Law, says the recent uptick in law school applications is probably not spread evenly across all law schools. So applicants to law schools with large applica-

new fields that now attract the best talent offering opportunities (technology opportunities being often cited as the most attractive ones). At the end, what matters is that fewer people choose law as a career long term, opting instead for other opportunities, be it as they are technologically more interesting, offer challenges and are linked to areas closer to their interests and aspirations, make them feel more impactful and / or allow for a better work—life balance. Who can blame them? However, I do worry about the legal profession (overall) not being able to recruit and retain among the most talented people, a worry which no doubt is shared by other industries these days too.

The composition of the law firms and legal departments is wrong, to start with. As many other areas, law is still dominated by white male practitioners. Changes have been happening, but not fast enough. This is evidenced by the current statistics as evidenced by an example on North American law firms' gender diversity.[5] Statistics vary from country to country and region to region, but the overall outcome is clear, the larger law firms have rarely progressed senior female representation above a quarter of the partners / general counsel population, and that is often only in countries / regions where gender diversity overall has progressed in the past decades. The problem perpetuates itself by

---

tion increases will face much stiffer competition, he says, but applicants to schools with minimal application increases won't feel much impact from this trend.»

5 *See* Marc Brodherson, Laura McGee & Mariana Pires dos Reis, *Women in law firms*, McKinsey & Company (October 2017), https://www.mckinsey.com/featured-insights/gender-equality/women-in-law-firms (last visited Feb. 3, 2019):

The article highlights the progress taking place in gender diversity in North American firms but also outlines the significant gap that remains to be addressed.

«Law firms have many of the right policies and programs in place to improve gender diversity, but more can be done to translate stated commitments into measurable outcomes.»

«As part of our broader Women in the Workplace 2017 research, we conducted a deep dive on women in law firms in North America… The survey finds that law firms are taking important steps to increase gender equality. They are providing senior-leadership support to advance attorneys' careers and offering programs that provide flexibility and address major work-life balance issues.

But these efforts have had limited success. Only 19 percent of equity partners are women, and women are 29 percent less likely to reach the first level of partnership than are men. We found that law firms face higher attrition among women than men at the equity partner level and that the gender gap is much wider in law firms than in other industries. Women of colour face an even steeper climb, with their representation dropping significantly at all levels in the pipeline. Female attorneys perceive less commitment to gender equality and a more uneven playing field at law firms than their male colleagues.

Law firms clearly have more work to do, not just in implementing policies and programs but also in fundamentally changing nonpartner attorneys' perceptions of their efforts. For example, female attorneys (and many of their male colleagues) fear that participating in flexible-work programs will damage their careers. The question now is how those firms that have invested in—and recognize—the benefits of gender equality translate their stated commitments into measurable outcomes.»

the lack of concerted desire of managers in the field to change and adapt new ways of operation to foster different types of diversity overall. After a long discussion of pros and cons on talent retention and development models at another forum, a senior partner questioned why this was discussed at all, whether we are not spending too much of an effort «on the millennials» and the need to «pamper» them (as, indeed «no one pampered us»). «*Maria, he said, as the client in the room,would you have accepted to be told that we cannot deal with your matter tonight, as the responsible lawyer needs to go and spend time with family / see his / her kids*». «*Oh, absolutely, I will accept that, I responded, I do know that there is only a very small minority of requests that require actually immediate attention. I would be happy with a delivery within a realistic deadline most of the time*». Having been in the profession for a very long time, I am well aware that very few things need to be done «now, immediately», most certainly can wait, if not for another day, then for a later moment that same day, perhaps after spending some precious time with family. The myth of «immediate delivery always needed» needs to be rebuked, by the clients and by the lawyers alike. Are all clients with that mind set already? No, they are not. But that is where law firm management and managers within the in-house function in charge of the task can interfere and correct the right time for delivery, to allow for lawyers to spend meaningfully personal time and, in that way, contribute to the overall atmosphere at the workplace. Many women abandon the legal profession, both in law firms and in-house because they do not have this flexibility at the work place to deliver and progress without having to do that with the old fashioned barriers of «time spent in the office». Men change too—the times of children not seeing their fathers during the week because of work and (often long) commute are going away. The new generation of fathers (my own husband being one of the shining examples of it) want to see their children also during the week, want to spend time with them not only on weekend or during holidays. The importance of time with family, of being able to have more control (or flexibility) over how you spend your time is moving up the value chain. The prestige of the legal profession is moving down. A work environment that does not cater to that dynamic keeps losing talent.

This is not necessarily a new phenomenon. The move of lawyers from the private practice to in-house teams that has resulted in more and more talented lawyers preferring the in-house path to the private practice is usually motivated by this desire to better control how they spend their time. That has increased the attractiveness of the in-house jobs over those of the law firms. The other major attraction for general counsel jobs is the overall shift of the in-house legal work away from the law firm advice work, more towards risk management, also perceived as a good proposition for those lawyers who want to be close to business and its strategy, be able to contribute in a more impactful and more diverse way (vs. simply «providing legal advice»). With the increased divergence between in-house and law firm legal roles, the in-house proposition has won over lawyers, who would otherwise have pursued the standard route of partnership. Women have also preferred the in-house departments for their greater flexibility and agile working opportunities. That shift doesn't help the in-house departments in long run, as they have been also slow to change, but it certainly demonstrates that loss of talent for the law firms is real and not from yesterday.

III. Different Work Environment

I was talking to newly qualified lawyers (it happened to be Germany in this particular case, but it is a conversation which I have had elsewhere on various occasions), we were in a relaxed environment post a successful project and I was joking about having to sleep for (as short as) 15 minutes under my desk when working for a law firm in London, sometimes even these 15 minutes being a luxury for stretches of 48 and more hours, when chasing deadlines on transactions. The looks on the younger lawyers' faces were showing their amazement. «*Maria, they explained politely, we have heard similar stories from other (older) colleagues too, but this is definitely not the type of jobs or work environment that we are seeking. Indeed, we do not want to work these long hours on what is, often repetitive work*». It is difficult to find people willing to spend a lot of hours at work, despite the still attractive remuneration offered—this is a complaint I hear often, by bankers and senior lawyers alike, when discussing challenges related to talent development. The millennials, generation Z, and those after them are often accused of not being willing to work hard and having a short attention (translate also, retention) span, looking for new excitements. Why wouldn't they? Being raised in an environment where information is as easily available as air, if not easier, where PlayStation, and other games, as well as internet overall allow for instant gratification and where communication happens outside phones and (remember those?) faxes (I have not had a land line at work or at home for years). Technology is what fascinates them, developing it further or using it in their jobs, using it to achieve the work life balance that they strive for. Perhaps they are not as willing as previous generations to spend long hours in (often) monotonous tasks (due diligence, anyone?). However, they do possess technological skills that keep developing at a rapid pace and that are the envy of the older generations (I do still know people who ask their assistants to print out their emails received during the day, so that they can write on each of them with a pen (!) what response the secretary should type back). In addition, with their increased ability to access and process information, with their knowledge range much more expanded because of the variety of info flows they have been exposed to since an early age, they also are much more used to operating in cognitive diverse groups. This is a huge advantage for the employers, as the ability to bring in different skills to problem solving is paramount; however it also underlines (even further) the need to have diverse teams that allow for that cognitive diversity to thrive. Putting it differently, the new generations crave working in a diverse environment that includes access to different intellectual angles, approaches, and perspectives (even more than generation of the past). The «one size fits all» environment of many institutions will not be right for many in the long term. Nor will these new generations wait for many years in a row to reach the next promotion level as set by rigid corporate prescriptions.

In addition, their different communication styles and expectations and the desire to express themselves in less restricted ways does not work with companies' (outdated often and certainly very restrictive) social media policies. This is an irreversible trend that we also see among many clients, notably in Asia, where the use of WeChat and similar channels now takes over as means of communications between institutions and clients, despite the challenges that it poses from a regulatory perspective for the companies.

Recently, *Riccarda Zezza*, CEO of MAAM said: «*Millennials are the new women. They do not fit.*».[6] This struck me as so correct, it nailed the point in its simplicity. Why hadn't I thought about it earlier? Exactly in the ways women did not exactly tick the boxes in the past, these new generations do not. Yet, they are judged by old standards, squeezed into parameters predetermined for them by previous generations, inclusive only for people who fit in the existing workforce mould. This creates barriers to progress. The inability to better integrate women is now becoming an inability to offer meaningful opportunities and a desired work environment for the new generations, irrespective of gender.

If we do not adapt the legal profession environment to cater to how they see it should be, we will keep losing them.

IV. Impact / Meaningfulness: On the Rise

Impact and meaningfulness of the job, moving away from how much time we clock and bill, away from «shuffling paper» becomes more and more important. This reflects the overall shift in interests between generations. We see this in the private banking industry also, for example—where the older generation is still very driven by wealth accumulation and optimization, the younger generations focus on sustainable investments and social impact. Same is valid for

---

6 Riccarda Zezza, CEO of MAAM (Maternity as a Master), Ashoka fellow since 2016, who works on redefining the work—life balance so parents can stop seeing their time off work spent with their children in conflict with their careers. For more information *see* https://www.maam.life.

our lawyers. The ability to influence causes close to their heart is often a determinant in which employer they want to work for and whether they can be retained long term. In my own experience in the banking industry, whilst in the past some of the most talented lawyers chose to move to the business side or smaller but more flexible players (e.g., on the buy side), but still staying in the industry, now they look to exit the industry all together, launching fintech, regtech or other enterprises, including such that aim to disrupt the traditional legal models. Many leave the profession altogether, to pursue teaching or writing, some friends who have pursued successful top chef careers, but in any event they leave to follow their passion. Some have been very successful in their new efforts, some less so, but most are content, if not happy, that they are doing something that is meaningful to them.

The search for a worthwhile impact does not remain a priority only for the younger talent. This is very relevant for people in my own generation too. Many senior lawyers choose to move into other fields in search of that stimulus and meaning, pursuing careers in administration, business or risk, some launching new enterprises using technology to alleviate regulatory and compliance burdens, developing operating models to cater for the agile and flexible working aspirations of the legal profession. With age and experience, I had myself thought that I will get more patient and adapt a more relaxed approach to work. The opposite has materialised. As one of my ex-bosses told me: «Time equals life». That could not be more true for me now. The time spent away from my young children needs to be meaningful and fulfilling. We need new challenges to stimulate us, to make our impact more meaningful.

V. Technology—Good News for Solution

The picture is bleak overall for the profession, but there is good news too. Technology is empowering lawyers to deliver without being slaves of the old work environment—without the necessity to be in the office, typing memos on an old fashioned computer, passing hand written comments to the secretary to produce comparisons with previous versions. Remote access options, voice driven technology, artificial intelligence have shifted the scope / substance of our work and the way we deliver it. Legal tasks (standard documentation, due diligence, investigative searches to mention only a few) are being performed with the help of technological solutions.

The legal profession itself is also being changed by technology; services are being digitalised and commoditised. Unfortunately, law firms are still charging huge fees for giving advice that is far from tailor made, that is often available already for other clients of theirs. The clients are somewhat of accomplices with their inertia in implementing new models and technology that would allow them to place less reliance on external advice. Indeed, unless it is advice related to new legislation, the big companies have already the advice in-house, i.e., they have already likely obtained that advice. It is not easy though to have fast access to it, without knowledge management systems. It is still faster to commission advice from externally anew instead of rummaging through the internal systems to dig it out. Artificial intelligence will change that though. It already allows for searches in smart and superfast ways (e.g., for due diligence purposes, developing easily accessible compliance «manuals», RegTech solutions, «ask Legal» AI and bots to name but only few), it is exciting to think about the opportunity of using it for know-how management and searches. Let me go even further—once AI starts searching the net for the advice that already almost certainly is available somewhere, the law firms will have their biggest competitor, for free. In-house pilots are being run with self-service portals (so that business can have easy, «google type» search access 24/7 to legal and compliance advice), bots, automated production of documentation, automated searches for litigation and investigation purposes, and applications providing legal advice that has previously been contained in hundreds of pages of documents. Employees fear the changes, as usual, not feeling prepared for the changes, not being ready to change themselves.

The big plus, though, is that these technology changes will assist with attracting more diverse lawyers to the teams, creating the environment that helps them thrive: an environment that is not based on selling hours and *presenteeism*, but value adding, with advice being able to be provided «on the go» and through advanced methods of communication. No one will be interested in *where* the adviser is when working, at home, in the office, in the same or another country or continent. As long as the work is done, clients will be happy. The lawyers will also be satisfied with the ability to work, without the old fashioned restrictions of when and where.

The automatization of lower level legal tasks will free capacity and refocus on expertise. With the advice on a legal position being readily available as information, the value of the lawyers ought to be in their ability to «join the dots», identify legal risks pertinent to specific businesses, help find mitigants, provide lessons learned and read-across, strategic work. This higher level work will hopefully make the work more attractive and also appeal to our desire to provide meaningful impact versus simply delivering advice.

This will be one more blow to the old fashioned model and, hopefully, another hope for changing the model.

The lawyers of the future will be well educated, experienced individuals with broad expertise, quick thinking, excellent understanding of the business, ability to change, adapt, and innovate with enthusiasm and drive. They will like what they are doing and feel impactful. Technology will support them and allow them to deliver better value and allow flexibility at the same time.

VI. Is Technology Though Enough?

OK, so far so good, most of you will say—we are aware of the issues, but how do we change the system versus blame it? And is technology enough? It is not that law firms and in-house legal departments have not tried, at least for the past decade or so, to ensure that diversity levels improve. Trying to stay away from naming which players or industries have been more successful than others, the focus, where there has been such, has been on creating diverse pipelines and adopting policies aiming at promoting diversity. Depending on the location, culture, and size of company, there are still numerous factors that are not considered when building up teams (most of these valid overall and not specifically for the legal profession). When recruiting, there is still not enough specific focus on minority groups, on candidates from less prestigious universities, concerted efforts to eliminate bias. Indeed, initiatives such as CV—blind recruitment are now being used, but these are usually only limited to some countries, whilst in many others hiring based on CVs that include a picture of the candidate and even a date of birth (!) is still *de rigueur*. Broadening the recruitment pool to include capable candidates from outside the «top school» range will increase significantly the cognitive skills of the team overall, at no cost. An option is to work with selected schools directly, but there are also already some recruiters who specialise in placing such law students for training contracts. Some of the most successful programmes in-house (with gender focus predominantly) have been the career-come-back programmes, assisting women (and, more rarely, men) who have taken a career break to re-enter the industry. I have had experience with such programmes at two different employers and can only praise them for they are fantastic opportunities to replenish the teams with (often senior) female employees, whose main objective is to go back to interesting and fulfilling jobs—after often acquiring other crucial skills as caretakers for families or trying their hand at something different. I find this such an easy «win» for the employers that I am really surprised that such programmes are not spread more widely yet.

Role models inspire. We need to create more role models of the diverse and inclusive work space. I was recently talking to a female partner from a prominent law firm in Switzerland, who was leaving the firm only a couple of years after making a partner (one of the very few female partners at that firm). She was moving to a much smaller firm where she felt she would have more impact in the management of the firm—hence more impact over the culture of the firm—and she could easier shape and influence the place. I was rather surprised by the news, as the firm my friend was coming from is known to be one of the more «progressive» firms in the country; but, evidently, even it had not been able to retain a highly talented and extremely well perceived in the market, female lawyer. This was a terrible blow in terms of losing a role model, too. Because whether we like it or not, we do become role models for our team members, evidence that someone who looks, sounds, behaves like them may make it to a higher level, proof that it is not impossible to go further. And when role models leave, or when there are no role models, there is no inspiration. I recall how shocked I was, when I was in my first general counsel role and a more junior lawyer asked me to mentor her. I had not mentored anyone (at least that I knew of) before and I hardly thought I knew something worth sharing with others about career advancement. It took me awhile to start perceiving myself as a role model, but I ultimately understood that just by being a woman, by not ticking a number of other «boxes» that were previously considered standard for the role I was in, I had attracted the curiosity of others. Since then, I have mentored, formally and informally, many, men and women, lawyers and non-lawyers, from the financial and other industries, including also kids from underprivileged schools, who had never been to the City before—a most rewarding experience, for the mentor at least as much as for the mentee, I find. Without that mentorship though, without the ability to guide and influence and show that there are other ways forward, outside the traditional ones, outside the «boys clubs», the roads of non-conformism and diversity will remain closed.

A big part of the solution for me lies in taking positive action overall though, not only for role models. We need to walk the talk and that is something that is, unfortunately, still lagging behind. And it is not going to change, until there is new leadership overall, by people of different generations, with different thinking, committed to the work-life balance and not seeing it as a «dirty word», committed to agile working and to having a diverse group of professionals on their team. Sometimes this means that one needs to force things, not go with the flow when replacing people, be serious about giving the «minority» quality candidate a chance, in order to demonstrate to the team that diverse structure and views are a priority. Only by leading by example will the senior managers influence really and foster the belief in change. But the lack of role models for diversity in the legal industry, together with the lack of constant positive action on part of senior managers to address the lack of diversity contributes to the huge disappointment of the team members—made even worse because of the perceived hypocrisy of senior management who lack of alignment of words and actions.

And another key element to contribute to the change is the inclusiveness, fight against bias, conscious and unconscious. Without that, we cannot achieve any diversity at all, as we will keep recruiting and retaining people who look and sound like us; we will keep promoting people in accordance with criteria that are perhaps outdated; we will not be able to connect to our employees because we do not understand them and evaluate them based on what are inappropriate parameters for them. I am not aware of any company that has managed to crack really the unconscious bias nut, despite many efforts in that regard recently. The companies, perceived as more modern and innovative by the new generations, are the ones that have managed to attract the most diverse employee groups, but that is due to their original design, progressive leadership, and relative short history, rather than a transformative effort. It is much more difficult to change existing institutions, with long standing cultures. Raising awareness of bias, building processes that foster inclusiveness and diversity, leading by example and role modelling, but most importantly, having a willingness to change—these must be the defining characteristics of legal leaders across the industry.

Coming back to the big opportunity though—technology will change the value proposition and will, therefore, change the operating models, empowering legal professionals, empowering change overall. In order to attract the best talent, the legal profession will need to need to offer interesting and challenging work, flexibility, social importance / responsibility. Just wait and see or, better, join the change.

VII. Bibliography

Online Sources

Brodherson, Marc, McGee, Laura & Pires dos Reis, Mariana, *Women in law firms*, McKinsey & Company (October 2017), https://www.mckinsey.com/featured-insights/gender-equality/women-in-law-firms (last visited Feb. 3, 2019).

Kowarski, Ilana, *Less Competitive Law School Admissions a Boon for Applicants* (Aug. 8, 2017, 8:30 AM), USNews, https://www.usnews.com/education/best-graduate-schools/top-law-schools/articles/2017-08-08/law-school-admissions-less-competitive-than-2008 (last visited Feb. 3, 2019).

Kowarski, Ilana, *Law School Applications Increased This Year* (Jan. 29, 2018, 8:00 AM), USNews, https://www.usnews.com/education/best-graduate-schools/top-law-schools/articles/2018-01-29/law-school-applications-increased-during-president-trumps-first-year (last visited Feb. 3, 2019).

Soergel, Andrew, *Hiring Outlook Bleak for New Law Grads* (Aug. 18, 2016, 4:19 PM), USNews, https://www.usnews.com/news/articles/2016-08-18/hiring-outlook-bleak-for-new-law-grads (last visited Feb. 3, 2019).

Jordan Furlong

Epilogue

The Rise of the Lawyer

TABLE OF CONTENT

I. Introduction

As I was preparing to write this epilogue, an email alert flashed into my inbox, a message from a legal technology company. It announced itself in breathless terms: «AI has once again triumphed over a human lawyer» at screening a non-disclosure agreement!

What an appropriate starting gun for this undertaking. The book you've just completed has catalogued in amazing detail the changes rippling along the foundations of the legal market worldwide, the technology that's rewriting the rulebook for practising law, and the market forces that are fundamentally changing the nature of legal demand. Enterprise legal services—that sector of the market devoted to the legal needs of large companies, corporations, institutions, and governments—will never be the same again.

Yet it's worth pausing to ponder the deeper implications of that message. Why does it say «triumphed»? Who is rooting for the machine here, and why root against the human? What benefit is being created by the application of this new technology, and who will ultimately reap that benefit? Are we celebrating because a human lawyer will be liberated from drudge work and assigned to deliver wise counsel to sophisticated clients? Or is it perhaps more likely that that lawyer will instead be liberated from a steady paycheque, and that fewer rather than more opportunities for human judgement will result?

We live in an age when the ultimate goal of many corporate activities is to «enhance shareholder value», a phrase that has become a mantra not just for corporate boards, but also for the equity shareholders of large law firms. But not everyone out there is a shareholder, and not everyone is seeing their value enhanced.

There are some people who instead characterize our era as «late capitalism», and who suggest that we are entering the decline phase of one system and the gradual emergence of something else, something new. Is either of these opinions correct? What mantras ought we to adopt in an enterprise legal market populated by blockchain, digitization, smart contracts, and Reg/Sup/PropTech? What is the real purpose of lawyers in the intelligent machine age?

For lawyers, these are not academic questions, and we should not act as if they are. If you are a lawyer whose career trajectory is likely to carry you to or past the midpoint of this century, I believe these questions are vital for you to contemplate. The answers you come up with will determine not just the sort of work you find yourself doing, but also the ultimate ends towards which your efforts lead you, your clients, and everyone else. This epilogue is intended to help you through that contemplation.

To my way of thinking, there are three critical considerations for you, the 21st-century lawyer, to ponder during this process of discernment—three factors that merit at least as much time and bandwidth as any other. These concepts are «System», «Service» and «Self». Here are my thoughts on each.

II. System

Now and for the foreseeable future, enterprise legal services will be created and delivered primarily through systems. For our purposes, we can define a system as «an organized, purposeful structure of interrelated and interdependent methods, procedures and routines, created to carry out an activity, perform a duty, or solve a problem.» If that concept interests or even thrills you, you're going to love this line of work. If it puzzles or bores you, you might have a problem.

The reason we're talking about systems is that we are long past the point where enterprise legal needs can be fulfilled by individual lawyers, sequentially and in single file, working in longhand and billing by the hour. As this book has made clear, both the sheer scale and the growing complexity of companies' legal and compliance challenges require equally scaled and complex solutions. Enterprise clients compete in high-pressure environments and operate according to unforgiving timeframes. They cannot be served in the same way you would serve a family business or a private client.

That's going to have a profound effect on the types of people who will be drawn to and who will thrive in this sector of the legal market. Systems analysts, software coders, design thinkers, and engineers of all kinds will be a natural fit for enterprise legal. People who can grasp the big picture of what the client needs, who can envision processes and flowcharts and logic statements that produce solutions to those needs, and who can build and maintain robust frameworks to contain and run those solutions rapidly, repeatedly, and reliably—those will be the architects and superstars of the enterprise legal market.

If you feel that the foregoing characteristics don't describe you, then it's quite possible that your legal career destiny lies in a different direction. But don't walk away yet! Because it is also possible, and maybe even likely, that there is a place for you in the enterprise legal market—an important place, in fact.

Analysts and coders and engineers can capture the big-picture needs of a major enterprise client and can design and build astonishingly complex systems to meet those needs in mere seconds. But there is still a role for human judgment here, because no matter how inspired and intricate a system might be, there are two questions that must constantly be asked of and about it:

1. Is the system doing what it's supposed to do?
2. Is what the system is supposed to do actually the right thing to be doing?

To be clear, many engineers and software architects have not only the skills required to envision and build effective systems, but also the talent required to monitor, scrutinize, and judge those systems. But not all of them do. The «how» of a system is not the same as the «why» of a system, and both of these inquiries need to be made of, and met by, a legal system on a regular basis. It will be useful to have different people with different skill sets making those inquiries.

Legal systems also age and atrophy and degrade over time. Minuscule errors inevitably crawl inside and start inaudibly misdirecting the intended flow of data or invisibly unraveling the logics underlying the processes.

Since we can't see or hear the initial errors, we need to watch the results, over and over again, and ask ourselves whether our incredible machines are delivering their intended solutions and client outcomes. That will require the attention of people who can detect patterns within a system and can find emerging variations therein, who have built strong relationships with clients that allow them to understand their goals and priorities, and who can integrate these two bodies of knowledge into an effective system assessment regime. Those are lawyer skills, and they will be needed in the enterprise legal market.

But there's more; there's also the need to ask whether a system that's doing what it was built to do is achieving what it *ought* to be doing.

A powerful and widespread misconception is that if a machine or a system is generating results, those results are necessarily good and trustworthy, because the machine or system is unbiased and objective; «It's all math, and the numbers don't lie.»

But it's not all math, of course, and it never has been. There are already countless examples of how sexism and racism is baked into algorithms and processes by programmers who don't believe they themselves are sexist or racist, but whose experiences and biases inevitably guide their «objective» decisions. This problem will become more pernicious, as machine learning and data-driven decision-making spreads to judicial, regulatory, and administrative systems (especially for poorer individuals who can't afford customized assistance). A system that performs exactly as it's designed, but that inadvertently yet consistently rejects valid compensation claims from people with non-Anglicized surnames, is a bad system. But will anyone notice?

The future of law, especially enterprise legal services, is without any doubt systemic. But systems need people to run them, to remedy them, and to remind everyone else that we build systems to serve people's interests. And that brings us to our next point.

III. Service

The law is a service profession. Both historically and etymologically, the very notion of «profession» is grounded in service towards others for the greater good. If you're a lawyer, your central purpose is to serve other people and make things better for them—principally your clients, but not exclusively, and not to the intentional detriment of others.

Now, if you're engaged (or you plan to engage) in the enterprise legal services market, where you're working with or for corporations and institutions and governments on a national or international scale, you might think that the foregoing homily doesn't apply to you. That kind of thing is for lawyers in family law, or wills and estates, or criminal defence—«People Law», as it's been described. By contrast, your job is to help grow shareholder value, or improve brand penetration, or eliminate unwanted efficiencies. You don't serve people so much as you serve productivity. Right?

Well, you'll make your own call on that question, of course. But if I might suggest something for your consideration, it would be this: No matter how massive and global your clients, no matter how complex and high-value the transactions, no matter how sophisticated and AI-driven the systems you're using, *it's all People Law.* Shareholders are people. Employees are people. Individuals whose lives are irrevocably altered by enterprise legal decisions are people. And you're not allowed to conveniently overlook them in pursuit of your legal duties.

I don't think it's deeply controversial to note that in many parts of the planet, perhaps including the location where you're reading this book, the quality of both public and private standards of living has noticeably deteriorated throughout the end of the 20th century and the start of the 21st. In a world where capital outperforms labour by a widening margin, the rewards of ever-greater productivity are shared by an ever-smaller number of people. It's now an article of faith in many respectable quarters that productivity is more important than people. These quarters seem to have forgotten that enterprises and institutions are supposed to serve people, not the other way around.

I have some news for you: One of your functions, as a lawyer for the people who've forgotten this truth, is to remind them of it.

When a corporation or an institution repeatedly crosses the line of acceptable conduct and ends up ruining itself and others, a question that invariably arises in the aftermath is, «Where were the lawyers?» The answer, in most cases, is that the lawyers were either helping to facilitate the client's actions on its road to ruin, or were studiously looking the other way, having persuaded themselves that it wasn't their job to challenge the sustainability or wisdom or even morality of their client's decisions. That the role of a lawyer is to make happen what the client decides should happen. That their job is to serve power, not speak truth to it.

That is the wrong conclusion to reach. It's wrong because it flies in the face of a lawyer's ultimate duty, which is not to his or her client but to the rule of law and the courts. It's wrong because it surgically removes ethical and societal factors from the lawyer's consideration, transforming the lawyer into a mindless enforcer or a random subroutine in the larger system. And it's wrong because many other people, both inside and outside the corridors of power, can sense when something the client is doing is not quite right, and they will look to the lawyers to see what they think—and if the lawyers are simply sitting quietly with their heads down, then that's what they'll do as well. People follow our lead in murky ethical situations, whether we want them to or not.

I'm not talking merely about the obvious kinds of scandal and self-dealing, which make even the most battle-hardened enterprise lawyer pause and think things over. I'm talking about the unexamined assumption that if the client wants to do something in order to enhance shareholder value, that is the highest and ultimately the only goal worth considering, regardless of the human or social or environmental consequences.

This challenge is made even greater by the rise of systems in the enterprise legal space. It's easier to call out misbehaviour by an individual than it is to call out bad programming in a system that «objectively» issues eviction notices to, or rejects loan applications from, the most vulnerable members of our community. There is a role for the lawyer of a commercial client to flag the negative social consequences of the enterprise's activities, to bring them to the attention of the client's leaders and to insist that they lock closely at the human cost of those activities. Maybe the lawyer's duties extend no farther than that. But they certainly do not extend any less.

Believe me when I tell you that enabling or tolerating socially corrosive activities is the most dangerous trap into which an enterprise lawyer can fall. And it is all the more dangerous because it disguises itself as «service to the client,» a salve to your conscience and a False North to your moral compass. Remember that people come before profitability or productivity. Remember the lawyer's foundational principle of professional service.

IV. Self

Early in my career as a legal magazine editor, I opined in an editorial that the most important person in your law practice was your client. I received a letter shortly afterwards from a lawyer health and wellness expert who took exception to that idea. The most important person in your law practice, he said, is you. Upon reflection, I've come to believe he was right.

It's easy to overlook this fact—and at times, it can even seem noble to do so. Haven't I just finished saying that the ultimate role of a lawyer is to serve others? Doesn't this suggest that a lawyer should strive to diminish herself or himself, to substitute the good of others for the good of ourselves? That certainly seems like it should be an attractive notion to a serving profession.

Yet self-diminishment and self-negation have proven to be destructive in all walks of life, and especially so in service-oriented professions like medicine and the law. What we need instead is a more fully developed sense of how

we should regard ourselves, and where we should place ourselves, within the dynamic array of needs and priorities of the 21st-century lawyer.

Technology makes this goal more important, not less. The first and longest-lasting promise of machines has been that they will make our lives better—that they will save us time and energy, allowing us to devote these precious resources to enhancing our freedom, leisure, and personal advancement. Raise your hand if you feel like technology has gifted you with these assets. Raise your other hand if you look forward to the rollout of a new technology in your office and how much you'll enjoy the extra time it will provide you.

The truth, of course, is that even those technologies that really do save us time and effort rarely do so to our benefit, but rather to the benefit of our employers. Think of all the amazing technologies that have arrived in the law over the last couple of decades, from document automation to contract drafting to e-discovery: Have lawyers enjoyed a windfall of unallocated hours and clear horizons with which to better ourselves and those around us, or to engage in more fulfilling and higher-value endeavours? Or have those «freed-up» hours been immediately captured by others and filled with more work, in service of «greater productivity»? Especially if you work for an employer who measures your productivity in hours billed, and for whom more «freed-up time» for you is the last thing they want?

Machine learning and artificial intelligence are going to amplify and accelerate these trends and concerns. Recall the email from the legal AI company quoted at the start of this article: «AI has once again triumphed over a human lawyer.»

So long as the prevailing philosophy of the corporate world is to prioritize productivity over people, it's going to be your responsibility to look out for yourself—and to look out for your *self*. There are two areas in particular in which you need to focus your efforts in this regard.

One is the broad category of your health and wellness. You must safeguard and strengthen them. Previous generations failed to do this, and they left countless unhappy lives, broken marriages, emotional breakdowns, and substance addictions in their wake. Probably you were raised in a home afflicted by these ills, or you know someone who was.

Now it's your turn to run this gauntlet—but you can do better. You can reject the proposition that your highest or only function is to be a cog in someone else's machine, to be constantly on call for those who pay your wages, or to substitute your client's judgment for your own on a daily basis. You can assert that your physical health, mental wellness, and emotional stability have value apart from, above, and beyond your work. You can invest in your health the way previous generations invested in CLEs and association memberships. This will pay off throughout the course of your legal career and your life.

But there is another way in which tending to your self will be important, and that is in understanding and applying your own unique value proposition as a lawyer. The ironic effect of the rise of automation and systems in the law is that lawyers' human qualities will become more important to employers and clients. Job interviews of the near future are likely to feature the question, «What can you do that our machines can't?» Previous generations of lawyers shared a common set of skills that have now largely been automated and systematized, such that a lawyer's distinctiveness will henceforth be highly personal and unique. Your humanity will be your selling point.

In a sense, this challenge will also be the great opportunity for your generation of lawyers. You will be able to re-engineer the blueprint or rewrite the DNA of what it means to be a lawyer. As systems and software proliferate, as we are tempted to serve the machines we created to serve us, as it becomes ever easier to prioritize productivity over people, the role of the lawyer will steadily evolve towards the enforcement of positive social norms, the enshrinement and protection of personal dignity, and the pursuit of service to the improvement of lives. That might be the greatest legacy of the 21st-century legal careers that you will build.

V. Conclusion

One last thought as we close this book. The greatest responsibility of being a lawyer is that what you do and say matters to many people beyond those who pay you for your services. That also happens to be the greatest privilege. This has always been true of the legal profession, but the clarity of that truth will be especially evident in the 2020s, 2030s, 2040s and 2050s—throughout the years of your legal career.

What you do matters. Who you are matters. When you speak out, it has an impact. When you fall silent, that has an impact too. Do not get lost in the complexity and delights of the machine; do not lose sight of the primacy and power of true service; do not lose who you are, and who you could be, amid the coming noise and confusion. Out of this chaos, you can forge new meaning and greater purpose. At the end of one era in the legal profession's history, you can launch the start of another.

Your time is coming; it's nearly here. The rise of the machines is almost over. Now it's time for the rise of the lawyer.

Eva A Kaili

Afterword

We can epitomize the main message of this book in ten words: *There is no such thing as «legal service as usual».* The co-curators of this book (Michele DeStefano and Guenther Dobrauz) and the amazing group of contributing authors bring together legal practice, innovation, and economics theory not merely to show how technology changes the work environment of the legal practitioner but also how it expands legal services by creating new value chains, a new business paradigm, and a new universe of client expectations.

The authors of this book warn the legal practitioner that the demand side for legal service has shifted. Thus, the supply side, in order to stay relevant, must shift accordingly to reach a new optimal equilibrium. LegalTech, which they see as an opportunity, becomes an instrument with strong economic significance. It urges the practitioner of our era to create (within in-house legal departments as well as law firms) the necessary infrastructure that supports a new «supply chain» of legal services and meets the needs of forward-looking organizations. Only with robust «exponential legal supply chains» can we move upwards on the S-curve.

However, it would be myopic to say that this book is only a «manual» for legal practitioners on how to find and grasp value in the unfolding reshaped market. I have worked with Guenther Dobrauz-Saldapenna who is one of my trusted advisors for some time now. From this I know that he continuously highlights the interplay between politics and legal work, the systemic effects of the transformation of legal service, and the use of exponential technologies as critical for the quality of regulation, law engineering and application, market design, culture and ethics of stakeholders, and ultimately the quality of our democratic institutions. Technological transformation in the legal marketplace is inherently good because, if used wisely, it can bring immense benefit to us (not only as clients but also as citizens) as it can impove access to justice. Guenther Dobrauz is a technology-enthusiast but he is also a highly esteemed legal practitioner who understands not only the pros but also the cons and the constraints of the use of technology. As such, I believe that this book will benefit legal practitioners and governments, (standard-setters and regulators) who significantly influence the framework against which the coming change will play out. It is also an important text for business analysts and technology specialists who want to explore how technology affects «traditional» and «conservative» industries.

As we have seen with the first machine age, radical change leads to significant social challenges. Therefore, we must attempt to mitigate this by fulfilling our ethical duty to 1) train students aspiring to be lawyers to meet the challenges and 2) retrain lawyers who are in their current careers as practicing lawyers. To this end, we must start at the very beginning—with education—which must also put on a «new suit» as Professor Michele DeStefano aptly points out in her two chapters in this book.

As such, it is my hope that this important book not only finds uptake with those considering a career in legal or those in charge of running law firms, legal departments, or business organisations, or those using legal services but also the professors who are in charge of educating law school students. As such, my hope is that this book will also inform the curricula of institutions of higher learning to help shape the thinking of those who will ultimately create our future.

Eva A Kaili
Member of the European Parliament
Chair of the European Parliament's Panel for the Future of Science and Technology

Appendix

TABLE OF CONTENT

Acknowledgements

From the very start of this book project, unsurprisingly, there was a lot of interest from publishers given the subject and the amazing line-up of authors. But with many publishers, we swiftly ended up in a discussion along the lines of «… so would you prefer the blue or the red cover?» When we shared our strong belief that a book about innovation and disruption shouldn't be packaged in either color or look like a casebook, we were met with raised eyebrows. Therefore, we consider ourselves more than lucky to finally have found **Stämpfli Verlag AG**, a publisher who not only shared but fully embraced our vision. A big thank you to visionary Stämpfli-CEO, **Dorothee Schneider**, for her trust in us! We cannot even begin to imagine how much conviction and persistence it must have taken to realize this at a publishing house with such longstanding tradition and repute! Kudos to that dear Dorothee!

A BIG thank you also to **Azmina Khimji** as the Stämpfli project manager for this book for her tireless work and help to make it come to life! We would also like to thank **Stephan Kilian** at Stämpfli for all his help with this book!

We are forever indebted to **Steve Hafner** and **Philipp Rosenauer** who have helped us with coordinating (and keeping track) of a group of more than 40 authors. Gentlemen—you are living proof that lawyers can be managers and that managers can work with lawyers!

We are proud beyond words that the one and only **Billy Morrison** created the cover art for this book. Who would ever have thought that a conversation with a rock guitarist just before he went on stage to perform in front of thousands of people at the world famous Montreux Jazz Festival would result in a book cover?!

Similarly, we would like to thank **Tom Jermann** of t42design in LA for taking charge of the overall cover design. This represents yet another case of the coming together of pieces that nobody would usually think of putting together which, in turn, is representative of how disruptive innovation usually occurs—outside of the established industry and by combining previously alien or entirely new elements in a novel way. In this case, a lunch in the wonderful garden of the Baur au Lac hotel in Zurich morphed into a dinner at the legendary Sunset Marquis Hotel in West Hollywood and resulted in the man behind more than 100 record covers and the logos of some of the world's most famous rock bands creating the packing of a book about the legal world and its way into an exciting future.

We are forever indebted to Zurich-based photographer, **Oliver Nanzig,** for his photography work for the cover image and portrait.

This book would never have happened without our friend the wonderful Professor **Leo Staub** and his amazing team—most notably **Bruno Mascello** and **Sabrina Weiss**—since it was at his *Conference on the Future of Legal Services* in St. Gallen where the curators and several of the contributing authors first met, and the idea for this book was born over the course of a traditional Swiss cheese fondue. Further input was generated and additional contributors added at the conference's second installment in Miami.

Thank you **Peter Würinger** for helping us with the graphical elements and formatting!

We would like to also thank **Robin Schard** and **Sarah Slinger** at the University of Miami School of Law for their great support.

Last but certainly not least, we would like to thank all the amazing authors who have contributed to this book and our families for their support and understanding throughout this project.

Co-Curators
Professor Michele DeStefano and Dr Guenther Dobrauz-Saldapenna
Coral Gables/Zurich, April 2019

List of Abbreviations

ABA	American Bar Association
ABS	Alternative Busines Structures
ACC	Association of Corporate Counsel
ACTUS	Algorithmic Contract Types Unified Standards
ADGM	Abu Dhabi Global Market
AFA	Alternative Fee Arrangements
AGI	Artificial General Intelligence
AI	Artificial Intelligence
AICPA	American Institute of Certified Public Accountants
AIFMD	(EU) Alternative Investment Fund Managers Directive
aka	also known as
ALSP	Alternative Legal Service Provider(s)
AMF	Autorité des marchés financiers Quebec
AML	Anti Money Laundering
API	Application Programing Interface
ASIC	Australian Securities & Investments Commission
AWS	Amazon Web Services
B2B	business-to-business
B2C	business-to-consumer
BCBS239	Basel Committee on Banking Supervision's standard number 239
BCFP	US Bureau of Consumer Financial Protection
BCG	Boston Consulting Group
BLIP	Brooklyn Law Incubator & Policy Clinic
BLP	Berwin Leighton & Paisner
BPA	Business Process Automation
CAGR	Compound Annual Growth Rate
CBB	Central Bank of Bahrain
CCBE	Council of Bars and Law Societies of Europe
CCM	Cloud Control Matrix
CEO	Chief Executive Officer
CESR	Committee of European Securities Regulators (CESR)
CGAP	Consultative Group to Assist the Poor
CJEU	Court of Justice of the European Union
COO	Chief Operations Officer
CLO	Chief Legal Officer

CPR	Civil Procedures Rules
CREtech	Commercial Real Estate Technology
CRM	Customer Relation Management
CSA	Cloud Security Alliance
CSP	Cloud Service Provider
DFSA	Dubai Financial Services Authority
DL	Deep Learning
DLT	Distributed Ledger Technology
DMCA	Digital Millenium Copyright Act
DMS	Document management systems
DNA	Deoxyribonucleic Acid
DOC	Department of Commerce
DRR	Digital Regulatory Reporting
DSG	Datenschutzgesetz
ECJ	European Court of Justice
Ed.	Editor(s)
EDP	Electronic Data Processing
EEA	European Economic Area
e-ID	Electronic Identity
e-KYC	eloctronic Know Your Customer
eIDAS	The Regulation on Electronic Identfication and Trust Services for Electronic Transactions in the Internal Market
EMIR	European Market Infrastructure Regulation
ERS	Entwurf einer Stellungnahme zur Rechnungslegung
ESFS	European System of Financial Supervision
ESIGN	Electronic Signatures in Global and National Commerce Act
ESMA	European Securities and Markets Authority
EU	European Union
EUD	End User Device
EUR	Euro
EY	Ernst & Young
FAIT	Fachausschuss für Informationstechnologie
FINMA	(Swiss) Financial Market Supervisory Authority
FinTech	Financial Technology
FISA	(US) Foreign Intelligence Surveillance Act
FMA	Financial Market Authority (Austria or Liechtenstein)
FSRA	Financial Regulatory Authority of the Abu Dhabi Global Market
FWA	Flexible Work Arrangement(s)
GB	gigabytes
GBT	General Business Terms
GC	General Counsel
GDP	Gross Domestic Product

GDPR	General Data Protection Regulation
GFC	Global Financial Crisis
GFIN	Global Financial Innovation Network
GFSC	Guernsey Financial Services Commission
GIS	Geographical Information System
GLBC	Global Legal Blockchain Consortium
GPL	General Public License
HDC	Hyperscale Data Centers
HKMA	Hong Kong Monetary Authority
HR	Human Ressources
IaaS	Infrastructure-as-a-Service
ICO	Initial Coin Offering
ICT	Information and Communication Technology
ID	Identitiy
ID-code	Personal Identification Code
IDW	Institut der Wirtschaftsprüfer Deutschland
IEC	International Electrotechnical Commission
IOSCO	International Organisation of Securities Commissions
IoT	Internet of Things
IP	Intellectual Property
IPA	Intelligent Process Automation
IPO	Initial Public Offering
IPSec	Internet Protocol Security
ISO	International Organization for Standardization
IT	Information Technology
JILA	Japan In-house Lawyers Association
KIS	The Court Information System
KPI	Key Performance Indicators
KYC	Know Your Customer
KR	Knowledge Representation
LegalTech	Legal Technology
LEI	Legal Entity Identifier
LL.M.	Masters in Law
LO	Legal Operations
LOD	Lawyers on Demand
LOM	Law Department Operations
LOI	Letter of Intent
LPO	Legal Process Outsourcing
LSP	Legal Service Provider
M&A	Mergers and Acquisitions
MAS	Monetary Authority of Singapore
MDP	Multidisciplinary Practice Firm(s)
MENA	Middle East and North Africa

MiFID	Markets in Financial Instruments Directive
MIFIR	Markets in Financial Instruments Reguation
MIT	Massachusetts Institute of Technology
ML	Machine Learning
MLS	Managed Legal Services
MoReq	Model Requirements for the Management of Electronic Records
MoU	Memorandum of Understanding
MMoU	Multilateral Memorandum of Understanding
NCSC	National Cyber Security Centre
NDA	Non-Dosclosure Agreement
NELIC	New and Emerging Legal Infrastructure Conference
NIST	National Institute of Standards and Technology
NLP	Natural Language Processing
NN	Neural Network
NSA	National Security Agency
ODR	Online Dispute Resolution
OECD	The Organisation for Economic Co-operation and Development
OGD	Open Government Data
OSC	Ontario Securities Commission
OSS	Open Source Software
OTC	Over-The-Counter
PaaS	Platform-as-a-Service
PIPA	PROTECT IP Act (PIPA
PoC	Proof of Concept
PLI	Practising Law Institute
PSD2	Revised Directive on Payment Services
PropTech	Property Technology
PwC	PricewaterhouseCoopers
RDG	Gesetz über außergerichtliche Rechtsdienstleistungen
RFP	Request for Proposal
RegTech	Regulatory Technology
ROI	Return on investment
RPA	Robotic Process Automation
SACO	Swiss Compliance Officers Association
SaaS	Software-as-a-Service
SBA	Swiss Bankers Association
SEC	(United States) Securities and Exchange Commission
SFTI	Swiss FinTech Innovations Association
SLA	Service Level Agreement
SME	Subject Matter Expert or Small and Medium-sized Enterprises
SOPA	Stop Online Piracy Act

SRA	Solicitors Regulation Authority
SSL	Secure Sockets Layer
SupTech	Supervisory Technology
TKG	Telekommunikationsgesetz 2003
TLS	Transport Layer Security
UCITS	Undertakings for Collective Investment in Transferable Securities Directive
UETA	Uniform Electronic Transactions Act
UK	United Kingdom
UNCITRAL	United Nations Commission on International Trade Law
US	United States
USA	United States of America
USD	US Dollar(s)
Vol	Volume
VPN	Virtual Private Network
WAN	Wide Area Network
WJP	World Justice Project
WWW	World Wide Web

Curators and Authors

I. Curators

Professor Michele DeStefano

Recognized by the ABA as a Legal Rebel and by the Financial Times Innovative Lawyers (North America) as one of top 20 most innovative lawyers, Michele DeStefano is a professor at the University of Miami School of Law, guest faculty at Harvard Law School Executive Education, and the founder of LawWithoutWalls, a multi-disciplinary, international think-tank of more than 2,000 lawyers, business professionals, entrepreneurs, and law and business students. Michele is an author, speaker, and consultant on innovation, culture creation, and teaming. Through her company MOVELΔW, Michele creates bespoke, experiential-learning workshops grounded in human-centered design to transform how lawyers collaborate and create culture change. Michele writes about the growing intersections between law, business, and legal innovation. Her book, *Legal Upheaval: A Guide to Creativity, Collaboration, and Innovation in Law* leverages more than 100 interviews with General Counsels at international corporations and Heads of Innovation at law firms.

Michele's work has been published in leading law journals and featured in a range of media including Time Magazine, the Financial Times (UK), Forbes Women, ABA Journal, National Law Journal, American Lawyer, Harvard Law Today, The National Jurist, Legal Futures (UK), Inside Counsel Magazine, Harvard Law The Practice, and Bloomberg News.

Professor DeStefano has been invited to speak about her work at a number of law conferences, leading law firms, and law schools including Stanford, Harvard, IE Business School, University of St. Gallen, and Fordham. And she has also delivered talks to legal departments within corporations and legal organizations such as Microsoft, Thomson Reuters, ABA, AALS, and NAFSA. She regularly consults on collaboration and culture change. She holds a J.D. from Harvard Law School (2002, magna cum laude) and a B.A. in English and Sociology from Dartmouth College (1991, magna cum laude).

Finally, Professor DeStefano is especially proud to be the mother of 3 wonderful children.

Dr Guenther Dobrauz-Saldapenna

Dr Guenther Dobrauz-Saldapenna is a Partner with PricewaterhouseCoopers in Zurich and Leader of PwC Legal Switzerland as well as a member of PwC's Global Legal Leadership team directing the firm's global legal practise comprising more than 4000 lawyers in more than 90 countries where his particular focus is on the firm's LegalTech efforts.

He is considered to be one of the leading European Banking, Investment and Blockchain/Crypto Law and Regulatory specialists. Before joining PwC, Guenther worked at another Big 4. Prior to this, Guenther was Legal Counsel of an international hedge fund group and has also served for a number of years as Managing Partner and Legal Counsel of a Swiss Venture Capital firm. Guenther has also practiced in court and with a leading business law firm.

Today Guenther specializes in supporting the structuring, authorization and ongoing lifecycle management of financial intermediaries and their products. In addition, he is focused on leading and supporting the implementation of large scale regulatory change and compliance alignment projects at Swiss and international financial institutions with particular focus on EU and Swiss regulations. Guenther is also the trusted advisor to several governments, international organisations and supervisory authorities. His passion is innovation, strategy, and working with the unfolding dynamics of LegalTech, RegTech, DLT and exponential technologies.

Guenther received his Master's and his PhD degree in law from Johannes Kepler University (Linz, Austria). Guenther also holds an MBA from the University of Strathclyde Graduate School of Business (Glasgow, UK) and has participated in Executive Education programs both at Harvard Business School and Harvard Law School.

Guenther is the author, co-author and editor of eight books mostly on the European, Swiss and Liechtenstein legal and regulatory frameworks as well as of books on innovation and tech venture investments. He is also the author of more than 100 articles in international expert magazines—many of them peer-reviewed and has, to date, spoke at more than 250 leading conferences in more than 30 countries all around the world and has been invited to present as an expert at the United Nations and the European Parliament.

Guenther is a permanent member of the Swiss Fund & Asset Management Association's Specialists Committee «Legal & Compliance Asset Management», of the ecomomiesuisse «Financial Market Regulation» working group, of the Regulatory Working Group at Swiss Fintech Innovations, a Member of the Advisory Board of the Swiss LegalTech Association and of the European Law Observatory on New Technologies (ELONTech), co-host of Legal Hackers Zurich and a lecturer at various universities around the world. In addition, Guenther is the host of education video series «Appetite For Disruption» and the founder of global exponential technologies enthusiasts movement «Disruption Disciples».

Guenther is both a Swiss and Austrian citizen, married and father of one son.

II. Authors

Luis Ackermann

As an IT architect and data scientist, Luis Ackermann has been designing and implementing various complex software projects for the last 10 years. In 2014, he co-founded Lex Ferenda, a Swiss LegalTech company specialising in robust and secure Machine Learning applications for legal experts (see lexferenda.ch). Alongside his work for Lex Ferenda, he is currently working on the publication of Switzerland's first natively digital legal commentary. Luis is an enthusiastic supporter and participant of hackathons and has given numerous international lectures and workshops on the subjects of Digitalisation and Machine Intelligence.

Simon Ahammer

Simon Ahammer has worked as a lawyer in Munich since 1998. During his studies, he programmed software programs for law firms. For more than 11 years, he was Head of software development at the international law firm Beiten Burkhardt. From 2017 to mid-2018, he was Head of the LegalTech department of publishing house C.H. Beck ohG. He is currently Head of business unit legal industry at smartwork solutions GmbH, a company offering a software solution, called SMASHDOCs, for collaborative document work. For several years, he has been intensively involved with the digitalization of the legal market and gives lectures and workshops on this topic.

Sebastian Ahrens

Sebastian Ahrens is a Director in the Forensics practice of PwC Switzerland and the innovation lead for PwC Europe Forensics. He specialises in innovative regulatory and compliance technology solutions and is the Financial Crime Technology subject matter expert for PwC in Switzerland. He has 15 years experience in the IT and security sector in public service, industry, law enforcement and professional services. Before joining PwC, Sebastian led the computer forensics team in the German Federal Cartel Office (BKartA) and was responsible for all IT dawn raids of the authority across Germany as well as for designing data analytics applications for sector enquiries in the Financial Service, Energy and Health Care sectors. In the last few years, he advised major banks in Financial Crime Technology matters and helped FIs to overcome their data issues preventing them from fully leveraging their existing information. As the PwC Europe Forensic Innovation Lead, he is continuously evaluating cutting edge technologies in the areas of AI and cognitive computing for regulatory matters.

Dr Eva Maria Baumgartner

Dr Eva Maria Baumgartner, MBA (UoT), GEMBA HSG is the founder of Baumgartner Attorneys at law in Vienna, Austria and a member of the faculty council of Sigmund Freud Private University Vienna, Austria (Faculty of law) where she lectures on legal methodology and innovation methods in the legal services industry. She is an experienced attorney at law with a demonstrated history of working in the legal services industry with a focus on M&A, litigation, corporate law and ADR in tier 1 firms in Austria, Liechtenstein and Switzerland. Eva´s entrepreneurial activities include investments in legal tech start-ups and advisory work for projects aiming to empower end-users dealing with legal problems. Eva graduated from University of Toronto (Rotman School of Management) (MBA), University of St. Gallen, Switzerland (HSG) (GEMBA) and University of Vienna (PhD and Masters).

Tom Braegelmann

Tom Braegelmann, LL.M. (Benjamin N. Cardozo School of Law) is admitted to the bars in Germany and New York. He is a business lawyer at BBL Bernsau Brockdorff & Partner Rechtsanwälte PartGmbB in Munich/Berlin, focusing on restructuring law, IT law, and legal technology. Formerly, he was General Counsel at the AI LegalTech/PropTech company Leverton GmbH in Berlin, he also worked for many years at DLA Piper Germany and before that he worked for more than three years in New York, in bankruptcy law and IP, at McLaughlin & Stern LLP with Alvin Deutsch and Paul Silverman.

Dr Micha-Manuel Buess

Dr Micha-Manuel Bues is founder and Managing Director of BRYTER GmbH, a leading provider of automation software. Previously, he was Managing Director at LEVERTON, a Legal AI company in Berlin. From 2013 to 2016, he was a business lawyer at the law firm Gleiss Lutz, where he specialized in antitrust and compliance law. He studied law in Passau, Bonn and Oxford. He earned his doctorate with a thesis on European law under Prof. Stephan Hobe in Cologne. He is also an Associate Member of St. Anne's College at Oxford University.

Micha is a member of the Task Force Legal Tech and Innovation within the Association of Lawyers (DAV) as well as a board member to the Executive Faculty at the Bucerius Center on the Legal Profession. He co-founded the European Legal Tech Association (ELTA).

Micha-Manuel Bues has worked in, advised on and studied the field of digital transformation and legal innovation for many years. He has co-published two major books on the subject. He studies which changes result from digital transformation and which opportunities, challenges and risks arise for law firms, legal departments and lawyers. He runs a blog (www.legal-tech-

blog.com) and is a sought-after speaker. He is a proud husband, father and a firm believer of making the world a better place.

David Bundi

David Bundi is the Head of RegTech and a Senior Manager at PwC Legal Switzerland. He has over 12 years of professional experience in Legal & Compliance, Innovation, and Project Management in the banking industry. David worked in Zurich and New York with the largest global Swiss bank and with multiple international private banks in Switzerland. Prior to joining PwC, he was Chief Compliance Officer at an innovative retail-bank and also an Advisory Board Member with two RegTech firms. One of David's particular strengths is the combination of leadership skills and expertise in the areas of Governance, Risk, Legal and Compliance related to innovation & new technologies. David has built a unique global network in the RegTech space and is considered a global thought-leader in RegTech. This is reflected in the fact that he is a judge at international regulatory technology competitions (e.g., FCA's TechSprint), RegTech Expert at economiesuisse, the Swiss FinTech Innovations Association, the International RegTech Association, and the President at the RegTechtalks Association. He is much in demand as a keynote speaker and panelist at major international RegTech conferences as well as a lecturer at universities in the US and Europe on RegTech, Legal & Compliance, AI/ML, Innovation and the latest technologies in the regulatory space. He received his Masters degree in law at the University of Fribourg (CH), in addition to studying in law at the University of Bristol (UK), and further education in law at the New York University School of Professional Studies (US). In his spare time, he is a passionate and active member of the global Disruption Disciples movement where he is the Co-Head of the Zurich Chapter and one of the key drivers of the entire initiative.

Dr Lena Campagna

Dr. Lena Campagna is Research and Education Director of the international trade organization, Buying Legal Council, and an Assistant Professor in the department of Sociology and Criminal Justice at Caldwell University in New Jersey. She has extensive experience in project coordination and community outreach, mixed methods research, and program evaluation. Lena has published in peer-reviewed academic journals in social science research as well as authored educational articles on the buying of legal services.

Lena holds a Ph.D. in Sociology from the University of Massachusetts Boston, a Master's degree in American Studies from the University of Massachusetts Boston, and a Bachelor's Degree in Marketing Communication from Emerson College.

Juan Crosby

Juan is a qualified lawyer who specializes in advising Fortune 500 and FTSE 100 law departments on legal strategy, operating models and workflow automation to manage costs and increase efficiency. He is a Partner at PwC and a co-founder of their New Law team where he designs and runs managed legal service offerings for clients that require a more cost-effective, technology enabled solutions to support high volume, recurring legal activities such as commercial contracting.

Jameson Dempsey

Jameson is a technology attorney and community builder who currently serves on the board of directors of Legal Hackers, a global movement that fosters creative problem-solving at the intersection of law and technology through education, prototyping, and policy discussions. In addition to his work with Legal Hackers, Jameson serves as a Residential Fellow at CodeX—The Stanford Center for Legal Informatics.

Jameson joined CodeX from Kelley Drye & Warren LLP, where he advised clients on federal and state privacy, information security, and communications issues. Prior to joining Kelley Drye, Jameson clerked for Magistrate Judge Roanne L. Mann in the U.S. District Court for the Eastern District of New York, and during law school he clerked for FCC Commissioner Robert M. McDowell. Before law school, Jameson worked in the litigation technology group of White & Case LLP, where he focused on eDiscovery and trial technology.

Jameson's work has earned him recommendations in Legal500 (Data Protection and Privacy), a 2016 «Fastcase 50» award, a fellowship with the Internet Law & Policy Foundry, as well as speaking engagements at SXSW, Mobile World Congress (4YFN), CTIA Super Mobility Week, the Legal Design Summit, and the Computers, Freedom & Privacy Conference.

Jameson earned a B.A. in political science and philosophy from Boston College, where he served as Production Director of WZBC-Newton, and a J.D. from Brooklyn Law School, where he served as Editor-in-Chief of the Brooklyn Law Review, a member of the Appellate Moot Court Honor Society, and a participant in the Brooklyn Law Incubator & Policy (BLIP) Clinic. Jameson enjoys writing sketch comedy and writing and playing music.

Corsin Derungs

Corsin Derungs is a Senior Legal Counsel in the legal department of Bank Julius Baer. He holds a Master's degree in law from the university in Freiburg i.Ue., Switzerland, and passed the bar exam in 2005 in the Canton of Zurich. Before joining Bank Julius Baer, Corsin worked for Deloitte in the Regulatory, Compliance and Legal department focusing on regulatory developments and project, primarily in the area of asset management. Corsin also worked for

Credit Suisse in the legal department, supporting the trading floor and the custody network management. Furthermore, Corsin worked on the trading floor at the structured products desk. He leads the Legal team specialized in collective investment schemes, private equity and hedge funds, investment management, advisory services, wealth planning, marketing and research. Corsin is author of several books and articles focusing on collective investment schemes and anti-money laundering.

Professor María José Esteban Ferrer

Professor María José Esteban holds a degree in Law from Universidad de Barcelona (1984) and a PhD (summa cum laude) in Economics and Business Administration from Universidad Ramon Llull (2010). She is a Numerary Member of the Royal European Academy of Doctors and an Officer of the International Bar Association Academic and Professional Development Committee.

Esteban combines her corporate Law practice as a partner at the Barcelona Law firm Escura with intense academic activity. Currently, she is a contract doctoral professor at ESADE Law School, Universidad Ramon Llull, an affiliated researcher at the Harvard Law School Center on the Legal Profession, and co-director of the Center's Big Four in Law Research Project. Her research is focused on the economic and regulatory analysis of the legal profession, with special emphasis in the evolution of the services offered by alternative legal services providers and their underlying business models.

David Fisher

David Fisher is the founder and CEO of Integra Ledger, which is the blockchain for the global legal industry, and the founder of the Global Legal Blockchain Consortium, which is the largest legal industry blockchain consortium in the world, with more than 240 major law firms, corporate legal departments, software companies, and universities. He also co-founded the Global Legal Hackathon, which is the largest legal technology innovation event in history. In its recently concluded second year, the GLH took place in 46 cities and 24 countries, drawing over 6,000 participants. Earlier in his career, he was the founder and CEO of Millennium Venture Group, and he is a former chairman of the board of Youthbiz, a Denver-based nonprofit focused on business education for inner city youth. He is a graduate of Rice University and Harvard Business School.

Professor John Flood

John Flood is a Professor of Law and Society at Griffith University in Brisbane, Austrialia and served as inaugural Director of its Law Futures Centre to focus on law, risk, and innovation, law and nature, law and global challenges, and lawyering and legal education. His research focuses on the legal profession, especially the role of large law firms in global transactions, the regulation of, and the role of technology legal services. He has published over 100 articles and chapters as well as two monographs. He studied law and sociolegal studies at the LSE (LL.B, 1975), Warwick (LL.M., 1978), Yale Law School (LL.M., 1981), and Northwestern University (PhD sociology, 1987). He is also Honorary Professor of Law at University College London and Research Fellow in the UCL Centre for Blockchain Technologies. Professor Flood advises a number of blockchain startups in Australia and the US.

Jordan Furlong

Jordan Furlong of Ottawa, Canada, is a legal market analyst, author, and consultant who forecasts the impact of changing market conditions on lawyers and law firms. He has given dozens of presentations to law firms and legal organizations throughout the United States, Canada, Europe, and Australia over the past several years, analyzing the rapidly evolving legal market and illuminating the forces and trends driving change in this environment. Jordan is a Fellow of the College of Law Practice Management and Co-Chair of the Board of Directors of Suffolk University Law School's Institute on Legal Innovation & Technology. He is the author, most recently, of *Law Is A Buyer's Market: Building a Client-First Law Firm,* and he writes regularly about the changing legal market at his website, law21.ca.

Dr Silke Graf

Dr Silke Graf is Senior Associate, attorney-at-law and Head of Legal Tech and Knowledge Management at PwC Legal Austria in Vienna. In 2018, she received the «Woman of Legal Tech» Award for her efforts in this area. Silke also advises on issues relating to Intellectual Property Rights and Unfair Competition. She publishes regularly in the area of Unfair Competition and Legal Tech. Silke previously worked in a renowned Viennese boutique law firm and gained experience in software development for the legal sector. Silke holds a doctoral and an LL.M. from the University of Vienna.

Pierson Grider

Pierson Grider is a Denver-based lawyer and technology enthusiast. At Integra, he educates, promotes, and develops blockchain solutions for law firms, legal corporate departments, and legal software companies. He is a global organizer of the Global Legal Blockchain Consortium, which is the world's largest legal blockchain organization. Pierson organizes and manages the Global Legal Hackathon, which in 2018 consisted of 5,000 participants in 40 cities across 22 countries. His work has appeared in various publications on legal technology, including The Colorado Lawyer and Legal IT Today. Pierson received his B.A. at Michigan State University James Madison College in International Relations and Technology Public Policy and his J.D. from Western Michigan University Cooley Law School.

Michael Grupp

Michael Grupp is a lawyer and entrepreneur. He is founder and Managing Director of BRYTER GmbH, a leading provider of automation software. Michael has founded, and successfully sold several companies: The academic research portal Thesius (2017) and the legal tech pioneer Lexalgo (2018), a provider of decision support systems, which has received several awards for its technology, developed in collaboration with the European Space Agency (ESA).

Michael is a member of the Task Force, Legal Tech and Innovation, within the Association of Lawyers (DAV) as well as a board member to the Executive Faculty of the leading German legal think tank Bucerius Center on the Legal Profession at the Bucerius Law School.

Michael studied in Germany and France, with legal clerkships in Frankfurt, London, Seoul and New York and has worked in commercial law firms in the field of dispute resolution. He publishes on legal technologies and data protection and is a lecturer at the Goethe University Frankfurt. Michael is a leading voice in the intersecting field of law, technology and digital business models and studies the effects on the legal market.

Steve Hafner

Steve Hafner is a Senior Manager with PwC in Zurich and Head Managed Legal Services & Legal Process Optimisation at PwC Legal Switzerland.

Steve has over 17 years of working experience and has in-depth knowledge about project and change management, conceptual design, and a very good comprehension of front-to-back banking processes. Before joining PwC, Steve worked at a big Swiss Bank as a Senior Business Project Leader in the department of International Business Management. There, he gained professional experience in managing various regulatory implementation projects. Steve was responsible for numerous multi-divisional implementation and migration projects on the senior management level in the legal and data governance area.

Today, he specialises in managing and supervising complex projects including the interaction in a multi-cultural SME-environment.

Steve holds a Master of Advanced Studies in Banking and Finance and has participated in various project and business innovation management programs.

Dr Silvia Hodges Silverstein

Dr. Silvia Hodges Silverstein is the executive director of the Buying Legal Council, the international trade organization for legal procurement, and she is adjunct professor at Columbia Law School.

She co-authored the Harvard Business School case studies «GlaxoSmithKline: Sourcing Complex Professional Services on the company's legal procurement initiative» and «Riverview Law: Applying Business Sense to the Legal Market on the new model law firm».

Silvia authored many articles on law firm management including The Georgetown Journal of Legal Ethics' «I didn't go to law school to become a salesperson», and in the South Caroline Law Review's «What we know and need to know about Legal procurement». She is also the author/editor of several books, including the *Legal Procurement Handbook* and *Buying Legal: Procurement Insights and Practice*. She is the publisher of *Winning Proposals-The Essential Guide for Law Firms and Legal Services Providers*.

She earned her PhD at Nottingham Law School (UK), holds a master's degree in business from Universität Bayreuth (Germany) and Warwick Business School (UK) and an undergraduate degree (economics) from Universität Bayreuth.

Salvatore Iacangelo

Salvatore Iacangelo is Head EAM Services/COO at Credit Suisse (Switzerland) Ltd. in Zurich/Switzerland. Prior to this, he was Chief Operating Officer and Chief Digital Officer at leading law firm Bär & Karrer, supporting the Board of Directors with the formulation and implementation of the strategic directives as well as with the operational management of the law firm. Salvatore has broad and well-founded expertise in the digitalization field and in the deployment of innovative technologies. His activity focuses predominantly on the transformation and redesign of processes and business models which he implements in combination with his experience as attorney-at-law and legal advisor. Salvatore Iacangelo publishes regularly and frequently lectures on digitalization related topics. He holds a law degree from the University of Zurich and an MBA from INSEAD.

Dr Ulf Klebeck

Dr Ulf Klebeck is the General Counsel at Montana Capital Partners AG. He is in charge of all legal, regulatory and compliance aspects of Montana Capital's private equity business, including fund structuring & regulatory governance of mcp's private equity investment platform.

Ulf joined Montana Capital Partners from Woodman Asset Management AG, an international multi-family office/asset manager with its headquarter in Zug, Switzerland. At Woodman he was in charge of all legal, regulatory and compliance aspects of its asset & wealth management as well as family

office business—including fund structuring & governance (AIF & UCITS in Luxembourg, Malta, Jersey, Guernsey, CH, Cayman Islands), Woodman's family office mandates and Woodman's M&A business division. He served as a board member on various funds (AIF & UCITS) as well as a director of Woodman's subsidiary in Denmark. Prior to working for Woodman, Ulf worked for Vontobel Asset Management where he was in charge of inter alia—dealing with all regulatory and governance issues of Vontobel's fund structures (CH, Luxembourg and Cayman Islands). He lead the AIFMD implementation project at Vontobel and was co-head of the FATCA project for the asset management division of Vontobel. Before Vontobel, Ulf worked as Legal Counsel for Capital Dynamics. He started his career as an attorney-at-law in the Munich office of Clifford Chance with a focus on private equity transactions.

While working on his doctoral thesis, he held the position of an assistant professor both at the University of Mannheim and Ludwig-Maximilians-University of Munich.

Ulf frequently acts as an editor and author of various law books, journals and articles as well as a speaker on financial market regulatory topics, including funds regulations, investment law and corporate law as well as digital financial services. He is an associate lecturer at the University of Liechtenstein and was a research visiting fellow at UNSW, Sydney/Australia.

Karl Koller

Karl Koller is a Partner at PwC Legal Austria where he leads the Real Estate & Construction practice. Prior to this, he held a similar role at leading law firm WolfTheiss in Vienna, Austria. He specializes in real estate and corporate law and is an expert in large-scale real estate transactions and real estate developments, particularly in connection with planning and construction agreements as well as with transactions in the hotel and leisure industry. He holds an LL.M. (2005) from the University of California School of Law in Los Angeles and a Mag. iur. (2000) from the University of Vienna Law School.

Dr Antonios Koumbarakis

Antonios Koumbarakis is a Senior Manager with PwC Zurich and a member of PwC Legal Switzerland's Legal FS Regulatory & Compliance Services practice. He is the Head of the PwC Regulatory Foresight and Macroprudentia intelligence Team in Switzerland and has deep knowledge regarding regulatory impact assessments. In this context, Antonios advises international financial institutions and regulatory authorities primarily in Switzerland, Europe, Middle East and East Asia. He has proven experience in program management, the management of teams, regulatory gap assessments and project execution. Given his background, Antonios is a Subject Matter Expert in the following areas: Sustainable Finance Regulation, MiFID II, Basel III, TBTF regulation such as capital requirements, liquidity requirements, recovery and resolution standards.

He holds a Master of Arts in Economics (lic.rer.pol) and he has written his Ph.D. thesis in the area of macroeconomics and monetary economics. He was a Visiting Research Fellow at the Max Planck Institute for Research on Collective Goods in Bonn with a research focus in monetary policy, financial stability and bank regulation. Moreover, he has participated in the London School of Economics' Executive Education Program. Furthermore, Antonios is author of several articles and books in the area of financial stability, bank regulation and monetary policy.

Christoph Küng

Christoph Küng is the Chief LegalTech Officer at leading Swiss law firm Kellerhals Carrard. He also serves as president and co-founder of the Swiss LegalTech Association (SLTA) and he is a LegalTech entrepreneur. Prior to this, he worked as a tax specialist and advisor with a leading Swiss law firm, a Big4 company and in the group tax department of Zurich Cantonal Bank. Christoph holds a degree in law from the University of Zurich and a degree in finance from University of Applied Sciences Northwestern Switzerland. He is a Swiss Certified Tax Expert.

Peter D Lederer

Peter Lederer's early life was in Vienna; he emigrated to the United States as a child, in 1938. Educated in the schools of Indianapolis, Indiana and Washington, DC, he attended college at the University of Chicago. Upon graduation in 1949, he spent two years as a community organizer for the United World Federalists, an organization seeking «world peace, through world law, through world government.» That was followed by two years in the United States army during the Korean War.

With its beginnings in the 1950s, his career in the law has spanned some seven decades. He attended the law school of the University of Chicago, receiving a JD in 1957, and an MCL in 1958 after further study at the University of Bern. While at law school, he worked as Professor Karl Llewellyn's research assistant for his book, *The Common Law Tradition*, and served as an editor of *The University of Chicago Law Review*. Upon return from Bern, he was appointed a *Law & Behavioral Science Research Fellow*, working for Professor Soia Mentschikoff on the Arbitration Project.

After joining the Chicago office of the global law firm Baker McKenzie in 1959, he opened the firm's Zurich office in 1960, and in 1966 returned to the United States. There, for many years, he led the firm's New York office and was actively engaged in the firm's global management. His practice ranged broadly: from counseling the aviation and utility industries on the organization of captive insurance companies, to serving as counsel for the former Yugosla-

via in its sovereign debt restructuring, to advising several of the former Big Eight accounting firms on structuring their global operations. As an outgrowth of the last, he served for several years as general counsel of Deloitte Touche Tohmatsu International. Upon retiring from law firm practice, he began strategic planning consulting for several major enterprises; he was also a co-founder and board chair of an Internet startup, CoverageConnect, Inc., an early web-based insurance broker.

Lederer has been a sometime lecturer in law at the law schools of Columbia, Georgetown, New York University and the University of Zurich. In recent years, he has pursued his interests in strategic planning, the Internet, and the future of the practice of law and legal education. He is a co-founder of the University of Miami School of Law's Law Without Walls project, and an Adjunct Professor of Law at Miami.

Maria Leistner

Maria Leistner was, until May 2019 the General Counsel for Global Wealth Management for UBS, based in Zurich. She will be pursuing other opportunities as of 2020. She joined UBS in May 2016 after spending 13 years with Credit Suisse in various roles in London including as General Counsel for EMEA, co-General Counsel for Investment Banking and General Counsel for International Wealth Management. Prior to that, she was in the private practice with leading international law firms. In addition to numerous awards for professional excellence for Maria and her teams, her activities to promote diversity and inclusion have been widely recognized too. Maria is on the 2014 and 2015 Financial Times / OUTstanding Top LGBT business allies lists, sponsors the LGBT Pride network at UBS Switzerland, has sponsored the Credit Suisse EMEA LGBT network, fronts a bank-wide initiative fighting unconscious bias and promoting inclusion at UBS, has organized, and participated in, numerous events promoting gender diversity, and is the co-founder of Women in Law in Switzerland.

Dr Marcel Lötscher

Dr Marcel Lötscher, LL.M. MBA studied law at the University of St. Gallen and the University of Bern. His initial professional training saw him complete a commercial banking apprenticeship at a major Swiss bank. He was admitted to the Lucerne bar and continued to study, becoming a Swiss Fund Officer FA/IAF and International Fund Officer FA. Marcel holds a doctoral degree in the field of collective investments. He also holds an Executive Master of Laws (LL.M.) in company, foundation and trust law awarded by the University of Liechtenstein and a Master of Business Administration (MBA) in General Management Competences awarded by the Danube University Krems. His appointments to various leading positions in the financial sphere include his role as a member of group executive management at a Swiss financial group.

In 2012, he was appointed Member of the Executive Board at the Financial Market Authority (FMA) Liechtenstein and Head of Securities and Markets Division (renamed January 1, 2017). The Securities and Markets Unit oversees asset management companies, funds and their management companies and the sector-specific markets regulation. Marcel is involved in various expert groups with respect to financial market law and regulation (inter alia ESMA and IOSCO) and regularly gives speeches on these topics.

Lauren Mack

Lauren Mack is co-founder of Legal Hackers and serves on its board of directors. As an organizer of the original New York Legal Hackers chapter, she has coordinated numerous events, including discussions around how the law may or should impact new technologies such as cryptocurrencies, 3D printing, eco-tech, and the sharing economy. Lauren has also assisted with various multi-chapter Legal Hackers events and helps keep the global community connected by managing the Legal Hackers' online presence.

In addition to her work with Legal Hackers, Lauren is a copyright, trademark, technology, and corporate law attorney at a boutique law firm in New York City. She particularly enjoys taking an active role in crafting thoughtful agreements related to new technologies. Lauren graduated *magna cum laude* with a B.S. from Drexel University and received her J.D. from the Benjamin N. Cardozo School of Law, where she served as a staff editor of the Cardozo Journal of Law & Gender and on the Executive Board of the Cardozo Intellectual Property Law Society as the Copyright Chair. In her spare time, Lauren loves music, art, writing, travel, and walking everywhere (within reason).

Priit Martinson

Priit Martinson leads the Government Technology & Digital Transformation practice of PwC Estonia. He is delivering Estonia's technology-driven e-government solutions as a one-stop shop and advising foreign nations on how to transform their public services. Priit has ten years of experience in international trade, foreign direct investment and business development in Europe and Asia. For five years, Priit served as a diplomat in China as the Head of the Commercial Section at the Consulate General of Estonia in Shanghai and as a Chief Representative in China at the Estonian Investment Agency. Priit holds the position of arbitrator at SHIAC (Shanghai International Economic and Trade Arbitration Commission), and he is a member of the PwC European China Business Group. Priit holds an LL.M. degree in Chinese Law from Tsinghua University.

Craig McKeown

Craig McKeown has over 15 years of experience delivering eDiscovery services to clients and has led on some of the largest matters to go through the UK

and Irish courts, as well as leading a number of complex multi-jurisdictional cases. Craig is a Partner in PwC's Forensic and Legal Technology practice, based in the UK. More recently, Craig has advised some of the world's largest organisations on their Legal Tech strategy and on the selection and implementation of Legal Tech solutions, including the use of machine learning, AI and robotics technology.

Dr Marc O Morant

Dr Marc O Morant is the Head of PwC's Flexible Legal Resources (FLR), a service of PwC Legal Switzerland. He is a Partner with PricewaterhouseCoopers Switzerland and possesses highly developed and detailed knowledge of the staff leasing and liquid resource business. Combined with a strong sense for innovation and entrepreneurship, he became a recognized partner in this field, offering thought leadership for all alternative legal and LegalTech/RegTech enthusiasts globally. Marc joined PwC from Axiom, the world's largest provider of tech-enabled legal, contracts and compliance solutions for large enterprises. Before Marc became an entrepreneur, he worked for Swiss Life International as Chief Counsel. Prior to Swiss Life, Marc was Senior Corporate Legal Counsel at XL Insurance, Senior Associate at Staiger, Schwald & Partner Attorneys at Law, and Corporate Legal Counsel at Novartis International.

Marc is a Swiss qualified lawyer and holds a Master of Law from the London School of Economics and Political Science (LSE) as well as a Doctoral degree in law (PhD) from the University of Basel, where he also earned his law degree. Additionally, he passed successfully a General Management Program at Harvard Business School.

Marc is a Member of the Advisory Board of the Swiss LegalTech Association and the RegTech start-up APIAX, a Member of the European Legal Technology Association and Member of the global exponential technologies enthusiasts movement «Disruption Disciples» and Founder of LegalHackers Zurich. Marc is also a passionate lecturer at various universities, law schools and conferences in Switzerland and the EU for topics around Law & Innovation, LegalTech/RegTech, Legal Procurement and Operation Models.

Finally, Marc is married and father of two children who keep him busy in his private life.

Dr Christian Öhner

Dr Christian Öhner is the Leader of PwC Legal Austria. Christian advises international and domestic clients, mainly on corporate and M&A matters and other legal aspects of high strategic importance. Christian is among Austria's leading M&A lawyers with more than 15 years of practice, including with leading law firms Freshfields Bruckhaus Deringer and Wolf Theiss as well as strategy consultant at The Boston Consulting Group (BCG). In recent years, Christian focused extensively on legal technology and the future of law. Christian holds a doctoral degree from the University Vienna and an LL.M. degree from the University of Chicago.

Karl J Paadam

Karl J Paadam leads PwC Legal in Central & Eastern Europe. After establishing PwC Legal in Estonia in 2012, Karl has led PwC Legal Estonia through unprecedented growth to becoming the 5th largest law firm nationally. During Karl's time with PwC Legal, the Estonian law firm has become the leading adviser for Estonian technology and FinTech companies. PwC Legal Estonia has leveraged its largest legal professionals network in the world to exporting Estonian technology business to over 40 countries across the globe. Karl has established himself as the preeminent banking and FinTech lawyer in the region. In addition to his work with banking, finance and technology clients, Karl took the role of managing partner of PwC Legal in the Central and Eastern Europe in July 2017 and is now leading the firm during its rapid growth. He is in charge of strategy and development of PwC Legal's operations in CEE through smart knowledge management and LegalTech.

Will Pangborn

Will Pangborn is marketing professional specializing in communications and public relations for the tech industry. He holds a Bachelor of Public Affairs (B.PAPM) from Carleton University and spent several years working with private sector clients on strategic communications initiatives across a variety of sectors. Now working with Kira Systems, one of Canada's top startups, Will manages content marketing, communications, and public relations.

Philipp Rosenauer

Philipp Rosenauer is a Senior Manager with PwC Legal in Zurich. His focus is on providing legal regulatory implementation support for financial intermediaries and on the set-up of legal functions. Before joining PwC, Philipp worked with the Financial Market Authority of Liechtenstein where he was primarily responsible for organizing and executing large-scale supervisory projects in the banking area. Prior to this Philipp was legal associate at two leading business law firms in the area of financial market law and M&A. Philipp also (for several years) worked as a Consultant at a management consultancy where he was as project manager responsible for the administration and coordination of various projects with particular focus on IT implementation. He received a Master's degree in Law and a Master degree in Business Administration from Johannes Kepler University (Linz, Austria). Because of his dual academic education and practical supervisory and consulting experience, he is competent in supporting Financial Intermediaries on regulatory, risk and process topics at the interface of legal and business and has strong project management capabilities with a proven track record of delivery and

stakeholder management. Philipp is also a permanent lecturer at the LLM and MBA program of the University of Liechtenstein and author of numerous articles in expert journals.

Michael Rowden

Michael Rowden has over 8 years of experience advising on and implementing technology solutions for large corporates and law firms, focused on utilizing data to improve legal strategy. Currently, he is a Senior Manager at PwC within the UK Forensics Legal Technology practice. Prior to joining PwC, he worked for a Toronto-based international law firm, leveraging technology to assist legal teams in responding to litigation, investigatory and regulatory matters.

Professor Mari Sako

Mari Sako is Professor of Management Studies at Saïd Business School and a Professorial Fellow of New College, University of Oxford. Her areas of expertise include global strategy, comparative institutional analysis, outsourcing and offshoring, and professional services.

Her research on the globalization of legal services and its impact on the professions has led to her becoming member of the UK Legal Services Board Research Strategy Group, and member of the advisory board of Thomson Reuters Legal Executive Institute. During 2011–12, she was President of the Society for the Advancement of Socio-Economics (SASE). Mari also earlier made a significant contribution to the understanding of the Japanese economy and Japanese firms. In the 1990s and 2000s, she was a researcher for the MIT International Motor Vehicle Program (IMVP), which gave her a valuable opportunity to be out in the field, observing and interviewing managers and workers at automakers and their suppliers in Japan, Europe and the USA. Insights from the fieldwork to understand lean production and quality control also inform her more recent work on what professionals, such as lawyers, do. Her research has been published in the form of five books and numerous journal articles.

Maurus Schreyvogel

As Chief Legal Innovation Officer, Maurus Schreyvogel drives peak in-house legal department performance and accelerates functional innovation. He focuses on corporate legal department best practices and future needs, and application of technologies to increase value to the business while driving down cost and fostering a globally connected culture. His responsibilities also include Legal operations, global processes and systems. He is a member of the Group Legal Leadership Team. In 2018, Maurus took over leadership for CLOC (Corporate Legal Operations Consortium) in continental Europe and he is a member of the editorial board of the International In-House Counsel Journal.

Maurus began his legal career at a Zurich law firm in 2002 and joined the Corporate IP department of Novartis in 2004. In 2007, Maurus transitioned to a two-year rotation in Finance and Audit and in 2009, he joined the Corporate Legal department as Program Manager. In this role, Maurus led strategic, cost-saving Legal and IP initiatives such as the implementation of a global spend management program, the establishment of preferred law firm panels and the introduction of legal knowledge and matter management. In 2013, Maurus assumed responsibility for Legal operations and operational excellence. Between 2015 and 2017, he served as Chief of Staff to the Group General Counsel.

Maurus received his law degree from the University of St. Gallen, Switzerland in 2002 and holds a Global Executive MBA from IE Business School in Spain.

Dr Matthias Trummer

Dr Matthias Trummer is a Senior Manager and attorney-at-law at PwC Legal Austria. Matthias advises industrial corporations, private equity and venture capital funds in complex buy-side and sell-side cross-border M&A transactions and restructuring matters. He has been working in the M&A practice group of leading international law firms based in Vienna and has more than 10 years working experience. Matthias holds a Masters degree in law from the University Graz and a doctoral degree in law from the University of Vienna. In 2014, his doctoral thesis focusing on Austrian and German corporate and insolvency law has been honored with the Austrian Bankers' Association Award. He has also received a Masters degree in Digital Innovation & Entrepreneurial Leadership from ESCP Europe. Through studying, researching and running digital innovation projects in Berlin, Paris, London, Shanghai and San Francisco/Silicon Valley Matthias has gained extensively deep knowledge in all aspects of digital technology and transformation processes.

Jordan Urstadt

Jordan Urstadt is the CEO and founder of PartnerVine. Before founding PartnerVine, Jordan was Managing Director, General Counsel and Head of Legal & Compliance at Capital Dynamics, a global asset management firm. Prior to that, he was a Vice President and Head of Legal & Compliance at LGT Capital Partners. He previously worked at White & Case. Jordan earned a Juris Doctor from New York University's School of Law and a Bachler of Arts Phi Beta Kappa from Dartmouth College.

Noah Waisberg

Noah co-founded Kira Systems in 2011 and launched the software, Kira, which is now the most used and trusted software for contract review and analysis, helping the world's largest corporations and professional service firms uncover relevant information from unstructured contracts and related documents. Prior to founding Kira Systems, Noah practiced at the law firm Weil,

Gotshal & Manges in New York, where he focused on private equity, M&A, and securities. Noah is an expert on contract analysis, legal technology, and artificial intelligence; has spoken at conferences including SXSW Interactive, ILTACON, and ReInvent Law; and was named 2016 ILTA Innovative Thought Leader of the Year. He is also the author of Robbie the Robot Learns to Read, the world's first ever children's book on machine learning. Noah holds a J.D. from the NYU School of Law, an A.M. from Brown University, and a B.A. with honours from McGill University.

Professor Rolf H Weber

Prof Dr Rolf H Weber studied law at the University of Zurich and at Harvard Law School. In 1979, he received his Doctorate of law (Ph. D. iur.) from the University of Zurich and, in 1986, he received his Habilitation from the same university in the field of Swiss and international civil and economic law.

Beginning in 1983, he has taught regularly at the University of St. Gallen (HSG). In 1995 he became a full professor for private, commercial and European law at the University of Zurich and in 2000 a visiting professor at the University of Hong Kong. Prof Weber has been an attorney with the law firm Bratschi AG in Zurich since 1982.

He is Director of the Center for Information Technology, Society, and Law, of the Europa Institute and of the Blockchain Center at the University of Zurich. From 2009 to 2011, he was employed as an expert by the European Council in the domain of Internet Governance and from 2010 to 2012, as an expert on the EU's Internet of Things Expert Group. Prof Weber has also served as the Vice Chairman of the Steering Committee of the Global Internet Governance Academic Network (GigaNet) from 2008 till 2015, and he has won awards for research contributions in numerous conferences. Since 1997, he has also been a member of the Appeal Commission of the SIX Swiss Exchange, where he became president in 2009.

Phil Weiss

Phil is a founder and director of Legal Hackers. He has spearheaded the coordination of dozens of local and global events for the organization, including the first Legal Hackers Annual Summit (aka the Legal Hackers Congress) and the New York Node of the first Computational Law and Blockchain Festival (CL+B).

When he is not serving the Legal Hackers community, Phil is a solo-practice attorney who serves as outside general counsel to startups, digital agencies, producers, and artists. Prior to that, Phil was Partner at Fridman Law Group PLLC, a boutique firm in New York City. Phil attended Brooklyn Law School where he graduated magna cum laude and served as Executive Articles Editor of the Brooklyn Law Review. Phil continues to lecture at Brooklyn Law

School, where he served as adjunct faculty from 2014 to 2018, and pressing students to adapt their legal training for the digital age.

Phil studied philosophy at Boston University as an undergraduate. His interest in tech, law, and policy extends to his love for coding, gaming, and writing.

Professor David B Wilkins

Professor David B Wilkins is the Lester Kissel Professor of Law, Vice Dean for Global Initiatives on the Legal Profession, and Faculty Director of the Center on the Legal Profession and the Center for Lawyers and the Professional Services Industry at Harvard Law School. He is also a Senior Research Fellow of the American Bar Foundation and a Fellow of the Harvard University Edmond J Safra Foundation Center for Ethics.

Professor Wilkins has written over 80 articles on the legal profession in leading scholarly journals and the popular press and is the co-author (along with his Harvard Law School colleague Andrew Kaufman) of one of the leading casebooks in the field. His current scholarly projects include Globalization, Lawyers, and Emerging Economies (where he directs over 50 researchers studying the impact of globalization on the market for legal services in rapidly developing countries in Asia, Africa, Latin America and Eastern Europe); After the JD (a ten-year nationwide longitudinal study of lawyers' careers); The Harvard Law School Career Study (examining, among other things, differences in the experiences of male and female graduates and the careers of lawyers who do not practice law); and The New Social Engineers (charting the historical development and current experiences of black lawyers in corporate law practice).

Professor Wilkins teaches several courses on lawyers including The Legal Profession, Legal Education for the Twenty-First Century, and Challenges of a General Counsel. In 2007, he co-founded Harvard Law School's Executive Education Program, where he teaches in several courses including Leadership in Law Firms and Leadership in Corporate Counsel.

Professor Wilkins has given over 40 endowed lectures at universities around the world and is a frequent speaker at professional conferences and law firm and corporate retreats. His recent academic honors include the 2012 Honorary Doctorate in Law from Stockholm University in Sweden, the 2012 Distinguished Visiting Mentor Award from Australia National University, the 2012 Genest Fellowship from Osgoode Hall Law School, the 2010 American Bar Foundation Scholar of the Year Award, the 2009 J. Clay Smith Award from Howard University School of Law, and the 2008 Order of the Coif Distinguished Visitor Fellowship. In 2012, Professor Wilkins was elected as a Member of the American Academy of Arts and Sciences.

CPSIA information can be obtained
at www.ICGtesting.com
Printed in the USA
BVHW040311030719
552379BV00033B/1718/P

9 783727 210396